S13   MISCELLANEOUS DO'S AND DON'TS

S13.1 Letter to Instructor	S13.2 Formal Announcements	S13.3 Speechmaking	S13.4 Hedging	S13.5 Blustering	S13.6 "You"	S13.7 Defining Terms
377	377	377	378	378	378	378–379

RESEARCH

R1 Bibliography Cards	R2 Note Cards	R3 QUOTATIONS		R4 Slug Outline	R5 FOOTNOTES		R6 Plagiarism	R7 Final Bibliography
		R3.1 On Cards	R3.2 In Paper		R5.1 Use	R5.2 Form		
298–303	303–307	307–308	312–315	309	315–316	318–322	316–318	322

HANDBOOK AND GLOSSARY

GRAMMAR—G

G1 Adjective–Adverb Confusion	G2 Comma Splice	G3 Comparative and Superlative Forms	G4 Comparisons: Logical and Complete	G5 Double Negative	G6 Sentence Fragment	G7 MODIFIERS		G8 Pronoun Agreement
						G7.1 Dangling	G7.2 Misplaced	
389–391	403–405	405–406	406–407	407–408	410–413	416	416–417	419–420

G9 Pronoun Case	G10 Pronoun Reference	G11 Run-on Sentence	G12 Tense Shift	G13 Shift in Person	G14 Subject–Verb Agreement	G15 Subjunctive	G16 Verbs: Principal Parts	G17 Verbs: Sequence of Tenses
420–423	423–424	425–426	427	427–428	430–434	434	435–437	437–440

PUNCTUATION—Pn

Pn1 APOSTROPHE			Pn2	Pn3
Pn1.1 Contractions	Pn1.2 Plurals	Pn1.3 Possessives	Brackets	Colon
391	391	391–393	394	396–397

Pn4 COMMA							
Pn4.1 List or Series	Pn4.2 Independent Clauses	Pn4.3 Introductory Elements	Pn4.4 Interrupting Elements	Pn4.5 Coordinate Adjectives	Pn4.6 Nonrestrictive Modifiers and Appositives	Pn4.7 Misreadings	Pn4.8 Other
397–398	398	398–399	399–400	400	400–401	402	402–403

Pn5 Dash	Pn6 Ellipsis	Pn7 Period Question Mark Exclamation Point	Pn8 Hyphen	Pn9 Parenthesis	Pn10 Quotation Mark	Pn11 Semicolon
407	408	408–410	413–414	418–419	424–425	426–427

OTHER CONVENTIONS—C

C1 Abbreviations	C2 Capitalization	C3 Italics	C4 Proofreading Symbols	C5 Numerals	C6 Spelling		Glos Glossary
388	394–396	414–415	415	418	428–430		442–468

STUDENT'S BOOK OF COLLEGE ENGLISH

SECOND EDITION

DAVID SKWIRE

FRANCES CHITWOOD

CUYAHOGA COMMUNITY COLLEGE
METROPOLITAN CAMPUS

GLENCOE PUBLISHING CO., INC.
Encino, California

Copyright © 1978 by Glencoe Publishing Co., Inc.

Earlier edition copyright © 1975 by Glencoe Press, a division of Benziger Bruce & Glencoe, Inc.

Printed in the United States of America

All rights reserved. No part of this book may be reproduced or transmitted in any form or by any means, electronic or mechanical, including photocopying, recording, or by any information storage and retrieval system, without permission in writing from the Publisher.

GLENCOE PUBLISHING CO., INC.
17337 Ventura Boulevard
Encino, California 91316
Collier Macmillan Canada, Ltd.

Library of Congress Catalog Card Number: 77-73258

4 5 6 7 8 9   81 80 79

ISBN 0-02-478330-7

ACKNOWLEDGMENTS

Acknowledgment is gratefully made to the following authors, agents, and publishers who have granted permission to use selections from their publications.

Ruth Banks, Ersa Poston, and the Estate of Theodore R. Poston for "The Revolt of the Evil Fairies." Reprinted by permission.

The Bettmann Archive, Inc., for photographs on pages ii–iii, xvi, 58, 286, 338, and 380. Reprinted by permission of The Bettmann Archive, Inc.

The Bodley Head, for "The Story Teller" by H. H. Munro, from THE COMPLETE SHORT STORIES OF SAKI (H. H. Munro) (THE BODLEY HEAD SAKI). Reprinted by permission of The Bodley Head; reprinted also by permission of The Viking Press.

Chatto and Windus Ltd., for "The Lottery Ticket" by Anton Chekhov, from THE WIFE AND OTHER STORIES by Anton Chekhov, translated by Constance Garnett. Copyright 1918 by Macmillan Publishing Co., Inc., renewed 1946 by Constance Garnett. Reprinted by permission of Chatto and Windus Ltd. and Mr. David Garnett; reprinted also by permission of Macmillan Publishing Co., Inc.; and for "Dulce et Decorum Est" from THE COLLECTED POEMS OF WILFRED OWEN: Edited by C. Day Lewis. Reprinted by permission of Chatto & Windus Ltd. and the Owen Estate. Reprinted also by permission of New Directions Publishing Corporation.

Delacorte Press for "Harrison Bergeron" by Kurt Vonnegut Jr., from WELCOME TO THE MONKEY HOUSE by Kurt Vonnegut Jr. Copyright 1961 by Kurt Vonnegut Jr. Reprinted by permission of Delacorte Press and Seymour Lawrence.

William Spooner Donald for "Will Someone Please Hiccup My Pat?" by William Spooner Donald. Copyright 1968. Reprinted by permission of William Spooner Donald.

Doubleday & Company, Inc., for THE FIRST FIVE YEARS (pp. 121–125) by Virginia E. Pomeranz with Dodi Schultz. Copyright 1973 by Virginia E. Pomeranz and Dodi Schultz. Reprinted by permission of Doubleday & Company, Inc.

E. P. Dutton, for "The Spires of Oxford" by Winifred M. Letts, from THE SPIRES OF OXFORD AND OTHER POEMS by Winifred M. Letts. Copyright 1917 by E. P. Dutton, renewal 1945 by Winifred M. Letts. Reprinted by permission of E. P. Dutton; reprinted also by permission of John Murray Ltd., London, England.

M. Evans and Company, Inc., for DANCING AZTECS (pp. 28–29) by Donald E. Westlake. Copyright 1976 by Donald E. Westlake. Reprinted by permission of M. Evans and Company, Inc.

Family Circle, Inc., for "How to Write a Letter That Will Get You a Job" by Nora Aguilar, copyright 1977; and for "Why Soap Operas Are So Popular" by Dan Wakefield, copyright, 1976. Reprinted by permission of The Family Circle, Inc.

Farrar, Straus & Giroux, Inc., for "Charles" by Shirley Jackson, from THE LOTTERY by Shirley Jackson. Copyright 1943, 1949 by Shirley Jackson; copyright renewed 1971 by Lawrence Hyman, Barry Hyman, Mrs. Sarah Webster, and Mrs. Joanne Schnurer. Reprinted by permission of Farrar, Straus & Giroux, Inc.

Field Newspaper Syndicate for "Sweet Mystery of Life—Children" by Erma Bombeck, from AT WIT'S END by Erma Bombeck, copyright 1975. Reprinted by permission of Field Newspaper Syndicate.

Harcourt Brace Jovanovich, Inc., for "Shooting an Elephant" by George Orwell, from SHOOTING AN ELEPHANT AND OTHER ESSAYS by George Orwell. Copyright 1945, 1946, 1949, 1950 by Sonia Brownell Orwell; renewed 1973, 1974, by Sonia Orwell; reprinted also by permission of A. M. Heath; and for "Grass" by Carl Sandburg, from CORNHUSKERS by Carl Sandburg. Copyright 1918 by Holt, Rinehart and Winston, Inc.; copyright 1946 by Carl Sandburg. Reprinted by permission of Harcourt Brace Jovanovich, Inc.

Harper & Row, Publishers, Inc., for "Letter from Birmingham Jail (April 16, 1973)" by Martin Luther King, Jr., from WHY WE CAN'T WAIT by Martin Luther King, Jr. Copyright 1963 by Martin Luther King, Jr. Reprinted by permission of Harper & Row, Publishers, Inc.

A. M. Heath and Company, Ltd., for "Shooting An Elephant" by George Orwell, from SHOOTING AN ELEPHANT AND OTHER ESSAYS by George Orwell. Reprinted by permission of A. M. Heath and Company Ltd. on behalf of the Orwell Estate; reprinted also by permission of Harcourt Brace Jovanovich, Inc.

William Heinemann Ltd., for "Quality" by John Galsworthy, from THE INN OF TRANQUILITY by John Galsworthy. Copyright 1912. Reprinted by permission of William Heinemann Ltd.; reprinted also by permission of Charles Scribner's Sons.

International Creative Management, for "The Portable Phonograph" by Walter Van Tilburg Clark, from THE WATCHFUL GODS AND OTHER STORIES. Copyright 1941, 1969 by Walter Van Tilburg Clark. Reprinted by permission of International Creative Management.

Alfred A. Knopf, Inc., for "The Landlady" by Roald Dahl, from KISS KISS by Roald Dahl. Copyright 1959 by Roald Dahl; and for "Her First Ball" by Katherine Mansfield, from THE SHORT STORIES OF KATHERINE MANSFIELD. Copyright 1922 by Alfred A. Knopf, Inc.; renewed 1950 by John Middleton Murry. Reprinted by permission of Alfred A. Knopf, Inc.

Macmillan Publishing Co., Inc., for "The Lottery Ticket" by Anton Chekhov, from THE WIFE AND OTHER STORIES by Anton Chekhov. Copyright 1918 by Macmillan Publishing Co., Inc.; renewed 1946 by Constance Garnett; reprinted also by permission of Chatto and Windus Ltd; for "There Will Come Soft Rains" by Sara Teasdale, from COLLECTED POEMS by Sara Teasdale. Copyright 1920 by Macmillan Publishing Co., Inc.; renewed 1948 by Mamie T. Wheless; and for "In Time of 'The Breaking of Nations' " by Thomas Hardy, from COLLECTED POEMS by Thomas Hardy. Copyright 1925 by Macmillan Publishing Co., Inc.; reprinted also by permission of Macmillan Company of Canada Ltd. Reprinted by permission of Macmillan Publishing Co., Inc.

The Macmillan Company of Canada Limited, for "In Time of 'The Breaking of Nations' " by Thomas Hardy, from COLLECTED POEMS OF THOMAS HARDY. Reprinted by permission of the Trustees of the Hardy Estate, Macmillan London and Basingstoke, and The Macmillan Company of Canada Limited; reprinted also by permission of Macmillan Publishing Co., Inc., New York.

Scott Meredith Literary Agency, for "Object Lesson" by Ellery Queen, from Q.E.D. Copyright 1968. Reprinted by permission of the author and the author's agents, Scott Meredith Literary Agency, Inc., 845 Third Avenue, New York, New York 10022.

John Murray Ltd., for "The Spires of Oxford" by Winifred M. Letts, from HALLOW-E'EN by Winifred Letts. Copyright 1917. Reprinted by permission of John Murray Publishers Ltd.; reprinted also by permission of E. P. Dutton.

Nash Publishing Corporation, for HOW TO PARENT (pp. 205–210) by Fitzhugh Dodson. Copyright 1970 by Fitzhugh Dodson. Reprinted by permission of the Nash Publishing Corporation.

National Wildlife Federation, for "With Legs Like These . . . Who Needs Wings?" by George E. Hollister. Copyright 1973 by National Wildlife Federation. Reprinted by permission of National Wildlife Federation.

New Directions Publishing Corporation, for "What Were They Like?" by Denise Levertov, from THE SORROW DANCE by Denise Levertov. Copyright 1966 by Denise Levertov; for "Dulce et Decorum Est" by Wilfred Owen, from COLLECTED POEMS by Wilfred Owen. Copyright 1946, 1963 by Chatto and Windus Ltd.; reprinted also by permission of Chatto and Windus Ltd.; for "The River Merchant's Wife: A Letter" by Ezra Pound, from PERSONAE by Ezra Pound. Copyright 1926 by Ezra Pound; for "Not Waving But Drowning" by Stevie Smith, from SELECTED POEMS by Stevie Smith. Copyright 1962, 1964 by Stevie Smith; and for "The Use of Force" by William Carlos Williams, from THE FARMERS' DAUGHTERS by William Carlos Williams. Copyright 1938 by William Carlos Williams. Reprinted by permission of New Directions Publishing Corporation.

Newsweek, for "Cruel Lib" by D. Keith Mano. Copyright 1975. Reprinted by permission of Newsweek.

Harold Ober Associates, for "Ballad of the Landlord" by Langston Hughes, from MONTAGE OF A DREAM DEFERRED. Copyright 1951 by Langston Hughes. Reprinted by permission of Harold Ober Associates Incorporated.

The Plain Dealer, for " 'Why' is Worse Than 'What' " by George E. Condon. Copyright 1975 by The Plain Dealer. Reprinted by permission of The Plain Dealer.

Robin Roberts, for "Strike Out Little League" by Robin Roberts. Copyright 1975 by Newsweek, Inc. Reprinted by permission of Newsweek.

George T. Sassoon, for "Base Details" by Siegfried Sassoon, from COLLECTED POEMS by Siegfried Sassoon. Reprinted by permission of George T. Sassoon; reprinted also by permission of The Viking Press.

Charles Scribner's Sons, for "Quality" by John Galsworthy, from THE INN OF TRANQUILITY by John Galsworthy. Copyright 1912 by Charles Scribner's Sons. Reprinted by permission of Charles Scribner's Sons; reprinted also by permission of William Heinemann Ltd.

Simon & Schuster, Inc., for A LAYMAN'S GUIDE TO PSYCHIATRY AND PSYCHOANALYSIS (pp. 25–28) by Eric Berne. Copyright 1947, 1957, 1968 by Eric Berne. Reprinted by permission of Simon & Schuster, Inc.

Squire-Reynolds Organization, Ltd., for "The Adventure of the Blue Carbuncle" by Sir Arthur Conan Doyle. Reprinted by permission of the Squire-Reynolds Organization, Ltd., New York.

Twayne Publishers, for "If We Must Die" by Claude McKay, from SELECTED POEMS OF CLAUDE MCKAY. Copyright 1953 by Twayne Publishers, Inc. Reprinted by permission of Twayne Publishers, a Division of G. K. Hall & Co.

University of Nebraska Press, for "Bridal Couch" by Donald G. Lloyd. Copyright 1947 by the University of Nebraska Press. Reprinted by permission of the University of Nebraska Press.

Vanguard Press, Inc., for "Where Are You Going, Where Have You Been?" by Joyce Carol Oates, from THE WHEEL OF LOVE by Joyce Carol Oates. Copyright 1965, 1966, 1967, 1968, 1970 by Joyce Carol Oates. Reprinted by permission of Vanguard Press, Inc.

The Viking Press, Inc., for "Base Details" by Siegfried Sassoon, from COLLECTED POEMS by Siegfried Sassoon. Copyright 1918 by E. P. Dutton & Co., 1946 by Siegfried Sassoon; reprinted also by permission of G. T. Sassoon; for "You Were Perfectly Fine" by Dorothy Parker, from THE PORTABLE DOROTHY PARKER. Copyright 1929, 1957 by Dorothy Parker; for THE GRAPES OF WRATH (Chapter 7) by John Steinbeck. Copyright 1939, 1967 by John Steinbeck; and for "The Story Teller" by H. H. Munro, from THE SHORT STORIES OF SAKI (H. H. Munro); reprinted also by permission of The Bodley Head. Reprinted by permission of The Viking Press, Inc.

Woman's Day, for "Drownproofing" by Carla Stephens. Copyright 1976 by Fawcett Publications, Inc. Reprinted by permission of Woman's Day Magazine.

CONTENTS

TO THE INSTRUCTOR

When the Lord finished the world, he pronounced it
good. That is what I said about my first work, too.
But Time, I tell you, Time takes the confidence out of
these incautious early opinions.
— *Mark Twain*

Without tampering with the strong points of the first edition of
Student's Book of College English, we have attempted to produce a true
second edition, not merely to perform cosmetic surgery on the first.

- An entirely new chapter on research papers broadens the scope
  of the original book.
- The handbook has been expanded and simplified to make it
  more immediately accessible to students with significant problems in basic skills.
- The number of student themes has been increased.
- Almost all of the original readings have been replaced. As good
  as many of the selections may have been, a living book—like a
  living teacher—must contend with the constant danger of
  going stale.

One of the unorthodox, possibly unique, features of the first
edition of *Student's Book* was the mix wherever practicable of readings for use as models and readings for use as subjects for compositions. We believe this mix significantly increased the versatility and
appeal of the book and helped account for its success. This principle
has been maintained in the second edition. Users will find, for
example, student and professional models of process writing, but
they will also find two short stories that can profitably be studied
and analyzed by students writing their own process papers.

We hope that clear prose and good sense also made their contributions to the success of the first edition. We have tried to keep
them constantly in mind in writing the second.

The authors wish to acknowledge with deep affection and
gratitude the help and cooperation of Raymond Ackley.

Special thanks for competence and devotion must go to Mae
Jordan, who did most of the typing, and Ida Skwire, who took care
of permissions.

We have tried to thank personally all the former students whose papers are part of this book, and we would like to take this opportunity to thank those students whom we were unable to contact before publication.

DAVID SKWIRE
FRANCES CHITWOOD
Cleveland, Ohio
January, 1978

TO THE STUDENT
Preface and First Lesson

This book is written for you. We don't say that simply to win your confidence or to make you think well of us. We've felt for a long time that most textbooks are written for your instructor.

Writing textbooks for your instructor instead of for you is natural enough, in a way. Instructors, after all, must teach from the books, and no book that makes them unhappy is going to find its way into the classroom. Still, this book is written for you. Its purpose is to help you become a better writer than you are now. We believe that if you read this book carefully and ask questions in class whenever there are points you have any trouble with, you can improve your writing significantly. Neither we nor anyone else knows how to teach you to be a great writer, but—with your active participation—we think we can teach you to handle competently any writing assignment you're likely to get.

We've tried to write this book in a straightforward, unfussy fashion. We've tried to concentrate as much as possible on being helpful about writing situations that you'll really be faced with in class. We've tried to pick reading selections that we think will interest you, as they have interested our own students, and that demonstrate writing principles you can apply to your own work. We've included a number of student writings, too, because we feel that comparing your work solely to that of experienced professionals is unprofitable and unfair. These writings were prepared by college students for classes similar to the one you're taking. Most of them are solid, honest pieces of work—but that's all. They are not intended to dazzle you with their genius, and they didn't all get A's in class either. We hope you'll use them as general points of reference, not as supreme models of excellence. We hope that you'll often outdo them in your own writing.

Now for your first lesson.

While this book will give you a great deal of information about writing, almost all of that information grows out of four simple ideas—ideas that are sufficiently important and usable to be thought of as rules. We're not peddling magic formulas, however, and we're not suggesting that a ready-made list of rules and regulations can substitute for the experiences and discoveries and sheer hard work by which writers educate themselves. No list ever made the pain of having nothing to say less painful. And people—not lists—write dramatic first sentences, come up with fresh insights, and choose the perfect word. Any rules we set down here or elsewhere are useful only because they can give direction and control to the inevitable hard work and thus increase the chances that the hard work will be worth the effort.

Don't approach the four simple ideas that follow, therefore, as representing more than important guidelines. They're starting points, but they're not eternal truths. George Orwell once drew up a list of rules for writing, the last of which was, "Break any of these rules rather than say anything outright barbarous." As a more immediate example, this book will advise you to write well-developed paragraphs and avoid sentence fragments. That's excellent advice, and we take it seriously, but just two paragraphs ago we deliberately wrote a five-word paragraph that also happened to be a sentence fragment. Enough said.

Here are the four ideas on which much of this book is based:

1. Except for a few commonsense exceptions such as recipes, technical manuals, encyclopedia articles, and certain kinds of stories, poems, and plays, *writing should state a central idea.* (We call that central idea—or position, or stand, or contention—the *thesis.*)
2. *The primary function of writing is to prove or support its thesis.*
3. *The most effective and interesting way to prove or support the thesis is to use specific facts presented in specific language.*
4. *Writing needs to be well organized. Every statement must be logically connected to the thesis.*

We'll be repeating and expanding and sometimes strongly qualifying these ideas throughout the book, but they are the heart of what we have to say. They are not obscure secrets or brand new discoveries. They are the assumptions about writing that nearly all good writers make. They are the principles that nearly all good writers try to put into practice in their own work.

In the chapters that follow, we will discuss in detail the full meaning and implications of these ideas and try to show you the most effective ways of applying them to common classroom writing assignments.

DAVID SKWIRE
FRANCES CHITWOOD

STUDENT'S
BOOK OF
COLLEGE
ENGLISH

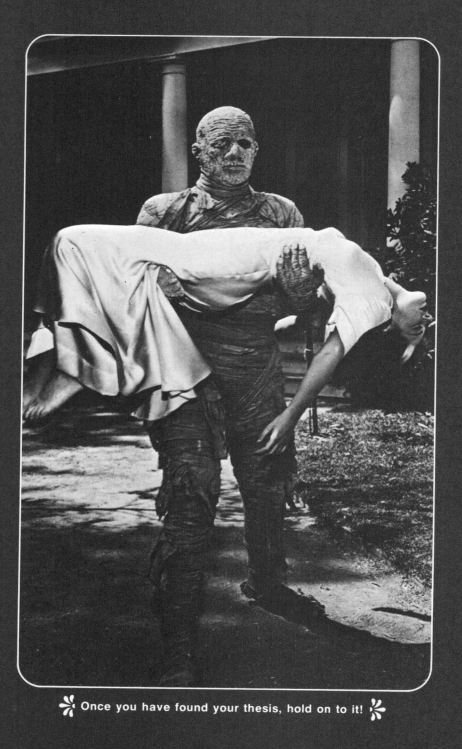

✿ Once you have found your thesis, hold on to it! ✿

PART 1

FUNDAMENTALS

The Principles of
Good Writing

1
FINDING A THESIS

2
SUPPORTING THE THESIS: LOGIC

3
PLANNING A PAPER: OUTLINING

4
WRITING A PAPER: AN OVERVIEW

CHAPTER 1
FINDING A THESIS

William Faulkner, who won a Nobel prize for literature, called writing "anguish and travail"—but he was probably just bragging. We don't mean to suggest that writing well is easy; it isn't. But we believe that following some well-chosen pieces of advice can make it easier than many freshman English students expect. Our first piece of advice is *think before you write*. Much of what makes any piece of writing good takes place before the writer ever puts pen to paper. In this chapter we will talk about the kind of thinking you should do before you begin to write.

Limiting the subject. Many college composition books begin by advising the student to choose a subject, but we won't do that because we think it's needless advice. After all, no one writes in a vacuum. If you choose to write, you do so because you're so interested in a subject—a sport, a vacation, a candidate, a book, a love affair, and so on—that you want to share your thoughts with others. Your enthusiasm selects your subject. If you don't actually "choose" to write but are told to do so by an instructor or employer, your general subject will usually be given to you. Your professor of world history will seldom simply tell you to write a paper; he will assign a ten-page paper on some effects of Islamic culture upon the Western world. Your employer won't merely ask for a report; she will ask for an analysis of your office's operations which includes recommendations for cutting costs and increasing productivity. Even when your assignment is an essay based on personal experience, your instructor will give you a general subject: a memorable journey, an influential person, a goal, a hobby, a favorite newspaper or magazine. Choosing the subject, then, isn't really a problem.

But most subjects need to be *limited*, and that sometimes is a problem. Suppose, for instance, that your instructor is an old-fashioned type and wants you to write about your vacation. No matter how short your vacation might have been, if you set out to discuss every detail of it, you could fill a book. Since most classroom assignments call for only three hundred to one thousand words, the subject must be limited. You must decide what part of the subject you will write about. A good way to begin is to jot down memorable moments, pleasant and unpleasant. Even that list may prove to be lengthy. You might remember dancing all night and then going for a swim at sunrise, or the day your foreign car broke down in a small town where the only mechanic would service nothing but American products, or eating your first lobster, or meeting a village character, or watching the sunset over the ocean, or sleeping out under the stars, or being stuck at the top of a Ferris wheel for two hours. You might have noticed differences among motels and restaurants, or various accents might have fascinated you. Any one of these memories could make a good paper. How do you choose?

Let your major interests decide for you. If you have a sense of the comic, you might decide to write about the mechanic who couldn't help you, or about sitting high in the air on a broken Ferris wheel, or about your first attempt to get meat from a lobster shell. If you like to study people, you might decide to write about the village character, or about the people you met when you danced all night, or about the personalities of the waitresses who served you. If the way people talk interests you, the accents or colorful expressions of those you met on your journey could make a good subject for a paper. If scenery appeals to you, describe that sunset or sunrise or those stars. If you should find that no one experience is more memorable than another—and that rarely happens—flip a coin and settle on one so you can get on with writing your paper. You will probably have other opportunities to write about the remaining memories.

"All right," you may protest, "it would be easy enough to settle on a subject if I never had to write about anything but my vacation. But what about my history paper?" As a beginning student of history (or sociology or economics), you may feel that your problem is finding enough to say about any given subject, not limiting the subject. Still, we will stick to our guns and say that almost every subject can and must be limited, even when some limiting has already been done by the instructor.

Take that assignment about the effects of Islamic culture on the West, for example. Your first reaction might well be to try to assemble any effects you could come up with, devoting one section of your paper to each effect—but that would lead to a very dull paper. Think a minute. If your instructor expects you to handle some part of that topic, it is because you have had some preparation for it. You've probably read part of a textbook and heard lectures on the subject; you've heard class discussions about it; perhaps you've been asked to do some supplementary reading in the library. From all of these sources, you've already begun to appreciate the vastness of the subject, even before doing any further research.

As with your vacation, you can still limit the subject, and again your special interests can determine how you limit it. If, for example, you have a good understanding of architecture, you may decide to explain how the Islamic culture, forbidden by its religion to use human images, contributed to modern architecture by exploring the possibilities of geometric forms. Or you might discuss the influence of geometric form as design on modern sculpture. If you're a nursing or pre-med student, you could trace the contributions of the Islamic world to medical science. If you're an interested observer of the political scene, you might discuss the effects on early Islamic cultures of the lack of a centralized government, comparing these cultures with others of the same period that were governed by a pope or emperor. Your interests could lead to other subjects—from military strategy to love poems—and still fulfill the assignment. Any subject, then, can and must be limited before you begin to write, and your personal interests can often determine the way you limit it.

Setting your purpose. Once you've limited your subject, you need to set your purpose; that is, you should decide how you will communicate with your reader. Will you *describe* a process—for example, how to pitch a tent? Will you *compare* two campsites? Will you *report* an event—what happened when you unwittingly pitched your tent in a cow pasture? Will you try to *convince* the reader that an opinion you hold is valid—that one can have an enjoyable yet inexpensive vacation by camping in state parks?

You can't hope to write a coherent paper until you set your purpose, because it is the purpose that gives focus to your paper. It determines what you include and what you leave out. If, for example, your purpose is to describe how to pitch a tent, you won't discuss the deep satisfaction to be gained by sleeping under the stars or the delicious taste of a fish that you've caught yourself and cooked over an open fire. Your purpose is to give instructions for a particular activity, and you will do just that in the clearest manner possible. If, on the other hand, your purpose is to convince a reader that camping in state parks is enjoyable, you might very well describe not only the joy of sleeping under the stars and cooking over an open fire, but also the conveniences provided to campers by the park system and the fun of meeting people in the relaxed atmosphere that a campfire creates.

Your purpose, in other words, controls the content of your paper. It keeps you from getting off the track and writing just a haphazard collection of impressions about your subject. In the paper below, for example, the writer's purpose was to describe the process for changing auto license plates. By setting that purpose for himself, he determined what he would leave out of his paper. He would not mention the colors or designs of plates in different states; he would not discuss methods of selling plates in different states; nor would he argue that the cost of plates discriminates against the poor. He would limit his efforts to giving the clearest possible set of instructions for changing plates. Here is what he wrote.

Changing Your Auto Plates
BRADLEY COMP

Every spring there are a good number of Americans who become frustrated, pull out their hair, and cut their hands on sharp, rusted edges trying to accomplish the simple task of changing their auto license plates. Yet this task can be performed without anguish if you follow a simple three-step process. The materials necessary are the new plates, a screwdriver, and common household oil. You might also want to use plastic screws, which may be purchased at a neighborhood hardware store. These screws will make the task easier the following year because plastic screws don't rust.

Step one involves the removal of the old plates. First, apply a few drops of oil on the screws that secure the front license plates. This will help loosen up the rust that has accumulated and will make the removal of the screws easier. Next, go to the rear of the car. Again apply a few drops of oil. By this time, the oil will have penetrated the screws in the front. Now, return to the front of the car and remove the plates. Place the blade of the screwdriver in the screw-slot and remove the screws securing the front plate by rotating the screwdriver in a counter-clockwise direction. After all the screws have been removed, the plate will fall off the car. If you have purchased the plastic screws, discard the metal screws. If not, place the metal screws in the envelope that the new plates came in so they will not get lost.

Step two is easy and optional. Some car owners prefer to prepare their new license plates before mounting them. This simple step is done by applying shellac or car wax to the surface of the plates. This will help prevent the plates from rusting and will keep the plates looking new for many months to come.

The final step involves easy mounting of the plate. First, position the screw holes of the plate with those of the car. Next, take the plastic (or metal) screws, place them in the holes, and turn them clockwise with the screwdriver until they are tight.

Now that the front plate is finished, return to the back plate, where the oil will have penetrated the screws. Repeat the same three easy steps. When you have finished and both plates are tightly secured, break the old plates in half to prevent the possibility of theft and reuse.

Questions for Writing or Discussion

1. Where does the author reveal his purpose?
2. Is the purpose sufficiently limited for the length of the paper?

Does the paper contain any extraneous material? That is, does the author depart from his purpose?

3. The paper consists of an introductory paragraph and four body paragraphs. Does each of the body paragraphs clearly advance the author's purpose? How?

4. The paper does not have a conclusion. Do you think it needs one?

5. Does the author provide enough information for one following his instructions to accomplish the task? If not, what did he leave out?

Stating a thesis. In preparing to write your hypothetical paper, you have so far limited your subject and determined your purpose. In a few cases, you could, at this point, begin organizing your material. The purpose of "Changing Your Auto Plates," for example, is to describe a process. This purpose simply calls for the division of the process into steps and a full description of each step. Similarly, some of the reports you must write, such as those for your chemistry class, often require merely a straightforward presentation of what happens when. Or a question on a psychology exam might call for a classification of types of schizophrenia, in which case you would put labels on each type and describe each fully. But apart from highly specialized kinds of papers such as technical descriptions and reports, we would argue that *most* good writing, even classification or process papers, benefits from a central idea. When the writer has an idea to push, the idea unifies the paper and gives it life.

Think, for example, how dull and rambling a report about spending Christmas day with the family would be if you should begin with rising early in the morning and continue through brushing your teeth and dressing and so on until you report retiring at midnight. But many of the details of the day can be given life if you settle on a central idea: *Having Christmas dinner at my family's house requires nerves of steel.* Now you have a focus for the details. Mother takes the joy out of eating by constantly reminding the family that she overcooked the turkey, undercooked the peas, and forgot to make the cranberry relish. Father won't let the family eat anyhow because every fifteen minutes they must smile for his new, expensive camera and then listen to him swear at the defective flash bulbs. Kid Brother must be restrained from injuring other members of the family by shooting rubber bullets from his new Super-Duper Killer Gun. Grandpa drones on about how this younger generation doesn't understand the true meaning of Christmas. Sister Suzy sulks because her boyfriend didn't give her the diamond ring she had expected, while Sister Josephine complains that helping with the dishes will simply ruin her manicure. Having a central idea enables you to select the details which make for a lively paper.

To be sure you have the kind of central idea that will lead to an interesting and unified paper, you still have one more step to take in the process of thinking before writing: *You must state a thesis.*

A *thesis* is the position a writer takes on an arguable point—one on which more than one opinion is possible. It is the main idea which the paper will prove. The writer's purpose is to convince the reader that this position or idea is valid. A thesis statement is a one-sentence summary of the idea the writer will defend: *Students in technical programs should be required to take some courses in the humanities, for example;* or *The registration procedure on our campus could be simplifed.*

With few exceptions, the papers you will be asked to write in college will benefit enormously from a thesis. Your professors will expect you to do more than merely arrange the facts you have gleaned from a course in some logical order; they are interested in what you think about the facts. They will expect you to make some statement about the facts, to show what point you think the facts add up to. A professor of American literature won't ask you to summarize *Huckleberry Finn.* He wants to know what conclusions you reached after a careful reading of the novel: *Mark Twain's* Huckleberry Finn *is an indictment of slavery,* let's say; or *Mark Twain in* Huckleberry Finn *criticizes the violence of the pre-Civil War South.* Until you can make that kind of statement, you aren't ready to write because you don't have clearly in mind the point you will defend in your paper. And if you aren't certain of what your idea is, you stand little chance of convincing a reader of its validity. It's important, therefore, to spend time thinking your idea through before you start writing. This will save you time and grief in the long run.

A good thesis has five characteristics. For one thing, *it can usually be stated in one complete sentence.* That doesn't mean that you must present the thesis statement, word for word, in the paper itself. In fact, once you start writing, you may find that you want to devote a paragraph or more to presenting the idea of your paper. Still, it's good to have a one-sentence statement in your own mind before you begin writing. Until you can state the idea in one sentence, you may not have it under control.

A good thesis makes a statement about the facts. To say that Brutus stabbed Shakespeare's Julius Caesar on the Ides of March is to state a fact. A thesis, a statement *about* the fact, might read as follows: *Brutus succeeds in killing Caesar on the Ides of March because Caesar has grown too arrogant and proud to protect himself.*

A good thesis is limited; that is, the one idea stated must be one which can be clearly explained, supported, and illustrated in the space called for. A long magazine article might have as its thesis, *Contemporary soap operas appeal to all levels of society because the directors employ sophisticated camera techniques, the writers deal with current social problems, the actors have time to develop characters who become as familiar as old friends, and the plots provide the kind of suspense which is missing from prime-time shows.* But this won't do for a thousand-word paper; the thesis could not be developed fully in that short a space. A better thesis for a short paper might read, *Contemporary soap operas are thought-provoking because they often deal with current social problems.* An even better thesis would be, *The realistic treatment in* Ryan's Hope *of withdrawing life support from terminally ill patients effectively presented the dilemma doctors face in such cases.*

A good thesis is unified. Consider the thesis, *Many in the women's liberation movement are too shrill and see every inconvenience as evidence of sexism, but genuine discrimination against women has made the movement necessary.* This thesis says three things about the women's liberation movement: (1) Some of its members are too shrill; (2) some of its members find sexism in every inconvenience; (3) the movement is necessary to combat genuine discrimination. A writer who begins with such a thesis runs the risk of writing a three-part paper which has no central control. The point of emphasis is not clear. To emphasize that the movement is necessary, the writer must subordinate the other points to that idea or even save the other points for another paper.

> Although many shrill-voiced women use the women's liberation movement as an excuse to find sexism in every inconvenience, the movement is necessary to combat the genuine discrimination against women practiced by our society.
>
> OR
>
> The women's liberation movement is necessary to combat the genuine discrimination against women practiced by our society.

To emphasize the silliness of some of the women in the movement, the writer should subordinate the idea of the movement's necessity or, again, save the other points for another paper.

> Although some genuine discrimination against women is practiced by our society, the shrill voices of many women who see every inconvenience as evidence of sexism have made the women's liberation movement a laughingstock.
>
> OR
>
> The shrill voices of many women who see every inconvenience as evidence of sexism have made the women's liberation movement a laughingstock.

A good thesis is precise. It lets the reader and the writer know exactly what the paper will contain. Words such as *good, interesting, impressive,* and *many* are too vague to do the job. They say nothing about the subject: what is interesting or good to one person may appear dull or offensive to another. Don't say, "Agatha Christie's detective stories are good." Say, instead, "Agatha Christie's detective stories appeal to those who enjoy solving puzzles." Don't say, "My history class is interesting." Say, "My history professor makes history easy to understand."

But enough of rules. Below is a student paper which illustrates a carefully defined thesis: *The highly organized celebration of today's Halloween deprives youngsters of the kind of joy I experienced during the Halloweens of my childhood.* As you read the paper, notice how the details help to support the thesis.

Too Bad About Ol' Halloween
SHIRLEY LYTTON-CANNON

As I was sitting at the kitchen table one morning last week having my second cup of coffee and staring, as usual, at the back of the cereal box which promised me that its breakfast plan could help me lose the extra ten-pound ball and chain I was dragging around with me, I noticed the note my fifth-grade son had brought home from school the day before. It gave instructions as to how Halloween is to be celebrated in our community this year. As I read it, I could just about hear his pinch-nosed principal dictating it.

1. Only children who are toddler age to the fourth grade are allowed to trick-or-treat. These children must be accompanied by a parent or another adult.
2. Trick-or-treating may be done from 5:00 P.M. to 6:00 P.M. only, and only at the houses where a porch light is burning.
3. Only manufacturer prewrapped and sealed treats may be given.
4. Children from the fifth grade and older should meet at the elementary school for a Halloween party. Admission 75 cents.

There was something that made me dislike the whole thing. It certainly didn't seem like much of a celebration to me, but then it dawned on me that Halloween is one more thing that has changed with time and circumstance. My experience of Halloween while growing up in a rural area of West Virginia was certainly different from the experience offered my son by this superorganized, unexciting little program I was about to thumbtack to our bulletin board.

There were certainly no age restrictions then. If you were too young to find your way after dark up and down the footpaths which led to the various houses, perhaps an older brother would take you out for an hour or so and then bring you home so he could get on with his own "Halloween-ing." In fact, many young-at-hearts would don masks belonging to the younger children and trick-or-treat homes of friends who were known for the quality of their hard cider.

A time restriction was also unknown then. If any poor soul had dared to suggest setting a time limit of 5:00 to 6:00 P.M., he would surely have been branded a sourpuss, stick-in-the-mud, spoilsport or tightwad, and probably would have paid dearly for his lack of sensitivity for many Halloween nights to come. It seems to me that the unspoken rule was that we confine our trick-or-treating to Halloween night after dark, although a few cheeky boys would occasionally make the rounds the night before also. As I remember, they didn't do too badly. It wouldn't have done much good for people to burn porch lights as a signal of some kind, for part of the fun was unscrewing light bulbs as we left.

And we would never have settled for the candy treats of today (if you care to call them treats), the generally tough little waxy-tasting blobs, all pre-wrapped and sealed, preferably by Price-Waterhouse, to ward off the growing number of "sickos" who hate children as well as Halloween. Our treats were mostly homemade cookies and candy, with the best being given by Mrs. Wright or Opal Morgan. Mrs. Wright gave us popcorn balls that were a deliciously sticky reminder that Christmas was near, and Opal Morgan made melt-in-your-mouth peanut butter fudge which she passed out in fat, soft, unwrapped squares to be devoured on the spot.

But I think it was item 4 of the Halloween instructions that saddened me most. As I reread the instructions telling us of the party for older children, I understood the principal's reasoning, but I was sorry that my son was probably never going to have memories of mischievous "tricking" on Halloween night. Parties are okay, but they're no match for the exhilarating feeling of sneaking around in the dark, going from house to house soaping windows, throwing handfuls of shelled corn on porches and roofs, and then running and laughing as the owners came out the door to try to catch us at our work. There were always a couple of outhouses that were tipped over on their sides each year, or sometimes we'd get black grease from the mines and paint a nice big line of grease around the seat hole. Someone painted grease on our seat one year, and if I could have found out who it was, I would have thanked him personally, because my oldest sister, Mary Lou, who was acting very grown-up and prissy in those days, made a trip to the outhouse just before her date arrived to take her out. Her screams of angry protest made a lovely Halloween.

As I recall it, we went pretty easy on the people we thought were nice and then stepped up our activity as we got to houses owned by people who were known for their contrary dispositions. Most of us kids had had run-ins with them at one time or another during the year, and since we always had to "respect our elders," Halloween was the only time to get even. There was one particular man, Ol' Will Honeycutt, who seemed always to take the brunt of the tricking, and for good reason. He was the most sour, narrow-minded, loud-mouthed human being I have ever come across to this day. Every year we'd all get together and try to outdo each other in thinking of ways to fix him. One year we got fresh cow manure from the field and put it into a paper bag. Without making a sound, about six of us tiptoed onto his front porch, lit the bag with a match, pounded on the door as hard as we could, and then ran off the porch like a herd of stampeding elephants. Ol' Will came rushing out the door, saw the burning bag, and immediately stamped it out with his work boots. Lucky for him that he always wore the kind with high tops! Some pretty colorful language followed us into the dark night that year.

I guess I have never heard of a Halloween trick more creative than the one pulled off by my teenage cousins, Billy Gene, Bobby Lee, Joey, and Frankie Wisenhunt. They were all big, husky farm boys who had worked at one time or another for Ol' Will, and they knew of his disposition firsthand. That particular year they waited until about eleven o'clock when they could be sure he was sleeping, and then, carrying a bucket of whitewash, started walking toward Ol' Will's barn and a long night's work. Now Ol' Will had a wagon and a team of four black horses which he cared more about than he did for his wife and kids. The boys very quietly and expertly, I must admit, disassembled the wagon, hoisted the pieces up the side of the barn to the roof, and then reassembled and tied it across the eaves of the barn roof. When Ol' Will walked out the next morning, he not only saw his wagon perched on the roof, but inside the barn he found a team of zebras with whitewash stripes! He never did find out who the culprits were, but when I read about the people who play horrible tricks on children on Halloween, I sometimes wonder if maybe Ol' Will is back and trying to get even.

Well, that was a long time ago, and things do change—sometimes for the better, and sometimes for the worse. It really is too bad about Ol' Halloween, but not about Ol' Will.

Questions for Writing or Discussion

1. What is the writer's purpose? Does the writer state her thesis in one sentence? If so, where?
2. Does the writer's mention of the text on her cereal box and her need to lose weight contribute to her idea? If not, do the opening sentences contribute to the development of the paper? If so, how?
3. In how many ways does the writer contrast her experience of Halloween with that of her son? Are the points of contrast clearly made? If so, how?
4. The writer devotes a disproportionate amount of her paper to the tricking which took place during her childhood. Do you feel that so much attention to tricking makes her paper seem unbalanced?
5. Do you believe the paper would have been stronger if the writer had restated her thesis in the last paragraph?

Now for another example. Below is a student paper about the instructions for assembly which come with many children's toys. What is the thesis of the paper?

Things Are Seldom What They Seem
JAY THOMPSON

Having three children under the age of six, I've given a lot of thought to a disturbing characteristic of children's toys: everything from bicycles to teetertotters is sold disassembled, and the parent must put all the parts together if he wants the product to resemble the picture on the cover of the box. I guess I wouldn't even mind assembling the toys if it weren't for the instructions that come with the boxes of parts. According to the manufacturers, there are basically three types of instructions included with today's toys: "Easy to Assemble," "Easy to Assemble in Minutes," and "So Easy a Child Can Do It." All these labels are misleading. They are dishonest. They misrepresent the task ahead of the unsuspecting parent.

Last week, for example, I attempted to assemble a Junior Olympic Jungle Gym by following instructions which informed me that the contraption would be "easy to assemble in minutes." Had the writer been honest, the heading would have read, "Infinite Patience Required for Assembly," and the instructions would have read something like this:

Step one consists of hiring three burly men to help you carry the box to the area of the yard where you wish to assemble your Junior Olympic Jungle Gym.

Having already armed yourself with the newest dictionary on the market, you are ready for step two. Remove the directions from the box and read them over carefully, locating each part as needed.

Step three requires that you get in your car and go back to the store to obtain all the parts that you found missing in step two.

The real fun begins with step four, the actual assembly. Following the directions, locate legs A(4) and place them inside corners D(2) after winding chain C around the backyard fence. Next unwrap chain C from the fence and fasten it to crossbar B by means of the large S hooks (20) and small eyebolts (4)—or was that the other way around? Remove leg A_1 from the top of your foot and repeat the process with remaining chains (3).

At this time you may wish to take a coffee break before tackling step five. Now take crossbar B and insert in side of corner D_1, fastening securely. Unfasten bolts and pull shirt-sleeve out of corner D and refasten. Repeat process with corner D_2, omitting shirt-sleeve episode.

If you have chased the children away or have at least put cotton in their ears, you are now ready for step six. Despite the instructions to anchor the Jungle Gym firmly, do not go to the local boat store; instead, take the bag of cement that did not come in the box, mix it according to its instructions, and pour around legs—the gym's, not yours. With this step accomplished, you are ready to put on the seats, the swings, and the trapeze. I strongly advise waiting until tomorrow to install the slide.

As you step back to admire the finished product, you will find that you are ready for step seven, hiring the same three burly men to help you move the gym to the place your wife wanted it all the time. Aren't you glad you waited until tomorrow to install the slide?

"Easy to assemble in minutes," indeed.

Questions for Writing or Discussion

1. What is the writer's thesis? Does he state it clearly in one sentence?
2. The writer tells us how the instructions should have read, but he does not tell us how they did read. Does that omission affect the credibility of his argument? Why? Or why not?
3. The writer uses only one example, his experience of assembling a jungle gym, to prove his point. Do you think his point would have been stronger if he had used examples of instructions for several toys which require assembly?
4. At the end of the first paragraph, the writer uses three sentences, each stating the same idea. Do you believe this repetition is justified? Why? Or why not?
5. The paper describes a process, but it has a thesis and is certainly more interesting to read than are the usual instructions which come with items requiring assembly. Do you think manufacturers should include instructions of this sort with their products? Why? Or why not?

Exercise A

Which of the following items are thesis statements and which are not? Revise those that are not into acceptable thesis statements. Which of the original thesis statements are too general or too lacking in unity to make a good paper?

1. How to buy a new car.
2. Television debates between political candidates are a waste of time.
3. Langston Hughes is a famous black poet.
4. Professor Smith is a terrible teacher.
5. Professor Smith grades unfairly.
6. Watching football on television is interesting.
7. The best way to prepare a turkey.
8. Helpful faculty and upperclass students made my first day at college much easier than I expected.
9. The vocabulary used by *Time* requires constant trips to the dictionary. *Time* slants its reports to suit its political bias. The reports in *Time* are entertaining and informative.
10. The trouble with newspapers is that they never report good news.

Exercise B _____

Read the following article carefully and then, by answering the questions at the end of the article, see if you can state the thesis.

Dan Wakefield
WHY SOAP OPERAS ARE SO POPULAR

One of the most popular pastimes in America is largely regarded as a secret shame. Despite a growing (if often grudging) acknowledgement by the media that this kind of entertainment may not be all bad, many of the 20 million citizens who enjoy it every day are still reluctant to admit their habit in polite society. And yet it is not illegal, illicit or immoral.

It's soap opera.

Since the days of *Ma Perkins* and *The Romance of Helen Trent* on radio to the present era of *The Young and the Restless* and *Another World* on television, soaps have been accused of causing a staggering number of maladies, including high blood pressure, un-Americanism, shrinking of the brain, vertigo and "perversity."

Even the increasing variety of people who admit and defend their "soap"-watching face the attitude described by author Beth Gutcheon, who wrote in *MS.* magazine that "the fact that you're watching soaps isn't the sort of thing you want to get around."

The image of the typical soap viewer is that of the cartoon housewife in her tattered bathrobe popping bonbons all day and nipping from a bottle of cooking sherry. No doubt there are fans of such description, but they can hardly be accounted representative of the vast and various audience that is tuned in to soaps today, an audience that includes men as well as women, college students and senior citizens, garage mechanics and economists, New York street-gang members and professors of literature, secretaries and civil servants (who watch on their lunch hours), artists and housewives, actors and salesmen.

If there's any more misleading cliché than that "typical" mindless, sherry-soaked fan, it's the cliché of the soap-opera programs themselves as interchangeable sagas of sobbing women wringing their dishpan hands over unrequited love for the doctor who saved their life with emergency surgery, played in the slowest drag-time dialogue with melodramatic organ music in the background and nothing but a steady supply of coffee to nourish the neurotic characters.

Most current soaps are far more sophisticated technically as well as thematically, with, for instance, "libraries" of tape-recorded orchestra music replacing the old organ trills, inventive camera work with fade-outs for flashbacks, story lines built around contemporary social and psychological problems such as child abuse, women's conflict with marriage and career, venereal disease, ecology, female frigidity and teen-age runaways.

Several years ago, *One Life to Live* shot scenes on location at New York City's Odyssey House for drug rehabilitation, letting real ex-addicts speak of their experiences, while an actress on the program played a troubled drug user. This year the new show, *Ryan's Hope,* built a moving story around the moral and legal questions of withdrawing life support from a patient who had lost all medical hope of being more than a human vegetable. But these new, more topical problems have not simply replaced the old heartaches in the teary twilight that once typified soap opera and is still believed to be its sole climate by critics who haven't watched the programs in the past five years. Certainly there are plenty of tears in the current daytime dramas, but there is also a pleasant new presence of laughter, fun and playfulness on many of the programs.

You can still find soaps that employ the old formula elements of the genre to greater or lesser degree. But the fact is there are now 14 soaps on the air, and they're as different and similar as, say, 14 popular novels might be. They share certain things in common due to limitations of time, budget, format and tradition, but their settings, themes and plots, their ambience and attitudes differ greatly and appeal to different sorts of people.

Some viewers are drawn to the social contrasts dramatized in *One Life to Live,* with its mixture of working-class Poles, socialite WASP's, middle-class blacks and Catholic nuns. Others prefer *Another World* of affluent Beautiful People elegantly dressed, discoursing about polo, painting and architecture as well as the inevitable personal problems of daily-life drama.

Soap fans today may choose, according to their own taste, the mystery-story aura of *The Edge of Night,* or the sense of home and roots reflected in *All My Children,* or the psychiatric orientation of *General Hospital,* with its convincing dramatizations of doctor-patient therapy sessions. Millions still love the more old-fashioned style and feeling of *As the World Turns,* whose focus on the familiar themes of love and marriage in smalltown Midwestern America still appeals to fans after 20 years on the air. Many new viewers are enthused about the youngest soap entry that debuted last summer, *Ryan's Hope,* the first serial to be set in New York City, built around an Irish-Catholic family whose parents run the local bar and grille, and their friends and neighbors who include politicians, reporters and a canny local underworld boss. . . .

Perhaps it's not the story per se that captivates a fan but a particular actor or actress. One of the factors that has raised the quality of soaps in the past five years or so is the caliber of the cast members, many of whom have experience in Hollywood or on Broadway and find in daytime drama one of the steadiest and most lucrative sorts of theater work today, with salaries for stars going as high as $100,000 a year—and the likelihood of highly paid commercial work deriving from their high visibility and popularity with viewers.

Ruth Warrick, the actress who originally gained fame playing the first wife of "Citizen Kane" opposite Orson Welles and has appeared in 31 movies, has worked on TV soaps since the late 1950's. She says that actors and actresses who once scoffed at her doing soaps have changed their attitude: *"Now* they ask if I can help *them* get on a soap!"

Ruth also finds she gets more recognition and enthusiasm from her soap-opera roles than for her work in movies and theater. At a fashionable cocktail party for the road-company cast of *Irene* in Chicago she was politely applauded for her role in the musical until one woman cried out in recognition, "That's 'Phoebe Tyler'!," the role she plays on *All My Children,* and the place went wild.

Fans regard actors on soaps as *being* the role they play, not because of stupidity or naïveté, but because a different, more intimate relationship exists between the audience and cast of a soap than with a movie or a play. In a movie or play you see an actress play a role, and no matter how well she does it or how many times you go back to see it, she'll say the same lines, behave the same way, and her fate in the story will be the same. On soaps, however, you watch an actress or actor several times to five times a week, and every day they'll say and do different things, and maybe even their personality will change in the months and years that the story continues. An inevitable intimacy develops between the fans and the characters, a sense of closeness and kinship that you would feel for a friend or neighbor whom you see in the course of your daily life.

When I go to a movie I come back and talk about seeing, say, Mia Farrow playing the role of "Daisy Buchanan" in *The Great Gatsby,* or Al Pacino playing the role of "Michael Corleone" in *The Godfather,* but I don't think of those actors as *being* those characters. Yet, even though I know Mary Fickett, the first person to win an Emmy for acting in a soap opera, when I watch her on *All My Children,* I don't think of her as Mary Fickett playing "Nurse Ruth Martin," I think of her as "Nurse Ruth Martin." Discussing the show with other fans, I say things such as, "Do you think anyone as loyal as 'Ruth Martin' would really leave her husband for that new young guy with the beard?"

Okay, I know in my mind the difference between the player and the role on a soap, just as I'm sure Sammy Davis Jr. knows, but I understand why, when he and his wife pulled up at a stop light on Sunset Boulevard and saw in the next car the young actor Nick Benedict who plays "Phil Brent" on *All My Children,* Davis yelled over, "Hey 'Phil,' don't marry 'Erica'!" . . .

Many people living alone find their favorite soaps provide a substitute family that serves not only as an entertainment but as a kind of nourishment, a human contact and connection. In our time of swift social change and uprootedness, people of all ages and backgrounds find in the continuing daytime dramas a sense of stability and support.

Soap watching amounts to a craze among college students, with fans gathering to watch their favorite serials in fraternity houses and dormitories and student unions on campuses as disparate as Columbia University, Wheaton College, the University of Northern Illinois, Brooklyn College, and the University of Texas. In the past few years, some soaps have even been taught as part of the curriculum in courses on popular culture at Princeton, and anthropology at Ohio State; but the students' interest isn't so much academic as social and personal. They find their favorite soaps entertaining—and fun. The fun isn't only in watching but in talking about them afterward, debating the age-old question of all good story-telling: What will happen next?

This question is one of the bases of the continuing appeal of the soaps, for if it is answered in one of the show's "story lines," it is raised in another; if one couple is reconciled, another is rudely torn asunder, posing anew the question of what will happen next. This is an element that prime-time shows can't employ, for by their very nature the answer to "what happens" must be given at the end of the half-hour or hour. Each episode is complete in itself, and each of the main characters remains the same for whatever challenge will be faced in the following week. There will be new criminals for "Kojak" to capture, but "Kojak" will remain "Kojak," just as "Mary Tyler Moore" will remain "Mary Tyler Moore," and "The Rookies" will remain "The Rookies" through all these shows, which are like a series of miniature movies starring the same character rather than like a serial. . . .

The serial form [has] . . . built-in problems . . . for . . . TV dramatists, for instance, in the recognition that for each new installment there may be new readers/viewers who are coming upon the story for the first time and so there has to be continual recapitulation of what has gone before, of what the relationships are among the characters. On the soaps this leads to a sometimes dreary retelling of events by one character to another, repetitive recitals of what happened yesterday or last week that many viewers already know. It is this necessity that leads to the frequency of those kaffeeklatsches where relatives or neighbors fill one another—and thus the audience—in as to what's going on.

Daytime serials on TV are also handicapped by low budgets, a lack of space and limited numbers of sets. One reason for the popularity of hospitals is that they provide a common, useful meeting place for a variety of characters. Many soaps now have their own restaurant where couples and friends and even large groups meet and talk. Soap producer Bud Kloss says people kid him that in Pine Valley, the fictional town of his show, "the main industry must be restaurants," because they often use a set designed as a restaurant for people to meet in.

The low budgets may handicap the producers of soaps, but they also help make them the most profitable shows on the networks. The three major networks spend an estimated $50 million a year on the 14 daily soaps in return for a gross of roughly $300 million. The lavish production of the prime-time shows means they often take a loss, and as any member of a daytime serial or its production staff is quick to point out, "We support the nighttime shows."

The nighttime dramas are flashier, prettier, more prestigious, and yet most of them come and go, are canceled quickly, replaced by another souped-up production, while the soaps plod along quietly year after year. Because they are economical to produce, and because the networks know it takes a serial a long time to build a following, they are given more time to become established—usually at least a year or two unless their initial ratings are unusually bad. All new soaps start at the bottom, and even the best take years to rise to the top (it took *All My Children* from January of 1970 until September of 1974 to gain a No. 1 rating in the Nielsens), but once they capture their audience, they're here to stay for years, maybe decades.

Because of budget restrictions, soaps rarely get to shoot outdoor scenes, which results in what both actors and writers call "dramatic claustrophobia." You often see people entering or leaving a room on a soap, but you'll wait a long time to see anyone *outside* of it, which sometimes gives *viewers* a sense of claustrophobia as well.

But once a fan is hooked, he becomes less aware and less critical of such limitations of the daytime serial. Once the viewer begins to wonder what will happen next, he tends to forget that most of the action is taking place in a series of little rooms, that the dialogue is often repetitive, that a "day" in the story may take three to five actual episodes in the program. The sets become familiar, even comforting. The habits and manners of the characters, as well as their problems, become interesting. Their moods, their reactions, the clothes they wear are recognizable and reassuring. Becoming involved in a soap is like moving to a new neighborhood. At first it's strange and confusing, but after a while you start to know the people and place, and you begin to feel at home.

Questions for Writing or Discussion

1. Soap operas were once characterized by deathbed scenes, trembling organ music, and unrealistic plots. What subject matter and techniques characterize today's soap operas?
2. What is the relationship between the actors and the viewers of soaps?
3. Why are the plots of soaps more satisfying than those of prime-time shows?
4. What are some of the built-in problems of the serial form?
5. What is the thesis of the article?

Exercise C

For a change of pace, here are two short stories. After you have read the stories, see if you can state a thesis about each story that could be developed into a brief paper. Depending on your own tastes, you could come up with theses about the serious ideas, if any, underlying the humor, the mixture of fantasy and realism, the conflicts between young people and adults, etc.

Saki (H. H. Munro)
THE STORY-TELLER

It was a hot afternoon, and the railway carriage was correspondingly sultry, and the next stop was at Templecombe, nearly an hour ahead. The occupants of the carriage were a small girl, and a smaller girl, and a small boy. An aunt belonging to the children occupied one corner seat, and the further corner seat on the opposite side was occupied by a bachelor who was a stranger to their party, but the small girls and the small boy emphatically occupied the compartment. Both the aunt and the children were conversational in a limited, persistent way, reminding one of the attentions of a housefly that refused to be discouraged. Most of the aunt's remarks seemed to begin with "Don't," and nearly all of the children's remarks began with "Why?" The bachelor said nothing out loud.

"Don't, Cyril, don't," exclaimed the aunt, as the small boy began smacking the cushions of the seat, producing a cloud of dust at each blow.

"Come and look out of the window," she added.

The child moved reluctantly to the window. "Why are those sheep being driven out of that field?" he asked.

"I expect they are being driven to another field where there is more grass," said the aunt weakly.

"But there is lots of grass in that field," protested the boy; "there's nothing else but grass there. Aunt, there's lots of grass in that field."

"Perhaps the grass in the other field is better," suggested the aunt fatuously.

"Why is the grass in the other field better?" persisted Cyril.

The frown on the bachelor's face was deepening to a scowl. He was a hard, unsympathetic man, the aunt decided in her mind. She was utterly unable to come to any satisfactory decision about the grass in the other field.

The smaller girl created a diversion by beginning to recite "On the Road to Mandalay." She only knew the first line, but she put her limited knowledge to the fullest possible use. She repeated the line over and over again in a dreamy but resolute and very audible voice; it seemed to the bachelor as though some one had had a bet with her that she could not repeat the line aloud two thousand times without stopping. Whoever it was who had made the wager was likely to lose his bet.

"Come over here and listen to a story," said the aunt, when the bachelor had looked twice at her and once at the communication cord.

The children moved listlessly towards the aunt's end of the carriage. Evidently her reputation as a story-teller did not rank high in their estimation.

In a low, confidential voice, interrupted at frequent intervals by loud, petulant questions from her listeners, she began an unenterprising and deplorably uninteresting story about a little girl who was good, and made friends with every one on account of her goodness, and was finally saved from a mad bull by a number of rescuers who admired her moral character.

"Wouldn't they have saved her if she hadn't been good?" demanded the bigger of the small girls. It was exactly the question that the bachelor had wanted to ask.

"Well, yes," admitted the aunt lamely, "but I don't think they would have run quite so fast to her help if they had not liked her so much."

"It's the stupidest story I've ever heard," said the bigger of the small girls, with immense conviction.

"I didn't listen after the first bit, it was so stupid," said Cyril.

The smaller girl made no actual comment on the story, but she had long ago recommenced a murmured repetition of her favourite line.

"You don't seem to be a success as a story-teller," said the bachelor suddenly from his corner.

The aunt bristled in instant defence at this unexpected attack.

"It's a very difficult thing to tell stories that children can both understand and appreciate," she said stiffly.

"I don't agree with you," said the bachelor, "there was a little girl called Bertha, who was extraordinarily good."

The children's momentarily-aroused interest began at once to flicker; all stories seemed dreadfully alike, no matter who told them.

"She did all that she was told, she was always truthful, she kept her clothes clean, ate milk puddings as though they were jam tarts, learned her lessons perfectly, and was polite in her manners."

"Was she pretty?" asked the bigger of the small girls.

"Not as pretty as any of you," said the bachelor, "but she was horribly good."

There was a wave of reaction in favour of the story; the word horrible in connection with goodness was a novelty that commended itself. It seemed to introduce a ring of truth that was absent from the aunt's tales of infant life.

"She was so good," continued the bachelor, "that she won several medals for goodness, which she always wore, pinned to her dress. There was a medal for obedience, another medal for punctuality, and a third for good behaviour. They were large metal medals and they clicked against one another as she walked. No other child in the town where she lived had as many as three medals, so everybody knew that she must be an extra good child."

"Horribly good," quoted Cyril.

"Everybody talked about her goodness, and the Prince of the country got to hear about it, and he said that as she was so very good she might be allowed once a week to walk in his park, which was just outside the town. It was a beautiful park and no children were ever allowed in it, so it was a great honour for Bertha to be allowed to go there."

"Were there any sheep in the park?" demanded Cyril.

"No," said the bachelor, "there were no sheep."

"Why weren't there any sheep?" came the inevitable question arising out of that answer.

The aunt permitted herself a smile, which might almost have been described as a grin.

"There were no sheep in the park," said the bachelor, "because the Prince's mother had once had a dream that her son would either be killed by a sheep or else by a clock falling on him. For that reason the Prince never kept a sheep in his park or a clock in his palace."

The aunt suppressed a gasp of admiration.

"Was the Prince killed by a sheep or by a clock?" asked Cyril.

"He is still alive so we can't tell whether the dream will come true," said the bachelor unconcernedly; "anyway, there were no sheep in the park, but there were lots of little pigs running all over the place."

"What colour were they?"

"Black with white faces, white with black spots, black all over, grey with white patches, and some were white all over."

The story-teller paused to let a full idea of the park's treasures sink into the children's imaginations; then he resumed:

"Bertha was rather sorry to find that there were no flowers in the park. She had promised her aunts, with tears in her eyes, that she would not pick any of the kind Prince's flowers, and she had meant to keep her promise, so of course it made her feel silly to find that there were no flowers to pick."

"Why weren't there any flowers?"

"Because the pigs had eaten them all," said the bachelor promptly. "The gardeners had told the Prince that you couldn't have pigs and flowers, so he decided to have pigs and no flowers."

There was a murmur of approval at the excellence of the Prince's decision; so many people would have decided the other way.

"There were lots of other delightful things in the park. There were ponds with gold and blue and green fish in them, and trees with beautiful parrots that said clever things at a moment's notice, and humming birds that hummed all the popular tunes of the day. Bertha walked up and down and enjoyed herself immensely, and thought to herself: 'If I were not so extraordinarily good I should not have been allowed to come into this beautiful park and enjoy all that there is to be seen in it,' and her three medals clinked against one another as she walked and helped to remind her how very good she really was. Just then an enormous wolf came prowling into the park to see if it could catch a fat little pig for its supper."

"What colour was it?" asked the children, amid an immediate quickening of interest.

"Mud-colour all over, with a black tongue and pale grey eyes that gleamed with unspeakable ferocity. The first thing that it saw in the park was Bertha; her pinafore was so spotlessly white and clean that it could be seen from a great distance. Bertha saw the wolf and saw that it was stealing towards her, and she began to wish that she had never been allowed to come into the park. She ran as hard as she could, and the wolf came after her with huge leaps and bounds. She managed to reach a shrubbery of myrtle bushes and she hid herself in one of the thickest of the bushes. The wolf came sniffing among the branches, its black tongue lolling out of its mouth and its pale grey eyes glaring with rage. Bertha was terribly frightened, and thought to herself: 'If I had not been so extraordinarily good I should have been safe in the town at this moment.' However, the scent of the myrtle was so strong that the wolf could not sniff out where Bertha was hiding, and the bushes were so thick that he might have hunted about in them for a long time without catching sight of her, so he thought he might as well go off and catch a little pig instead. Bertha was trembling very much at having the wolf prowling and sniffing so near her, and as she trembled the medal for obedience clinked against the medals for good conduct and punctuality. The wolf was just moving away when he heard the sound of the medals clinking and stopped to listen; they clinked again in a bush quite near him. He dashed into the brush, his pale grey eyes gleaming with ferocity and triumph, and dragged Bertha out and devoured her to the last morsel. All that were left of her were her shoes, bits of clothing, and the three medals for goodness."

"Were any of the little pigs killed?"

"No, they all escaped."

"The story began badly," said the smaller of the small girls, "but it had a beautiful ending."

"It is the most beautiful story I ever heard," said the bigger of the ⸲ girls, with immense decision.

"It is the only beautiful story I have ever heard," said Cyril.

A dissentient opinion came from the aunt.

"A most improper story to tell to young children! You have undermined the effect of years of careful teaching."

"At any rate," said the bachelor, collecting his belongings preparatory to leaving the carriage, "I kept them quiet for ten minutes, which was more than you were able to do."

"Unhappy woman!" he observed to himself as he walked down the platform of Templecombe station; "for the next six months or so those children will assail her in public with demands for an improper story!"

Questions for Writing or Discussion

1. What is the point of the bachelor's story?
2. What details create an unfavorable impression of Bertha?
3. The wolf had been planning on pig and would have settled for pig. What brought about Bertha's doom?
4. How does the answer to the previous question support the point of the bachelor's story?
5. Why does the bachelor tell his story? Do his reasons fit in with the point of the story?
6. Does "The Story-Teller" as a whole have a central idea? If so, what is it?

Kurt Vonnegut, Jr.
HARRISON BERGERON

The year was 2081, and everybody was finally equal. They weren't only equal before God and the law. They were equal every which way. Nobody was smarter than anybody else. Nobody was better looking than anybody else. Nobody was stronger or quicker than anybody else. All this equality was due to the 211th, 212th, and 213th Amendments to the Constitution, and to the unceasing vigilance of agents of the United States Handicapper General.

Some things about living still weren't quite right, though. April, for instance, still drove people crazy by not being springtime. And it was in that clammy month that the H-G men took George and Hazel Bergeron's fourteen-year-old son, Harrison, away.

It was tragic, all right, but George and Hazel couldn't think about it very hard. Hazel had a perfectly average intelligence, which meant she couldn't think about anything except in short bursts. And George, while his intelligence was way above normal, had a little mental handicap radio in his ear. He was required by law to wear it at all times. It was tuned to a government transmitter. Every twenty seconds or so, the transmitter would send out some sharp noise to keep people like George from taking unfair advantage of their brains.

George and Hazel were watching television. There were tears on Hazel's cheeks, but she'd forgotten for the moment what they were about.

On the television screen were ballerinas.

A buzzer sounded in George's head. His thoughts fled in panic, like bandits from a burglar alarm.

"That was a real pretty dance, that dance they just did," said Hazel.

"Huh?" said George.

"That dance—it was nice," said Hazel.

"Yup," said George. He tried to think a little about the ballerinas. They weren't really very good—no better than anybody else would have been, anyway. They were burdened with sashweights and bags of birdshot, and their faces were masked, so that no one, seeing a free and graceful gesture or a pretty face, would feel like something the cat drug in. George was toying with the vague notion that maybe dancers shouldn't be handicapped. But he didn't get very far with it before another noise in his ear radio scattered his thoughts.

George winced. So did two out of the eight ballerinas.

Hazel saw him wince. Having no mental handicap herself, she had to ask George what the latest sound had been.

"Sounded like somebody hitting a milk bottle with a ball peen hammer," said George.

"I'd think it would be real interesting, hearing all the different sounds," said Hazel, a little envious. "All the things they think up."

"Um," said George.

"Only, if I was Handicapper General, you know what I would do?" said Hazel. Hazel, as a matter of fact, bore a strong resemblance to the Handicapper General, a woman named Diana Moon Glampers. "If I was Diana Moon Glampers," said Hazel, "I'd have chimes on Sunday—just chimes. Kind of in honor of religion."

"I could think, if it was just chimes," said George.

"Well—maybe make 'em real loud," said Hazel. "I think I'd make a good Handicapper General."

"Good as anybody else," said George.

"Who knows better'n I do what normal is?" said Hazel.

"Right," said George. He began to think glimmeringly about his abnormal son who was now in jail, about Harrison, but a twenty-one-gun salute in his head stopped that.

"Boy!" said Hazel, "that was a doozy, wasn't it?"

It was such a doozy that George was white and trembling, and tears stood on the rims of his red eyes. Two of the eight ballerinas had collapsed to the studio floor, were holding their temples.

"All of a sudden you look so tired," said Hazel. "Why don't you stretch out on the sofa, so's you can rest your handicap bag on the pillows, honeybunch." She was referring to the forty-seven pounds of birdshot in a canvas bag, which was padlocked around George's neck. "Go on and rest the bag for a little while," she said. "I don't care if you're not equal to me for a while."

George weighed the bag with his hands. "I don't mind it," he said. "I don't notice it any more. It's just a part of me."

"You been so tired lately—kind of wore out," said Hazel. "If there was just some way we could make a little hole in the bottom of the bag, and just take out a few of them lead balls. Just a few."

"Two years in prison and two thousand dollars fine for every ball I took out," said George. "I don't call that a bargain."

"If you could just take a few out when you came home from work," said Hazel. "I mean—you don't compete with anybody around here. You just set around."

"If I tried to get away with it," said George, "then other people'd get away with it—and pretty soon we'd be right back to the dark ages again, with everybody competing against everybody else. You wouldn't like that, would you?"

"I'd hate it," said Hazel.

"There you are," said George. "The minute people start cheating on laws, what do you think happens to society?"

If Hazel hadn't been able to come up with an answer to this question, George couldn't have supplied one. A siren was going off in his head.

"Reckon it'd fall all apart," said Hazel.

"What would?" said George blankly.

"Society," said Hazel uncertainly. "Wasn't that what you just said?"

"Who knows?" said George.

The television program was suddenly interrupted for a news bulletin. It wasn't clear at first as to what the bulletin was about, since the announcer, like all announcers, had a serious speech impediment. For about half a minute, and in a state of high excitement, the announcer tried to say, "Ladies and gentlemen—"

He finally gave up, handed the bulletin to a ballerina to read.

"That's all right—" Hazel said of the announcer, "he tried. That's the big thing. He tried to do the best he could with what God gave him. He should get a nice raise for trying so hard."

"Ladies and gentlemen—" said the ballerina, reading the bulletin. She must have been extraordinarily beautiful, because the mask she wore was hideous. And it was easy to see that she was the strongest and most graceful of all the dancers, for her handicap bags were as big as those worn by two-hundred-pound men.

And she had to apologize at once for her voice, which was a very unfair voice for a woman to use. Her voice was a warm, luminous, timeless melody. "Excuse me—" she said, and she began again, making her voice absolutely uncompetitive.

"Harrison Bergeron, age fourteen," she said in a grackle squawk, "has just escaped from jail, where he was held on suspicion of plotting to overthrow the government. He is a genius and an athlete, is under-handicapped, and should be regarded as extremely dangerous."

A police photograph of Harrison Bergeron was flashed on the screen upside down, then sideways, upside down again, then right side up. The picture showed the full length of Harrison against a background calibrated in feet and inches. He was exactly seven feet tall.

The rest of Harrison's appearance was Halloween and hardware. Nobody had ever born heavier handicaps. He had outgrown hindrances faster than the H-G men could think them up. Instead of a little ear radio for a mental handicap, he wore a tremendous pair of earphones, and spectacles with thick wavy lenses. The spectacles were intended to make him not only half blind, but to give him whanging headaches besides.

Scrap metal was hung all over him. Ordinarily, there was a certain symmetry, a military neatness to the handicaps issued to strong people, but Harrison looked like a walking junkyard. In the race of life, Harrison carried three hundred pounds.

And to offset his good looks, the H-G men required that he wear at all times a red rubber ball for a nose, keep his eyebrows shaved off, and cover his even white teeth with black caps at snaggle-tooth random.

"If you see this boy," said the ballerina, "do not—I repeat, do not—try to reason with him."

There was a shriek of a door being torn from its hinges.

Screams and barking cries of consternation came from the television set. The photograph of Harrison Bergeron on the screen jumped again and again, as though dancing to the tune of an earthquake.

George Bergeron correctly identified the earthquake, and well he might have—for many was the time his own home had danced to the same crashing tune. "My God—" said George, "that must be Harrison!"

The realization was blasted from his mind instantly by the sound of an automobile collision in his head.

When George could open his eyes again, the photograph of Harrison was gone. A living, breathing Harrison filled the screen.

Clanking, clownish, and huge, Harrison stood in the center of the studio. The knob of the uprooted studio door was still in his hand. Ballerinas, technicians, musicians, and announcers cowered on their knees before him, expecting to die.

"I am the Emperor!" cried Harrison. "Do you hear? I am the Emperor! Everybody must do what I say at once!" He stamped his foot and the studio shook.

"Even as I stand here—" he bellowed, "crippled, hobbled, sickened—I am a greater ruler than any man who ever lived! Now watch me become what I *can* become!"

Harrison tore the straps of his handicap harness like wet tissue paper, tore straps guaranteed to support five thousand pounds.

Harrison's scrap-iron handicaps crashed to the floor.

Harrison thrust his thumbs under the bar of the padlock that secured his head harness. The bar snapped like celery. Harrison smashed his headphones and spectacles against the wall.

He flung away his rubber-ball nose, revealed a man that would have awed Thor, the god of thunder.

"I shall now select my Empress!" he said, looking down on the cowering people. "Let the first woman who dares rise to her feet claim her mate and her throne!"

A moment passed, and then a ballerina arose, swaying like a willow.

Harrison plucked the mental handicap from her ear, snapped off her physical handicaps with marvelous delicacy. Last of all, he removed her mask.

She was blindingly beautiful.

"Now—" said Harrison, taking her hand, "shall we show the people the meaning of the word dance? Music!" he commanded.

The musicians scrambled back into their chairs, and Harrison stripped them of their handicaps, too. "Play your best," he told them, "and I'll make you barons and dukes and earls."

The music began. It was normal at first—cheap, silly, false. But Harrison snatched two musicians from their chairs, waved them like batons as he sang the music as he wanted it played. He slammed them back into their chairs.

The music began again and was much improved.

Harrison and his Empress merely listened to the music for a while— listened gravely, as though synchronizing their heartbeats with it.

They shifted their weights to their toes.

Harrison placed his big hands on the girl's tiny waist, letting her sense the weightlessness that would soon be hers.

And then in an explosion of joy and grace, into the air they sprang!

Not only were the laws of the land abandoned, but the law of gravity and the laws of motion as well.

They reeled, whirled, swiveled, flounced, capered, gamboled, and spun.

They leaped like deer on the moon.

The studio ceiling was thirty feet high, but each leap brought the dancers nearer to it.

It became their obvious intention to kiss the ceiling.

They kissed it.

And then, neutralizing gravity with love and pure will, they remained suspended in air inches below the ceiling, and they kissed each other for a long, long time.

It was then that Diana Moon Glampers, the Handicapper General, came into the studio with a double-barreled ten-gauge shotgun. She fired twice, and the Emperor and the Empress were dead before they hit the floor.

Diana Moon Glampers loaded the gun again. She aimed it at the musicians and told them they had ten seconds to get their handicaps back on.

It was then that the Bergerons' television tube burned out.

Hazel turned to comment about the blackout to George. But George had gone out into the kitchen for a can of beer.

George came back in with the beer, paused while a handicap signal shook him up. And then he sat down again.

"You been crying?" he said to Hazel.

"Yup," she said.

"What about?" he said.

"I forget," she said. "Something real sad on television."

"What was it?" he said.

"It's all kind of mixed up in my mind," said Hazel.

"Forget sad things," said George.

"I always do," said Hazel.

"That's my girl," said George. He winced. There was the sound of a rivetting gun in his head.

"Gee—I could tell that one was a doozy," said Hazel.

"You can say that again," said George.

"Gee—" said Hazel, "I could tell that one was a doozy."

Questions for Writing or Discussion

1. The author writes a story of the future in which he looks at trends today that disturb him and asks what life would be like if they continue for a hundred years or so. What other stories, novels, movies, and television programs can you think of that use the same approach?
2. What specifically is the author satirizing in modern America? Do you feel he has good cause to be upset?
3. What would the author feel is a correct definition of equality? How would Diana Moon Glampers define equality?
4. Why is the name Harrison Bergeron a better choice than a name such as John Smith or Bill Jones?
5. Name all the different kinds of handicaps in the story. Does each attempt to solve a different problem?
6. Specifically, what are the bad results of the misunderstanding of equality?
7. What is symbolized by the soaring of Harrison and the ballerina to the ceiling?
8. Does the fact that Harrison declares himself an emperor justify the society's fear of him?

CHAPTER 2

SUPPORTING
THE THESIS: LOGIC

The best way to convince a reader that your idea is worth considering is to offer logical support for your thesis. Although lengthy
books have been written about logic, we believe the subject doesn't
need to be as intimidating as these elaborate treatments suggest.
Common sense and fair play are the basic tools—and sometimes the
only tools—that conscientious writers need. As far as possible, then,
we will avoid fine philosophical distinctions and concentrate on the
most common logical pitfalls—the basic errors in thinking that can
turn up in anyone's writing.

To check your own logic and that of others, a knowledge of the
two kinds of logical thinking, *induction* and *deduction,* and of the
errors in logic, the *fallacies,* will be helpful.

Induction is the process of reasoning from the particular to the
general. It is the process of arriving at a general conclusion about all
the members of a class after examining some members of the class.
Induction is a useful tool because it isn't always practical or possible
to check every member of a class before drawing a conclusion about
that class. If, for example, you develop a stomach ache every time
you eat green apples, you may, without sampling every green apple
in the world, safely conclude that green apples give you a stomach
ache. You've made a generalization about all the members of the
class *green apples* after examining some of its members. Or maybe
you've noticed that for four Fridays in a row, Professor Hadley has
given a pop quiz. You may draw the useful conclusion that Professor Hadley is likely to give pop quizzes on Friday without waiting
until the end of the term to see if indeed he does give a quiz every
Friday.

But induction is useful only if the conclusion about a class is
drawn from a fair sampling of that class. What's fair depends on the
class. You don't need to stick your hand into twenty fires to
conclude that fire burns; one or two fires will do. Other classes
should be sampled more broadly. Conclusions about groups of

people, for example, should always be drawn from a representative sampling and even then should be qualified with words like *tend, may, are likely,* etc. (See Hasty Generalization and Overgeneralization, pp. 33–34; see also Chapter 5, "Writing an Example Paper.")

Deduction is the process of reasoning from the general to the particular. A generalization already established—by oneself or by someone else—is applied to a specific case. Deduction, like induction, is a useful tool. You've concluded, for example, that Professor Hadley is likely to give pop quizzes on Friday. When your roommate suggests one Friday morning that you cut classes and spend the day in the park, you say, "No, I can't go today. Professor Hadley is likely to give a pop quiz, and my average can't stand a zero." You've applied your generalization (Fridays are likely days for quizzes) to a specific case (this Friday) and just may have assured yourself a passing grade in Professor Hadley's class.

In its simplest form, the deductive process is stated as a syllogism: an argument consisting of a *major premise,* a *minor premise,* and a *conclusion.*

Major premise: Fridays are likely days for pop quizzes.

Minor premise: Today is Friday.

Conclusion: Therefore, today is a likely day for a pop quiz.

Perhaps a more sophisticated example is the syllogism implicit in the Declaration of Independence (p. 222):

Major premise: Rulers who violate basic human rights should be overthrown.

Minor premise: King George III has violated basic human rights.

Conclusion: Therefore, King George III should be overthrown.

Syllogisms rarely appear in writing or conversation in their pure three-part form. It is far more common to find *enthymemes,* condensed syllogisms in which one or more parts are missing, the writer assuming that the missing parts are clearly understood and don't need to be stated directly.

It's Friday, so I'd better go to Professor Hadley's class. (*Missing premise:* Fridays are likely days for quizzes in Professor Hadley's class.)

I don't trust him because he's sneaky. (*Missing premise:* Sneaky people should not be trusted.)

I hate movies with violence, and this movie is teeming with violence. (*Missing conclusion:* Therefore, I hate this movie.)

Syllogisms are worth serious study primarily because they enable readers and writers to examine the often unstated, and sometimes shaky, assumptions behind otherwise convincing arguments.

For a syllogism to be taken seriously, of course, both premises must be true. It's hard to imagine a syllogism that begins with the premise "The earth is flat" leading to any valid conclusion. But even if both premises are true, the reasoning process itself may be faulty and the conclusion invalid. Consider this syllogism:

> *Major premise:* English majors read a lot of books.
>
> *Minor premise:* David reads a lot of books.
>
> *Conclusion:* Therefore, David is an English major.

Despite the true premises, the conclusion still doesn't follow. The major premise merely says, "English majors read a lot of books"; it says nothing about other people who may also read books. Logically, David *may* be an English major, but he may also be a merchant marine who kills time on shipboard by reading, an invalid who doesn't enjoy television, a desk clerk whose job is boring, or just someone who likes to read for no particular reason. The logical structure of the argument makes no more sense than this syllogism: Grass is green; her hat is green; therefore, her hat is grass.

So far, we have talked about induction and deduction as if the processes were mutually exclusive, but, in practice, they aren't. You will seldom engage in one kind of thought without using the other. When you use induction, you usually have a hunch about what generalization the facts will add up to. If you didn't, you wouldn't have a guideline for handling the facts. Consider, for example, that observation about Professor Hadley's quiz-giving tendency. If you hadn't already suspected that Hadley was a Friday-quiz-giver, you might not have noticed that the pop quizzes did occur on Friday. Some deduction, therefore, was involved in the process of reaching the generalization about pop quizzes on Friday.

Similarly, in deductive reasoning you must also employ induction. A syllogism is only as valid as both its premises. To assure sound premises, you must be sure that your evidence is both adequate and fair, and that involves induction. Induction is important, too, when you present your material. Even if yours is the best of syllogisms, you probably won't convince a reader of its worth unless you offer support for it—reasons, statistics, facts, opinions of authorities, examples. The reader's agreement or approval depends on the case you build; it depends on evidence. In the Declaration of Independence, for example, Thomas Jefferson supported his case against George III by citing twenty-eight instances in which the king had violated basic human rights. The instances came from induction.

Whether your primary tool is induction or deduction, you need to make certain that the evidence you offer isn't based on errors in logic. In other words, you should avoid the following fallacies.

POST HOC, ERGO PROPTER HOC

This impressive Latin phrase means "after this, therefore because of this." The *post hoc* fallacy takes for a cause an event which merely happened earlier: for example, *A black cat crossed my path and ten minutes later I broke my ankle; therefore, the black cat caused my broken ankle.* Unless the speaker tripped over the cat, such a statement is as unreasonable as *Night follows day; therefore, day causes night.*

The *post hoc* fallacy often appears in political discussions. Haven't you heard people say things like, "The crime rate has increased since the governor took office; I'm certainly not going to vote for him again"? Possibly the governor could be held responsible for the increased crime, but before he could logically be blamed for it, a direct connection between his policies and the crime rate would have to be proved.

To avoid the *post hoc* fallacy in your own writing, think carefully about the events which immediately precede an outcome. They may have little or nothing to do with the real causes of the outcome. In Chekhov's "The Lottery Ticket" (p. 145), for example, Ivan Dmitritch, shortly after discovering that his wife does not hold the winning lottery ticket, threatens to hang himself. His despair, however, is not caused by that discovery. It is caused by new realizations about his life which have been prompted by his daydreams of great wealth. To attribute his despair to the loss of the lottery is to commit a *post hoc* fallacy.

CARD STACKING

Card stacking means using only the evidence which supports a thesis and ignoring that which contradicts or weakens it. Card stacking is dishonest and can sometimes do serious damage. Suppose, for instance, that a newspaper editor dislikes the mayor of the city. The editor could prevent the mayor's reelection simply by emphasizing reports of the administration's mistakes and playing down reports of its accomplishments. Soon, the readers of the newspaper would begin to think of the mayor as a bungler who shouldn't be reelected.

Unfair? Of course. It's also unnecessary. A reasonable thesis doesn't require card stacking. A writer can make concessions and still advance the argument: *Although the mayor has made some attempts to attract convention business, the efforts have been too few and too late,* for example. If a thesis isn't reasonable, if it requires card stacking for support, it probably isn't worth defending. A person writing about Williams's "The Use of Force" (p. 151), for example would have to resort to card stacking to prove the thesis, *The doctor's sole reason for injuring the child is to protect her and the community from diphtheria.* The doctor wants to do that, of course, but to say that is the *only* reason for his actions is to ignore his own admission that he enjoyed hurting the child. The thesis isn't worth defending and should be changed.

SLANTING

A variation of card stacking is *slanting,* using words whose connotations suggest approval or disapproval of the subject. A woman may be "skinny," or she may have "a model's figure." In both cases, she is underweight, but one term suggests scorn and the other approval. Similarly, George Washington may be described as "a militant revolutionary who was responsible for the death of many people." Or he may be characterized as "a great military genius who led his freedom-loving people in a victorious battle against tyranny." The conscious use of slanting to sway opinion usually occurs when a writer lacks enough logical evidence to support the thesis. Slanting, like card stacking, is dishonest and misleading when it is used as a substitute for logical argument. But slanting should not be confused with a writer's legitimate efforts to convey admittedly personal impressions and emotions.

HASTY GENERALIZATION

One snowflake doesn't make a blizzard, nor does one experience make a universal law. That one student has cheated on the last five psychology quizzes doesn't mean that all psychology students in the school are cheaters; to say so is to make a *hasty generalization,* to draw a conclusion about a group which is based on insufficient evidence. Establishing a thesis on the basis of a hasty generalization can make an entire paper unacceptable.

OVERGENERALIZATION

Overgeneralizations are similar to hasty generalizations. A hasty generalization results from drawing a conclusion about a large number on the basis of very limited evidence. Overgeneralization occurs, regardless of how much "evidence" is available, when one assumes that *all* members of a group, nationality, race, or sex have the characteristics observed in some members of that group: *"all* feminists are bra-burners"; *"all* blacks have rhythm"; *"all* Italians like spaghetti"; "the English are *always* cold and reserved"; *"never* trust a used-car salesman." Surely it's possible that some feminists wear undergarments, that some blacks can't dance, that some Italians prefer green salads, that some English people are volatile, and that at least one or two used-car salesmen are trustworthy. Words such as *all, never, always, every, true,* and *untrue* are seldom justified when dealing with the complexities of human beings and human institutions. You would do well in writing your papers to qualify potentially troublesome generalizations with words such as *some, seldom, tend, sometimes, frequently, seem, appear, often, perhaps,* and *many.* Both hasty generalizations and overgeneralizations lead to prejudice and superstition and to theses which cannot be developed logically and effectively.

NON SEQUITUR

The term means, "It does not follow." A *non sequitur* is a conclusion which does not follow from the premise:

> I always vote the Republican ticket because my great-great grandfather fought in the Union army.

Usually, *non sequiturs* occur because the writer or speaker believes there is a connection between the premise and the conclusion. In the above instance, the writer's thinking probably goes something like this:

1. The Union army served under President Abraham Lincoln, the first Republican president.
2. I believe in supporting the traditions of my ancestors.
3. Since one of my ancestors served a Republican administration, I support that tradition by voting Republican.

The writer does see a connection, to be sure, but is it a connection worth making? One might as well argue that since our earliest ancestors ate their meat raw, we should also eat raw meat to honor family tradition.

Not all non sequiturs are so obviously foolish.

We all know what happened at Hiroshima. We must vote against nuclear power plants.

Here, as in the earlier example, the writer draws a conclusion without revealing the steps in the thought process which led to that conclusion, and if the audience doesn't fill in the missing steps, it may be taken in by the argument and rush out to vote down nuclear plants. The steps in the process are as follows:

1. The bomb exploded over Hiroshima produced greater man-made destruction than the world had ever known before.
2. The bomb's power derived from energy produced by the nuclear fission of atoms.
3. Nuclear plants derive their power from energy produced by the nuclear fission of atoms.
4. Nuclear power plants could explode like the atomic bomb and produce the same kind of destruction which occurred at Hiroshima.
5. Therefore, the construction of such plants should be prevented.

Once the thought process has been revealed, the audience can consider the logic of the argument. *Can* nuclear plants explode like atomic bombs? If not, the writer's conclusion is questionable and perhaps should be rejected.

In your own writing, you can avoid non sequiturs by revealing the connection between the premise and the conclusion and by making certain that the connection is defensible.

IGNORING THE QUESTION

In ignoring the question, the writer or speaker deliberately or unintentionally shifts emphasis from the topic under discussion. As you will see below, the question can be ignored in several ways.

Ad hominem argument. Arguing "against the man" means making an irrelevant attack on a person rather than dealing with the actual issue under discussion. Suppose, for example, that Senator Goodfellow, who has admitted to cheating on his income tax for the past five years, proposes a bill for national health insurance. It would be a fallacy to attack the bill by arguing that its proponent is guilty of tax evasion. The bill may be logical, humane, and in the best interest of the country. If it is not, what are its weaknesses? The bill, not Senator Goodfellow's problems with the Internal Revenue Service, should be the subject of discussion.

Not all personal attacks, of course, are necessarily irrelevant. If Senator Goodfellow were seeking reelection, one could logically approve of his ideas and still vote against him because his character defects indicate the danger of trusting him in a position of power and responsibility.

Students sometimes employ the ad hominem fallacy in discussing literary works by rejecting a work whose author does not fulfill their idea of a good person:

> One cannot be expected to take "Kubla Khan" seriously. Coleridge admitted to writing it after he had taken dope.
>
> It is well known that Edgar Allan Poe was an alcoholic. His stories are nothing but the fantasies of a drunken mind.

Such a practice indicates little understanding of the artistic process or of human nature. Writers of questionable character have produced inspiring works which affirm the highest values of civilization, and those affirmations deserve consideration. After all, most of us are such a mixture of good and evil, of wisdom and folly, of generosity and greed that if we waited until we found a good idea proposed by a perfect person, we should wait long indeed.

Straw man argument. The writer or speaker attributes to the opposition actions or beliefs of which the opposition is not guilty and then attacks the opposition for those actions or beliefs.

> Parents who boast of never having to spank their children should feel shame instead of pride. Discipline and socially responsible behavior are vitally important, and people who sneer at such things deserve the condemnation of all concerned citizens.

Some parents might very well be able to boast of not having to spank their children and yet also demand of their children discipline and socially responsible behavior.

Begging the question. The writer or speaker assumes in the thesis something which really needs to be proved.

> Since students learn to write in high school, the college composition course is a waste of time and should be replaced by a more useful and stimulating course.

One who chooses to write a paper with that thesis has the obligation to prove that the students do learn how to write in high school before presenting plans for a new course.

Shifting the burden of proof. Logic requires that *he who asserts must prove.* It is not logical to say,

> I believe the flu epidemic was caused by a communist conspiracy, and you can't prove it wasn't.

For the assertion to be taken seriously, reasonable proof of a conspiracy must be offered.

Circular argument. Arguing in a circle means simply restating the premise instead of giving a reason for holding the premise.

> I like detective novels because mystery stories always give me great pleasure.

All that sentence says is, "I like detective novels because I like detective novels." One who begins a paper that way will be hard pressed to continue. Of greater interest would be the characteristics of the detective novels the speaker does like. Some readers like Agatha Christie's novels. How do her works differ from, say, Mickey Spillane's detective novels? Or Erle Stanley Gardner's? Surely one's taste for detective novels isn't indiscriminate. In other words, one needs a reason for liking detective novels, and to say that one likes mysteries because they give pleasure is not to give a reason. *Why* do the novels give pleasure? An honest answer to that question will provide a workable thesis and prevent a circular argument.

EITHER/OR

In this fallacy, the writer or speaker suggests that there are only two alternatives when, in fact, there may be more.

> Although I am quite ill, I must turn my term paper in tomorrow, or I will fail the course.

The writer presents only two alternatives; however, it is also possible that the instructor, recognizing the student's illness, might accept a late paper. Of course, if one is cursed with a professor who accepts no late papers, regardless of circumstances, then one actually has only two alternatives, and no fallacy exists.

ARGUMENT FROM ANALOGY

An analogy is an extended comparison. It is useful because it can clarify a difficult concept or dramatize an abstraction by comparing the unfamiliar with the familiar. But an analogy doesn't prove anything, because, regardless of the number of similarities between two things, there are always some differences. One can't assume that because two things are alike in some respects, they are alike in all respects.

> Learning to write a good essay is like learning to drive a car. Beginning drivers feel overwhelmed by the number of operations they must perform to keep a car moving—controlling the brake and the accelerator, staying in their lane, watching the cars in front of them while keeping an eye on the rear-view mirror. In addition, they must observe all traffic laws. The tasks seem insurmountable. Yet, in time, some of the operations become almost automatic and the drivers relax enough that they can even look at the scenery now and then. So it is with beginning writers. At first, they wonder how they can make an outline for a paper, write clear topic sentences, develop paragraphs, provide transitions, write good introductions and conclusions, and still observe all the rules of English grammar. As with driving, part of the process eventually becomes automatic, and the writers relax enough to concentrate primarily on the ideas they wish to develop.

That comparison deals only with the similarities of feelings resulting from the two experiences and is a successful analogy because it clarifies for the beginner the experience of writing. But if one extends the comparison to encompass other demands on drivers— checking antifreeze, acquiring new windshield wipers, mounting snow tires, repairing flats, maintaining brake fluid—the analogy breaks down.

Historical analogies present a similar problem. Certainly, we can learn from history, but we can't assume that because two events are alike in some respects, the outcomes will inevitably be the same. You have probably heard the argument that the United States is on the verge of collapse because conditions here—relaxed sexual mores, widespread demand for immediate pleasure, and political corruption—parallel those of the Roman Empire just before its fall. The argument doesn't consider that the forms of government differ, that the bases for the economy differ, or that the means of educating the population differ. The differences between the two societies don't justify the conclusion that the societies will take exactly the same course.

Analogy is useful for clarifying an idea; argument by analogy is usually dangerous because it may lead the writer to invalid conclusions.

Exercise

Following is a list of statements containing logical fallacies. Read them over and determine what type of fallacy each most strongly represents.

1. Every day after my two o'clock class, I develop a headache. Therefore, the professor of my two o'clock class causes my headaches.
2. Over fifty percent of the students in my college English class failed the diagnostic grammar test. High school teachers never teach grammar any more.
3. Of course he'll like the tacos. He's Mexican, isn't he?
4. Bill's father worked in the steel mills most of his life; that's why Bill organized a teacher's union.
5. You should never change horses in the middle of the stream; therefore, we should keep the incumbent president in office until the recession is over.
6. Senator Jones's bill proposing the government's financial support of public housing projects should be rejected because Jones has admitted to beating his wife.
7. I enjoy reading Shakespeare's sonnets because I just love poetry.
8. Because the university is not meeting its responsibilities to the students, it should be restructured in several ways.
9. If you don't approve my plan, I must assume you don't like me.
10. I don't understand why Abraham Lincoln is considered a great president. He was a warmonger who, by government proclamation, took away the property of a large number of citizens.
11. My opponent urges a review of the parole board. People like him, who want to free rapists and killers, are responsible for our unsafe cities.
12. Of course, he's the thief. He hasn't proved that he isn't, has he?

CHAPTER 3

PLANNING A PAPER: OUTLINING

Once you have a thesis and a general notion of how it can be supported logically, your next step is to plan the order of its development. What proof will you give first? What next? What examples will you use? Where? In some cases, the plan for your paper is set by your purpose. If, for example, you plan to describe a process, such as changing auto plates, all you have to do is to arrange the steps in the process in chronological order. Some reports of events also call for chronological order, and the planning involves simply grouping the details of the event under major headings: for example, discovering the fire, sounding the alarm, fighting the fire, and cleaning up the debris. If, however, your purpose is to convince, to develop a thesis, the plan may not be so obvious, and you will want to think carefully about the order in which you need to arrange your material.

Whatever the case, it's a good idea to plan your paper before you begin writing because if you don't, you may get so involved in choosing the right words that you forget where you want to go with the idea. An outline will keep you moving in the right direction. Part 2 of this text will show you many different methods of organization and will help you write papers using each method. For the time being, let's consider the general rules of outlining, of planning a paper.

The form of an outline gives a picture of the logical relationship of the parts of a paper to the thesis or purpose. So begin by stating the thesis or purpose. Then indicate all major divisions of the paper with Roman numerals. Mark the support for the major divisions with capital letters and support for the subheadings with Arabic numerals. If you are planning a very long paper, you may want to make further subdivisions. To do so, next use small letters—a, b, c—and then Arabic numerals in parentheses—(1), (2)—then small letters in parentheses—(a), (b). For short papers, the major divisions and two or three subdivisions for each will probably be adequate. Here, for example, is an outline for "Changing Your Auto Plates," which you read in Chapter 1.

Purpose: To show how to change auto license plates.

    I. Assemble materials
       A. Find screw driver
       B. Find household oil
       C. Buy plastic screws (optional)

    II. Remove old plates
       A. Oil screws
       B. Unscrew plates
       C. Discard metal screws (optional)

    III. Prepare new plates (optional)

    IV. Mount new plates
       A. Position plate with screw holes
       B. Screw on plates

    V. Break old plates

The outline for a longer, more complex paper might look like this:

Purpose: To illustrate the outline for a complex paper.

    I. Major division
       A. First-level subdivision
          1. Second-level subdivision
          2. Second-level subdivision
             a. Third-level subdivision
             b. Third-level subdivision
                (1) Fourth-level subdivision
                (2) Fourth-level subdivision
       B. First-level subdivision
          1. Second-level subdivision
          2. Second-level subdivision

    II. Major division
       A. First-level subdivision
          1. Second-level subdivision
          2. Second-level subdivision
       B. First-level subdivision
          1. Second-level subdivision
             a. Third-level subdivision
             b. Third-level subdivision
          2. Second-level subdivision
             a. Third-level subdivision
             b. Third-level subdivision

          (1) Fourth-level subdivision
          (2) Fourth-level subdivision
             (a) Fifth-level subdivision
             (b) Fifth-level subdivision

Outlines are of two types, *topic outlines* or *sentence outlines.* The outline of "Changing Your Auto Plates" is a topic outline, one in which the writer uses just a few words or phrases to indicate the topics and subtopics which the paper covers. Topic outlines are sufficient for many short papers, especially for papers which classify or present a process. Longer papers and those which develop theses often profit from sentence outlines.

To write a *sentence outline,* you must sum up in one sentence what you want to say on each topic and subtopic. The sentence doesn't merely indicate the topic; it states what is to be said about the topic. This kind of outline forces you to think through exactly what you want to say before you begin to write. By constructing a sentence outline, you will find out whether you really have proof for your position.

Below is a sentence outline for a paper which argues that the Christmas season, though commercialized, still is a time of good will.

Thesis: Although Christmas has become commercialized, the spirit of the season nevertheless survives.

   I. Christmas has become commercialized.
      A. Media advertising suggests that viewers lack Christmas spirit if they don't buy, buy, buy.
         1. Commercials on children's shows imply that good parents buy expensive toys for children.
         2. Commercials on family shows imply that good friends deserve expensive gifts.
         3. Commercials on adult shows imply that affection from the opposite sex can only be gained or kept by giving expensive presents.
      B. Merchants, as early as Halloween, stand ready to satisfy desires created by advertising.
  II. The spirit of Christmas survives.
      A. The desire to help the unfortunate increases at Christmas.
         1. Shoppers toss coins into Salvation Army kettles.
         2. Readers respond to newspaper pleas for aid to the needy.
         3. Schools and clubs collect food and clothing for the needy.

B. The desire to share with friends increases at Christmas.
  1. People entertain at home with food and gifts.
  2. Clubs have parties at which members exchange gifts.
  3. Fellow workers share food and gifts at office parties.
C. The desire to share with family increases at Christmas.
  1. Families travel great distances to be with each other at Christmas.
  2. Families who are apart mail gifts and telephone each other at Christmas.

The outlines you have looked at so far show that whether your outline is topic or sentence, it should include a statement of the thesis or purpose of the paper and an indication by means of Roman numerals of the main points to be covered in the paper. Major and minor subdivisions, indicated by letters and Arabic numerals respectively, should show how the main points will be developed. The outlines also fulfill four other requirements:

1. *Do not make single subdivisions.* If you decide to subdivide a point, you must have at least two subdivisions. If there is an A, there must be a B; if there is a I, there must be a II. If you cannot think of two divisions, rephrase the heading so that no division is necessary.
2. *Use parallel grammatical form for headings of equal importance* to show their relationship to one another. If I reads "Assembling the ingredients," II should read "Mixing the ingredients," not "Stir up the ingredients."
3. *Make sure the divisions of an outline do not overlap and that you stick to a single principle of division.* You should not, for example, discuss books in terms of *fiction, nonfiction,* and *novels* because novels are logically a subdivision of fiction. You should not discuss the branches of government in terms of *legislative, judicial, executive,* and *crooked politicians* because one might find crooked politicians in any of the branches. You should not discuss people in terms of *overweight, underweight, normal weight,* and *handsome.* Obviously, *handsome* does not belong in a division which is based on a principle of weight.
4. *Make sure that headings and subheadings show a proper logical relationship.* In discussing athletes, you should not establish *Babe Ruth* as one major division and *baseball players* as a second. You might, however, have *great home-run hitters* as a major division, and *Babe Ruth* and *Hank Aaron* as subdivisions.

Exercise A

Point out the faults in the following outlines:

Purpose: To classify country music.
I. Folk music
II. Western music
III. Guitar music
IV. Hillbilly music

Thesis: The major political parties in America represent the prevailing attitudes of the public.
I. Democrats
A. Moderate
B. Liberal
II. Republicans
A. Moderate
B. Conservative
III. Skeptics
A. Disillusioned
B. Cynical

Purpose: To classify the divisions of the federal government.
I. The executive
A. President
II. Legislative
A. House of Representatives
B. Senate
C. Lawyers
III. Judicial
A. Supreme Court
B. Judges

Thesis: Foolish stereotypes about different nationalities distort our thinking.
I. Italians
A. Fat
II. French
A. Romantic
B. Charming
III. Asians
A. Chinese
B. Japanese

Thesis: Both Christmas and Easter are religious holidays which also provide an opportunity for secular pleasures.

I. Both are religious holidays.
   A. Christmas observes the birth of Christ.
   B. Easter observes the Resurrection of Christ.
   C. Halloween is the eve of All Saints Day.
II. Both provide opportunities for secular pleasures.
   A. Christmas is a time for parties and gifts.
      1. Families decorate trees.
      2. Children sing carols.
   B. Easter is a time for new clothes and egg hunts.
      1. The bunny rabbit is a symbol of Easter.
      2. Baskets are beautifully decorated.
      3. The President of the United States sponsors an egg roll on the White House lawn.

Exercise B

Below are nine statements which, if properly grouped, will develop the thesis, *Television commercials are a curse to be endured.* Decide which statements should be indicated by Roman numerals and which by capital letters. Then reconstruct the entire outline.

1. Some commercials detail the unpleasantness of irregularity.
2. Some commercials present husband and wife embracing their new car.
3. Some commercials raise false hopes.
4. Some commercials present mother and daughter listing the virtues of fabric softeners.
5. Some commercials offend the sensibilities of viewers.
6. Some commercials imply that the right deodorant can ensure social poise.
7. Some commercials detail the difficulty of keeping false teeth in the mouth.
8. Some commercials misrepresent family life.
9. Some commercials imply that the right toothpaste assures sexual success.

Exercise C

Write a topic outline of "Too Bad About Ol' Haloween" (p. 10).

CHAPTER 4

WRITING A PAPER: AN OVERVIEW

We will show you in Part 2 of this book how to develop different kinds of papers—comparison, classification, process, etc. But first, a few words about the characteristics of *all* papers seem to be in order.

THE INTRODUCTION

To begin, you need a beginning, or *introduction*. The simplest introduction identifies the subject and states the thesis. This is not to say that the bare thesis statement at the top of the outline must necessarily appear in the same (and often drab) form in the actual introduction. For example, the thesis statement for the outline of "Too Bad about Ol' Halloween" (p. 10) read, *The highly organized celebration of today's Halloween deprives youngsters of the kind of joy I experienced during the Halloweens of my childhood.* In the paper itself, the author stated her thesis this way:

> My experience of Halloween while growing up in a rural area of West Virginia was certainly different from the experience offered my son by this super-organized, unexciting little program I was about to thumbtack to our bulletin board.

Here's another example from a second student's theme. The thesis statement on the outline read, *The current resistance to enlistment, a reaction to the army's long involvement in Vietnam, should not prevent a young man planning his career from seriously considering the numerous advantages offered by today's volunteer army.* In the paper, the author wrote the following:

> One major change in attitude brought about by the Vietnam War is the feeling of antimilitarism prevalent among today's youth. After a decade of conscription to fight a war to which many were strongly opposed, it

has become unfashionable to express any opinion of military service but a negative one. Thus, many young men who might consider enlisting in the army are discouraged from doing so by peer pressure. But in view of the many benefits to be obtained by serving in the military, every young man should consider the facts objectively.

What matters is to present the *idea* of the thesis in the most interesting manner possible.

Here is yet another example of an introduction that simply identifies the subject and states the thesis:

> Ted Poston's "The Revolt of the Evil Fairies" (p. 154) tells of a little boy in an all-black school who, because of his dark skin, is forced to take the undesirable role of an evil fairy in the school's annual presentation of "Prince Charming and the Sleeping Beauty"; on the night of the production, he gets revenge by wrecking the play when he lands a strong right on the chin of Prince Charming, a light-skinned child. Although the tale is amusing, under its comedy lies a serious criticism of a culture in which white is seen as good and black as evil.

That introduction immediately identifies the subject: the first sentence gives the author and title of the story and a brief description of its content. The next sentence states the thesis of the paper.

Sometimes, in addition to identifying the subject and stating the thesis, the introduction actually lists the divisions of the rest of the paper.

> In this day of the liberated female, any woman who admits to attending college to catch a husband risks alienation, hostility, and ridicule. I'm not sure that's fair. Although I firmly believe that a woman, while she is in college, should get the best education possible, I see no harm in her looking for a husband at the same time. I believe that college is the ideal place for an intelligent woman to look for a mate. For one thing, it's easy to meet men in college. Then, too, college provides a setting in which friendships can grow freely and naturally into love. Besides, an educated woman surely wants a husband who shares her interests and tastes. What better place to find him than in college?

Here, the introduction identifies the subject, finding a husband while in college, and then states the thesis: *College is the ideal place for an intelligent woman to look for a mate.* The sentences following the thesis statement let you know how the argument will be advanced in the rest of the paper. You are prepared to expect the three reasons to be developed in such a way as to prove that college is the ideal place to find a husband.

In short papers, the one-paragraph introduction is common, but don't feel that you are always limited to one paragraph. Consider this introduction:

"I don't like to do my Christmas shopping early. I enjoy the bustle of last-minute crowds."

"Why should I start research for my term paper this early? I work best under pressure."

"I'll replace the washer on the bathroom sink Saturday when I have time to do it properly."

We recognize such statements, even when they are our own, for what they are—excuses for procrastination. We have, of course, been told from childhood that putting off until tomorrow what we can do today is bad practice, and we feel guilty about not following such good advice, so we make up excuses to justify our tendency to delay performing unpleasant tasks. Away with guilt. Away with excuses. Procrastination, far from being evil, can, in many cases, have positive effects.

The first three paragraphs give examples of the subject, procrastination. The fourth paragraph explains the examples and then, about the time the reader probably expects a humdrum list of ways to avoid putting off tasks, states a surprising thesis: Procrastination may be a good thing.

In a few instances, the introduction may not even declare the thesis at all. Consider the following introduction to "When I Get Rich" (p. 148):

Most of us sometimes dream about what we would do if we suddenly had a lot of money. The clothes we would buy! The gifts we would bestow upon our friends and loved ones! The trips we would take—first class all the way! When we engage in one of these flights of fancy, we dream only of gratifying every desire we have ever held. We don't dream of problems. How can there be problems with so much money?

Yet, sharing just a dream of money can cause dissension. Anton Chekhov's "The Lottery Ticket," for example, tells the story of a husband and wife who, when they believe the wife may have a winning lottery ticket, dream about money—and end up hating each other. Why should a few daydreams result in hatred?

This introduction, consisting of two paragraphs, identifies the subject—Chekhov's treatment of dreams of money in "The Lottery Ticket"—but it doesn't state the thesis. Instead, it asks a question. The answer to the question will make up the body of the paper, and the summary of the answer in the concluding paragraph will state the thesis.

In other words, many kinds of introductions are effective. You might, for example, occasionally try dramatizing a situation:

Sheila felt light-headed: her eyes would not focus and there was a slight hum in her ears. Her hands, wet and clammy now, shook so that she could hardly write. She could not concentrate. She wanted only to run, to be away from that terrible scene.

Sheila has not just witnessed some horrible accident which she must report. She is a freshman composition student who has just been told to write her first "in-class" composition. Many students will recognize Sheila's symptoms. Perhaps the following tips about writing a composition under pressure will help alleviate their pain.

The dramatization in the first paragraph attracts the reader's attention. The second paragraph explains the situation and anticipates the rest of the paper, which offers tips on writing a theme under pressure.

Or you could sometimes use an anecdote to illustrate the subject:

Mrs. Peters was busy talking to a neighbor over the telephone one afternoon when she suddenly experienced the frightening sensation that her baby son was hurt. She told her neighbor about her feeling and ran to check the baby, who was supposedly napping in his crib upstairs. To her horror, she found her son lying unconscious on the floor. Evidently he had tried to climb out of the crib but, in the attempt, had fallen on his head. Mrs. Peters' "knowing" that her baby was in danger is the kind of experience many of us have had at one time or another. Yesterday, for example, I dialed a friend and, just before his telephone rang, he had picked up the receiver to call me. Both of these incidents are illustrations of the kind of thought transference known as *telepathy*.

The two anecdotes illustrate the way telepathy, the subject of the paper, functions. The remainder of the paper will contain an extended definition of the term.

As you can see, introductions take various forms. The examples here by no means exhaust the possibilities, but they do illustrate some ways of getting into a subject. Whatever form you choose, it's important to remember that the introduction must interest your readers—after all, you do want them to read the remainder of the paper—and it should in some way prepare readers for what will follow.

THE BODY

You have learned from your study of outlining that the development of your purpose must be carefully planned. The body of your paper is the realization of that plan. In a sense, the outline serves as the table of contents for the body of your paper. It is not, however, enough simply to discuss each division of your outline, although that is essential. You must also *lead* your readers from one section to another in such a way that they don't become confused about what you are saying.

Topic sentences. One method of leading your reader is to write clear topic sentences for each paragraph. A topic sentence is to a paragraph what a thesis is to a paper: it expresses the central idea of the paragraph. The remainder of the paragraph will give proof of the topic sentence. If you work from a sentence outline, you may find that the sentences indicating major divisions serve very well as topic sentences. But whether you use sentences from your outline or make up new ones, you need topic sentences which clearly let the reader know what the idea of each paragraph is.

To illustrate, below is a student paper which develops the thesis *Attending college exposes a person to a unique set of frustrating experiences.* The writer supports his thesis by mentioning different kinds of frustrations students encounter and giving examples of each kind. His topic sentences (indicated by *italics*) identify the kind of frustration to be discussed in each paragraph.

The Frustrations of the College Student
R. B. CAMPBELL

Life is never simple. For the businessman, the housewife, the factory worker, and even (or perhaps especially) the young child, each day is filled with its share of frustrations and disappointments. The college student is not exempt from these incidents; in fact, attending college exposes a person to a unique set of such experiences.

Registration is an occasion which often gives rise to frustrating circumstances. Classes which are closed because they are filled, or due to lack of registrants, can destroy the most carefully planned schedule. Even if the desired classes are available, clerical errors can wreak havoc. A computer mix-up at Miami University during the fall quarter of last year sent an estimated 5,000 of the school's 11,000 students to the drop/add line on the first day of classes. To view such a line from near the end, as I did, can indeed be a frustrating experience.

Even if the desired class is obtained, *the instructor can make it seem as if it would have been more profitable to take some other course.* College professors are often chosen for their ability to learn rather than their ability to teach. Every student can tell of at least one professor who, although more than competent in his field, could not effectively communicate his knowledge to the class. Also, the more able a man is in his discipline, the greater the demands on his time. My cousin, a student at a small, private college, once took a nonrequired psychology course specifically because a well-known doctor was listed as the professor. The doctor, however, was rarely seen. Most of the classes were given by a graduate assistant, who also marked the papers and made up the tests. The much-hailed doctor was too busy to actually teach.

Perhaps the most frustrating experience for a college student is the realization that he has been following a course of study for which he is not suited. During my first five quarters of college, I was a chemistry major. It was not until after I had received failing grades in that subject from three different institutions that I finally came to the conclusion that it would perhaps be better if I studied a different subject. A friend of mine, an education major at Kent State, was not so lucky. It was not until he completed his student teaching experience, fifteen hours short of graduation, that he found he had no desire to teach. He will graduate at the end of the present quarter with a highly specialized degree in a field he has no desire to pursue.

College can be and should be a highly adventurous, rewarding period in the student's life. But like all other situations in life, it can often be fraught with frustration.

Topic sentences usually appear at the beginning of a paragraph, but they don't have to. They may appear anywhere in the paragraph. In fact, sometimes a writer can create suspense by placing the topic sentence at the end of the paragraph.

He drank noisily and chewed with his mouth open. He stuffed food into his mouth with his fingers and wiped his chin with the sleeve of his coat. He made loud, vulgar comments to the waitress, who had difficulty hiding her anger as other customers turned to stare. His idea of conversation was to regale his date with statistics about the World Series or facts about his expensive new car—especially its expense. *An hour with Bruce in the city's most costly restaurant made Jane wish she had dined at home alone on a tuna fish sandwich.*

You can put the topic sentence anywhere in the paragraph you want to, but you must make certain the idea of the paragraph is clear to the reader. That means making every sentence in the paragraph relate to the topic sentence. Such care will give clarity to your paper.

Exercise

Below is a group of short paragraphs without topic sentences. Suggest a logical topic sentence for each paragraph.

1. My sister wants to spend the family vacation at some expensive resort. Dad wants only a mountain stream and good fishing gear. Mom likes to visit old friends and sit and reminisce. I would like to say good-bye to all of them and hitchhike to California, but then we wouldn't have a family vacation.

2. Jim likes to listen to classical music while he reads a good book. His brother John snaps his fingers to country and western and

has to be forced to read anything more demanding than the sports page. Jim, a junior, is an "A" student; John, a senior, may not graduate this year unless he pulls up his math grade. Jim is considerate of the rest of the family: he doesn't monopolize the shower; if he comes in late, he does so quietly; he remembers birthdays with carefully selected gifts. John believes the family exists for his convenience: he stays in the shower for hours, singing off-key at the top of his voice; when he comes in late, which he often does, he slams doors and turns up the radio, and he never—but never—even sends a birthday card to another member of the family.

3. Two weeks after I bought my car, I parked it in front of a friend's house, and her neighbor's daughter backed into it, demolishing the left door. A month later, another friend's babysitter backed into it, demolishing the right door. After two months of calm, a harried housewife ran a red light as I was crossing the intersection and removed my right fender. A few weeks later, I discovered that a hit-and-run driver had banged into the left tail light during the car's stay in a parking lot.

4. The tuition at this college is the lowest in the state, but the quality of instruction is among the highest: the professors, who emphasize their roles as teachers rather than as researchers, seem genuinely dedicated to making their students learn. In addition to traditional courses, the college offers community-related courses in everything from cutting fur to reading income-tax forms. Finally, the college is located in the center of downtown so that it can easily be reached by public transportation.

5. The acting in opera is atrocious. The plots are absurd. The lyrics are abominable. Tickets cost a small fortune. Yet year after year, century after century, people by the tens of thousands find some reason to adore it.

Transitions. Another method of maintaining clarity and helping your reader follow your line of thought is the use of *transitional words and phrases.* Such words as *first, second, finally, consequently, thus, therefore, however, similarly, conversely,* and *furthermore* can show the logical connection between the parts of your paper. Some phrases serve a similar function. *In the first place, in the second place, in conclusion, in addition, on the other hand,* and *as a result* also help the reader see connections between one part of the paper and another.

Often the *topic sentence* serves both as a transition and as an indicator of the central idea of the paragraph.

Besides making life difficult for his parents, Charles sent his first-grade teacher home with a nightly headache.

Although the Puritans observed a strict code of behavior, their lives were often filled with great joy.

In sentences of this kind, the introductory adverbial phrase or clause points back to the preceding paragraph to provide a transition. At the same time, the rest of the sentence points forward to the subject matter of the paragraph for which it is the topic sentence.

Particularly in long papers, you may want to use a *transitional paragraph.* The following paragraph is taken from a paper on J. D. Salinger's *The Catcher in the Rye.* Up to this point in the paper, the writer has shown that the main character, Holden Caulfield, could be dismissed as simply a disturbed adolescent. In this transitional paragraph, the writer summarizes what has gone before and prepares for the second part of the paper, in which she will show that Holden may be disturbed, but that his disturbance has been caused by a society which he judges accurately. The italicized sentences indicate the beginning of the second section.

Holden, then, chooses fantasy over reality and rejects the real world, apparently without good reason. His negative attitudes are often unjustified. He expects perfection in others; he expects others to understand and cater to his desires, while he ignores the desires of others. He becomes greatly disturbed over minor problems. All of these ways of thinking are characteristically adolescent. *But before one dismisses Holden as being simply a disturbed adolescent, one must examine those aspects of the society which Holden finds objectionable. That examination will show that although Holden's method of expressing his disapproval is adolescent, he has, nevertheless, accurately judged the society which has made him its victim.*

Other effective transitional paragraphs may require only a few words:

So much for the preparation of the surface. Now we are ready to paint.

Thus, Jackie Robinson had to confront a long tradition of bigotry in the major leagues. How did he meet this challenge?

With all these arguments in favor of state-run lotteries, opponents of such lotteries can still raise some valid points.

Paragraph development. Besides leading your reader from one paragraph to another, you must be certain that each paragraph is adequately developed, that the idea of each paragraph is clear and complete. To do so, you can give facts, details, examples, or quotations of authorities to support the generalizations you make in the paragraph. Consider, for example, the difference between the following two paragraphs:

> Until a few years ago, there was a myth that the divorced woman, because of a generous alimony and child-support check, enjoyed a life of luxury and excitement. I wish that were so.

> The good life is supposed to begin as soon as a woman regains her freedom, or so I've been told. According to the script of the good life, a fat alimony and child-support check will carry the divorcee until she walks into a glamorous new job filled with challenge, excitement, and a fabulous salary. She will enjoy a spacious suite of rooms in an exclusive neighborhood. Her closet will bulge with expensive clothes from the finest boutiques. A classic automobile, perhaps an El Dorado, will wait for her to turn the key and carry her to exotic places and adventures with exciting new friends. My experience has not quite hit all these high spots.

Obviously, the second paragraph is more fully developed than the first, which contains nothing but the barest statement of the idea. The second paragraph brings the idea to life by spelling out the myth of the divorced woman.

Now consider the following descriptive paragraphs:

> My roommate's desk is a mess. It is covered with food, papers, clothing, and books. It is so cluttered that it took me three weeks to find my biology book, which she borrowed a month ago.

> My roommate's desk is a study in chaos. An ancient Royal typewriter with a sheet of paper in the carriage dominates the desk, but it has considerable company. The remains of three wild roses, picked two weeks ago during a walk with her boyfriend, droop from a Coke bottle. The petals have long since fallen on her open dictionary where they punctuate the definitions of words beginning with "I." A box of Ritz crackers and a jar of peanut butter serve as one bookend for her textbooks; a stained coffee cup with a spoon in it and a jar of instant coffee serve as the other. A rolled-up sweat shirt leans wearily against a stack of overdue library books. A sheaf of notebook paper containing many scrawls is, she says, the rough draft for her term paper in history. A manual for writing term papers is opened to the page on footnotes, where a McDonald's hamburger wrapper acts as a bookmark, and mustard from its former contents has stained the pages. A jar which once contained cold cream now holds ten or fifteen pencils and ball-point pens. Cigarette butts overflow a large green ashtray. Under the ashtray is my biology book, which she borrowed a month ago.

As in the earlier example, the second paragraph brings the description to life by providing specific details. The vivid description of the roommate's desk enables the reader to visualize it and even to make some inferences about the character of the girls. For these reasons, the fully developed second paragraph is more convincing than the first.

Not every paragraph need be so long, of course. The length of a paragraph is determined by its topic sentence. You have to decide how much material you need to develop the idea of the paragraph. Some ideas simply require more development than others. In every case, the material you include should relate to your point and should be as concisely stated as possible. In other words, you should never *pad* your writing. An intelligent reader can tell immediately if you are using words simply to fill up space and will probably reject your arguments, however worthy, because of your manner of presenting them. You should, then, use as many facts, details, examples, quotations, or reasons as you need to develop your point, but no more. You should not use words just to fill up space.

THE CONCLUSION

If you have written a thoughtful introduction and have led your reader, by means of topic sentences and transitions, through a logically and adequately developed body, your conclusion should be easy to write. A good conclusion gives a sense of finality, which may be achieved in one of several ways.

The easiest way to conclude a paper is to summarize its major ideas. The following paragraph concludes a paper in which the writer explains why he belongs to a book club:

> Convenience, variety, and economy—these were my reasons for joining a book club. I have not been disappointed.

Some conclusions merely restate the thesis, although in different words to avoid monotony. This is the case in " 'Why' Is Worse than 'What' " (p. 67):

> There's an explanation for everything, it's true, but some explanations are more readily acceptable than others. That's the way it is.

Some conclusions interpret the significance of the material presented in the body of the paper, as is the case in "Cruel Lib" (p. 69):

> In this country, circa 1975, lib has become a growth industry. Many who are otherwise talentless have made it their profession. But what Ralph Nader will hold them accountable for the Freds and the Gwens, for those who have been dispirited by a society that no longer prizes sexual

restraint or menial labor or the nuclear family? We have, I hold it self-evident, an inalienable right to be unliberated. This nation—another unattractive truth—doesn't need more personal freedom. The human spirit can be an unruly beast; a little restraint is wholesome. Let people be cherished for what they are, not for ambiguous thwarted gifts, or for the social responsibilities they default on. The men and women of Middle America have earned that small consideration. Really "creative" people will surface anyway. They usually do. And they will have their great rewards.

Other conclusions make predictions based on the material in the body of the paper.

Pollution is a major world-wide problem against which many powerful interests are being marshaled. From the private citizens who are concerned with the type of detergent or pesticide they use to the leaders of great nations, all thinking people are involved in the environmental crisis. There is still time for humanity to resolve this problem, as people are creative, inventive, and ambitious. These qualities, which are responsible for precipitating this crisis, will be the very means for humanity's salvation.

An anecdote sometimes effectively concludes a paper. The following is a conclusion to a paper about the rewards given Dr. Salk, inventor of the polio vaccine:

Probably the greatest tribute Dr. Salk has received for his work was unwittingly paid by a small boy whose father, having shown his son the research center, told him that Dr. Salk invented the polio vaccine. The boy, looking puzzled, said, "Daddy, what's polio?"

Quotations and questions can serve to conclude papers. Both devices are used in the conclusion to a paper urging support of the United Torch Drive:

Samuel Johnson defined a patron as "one who looks with unconcern on a man struggling for life in the water, and when he has reached ground encumbers him with help." Shall we be merely patrons of the needy?

Forms of conclusions, like forms of introductions, vary. All conclusions, however, should be related to what has gone before. In writing your own conclusions, be sure that you don't present irrelevant material—ideas which have not been prepared for in the body of the paper. Furthermore, all conclusions should be consistent in tone with the body of the paper. Don't let a strong argument just dwindle away because of a weak conclusion. If Patrick Henry, for example, had concluded his speech to the House of Burgesses with,

"Thus, Gentlemen, now that you have heard my arguments, I am sure you will agree with me that we should oppose the British crown," his words would not have been remembered. Instead, he said,

> Is life so dear, or peace so sweet, as to be purchased at the price of chains and slavery? Forbid it, Almighty God! I know not what course others may take; but as for me, give me liberty or give me death!

And all conclusions should be brief. Make the important points in the body of your paper. The conclusion should simply drive the points home.

A BRIEF NOTE ON STYLE

Finally, the style of the paper should be readable. We realize, of course, that a polished style doesn't just happen because some English teacher calls for it, and we have devoted an entire section of this book to a discussion of style. But for starters—even before your teacher subjects you to a rigorous consideration of stylistic elements—you would do well to study "Miscellaneous Do's and Don'ts" (pp. 377–379). Observing the suggestions given there should help assure that even your first papers will be readable.

❧ Good ideas can seldom be communicated ❧
without good organization.

PART 2

METHODS OF DEVELOPMENT

INTRODUCTORY NOTE:
WHY DIFFERENT METHODS?

5
WRITING AN EXAMPLE PAPER

6
WRITING A CLASSIFICATION PAPER

7
WRITING A PROCESS PAPER

8
WRITING A DEFINITION PAPER

9
WRITING A CAUSE AND EFFECT PAPER

10
WRITING A COMPARISON
AND CONTRAST PAPER

11
WRITING AN ARGUMENTATIVE PAPER

12
WRITING A DESCRIPTIVE PAPER

13
WRITING AN ANALYSIS OF LITERATURE

INTRODUCTORY NOTE
Why Different Methods?

So far, we have considered the general requirements for a good paper: every paper must have a purpose or a thesis; every paper must be logical; every paper must be organized. Now, we want to look at some requirements for particular kinds of papers.

Many writing assignments call for specific methods of development. In a psychology class, for example, you might be asked to *compare and contrast* psychosis and neurosis. In a history class, you might be asked to trace the *process* by which the Bolsheviks took power after the Russian Revolution. In a sociology class, you might be asked to *classify* the groups which make up a community, taking into consideration the level of income, education, taste, and social practices of each group. Each of these assignments requires a specific method of development, and this section of the text will show you how to meet those requirements.

Other writing assignments, though they may not call for specific methods, will profit from an intelligent combination of the methods discussed here. A definition, for instance, might require the use of comparisons, examples, and cause-and-effect methods. Thus, even though we have, for the purposes of discussion, arbitrarily established separate methods, we recognize that, more often than not, these methods will be combined.

We recognize, also, that our "rules" about methods of development are not sacred, even though we often deliver them as if we believe they were handed down by God to Moses along with the Ten Commandments. But we have discovered from our own students that at least some clearly stated guidelines are helpful to beginning writers. As you gain practice in writing, you will discover the exceptions to these guidelines that work for you.

CHAPTER 5

WRITING
AN EXAMPLE
PAPER

An example or illustration is a specific instance in which a generalization proves to be true. An example paper is one which relies almost solely on illustration for support of its thesis. An example paper, in many respects, can be thought of as a foundation for all the kinds of papers you will do. In a definition paper, for instance, a writer may use illustrations to clarify the definition. The writer of a classification paper may give examples of members of each category, but the primary purpose of the paper is to establish categories. An example paper, however, depends almost exclusively on a fully developed string—a kind of sophisticated list—of illustrations as its way of supporting its thesis.

Virtually all good writing depends heavily on examples as an important means of supporting ideas—and for very sound reasons. Examples give concreteness and therefore clarity to ideas. A writer might say, for instance, that the college student experiences many frustrations (as did the author of "The Frustrations of the College Student" [p. 50]), and, as a student, you may nod your head in agreement. But are you sure that you and the writer have the same understanding of *frustration?* If you supply your own examples for the word, aren't you likely to give it a meaning that the writer didn't intend? You might decide, for instance, that frustration comes from having to read so much. When, however, the writer exemplifies the idea with one story of standing at the end of a long drop/add line because of a computer mix-up, and another about disillusionment with professors, you gain a clear understanding of what *that* writer means by frustration. By making ideas concrete, examples also give them interest.

Even the smallest sentence sequence, therefore, will often be shaped by example:

> To convince a reader, the author must offer proof of any generalizations. In the Declaration of Independence, for example, Thomas Jefferson cites twenty-eight violations of basic human rights to support his assertion that George III is a tyrant.

Indeed, a writer may develop an entire paragraph by example, sometimes in a chatty and informal manner:

> I can do anything to keep myself from writing. I can sharpen pencils. I can dust my desk. I can consider whether to use white or yellow paper. I can arrange my dictionary at a neat 45-degree angle to the wall. I can stare vacantly out the window, praying for inspiration. I can sharpen my pencils all over again.

In a more formal paragraph, the writer may even choose to number the examples:

> Some of the greatest scientific discoveries are the result of inspirations caused by chance occurrences. Three brief examples can demonstrate this point. First, Archimedes' noticing the rise of the water level as he submerged himself in a tub led to the formulation of the laws of liquid displacement which are the foundation of many of the laws of modern physics. Second, Sir Isaac Newton discovered the law of gravity because an apple fell on his head while he sat under a tree. Third, after being caught in a strong current of hot rising air while flying his gas balloon, George Alexander Whitehead thought about this occurrence and developed the fundamental principles of meteorology. These and other incidents show that many of the greatest scientific developments spring from lucky accidents that stimulate work in a specific direction.

But our concern in this chapter is to look at an entire paper developed by example. In such a paper, the writer offers well-developed illustrations to support a thesis. The success of the paper depends largely on the quality of the illustrations and on their arrangement. We have a few tips that may help you select and arrange illustrations which will contribute to the success of your paper.

First of all, when the subject allows, you should try to select examples that represent a fair cross section of your subject. If, for example, you decide to write a paper to demonstrate that good manners are disappearing, don't wind up with all your examples about rude teenage boys. Try to distribute the examples among teenagers, middle-aged persons, and elderly persons. Try to find examples of both men and women who are rude. If you want to show that most of the teachers in a particular school are boring lecturers, try to find examples of some who are young, some who are middle-aged, and some who need to retire. Again, some of your examples should be women and some men, some perhaps single teachers and some married. Your examples should also indicate a fair distribution among departments. You don't want your examples to suggest that all boring teachers are single young women who wear glasses and teach English; the idea is that boring teachers pop up everywhere in this particular school, reflecting many different ages and backgrounds and subject areas and even ways of being boring.

Secondly, you should think about the arrangement of your examples. Many writers like to save their best example for last in order to achieve a dramatic conclusion. Others like to use their best example first to awaken interest. Certainly, the first and last positions in a paper are likely to get the most attention from a reader. Since some examples are more dramatic and convincing than others, you would do well to bury the weaker ones in the middle of the paper. Of course, if all your examples are excellent, you have nothing to worry about.

See what you think of the choice and arrangement of the examples in the following paper.

Winter Wonderland?

LUCILLE JORDAN

Irving Berlin dreamed of a White Christmas. Skiers' cars sport bumper stickers reading, "Think snow." Thousands who have never even seen a horse believe going over the hill and through the woods by sleigh would be the ideal means of travel. And certainly winter has its good points. For many, however, winter is a time of inconveniences, if not dangers.

To the mother, for example, severely cold and snowy days present a number of problems. She must see that her children are dressed warmly enough to withstand the chill of lowered thermostats in these days of fuel shortages. She must nurse them through colds and sore throats and occasionally break up snowball fights. In addition, she faces a never-ending supply of wet socks, wet snow suits, wet slacks, wet mittens, wet scarves, and wet jackets—all of which must go in the dryer. In her spare time, she mops up mud left on the kitchen floor by wet boots. If the mother can stay at home, however, her problems are few compared with those of the commuter.

To the suburbanite who commutes to work, winter offers the inconveniences and dangers of driving. On cold, snowy mornings, rear windows frost over, traffic crawls, and batteries die. Then, too, there are the dangers of the road. Chuck holes, hidden by fresh snow, can knock wheels out of alignment or break tie rods. On days when snow reduces visibility, some driver can be depended upon to maintain his usual speed and hit the car in front of him because he didn't see it. And even the most careful driver can hit a patch of ice and slide into a wall, a fence, or another car.

The commuter, if he is a homeowner, meets another set of inconveniences and hazards at home. Pipes freeze and break, leaking water all over the new carpet. Pilot lights go out, and the gas company can't send a repairman until tomorrow. Unless he wants to risk a lawsuit from a pedestrian who has fallen in front of his house, the homeowner must shovel walks and driveways. In avoiding a lawsuit, however, he runs the risk of frostbite or, if he is over forty, a heart attack brought on by over-exertion.

Sleigh bells make a pleasing sound, and fresh snow on the evergreens is a lovely sight. But such little pleasures do not make up for the inconveniences and dangers of winter.

Questions for Writing or Discussion

1. What is the thesis of the paper?
2. Does each of the examples help to clarify the thesis? If so, how?
3. Do the examples represent a fair enough cross section of the subject to justify the thesis?
4. Are the examples convincing? Why, or why not?
5. Could the examples be better arranged, or are they placed just right?
6. Can you think of other examples to support the thesis?

Readings

The following newspaper articles show how examples can be used to achieve humor.

Erma Bombeck
SWEET MYSTERY OF LIFE—CHILDREN

My goodness, the children have only been out of school for six weeks. Time flies when you're under sedation, doesn't it?

As I was hiding from them in the back seat of the car just last week it occurred to me that I don't know children at all. I'm raising three of them and yet they remain one of life's greatest mysteries.

For example, I don't understand how come a child can climb up on the roof, scale the TV antenna and rescue the cat . . . yet cannot walk down the hallway without grabbing both walls with his grubby hands for balance.

Or how come a child can eat yellow snow, kiss the dog on the lips, chew gum that he has found in the ashtray, put his mouth over a muddy garden hose nozzle . . . and refuse to drink from a glass his brother has just used.

Why is it he can stand with one foot on first base while reaching out and plucking a baseball off the ground with the tips of his fingers . . . yet cannot pick up a piece of soap before it melts into the drain.

Explain to me how he can ride a bicycle, run, play ball, set up a camp, swing, fight a war, swim and race for eight hours . . . and has to be driven to the garbage can.

It puzzles me how a child can see a dairy bar three miles away, but cannot see a 4 x 6 rug that has scrunched up under his feet and has been dragged through two rooms.

Why is it a child can reject a hot dog with mustard served on a soft bun at home . . . yet eat six of them two hours later at 50 cents each.

How come I can trip over a kid's shoes under the kitchen sink, in the bathroom, on the front porch, under the coffee table, in the sandbox, in the car, in the clothes hamper and on the washer . . . but we can never find them when it is time to cut the grass.

Why is the sun hotter delivering papers than it is goofing around . . . when it is the same sun?

How come they can't remember what time they're supposed to be home, but they remember they did dishes a week ago Wednesday two nights in a row because we had spaghetti and a spoon got caught in the disposal and they traded off.

I'll never understand how a child can't even find his English book when it is under his right hand, but can find his mother hiding out in the back seat of a car.

Questions for Writing or Discussion

1. What is Bombeck's thesis? Is the thesis stated directly?
2. Are the examples varied enough to make the thesis believable?
3. How does the use of phrases such as "how come," "I don't understand," "why is it," and "explain to me" contribute to the development of the thesis?
4. Are any of the examples weaker than the others? If so, which ones?
5. Could the order of the examples be changed without altering the effect of the article?
6. A good writing exercise might be to try to develop a paper by example which supports a gentler thesis about children.

George E. Condon
"WHY" IS WORSE THAN "WHAT"

To quote one of the comforting cliches that puzzled people have been falling back on for many, many years, "There's an explanation for everything." Truer aphorism was never circulated. It is also true that sometimes the explanation is just as incredible as the actual happening.

Take the experience of the couple from Lorain [Ohio] who bought a house trailer and went on a vacation trip to Florida. All went well until the return trip home. The husband grew weary after many hours at the wheel and finally abdicated the driver's seat in favor of his wife, while he went back to the trailer and fell asleep.

It was a nervous sleep, to be sure. He had never before trusted his wife at the wheel, and he was naturally uneasy over the risks involved. When the vehicle suddenly came to an abrupt, screeching stop, he immediately assumed the worst and leaped out the back of the house trailer to see what had gone wrong.

All that had happened, actually, was that a traffic signal suddenly had turned red and the wife had found it necessary to slam on the brake. By the time the husband, dressed only in his underwear, made his exit to the street and in his slow, sleep-fogged way sized up the situation, the light had turned green and the wife blithely drove away, leaving him in the middle of the intersection in his underdrawers. That's where a police cruiser came upon him a few minutes later.

"I can explain it all, officer!" said the husband to the policeman as his shivering shanks were hustled into the cop car. No doubt he did, in time, but the explanation could not possibly have been an easy one.

Which brings us around to a related dilemma that faced a woman in Clearwater, Fla., a few weeks ago when she drove her new luxury car with less than 1,000 miles on it to Sarasota, not far away.

Sarasota is the permanent home of the Ringling Circus, of course, and she parked her car in a lot near circus headquarters while she visited an art show. When she returned to her car it immediately occurred to her that there was something different about her new automobile. The roof, so to speak, had caved in.

But the mystery was quickly cleared up by a man who had come upon the scene.

"This your car, lady? Ah, you're probably wondering what happened to the old buggy to flatten it that way, eh? Well, you see, we were moving some elephants through the lot and one of them decided to sit down."

On top of her car, of course.

But the representative of the parking lot hastened to assure her that the Ringling people would repair the car. He noted that while the car looked rather bad, most of the damage was in the rear, and it could be driven. He gave her instructions on the repair procedure to follow and she got in the battered new car and swung it toward its Clearwater home.

On the way, however, a bad traffic accident caused considerable congestion at an intersection, and the woman decided on a short cut through a shopping center's parking lot. She was making this shrewd move when a police car cornered her and an officer leaped out and approached.

"Why are you leaving the scene of that accident?" he demanded to know.

"I'm not trying to leave an accident," she replied. "I'm trying to drive around one."

The policeman nodded. He was a reasonable man.

"Uh-huh," he said agreeably, "then you wouldn't mind telling me how that car of yours got smashed flat, would you?"

Now, then, all she had to do was tell the copper that an elephant had come by and sat on her car. A simple enough explanation, surely, but one that would take a bit of telling. "It was this way, officer. You see, an elephant came along and . . ."

There's an explanation for everything, it's true, but some explanations are more readily acceptable than others. That's the way it is.

Questions for Writing or Discussion

1. Condon states the thesis of the article twice. Find both statements. Do you think repeating the thesis is a good idea? Why, or why not?

2. Bombeck uses ten examples to support her thesis; Condon uses only two. Does Condon's limited use of examples affect the credibility of his thesis? Why, or why not?

3. Discuss the effect of the paragraph consisting of only a sentence fragment, "On top of her car, of course."

4. Why does Condon not complete the sentence, "You see, an elephant came along and . . ." (See *ellipsis*, p. 408.)

5. Can you think of two well-developed examples for a humorous paper with the thesis, "Life is filled with awkward (or embarrassing) moments"?

A long paper can be developed entirely by example. Most long papers, however, even those which make example the primary means of support, tend to combine example with other methods of development. An example paper is, at best, a list, and a list can't go on forever. Many writers, therefore, prefer to use examples in combination with other methods of development. D. Keith Mano's essay "Cruel Lib" is an argumentative paper. But as you read it, notice how heavily the author relies on examples to advance his argument. In fact, without examples, the essay would lose much of its appeal.

D. Keith Mano
CRUEL LIB

Let's call him Fred. I met Fred during his junior year at college. All Fred wanted was love and a rewarding sexual relationship—is that not an inalienable right by now? Fred was purposelessly big, overweight. His arm flesh hung down, white as a brandy Alexander, full of stretch marks. His face, in contrast, was bluish: acne scars that might have been haphazard tattooing. A nice guy, intelligent enough, but the coeds were put off. Fred wooed them at mixers with his face half-averted, as if it were an illicit act.

Fred was without sexual prejudice: as they say, he could go both ways. There was a militant gay-lib branch on campus. For months, struck out at mixers, he had considered joining. It was a painful decision: if he came out of the closet, Fred knew, his mother and father would probably go in—hidden there for shame. Yet mimeo sheets from gay lib offered a tacit, thrilling promise: new life, freedom. I remember the day Fred told me he had come out: he was relieved, optimistic. But being gay and free didn't cosmetize his face. When Fred let it all hang out, it just dangled there. After a while he noticed the good-looking gays dated the good-looking gays, as a first-string quarterback goes out with a home-coming queen. Fred had caused his family anguish for small compensation: he was now a wallflower in both sexes. Liberation. The tacit promise had been empty, and it had cracked his fragile spirit. Three months later Fred committed suicide.

Uncreative. Let's call her Gwen. The usual: $40,000 bilevel house, three kids, married to a good provider. Her unwed sister-in-law, however, ran the local women's-lib cell. Gwen's sister-in-law made fun of the drudgery: dishes; that unending double-play combo, hamper to washer to dryer; the vacuum she used and the one she lived in. It seemed so *uncreative*. Creativity, you know, is another inalienable American right. Gwen was 34 and, good grief, only a housewife. There were wonderful, though unspecified, resources inside her. After some time marriage, in Gwen's mind, became a kind of moth closet.

Ms. Gwen is divorced now. Mr. Gwen still loves her; he has taken the children. Gwen enrolled in a community college, but she didn't do well. Term papers were drudgery. For some time she made lopsided ashtrays at a Wednesday-night ceramics class. She was free and bored to death with herself. Now Gwen drinks a lot; she has some talent in that direction. Her children, well . . . all three understand, of course, that they were exploiting Gwen for twelve and nine and seven years respectively.

Nothing There. It's an unattractive human truth, but every now and then someone should put it on record: most people—Christians used to acknowledge this fact without embarrassment—most people are not particularly talented or beautiful or charismatic. Set free to discover "the true self," very often they find nothing there at all. Men and women who determine "to do their own thing" commonly learn that they have little of note to do. Yet these people are harassed, shamed by the Zeitgeist[1] and its glib armies into

Copyright 1975 by Newsweek, Inc. All rights reserved. Reprinted by permission.

1. Spirit of the times

disparaging their conventional roles. The bubble-gum tune goes like this: American civilization, through some spiteful, stupid conspiracy, means to thwart self-expression. We are all frustrated painters, explorers, starlets, senators. But there are times when it's more healthful to be frustrated than to have one's mediocrity confirmed in the light of common day.

Roles don't limit people; roles protect them. And, yes, most people need protection: deserve it. Not so long ago our society honored the husband and the wife, the mother and the father. These were titles that carried merit enough to justify a full human life. Remember the phrase? "It's like attacking motherhood." Times have changed. On the lecture circuit today, you can pull down a nice income plus expenses attacking motherhood.

Yet probably the cruelest of libs is education lib. Ed lib hasn't been formally incorporated, but it's very well sustained by an immense bureaucracy of teachers, professors, administrators, foundations, Federal agencies. Strike a match and you learn inside the pad how John earned respect from his bowling team as a correspondence-school computer executive. And on the crosstown bus they tell you DON'T PREPARE FOR TOMORROW WITH YESTERDAY'S SKILLS (picture of a wheelbarrow). Or, A MIND IS A TERRIBLE THING TO WASTE. Sure. But what about a pair of hands, damn it? Even at fifteen bucks per hour, we humiliate our labor force in a programmatic way. The elitism of it all is pernicious and disgusting.

Some few centuries ago another kind of lib prevailed. Christianity, they called it. Christian lib isn't a "now" item; it comes due in another life. Prerequisites are faith, works, humility: children are raised, things are made, to God's glory. Christians know personal gratification for what it is: a brummagem trinket. And this has been the shrewd beauty of Communism. Lenin cribbed his tactics from the New Testament. Liberation is promised through an arduous class struggle—but not in anyone's lifetime. This lib movement, moreover, functions within a powerfully structured, oppressive social system. Not only do totalitarian governments curtail personal liberty, but they are downright prissy when it comes to permissive sex. Yet people, in general, accept. Their roles are clear, and those roles are esteemed.

Unruly Beast. In this country, circa 1975, lib has becomes a growth industry. Many who are otherwise talentless have made it their profession. But what Ralph Nader will hold them accountable for the Freds and the Gwens, for those who have been dispirited by a society that no longer prizes sexual restraint or menial labor or the nuclear family? We have, I hold it self-evident, an inalienable right to be unliberated. This nation—another unattractive truth—doesn't need more personal freedom. The human spirit can be an unruly beast; a little restraint is wholesome. Let people be cherished for what they are, not for ambiguous thwarted gifts, or for the social responsibilities they default on. The men and women of Middle America have earned that small consideration. Really "creative" people will surface anyway. They usually do. And they will have their great rewards.

Questions for Writing or Discussion

1. What is the thesis of the article? Does the title accurately reflect the thesis?

2. Mano presents two fully developed examples, the stories of Fred and Gwen, before he begins to argue his point. Do you think he has chosen a good way to open his article? Why, or why not?

3. Mano implies that neither Fred's suicide nor Gwen's broken marriage would have occurred if it had not been for the gay and women's liberation movements. What logical fallacy might opponents of the author's position accuse him of?

4. In discussing "education lib," Mano uses three brief examples. Do you think they make his point as well as did the two fully developed examples at the beginning? Why, or why not?

5. With two or three well developed examples, oppose Mano's attack on "education lib."

Exercise

Develop a thesis which could enable you to use at least four of the following "wise sayings" as examples in a paragraph of about a hundred words or a brief essay.

Do unto others as you would have them do unto you.

Charity begins at home.

* * *

Still waters run deep.

A rolling stone gathers no moss.

* * *

A bird in the hand is worth two in the bush.

Nothing ventured, nothing gained.

* * *

A soft answer turneth away wrath.

The squeaking wheel gets the grease.

* * *

Better to be thought a fool than to open your mouth and remove all doubt.

Have the courage of your convictions.

* * *

Look before you leap.

He who hesitates is lost.

* * *

Leave well enough alone.

If at first you don't succeed, try, and try again.

* * *

You can't judge a book by its cover.

What you see is what you get.

Haste makes waste.

Seize the moment.

      * * *

Winning isn't everything; it's the only thing.

For when the One Great Scorer comes
To write against your name,
He marks—not that you won or lost—
But how you played the game.

      * * *

Many hands make light work.

Too many cooks spoil the broth.

      * * *

Absence makes the heart grow fonder.

Out of sight, out of mind.

      * * *

Patriotism is the last refuge of a scoundrel.

Breathes there a man with soul so dead
Who never to himself has said,
"This is my own,
My native land."

CHAPTER 6

WRITING
A CLASSIFICATION
OR DIVISION PAPER

In writing an example paper, you discovered that you need a thesis which is illustrated by a few examples. You enumerated, or made a list of, examples. Not all ideas or writing tasks lend themselves to list making, however sophisticated the list. Many subjects must be broken down into parts before they can be treated effectively; that is, the subjects must be *analyzed*. Two important techniques of analysis are *classification* and *division*.

CLASSIFICATION

You go to the library to get a book about Ernest Hemingway's novels. You find it shelved with other books of criticism on American authors. You turn to the want ads to see if there are any openings for a bookkeeper. You find notices of such jobs under the heading "Help Wanted." You want to send flowers to Aunt Mathilda, but you don't know where to call. You look in the Yellow Pages under "Florists." You want to buy cottage cheese at the grocery. You find it in the dairy section. You aren't sure whether to let your six-year-old child go to a movie with her older brother. You check the entertainment section of the paper and, finding that the film is rated "G," decide to let her go.

You can easily find your book or job listing or cottage cheese or information about movies and florists because someone has *classified* the subjects for you. *Classification* is the process by which one assigns members of a large group—ideas, people, plants, animals, books, poems, groceries, etc.—to categories on the basis of a single principle. A credit office, for example, might assign all applicants for credit (large group) to one of three categories: excellent risk, fair risk, poor risk. The assignment would be made on the basis of each applicant's ability and readiness to pay the bills when they come due (principle of classification).

Clearly, classification is essential to the credit office if the company is to remain in business. Classification is useful to others, too, because it enables them to cope with a large body of material by placing it in pigeonholes. Besides, we all like to classify. We do it naturally. Students classify their professors as boring or stimulating. Homemakers classify their cooking utensils, perhaps as those used often and those used occasionally, and place them in drawers and cupboards accordingly. But whether used for fun or for profit, classification has certain requirements, most of which you have already employed in developing outlines.

Decide what the basis for classification is and then apply it consistently. If you decide to classify the war poems in this chapter (pp. 85–94), you shouldn't establish as your categories realistic poems, brave warriors, and free verse. The first class is based on attitude, the second on subject matter, and the third on literary form. A logical principle would be attitudes toward war; then, the categories might be poems which glorify war, poems which attack war, and poems which assert that war does not significantly affect man or nature. If you wanted to classify the courses you are taking according to level of interest, you shouldn't establish as the categories *dull, moderately interesting,* and *difficult. Difficult* violates the principle of classification.

Keep the categories mutually exclusive. It would not be advisable to classify drivers as male drivers, female drivers, and truck drivers. Truck drivers may be male or female. Nor should you classify women as shy, pretty, and bold. Pretty women can be shy or bold.

In some cases, it is necessary to define terms. *You should, of course, define any terms which might be unfamiliar to the audience or which are used in a special way.* Eric Berne (p. 78) finds that *mesomorphs, ectomorphs,* and *endomorphs* have distinct personalities. Since these terms are not household words, they must be defined. Similarly, suppose you make up names of categories of customers in a store. Let's say you call them *impatients, nitpickers,* and *no-shows.* You must share with your reader your understanding of these made-up terms.

Decide whether you need only describe each category fully or whether, in addition to discussing the characteristics of each category, you need to list all or nearly all of its members. A classification of people as overweight, underweight, and normal, for example, would require merely a complete description of each type. Readers could, on the basis of the description, decide which category the various people they meet belong to. On the other hand, a classification of the present Supreme Court justices as liberals or conservatives, besides giving the characteristics of a liberal and a conservative justice, should also give the names of the justices who belong to each category and some explanation of why they have been placed there.

Have a thesis. In one sense, of course, the classification itself provides a thesis. One writer says there are three types, while another writer might see five types in the group. The point is therefore arguable. But as a classifier, you can take even stronger positions: *Unfortunately, most theology classes in Catholic high schools are a waste of time because all three kinds of instructors who present them are poor teachers,* for example. (See "Say Goodnight through the Screen Door," p. 75.) Or you could show that one of the categories is preferable to the others, or that all the categories are silly or despicable or admirable. Having a thesis will give force to your categories.

Establish some kind of order. In a few cases, you could order your categories according to time, from earliest to latest. Or, depending on your thesis, several other possibilities for ordering the categories present themselves: you might order the categories from worst to best, best to worst, least enjoyable to most enjoyable, or weakest to strongest, for example. In most listings, some members of the list are stronger or more interesting or more amusing than the others. Arrange your categories so that the weaker ones are in the middle of your paper. Hook your readers with a strong first category and leave them satisfied with an even stronger last category. The practice of ordering categories will make an important contribution to your classification papers.

See what you think of this student effort at classification.

Say Goodnight Through the Screen Door
DIANNA ESTOK

Most parents are under the impression that the purpose of a Catholic high school theology class is to teach students about God and to give them some understanding of their faith. These parents have the wrong idea. Throughout their high school years, many students are plagued with teachers who know shockingly little about religious topics. These so-called "religion teachers" make many high-school theology classes a total waste of time.

I suspect that almost every Catholic high school is furnished with at least one teacher from the category of Sister M. Sex Expert. (She is usually about eighty-five years old and probably never had a date in her life. If she did, Lord knows she didn't have him for long!) No matter what topic the class is supposedly discussing, whether it be "How we can fight poverty" or "Jesus

Christ is the Savior of mankind," after ten minutes, the discussion leads to advice on "sex" or dating. Some of her comments go like this:

> "Now, girls, never ever give your boyfriend a goodnight kiss on the first date. He might get the wrong idea and think you're cheap. Just go in the house and tell him goodnight through the screen door."
>
> "Boys, always marry a girl at least four years older than you. That way you'll both die at about the same time."

Usually her comments leave the class in hysterical laughter. If high school students don't know what dating is about by now, they're in big trouble. And what loving male wants to marry somebody just to be able to die with her? When the class decides to ask a serious question about sex, Sister M. Sex Expert gets all flushed and avoids answering the question directly. The course goes on like this all year, leaving the students no more knowledgeable about their religion than they were before entering the course. The class is great for a good laugh and an easy "A," since there aren't any tests and the grade is earned by class participation and hand-made posters.

The next type of teacher is a Mr. Work-on-Your-Own. He usually lets students pick out a quarter project of their choice, whether it be "A picture album of what love means to me" or "An interpretation of the current top ten, and how these songs relate to me." When the students finish these projects, he asks them to evaluate the projects and grades the students according to their evaluations. Naturally, most of the students think they deserve "A's" on their projects, and since this is the only grade the teacher has for each student, the majority of the students receive "A's" on their report cards.

In class, Mr. Work-on-Your-Own usually sits at his desk attentively reading a newspaper or some religious book. The class, on the other hand, learns to become expert on subjects such as spitball fighting, squirt-gun shooting, and just plain time wasting. Once in a while, there's a discussion, but the teacher seldom knows what he's talking about and loses control of the members of the class, leaving them to their own little discussions of sports, who's dating whom, and what's on the fourth-period algebra exam.

The last kind of teacher is Mr. Boring. He is usually very well versed in his subject, but his students need a Ph.D. to understand him. He requires students to take notes and gives so many that a student needs to be a shorthand expert to keep up. Students are never permitted to ask questions. Nonsense, such as questions, is definitely out in his class. After all, high school students should understand everything. He makes his class as dull and drawn out as possible, putting the majority of students to sleep. Mr. Boring's tests are as hard and as picky as he can make them. Usually everybody receives "D's" and "F's" on the tests and hence "D's" and "F's" in the course, showing once again that students have learned nothing.

With "teachers" such as these, Catholic students are destined just to float through life with no idea of what their faith is really about. In far too many schools, a religion class is nothing but a "hygiene" class, a free-for-all study hall, or a sleeping area, and unless the Church can provide better teachers, religion courses should be dropped all together.

Questions for Writing or Discussion

1. What is the group classified in this paper?
2. What is the principle of classification?
3. What is the thesis of the paper? Is it stated directly?
4. Which of the categories is the most interesting? Do you think the writer should have organized her categories differently? Why, or why not?
5. Select at least six good, specific details and discuss how these details help clarify the different types.
6. Think of a group of people you have observed—bus riders, or speech teachers, perhaps—and classify the group.

Division

In analysis by classification, a large group is broken down into smaller groups. In analysis by *division,* a subject usually thought of as a single unit is broken down into each one of its parts. An analysis of a stereo system, for example, requires naming and describing each of its components. An analysis of a poem requires studying each element in the poem—rhyme, meter, figures of speech, diction, image patterns, etc. An analysis of the federal government requires description of the three branches—legislative, executive, and judicial. In analysis by division, then, each element which helps to make up the whole is treated separately.

Despite the differences between classification and division, the rules for writing the two kinds of papers are almost the same, but they are so important that they can bear repeating here:

1. Decide what the basis for division is and then apply it consistently.
2. Keep the divisions mutually exclusive.
3. Define unfamiliar terms or those which are used in a special way.
4. Have a thesis.
5. Establish some kind of order.

Readings

Following are two essays composed by professional writers. The first is presented as an example of classification and the second as an example of division. Do the writers observe the rules for classification and division laid down in this chapter?

Eric Berne
CAN PEOPLE BE JUDGED BY THEIR APPEARANCE?

Everyone knows that a human being, like a chicken, comes from an egg. At a very early stage, the human embryo forms a three-layered tube, the inside layer of which grows into the stomach and lungs, the middle layer into bones, muscles, joints, and blood vessels, and the outside layer into the skin and nervous sytem.

Usually these three grow about equally, so that the average human being is a fair mixture of brains, muscles, and inward organs. In some eggs, however, one layer grows more than the others, and when the angels have finished putting the child together, he may have more gut than brain, or more brain than muscle. When this happens, the individual's activities will often be mostly with the overgrown layer.

We can thus say that while the average human being is a mixture, some people are mainly "digestion-minded," some "muscle-minded," and some "brain-minded," and correspondingly digestion-bodied, muscle-bodied, or brain-bodied. The digestion-bodied people look thick; the muscle-bodied people look wide; and the brain-bodied people look long. This does not mean the taller a man is the brainier he will be. It means that if a man, even a short man, looks long rather than wide or thick, he will often be more concerned about what goes on in his mind than about what he does or what he eats; but the key factor is slenderness and not height. On the other hand, a man who gives the impression of being thick rather than long or wide will usually be more interested in a good steak than in a good idea or a good long walk.

Medical men use Greek words to describe these types of bodybuild. For the man whose body shape mostly depends on the inside layer of the egg, they use the word *endomorph.* If it depends mostly upon the middle layer, they call him a *mesomorph.* If it depends upon the outside layer, they call him an *ectomorph.* We can see the same roots in our English words "enter," "medium," and "exit," which might just as easily have been spelled, "ender," "mesium," and "ectit."

Since the inside skin of the human egg, or endoderm, forms the inner organs of the belly, the viscera, the endomorph is usually belly-minded; since the middle skin forms the body tissues, or soma, the mesomorph is usually muscle-minded; and since the outside skin forms the brain, or cerebrum, the ectomorph is usually brain-minded. Translating this into Greek, we have the viscerotonic endomorph, the somatotonic mesomorph, and the cerebrotonic ectomorph.

Words are beautiful things to a cerebrotonic, but a viscerotonic knows you cannot eat a menu no matter what language it is printed in, and a somatotonic knows you cannot increase your chest expansion by reading a dictionary. So it is advisable to leave these words and see what kinds of people they actually apply to, remembering again that most individuals are fairly equal mixtures and that what we have to say concerns only the extremes. Up to the present, these types have been thoroughly studied only in the male sex.

Viscerotonic Endomorph. If a man is definitely a thick type rather than a broad or long type, he is likely to be round and soft, with a big chest but a bigger belly. He would rather eat than breathe comfortably. He is likely to have a wide face, short, thick neck, big thighs and upper arms, and small hands and feet. He has over-developed breasts and looks as though he were blown up a little like a balloon. His skin is soft and smooth, and when he gets bald, as he does usually quite early, he loses the hair in the middle of his head first.

The short, jolly, thickset, red-faced politician with a cigar in his mouth, who always looks as though he were about to have a stroke, is the best example of this type. The reason he often makes a good politician is that he likes people, banquets, baths, and sleep; he is easygoing, soothing, and his feelings are easy to understand.

His abdomen is big because he has lots of intestines. He likes to take in things. He likes to take in food, and affection and approval as well. Going to a banquet with people who like him is his idea of a fine time. It is important for a psychiatrist to understand the natures of such men when they come to him for advice.

Somatotonic Mesomorph. If a man is definitely a broad type rather than a thick or long type, he is likely to be rugged and have lots of muscle. He is apt to have big forearms and legs, and his chest and belly are well formed and firm, with the chest bigger than the belly. He would rather breathe than eat. He has a bony head, big shoulders, and a square jaw. His skin is thick, coarse, and elastic, and tans easily. If he gets bald, it usually starts on the front of the head.

Dick Tracy, Li'l Abner, and other men of action belong to this type. Such people make good lifeguards and construction workers. They like to put out energy. They have lots of muscles and they like to use them. They go in for adventure, exercise, fighting, and getting the upper hand. They are bold and unrestrained, and love to master the people and things around them. If the psychiatrist knows the things which give such people satisfaction, he is able to understand why they may be unhappy in certain situations.

Cerebrotonic Ectomorph. The man who is definitely a long type is likely to have thin bones and muscles. His shoulders are apt to sag and he has a flat belly with a dropped stomach, and long, weak legs. His neck and fingers are long, and his face is shaped like a long egg. His skin is thin, dry, and pale, and he rarely gets bald. He looks like an absent-minded professor and often is one.

Though such people are jumpy, they like to keep their energy and don't fancy moving around much. They would rather sit quietly by themselves and keep out of difficulties. Trouble upsets them, and they run away from it. Their friends don't understand them very well. They move jerkily and feel jerkily. The psychiatrist who understands how easily they become anxious is often able to help them get along better in the sociable and aggressive world of endomorphs and mesomorphs.

In the special cases where people definitely belong to one type or another, then, one can tell a good deal about their personalities from their appearance. When the human mind is engaged in one of its struggles with itself or with the world outside, the individual's way of handling the struggle will be partly determined by his type. If he is viscerotonic he will often want to go to a party where he can eat and drink and be in good company at a time when he might be better off attending to business; the somatotonic will want to go out and do something about it, master the situation, even if what he does is foolish and not properly figured out, while the cerebrotonic will go off by himself and think it over, when perhaps he would be better off doing something about it or seeking good company to try to forget it.

Since these personality characteristics depend on the growth of the layers of the little egg from which the person developed, they are very difficult to change. Nevertheless, it is important for the individual to know about these types, so that he can have at least an inkling of what to expect from those around him, and can make allowances for the different kinds of human nature, and so that he can become aware of and learn to control his own natural tendencies, which may sometimes guide him into making the same mistakes over and over again in handling his difficulties.

Questions for Writing or Discussion

1. Berne says that most people don't exactly fit into any one of these categories. In that case, is his classification justified?
2. Berne names each type and gives examples of each in his introduction. Do you find his introduction helpful to your understanding the subject, or do you find it repetitious?
3. Berne uses a number of Greek words in an essay written for lay readers. Does he provide adequate definitions of the terms?
4. Does Berne have a thesis in his article; that is, does he say something *about* the types?
5. At the end of each section, Berne explains why an understanding of each type is useful to a psychiatrist; the article, however, was written for lay readers, not psychiatrists. In this case, should Berne have included these explanations? Why, or why not?
6. Using Berne's categories, try your hand at classifying the members of your gym class.

Nona Aguilar
HOW TO WRITE A LETTER THAT WILL GET YOU A JOB

Whether you're just getting back into the job market after years out of it or you're looking for a better job to advance your career, you can double your chances of success by using a "tailored" letter.

What's a tailored letter? It's simply a brief letter highlighting background elements which most relate to the needs of a prospective employer. In other words, you "tailor" your experience to meet the needs of the person or company you want to work for. By following our simple guidelines, you can write a persuasive, concise letter that gets results.

Here's an example of the power of a tailored letter: My friend's mother, Mrs. Kinley, had been widowed for almost three years. She was 54 years old, her children were grown and she hadn't worked during the 29 years of her marriage. Now, with time on her hands, she wanted a job, but employment agencies discouraged her because, she was told, she didn't have skills or work experience.

Since she knew that I had always managed to rustle up a job no matter what or where, she talked to me about her problem. She realized that she didn't really want a full-time job; she had looked for one because it was the only type of work available through the agencies. And her only work experience was the hospital and Red Cross volunteer work she'd done throughout her marriage. We used that experience in composing her tailored letter, which she sent to 30 doctors (found in the "Physicians" section of the Yellow Pages).

What Were the Results? Within three days of mailing the letter, Mrs. Kinley had received four telephone calls. One wanted someone to work full time for five doctors in practice together; she declined that interview request but went on the other three.

While trying to decide which of two opportunities she might take—one of the positions wasn't offered to her after the interview—the mail brought a written reply asking her to call for an interview. On a hunch, she decided to make the call. That last interview turned out to be THE job: four days a week, from 9 to 1:30.

A postscript to the story: She received two more calls after she started working. She also got a few P.B.-O.s (Polite Brush-Offs) in the mail plus a "not right now but maybe in six months" letter. *That* is what I mean about the power of a tailored letter!

Measurable Accomplishments. Take a look at the letter Mrs. Kinley wrote. She used the Four Elements that form the basic structure of a good tailored letter: (1) an opening grabber, (2) an appeal to the self-interest of the reader, (3) a number of examples of her experience and (4) a good closing. The Four Elements are detailed . . . here, but as you can see, *specific accomplishments* are at the letter's heart. If your accomplishments are measurable in any way, you will look that much more impressive.

Here's what I mean by measurable. I landed a job teaching English in a language school in Italy. I was not a professional teacher; I had never taught in a school—obviously I had never been certified! However, one summer while I was still in high school, I started a little brush-up school in our family dining room to help three of my kid brothers and sisters. Four neighborhood kids joined my "class" and, through tutoring, I literally boosted English grades by about 13%.

The opening line of my tailored letter to the directress of the language school—the "grabber"—read: "I raised students' grades in English an average of 13% during a summer-school program which I began in my neighborhood." The letter made an impression, sailing past almost 100 weighty epistles and résumés sent by teaching professionals listing schools, courses, degrees and experience in abundance. When I came in for my interview, the directress was already anxious to meet me. My letter had shown an awareness of her major problem: Finding teachers who could actually teach—and could then prove it.

Mrs. Kinley's letter

```
March 1, 197-

Marvin Willis, M.D.
488 Madison Avenue
New York, NY ]0022

Dear Dr. Willis:

In the past several years, I have worked  (1)
over 6,000 hours in hospitals handling
bookkeeping and billing.

       I am writing to you because your office may
(2)   be in need of a woman with my background and
       experience to work on a part-time basis.  If
       so, you may be interested in some of the
       things I have done.

For example, I was responsible for handling
Wednesday receipts for a volunteer-operated
hospital gift shop.

I sorted 500 pieces of patient mail per week.  (3)

I handled all bookkeeping for the gift shop,
insuring payment of suppliers and disbursement
of profits to the hospital by the 30th
of each month.

       If such experience would be valuable to your
(4)   office to help with bookkeeping or billing, I
       would be happy to talk to you in more detail.
       My telephone number is EL 6-0000.

Sincerely yours,
```

THE FOUR ELEMENTS

1. AN OPENING GRABBER

Mrs. Kinley's letter begins with a short sentence listing a memorable figure: 6,000 hours of work experience in a hospital. This grabs the reader's interest.

2. SELF-INTEREST APPEAL

She appeals to his self-interest right away in her second sentence by letting the doctor know that those 6,000 hours are part of valuable experience which might be useful to him.

3. EXAMPLES

Mrs. Kinley gives three specific examples of accomplishments to further appeal to the self-interest of a would-be employer.

4. THE CLOSING

Mrs. Kinley does not plead for an interview. She doesn't even ask for one. Rather, she lets the recipient know she's a worthwhile professional person and that "if such experience would be valuable to your office . . ." she'd be happy to discuss it in an interview.

Specific Accomplishments. So I can't stress it enough: *The heart of a successful tailored letter is specific accomplishments.* When your accomplishments are measurable, you look even more impressive—but don't equate *paid* with *measurable.* Mrs. Kinley does not apologize for her lack of paid business experience. That isn't even mentioned, nor is the fact that her work had been on a volunteer basis. Instead she casts all her experience in terms of *accomplishment.* Each separate accomplishment that relates to working in a medical environment is placed in its own brief, one-sentence paragraph. Indeed, the whole letter is brief, only eight sentences in all, so busy recipients—in this case doctors—are more inclined to read the letter straight through to the end.

It's important that your letter be short and crisp. Work and rework the letter so that your grabber is brief and punchy. Appeal right away to the self-interest of the recipient. In the Examples section of your letter, cover each accomplishment in one short sentence in its own paragraph. The succession of short, accomplishment-laden paragraphs makes a greater impact on the reader than long, cumbersome prose. Make your closing sharp and clean. And *don't beg* for an interview.

Finding Job Prospects. Of course, you have to find prospects for your letter!

It was easy with Mrs. Kinley: We just opened the phone book and picked physicians whose offices were convenient to her home.

If you already have a job but want a better one, you're probably aware of where and for whom you want to work. All you have to do is send letters to the companies on your "list".

If you use the help-wanted ads in the paper, send a tailored letter *instead* of a résumé, even if a résumé is asked for. All résumés tend to look alike, so your letter will stand out, considerably increasing your chances of getting an interview—*the* crucial first step toward getting a new job.

If you're interested in a particular business or industry, check with your librarian to see if a directory exists for it. There you'll find listings complete with spellings, business titles and addresses. You can also pick up your telephone and call companies or businesses. Ask for the name and correct spelling of the owner or president—if it's a small company—or the district manager, if it's a large company and you're calling the regional office in your city. If a secretary insists on knowing why you're calling before she gives the information, simply say that you're writing the man or woman a letter and need the information.

How many letters will you have to send out? That's hard to say.

When you send letters to companies that aren't specifically advertising or looking for someone, you can expect to send a lot. I did that some years ago; I sent over 60 letters to advertising agencies. Some of the letters drew interviews; only one interview finally resulted in a job. But I only needed *one* job, and I got the job I wanted!

As a general rule, your letter is a good one when requests for an interview run about 8% to 10%. If Mrs. Kinley had received just two or three interview requests, she would have been doing fine. If she had received only one reply, or none, we'd have reworked the letter. As it turned out, she got six interview requests out of 30 letters—that's an exceptionally high 20%.

If you send a tailored letter when you know a company is hiring—for instance, in reply to a help-wanted ad—you will increase your chances of being called for an interview at least 30% to 50%, sometimes more. Once I was the only person called for an interview for an advertised editorial job, even though I had never worked on either a newspaper or a magazine in my life—there's the power of a tailored letter!

Look Professional! Once you've composed your short, punchy, accomplishment-laden letter and decided who's going to get it, make sure you're careful about three things:

First, *type*—don't handwrite—the letter, following standard business form; a secretarial handbook in your library will show you examples. Or follow the form Mrs. Kinley used.

Second, use plain white or ivory-colored stationery. Very pale, almost neutral, colors are okay too, but nothing flashy or brightly colored. I've found that it is helpful to write on monarch-sized stationery, which is smaller than the standard 8½"x11" paper; the letter looks much more personal and invites a reading.

Finally, do *not* do anything gimmicky or "cute." I remember the laughter that erupted in an office when a job-seeking executive sent a letter with a small, sugar-filled bag carefully stapled to the top of the page. His opening line was: "I'd like to sweeten your day just a little." He came across looking foolish . . . and the boss didn't sweeten his day by calling him for an interview.

These are the basics that add up to a professional business letter. I've worked in a lot of offices and seen some pretty silly letters tumble out of the mail bag. Don't let yours be one of them; especially not if you're a woman of specific accomplishments who 's ready for a job!

Questions for Writing or Discussion

1. What is the thesis of the article?
2. What is the subject that is divided?
3. What are the divisions?
4. Is each of these divisions fully developed in the article? If not, does the author find other ways of making the divisions clear?
5. Which of the divisions receives the greatest amount of attention? Why?
6. The early sections of the article make clear use of division. At what point does the article stop discussing divisions and become concerned with other issues? Now check the table of contents for this part of the book. What other "method" or methods is the author using?
7. Do you believe the section headed "Look Professional!" should have appeared before the section headed "Finding Job Prospects"? If so, why?

Exercise A ————————————————————————————

Select a person you admire—a teacher or public figure, perhaps—and write a paper in which you divide the person's appeal into its separate elements.

Exercise B ————————————————————————————

Following is a group of poems on the theme of war. By establishing a single principle, you can classify these poems. Devise a system of classification that makes sense—that works—and write a paper showing how each poem fits into one of the categories.

A Group of War Poems for Classification

From HENRY V, Act IV, Scene 3

Westmoreland.   Oh, that we now had here
But one ten thousand of those men in England
That do no work today!

King Henry.   What's he that wishes so?
My cousin Westmoreland? No, my fair cousin.
If we are marked to die, we are enow[1]
To do our country loss, and if to live,
The fewer men, the greater share of honor.
God's will! I pray thee wish not one man more.
By Jove, I am not covetous for gold,
Nor care I who doth feed upon my cost.[2]
It yearns[3] me not if men my garments wear,
Such outward things dwell not in my desires.
But if it be a sin to covet honor,
I am the most offending soul alive.
No, faith, my coz,[4] wish not a man from England.
God's peace! I would not lose so great an honor
As one man more, methinks, would share from me
For the best hope I have. Oh, do not wish one more!
Rather proclaim it, Westmoreland, through my host,[5]

1. enough 2. at my expense 3. grieves 4. cousin 5. army

That he which hath no stomach to this fight,
Let him depart. His passport shall be made
And crowns for convoy put into his purse.
We would not die in that man's company
That fears his fellowship to die with us.
This day is called the feast of Crispian.
He that outlives this day and comes safe home
Will stand a-tiptoe when this day is named
And rouse him at the name of Crispian.
He that shall live this day and see old age
Will yearly on the vigil feast his neighbors
And say, "Tomorrow is Saint Crispian."
Then will he strip his sleeve and show his scars,
And say, "These wounds I had on Crispin's Day."
Old men forget, yet all shall be forgot,
But he'll remember with advantages
What feats he did that day. Then shall our names,
Familiar in his mouth as household words,
Harry the King, Bedford and Exeter,
Warwick and Talbot, Salisbury and Gloucester,
Be in their flowing cups freshly remembered.
This story shall the good man teach his son,
And Crispin Crispian shall ne'er go by,
From this day to the ending of the world,
But we in it shall be remembered—
We few, we happy few, we band of brothers.
For he today that sheds his blood with me
Shall be my brother. Be he ne'er so vile,
This day shall gentle his condition.[6]
And gentlemen in England now abed
Shall think themselves accursed they were not here,
And hold their manhoods cheap while any speaks
That fought with us upon Saint Crispin's Day.

—*William Shakespeare*

6. make a gentleman of him

DULCE ET DECORUM EST

Bent double, like old beggars under sacks,
Knock-kneed, coughing like hags, we cursed through sludge,
Till on the haunting flares we turned our backs
And towards our distant rest began to trudge.
Men marched asleep. Many had lost their boots
But limped on, blood-shod. All went lame; all blind;
Drunk with fatigue; deaf even to the hoots
Of tired, outstripped Five-Nines that dropped behind.

Gas! Gas! Quick, boys!—An ecstasy of fumbling,
Fitting the clumsy helmets just in time,
But someone still was yelling out and stumbling
And flound'ring like a man in fire or lime . . .
Dim through the misty panes and thick green light,
As under a green sea, I saw him drowning.

In all my dreams, before my helpless sight,
He plunges at me, guttering, choking, drowning.

If in some smothering dreams you too could pace
Behind the wagon that we flung him in,
And watch the white eyes writhing in his face,
His hanging face, like a devil's sick of sin;
If you could hear, at every jolt, the blood
Come gargling from the froth-corrupted lungs
Obscene as cancer, bitter as the cud
Of vile, incurable sores on innocent tongues,—
My friend, you would not tell with such high zest
To children ardent for some desperate glory,
The old lie: *Dulce et decorum est
Pro patria mori.* [1]

—*Wilfred Owen*

1. "It is sweet and fitting to die for one's country."

"THERE WILL COME SOFT RAINS"
(WAR TIME)

There will come soft rains and the smell of the ground,
And swallows circling with their shimmering sound;

And frogs in the pools singing at night,
And wild plum-trees in tremulous white;

Robins will wear their feathery fire
Whistling their whims on a low fence-wire;

And not one will know of the war, not one
Will care at last when it is done.

Not one would mind, neither bird nor tree
If mankind perished utterly;

And Spring herself, when she woke at dawn,
Would scarcely know that we were gone.

—*Sara Teasdale*

THE CHARGE OF THE LIGHT BRIGADE

I

Half a league, half a league,
Half a league onward,
All in the valley of Death
  Rode the six hundred.
"Forward the Light Brigade!
Charge for the guns!" he said.
Into the valley of Death
  Rode the six hundred.

II

"Forward the Light Brigade!"
Was there a man dismayed?
Not though the soldier knew
  Someone had blundered.
Theirs not to make reply,
Theirs not to reason why,
Theirs but to do and die.
Into the valley of Death
  Rode the six hundred.

III

Cannon to right of them,
Cannon to left of them,
Cannon in front of them,
  Volleyed and thundered;
Stormed at with shot and shell,
Boldly they rode and well,
Into the jaws of Death,
Into the mouth of hell
  Rode the six hundred.

IV

Flashed all their sabres bare,
Flashed as they turned in air
Sabring the gunners there,
Charging an army, while
  All the world wondered.
Plunged in the battery-smoke
Right through the line they broke;
Cossack and Russian
Reeled from the sabre-stroke
  Shattered and sundered.
Then they rode back, but not,
  Not the six hundred.

V

Cannon to right of them,
Cannon to left of them,
Cannon behind them
   Volleyed and thundered;
Stormed at with shot and shell,
While horse and hero fell,
They that had fought so well
Came through the jaws of hell,
All that was left of them,
   Left of six hundred.

VI

When can their glory fade?
O the wild charge they made!
   All the world wondered.
Honor the charge they made!
Honor the Light Brigade,
   Noble six hundred!

—*Alfred, Lord Tennyson*

Through foolish orders blindly followed, the British "Light Brigade" charged entrenched Russian artillery positions in the Crimean War on October 25, 1854. About half the officers and men were killed or wounded.

THE BATTLE OF BLENHEIM

It was a summer evening,
   Old Kaspar's work was done,
And he before his cottage door
   Was sitting in the sun,
And by him sported on the green
His little grandchild Wilhelmine.

She saw her brother Peterkin
   Roll something large and round,
Which he beside the rivulet
   In playing there had found;
He came to ask what he had found,
That was so large, and smooth, and round.

Old Kaspar took it from the boy,
   Who stood expectant by;
And then the old man shook his head,
   And, with a natural sigh,
"'Tis some poor fellow's skull," said he,
"Who fell in the great victory.

"I find them in the garden,
  For there's many here about;
And often when I go to plough,
  The ploughshare turns them out!
For many a thousand men," said he,
"Were slain in that great victory."

"Now tell us what 'twas all about,"
  Young Peterkin, he cries;
And little Wilhelmine looks up
  With wonder-waiting eyes;
"Now tell us all about the war,
And what they fought each other for."

"It was the English," Kaspar cried,
  "Who put the French to rout;
But what they fought each other for,
  I could not well make out;
But everybody said," quoth he,
"That 'twas a famous victory.

"My father lived at Blenheim then,
  Yon little stream hard by;
They burnt his dwelling to the ground,
  And he was forced to fly;
So with his wife and child he fled,
Nor had he where to rest his head.

"With fire and sword the country round
  Was wasted far and wide,
And many a childing mother then,
  And new-born baby died;
But things like that, you know, must be
At every famous victory.

"They say it was a shocking sight
  After the field was won;
For many thousand bodies here
  Lay rotting in the sun;
But things like that, you know, must be
After a famous victory.

"Great praise the Duke of Marlbro' won,
  And our good Prince Eugene."
"Why 'twas a very wicked thing!"
  Said little Wilhelmine.
"Nay, nay, my little girl," quoth he,
"It was a famous victory.

"And everybody praised the Duke
  Who this great fight did win."
"But what good came of it at last?"
  Quoth little Peterkin.
"Why that I cannot tell," said he.
"But 'twas a famous victory."

—*Robert Southey*

Blenheim (pronounced Blen'm) is in Bavaria. The battle took place in 1704; France was defeated by the armies of England, Austria, and the Netherlands under the command of the Duke of Marlborough and Prince Eugene of Austria.

WHAT WERE THEY LIKE?

1) Did the people of Viet Nam
   use lanterns of stone?
2) Did they hold ceremonies
   to reverence the opening of buds?
3) Were they inclined to quiet laughter?
4) Did they use bone and ivory,
   jade and silver, for ornament?
5) Had they an epic poem?
6) Did they distinguish between speech and singing?

1) Sir, their light hearts turned to stone.
   It is not remembered whether in gardens
   stone lanterns illumined pleasant ways.
2) Perhaps they gathered once to delight in blossom,
   but after the children were killed
   there were no more buds.
3) Sir, laughter is bitter to the burned mouth.
4) A dream ago, perhaps. Ornament is for joy.
   All the bones were charred.
5) It is not remembered. Remember,
   most were peasants; their life
   was in rice and bamboo.
   When peaceful clouds were reflected in the paddies
   and the water buffalo stepped surely along terraces,
   maybe fathers told their sons old tales.
   When bombs smashed those mirrors
   there was time only to scream.

6) There is no echo yet
   of their speech which was like a song.
   It was reported their singing resembled
   the flight of moths in moonlight.
   Who can say? It is silent now.

—*Denise Levertov*

GRASS

Pile the bodies high at Austerlitz and Waterloo.[1]
Shovel them under and let me work—
   I am the grass; I cover all.

And pile them high at Gettysburg
And pile them high at Ypres and Verdun.[2]
Shovel them under and let me work.
Two years, ten years, and passengers ask the conductor:
   What place is this?
   Where are we now?

   I am the grass.
   Let me work.

—*Carl Sandburg*

1. Austerlitz is the scene of one of Napoleon's greatest victories, Waterloo the scene of his final defeat.
2. Major battles of World War I.

TO LUCASTA, GOING TO THE WARS

Tell me not, sweet, I am unkind
   That from the nunnery
Of thy chaste breast and quiet mind,
   To war and arms I fly.

True, a new mistress now I chase,
   The first foe in the field;
And with a stronger faith embrace
   A sword, a horse, a shield.

Yet this inconstancy is such
   As you too shall adore;
I could not love thee, dear, so much,
   Loved I not Honor more.

—*Richard Lovelace*

BASE DETAILS

If I were fierce, and bald, and short of breath,
   I'd live with scarlet Majors at the Base,
And speed glum heroes up the line to death.
   You'd see me with my puffy petulant face,
Guzzling and gulping in the best hotel,
   Reading the Roll of Honour. "Poor young chap,"
I'd say—"I used to know his father well;
   Yes, we've lost heavily in this last scrap."
And when the war is done and youth stone dead,
I'd toddle safely home and die—in bed.

—*Siegfried Sassoon*

THE SPIRES OF OXFORD

I saw the spires of Oxford
   As I was passing by,
The gray spires of Oxford
   Against the pearl-gray sky.
My heart was with the Oxford men
   Who went abroad to die.

The years go fast in Oxford,
   The golden years and gay,
The hoary[1] Colleges look down
   On careless boys at play.
But when the bugles sounded war
   They put their games away.

They left the peaceful river,
   The cricket-field, the quad,
The shaven lawns of Oxford,
   To seek a bloody sod—
They gave their merry youth away
   For country and for God.

God rest you, happy gentlemen,
   Who laid your good lives down,
Who took the khaki and the gun
   Instead of cap and gown.
God bring you to a fairer place
   Than even Oxford town.

—*Winifred M. Letts*

1. gray

IN TIME OF "THE BREAKING OF NATIONS"

1

Only a man harrowing clods
    In a slow silent walk
With an old horse that stumbles and nods
    Half asleep as they stalk.

2

Only thin smoke without flame
    From the heaps of couch-grass;
Yet this will go onward the same
    Though Dynasties pass.

3

Yonder a maid and her wight[1]
    Come whispering by;
War's annals will cloud into night
    Ere their story die.

—*Thomas Hardy*

The poem was published during World War I. The title alludes to Jeremiah 5:20:
"Thou art my battle ax and weapons of war: for with thee will I break in pieces
the nations, and with thee will I destroy kingdoms."

1. boy friend

CHAPTER 7

WRITING
A PROCESS PAPER

The *process* paper describes a series of actions, changes, or functions that bring about an end or result. Probably the most familiar kind of process paper is the "how-to" paper, a step-by-step set of instructions on how to complete a particular task—how to change a tire, how to bake a cake, how to install storm windows, how to assemble a bicycle.

Although the rules for this kind of paper are simple and obvious, you should check your paper to see that you have observed them, because if you haven't, your description of the process may be useless to the reader. The rules follow.

Make certain that the explanation is complete and accurate. If, for example, you want to describe the process for baking a cake, you would mislead your reader if you omitted the instruction to grease and flour the pan. It's surprisingly easy to leave out important steps. You will be writing about a process you know extremely well, and you probably perform some steps—such as greasing a pan—without consciously thinking about them at all.

Maintain strict chronological order. Once the cake is in the oven, it is too late to tell the reader that walnuts should have been stirred into the batter.

If a particular kind of performance is called for in any part of the process, indicate the nature of the action. Should the batter be stirred vigorously or gently? Should an applicant for a job approach the interviewer humbly or aggressively? Besides indicating the nature of the action, you should also tell the reader why such action is called for. Readers are more likely to follow instructions if they understand the reason for them.

Group the steps in the process. A process may include many steps, but they can usually be grouped under logical headings—for example, *assembling ingredients, assembling utensils, mixing ingredients, cooking ingredients.* A number of steps may be involved in each of these divisions, but reading the steps in groups is far less frightening and confusing to a reader than beginning with step one and ending with step nineteen.

Define any terms which might be unfamiliar to the reader or which may have more than one meaning. To most of us, *conceit* means extreme self-love, but to a literary scholar, it means an elaborate and extended metaphor. The scholar, when writing instructions for first-year students on how to analyze a poem, would have to define the term.

Have a thesis. It's possible just to present a clear set of instructions and stop. But the most interesting process papers do have theses. Few of us read car manuals or recipe books for pleasure, but we might well read the student paper "Porch Scrubbing with the Best" (p. 98) more than once, just for the pleasure of it. Part of the pleasure comes from the thesis of the paper, which gives the paper focus and charm. It's a good idea, then, to try for a thesis.

> My way of changing license plates will save you time and frustration. (See p. 6.)
>
> Writing a term paper can be simplified by breaking the work up into steps.
>
> Cleaning chitterlings is a nauseating task. (See p. 97.)

Anticipate difficulties. One way to anticipate difficulties is to warn the reader in advance when to expect problems:

> This step requires your constant attention.
>
> Now you will need all the strength you can muster.
>
> You'd better have a friend handy to help with this step.

Another way to anticipate difficulties is to give the reader advice on how to make the process easier or more pleasant. You're the authority on the subject, and you want to pass on to the novice any helpful tips you've gained from experience. Wearing old clothes isn't essential to the process of shampooing a carpet, of course, but you've learned from experience that dirty suds can fly and soil clothing, and you want to pass that information on to the reader. Similarly, it's possible to erase a typing error without moving the carriage away from the keys. But you've learned that this practice can lead to gummy keys and, in the case of an electric typewriter, a broken fan belt. Naturally, you want to warn the reader against erasing over the keys.

Finally, *tell the reader what to do if something goes wrong.* In many processes, one can follow the instructions faithfully and still have problems. Prepare your reader for such cases.

If, at this point, the pecan pie is not firm when you test the center, reduce the heat to 250 degrees and cook it fifteen minutes longer.

If, even after careful proofreading, you find a misspelled word at the last minute, carefully erase the word and neatly print the correction by hand.

An introduction to a how-to paper, in addition to presenting the thesis, might state when and by whom the process would be performed. It could also list any equipment needed for performing the process, and it might briefly list the major headings or divisions of the process. Don't forget about the need for a conclusion. You want the last thought in your reader's mind to be about the process as a whole, not about the comparatively trivial final step.

Below is an amusing how-to paper. Study it and determine whether the writer has given clear instructions on how to perform the task.

Cleaning Pork Chitterlings
ETHELYN HOWARD

Among soul food connoisseurs, there is much discussion concerning the delectable main dish known as chitterlings, more frequently called and spelled *chitlins*. For those of you who have not as yet experienced the joy of cleaning the foul-smelling, disgustingly slimy intestines of a hog, you're in for a real experience.

To begin, you must purchase the chitterlings. The brand name is not as important as getting intestines that are already as clean as possible. After all, the cleaner they are, the less work for you, and the sooner your nostrils will get relief from the stench of hog's stool. So look at the intestines. Have the butcher remove the lid from the carton and display the contents for your inspection. Stay away from intestines so covered by thick white fat that you can barely see the pink tube that is the edible portion. Ten pounds of intestines will serve four people. Fresh or frozen is a matter of personal choice, depending on whether you want to dig right in or wait about twelve hours for thawing.

When you are ready to begin cleaning, roll up your sleeves, hold your breath, and thrust your hands into the bucket of slippery guts. Taking a firm hold on a section, pull the intestine from the tangle in the carton and begin the tedious task of peeling off the lumps of fat with a paring knife. Once this has been completed, skin the thin, transluscent membrane from the inside of the section and discard it along with the fat.

The worst is over when the last section of intestine is peeled and skinned. Now all that remains is washing and bleaching. Fill a clean wash pan with intestines and water. By now the sections are considerably smoother and easier to handle. Rub each section vigorously, dunking it into the water frequently. Drain all water from the pan, and refill with fresh, cold water, adding four tablespoons of salt. Soak overnight or six to eight hours, until the intestines are nearly white in appearance.

By now you have devoted about four hours to cleaning and at least six hours to soaking. As you wearily scrub the remaining odor from your hands with baking soda, think about what you have just experienced and resolve to take the family to Kentucky Fried Chicken the next time.

Questions for Writing or Discussion

1. What is the thesis of the paper? Is the thesis stated in one sentence? Should it be?
2. Consider the writer's diction. Does her choice of words such as *slimy, hog's stool,* and *guts* reinforce her thesis? Is her language too strong?
3. The writer uses the word *chitterlings* (or *chitlins*) only twice. Otherwise, she uses the word *intestines.* Does her choice make a value judgment on the dish fancied by "soul food connoisseurs"?
4. Does the writer observe all the requirements of a good process paper?
5. If you are well acquainted with a dish which is characteristic of your ethnic group, neighborhood, or some member of your family, write a process paper telling how to prepare the dish or how best to eat it. Do not, however, just give a recipe in cook-book style.

Not all process papers simply give instructions. Some tell "how it works." Such papers explain the functioning of anything from an electric blender to the system by which congressional legislation is passed. Still other process papers describe "how it was done." This kind of paper could trace the process by which Walter Reed discovered the cause of yellow fever or, as in the popular *Making of the President* books, how a man came to be president. A how-it-was-done paper could even trace the process by which a person achieved a certain kind of awareness, as is the case in the following student paper.

Porch Scrubbing with the Best
SHIRLEY LYTTON-CANNON

There are a lot of famous experts around from whom we can learn a great deal, just by watching them or listening to what they have to say about their special techniques, style, or sources of information. Depending on what we want to learn, we usually give most of our attention to the how-to-do-it people who have at one time or another made their way into a newspaper column or perhaps have written a little manual or not-so-little book on how to do something. But if you want to know about scrubbing porches, your best bet is to take on-the-job training with Elizabeth Lytton.

Now, I know that as far as the media are concerned, Elizabeth Lytton doesn't even exist. But when you live in a mining camp such as National, West Virginia, it's darn hard to make a name for yourself, especially if you come from a family of twelve children, have only a fourth-grade education, and don't know much about anything except hard work, empty cupboards and cold houses. Nonetheless, make a name for herself she did. Everyone in National, as well as in the surrounding mining camps such as Riverseam, Flaggy Meadow, Edna Gas and Harmony Grove, knows that Elizabeth Lytton has the house with the greenest lawn, the most beautiful flower garden, the earliest lettuce, and most important, the cleanest porches.

It wasn't until I was about twelve years old and had my first porch-scrubbing lesson with her that I realized why clean porches were so highly respected. We were cleaning our big grey-painted cement porch with the white enamel bannisters and porch-green enamel flower boxes. She told me that the houses in the camps all have coal furnaces, so between the soot and gritty dirt pouring out of the chimneys of the houses, and the smoky fumes seeping out of the mine's slate dump, which was always burning nearby, a person really has to know what he's doing if he expects to sit on a porch and not feel as if he'll have to take a bath afterward.

We began by dragging the glider, chaise lounge, rocking chair, grass rug, and a couple of miscellaneous tables out into the back yard, during which time she minced no words in telling me exactly what she thought of certain people who smear dirt around with a damp mop and call a porch clean.

When we went into the basement to get the cleaning supplies, I expected her to whip out some magic cleaning solutions and mix her own concoction, but that wasn't exactly the case. Instead, she opened a giant-sized box of Spic-n-Span, which didn't look like a miracle worker to my inexperienced eyes, and then added triple the amount called for on the label to the biggest, hottest bucket of water into which I have ever had the ill fortune of dunking my hands. I asked her if she wanted me to get some rubber gloves, but she said something about the fact that cracks and grooves weren't about to move aside for fat rubber fingers! I think I began suspecting then that this was going to be no ordinary cleaning day.

We carried the bucket of Spic-n-Span water outside to the porch, along with two stiff-bristled scrub brushes, two mops, two brooms, and two old towels to be used for scrub rags. She hooked up the garden hose nearby, turned on the faucet, and we were ready to begin.

I guess at that point your average, everyday porch scrubber would have cleaned the floor of the porch after having wiped off the bannisters a little, and then been done with it. But not Elizabeth. She had a reputation to uphold, and she didn't get that reputation by doing things "with a lick and a promise." She told me to dip my brush into the bucket and bring as much hot cleaning water up with it as possible and start scrubbing the ceiling

boards of the porch first, continuing to dip the brush into the bucket often
enough to keep plenty of water on the boards. Well, we dipped and
scrubbed until we cleaned not only the ceiling boards, but also the side of
the house leading from the porch to the inside, as well as the carved posts
that make up the bannister. That's a lot of dunking and scrubbing! We used
our brooms and what was left of the water to scrub the floor of the porch. I
noticed that my hands grew accustomed to the water temperature just about
the time some of the skin between my fingers began to get cracked and flaky
looking.

The fun part of the training came when we used the hose to rinse
everything—fun, that is, until the ice cold water soaked through my penny
loafers and white cotton socks.

Just about the time I figured we had to be pretty close to finished, she
brought out another huge bucket of plain hot water, and we began to dip
the towels into the bucket, squeeze the water out of them as much as
possible, and then wipe each board clean and dry, making sure, if you
please, to get all the cracks, grooves and crannies clean also. We used our
mops in the same manner as the towels to finish cleaning the floor.

Finally, we repeated the whole ritual on the porch furniture and then put
everything back in its proper place.

We sat down together for a while on the glider, just talking about how
nice everything looked and how hard we had worked. It seemed to me that
she felt more pleased with the work we had done than with the fact that it
was finally finished.

During our lifetime together we were always working on something or
other, and the one thing that I always noticed about her was that she never
did anything halfway—whether it was sewing a dress, growing a garden,
caring for a lawn, or scrubbing a porch. It was just her way to do the best
she could, no matter how menial the task. She thrived on the pride that
came from being the best at it. Maybe that's the secret of all experts such as
Elizabeth.

Questions for Writing or Discussion

1. Besides learning how to scrub a porch, what is the more important lesson the writer learned?
2. Considering the lesson the writer learned, discuss the importance
of paragraph 2.
3. How does the first sentence in the fifth paragraph help characterize the writer? Can you find other sentences which support
that characterization?
4. Why is porch scrubbing a better subject to make the writer's point
than, say, learning to appreciate the symbolism of *Moby-Dick* from
a dedicated high school English teacher?
5. Perhaps you have had an experience which taught you something about yourself, a member of your family, or the nature of
life. Trace the process by which you made the discovery.

Process writing can also be an effective tool of literary analysis. In the student paper below, the author finds a process in "The River Merchant's Wife: A Letter."

THE RIVER MERCHANT'S WIFE: A LETTER

While my hair was still cut straight across my forehead
I played about the front gate, pulling flowers.
You came by on bamboo stilts, playing horse,
You walked about my seat, playing with blue plums,
And we went on living in the village of Chokan:
Two small people, without dislike or suspicions.

At fourteen I married My Lord you.
I never laughed, being bashful.
Lowering my head, I looked at the wall.
Called to, a thousand times, I never looked back.

At fifteen I stopped scowling,
I desired my dust to be mingled with yours
Forever and forever and forever.
Why should I climb the lookout?

At sixteen you departed,
You went into far Ku-to-yen, by the river of swirling eddies,
And you have been gone five months.
The monkeys make sorrowful noise overhead.

You dragged your feet when you went out.
By the gate now, the moss is grown, the different mosses.
Too deep to clear them away!
The leaves fall early this autumn, in wind.
The paired butterflies are already yellow with August.
They hurt me. I grow older.

If you are coming down through the narrows of the river Kiang,
Please let me know before hand,
And I will come out to meet you
    As far as Cho-fu-sa.

—Li T'ai Po
(Tr. by Ezra Pound)

The Growth of Love
ARLENE CHMIELEWSKI

I've always wondered if two people thrown together in a prearranged marriage could ever grow to love each other. Could a young Chinese girl, for example, love her husband when she is taught that the choice is not hers—or his, for that matter? "The River Merchant's Wife: A Letter," by Li T'ai Po, answers my question. The poem is a letter written by a young Chinese wife to her husband. It is actually a beautiful love letter telling of how her love has grown.

She admits to him in the letter that there was no emotion at first. She writes her impressions of their first meeting. As a young child, whether she knew of an impending marriage, she was too young to realize any feeling for him. The meeting left them "without dislike or suspicions." She reports in the second stanza that as a young girl of fourteen she was married to her "Lord." She tells him she wasn't comfortable with him then.

Something in her changes in the third stanza. The young bride is fifteen and has "stopped scowling." A great desire for her husband exists, but she still cannot show any loving concern, for she writes, "Why should I climb the lookout?" Even though she doesn't have the need to show her feelings for him, there is the beginning of emotion.

The last three stanzas of the poem illustrate the young wife's realization of her need to show her love for her husband. She has turned sixteen. They have been separated for five months, possibly because of his job. She writes to him of how deeply he is missed: "The monkeys make sorrowful noise overhead." Her love seems to have grown as "the different mosses. Too deep to clear them away!" Her love has also matured, for she writes, "I grow older."

Finally, she asks him to let her know when he's coming home so she can meet him "As far as Cho-fu-Sa"—possibly halfway.

Questions for Writing or Discussion

1. What is the thesis of the paper? Is the thesis stated in one sentence?
2. What is the process traced in the paper?
3. Would you have divided the process into the same steps as the author did?
4. Do you think the paper needs a concluding paragraph which summarizes the steps in the process? Do you think the paper ends too abruptly?
5. Do you believe the sections of the poem which the author quotes effectively support her generalizations? Can you find other lines which might be more effective?

Readings

In the first of the readings that follow, the author, Carla Stephens, describes the process by which one can stay afloat in water.

Carla Stephens
DROWNPROOFING

If your warm-weather plans include water sports, there's one thing you should do to make this summer safe as well as enjoyable for your family: Drownproof them!

Drowning is the second leading cause of accidental death for people between the ages of 4 and 44, according to the American National Red Cross. Twenty-eight percent of those drowned are children under 15 years old. Seven out of ten of them are boys.

Even more shocking is the fact that many of the seven thousand annual drowning victims *know how to swim.* In fact, swimmers face several hazards that non-swimmers don't. First, they may overexert themselves—especially in May and June when they're likely to expect out-of-condition bodies to perform as well as in summers past. They may also get into a situation beyond their skills. If panic takes over, tragedy may follow.

With drownproofing, on the other hand, a poor swimmer or even a non-swimmer can survive in the water twelve hours or more—even when fully clothed and in rough water.

Developed by the late Fred Lanoue, drownproofing relies on the body's ability to float when air fills the lungs. Picture yourself bobbing restfully just under the surface of the water. With a few easy movements you come up to breathe as often as necessary. That's the basic idea of drownproofing, a technique endorsed by the Red Cross, the National Safety Council and the YMCA. It's easy to learn, even for some three-year-olds. You can teach yourself and your family.

Here's how it's done: First, take a breath through your mouth. Then, holding your breath, put your face into the water and float vertically with your arms and legs dangling. Don't try to keep your head up; it weighs fifteen pounds.

When you're ready for another breath, slowly raise your arms to shoulder height. At the same time bring one leg a little forward and the other back into a position somewhat like the scissors kick. (If injury makes it necessary, drownproofing can be done with either the arm or the leg movements.) Then gently press your arms down to your sides (not backward) and bring your legs together. Keep your eyes open and raise your head until your mouth is out of the water. Exhale through your nose, your mouth or both.

Inhale through your mouth while continuing to press your arms down. But don't press too hard, for you want to keep your chin at, not above, the surface of the water. Finally, return to the resting position with your face in the water. If you sink too far, a small kick or a slight downward push of your arms will return you to the surface.

When teaching your children, it's advisable to stand with them in shoulder-deep water. Have them bend forward to practice the breathing and arm movements. If they swallow water, be patient and encourage them to try again. Once they're comfortable with the procedure, move into deeper water near the side of the pool to coordinate the floating, breathing and body movements. Water just deep enough for them to go under is sufficient. Remember, all movements should be easy and relaxed.

If your child needs to work at the vertical float, let him practice at the side of a pool or some other spot where he'll be able to hold on. At first you might even help hold him up by placing a hand just beneath his shoulder. Have him take a breath, put his face into the water and then remove his hands from the side. As soon as he has some experience in floating remove your hand and watch.

While practicing, youngsters usually spend only about three seconds under water at first. That time should gradually increase—depending, of course, on their age. Older children may reach ten seconds, the period recommended for adults.

With a little practice your family will be drownproofed and truly ready for fun in the water.

Questions for Writing or Discussion

1. What is the thesis of the article?
2. How many steps are involved in the process of staying afloat?
3. Does the author describe more than one process? If so, what process or processes are described besides that of staying afloat?
4. What rule of a good process paper do paragraphs two and three fulfill?
5. Do you believe you could follow these instructions, or do you think pictures would help make the process clearer?
6. Write a paper in which you describe a process which could be of benefit to someone else.

In the following story, Walter Van Tilburg Clark looks into the future and sees a process repeating itself.

Walter Van Tilburg Clark
THE PORTABLE PHONOGRAPH

The red sunset, with narrow black cloud strips like threats across it, lay on the curved horizon of the prairie. The air was still and cold, and in it settled the mute darkness and greater cold of night. High in the air there was wind, for through the veil of the dusk the clouds could be seen gliding rapidly south and changing shapes. A queer sensation of torment, of two-sided, unpredictable nature, arose from the stillness of the earth air beneath the violence of the upper air. Out of the sunset, through the dead, matted grass and isolated weed stalks of the prairie, crept the narrow and deeply rutted remains of a road. In the road, in places, there were crusts of shallow, brittle ice. There were little islands of an old oiled pavement in the road too, but most of it was mud, now frozen rigid. The frozen mud still bore the toothed impress of great tanks, and a wanderer on the neighboring undulations might have stumbled, in this light, into large, partially filled-in and weed-grown cavities, their banks channeled and beginning to spread into bad-lands. These pits were such as might have been made by falling meteors, but they were not. They were the scars of gigantic bombs, their rawness already made a little natural by rain, seed, and time. Along the road there were rakish remnants of fence. There was also, just visible, one portion of tangled and multiple barbed wire still erect, behind which was a shelving ditch with small caves, now very quiet and empty, at intervals in its back wall. Otherwise there was no structure or remnant of a structure visible over the dome of the darkling earth, but only, in sheltered hollows, the darker shadows of young trees trying again.

Under the wuthering arch of the high wind a V of wild geese fled south. The rush of their pinions sounded briefly, and the faint, plaintive notes of their expeditionary talk. Then they left a still greater vacancy. There was the smell and expectation of snow, as there is likely to be when the wild geese fly south. From the remote distance, towards the red sky, came faintly the protracted howl and quick yap-yap of a prairie wolf.

North of the road, perhaps a hundred yards, lay the parallel and deeply intrenched course of a small creek, lined with leafless alders and willows. The creek was already silent under ice. Into the bank above it was dug a sort of cell, with a single opening, like the mouth of a mine tunnel. Within the cell there was a little red of fire, which showed dully through the opening, like a reflection or a deception of the imagination. The light came from the chary burning of four blocks of poorly aged peat, which gave off a petty warmth and much acrid smoke. But the precious remnants of wood, old fenceposts and timbers from the long-deserted dugouts, had to be saved for the real cold, for the time when a man's breath blew white, the moisture in his nostrils stiffened at once when he stepped out, and the expansive blizzards paraded for days over the vast open, swirling and settling and thickening, till the dawn of the cleared day when the sky was thin blue-green and the terrible cold, in which a man could not live for three hours unwarmed, lay over the uniformly drifted swell of the plain.

Around the smoldering peat four men were seated cross-legged. Behind them, traversed by their shadows, was the earth bench, with two old and dirty army blankets, where the owner of the cell slept. In a niche in the opposite wall were a few tin utensils which caught the glint of the coals. The host was rewrapping in a piece of daubed burlap four fine, leather-bound books. He worked slowly and very carefully and at last tied the bundle securely with a piece of grass-woven cord. The other three looked intently upon the process, as if a great significance lay in it. As the host tied the cord he spoke. He was an old man, his long, matted beard and hair gray to nearly white. The shadows made his brows and cheekbones appear gnarled, his eyes and cheeks deeply sunken. His big hands, rough with frost and swollen by rheumatism, were awkward but gentle at their task. He was like a prehistoric priest performing a fateful ceremonial rite. Also his voice had in it a suitable quality of deep, reverent despair, yet perhaps at the moment a sharpness of selfish satisfaction.

"When I perceived what was happening," he said, "I told myself, 'It is the end. I cannot take much; I will take these.'"

"Perhaps I was impractical," he continued. "But for myself, I do not regret, and what do we know of those who will come after us? We are the doddering remnant of a race of mechanical fools. I have saved what I love; the soul of what was good in us is here; perhaps the new ones will make a strong enough beginning not to fall behind when they become clever."

He rose with slow pain and placed the wrapped volumes in the niche with his utensils. The others watched him with the same ritualistic gaze.

"Shakespeare, the Bible, *Moby-Dick*, the *Divine Comedy*," one of them said softly. "You might have done worse, much worse."

"You will have a little soul left until you die," said another harshly. "That is more than is true of us. My brain becomes thick, like my hands." He held the big, battered hands, with their black nails, in the glow to be seen.

"I want paper to write on," he said. "And there is none."

The fourth man said nothing. He sat in the shadow farthest from the fire, and sometimes his body jerked in its rags from the cold. Although he was still young, he was sick and coughed often. Writing implied a greater future than he now felt able to consider.

The old man seated himself laboriously and reached out, groaning at the movement, to put another block of peat on the fire. With bowed heads and averted eyes his three guests acknowledged his magnanimity.

"We thank you, Dr. Jenkins, for the reading," said the man who had named the books.

They seemed then to be waiting for something. Dr. Jenkins understood but was loath to comply. In an ordinary moment he would have said nothing. But the words of *The Tempest,* which he had been reading, and the religious attention of the three made this an unusual occasion.

"You wish to hear the phonograph," he said grudgingly.

The two middle-aged men stared into the fire, unable to formulate and expose the enormity of their desire.

The young man, however, said anxiously, between suppressed coughs, "Oh, please," like an excited child.

The old man rose again in his difficult way and went to the back of the cell. He returned and placed tenderly upon the packed floor, where the firelight might fall upon it, an old portable phonograph in a black case. He smoothed the top with his hand and then opened it. The lovely green-felt-covered disk became visible.

"I have been using thorns as needles." he said. "But tonight, because we have a musician among us"—he bent his head to the young man, almost invisible in the shadow—"I will use a steel needle. There are only three left."

The two middle-aged men stared at him in speechless adoration. The one with the big hands, who wanted to write, moved his lips, but the whisper was not audible.

"Oh, don't!" cried the young man, as if he were hurt. "The thorns will do beautifully."

"No," the old man said. "I have become accustomed to the thorns, but they are not really good. For you, my young friend, we will have good music tonight."

"After all," he added generously, and beginning to wind the phonograph, which creaked, "they can't last forever."

"No, nor we," the man who needed to write said harshly. "The needle, by all means."

"Oh, thanks," said the young man. "Thanks," he said again in a low, excited voice, and then stifled his coughing with a bowed head.

"The records, though," said the old man when he had finished winding, "are a different matter. Already they are very worn. I do not play them more than once a week. One, once a week, that is what I allow myself."

"More than a week I cannot stand it; not to hear them," he apologized.

"No, how could you?" cried the young man. "And with them here like this."

"A man can stand anything," said the man who wanted to write, in his harsh, antagonistic voice.

"Please, the music," said the young man.

"Only the one," said the old man. "In the long run, we will remember more that way."

He had a dozen records with luxuriant gold and red seals. Even in that light the others could see that the threads of the records were becoming worn. Slowly he read out the titles and the tremendous, dead names of the composers and the artists and the orchestras. The three worked upon the names in their minds, carefully. It was difficult to select from such a wealth what they would at once most like to remember. Finally the man who wanted to write named Gershwin's "New York."

"Oh, no!" cried the sick young man, and then could say nothing more because he had to cough. The others understood him, and the harsh man withdrew his selection and waited for the musician to choose.

The musician begged Dr. Jenkins to read the titles again, very slowly, so that he could remember the sounds. While they were read he lay back against the wall, his eyes closed, his thin, horny hand pulling at his light beard, and listened to the voices and the orchestras and the single instruments in his mind.

When the reading was done he spoke despairingly. "I have forgotten," he complained. "I cannot hear them clearly."

"There are things missing," he explained.

"I know," said Dr. Jenkins. "I thought that I knew all of Shelley by heart. I should have brought Shelley."

"That's more soul than we can use," said the harsh man. "*Moby-Dick* is better.

"By God, we can understand that," he emphasized.

The Doctor nodded.

"Still," said the man who had admired the books, "we need the absolute if we are to keep a grasp on anything.

"Anything but these sticks and peat clods and rabbit snares," he said bitterly.

"Shelley desired an ultimate absolute," said the harsh man. "It's too much," he said. "It's no good; no earthly good."

The musician selected a Debussy nocturne. The others considered and approved. They rose to their knees to watch the Doctor prepare for the playing, so that they appeared to be actually in an attitude of worship. The peat glow showed the thinness of their bearded faces, and the deep lines in them, and revealed the condition of their garments. The other two continued to kneel as the old man carefully lowered the needle onto the spinning disk, but the musician suddenly drew back against the wall again, with his knees up, and buried his face in his hands.

At the first notes of the piano the listeners were startled. They stared at each other. Even the musician lifted his head in amazement but then quickly bowed it again, strainingly, as if he were suffering from a pain he might not be able to endure. They were all listening deeply, without movement. The wet, blue-green notes tinkled forth from the old machine and were individual, delectable presences in the cell. The individual, delectable presences swept into a sudden tide of unbearably beautiful dissonance and then continued fully the swelling and ebbing of that tide, the dissonant inpourings, and the resolutions, and the diminishments, and the little, quiet wavelets of interlude lapping between. Every sound was piercing and singularly sweet. In all the men except the musician there occurred rapid sequences of tragically heightened recollection. He heard nothing but what was there. At the final, whispering disappearance, but moving quietly so that the others would not hear him and look at him, he let his head fall back in agony, as if it were drawn there by the hair, and clenched the fingers of one hand over his teeth. He sat that way while the others were silent and until they began to breathe again normally. His drawn-up legs were trembling violently.

Quickly Dr. Jenkins lifted the needle off, to save it and not to spoil the recollection with scraping. When he had stopped the whirling of the sacred disk he courteously left the phonograph open and by the fire, in sight.

The others, however, understood. The musician rose last, but then abruptly, and went quickly out of the door without saying anything. The others stopped at the door and gave their thanks in low voices. The Doctor nodded magnificently.

"Come again," he invited, "in a week. We will have the 'New York.'"

When the two had gone together, out towards the rimed road, he stood in the entrance, peering and listening. At first there was only the resonant boom of the wind overhead, and then far over the dome of the dead, dark plain the wolf cry lamenting. In the rifts of clouds the Doctor saw four stars flying. It impressed the Doctor that one of them had just been obscured by the beginning of a flying cloud at the very moment he heard what he had been listening for, a sound of suppressed coughing. It was not near by, however. He believed that down against the pale alders he could see the moving shadow.

With nervous hands he lowered the piece of canvas which served as his door and pegged it at the bottom. Then quickly and quietly, looking at the piece of canvas frequently, he slipped the records into the case, snapped the lid shut, and carried the phonograph to his couch. There, pausing often to stare at the canvas and listen, he dug earth from the wall and disclosed a piece of board. Behind this there was a deep hole in the wall, into which he put the phonograph. After a moment's consideration he went over and reached down his bundle of books and inserted it also. Then, guardedly, he once more sealed up the hole with the board and the earth. He also changed his blankets and the grass-stuffed sack which served as a pillow, so that he could lie facing the entrance. After carefully placing two more blocks of peat upon the fire he stood for a long time watching the stretched canvas, but it seemed to billow naturally with the first gusts of a lowering wind. At last he prayed, and got in under his blankets, and closed his smoke-smarting eyes. On the inside of the bed, next to the wall, he could feel with his hand the comfortable piece of lead pipe.

Questions for Writing or Discussion

1. What has happened before the story opens to make the surroundings so bleak?
2. Your first reaction to Dr. Jenkins's going to sleep with a "comfortable piece of lead pipe" in his hand might be surprise. As you read the story again, look for clues that Dr. Jenkins is not really as generous and gentle as he appears at first.
3. Dr. Jenkins says, "We are the doddering remnant of a race of mechanical fools. I have saved what I love; the soul of what was good in us is here; perhaps the new ones will make a strong enough beginning not to fall behind when they become clever." Yet consider:
   a. "The three looked intently upon the process [of tying the leather bound books] as if a great significance lay in it."
   b. Dr. Jenkins has devised a way to use thorns as needles for the phonograph.
   c. Dr. Jenkins cannot remember Shelley, who wanted absolutes, and the writer rejects Shelley because "that's more soul than we can use."
   d. The group kneels around the phonograph as if at worship.
   e. The records are in jackets of red and gold.
   What do these facts reveal about the true soul of the group? Will the "new ones . . . fall behind when they become clever"?
4. The writer, who rejects Shelley and prefers *Moby-Dick*, always speaks harshly. Why is that characterization significant?
5. Write a paper in which, by using the evidences of human nature revealed in the story, you trace the process by which the four men came to their present state and then predict what will happen later.

The following story by Willa Cather ends in tragedy. One can see the friends and relatives asking, "Where did it all begin?" And the answer to that question can lead you into an excellent process paper.

Willa Cather
PAUL'S CASE

It was Paul's afternoon to appear before the faculty of the Pittsburgh High School to account for his various misdemeanours. He had been suspended a week ago, and his father had called at the Principal's office and confessed his perplexity about his son. Paul entered the faculty room suave and smiling. His clothes were a trifle outgrown and the tan velvet on the collar of his open overcoat was frayed and worn; but for all that there was something of the dandy about him, and he wore an opal pin in his neatly knotted black four-in-hand, and a red carnation in his button-hole. This latter adornment the faculty somehow felt was not properly significant of the contrite spirit befitting a boy under the ban of suspension.

Paul was tall for his age and very thin, with high, cramped shoulders and a narrow chest. His eyes were remarkable for a certain hysterical brilliancy and he continually used them in a conscious, theatrical sort of way, peculiarly offensive in a boy. The pupils were abnormally large, as though he were addicted to belladonna, but there was a glassy glitter about them which that drug does not produce.

When questioned by the Principal as to why he was there, Paul stated, politely enough, that he wanted to come back to school. This was a lie, but Paul was quite accustomed to lying; found it, indeed, indispensable for overcoming friction. His teachers were asked to state their respective charges against him, which they did with such a rancour and aggrievedness as evinced that this was not a usual case. Disorder and impertinence were among the offences named, yet each of his instructors felt that it was scarcely possible to put into words the real cause of the trouble, which lay in a sort of hysterically defiant manner of the boy's; in the contempt which they all knew he felt for them, and which he seemingly made not the least effort to conceal. Once, when he had been making a synopsis of a paragraph at the blackboard, his English teacher had stepped to his side and attempted to guide his hand. Paul had started back with a shudder and thrust his hands violently behind him. The astonished woman could scarcely have been more hurt and embarrassed had he struck at her. The insult was so involuntary and definitely personal as to be unforgettable. In one way and another, he had made all his teachers, men and women alike, conscious of the same feeling of physical aversion. In one class he habitually sat with his hand shading his eyes; in another he always looked out of the window during the recitation; in another he made a running commentary on the lecture, with humorous intention.

His teachers felt this afternoon that his whole attitude was symbolized by his shrug and his flippantly red carnation flower, and they fell upon him without mercy, his English teacher leading the pack. He stood through it smiling, his pale lips parted over his white teeth. (His lips were continually twitching, and he had a habit of raising his eyebrows that was contemptuous and irritating to the last degree.) Older boys than Paul had broken down and shed tears under that baptism of fire, but his set smile did not once desert him, and his only sign of discomfort was the nervous trembling of the fingers that toyed with the buttons of his overcoat, and an occasional jerking of the other hand that held his hat. Paul was always smiling, always glancing about him, seeming to feel that people might be watching him and trying to detect something. This conscious expression, since it was as far as possible from boyish mirthfulness, was usually attributed to insolence or "smartness."

As the inquisition proceeded, one of his instructors repeated an impertinent remark of the boy's, and the Principal asked him whether he thought that a courteous speech to have made a woman. Paul shrugged his shoulders slightly and his eyebrows twitched.

"I don't know," he replied. "I didn't mean to be polite or impolite, either. I guess it's a sort of way I have of saying things regardless."

The Principal, who was a sympathetic man, asked him whether he didn't think that a way it would be well to get rid of. Paul grinned and said he guessed so. When he was told that he could go, he bowed gracefully and went out. His bow was but a repetition of the scandalous red carnation.

His teachers were in despair, and his drawing master voiced the feeling of them all when he declared there was something about the boy which none of them understood. He added: "I don't really believe that smile of his comes altogether from insolence; there's something sort of haunted about it. The boy is not strong, for one thing. I happen to know that he was born in Colorado, only a few months before his mother died out there of a long illness. There is something wrong about the fellow."

The drawing master had come to realize that, in looking at Paul, one saw only his white teeth and the forced animation of his eyes. One warm afternoon the boy had gone to sleep at his drawing-board, and his master had noted with amazement what a white, blue-veined face it was; drawn and wrinkled like an old man's about the eyes, the lips twitching even in his sleep, and stiff with a nervous tension that drew them back from his teeth.

His teachers left the building dissatisfied and unhappy; humiliated to have felt so vindictive toward a mere boy, to have uttered this feeling in cutting terms, and to have set each other on, as it were, in the gruesome game of intemperate reproach. Some of them remembered having seen a miserable street cat set at bay by a ring of tormentors.

As for Paul, he ran down the hill whistling the Soldiers' Chorus from *Faust* looking wildly behind him now and then to see whether some of his teachers were not there to writhe under his light-heartedness. As it was now late in the afternoon and Paul was on duty that evening as usher at Carnegie Hall, he decided that he would not go home to supper. When he reached the concert hall the doors were not yet open and, as it was chilly outside, he decided to go up into the picture gallery—always deserted at this hour—where there were some of Raffelli's gay studies of Paris streets and an airy blue Venetian scene or two that always exhilarated him. He was delighted to find no one in the gallery but the old guard, who sat in one corner, a newspaper on his knee, a black patch over one eye and the other closed. Paul possessed himself of the place and walked confidently up and down, whistling under his breath. After a while he sat down before a blue Rico and lost himself. When he bethought him to look at his watch, it was after seven o'clock, and he rose with a start and ran downstairs, making a face at Augustus, peering out from the castroom, and an evil gesture at the Venus of Milo as he passed her on the stairway.

When Paul reached the ushers' dressing-room half-a-dozen boys were there already, and he began excitedly to tumble into his uniform. It was one of the few that at all approached fitting, and Paul thought it very becoming—though he knew that the tight, straight coat accentuated his narrow chest, about which he was exceedingly sensitive. He was always considerably excited while he dressed, twanging all over to the tuning of the strings and the preliminary flourishes of the horns in the music-room; but to-night he seemed quite beside himself, and he teased and plagued the boys until, telling him that he was crazy, they put him down on the floor and sat on him.

Somewhat calmed by his suppression, Paul dashed out to the front of the house to seat the early comers. He was a model usher; gracious and smiling he ran up and down the aisles; nothing was too much trouble for him; he carried messages and brought programmes as though it were his greatest pleasure in life, and all the people in his section thought him a charming boy, feeling that he remembered and admired them. As the house filled, he grew more and more vivacious and animated, and the colour came to his cheeks and lips. It was very much as though this were a great reception and Paul were the host. Just as the musicians came out to take their places, his English teacher arrived with checks for the seats which a prominent man-ufacturer had taken for the season. She betrayed some embarrassment when she handed Paul the tickets, and a *hauteur* which subsequently made her feel very foolish. Paul was startled for a moment, and had the feeling of wanting to put her out; what business had she here among all these fine people and gay colours? He looked her over and decided that she was not appropriately dressed and must be a fool to sit downstairs in such togs. The tickets had probably been sent her out of kindness, he reflected as he put down a seat for her, and she had about as much right to sit there as he had.

When the symphony began Paul sank into one of the rear seats with a long sigh of relief, and lost himself as he had done before the Rico. It was not that symphonies, as such, meant anything in particular to Paul, but the first sigh of the instruments seemed to free some hilarious and potent spirit within him; something that struggled there like the Genius in the bottle found by the Arab fisherman. He felt a sudden zest of life; the lights danced before his eyes and the concert hall blazed into unimaginable splendour. When the soprano soloist came on, Paul forgot even the nastiness of his teacher's being there and gave himself up to the peculiar stimulus such personages always had for him. The soloist chanced to be a German woman, by no means in her first youth, and the mother of many children; but she wore an elaborate gown and a tiara, and above all she had that indefinable air of achievement, that world-shine upon her, which, in Paul's eyes, made her a veritable queen of Romance.

After a concert was over Paul was always irritable and wretched until he got to sleep, and to-night he was even more than usually restless. He had the feeling of not being able to let down, of its being impossible to give up this delicious excitement which was the only thing that could be called living at all. During the last number he withdrew and, after hastily changing his clothes in the dressing-room, slipped out to the side door where the soprano's carriage stood. Here he began pacing rapidly up and down the walk, waiting to see her come out.

Over yonder the Schenley, in its vacant stretch, loomed big and square through the fine rain, the windows of its twelve stories glowing like those of a lighted card-board house under a Christmas tree. All the actors and singers of the better class stayed there when they were in the city, and a number of the big manufacturers of the place lived there in the winter. Paul had often hung about the hotel, watching the people go in and out, longing to enter and leave school-masters and dull care behind him forever.

At last the singer came out, accompanied by the conductor, who helped her into her carriage and closed the door with a cordial *auf wiedersehen* which set Paul to wondering whether she were not an old sweetheart of his. Paul followed the carriage over to the hotel, walking so rapidly as not to be far from the entrance when the singer alighted and disappeared behind the swinging glass doors that were opened by a negro in a tall hat and a long coat. In the moment that the door was ajar it seemed to Paul that he, too, entered. He seemed to feel himself go after her up the steps, into the warm, lighted building, into an exotic, a tropical world of shiny, glistening surfaces and basking ease. He reflected upon the mysterious dishes that were brought into the dining-room, the green bottles in buckets of ice, as he had seen them in the supper party pictures of the *Sunday World* supplement. A quick gust of wind brought the rain down with sudden vehemence, and Paul was startled to find that he was still outside in the slush of the gravel driveway; that his boots were letting in the water and his scanty overcoat was clinging wet about him; that the lights in front of the concert hall were out, and that the rain was driving in sheets between him and the orange glow of the windows above him. There it was, what he wanted—tangibly before him, like the fairy world of a Christmas pantomime, but mocking spirits stood guard at the doors, and, as the rain beat in his face, Paul wondered whether he were destined always to shiver in the black night outside, looking up at it.

He turned and walked reluctantly toward the car tracks. The end had to come sometime; his father in his night-clothes at the top of the stairs, explanations that did not explain, hastily improvised fictions that were forever tripping him up, his upstairs room and its horrible yellow wall-paper, the creaking bureau with the greasy plush collar-box, and over his painted wooden bed the pictures of George Washington and John Calvin, and the framed motto, "Feed my Lambs," which had been worked in red worsted by his mother.

Half an hour later, Paul alighted from his car and went slowly down one of the side streets off the main thoroughfare. It was a highly respectable street, where all the houses were exactly alike, and where business men of moderate means begot and reared large families of children, all of whom went to Sabbath-school and learned the shorter catechism, and were interested in arithmetic; all of whom were as exactly alike as their homes, and of a piece with the monotony in which they lived. Paul never went up Cordelia Street without a shudder of loathing. His home was next to the house of the Cumberland minister. He approached it to-night with the nerveless sense of defeat, the hopeless feeling of sinking back forever into ugliness and commonness that he had always had when he came home. The moment he turned into Cordelia Street he felt the waters close above his head. After each of these orgies of living, he experienced all the physical depression which follows a debauch; the loathing of respectable beds, of common food, of a house penetrated by kitchen odours; a shuddering repulsion for the flavourless, colourless mass of every-day existence; a morbid desire for cool things and soft lights and fresh flowers.

The nearer he approached the house, the more absolutely unequal Paul felt to the sight of it all; his ugly sleeping chamber; the cold bathroom with the grimy zinc tub, the cracked mirror, the dripping spiggots; his father, at the top of the stairs, his hairy legs sticking out from his night-shirt, his feet thrust into carpet slippers. He was so much later than usual that there would certainly be inquiries and reproaches. Paul stopped short before the door. He felt that he could not be accosted by his father to-night; that he could not toss again on that miserable bed. He would not go in. He would tell his father that he had no car fare, and it was raining so hard he had gone home with one of the boys and stayed all night.

Meanwhile, he was wet and cold. He went around to the back of the house and tried one of the basement windows, found it open, raised it cautiously, and scrambled down the cellar wall to the floor. There he stood, holding his breath, terrified by the noise he had made, but the floor above him was silent, and there was no creak on the stairs. He found a soap-box, and carried it over to the soft ring of light that streamed from the furnace door, and sat down. He was horribly afraid of rats, so he did not try to sleep, but sat looking distrustfully at the dark, still terrified lest he might have awakened his father. In such reactions, after one of the experiences which made days and nights out of the dreary blanks of the calendar, when his senses were deadened, Paul's head was always singularly clear. Suppose his father had heard him getting in at the window and had come down and shot him for a burglar? Then, again, suppose his father had come down, pistol in hand, and he had cried out in time to save himself, and his father had been horrified to think how nearly he had killed him? Then, again, suppose a day should come when his father would remember that night, and wish there had been no warning cry to stay his hand? With this last supposition Paul entertained himself until daybreak.

The following Sunday was fine; the sodden November chill was broken by the last flash of autumnal summer. In the morning Paul had to go to church and Sabbath-school, as always. On seasonable Sunday afternoons the burghers of Cordelia Street always sat out on their front "stoops," and talked to their neighbours on the next stoop, or called to those across the street in neighbourly fashion. The men usually sat on gay cushions placed upon the steps that led down to the sidewalk, while the women, in their Sunday "waists," sat in rockers on the cramped porches, pretending to be greatly at their ease. The children played in the streets; there were so many of them that the place resembled the recreation grounds of a kindergarten. The men on the steps—all in their shirt sleeves, their vests unbuttoned—sat with their legs well apart, their stomachs comfortably protruding, and talked of the prices of things, or told anecdotes of the sagacity of their various chiefs and overlords. They occasionally looked over the multitude of squabbling children, listened affectionately to their high-pitched, nasal voices, smiling to see their own proclivities reproduced in their offspring, and interspersed their legends of the iron kings with remarks about their sons' progress at school, their grades in arithmetic, and the amounts they had saved in their toy banks.

On this last Sunday of November, Paul sat all the afternoon on the lowest step of his "stoop," staring into the street, while his sisters, in their rockers, were talking to the minister's daughters next door about how many shirt-waists they had made in the last week, and how many waffles some one had eaten at the last church supper. When the weather was warm, and his father was in a particularly jovial frame of mind, the girls made lemonade, which was always brought out in a red-glass pitcher, ornamented with forget-me-nots in blue enamel. This the girls thought very fine, and the neighbours always joked about the suspicious colour of the pitcher.

To-day Paul's father sat on the top step, talking to a young man who shifted a restless baby from knee to knee. He happened to be the young man who was daily held up to Paul as a model, and after whom it was his father's dearest hope that he would pattern. This young man was of a ruddy complexion, with a compressed, red mouth, and faded, nearsighted eyes, over which he wore thick spectacles, with gold bows that curved about his ears. He was clerk to one of the magnates of a great steel corporation, and was looked upon in Cordelia Street as a young man with a future. There was a story that, some five years ago—he was now barely twenty-six—he had been a trifle dissipated but in order to curb his appetites and save the loss of time and strength that a sowing of wild oats might have entailed, he had taken his chief's advice, oft reiterated to his employees, and at twenty-one had married the first woman whom he could persuade to share his fortunes. She happened to be an angular schoolmistress, much older than he, who also wore thick glasses, and who had now borne him four children, all near-sighted, like herself.

The young man was relating how his chief, now cruising in the Mediterranean, kept in touch with all the details of the business, arranging his office hours on his yacht just as though he were at home, and "knocking off work enough to keep two stenographers busy." His father told, in turn, the plan his corporation was considering, of putting in an electric railway plant at Cairo. Paul snapped his teeth; he had an awful apprehension that they might spoil it all before he got there. Yet he rather liked to hear these legends of the iron kings, that were told and retold on Sundays and holidays; these stories of palaces in Venice, yachts on the Mediterranean, and high play at Monte Carlo appealed to his fancy, and he was interested in the triumphs of these cash boys who had become famous, though he had no mind for the cash-boy stage.

After supper was over, and he had helped to dry the dishes, Paul nervously asked his father whether he could go to George's to get some help in his geometry, and still more nervously asked for car fare. This latter request he had to repeat, as his father, on principle, did not like to hear requests for money, whether much or little. He asked Paul whether he could not go to some boy who lived nearer, and told him that he ought not to leave his school work until Sunday; but he gave him the dime. He was not a poor man, but he had a worthy ambition to come up in the world. His only reason for allowing Paul to usher was, that he thought a boy ought to be earning a little.

Paul bounded upstairs, scrubbed the greasy odour of the dish-water from his hands with the ill-smelling soap he hated, and then shook over his fingers a few drops of violet water from the bottle he kept hidden in his drawer. He left the house with his geometry conspicuously under his arm, and the moment he got out of Cordelia Street and boarded a downtown car, he shook off the lethargy of two deadening days, and began to live again.

The leading juvenile of the permanent stock company which played at one of the downtown theatres was an acquaintance of Paul's, and the boy had been invited to drop in at the Sunday-night rehearsals whenever he could. For more than a year Paul had spent every available moment loitering about Charley Edwards's dressing-room. He had won a place among Edwards's following not only because the young actor, who could not afford to employ a dresser, often found him useful, but because he recognized in Paul something akin to what churchmen term "vocation."

It was at the theatre and at Carnegie Hall that Paul really lived; the rest was but a sleep and a forgetting. This was Paul's fairy tale, and it had for him all the allurement of a secret love. The moment he inhaled the gassy, painty, dusty odour behind the scenes, he breathed like a prisoner set free, and felt within him the possibility of doing or saying splendid, brilliant, poetic things. The moment the cracked orchestra beat out the overture from *Martha*, or jerked at the serenade from *Rigoletto*, all stupid and ugly things slid from him, and his senses were deliciously, yet delicately fired.

Perhaps it was because, in Paul's world, the natural nearly always wore the guise of ugliness, that a certain element of artificiality seemed to him necessary in beauty. Perhaps it was because his experience of life elsewhere was so full of Sabbath-school picnics, petty economies, wholesome advice as to how to succeed in life, and the unescapable odours of cooking that he found this existence so alluring, these smartly-clad men and women so attractive, that he was so moved by these starry apple orchards that bloomed perennially under the lime-light.

It would be difficult to put it strongly enough how convincingly the stage entrance of that theatre was for Paul the actual portal of Romance. Certainly none of the company ever suspected it, least of all Charley Edwards. It was very like the old stories that used to float about London of fabulously rich Jews, who had subterranean halls there, with palms, and fountains, and soft lamps and richly apparelled women who never saw the disenchanting light of London day. So, in the midst of that smoke-palled city, enamoured of figures and grimy toil, Paul had his secret temple, his wishing carpet, his bit of blue-and-white Mediterranean shore bathed in perpetual sunshine.

Several of Paul's teachers had a theory that his imagination had been perverted by garish fiction, but the truth was that he scarcely ever read at all. The books at home were not such as would either tempt or corrupt a youthful mind, and as for reading the novels that some of his friends urged upon him—well, he got what he wanted much more quickly from music; any sort of music, from an orchestra to a barrel organ. He needed only the spark, the indescribable thrill that made his imagination master of his senses, and he could make plots and pictures enough of his own. It was equally true that he was not stage struck—not, at any rate, in the usual acceptation of that expression. He had no desire to become an actor, any more than he had to become a musician. He felt no necessity to do any of these things; what he wanted was to see, to be in the atmosphere, float on the wave of it, to be carried out, blue league after blue league, away from everything.

After a night behind the scenes, Paul found the school-room more than ever repulsive; the bare floors and naked walls; the prosy men who never wore frock coats, or violets in their buttonholes; the women with their dull gowns, shrill voices, and pitiful seriousness about prepositions that govern the dative. He could not bear to have the other pupils think, for a moment, that he took these people seriously; he must convey to them that he considered it all trivial, and was there only by way of a jest, anyway. He had autographed pictures of all the members of the stock company which he showed his classmates, telling them the most incredible stories of his familiarity with these people, of his acquaintance with the soloists who came to Carnegie Hall, his suppers with them and the flowers he sent them. When these stories lost their effect, and his audience grew listless, he became desperate and would bid all the boys good-bye, announcing that he was going to travel for a while; going to Naples, to Venice, to Egypt. Then, next Monday, he would slip back, conscious and nervously smiling; his sister was ill, and he should have to defer his voyage until spring.

Matters went steadily worse with Paul at school. In the itch to let his instructors know how heartily he despised them and their homilies, and how thoroughly he was appreciated elsewhere, he mentioned once or twice that he had no time to fool with theorems; adding—with a twitch of the eyebrows and a touch of that nervous bravado which so perplexed them— that he was helping the people down at the stock company; they were old friends of his.

The upshot of the matter was that the Principal went to Paul's father, and Paul was taken out of school and put to work. The manager at Carnegie Hall was told to get another usher in his stead; the doorkeeper at the theatre was warned not to admit him to the house; and Charley Edwards remorsefully promised the boy's father not to see him again.

The members of the stock company were vastly amused when some of Paul's stories reached them—especially the women. They were hardworking women, most of them supporting indigent husbands or brothers, and they laughed rather bitterly at having stirred the boy to such fervid and florid inventions. They agreed with the faculty and with his father that Paul's was a bad case.

The east-bound train was ploughing through a January snow-storm; the dull dawn was beginning to show grey when the engine whistled a mile out of Newark. Paul started up from the seat where he had lain curled in uneasy slumber, rubbed the breath-misted window glass with his hand, and peered out. The snow was whirling in curling eddies above the white bottom lands, and the drifts lay already deep in the fields and along the fences, while here and there the long dead grass and dried weed stalks protruded black above it. Lights shone from the scattered houses, and a gang of labourers who stood beside the track waved their lanterns.

Paul had slept very little, and he felt grimy and uncomfortable. He had made the all-night journey in a day coach, partly because he was ashamed, dressed as he was, to go into a Pullman, and partly because he was afraid of being seen there by some Pittsburgh business man, who might have noticed him in Denny & Carson's office. When the whistle awoke him, he clutched quickly at his breast pocket, glancing about him with an uncertain smile. But the little, clay-bespattered Italians were still sleeping, the slatternly women across the aisle were in open-mouthed oblivion, and even the crumby, crying babies were for the nonce stilled. Paul settled back to struggle with his impatience as best he could.

When he arrived at the Jersey City station, he hurried through his breakfast, manifestly ill at ease and keeping a sharp eye about him. After he reached the Twenty-third Street station, he consulted a cabman, and had himself driven to a men's furnishing establishment that was just opening for the day. He spent upward of two hours there, buying with endless reconsidering and great care. His new street suit he put on in the fitting-room; the frock coat and dress clothes he had bundled into the cab with his linen. Then he drove to a hatter's and a shoe house. His next errand was at Tiffany's, where he selected his silver and a new scarf-pin. He would not wait to have his silver marked, he said. Lastly, he stopped at a trunk shop on Broadway, and had his purchases packed into various travelling bags.

It was a little after one o'clock when he drove up to the Waldorf, and after settling with the cabman, went into the office. He registered from Washington; said his mother and father had been abroad, and that he had come down to await the arrival of their steamer. He told his story plausibly and had no trouble, since he volunteered to pay for them in advance, in engaging his rooms; a sleeping-room, sitting-room and bath.

Not once, but a hundred times Paul had planned this entry into New York. He had gone over every detail of it with Charley Edwards, and in his scrap book at home there were pages of description about New York hotels, cut from the Sunday papers. When he was shown to his sitting-room on the eighth floor, he saw at a glance that everything was as it should be; there was but one detail in his mental picture that the place did not realize, so he rang for the bell boy and sent him down for flowers. He moved about nervously until the boy returned, putting away his new linen and fingering it delightedly as he did so. When the flowers came, he put them hastily into water, and then tumbled into a hot bath. Presently he came out of his white bath-room, resplendent in his new silk underwear, and playing with the tassels of his red robe. The snow was whirling so fiercely outside his windows that he could scarcely see across the street, but within the air was deliciously soft and fragrant. He put the violets and jonquils on the taboret beside the couch, and threw himself down, with a long sigh, covering himself with a Roman blanket. He was thoroughly tired; he had been in such haste, he had stood up to such a strain, covered so much ground in the last twenty-four hours, that he wanted to think how it had all come about. Lulled by the sound of the wind, the warm air, and the cool fragrance of the flowers, he sank into deep, drowsy retrospection.

It had been wonderfully simple; when they had shut him out of the theatre and concert hall, when they had taken away his bone, the whole thing was virtually determined. The rest was a mere matter of opportunity. The only thing that at all surprised him was his own courage—for he realized well enough that he had always been tormented by fear, a sort of apprehensive dread that, of late years, as the meshes of the lies he had told closed about him, had been pulling the muscles of his body tighter and tighter. Until now, he could not remember the time when he had not been dreading something. Even when he was a little boy, it was always there— behind him, or before, or on either side. There had always been the shadowed corner, the dark place into which he dared not look, but from which something seemed always to be watching him—and Paul had done things that were not pretty to watch, he knew.

But now he had a curious sense of relief, as though he had at last thrown down the gauntlet to the thing in the corner.

Yet it was but a day since he had been sulking in the traces; but yesterday afternoon that he had been sent to the bank with Denny & Carson's deposit, as usual—but this time he was instructed to leave the book to be balanced. There was above two thousand dollars in checks, and nearly a thousand in the bank notes which he had taken from the book and quietly transferred to his pocket. At the bank he had made out a new deposit slip. His nerves had been steady enough to permit of his returning to the office, where he had finished his work and asked for a full day's holiday to-morrow, Saturday, giving a perfectly reasonable pretext. The bank book, he knew, would not be returned before Monday or Tuesday, and his father would be out of town for the next week. From the time he slipped the bank notes into his pocket until he boarded the night train for New York, he had not known a moment's hesitation. It was not the first time Paul had steered through treacherous waters.

How astonishingly easy it had all been; here he was, the thing done; and this time there would be no awakening, no figure at the top of the stairs. He watched the snow flakes whirling by his window until he fell asleep.

When he awoke, it was three o'clock in the afternoon. He bounded up with a start; half of one of his precious days gone already! He spent more than an hour in dressing, watching every stage of his toilet carefully in the mirror. Everything was quite perfect; he was exactly the kind of boy he had always wanted to be.

When he went downstairs, Paul took a carriage and drove up Fifth Avenue toward the Park. The snow had somewhat abated; carriages and tradesmen's wagons were hurrying soundlessly to and fro in the winter twilight; boys in woollen mufflers were shovelling off the doorsteps; the avenue stages made fine spots of colour against the white street. Here and there on the corners were stands, with whole flower gardens blooming under glass cases, against the sides of which the snow flakes stuck and melted; violets, roses, carnations, lilies of the valley—somehow vastly more lovely and alluring that they blossomed thus unnaturally in the snow. The Park itself was a wonderful stage winterpiece.

When he returned, the pause of the twilight had ceased, and the tune of the streets had changed. The snow was falling faster, lights streamed from the hotels that reared their dozen stories fearlessly up into the storm, defying the raging Atlantic winds. A long, black stream of carriages poured down the avenue, intersected here and there by other streams, tending horizontally. There were a score of cabs about the entrance of his hotel, and his driver had to wait. Boys in livery were running in and out of the awning stretched across the sidewalk, up and down the red velvet carpet laid from the door to the street. Above, about, within it all was the rumble and roar, the hurry and toss of thousands of human beings as hot for pleasure as himself, and on every side of him towered the glaring affirmation of the omnipotence of wealth.

The boy set his teeth and drew his shoulders together in a spasm of realization; the plot of all dramas, the text of all romances, the nerve-stuff of all sensations was whirling about him like the snow flakes. He burnt like a faggot in a tempest.

When Paul went down to dinner, the music of the orchestra came floating up the elevator shaft to greet him. His head whirled as he stepped into the thronged corridor, and he sank back into one of the chairs against the wall to get his breath. The lights, the chatter, the perfumes, the bewildering medley of colour—he had, for a moment, the feeling of not being able to stand it. But only for a moment; these were his own people, he told himself. He went slowly about the corridors, through the writing-rooms, smoking-rooms, reception-rooms, as though he were exploring the chambers of an enchanted palace, built and peopled for him alone.

When he reached the dining-room he sat down at a table near a window. The flowers, the white linen, the many-coloured wine glasses, the gay toilettes of the women, the low popping of corks, the undulating repetitions of the *Blue Danube* from the orchestra, all flooded Paul's dream with bewildering radiance. When the roseate tinge of his champagne was added—that cold, precious, bubbling stuff that creamed and foamed in his glass—Paul wondered that there were honest men in the world at all. This was what all the world was fighting for, he reflected; this was what all the struggle was about. He doubted the reality of his past. Had he ever known a place called Cordelia Street, a place where fagged-looking businessmen got on the early car; mere rivets in a machine they seemed to Paul—sickening men, with combings of children's hair always hanging to their coats, and the smell of cooking in their clothes. Cordelia Street—Ah! that belonged to another time and country; had he not always been thus, had he not sat here night after night, from as far back as he could remember, looking pensively over just such shimmering textures, and slowly twirling the stem of a glass like this one between his thumb and middle finger? He rather thought he had.

He was not in the least abashed or lonely. He had no especial desire to meet or to know any of these people; all he demanded was the right to look on and conjecture, to watch the pageant. The mere stage properties were all he contended for. Nor was he lonely later in the evening, in his loge at the Metropolitan. He was now entirely rid of his nervous misgivings, of his forced aggressiveness, of the imperative desire to show himself different from his surroundings. He felt now that his surroundings explained him. Nobody questioned the purple; he had only to wear it passively. He had only to glance down at his attire to reassure himself that here it would be impossible for anyone to humiliate him.

He found it hard to leave his beautiful sitting-room to go to bed that night, and sat long watching the raging storm from his turret window. When he went to sleep it was with the lights turned on in his bedroom; partly because of his old timidity, and partly so that, if he should wake in the night, there would be no wretched moment of doubt, no horrible suspicion of yellow wall-paper, or of Washington and Calvin above his bed.

Sunday morning the city was practically snow-bound. Paul breakfasted late, and in the afternoon he fell in with a wild San Francisco boy, a freshman at Yale, who said he had run down for a "little flyer" over Sunday. The young man offered to show Paul the night side of the town, and the two boys went out together after dinner, not returning to the hotel until seven o'clock the next morning. They had started out in the confiding warmth of a champagne friendship, but their parting in the elevator was singularly cool. The freshman pulled himself together to make his train, and Paul went to bed. He awoke at two o'clock in the afternoon, very thirsty and dizzy, and rang for ice-water, coffee, and the Pittsburgh papers.

On the part of the hotel management, Paul excited no suspicion. There was this to be said for him, that he wore his spoils with dignity and in no way made himself conspicuous. Even under the glow of his wine he was never boisterous, though he found the stuff like a magician's wand for wonder-building. His chief greediness lay in his ears and eyes, and his excesses were not offensive ones. His dearest pleasures were the grey winter twilights in his sitting-room; his quiet enjoyment of his flowers, his clothes, his wide divan, his cigarette and his sense of power. He could not remember a time when he had felt so at peace with himself. The mere release from the necessity of petty lying, lying every day and every day, restored his self-respect. He had never lied for pleasure, even at school; but to be noticed and admired, to assert his difference from other Cordelia Street boys; and he felt a good deal more manly, more honest, even, now that he had no need for boastful pretensions, now that he could, as his actor friends used to say, "dress the part." It was characteristic that remorse did not occur to him. His golden days went by without a shadow, and he made each as perfect as he could.

On the eighth day after his arrival in New York, he found the whole affair exploited in the Pittsburgh papers, exploited with a wealth of detail which indicated that local news of a sensational nature was at a low ebb. The firm of Denny & Carson announced that the boy's father had refunded the full amount of the theft, and that they had no intention of prosecuting. The Cumberland minister had been interviewed, and expressed his hope of yet reclaiming the motherless lad, and his Sabbath-school teacher declared that she would spare no effort to that end. The rumour had reached Pittsburgh that the boy had been seen in a New York hotel, and his father had gone East to find him and bring him home.

Paul had just come in to dress for dinner; he sank into a chair, weak to the knees, and clasped his head in his hands. It was to be worse than jail, even; the tepid waters of Cordelia Street were to close over him finally and forever. The grey monotony stretched before him in hopeless, unrelieved years; Sabbath-school, Young People's Meeting, the yellow-papered room, the damp dish-towels; it all rushed back upon him with a sickening vividness. He had the old feeling that the orchestra had suddenly stopped, the sinking sensation that the play was over. The sweat broke out on his face, and he sprang to his feet, looked about him with his white, conscious smile, and winked at himself in the mirror. With something of the old childish belief in miracles with which he had so often gone to class, all his lessons unlearned, Paul dressed and dashed whistling down the corridor to the elevator.

He had no sooner entered the dining-room and caught the measure of the music than his remembrance was lightened by his old elastic power of claiming the moment, mounting with it, and finding it all sufficient. The glare and glitter about him, the mere scenic accessories had again, and for the last time, their old potency. He would show himself that he was game, he would finish the thing splendidly. He doubted, more than ever, the existence of Cordelia Street, and for the first time he drank his wine recklessly. Was he not, after all, one of those fortunate beings born to the purple, was he not still himself and in his own place? He drummed a nervous accompaniment to the Pagliacci music and looked about him, telling himself over and over that it had paid.

He reflected drowsily, to the swell of the music and the chill sweetness of his wine, that he might have done it more wisely. He might have caught an outbound steamer and been well out of their clutches before now. But the other side of the world had seemed too far away and too uncertain then; he could not have waited for it; his need had been too sharp. If he had to choose over again, he would do the same thing to-morrow. He looked affectionately about the dining-room, now gilded with a soft mist. Ah, it had paid indeed!

Paul was awakened next morning by a painful throbbing in his head and feet. He had thrown himself across the bed without undressing, and had slept with his shoes on. His limbs and hands were lead heavy, and his tongue and throat were parched and burnt. There came upon him one of those fateful attacks of clear-headedness that never occurred except when he was physically exhausted and his nerves hung loose. He lay still and closed his eyes and let the tide of things wash over him.

His father was in New York; "stopping at some joint or other," he told himself. The memory of successive summers on the front stoop fell upon him like a weight of black water. He had not a hundred dollars left; and he knew now, more than ever, that money was everything, the wall that stood between all he loathed and all he wanted. The thing was winding itself up; he had thought of that on his first glorious day in New York, and had even provided a way to snap the thread. It lay on his dressing-table now; he had got it out last night when he came blindly up from dinner, but the shiny metal hurt his eyes, and he disliked the looks of it.

He rose and moved about with a painful effort, succumbing now and again to attacks of nausea. It was the old depression exaggerated; all the world had become Cordelia Street. Yet somehow he was not afraid of anything, was absolutely calm; perhaps because he had looked into the dark corner at last and knew. It was bad enough, what he saw there, but somehow not so bad as his long fear of it had been. He saw everything clearly now. He had a feeling that he had made the best of it, that he had lived the sort of life he was meant to live, and for half an hour he sat staring at the revolver. But he told himself that was not the way, so he went downstairs and took a cab to the ferry.

When Paul arrived at Newark, he got off the train and took another cab, directing the driver to follow the Pennsylvania tracks out of the town. The snow lay heavy on the roadways and had drifted deep in the open fields. Only here and there the dead grass or dried weed stalks projected, singularly black, above it. Once well in the country, Paul dismissed the carriage and walked, floundering along the tracks, his mind a medley of irrelevant things. He seemed to hold in his brain an actual picture of everything he had seen that morning. He remembered every feature of both his drivers, of the toothless old woman from whom he had bought the red flowers in his coat, the agent from whom he had got his ticket, and all of his fellow-passengers on the ferry. His mind, unable to cope with vital matters near at hand, worked feverishly and deftly at sorting and grouping these images. They made for him a part of the ugliness of the world, of the ache in his head, and the bitter burning on his tongue. He stooped and put a handful of snow into his mouth as he walked, but that, too, seemed hot. When he reached a little hillside, where the tracks ran through a cut some twenty feet below him, he stopped and sat down.

The carnations in his coat were drooping with the cold, he noticed; their red glory all over. It occurred to him that all the flowers he had seen in the glass cases that first night must have gone the same way, long before this. It was only one splendid breath they had, in spite of their brave mockery at the winter outside the glass; and it was a losing game in the end, it seemed, this revolt against the homilies by which the world is run. Paul took one of the blossoms carefully from his coat and scooped a little hole in the snow, where he covered it up. Then he dozed a while, from his weak condition, seemingly insensible to the cold.

The sound of an approaching train awoke him, and he started to his feet, remembering only his resolution, and afraid lest he should be too late. He stood watching the approaching locomotive, his teeth chattering, his lips drawn away from them in a frightened smile; once or twice he glanced nervously sidewise, as though he were being watched. When the right moment came, he jumped. As he fell, the folly of his haste occurred to him with merciless clearness, the vastness of what he had left undone. There flashed through his brain, clearer than ever before, the blue of Adriatic water, the yellow of Algerian sands.

He felt something strike his chest, and that his body was being thrown swiftly through the air, on and on, immeasurably far and fast, while his limbs were gently relaxed. Then, because the picture making mechanism was crushed, the disturbing visions flashed into black, and Paul dropped back into the immense design of things.

Questions for Writing or Discussion

1. Paul seems to irritate all the people who know him. Do we understand the reasons for their irritation? Do we sympathize at all with their reasons, or do we feel only sorrow and pity for Paul?
2. Is Paul's suicide in character, or is it an unconvincingly melodramatic conclusion?
3. What basic dissatisfaction explains Paul's various feelings and actions: the clothes he wears, the problems he helps create at school, his attitude toward music, and so on?
4. Using your answer to the previous question as a thesis, trace the process leading up to Paul's suicide. Do not write a mere plot summary. The process begins long before the first scene of the story. The reader of your paper should be able to understand not only *what* happened, but *why*.

CHAPTER 8

WRITING A DEFINITION PAPER

From time to time, you've probably found yourself engaged in a shouting match with one or more acquaintances over a question such as, which is the better disco group—Eddie Kendricks or K C and the Sunshine Band. Eventually, some wise soul says, "Hey, wait a minute. What's your idea of a good disco group?" The speaker has demanded a definition of the term which is at the heart of the debate. When you and your friends explain what you're shouting about, you may find that one person's standard for *good* is the degree of amplification the group possesses. Another may respond to the subtlety with which the group improvises on a theme. Then you realize, perhaps, either that your respective ideas of a good group are so different that you can't have a discussion or that, once a definition is understood, you have no real disagreement.

When writing, you won't have the advantage of another party's saying, "Hey, wait a minute. Don't you think you'd better define your terms?" If you want to appear reasonable in your presentation of an idea, you will sometimes have to define terms. Often, the dictionary won't be much help. It may be a good place to start, but there are times when a dictionary definition won't give a full understanding of a term. Take that word *good,* for example. A dictionary tells you that it means "having positive or desirable qualities," and so it does, but how does such a definition help you distinguish between one disco group and another? To do so, you could *begin* with the dictionary definition, to be sure, but you must let your reader know what you believe the positive or desirable qualities of a disco group are. You must write an *extended* definition.

No matter how solid your reasons for approving or disapproving of a person, place, thing, group, or idea, those reasons are unlikely to find acceptance with a reader if you don't define your terms. In writing the Declaration of Independence (p. 222), for example,

Thomas Jefferson clearly understood the need to define a *good* government—one which secures the natural rights of "life, liberty, and the pursuit of happiness" and which derives its powers "from the consent of the governed"—before arguing that George III's government failed to meet those standards. Without the carefully stated definition of a good government, the long list of complaints against the British government might well have been viewed as merely an expression of dissatisfaction by a group of malcontents.

Certain kinds of terms, then, require a more extended definition than the dictionary will give. The burden is on you to explain what you mean by the term. Sometimes this extended definition may appear as a paragraph or two of a long paper. Occasionally, a definition can become a paper in itself.

What kinds of terms need defining?

Judgmental words, words which reflect opinions, need definitions. Whether subjects being discussed are *good, better, best; bad, worse, worst; beautiful, ugly; friendly, unfriendly; wise, foolish; fair, unfair;* etc. is a matter of opinion.

Specialized terms, terms which have a special meaning to a given group, need definition. Almost every professional or occupational group uses specialized terms which the members of the group understand but which require explanation for those outside the group: for example, *psychosis,* a psychological term; *neoclassicism,* a literary term; *writ,* a legal term; and *gig,* a show business term.

Abstractions, general words like *love, democracy, justice, freedom,* and *quality,* need definition.

Controversial terms like *male chauvinist, nuclear build-up,* and *affirmative action* need definition.

Slang terms like *right on, with it, cool,* and *out to lunch* may need definition for many audiences.

You can present your extended definition in one of two ways—formally or informally. The *formal* definition contains the three parts of a dictionary definition: the *term*—the word or phrase to be defined; the *class*—the large group to which the object or concept belongs; and the *differentiation*—those characteristics which distinguish it from all others in its class.

Term	Class	Differentiation
A garden	is a small plot of land	used for the cultivation of flowers, vegetables, or fruits.
Beer	is a fermented alcoholic beverage	brewed from malt and flavored with hops.
Lunch	is a meal	eaten at midday.

To write an extended formal definition, you would first need to develop a one-sentence definition of the term. In doing so, keep the following cautions in mind:

1. *Keep the class restricted.* Speak of a sonnet not as a kind of literature, but as a kind of poem.
2. *Include no important part of the term itself or its derivatives in the class or differentiation.* Don't say that "a definition is that which defines."
3. *Make certain that the sentence defines and does not simply make a statement about the term.* "Happiness is a dry martini" doesn't have the essential parts of a definition.
4. *Provide adequate differentiation to clarify the meaning.* Don't define a traitor as "one who opposes the best interests of his or her country." That definition doesn't exclude the well-meaning person who misunderstands the country's best interests and opposes from ignorance. Try, "A traitor is one who opposes the best interests of his or her country with malicious intent."
5. *Don't make the definition too restrictive.* Don't define a matinee as "a drama presented during the day." That definition doesn't include other forms of entertainment, such as concerts, which could also be held during the daytime.
6. *Make sure to include the class.* Don't write, "Baseball is when nine players . . . ." Write, "Baseball is *a sport* in which nine players . . . ." Remember that a term must always be placed in a class. The differentiation will then tell how this term (baseball) is different from all other items in that class (sport). Baseball must be differentiated from other sports such as basketball and football.

Once you have composed a one-sentence formal definition, its three parts could become the major divisions of your paper. The introduction to your paper might contain the term and its one-sentence definition. That sentence could become the thesis for your paper, or, in addition to providing a one-sentence definition, you could also express an attitude toward the term: "Equality *ought to be* a philosophy and set of laws in which all people are given the same opportunity to achieve their own individual potential." (See "Everyone is Equal in the Grave," [p. 128].)

The first division of your paper could discuss the class, and the second the differentiation. In those discussions, you can make your idea clear by using specific details, by using analogies, by giving examples or telling anecdotes, and sometimes by tracing the history of the term. Often you will be able to quote or refer to the definitions others have given the term. This technique is particularly useful if experts disagree over the meaning of the term. An especially effective tool of definition is *exclusion*, showing what the term is *not:*

> *Gourmet* cooking does not mean to me the preparation of food in expensive wines; it does not mean the preparation of exotic dishes like octopus or rattlesnake; it does not mean the smothering of meat with highly caloric sauces. *Gourmet* cooking to me means the preparation of any food—whether black-eyed peas or hollandaise sauce—in such a way that the dish will be as tasty and attractive as it can be made.

In advancing your discussions of class and differentiation, you can use any method or combination of methods of development which you have studied. You might, for instance, make your idea clear by *classifying* your term. For example, Martin Luther King, Jr., in "Letter from Birmingham Jail" (p. 225), classifies laws as *just* and *unjust.* Or you might *compare and contrast* your understanding of the term with another conception of the term. In the student paper "Everyone Is Equal in the Grave," for example, the author contrasts his understanding of *equality* with that of the futuristic society represented in Vonnegut's short story "Harrison Bergeron." You could also trace a *process.* A definition of *alcoholism,* for instance, could contain a step-by-step analysis of the process by which one becomes an alcoholic. Finally, you could, in some instances, show cause-and-effect relationships. If you were defining a *ghetto,* for example, you could make the definition more insightful by analyzing the reasons ghettos come into existence.

In the paper below, the student derives a formal definition of *equality* from his reading of "Harrison Bergeron" (p. 23).

Everyone Is Equal in the Grave
FREDERICK SPENSE

Kurt Vonnegut, Jr.'s short story "Harrison Bergeron" contrasts the misunderstanding and perversion of equality with the true meaning of the word. Equality ought to be a philosophy and set of laws in which all people are given the same opportunity to achieve their own individual potential. In the U.S.A. of 2081, equality has become a philosophy and set of laws in which everyone is forced to be the same.

The Declaration of Independence presents the principle that "all men are created equal," and various laws attempt to put the principle into practice— laws about voting, employment, housing, and so on. "Equal before God and the law" in the second sentence of the story seems to show Vonnegut's approval of this approach. "Equal every which way" is another problem, though, and the story attempts to show that a government that interprets equality in that manner is going to be a slave state.

Giving people an equal opportunity to be the best they can be is not the same as forcing people to be like everyone else. Any girl who wants to should have the chance to study ballet. That represents equality. Letting poor dancers join the ballet company and "handicapping" good dancers so everyone will be the same is the corruption of equality that has taken place in 2081.

Instead of everyone with a good voice having the same chance to become an announcer if he or she wants to, all the announcers in the world of 2081 have speech impediments. Instead of the most skilled technicians competing for jobs on the television crews so that the best person will be chosen, the crews consist of people who cannot even hold cards right side up. Instead of admitting that smart people and dumb people are different even though they have the same worth as human beings, the government installs electronic equipment to prevent the smart people using their brains for more than a few seconds at a time. Good-looking people wear masks to make them "equal" to ugly people. Strong people wear weights to make them "equal" to weak people.

Vonnegut's point is that this is not true equality, but tyranny. It is not just stupid to stifle exceptional people and create a world where being outstanding is a sin, but to do so requires a tremendous government agency whose job is to snoop and to control the smallest aspects of people's private lives. The Constitution has to be amended to make all this possible, and the Handicapper General has the authority to shoot criminals—that is, individuals—on sight.

Equality is and ought to be one of our most precious ideals. If it ever comes to mean sameness and conformity, it will not really be equality at all, only obedience and regimentation. Equality like that is the equality of the grave.

Questions for Writing or Discussion

1. What is the thesis of the paper?
2. Does the writer successfully achieve a one-sentence formal definition of the term? If so, what is it?
3. What methods of development does the writer use in advancing
   his definition? Could he make his idea clear without using these
   methods?
4. From your reading of the story, do you believe that the definition
   of *equality* presented in this paper is one that Vonnegut would
   approve?

Not all terms lend themselves to the three-part formal definition. Some are better explained by *informal* definition. What is a *good teacher*, for example? Or a *bad marriage*? Or an *ideal home*? Clearly, such topics can only be defined in a subjective or personal way; your purpose is to show what the term means to you. In such instances, it is probably wise to get away from the rigidity of the formal definition and just do a good job of making your conception of the term clear, usually by describing the subject as fully as you can. By the time readers finish the paper, they should understand what the term means to you.

As with formal definitions, you can employ any method or combination of methods of development you have studied. *Examples* and *anecdotes* are especially good for explaining a term. So are *comparison, process, classification,* and *cause and effect.* The idea is to use whatever techniques come in handy to put the idea across.

One good subject for an informal definition is a word or phrase used by a group or a region of the country. In the student paper below, the author explains a term used only by members of her family.

The Grinnies

HELEN FLEMING

Until I was twelve years old, I thought everyone in the world knew about the grinnies, if I thought about the term at all—which is unlikely. After all, everyone in my family used the word quite naturally, and we understood each other. So far as I knew, it was a word like any other word—like *bath,* or *chocolate,* or *homework.* But it was my homework which led to my discovery that *grinnies* was a word not known outside my family.

My last report card had said that I was a "C" student in English, and my parents, both teachers, decided that no child of theirs would be just an average student of anything. So nightly I spelled words aloud and answered questions about the fine points of grammar. I wrote and rewrote and rewrote every composition until I convinced my mother that I could make no more improvements. And the hard work paid off. One day the teacher returned compositions, and there it was—a big, fat, bright red "A" on the top of my paper. Naturally, I was delighted, but I didn't know I was attracting attention until the teacher snapped, "Helen, what *are* you doing?"

Called suddenly out of my happy thoughts, I said, "Oh, I've got the grinnies!" The teacher and my classmates burst into laughter, and then I understood that grinnies were confined to my family. Other people were not so privileged.

And it is a privilege to have the grinnies, an uncontrollable, spontaneous state of ecstasy. Grinnies are demonstrated on the outside by sparkling eyes and a wide, wide smile—not just any smile, but one that shows the teeth and stretches the mouth to its limits. A person experiencing the grinnies appears to be all mouth. On the inside, grinnies are characterized by a feeling of joyful agitation, almost a bubbly sensation. Grinnies usually last just a few seconds, but they can come and go. Sometimes, when life seems just perfect, I have intermittent attacks of the grinnies for a whole day.

The term originated in my mother's family. Her youngest sister, Rose, who had deep dimples, often expressed her pleasure with such a grin that the dimples appeared to become permanent. When Rose was about four, she started explaining her funny look by saying, "I have the grinnies." The term caught on, and it has been an important word in our family now for two generations.

The occasion doesn't matter. Anything can bring on the grinnies—just so long as one feels great delight. When my brother finally pumped his bicycle—without training wheels—from our house to the corner and back, he came home with the grinnies. When I was little, my mother's announcement that we would have homemade ice cream for dessert always gave me the grinnies. My father had the grinnies when I was valedictorian. Grinnies can be brought on by a good meal, a sense of pride, a new friend, a telephone call from someone special, an accomplishment. Or sometimes one gets the grinnies for no reason at all: just a sudden sense of well-being can bring on a case. Whatever brings them on, an attack of the grinnies is among life's greatest pleasures.

In fact, now that I look back on the experience, I feel sorry for my seventh-grade teacher. I think it's a pity she didn't know the word *grinnies*. It's such a useful term for saying, "I'm really, really pleased!"

Questions for Writing or Discussion

1. What is the author's attitude toward her subject?
2. Could a comprehensive understanding of the term be accomplished by a three-part formal definition of the word? Why, or why not?
3. What methods of development does the writer use in defining the term?
4. Do you understand the meaning of the term well enough to give examples—other than those used by the author—of situations which could produce the grinnies?

Readings

The reading selections that follow are examples of informal definitions. As you study them, see if you can identify the methods of development which help make them good definitions.

William Spooner Donald
WILL SOMEONE PLEASE HICCUP MY PAT?

One afternoon nearly a hundred years ago the October wind gusted merrily down Oxford's High Street. Hatless and helpless, a white-haired clergyman with pink cherubic features uttered his plaintive cry for aid. As an athletic youngster chased the spinning topper, other bystanders smiled delightedly—they had just heard at first hand the latest "Spoonerism."

My revered relative William Archibald Spooner was born in 1844, the son of a Staffordshire county court judge. As a young man, he was handicapped by a poor physique, a stammer, and weak eyesight; at first, his only possible claim to future fame lay in the fact that he was an albino, with very pale blue eyes and white hair tinged slightly yellow.

But nature compensated the weakling by blessing him with a brilliant intellect. By 1868 he had been appointed a lecturer at New College, Oxford. Just then he would have been a caricaturist's dream with his freakish looks, nervous manner, and peculiar mental kink that caused him—in his own words—to "make occasional felicities in verbal diction."

Victorian Oxford was a little world of its own where life drifted gently by; a world where splendid intellectuals lived in their ivory towers of Latin, Euclid, and Philosophy; a world where it was always a sunny summer afternoon in a countryside, where Spooner admitted he loved to "pedal gently round on a well-boiled icicle."

As the years passed, Spooner grew, probably without himself being aware of the fact, into a "character." A hard worker himself, he detested idleness and is on record as having rent some lazybones with the gem, "You have hissed all my mystery lessons, and completely tasted two whole worms."

With his kindly outlook on life, it was almost natural for him to take holy orders; he was ordained a deacon in 1872 and a priest in 1875. His unique idiosyncrasy never caused any serious trouble and merely made him more popular. On one occasion, in New College chapel in 1879, he announced smilingly that the next hymn would be "Number one seven five—Kinkering Kongs their Titles Take." Other congregations were treated to such jewels as ". . . Our Lord, we know, is a shoving Leopard . . ." and ". . . All of us have in our hearts a half-warmed fish to lead a better life. . . ."

Spooner often preached in the little village churches around Oxford and once delivered an eloquent address on the subject of Aristotle. No doubt the sermon contained some surprising information for his rustic congregation. For after Spooner had left the pulpit, an idea seemed to occur to him, and he hopped back up the steps again.

"Excuse me, dear brethren," he announced brightly, "I just want to say that in my sermon whenever I mentioned Aristotle, I should have said Saint Paul."

By 1885 the word "Spoonerism" was in colloquial use in Oxford circles, and a few years later, in general use all over England. If the dividing line between truth and myth is often only a hairsbreadth, does it really matter? One story that has been told concerns an optician's shop in London.

Spooner is reputed to have entered and asked to see a "signifying glass." The optician registered polite bewilderment.

"Just an ordinary signifying glass," repeated Spooner, perhaps surprised at the man's obtuseness.

"I'm afraid we haven't one in stock, but I'll make inquiries right away, sir," said the shopkeeper, playing for time.

"Oh, don't bother, it doesn't magnify, it doesn't magnify," said Spooner airily, and walked out.

Fortunately for Spooner, he made the right choice when he met his wife-to-be. He was thirty-four years old when he married Frances Goodwin in 1878. The marriage was a happy one, and they had one son and four daughters. Mrs. Spooner was a tall, good-looking girl, and on one occasion the family went on a short holiday in Switzerland. The "genial Dean," as he was then called, took a keen interest in geology, and in no time at all he had mastered much information and many technical definitions on the subject of glaciers.

One day at lunchtime the younger folk were worried because their parents had not returned from a long walk. When Spooner finally appeared with his wife, his explanation was: "We strolled up a long valley, and when we turned a corner we found ourselves completely surrounded by erotic blacks."

He was, of course, referring to "erratic blocks," or large boulders left around after the passage of a glacier.

In 1903 Spooner was appointed Warden of New College, the highest possible post for a Fellow. One day walking across the quadrangle, he met a certain Mr. Casson, who had just been elected a Fellow of New College.

"Do come to dinner tonight," said Spooner, "we are welcoming our new Fellow, Mr. Casson."

"But, my dear Warden, I *am* Casson," was the surprised reply.

"Never mind, never mind, come along all the same," said Spooner tactfully.

On another occasion in later years when his eyesight was really very bad, Spooner found himself seated next to a most elegant lady at dinner. In a casual moment the latter put her lily-white hand onto the polished table, and Spooner, in an even more casual manner, pronged her hand with his fork, remarking genially, "My bread, I think."

In 1924 Spooner retired as Warden. He had established an astonishing record of continuous residence at New College for sixty-two years first as undergraduate, then as Fellow, then Dean, and finally as Warden. His death in 1930, at the age of eighty-six, was a blushing crow to collectors of those odd linguistic transpositions known by then throughout the English-speaking world as Spoonerisms.

Questions for Writing or Discussion

1. What is a Spoonerism? Does a one-sentence definition of the term appear in the article? Where?

2. At what point in the article did you begin to catch on to what a Spoonerism is? Why, do you suppose, did the author not just tell us at the beginning what the term means?
3. Did the other examples of amusing remarks made by Spooner interfere with your understanding of the term Spoonerism?
4. What is the primary method of development used in this article?
5. If the author's purpose is to define *Spoonerism*, why does he give so many details about Spooner's life?
6. Write an informal paper in which you define an *Archie Bunker*, a *James Bond*, a *Marlboro man*, or a *Mona Lisa smile*.

George E. Hollister
WITH LEGS LIKE THESE . . . WHO NEEDS WINGS?

He's half tail and half feet. The rest of him is head and beak. When he runs, he moves on blurring wheels. He can turn on a dime and leave change. He doesn't need to fly because he can run faster. He kicks dirt in a snake's face, and then eats the snake. He chases lizards, and watches hawks with one eye.

He's "Meep-meep" and a cartoon favorite of three generations. He's an odd bird, but a real one—the roadrunner.

Early southwestern settlers were surprised to see a wildly colored bird dart onto a trail, race ahead of a lone horse and rider, slide to a dusty halt and then bob and bow in salute. Scientists later labeled him *Geococcyx californianus,* a member of the cuckoo family, but settlers aptly named him "roadrunner."

Because of his foot structure, Indians of the Southwest believed he had special power. His toes form an X, with two pointed forward and two backward. This arrangement held special meaning to the Indians, who scratched duplicate X figures near new graves and, for extra protection from evil spirits, decorated infant cradleboards with roadrunner feathers.

The footprint X's are unique in a more concrete way—they show the roadrunner may take 22-inch strides in high gear. He's been clocked at fifteen miles per hour (the rate of a four-minute miler). This means his thin muscular legs are taking 12 steps every second.

The combination of fast feet and a flat, wide tail serving as rudder gives the roadrunner a double advantage over lizards and low-flying insects. He simply darts and twists after his prey, screeching into ninety-degree turns, careening around sagebrush and spurting into a straightaway as he catches his meals on the run.

In the roadrunner's hot, dry desert environment, all this hyper-activity would seem likely to dehydrate the bird. (He also frequents many plains, prairies and oak-hickory forests.) But he has adapted remarkably well to temperatures over one hundred degrees and dry winds. His biggest problem—water—is solved by careful budgeting. He rests in the shade during the hottest part of the day, and replenishes body water through his diet; he eats things like lizards, whose bodies have a high water content, and then manufactures liquid by oxidation of the food into carbon dioxide.

The remainder of his diet is no problem, mainly because he eats most anything he can catch that's smaller than he is. He prefers insects (high water content), plants, lizards, snakes, and mammals like mice and rats.

His manner of catching a snake is especially noteworthy. He dashes in circles around a coiled snake, stops within striking distance, shuffles his feet, swishes his tail in the dirt and stirs up a blinding cloud of dust.

Then begins Act II. Roadrunner ruffles his feathers to reduce penetration from a direct strike, and leaps back into a dizzying series of circles around the bewildered snake. He often reverses directions in mid-stride, catches the snake going the other way, and clouts him with his long, sharp beak. Finally, the tired, wounded snake catches several pecks to the brain and succumbs.

Eating the snake requires almost as much talent as catching it; the bird is dealing with a dinner frequently longer than itself. Roadrunner swallows his prey headfirst, forcing the snake as far down his gullet as possible. If there is excess snake, the bird simply waits for his superactive digestive juices to do their part, and in a matter of hours the snake is completely eaten.

Compared to snakes, insects are easy pickings. Most are simply snapped off mesquite and cacti, or flushed from under rocks with a tail flick. To catch cicadas, so erratic in flight that man can hardly catch them, Roadrunner simply dogs their odd flight pattern.

Roadrunner's eyesight is spectacular. He can spot a lizard skittering out of reach and watch an enemy hawk overhead at the same time. When he really wants to concentrate, he can focus all attention through one eye. Roadrunners have been observed standing entranced with head tilted sideways, one eye focused on the ground, and the other scanning the sky for airborne enemies.

In the spring, Roadrunner gets restless, grows a few sporty new feathers in his head crest and begins stepping out. When he finds a likely prospect for his affections, he starts acting like a normal roadrunner—odd. His call to establish territory is normal: his series of six or eight calls descends in pitch until the last one resembles a mourning dove's plaintive coo.

He'll offer some food, flutter his tail, shuffle his feet in another dust-stirring dance, then end the performance with a graceful bow and more coos. If the hen thinks he's acceptable, she takes the food, they dance and bow, then begin to look for a suitable place to build a nest.

Nest building, roadrunner style, usually results in a disorganized pile of sticks, feathers, old snake skins and rubble. The hen tramples a slight hollow in the center of this debris and lays three to eight white eggs at infrequent intervals. This haphazardly planned parenthood usually results in the first hatched young stumbling over a freshly laid egg or two.

It remained for Warner Brothers to enshrine the incredible roadrunner. From cartoons, the screwball bird and "meep-meep" branched out to emblems, decals and patches. And not only for the toddler set—unofficial military insignia also bear his picture.

And he's not done yet. Next time you see a whirling cloud of dust, watch for some fast soft-shoe, a little artful bobbing and weaving. In the center of that cloud will be a roadrunner, the king of the cuckoos, doing his bit to enliven your hours on the road.

Questions for Writing or Discussion

1. A bird which is half tail and half feet would have no body. What is the effect of such an exaggeration in the opening of the article?
2. Hollister discusses the bird as if it were a person. What personality does he give the bird? Does that technique help you to understand what a roadrunner is?
3. Hollister uses several methods of development in this highly informal definition. What are they?
4. What is the advantage to the reader of being told that Warner Brothers has enshrined the roadrunner?
5. Write an informal paper in which you define *law of the jungle, rat race, mutt,* or another phrase that involves animals or terms associated with animals.

Here is a story which you can use as the basis of a definition paper. As you read the story, try to decide why Galsworthy called it "Quality."

John Galsworthy
QUALITY

I knew him from the days of my extreme youth, because he made my father's boots; inhabiting with his elder brother two little shops let into one, in a small by-street—now no more, but then most fashionably placed in the West End.

That tenement had a certain quiet distinction; there was no sign upon its face that he made for any of the Royal Family—merely his own German name of Gessler Brothers; and in the window a few pairs of boots. I remember that it always troubled me to account for those unvarying boots in the window, for he made only what was ordered, reaching nothing down, and it seemed so inconceivable that what he made could ever have failed to fit. Had he bought them to put there? That, too, seemed inconceivable. He would never have tolerated in his house leather on which he had not worked himself. Besides, they were too beautiful—the pairs of pumps, so inexpressibly slim, the patent leathers with cloth tops, making water come into one's mouth, the tall brown riding-boots with marvelous sooty glow, as if, though new, they had been worn a hundred years. Those pairs could only have been made by one who saw before him the Soul of

Boot—so truly were· they prototypes, incarnating the very spirit of all footwear. These thoughts, of course, came to me later, though even when I was promoted to him, at the age of perhaps fourteen, some inkling haunted me of the dignity of himself and brother. For to make boots—such boots as he made—seemed to me then, and still seems to me, mysterious and wonderful.

I remember well my shy remark, one day, while stretching out to him my youthful foot:

"Isn't it awfully hard to do, Mr. Gessler?"

And his answer, given with a sudden smile from out of the sardonic redness of his beard: "Id is an Ardt!"

Himself, he was a little as if made of leather, with his yellow crinkly face, and crinkly reddish hair and beard, and neat folds slanting down his cheeks to the corners of his mouth, and his guttural and one-toned voice; for leather is a sardonic substance, and stiff and slow of purpose. And that was the character of his face, save that his eyes, which were gray-blue, had in them the simple gravity of one secretly possessed by the Ideal. His elder brother was so very like him—though watery, paler in every way, with a great industry—that sometimes in early days I was not quite sure of him until the interview was over. Then I knew that it was he, if the words, "I will ask my brudder," had not been spoken, and that, if they had, it was the elder brother.

When one grew old and wild and ran up bills, one somehow never ran them up with Gessler Brothers. It would not have seemed becoming to go in there and stretch out one's foot to that blue iron-spectacled face, owing him for more than—say—two pairs, just the comfortable reassurance that one was still his client.

For it was not possible to go to him very often—his boots lasted terribly, having something beyond the temporary—some, as it were, essence of boot stitched into them.

One went in, not as into most shops, in the mood of: "Please serve me, and let me go!" but restfully, as one enters a church; and, sitting on the single wooden chair, waited—for there was never anybody there. Soon—over the top edge of that sort of well—rather dark, and smelling soothingly of leather—which formed the shop, there would be seen his face, or that of his elder brother, peering down. A guttural sound, and the tip-tap of bast slippers beating the narrow wooden stairs, and he would stand before one without coat, a little bent, in leather apron, with sleeves turned back, blinking—as if awakened from some dream of boots, or like an owl surprised in daylight and annoyed at this interruption.

And I would say: "How do you do, Mr. Gessler? Could you make me a pair of Russia leather boots?"

Without a word he would leave me, retiring whence he came, or into the other portion of the shop, and I would continue to rest in the wooden chair, inhaling the incense of his trade. Soon he would come back, holding in his thin, veined hand a piece of gold-brown leather. With eyes fixed on it, he would remark: "What a beaudiful biece!" When I, too, had admired it, he would speak again: "When do you wand dem?" And I would answer: "Oh! As soon as you conveniently can." And he would say: "Tomorrow fordnighd?" Or if he were his elder brother: "I will ask my brudder!"

Then I would murmur: "Thank you! Good-morning, Mr. Gessler."
"Goot-morning!" he would reply, still looking at the leather in his hand.
And as I moved to the door, I would hear the tip-tap of his bast slippers
restoring him, up the stairs, to his dream of boots. But if it were some new
kind of footgear that he had not yet made me, then indeed he would observe
ceremony—divesting me of my boot and holding it long in his hand,
looking at it with eyes at once critical and loving, as if recalling the glow
with which he had created it, and rebuking the way in which one had
disorganized this masterpiece. Then, placing my foot on a piece of paper, he
would two or three times tickle the outer edges with a pencil and pass his
nervous fingers over my toes, feeling himself into the heart of my requirements.

I cannot forget that day on which I had occasion to say to him: "Mr.
Gessler, that last pair of town walking-boots creaked, you know."

He looked at me for a time without replying, as if expecting me to
withdraw or qualify the statement, then said:

"Id shouldn'd 'ave greaked."

"It did, I'm afraid."

"You goddem wed before dey found demselves?"

"I don't think so."

At that he lowered his eyes, as if hunting for memory of those boots, and
I felt sorry I had mentioned this grave thing.

"Zend dem back!" he said; "I will look at dem."

A feeling of compassion for my creaking boots surged up in me, so well
could I imagine the sorrowful long curiosity of regard which he would bend
on them.

"Zome boods," he said slowly, "are bad from birdt. If I can do noding
wid dem, I dake dem off your bill."

Once (once only) I went absentmindedly into his shop in a pair of boots
bought in an emergency at some large firm's. He took my order without
showing me any leather, and I could feel his eyes penetrating the interior
integument of my foot. At last he said:

"Dose are nod my boods."

The tone was not one of anger, nor of sorrow, not even of contempt, but
there was in it something quiet that froze the blood. He put his hand down
and pressed a finger on the place where the left boot, endeavoring to be
fashionable, was not quite comfortable.

"Id 'urds you dere," he said. "Dose big virms 'ave no self-respect.
Drash!" And then, as if something had given way within him, he spoke
long and bitterly. It was the only time I ever heard him discuss the
conditions and hardships of his trade.

"Dey get id all," he said, "dey get id by advertisement, nod by work.
Dey dake id away from us, who lofe our boods. Id gomes to this—bresently
I haf no work. Every year id gets less—you will see." And looking at his
lined face I saw things I had never noticed before, bitter things and bitter
struggle—and what a lot of gray hairs there seemed suddenly in his red
beard!

As best I could, I explained the circumstances of the purchase of those
ill-omened boots. But his face and voice made a so deep impression that

during the next few minutes I ordered many pairs! Nemesis fell! They lasted more terribly than ever. And I was not able conscientiously to go to him for nearly two years.

When at last I went I was surprised that outside one of the two little windows of his shop another name was painted, also that of a bootmaker—making, of course, for the Royal Family. The old familiar boots, no longer in dignified isolation, were huddled in the single window. Inside, the now contracted well of the one little shop was more scented and darker than ever. And it was longer than usual, too, before a face peered down, and the tip-tap of the bast slippers began. At last he stood before me, and, gazing through those rusty iron spectacles, said:

"Mr. —— , isn'd id?"

"Ah! Mr. Gessler," I stammered, "but your boots are really *too* good, you know! See, these are quite decent still!" And I stretched out to him my foot. He looked at it.

"Yes," he said, "beople do nod wand good boods, id seems."

To get away from his reproachful eyes and voice I hastily remarked: "What have you done to your shop?"

He answered quietly: "Id was too exbensif. Do you wand some boods?"

I ordered three pairs, though I had wanted only two, and quickly left. I had, I know not quite what feeling of being part, in his mind, of a conspiracy against him; or not perhaps so much against him as against his idea of boot. One does not, I suppose, care to feel like that; for it was again many months before my next visit to his shop, paid, I remember, with the feeling: "Oh! well, I can't leave the old boy—so here goes! Perhaps it'll be his elder brother!"

For his elder brother, I knew, had not character enough to reproach me, even dumbly.

And, to my relief, in the shop there did appear to be his elder brother, handling a piece of leather.

"Well, Mr. Gessler," I said, "how are you?"

He came close, and peered at me.

"I am breddy well," he said slowly; "but my elder brudder is dead."

And I saw that it was indeed himself—but how aged and wan! And never before had I heard him mention his brother. Much shocked, I murmured: "Oh! I am sorry!"

"Yes," he answered, "he was a good man, he made a good bood; but he is dead." And he touched the top of his head, where the hair had suddenly gone as thin as it had been on that of his poor brother, to indicate, I suppose, the cause of death. "He could nod get over losing de oder shop. Do you wand any boods?" And he held up the leather in his hand: "Id's a beaudiful biece."

I ordered several pairs. It was very long before they came—but they were better than ever. One simply could not wear them out. And soon after that I went abroad.

It was over a year before I was again in London. And the first shop I went to was my old friend's. I had left a man of sixty, I came back to find one of seventy-five, pinched and worn and tremulous, who genuinely, this time, did not at first know me.

"Oh! Mr. Gessler," I said, sick at heart: "how splendid your boots are! See, I've been wearing this pair nearly all the time I've been abroad; and they're not half worn out, are they?"

He looked long at my boots—a pair of Russia leather, and his face seemed to regain its steadiness. Putting his hand on my instep, he said:

"Do dey vid you here? I 'ad trouble wid dat bair, I remember."

I assured him that they had fitted beautifully.

"Do you wand any boods?" he said. "I can make dem quickly; id is a slack dime."

I answered: "Please, please! I want boots all round—every kind!"

"I vill make a vresh model. You food must be bigger." And with utter slowness, he traced round my foot, and felt my toes, only once looking up to say:

"Did I dell you my brudder was dead?"

To watch him was quite painful, so feeble had he grown; I was glad to get away.

I had given those boots up, when one evening they came. Opening the parcel, I set the four pairs out in a row. Then one by one I tried them on. There was no doubt about it. In shape and fit, in finish and quality of leather, they were the best he had ever made me. And in the mouth of one of the town walking-boots I found his bill. The amount was the same as usual, but it gave me quite a shock. He had never before sent it in until quarter day. I flew downstairs and wrote a check, and posted it at once with my own hand.

A week later, passing the little street, I thought I would go in and tell him how splendidly the new boots fitted. But when I came to where his shop had been, his name was gone. Still there, in the window, were the slim pumps, the patent leathers with cloth tops, the sooty riding-boots.

I went in, very much disturbed. In the two little shops—again made into one—was a young man with an English face.

"Mr. Gessler in?" I said.

He gave me a strange, ingratiating look.

"No, sir," he said, "no. But we can attend to anything with pleasure. We've taken the shop over. You've seen our name, no doubt, next door. We make for some very good people."

"Yes, yes," I said, "but Mr. Gessler?"

"Oh!" he answered; "dead."

"Dead! But I received these boots from him only last Wednesday week."

"Ah!" he said; "a shockin' go. Poor old man starved 'imself."

"Good God!"

"Slow starvation, the doctor called it! You see he went to work in such a way! Would keep the shop on; wouldn't have a soul touch his boots except himself. When he got an order, it took him such a time. People won't wait. He lost everybody. And there he'd sit, goin' on and on—I will say that for him—not a man in London made a better boot! But look at the competition! He never advertised! Would 'ave the best leather, too, and do it all 'imself. Well, there it is. What could you expect with his ideas?"

"But starvation—!"

"That may be a bit flowery, as the sayin' is—but I know myself he was sittin' over his boots day and night, to the very last. You see, I used to watch him. Never gave 'imself time to eat; never had a penny in the house. All went in rent and leather. How he lived so long I don't know. He regular let his fire go out. He was a character. But he made good boots."

"Yes," I said, "he made good boots."

Questions for Writing or Discussion

1. Why did the Gessler brothers not advertise that they made boots for the Royal Family?
2. How sympathetic do you think the author wants readers to be toward Mr. Gessler? Does the fact that he makes shoes that last forever make him more admirable or simply foolish?
3. What is the difference between the boots made by Mr. Gessler and those bought by the narrator at a larger store?
4. The only facts we learn directly about the Gessler brothers tell us that they made good shoes. What other facts are strongly implied?
5. Write a paper with specific references to the story in which you define the author's conception of "quality."

CHAPTER 9

WRITING A CAUSE AND EFFECT PAPER

Many of the papers you will be asked to write while in college will require the analysis of the causes or circumstances which led to a given situation: Why did the Women's Liberation Movement come into being? Why, after the Norman Conquest, did England not become a French-speaking nation? Why does the cost of living continue to rise? In questions of this type, the *effect* or result is given, at least briefly. Your job as a student is to determine the causes which produced that effect.

Other papers will require that you discuss the results of a particular cause: What are the positive and negative effects of legalizing lotteries? Discuss the effect of Upton Sinclair's *The Jungle* on the establishment of the Food and Drug Administration. How can noise pollution have a dangerous effect on our bodies? In questions of this type, the *cause* is given, and you must determine the effects which might result or have resulted from that cause.

Cause-and-effect papers do not call for the rigid structure demanded of classification, process, and definition papers. Nevertheless, some logical demands must be met:

Do not confuse cause with process. A process paper tells *how* an event or product came about; a cause-and-effect paper tells *why* something happened.

Avoid the post hoc *fallacy* (p. 32). That a man lost his billfold shortly after walking under a ladder does not mean that walking under the ladder caused his loss. Similarly, that a woman lost her hearing shortly after attending an especially loud rock concert does not necessarily prove that her deafness is a direct result of the band's decibel level.

Do not oversimplify causes. Getting a good night's sleep before an exam doesn't cause a student to receive the highest grade in the

142

class. The rest certainly won't do any harm, but familiarity with the material covered on the exam, intelligence, and ability to write also have something to do with the grade. Almost all effects worth writing about have more than one cause.

Do not oversimplify effects. Even though it may be true that many people lose a lot of money by gambling on lotteries, that does not mean legalizing lotteries will result in nationwide bankruptcy.

Once you have determined the causes or effects you wish to discuss, you can organize your paper in several ways. In a paper devoted primarily to cause, the simplest pattern is to open by describing the *effect* in some detail, then to develop the reasons for that effect in the body of the paper. Thus, if you are trying to explain a recent rise in the cost of living, you begin with a description of the rise (effect)—the cost of living has risen 37.5% during the past three years and promises to go even higher in the coming year—before dealing with its causes. Similarly, a paper devoted primarily to effect will begin with a description of the *cause*. If your subject is the probable effects of the proposed state lottery, you begin with a description of the proposal (cause) before discussing its effects.

In some cases, as when cause and effect are of approximately equal concern, you may want to present one dramatic instance of an effect to open the paper. For example, you might begin a paper on ocean pollution with a description of the sludge mass off the coast of New York, a striking example of the effects of this kind of pollution. The rest of the introduction would lead into the causes of ocean pollution in general. The first major division of the body might list several important causes, and the second major division might detail the effects of those causes: extermination of sea life, danger to public water supplies and hence to public health, and so on.

What pattern of organization does the student use in the following paper?

The Popcorn Habit
MICHAEL BARTKO

It was Friday night. I had been ill, but I was beginning to recover. I knew what I had to do. I did not want this to happen again. I wished that I could avail myself of the twelve steps of Alcoholics Anonymous, but somehow they did not apply; neither could I find an addict's halfway house. I had no problem with drugs. I was not an alcoholic. There was no one to understand me or to commiserate with me. I was a popcorn freak, and I was getting sick of it. I had to try to break the habit, but how?

I know now that I must try to understand my affliction. What purpose does it serve? Why do I enjoy it so much? My life has so many problems.

The way I usually deal with problems is to sit in as near a fetal position as I can, knit my brow, grind my teeth together, and worry. I sometimes need a break from this response to problems. With popcorn, I can forget everything and enjoy the many pleasurable aspects of gluttony. First, I can think of popcorn. Next, I can buy the popcorn. I can then make the popcorn. I can listen to it pop, slowly at first, building to an intense climax as the corn forces open the lid of the pan. I can smell the enticing corn fragrance. Then, I can salt the popcorn. Finally, at last, I can eat the popcorn. Yes, it is good to lose myself in food. This is part of the answer, but why just popcorn?

There are many beautiful things about popcorn itself which cause me to love it: the way it looks, gold and white in the pan, the tempting way it smells, its flavor. It is easy to eat, but its crispness gives the illusion of chewing something solid. It is salty. It is hot.

There is yet another reason I love popcorn so much: happy memories. When I was small, my family used to gather around the radio on Sunday night and listen to the then common mystery and comedy shows. As an extra treat my father would make for us huge bowls of fresh, hot popcorn. This was his way of showing love, of making an exception to his cool deportment. We loved him for it.

The usefulness and pleasure of gluttony, the intrinsic qualities of popcorn, and the fond memories I have about it are strong reasons for continuing the habit, just as they have been strong causes for starting it. Maybe I can learn to live with it. Maybe I'll have to.

Questions for Writing or Discussion

1. What is the thesis of the paper? Where is it stated?
2. What pattern of organization does the writer employ?
3. Look for good transitional devices which help give the paper coherence.
4. Do the causes the student gives appear to be reasonable explanations for how the habit developed?
5. Think about a habit or a prejudice or an unreasonable fear that you have and write a paper which analyzes its causes.

You may find that cause-and-effect analysis is a useful tool for writing about fiction. You look at a character and say, "Why is he like that, exactly?" Then you examine the work to discover the causes for the character traits you have observed. Or you may trace the causes that led to a crisis in a story.

Following is a story by Anton Chekhov, "The Lottery Ticket." After you have read the story, study the paper that follows it.

Anton Chekhov
THE LOTTERY TICKET

Ivan Dmitritch, a middle-class man who lived with his family on an income of twelve hundred a year and was very well satisfied with his lot, sat down on the sofa after supper and began reading the newspaper.

"I forgot to look at the newspaper today," his wife said to him as she cleared the table. "Look and see whether the list of drawings is there."

"Yes, it is," said Ivan Dmitritch; "but hasn't your ticket lapsed?"

"No; I took the interest on Tuesday."

"What is the number?"

"Series 9,499, number 26."

"All right . . . we will look . . . 9,499 and 26."

Ivan Dmitritch had no faith in lottery luck, and would not, as a rule, have consented to look at the lists of winning numbers, but now, as he had nothing else to do and as the newspaper was before his eyes, he passed his finger downwards along the column of numbers. And immediately, as though in mockery of his scepticism, no further than the second line from the top, his eye was caught by the figure 9,499! Unable to believe his eyes, he hurriedly dropped the paper on his knees without looking to see the number of the ticket, and, just as though some one had given him a douche of cold water, he felt an agreeable chill in the pit of the stomach; tingling and terrible and sweet!

"Masha, 9,499 is there!" he said in a hollow voice.

His wife looked at his astonished and panic-stricken face, and realized that he was not joking.

"9,499?" she asked, turning pale and dropping the folded tablecloth on the table.

"Yes, yes . . . it really is there!"

"And the number of the ticket?"

"Oh, yes! There's the number of the ticket too. But stay . . . wait! No, I say! Anyway, the number of our series is there! Anyway, you understand. . . ."

Looking at his wife, Ivan Dmitritch gave a broad, senseless smile, like a baby when a bright object is shown it. His wife smiled too; it was as pleasant to her as to him that he only mentioned the series, and did not try to find out the number of the winning ticket. To torment and tantalize oneself with hopes of possible fortune is so sweet, so thrilling!

"It is our series," said Ivan Dmitritch, after a long silence. "So there is a probability that we have won. It's only a probability, but there it is!"

"Well, now look!"

"Wait a little. We have plenty of time to be disappointed. It's on the second line from the top, so the prize is seventy-five thousand. That's not money, but power, capital! And in a minute I shall look at the list, and there—26! Eh? I say, what if we really have won?"

The husband and wife began laughing and staring at one another in silence. The possibility of winning bewildered them; they could not have said, could not have dreamed, what they both needed that seventy-five thousand for, what they would buy, where they would go. They thought only of the figures 9,499 and 75,000 and pictured them in their imagination, while somehow they could not think of the happiness itself which was so possible.

Ivan Dmitritch, holding the paper in his hand, walked several times from corner to corner, and only when he had recovered from the first impression began dreaming a little.

"And if we have won," he said—"why, it will be a new life, it will be a transformation! The ticket is yours, but if it were mine I should, first of all, of course, spend twenty-five thousand on real property in the shape of an estate; ten thousand on immediate expenses, new furnishing . . . travelling . . . paying debts, and so on. . . . The other forty thousand I would put in the bank and get interest on it."

"Yes, an estate, that would be nice," said his wife, sitting down and dropping her hands in her lap.

"Somewhere in the Tula or Oryol provinces. . . . In the first place we shouldn't need a summer villa, and besides, it would always bring in an income."

And pictures came crowding on his imagination, each more gracious and poetical than the last. And in all these pictures he saw himself well-fed, serene, healthy, felt warm, even hot! Here, after eating a summer soup, cold as ice, he lay on his back on the burning sand close to a stream or in the garden under a lime-tree. . . . It is hot. . . . His little boy and girl are crawling about near him, digging in the sand or catching ladybirds in the grass. He dozes sweetly, thinking of nothing, and feeling all over that he need not go to the office today, tomorrow, or the day after. Or, tired of lying still, he goes to the hayfield, or to the forest for mushrooms, or watches the peasants catching fish with a net. When the sun sets he takes a towel and soap and saunters to the bathing-shed, where he undresses at his leisure, slowly rubs his bare chest with his hands, and goes into the water. And in the water, near the opaque soapy circles, little fish flit to and fro and green water-weeds nod their heads. After bathing there is tea with cream and milk rolls. . . . In the evening a walk or *vint* with the neighbors.

"Yes, it would be nice to buy an estate," said his wife, also dreaming, and from her face it was evident that she was enchanted by her thoughts.

Ivan Dmitritch pictured to himself autumn with its rains, its cold evenings, and its St. Martin's summer. At that season he would have to take longer walks about the garden and beside the river, so as to get thoroughly chilled, and then drink a big glass of vodka and eat a salted mushroom or a soused cucumber, and then—drink another. . . . The children would come running from the kitchen-garden, bringing a carrot and a radish smelling of fresh earth. . . . And then, he would lie stretched full length on the sofa, and in leisurely fashion turn over the pages of some illustrated magazine, or, covering his face with it and unbuttoning his waistcoat, give himself up to slumber.

The St. Martin's summer is followed by cloudy, gloomy weather. It rains day and night, the bare trees weep, the wind is damp and cold. The dogs, the horses, the fowls—all are wet, depressed, downcast. There is nowhere to walk; one can't go out for days together; one has to pace up and down the room, looking despondently at the grey window. It is dreary!

Ivan Dmitritch stopped and looked at his wife.

"I should go abroad, you know, Masha," he said.

And he began thinking how nice it would be in late autumn to go abroad somewhere to the South of France . . . to Italy . . . to India!

"I should certainly go abroad too," his wife said. "But look at the number of the ticket!"

"Wait, wait!"

He walked about the room and went on thinking. It occurred to him: what if his wife really did go abroad? It is pleasant to travel alone, or in the society of light, careless women who live in the present, and not such as think and talk all the journey about nothing but their children, sigh, and tremble with dismay over every farthing. Ivan Dmitritch imagined his wife in the train with a multitude of parcels, baskets, and bags; she would be sighing over something, complaining that the train made her head ache, that she had spent so much money. . . . At the stations he would continually be having to run for boiling water, bread and butter. . . . She wouldn't have dinner because of its being too dear. . . .

"She would begrudge me every farthing," he thought, with a glance at his wife. "The lottery ticket is hers, not mine! Besides, what is the use of her going abroad? What does she want there? She would shut herself up in the hotel, and not let me out of her sight . . . I know!"

And for the first time in his life his mind dwelt on the fact that his wife had grown elderly and plain, and that she was saturated through and through with the smell of cooking, while he was still young, fresh, and healthy, and might well have got married again.

"Of course, all that is silly nonsense," he thought; "but . . . why should she go abroad? What would she make of it? And yet she would go, of course. . . . I can fancy. . . . In reality it is all one to her, whether it is Naples or Klin. She would only be in my way. I should be dependent upon her. I can fancy how, like a regular woman, she will lock the money up as soon as she gets it. . . . She will look after her relations and grudge me every farthing."

Ivan Dmitritch thought of her relations. All those wretched brothers and sisters and aunts and uncles would come crawling about as soon as they heard of the winning ticket, would begin whining like beggars, and fawning upon them with oily, hypocritical smiles. Wretched, detestable people! If they were given anything, they would ask for more; while if they were refused, they would swear at them, slander them, and wish them every kind of misfortune.

Ivan Dmitritch remembered his own relations, and their faces, at which he had looked impartially in the past, struck him now as repulsive and hateful.

"They are such reptiles!" he thought.

And his wife's face, too, struck him as repulsive and hateful. Anger surged up in his heart against her, and he thought malignantly:

"She knows nothing about money, and so she is stingy. If she won it she would give me a hundred rubles, and put the rest away under lock and key."

And he looked at his wife, not with a smile now, but with hatred. She glanced at him too, and also with hatred and anger. She had her own daydreams, her own plans, her own reflections; she understood perfectly well what her husband's dreams were. She knew who would be the first to try to grab her winnings.

"It's very nice making daydreams at other people's expense!" is what her eyes expressed. "No, don't you dare!"

Her husband understood her look; hatred began stirring again in his breast, and in order to annoy his wife he glanced quickly, to spite her, at the fourth page of the newspaper and read out triumphantly:

"Series 9,499, number 46! Not 26!"

Hatred and hope both disappeared at once, and it began immediately to seem to Ivan Dmitritch and his wife that their rooms were dark and small and low-pitched, that the supper they had been eating was not doing them good, but lying heavy on their stomachs, that the evenings were long and wearisome. . . .

"What the devil's the meaning of it?" said Ivan Dmitritch, beginning to be ill-humored. "Wherever one steps there are bits of paper under one's feet, crumbs, husks. The rooms are never swept! One is simply forced to go out. Damnation take my soul entirely! I shall go and hang myself on the first aspen-tree!"

Questions for Writing or Discussion

1. The "effect" in this story is clear. The characters end up hating their lives and each other. Could this effect result only from the possibility of holding a winning lottery ticket?

2. What are the other causes behind the couple's emotions, if any? Why does the author not discuss these other causes directly? Write a paper on the underlying causes for Ivan Dmitritch's unhappiness. (See the student paper that follows for some possibilities.)

When I Get Rich

REBECCA HUNT

Most of us sometimes dream about what we would do if we suddenly had a lot of money. The clothes we would buy! The gifts we would bestow upon our friends and loved ones! The trips we would take—first class all the way! When we engage in one of these flights of fancy, we dream only of gratifying every desire we have ever held. We don't dream of problems. How can there be problems with so much money?

Yet, sharing just the dream of money can cause dissension. Anton Chekhov's "The Lottery Ticket," for example, tells the story of a husband and wife who, when they believe the wife may have a winning lottery ticket, dream about money—and end up hating each other. Why should a few daydreams result in hatred?

The answer lies in the dreams themselves. They tell us a great deal about the way the husband and wife see each other and themselves. Ivan Dmitritch, the husband, at first dreams, as we all might, about a beautiful home with a place for the children to play, of good food and liquor and comfortable surroundings. But when he tells his wife that he would like to travel and she agrees that travel would be nice, his thoughts about the money change. He decides that his wife is stingy. "She would begrudge me every farthing," he says. He realizes, too, that she is old and plain while *he* is "still young, fresh, and healthy, and might well have got married again." He feels that travel wouldn't mean anything to her because she is not adventurous; she would never leave the hotel room. But *he* knows the difference between Naples and Klin. She knows nothing about money and would probably lock it up, whereas *he* knows how to invest in "real property in the shape of an estate." She would probably give the money to her "wretched" relations, but *he* can now regard even his own relations as "reptiles." Ivan Dmitritch sees himself as a shrewd business man, a candidate for remarriage, a world traveler, and an astute judge of personalities. He sees his wife as stingy, ugly, unadventurous, lacking in financial judgment, and a soft touch. He sees her as someone who would spoil his fun if he had money, and he hates her for being that kind of person.

We are not told much about the wife's dreams except that she had her own plans. But we are told that "she knew who would be the first to try to grab her winnings," and that she understood what her husband had been dreaming. This shows that she knows what he thinks of her and that she doesn't like it.

The narrator tells us at the beginning of the story that Ivan Dmitritch "was very well satisifed with his lot." Later we learn that "for the first time in his life" he saw that his wife was old and plain. But no one just suddenly changes from a contented person to one with the number of complaints about his wife that Ivan makes. That kind of discontent had to build; it has been there for a long time. The fact that his wife so quickly understands what he has been dreaming shows that she has been aware of his discontent for some time, too. She hates him for his discontent with her.

Thus, dreaming about money did not cause the mutual hatred with which the story ends. The possibility of having money merely brought to the surface the unhappiness which had existed for a long time.

Questions for Writing or Discussion

1. What causes does the writer give for the mutual hatred at the end of the story? Do you think these are the real causes?
2. Does the writer ignore any significant parts of the story which might contradict her assertions about the husband and wife?
3. Does the introduction clearly call for an analysis of causes?

Readings

Here is a group of readings in which the writers dramatize several cause-and-effect relationships. Notice what a diversity of subjects lend themselves to this approach.

BALLAD OF THE LANDLORD

Landlord, landlord,
My roof has sprung a leak.
Don't you 'member I told you about it
Way last week?

Landlord, landlord,
The steps is broken down.
When you come up yourself
It's a wonder you don't fall down.

Ten bucks you say I owe you?
Ten bucks you say is due?
Well, that's ten bucks more'n I'll pay you
Till you fix this house up new.

What? You gonna get eviction orders?
You gonna cut my heat?
You gonna take my furniture and
Throw it in the street?

Um-huh! You talking high and mighty.
Talk on—till you get through.
You ain't gonna be able to say a word
If I land my fist on you.

Police! Police!
Come and get this man!
He's trying to ruin the government
And overturn the land!

Copper's whistle!
Patrol bell!
Arrest.

Precinct Station.
Iron cell.
Headlines in press:

MAN THREATENS LANDLORD

* * *

TENANT HELD NO BAIL

* * *

JUDGE GIVES NEGRO 90 DAYS IN COUNTY JAIL

—*Langston Hughes*

Questions for Writing or Discussion

1. Outline the sequence of happenings. Several causes bring about the first effect, and that effect in turn becomes a cause for another effect, and so on.
2. How does the author's selection of details and language make us side with the tenant rather than the landlord?

William Carlos Williams
THE USE OF FORCE

They were new patients to me, all I had was the name, Olson. Please come down as soon as you can, my daughter is very sick.

When I arrived I was met by the mother, a big startled looking woman, very clean and apologetic who merely said, Is this the doctor? and let me in. In the back, she added. You must excuse us, doctor, we have her in the kitchen where it is warm. It is very damp here sometimes.

The child was fully dressed and sitting on her father's lap near the kitchen table. He tried to get up, but I motioned for him not to bother, took off my overcoat and started to look things over. I could see that they were all very nervous, eyeing me up and down distrustfully. As often, in such cases, they weren't telling me more than they had to, it was up to me to tell them; that's why they were spending three dollars on me.

The child was fairly eating me up with her cold, steady eyes, and no expression to her face whatever. She did not move and seemed, inwardly, quiet; an unusually attractive little thing, and as strong as a heifer in appearance. But her face was flushed, she was breathing rapidly, and I realized that she had a high fever. She had magnificent blonde hair, in profusion. One of those picture children often reproduced in advertising leaflets and the photogravure sections of the Sunday papers.

She's had a fever for three days, began the father and we don't know what it comes from. My wife has given her things, you know, like people do, but it don't do no good. And there's been a lot of sickness around. So we tho't you'd better look her over and tell us what is the matter.

As doctors often do I took a trial shot at it as a point of departure. Has she had a sore throat?

Both parents answered me together, No . . . No, she says her throat don't hurt her.

Does your throat hurt you? added the mother to the child. But the little girl's expression didn't change nor did she move her eyes from my face.

Have you looked?

I tried to, said the mother, but I couldn't see.

As it happens we had been having a number of cases of diphtheria in the school to which this child went during that month and we were all, quite apparently, thinking of that, though no one had as yet spoken of the thing.

Well, I said, suppose we take a look at the throat first. I smiled in my best professional manner and asking for the child's first name I said, come on, Mathilda, open your mouth and let's take a look at your throat.

Nothing doing.

Aw, come on, I coaxed, just open your mouth wide and let me take a look. Look, I said opening both hands wide, I haven't anything in my hands. Just open up and let me see.

Such a nice man, put in the mother. Look how kind he is to you. Come on, do what he tells you to. He won't hurt you.

At that I ground my teeth in disgust. If only they wouldn't use the word "hurt" I might be able to get somewhere. But I did not allow myself to be hurried or disturbed but speaking quietly and slowly I approached the child again.

As I moved my chair a little nearer suddenly with one catlike movement both her hands clawed instinctively for my eyes and she almost reached them too. In fact she knocked my glasses flying and they fell, though unbroken, several feet away from me on the kitchen floor.

Both the mother and father almost turned themselves inside out in embarrassment and apology. You bad girl, said the mother, taking her and shaking her by one arm. Look what you've done. The nice man . . .

For heaven's sake, I broke in. Don't call me a nice man to her. I'm here to look at her throat on the chance that she might have diphtheria and possibly die of it. But that's nothing to her. Look here, I said to the child, we're going to look at your throat. You're old enough to understand what I'm saying. Will you open it now by yourself or shall we have to open it for you?

Not a move. Even her expression hadn't changed. Her breaths however were coming faster and faster. Then the battle began. I had to do it. I had to have a throat culture for her own protection. But first I told the parents that it was entirely up to them. I explained the danger but said that I would not insist on a throat examination so long as they would take the responsibility.

If you don't do what the doctor says you'll have to go to the hospital, the mother admonished her severely.

Oh yeah? I had to smile to myself. After all, I had already fallen in love with the savage brat, the parents were contemptible to me. In the ensuing struggle they grew more and more abject, crushed, exhausted while she surely rose to magnificent heights of insane fury of effort bred of her terror of me.

The father tried his best, and he was a big man but the fact that she was his daughter, his shame at her behavior and his dread of hurting her made him release her just at the critical times when I had almost achieved success, till I wanted to kill him. But his dread also that she might have diphtheria made him tell me to go on, go on though he himself was almost fainting, while the mother moved back and forth behind us raising and lowering her hands in an agony of apprehension.

Put her in front of you on your lap, I ordered, and hold both her wrists.

But as soon as he did the child let out a scream. Don't, you're hurting me. Let go of my hands. Let them go I tell you. Then she shrieked terrifyingly, hysterically. Stop it! Stop it! You're killing me!

Do you think she can stand it, doctor! said the mother.

You get out, said the husband to his wife. Do you want her to die of diphtheria?

Come on now, hold her, I said.

Then I grasped the child's head with my left hand and tried to get the wooden tongue depressor between her teeth. She fought, with clenched teeth, desperately! But now I also had grown furious—at a child. I tried to hold myself down but I couldn't. I know how to expose a throat for inspection. And I did my best. When finally I got the wooden spatula behind the last teeth and just the point of it into the mouth cavity, she opened up for an instant but before I could see anything she came down again and gripping the wooden blade between her molars she reduced it to splinters before I could get it out again.

Aren't you ashamed, the mother yelled at her. Aren't you ashamed to act like that in front of the doctor?

Get me a smooth-handled spoon of some sort, I told the mother. We're going through with this. The child's mouth was already bleeding. Her tongue was cut and she was screaming in wild hysterical shrieks. Perhaps I should have desisted and come back in an hour or more. No doubt it would have been better. But I have seen at least two children lying dead in bed of neglect in such cases, and feeling that I must get a diagnosis now or never I went at it again. But the worst of it was that I too had got beyond reason. I could have torn the child apart in my own fury and enjoyed it. It was a pleasure to attack her. My face was burning with it.

The damned little brat must be protected against her own idiocy, one says to one's self at such times. Others must be protected against her. It is a social necessity. And all these things are true. But a blind fury, a feeling of adult shame, bred of a longing for muscular release are the operatives. One goes on to the end.

In a final unreasoning assault I overpowered the child's neck and jaws. I forced the heavy silver spoon back of her teeth and down her throat till she gagged. And there is was—both tonsils covered with membrane. She had fought valiantly to keep me from knowing her secret. She had been hiding that sore throat for three days at least and lying to her parents in order to escape just such an outcome as this.

Now truly she was furious. She had been on the defensive before but now she attacked. Tried to get off her father's lap and fly at me while tears of defeat blinded her eyes.

Questions for Writing or Discussion

1. Several of the doctor's comments reveal something about his character.

a. He says of the mother and father, ". . . they weren't telling me more than they had to, it was up to me to tell them; that's why they were spending three dollars on me."
b. "At that I ground my teeth in disgust. If only they wouldn't use the word 'hurt' I might be able to get somewhere."
c. "I had already fallen in love with the savage brat, the parents were contemptible to me."
d. ". . . I wanted to kill him" (the father).
What do these quotations and the events of the last part of the story reveal about the man?
2. Why does the doctor say he was in love with the child and also call her a "damned little brat"?
3. Keeping your answers to the above questions in mind, write a paper which explains why the doctor tore the child's mouth. Fear that the child had diphtheria is only one cause.

Ted Poston
THE REVOLT OF THE EVIL FAIRIES

The grand dramatic offering of the Booker T. Washington Colored Grammar School was the biggest event of the year in our social life in Hopkinsville, Kentucky. It was the one occasion on which they let us use the old Cooper Opera House, and even some of the white folks came out yearly to applaud our presentation. The first two rows of the orchestra were always reserved for our white friends, and our leading colored citizens sat right behind them—with an empty row intervening, of course.

Mr. Ed Smith, our local undertaker, invariably occupied a box to the left of the house and wore his cutaway coat and striped breeches. This distinctive garb was usually reserved for those rare occasions when he officiated at the funerals of our most prominent colored citizens. Mr. Thaddeus Long, our colored mailman, once rented a tuxedo and bought a box too. But nobody paid him much mind. We knew he was just showing off.

The title of our play never varied. It was always Prince Charming and the Sleeping Beauty, but no two presentations were ever the same. Miss H. Belle LaPrade, our sixth-grade teacher, rewrote the script every season, and it was never like anything you read in the storybooks.

Miss LaPrade called it "a modern morality play of conflict between the forces of good and evil." And the forces of evil, of course, always came off second best.

The Booker T. Washington Colored Grammar School was in a state of ferment from Christmas until February, for this was the period when parts were assigned. First there was the selection of the Good Fairies and the Evil Fairies. This was very important, because the Good Fairies wore white costumes and the Evil Fairies black. And strangely enough most of the Good Fairies usually turned out to be extremely light in complexion, with straight hair and white folks' features. On rare occasions a darkskinned girl might be lucky enough to be a Good Fairy, but not one with a speaking part.

There never was any doubt about Prince Charming and the Sleeping Beauty. They were always lightskinned. And though nobody ever discussed those things openly, it was an accepted fact that a lack of pigmentation was a decided advantage in the Prince Charming and Sleeping Beauty sweepstakes.

And therein lay my personal tragedy. I made the best grades in my class, I was the leading debater, and the scion of a respected family in the community. But I could never be Prince Charming, because I was black.

In fact, every year when they started casting our grand dramatic offering my family started pricing black cheesecloth at Franklin's Department Store. For they knew that I would be leading the forces of darkness and skulking back in the shadows—waiting to be vanquished in the third act. Mamma had experience with this sort of thing. All my brothers had finished Booker T. before me.

Not that I was alone in my disappointment. Many of my classmates felt it too. I probably just took it more to heart. Rat Joiner, for instance, could rationalize the situation. Rat was not only black; he lived on Billy Goat Hill. But Rat summed it up like this:

"If you black, you black."

I should have been able to regard the matter calmly too. For our grand dramatic offering was only a reflection of our daily community life in Hopkinsville. The yallers had the best of everything. They held most of the teaching jobs in Booker T. Washington Colored Grammar School. They were the Negro doctors, the lawyers, the insurance men. They even had a "Blue Vein Society," and if your dark skin obscured your throbbing pulse you were hardly a member of the elite.

Yet I was inconsolable the first time they turned me down for Prince Charming. That was the year they picked Roger Jackson. Roger was not only dumb; he stuttered. But he was light enough to pass for white, and that was apparently sufficient.

In all fairness, however, it must be admitted that Roger had other qualifications. His father owned the only colored saloon in town and was quite a power in local politics. In fact, Mr. Clinton Jackson had a lot to say about just who taught in the Booker T. Washington Colored Grammar School. So it was understandable that Roger should have been picked for Prince Charming.

My real heartbreak, however, came the year they picked Sarah Williams for Sleeping Beauty. I had been in love with Sarah since kindergarten. She had soft light hair, bluish-gray eyes, and a dimple which stayed in her left cheek whether she was smiling or not.

Of course Sarah never encouraged me much. She never answered any of my fervent love letters, and Rat was very scornful of my one-sided love affairs. "As long as she don't call you a black baboon," he sneered, "you'll keep on hanging around."

After Sarah was chosen for Sleeping Beauty, I went out for the Prince Charming role with all my heart. If I had declaimed boldly in previous contests, I was matchless now. If I had bothered Mamma with rehearsals at home before, I pestered her to death this time. Yes, and I purloined my sister's can of Palmer's Skin Success.

I knew the Prince's role from start to finish, having played the Head Evil Fairy opposite it for two seasons. And Prince Charming was one character whose lines Miss LaPrade never varied much in her many versions. But although I never admitted it, even to myself, I knew I was doomed from the start. They gave the part to Leonardius Wright. Leonardius, of course, was yaller.

The teachers sensed my resentment. They were most apologetic. They pointed out that I had been such a splendid Head Evil Fairy for two seasons that it would be a crime to let anybody else try the role. They reminded me that Mamma wouldn't have to buy any more cheesecloth because I could use my same old costume. They insisted that the Head Evil Fairy was even more important than Prince Charming because he was the one who cast the spell on Sleeping Beauty. So what could I do but accept?

I had never liked Leonardius Wright. He was a goody-goody, and even Mamma was always throwing him up to me. But, above all, he too was in love with Sarah Williams. And now he got a chance to kiss Sarah every day in rehearsing the awakening scene.

Well, the show must go on, even for little black boys. So I threw my soul into my part and made the Head Evil Fairy a character to be remembered. When I drew back from the couch of Sleeping Beauty and slunk away into the shadows at the approach of Prince Charming, my facial expression was indeed something to behold. When I was vanquished by the shining sword of Prince Charming in the last act, I was a little hammy perhaps—but terrific!

The attendance at our grand dramatic offering that year was the best in its history. Even the while folks overflowed the two rows reserved for them, and a few were forced to sit in the intervening one. This created a delicate situation, but everybody tactfully ignored it.

When the curtain went up on the last act, the audience was in fine fettle. Everything had gone well for me too—except for one spot in the second act. That was where Leonardius unexpectedly rapped me over the head with his sword as I slunk off into the shadows. That was not in the script, but Miss LaPrade quieted me down by saying it made a nice touch anyway. Rat said Leonardius did it on purpose.

The third act went on smoothly, though, until we came to the vanquishing scene. That was where I slunk from the shadows for the last time and challenged Prince Charming to mortal combat. The hero reached for his shining sword—a bit unsportsmanlike, I always thought, since Miss LaPrade consistently left the Head Evil Fairy unarmed—and then it happened!

Later I protested loudly—but in vain—that it was a case of self-defense. I pointed out that Leonardius had a mean look in his eye. I cited the impromptu rapping he had given my head in the second act. But nobody would listen. They just wouldn't believe that Leonardius really intended to brain me when he reached for his sword.

Anyway, he didn't succeed. For the minute I saw that evil gleam in his eye—or was it my own?—I cut loose with a right to the chin, and Prince Charming dropped his shining sword and staggered back. His astonishment lasted only a minute, though, for he lowered his head and came charging in, fists flailing. There was nothing yellow about Leonardius but his skin.

The audience thought the scrap was something new Miss LaPrade had written in. They might have kept on thinking so if Miss LaPrade hadn't been screaming so hysterically from the sidelines. And if Rat Joiner hadn't decided that this was as good a time as any to settle old scores. So he turned around and took a sock at the male Good Fairy nearest him.

When the curtain rang down, the forces of Good and Evil were locked in combat. And Sleeping Beauty was wide awake and streaking for the wings.

They rang the curtain back up fifteen minutes later, and we finished the play. I lay down and expired according to specifications but Prince Charming will probably remember my sneering corpse to his dying day. They wouldn't let me appear in the grand dramatic offering at all the next year. But I didn't care. I couldn't have been Prince Charming anyway.

Questions for Writing or Discussion

1. To what race does Miss LaPrade belong?
2. Why is it significant that the narrator made the best grades, was the leading debater, and was the son of a respected family?
3. Why do the "yallers" have the best of everything in the community?
4. Why is the Head Evil Fairy unarmed?
5. Write a paper in which you explain why the narrator "couldn't have been Prince Charming anyway."

George Orwell
SHOOTING AN ELEPHANT

In Moulmein, in Lower Burma, I was hated by large numbers of people—the only time in my life that I have been important enough for this to happen to me. I was sub-divisional police officer of the town, and in an aimless, petty kind of way anti-European feeling was very bitter. No one had the guts to raise a riot, but if a European woman went through the bazaars alone somebody would probably spit betel juice over her dress. As a police officer I was an obvious target and was baited whenever it seemed safe to do so. When a nimble Burman tripped me up on the football field and the referee (another Burman) looked the other way, the crowd yelled with hideous laughter. This happened more than once. In the end the sneering yellow faces of young men that met me everywhere, the insults hooted after me when I was at a safe distance, got badly on my nerves. The young Buddhist priests were the worst of all. There were several thousands of them in the town and none of them seemed to have anything to do except stand on street corners and jeer at Europeans.

All this was perplexing and upsetting. For at that time I had already made up my mind that imperialism was an evil thing and the sooner I chucked up my job and got out of it the better. Theoretically—and secretly, of course—I was all for the Burmese and all against their oppressors, the British. As for the job I was doing, I hated it more bitterly than I can perhaps make clear. In a job like that you see the dirty work of Empire at close quarters. The wretched prisoners huddling in the stinking cages of the lock-ups, the grey, cowed faces of the long-term convicts, the scarred buttocks of the men who had been flogged with bamboos—all these oppressed me with an intolerable sense of guilt. But I could get nothing into perspective. I was young and ill-educated and I had had to think out my problems in the utter silence that is imposed on every Englishman in the East. I did not even know that the British Empire is dying, still less did I know that it is a great deal better than the younger empires that are going to supplant it. All I knew was that I was stuck between my hatred of the empire I served and my rage against the evil-spirited little beasts who tried to make my job impossible. With one part of my mind I thought of the British Raj as an unbreakable tyranny, as something clamped down, *in saecula saeculorum*,[1] upon the will of prostrate peoples; with another part I thought that the greatest joy in the world would be to drive a bayonet into a Buddhist priest's guts. Feelings like these are the normal by-products of imperialism; ask any Anglo-Indian official, if you can catch him off duty.

One day something happened which in a roundabout way was enlightening. It was a tiny incident in itself, but it gave me a better glimpse than I had had before of the real nature of imperialism—the real motives for which despotic governments act. Early one morning the sub-inspector at a police station the other end of the town rang me up on the phone and said that an elephant was ravaging the bazaar. Would I please come and do something about it? I did not know what I could do, but I wanted to see what was happening and I got on to a pony and started out. I took my rifle, an old .44 Winchester and much too small to kill an elephant, but I thought the noise might be useful *in terrorem*.[2] Various Burmans stopped me on the way and told me about the elephant's doings. It was not, of course, a wild elephant, but a tame one which had gone "must." It had been chained up as tame elephants always are when their attack of "must" is due, but on the previous night it had broken its chain and escaped. Its mahout,[3] the only person who could manage it when it was in that state, had set out in pursuit, but he had taken the wrong direction and was now twelve hours' journey away, and in the morning the elephant had suddenly reappeared in the town. The Burmese population had no weapons and were quite helpless against it. It had already destroyed somebody's bamboo hut, killed a cow and raided some fruit-stalls and devoured the stock; also it had met the municipal rubbish van, and, when the driver jumped out and took to his heels, had turned the van over and inflicted violence upon it.

---

1. Latin for "time out of mind"
2. Latin for "as a warning"
3. trainer and rider

The Burmese sub-inspector and some Indian constables were waiting for me in the quarter where the elephant had been seen. It was a very poor quarter, a labyrinth of squalid bamboo huts, thatched with palm-leaf, winding all over a steep hillside. I remember that it was a cloudy stuffy morning at the beginning of the rains. We began questioning the people as to where the elephant had gone, and, as usual, failed to get any definite information. That is invariably the case in the East; a story always sounds clear enough at a distance, but the nearer you get to the scene of events the vaguer it becomes. Some of the people said that the elephant had gone in one direction, some said that he had gone in another, some professed not even to have heard of any elephant. I had almost made up my mind that the whole story was a pack of lies, when we heard yells a little distance away. There was a loud, scandalised cry of "Go away, child! Go away this instant!" and an old woman with a switch in her hand came round the corner of a hut, violently shooing away a crowd of naked children. Some more women followed, clicking their tongues and exclaiming; evidently there was something there that the children ought not to have seen. I rounded the hut and saw a man's dead body sprawling in the mud. He was an Indian, a black Dravidian coolie, almost naked, and he could not have been dead many minutes. The people said that the elephant had come suddenly upon him round the corner of the hut, caught him with its trunk, put its foot on his back and ground him into the earth. This was the rainy season and the ground was soft, and his face had scored a trench a foot deep and a couple of yards long. He was lying on his belly with arms crucified and head sharply twisted to one side. His face was coated with mud, the eyes wide open, the teeth bared and grinning with an expression of unendurable agony. (Never tell me, by the way, that the dead look peaceful. Most of the corpses I have seen looked devilish.) The friction of the great beast's foot had stripped the skin from his back as neatly as one skins a rabbit. As soon as I saw the dead man I sent an orderly to a friend's house nearby to borrow an elephant rifle. I had already sent back the pony, not wanting it to go mad with fright and throw me if it smelled the elephant.

The orderly came back in a few minutes with a rifle and five cartridges, and meanwhile some Burmans had arrived and told us that the elephant was in the paddy fields below, only a few hundred yards away. As I started forward practically the whole population of the quarter flocked out of their houses and followed me. They had seen the rifle and were all shouting excitedly that I was going to shoot the elephant. They had not shown much interest in the elephant when he was merely ravaging their homes, but it was different now that he was going to be shot. It was a bit of fun to them, as it would be to an English crowd; besides, they wanted the meat. It made me vaguely uneasy. I had no intention of shooting the elephant—I had merely sent for the rifle to defend myself if necessary—and it is always unnerving to have a crowd following you. I marched down the hill, looking and feeling a fool, with the rifle over my shoulder and an ever-growing army of people jostling at my heels. At the bottom, when you got away from the huts, there was a metalled road and beyond that a miry waste of paddy fields a thousand yards across, not yet ploughed but soggy from the first rains and dotted with coarse grass. The elephant was standing eighty yards from the road, his left side towards us. He took not the slightest notice of the crowd's approach. He was tearing up bunches of grass, beating them against his knees to clean them and stuffing them into his mouth.

I had halted on the road. As soon as I saw the elephant I knew with perfect certainty that I ought not to shoot him. It is a serious matter to shoot a working elephant—it is comparable to destroying a huge and costly piece of machinery—and obviously one ought not to do it if it can possibly be avoided. And at that distance, peacefully eating, the elephant looked no more dangerous than a cow. I thought then and I think now that his attack of "must" was already passing off; in which case he would merely wander harmlessly about until the mahout came back and caught him. Moreover, I did not in the least want to shoot him. I decided that I would watch him for a little while to make sure that he did not turn savage again, and then go home.

But at that moment I glanced round at the crowd that had followed me. It was an immense crowd, two thousand at the least and growing every minute. It blocked the road for a long distance on either side. I looked at the sea of yellow faces above the garish clothes—faces all happy and excited over this bit of fun, all certain that the elephant was going to be shot. They were watching me as they would watch a conjuror about to perform a trick. They did not like me, but with the magical rifle in my hands I was momentarily worth watching. And suddenly I realised that I should have to shoot the elephant after all. The people expected it of me and I had got to do it; I could feel their two thousand wills pressing me forward, irresistibly. And it was at this moment, as I stood there with the rifle in my hands, that I first grasped the hollowness, the futility of the white man's dominion in the East. Here was I, the white man with his gun, standing in front of the unarmed native crowd—seemingly the leading actor of the piece; but in reality I was only an absurd puppet pushed to and fro by the will of those yellow faces behind. I perceived in this moment that when the white man turns tyrant it is his own freedom that he destroys. He becomes a sort of hollow, posing dummy, the conventionalised figure of a sahib.[4] For it is the condition of his rule that he shall spend his life in trying to impress the "natives" and so in every crisis he has got to do what the "natives" expect of him. He wears a mask, and his face grows to fit it. I had got to shoot the elephant. I had committed myself to doing it when I sent for the rifle. A sahib has got to act like a sahib; he has got to appear resolute, to know his own mind and do definite things. To come all that way, rifle in hand, with two thousand people marching at my heels, and then to trail feebly away, having done nothing—no, that was impossible. The crowd would laugh at me. And my whole life, every white man's life in the East, was one long struggle not to be laughed at.

But I did not want to shoot the elephant. I watched him beating his bunch of grass against his knees, with that preoccupied grandmotherly air that elephants have. It seemed to me that it would be murder to shoot him. At that age I was not squeamish about killing animals, but I had never shot an

---

4. master

elephant and never wanted to. (Somehow it always seems worse to kill a *large* animal.) Besides, there was the beast's owner to be considered. Alive, the elephant was worth at least a hundred pounds; dead, he would only be worth the value of his tusks—five pounds, possibly. But I had got to act quickly. I turned to some experienced-looking Burmans who had been there when we arrived, and asked them how the elephant had been behaving. They all said the same thing: he took no notice of you if you left him alone, but he might charge if you went too close to him.

It was perfectly clear to me what I ought to do. I ought to walk up to within, say, twenty-five yards of the elephant and test his behaviour. If he charged I could shoot, if he took no notice of me it would be safe to leave him until the mahout came back. But also I knew that I was going to do no such thing. I was a poor shot with a rifle and the ground was soft mud into which one would sink at every step. If the elephant charged and I missed him, I should have about as much chance as a toad under a steam-roller. But even then I was not thinking particularly of my own skin, only the watchful yellow faces behind. For at that moment, with the crowd watching me, I was not afraid in the ordinary sense, as I would have been if I had been alone. A white man mustn't be frightened in front of "natives"; and so, in general, he isn't frightened. The sole thought in my mind was that if anything went wrong those two thousand Burmans would see me pursued, caught, trampled on and reduced to a grinning corpse like that Indian up the hill. And if that happened it was quite probable that some of them would laugh. That would never do. There was only one alternative. I shoved the cartridges into the magazine and lay down on the road to get a better aim.

The crowd grew very still, and a deep, low, happy sigh, as of people who see the theatre curtain go up at last, breathed from innumerable throats. They were going to have their bit of fun after all. The rifle was a beautiful German thing with cross-hair sights. I did not then know that in shooting an elephant one should shoot to cut an imaginary bar running from ear-hole to ear-hole. I ought therefore, as the elephant was sideways on, to have aimed straight at his ear-hole; actually I aimed several inches in front of this, thinking the brain would be further forward.

When I pulled the trigger I did not hear the bang or feel the kick—one never does when a shot goes home—but I heard the devilish roar of glee that went up from the crowd. In that instant, in too short a time, one would have thought, even for the bullet to get there, a mysterious, terrible change had come over the elephant. He neither stirred nor fell, but every line of his body had altered. He looked suddenly stricken, shrunken, immensely old, as though the frightful impact of the bullet had paralysed him without knocking him down. At last, after what seemed a long time—it might have been five seconds, I dare say—he sagged flabbily to his knees. His mouth slobbered. An enormous senility seemed to have settled upon him. One could have imagined him thousands of years old. I fired again into the same spot. At the second shot he did not collapse but climbed with desperate slowness to his feet and stood weakly upright, with legs sagging and head drooping. I fired a third time. That was the shot that did for him. You could see the agony of it jolt his whole body and knock the last remnant of strength from his legs. But in falling he seemed for a moment to rise, for as his hind legs collapsed beneath him he seemed to tower upwards like a huge rock toppling, his trunk reaching skyward like a tree. He trumpeted, for the first and only time. And then down he came, his belly towards me, with a crash that seemed to shake the ground even where I lay.

I got up. The Burmans were already racing past me across the mud. It was obvious that the elephant would never rise again, but he was not dead. He was breathing very rhythmically with long rattling gasps, his great mound of a side painfully rising and falling. His mouth was wide open—I could see far down into caverns of pale pink throat. I waited a long time for him to die, but his breathing did not weaken. Finally I fired my two remaining shots into the spot where I thought his heart must be. The thick blood welled out of him like red velvet, but still he did not die. His body did not even jerk when the shots hit him, the tortured breathing continued without a pause. He was dying, very slowly and in great agony, but in some world remote from me where not even a bullet could damage him further. I felt that I had got to put an end to that dreadful noise. It seemed dreadful to see the great beast lying there, powerless to move and yet powerless to die, and not even to be able to finish him. I sent back for my small rifle and poured shot after shot into his heart and down his throat. They seemed to make no impression. The tortured gasps continued as steadily as the ticking of a clock.

In the end I could not stand it any longer and went away. I heard later that it took him half an hour to die. Burmans were arriving with dahs[5] and baskets even before I left, and I was told they had stripped his body almost to the bones by the afternoon.

Afterwards, of course, there were endless discussions about the shooting of the elephant. The owner was furious, but he was only an Indian and could do nothing. Besides, legally I had done the right thing, for a mad elephant has to be killed, like a mad dog, if its owner fails to control it. Among the Europeans opinion was divided. The older men said I was right, the younger men said it was a damn shame to shoot an elephant for killing a coolie, because an elephant was worth more than any damn Coringhee coolie. And afterwards I was very glad that the coolie had been killed; it put me legally in the right and it gave me a sufficient pretext for shooting the elephant. I often wondered whether any of the others grasped that I had done it solely to avoid looking a fool.

Questions for Writing or Discussion

1. What insight about the real nature of imperialism did Orwell gain from the incident?
2. Why did Orwell shoot the elephant?
3. Why did he not want to shoot the elephant?

---

5. knives

4. Why, if Orwell's purpose is to explain his hatred of imperialism, does he devote so much space to his hatred of the Burmese?
5. In view of the insight Orwell gained, do you find the last paragraph ironic?
6. Does Orwell's statement that he had killed the elephant solely to avoid looking a fool have greater meaning than merely trying to avoid an embarrassing moment? If so, what other meaning do you find in the statement?
7. Write a paper in which you analyze the causes for Orwell's shooting the elephant. Why did he feel he *had* to shoot the elephant?

CHAPTER 10

WRITING A COMPARISON AND CONTRAST PAPER

A comparison shows the similarities between two or more things; a contrast shows the differences between two or more things; a comparison-contrast shows both similarities and differences. The most common kind of essay question given on examinations calls for comparison-contrast. You would do well, therefore, to master the techniques of that pattern of development.

Comparison and contrast are both useful because they enable us to comprehend our world. A small boy asks his mother what an apartment is. The mother responds, "It's like our house. It has a living room, kitchen, bathroom, and bedroom. Some apartments have dining rooms and more than one bedroom—just as we do. But it's not exactly like our house. You wouldn't have your own yard to play in. And there are lots of apartments in one building, so many families live close together. An apartment is usually much smaller than a house. And you are not as free in an apartment as in a house. You wouldn't be able to run in the living room because you might bother the neighbors beneath you." The mother, by comparing and contrasting the familiar with the unfamiliar, has been able to give the child some idea of what an apartment is; she has enlarged his comprehension of the world.

Everyone uses comparisons, sometimes to explain the unfamiliar, and sometimes just to establish a superficial similarity: "He is as slow as a snail," for example. But to produce papers of significant worth, a writer should apply logical principles to the consideration of similarities and differences.

Compare and contrast according to a single principle. The average citizen might compare or contrast automobiles and airplanes as means of transportation. An engineer might deal with the same subjects in an attempt to solve the problem of air pollution. The principle in the first instance could be ease of travel; in the second, pollution. The principle, in each case, determines the similarities and differences which would be discussed in the paper. The citizen concerned with ease of travel need not mention the variety of colors which both airplanes and automobiles can be painted. The engineer concerned with pollution need not mention the presence of stewardesses on the plane.

In a sense, this means developing a thesis. However, a principle for comparison-contrast would probably need to be established before the writer could arrive at a thesis: the meaning of the similarities and differences. In the first instance, a writer might, after examination of the similarities and differences according to the principle of ease of travel, establish as a thesis that travel by air is more convenient than travel by automobile.

Compare and contrast according to a single purpose. One useful purpose is to *clarify* by pointing out the similarities in apparently dissimilar things and the differences in apparently similar things. One might, for example, discuss a novel like *The Great Gatsby* and the movie version of that novel, which starred Robert Redford and Mia Farrow. The novel is generally regarded as a classic of our literature; the movie, which was extraordinarily faithful to the book, is thought by most critics to be a catastrophe. An effective paper on the two could help clarify the reasons for the success of one and the failure of the other.

A second purpose of comparison-contrast is to show the superiority of one thing over another. The writer who concludes that travel by air is more convenient than travel by automobile does that.

A third purpose of comparison-contrast is to use the two items as examples of a generalization: for instance, "That black people in America want to be thought of as individuals rather than as stereotyped representatives of causes or groups is shown in the writings of Ralph Ellison and James Baldwin."

Be fair with your comparison-contrasts. If you see an exception to the comparison you have made, mention it. This is known as *qualification,* and can often be a most effective means of winning the reader's respect and confidence.

A comparison-contrast paper can be organized in one of three ways: subject-by-subject, point-by-point, or a combination of the two.

For short papers, one of the clearest patterns of organization—for comparison *or* contrast—is the subject-by-subject pattern. If you select this pattern, you first discuss one side of the subject completely, and then you discuss the other side. You must, of course, stress the same points in discussing each side of the subject; otherwise there will be no comparison. The following outline and paper will illustrate this pattern of development.

The Gay Divorcée

BARBARA GROSS

Thesis: The life of the divorced woman is vastly different from what is represented in the myth of the gay divorcée.

    I. Elements of the myth
        A. Support
        B. Living quarters
        C. Clothes
        D. Transportation
        E. Entertainment
   II. Reality of the situation
        A. Support
        B. Living quarters
        C. Clothes
        D. Transportation
        E. Entertainment

It took twenty-five minutes to get married, and after five years, only fifteen minutes to get unmarried. "La Dolce Vita" is supposed to begin as soon as a woman regains her freedom, or so I've been told.

According to the script of "La Dolce Vita," a fat alimony-and-child-support check will carry the divorcée until she walks into a glamorous new job filled with challenge, excitement, and a fabulous salary. She will enjoy a spacious suite of rooms in an exclusive neighborhood. Her closet will bulge with expensive clothes from the very finest boutiques. A classic automobile, perhaps an El Dorado, will wait for her to turn the key and carry her to exotic places and adventures with exciting new friends.

My experience has not quite hit all these high points. When my ex and I parted company, I got the kids, the furniture, the cat and a nonexistent monthly support check.

Glamour is one word I would not use when talking about that first job I "walked into" in my newly awarded freedom. (And *grabbed* is probably a better term than *walked into!*) I was not the best prepared person to have to shoulder the support of two small children. Two and a half years as a girl Friday in a department store's accounts payable department coupled with a high school diploma and interrupted by a five-year marriage does not put one in the five-figure salary bracket; it barely gets one into the middle of four! After forty-seven interviews in which I was either overqualified for low pay jobs or underqualified for decent pay jobs, I accepted the intriguing opportunity to become a bookkeeper for a fish house. The fabulous salary I acquired with my new position barely put me over the poverty level.

Consequently, my plush apartment is a relatively comfortable upstairs of an aging two-family on the west side. It's not the Gold Coast, but then someone has to live in the inner city. And my wardrobe consists largely of leftovers from the last eight years and some hand-me-downs from a second cousin.

Six months after I was divorced, I took the plunge and learned to drive. My first car was an adventure in itself. My father purchased the marvel on wheels for fifteen dollars and after he made some "minor" repairs, he turned me loose. It took me one month and a rainy day to wreck it, and the public transportation system chauffeured me about for nearly a year afterwards.

The fish house is hardly exotic, and the bus drivers and truckers from the fish house hardly comprise a group of exciting new friends, nice folks though they are, but I've gone back to college now, and I enjoy my courses.

I've had two raises in pay since I started at the fish house, and I feel pretty good about life. Looking back over the past three years since I began "La Dolce Vita," I must say things have improved, but I still have a long way to go, Baby!

A second pattern of development is the point-by-point pattern. This pattern is most frequently used in writing long papers, but it can be employed even in a short paragraph. In it, the writer establishes one or more points of comparison or contrast and then applies those points to each side of a subject.

Having It My Way
JOHN KERMAVNER

Thesis: McDonald's is a better fast-food restaurant than Burger King.

    I. Service to customers
       A. Burger King
       B. McDonald's

   II. Taste of burgers
       A. Burger King
       B. McDonald's

To some people, all hamburgers are alike. To me, a connoisseur of hamburgers in fast-food restaurants, there is a world of difference. Burger King and McDonald's are two such fast-food chains that differ in quality. About the only thing Burger King and McDonald's have in common is that they both serve giant hamburgers. Burger King calls its giant hamburger the Whopper. McDonald's offers the Big Mac.

The obvious differences are those of service and taste of the burgers. Whenever I enter Burger King there is always a single line which snakes its way up to the front where the cashier takes my order. This is a long and slow procedure. When I go into McDonald's, the lines are usually short, because there are many friendly cashiers who take the orders quickly.

Burger King makes a bland Whopper which consists of a large patty of beef with lettuce, mayonnaise, mustard, ketchup, onions, and pickles thrown on top. All of this is put between a cold bun. McDonald's uses two freshly fried beef patties, smothered with a special sauce which enhances the flavor of the meat. Added to this sandwich are crisp lettuce, mild onions, juicy pickles, tasty cheese, and a warm sesame seed bun.

The food and service at McDonald's are superb. I'm sure glad they're doing it all for me.

The point-by-point pattern and the subject-by-subject pattern are most useful if you wish to stress only the similarities between two items or only the differences between two items. Sometimes, however, you will want to give approximately equal weight to similarities *and* differences. To do that, you will combine the above patterns, as the outline and paper below illustrate.

A Tropical Christmas
SANDRA LYNN

Thesis: It is not necessary to spend the Christmas holidays at home to enjoy them.

I. Similarities
   A. Waking up
   B. Opening the gifts
   C. Going to church

II. Differences
   A. Weather
      1. In Olmsted Falls, Ohio
      2. In Ft. Myers Beach, Florida
   B. Christmas Tree
      1. In Olmsted Falls, Ohio
      2. In Ft. Myers Beach, Florida
   C. Christmas Dinner
      1. In Olmsted Falls, Ohio
      2. In Ft. Myers Beach, Florida

For the past few years, my family and I have spent the holiday season in Florida. Many foolish people actually presume that we miss being home on Christmas Day. Nothing could be farther from the truth. It is not necessary to be at home to enjoy Christmas. To be blunt and to risk seeming snooty, Christmas in a rented condominium in Ft. Myers Beach, Florida, is the best place to be on Christmas Day.

As at home, the children are up with the first ray of light that filters through the drapes. They giggle and whisper just loudly enough not to aggravate my husband and me but loudly enough to wake us up for their big event of the day—the opening of the gifts.

As at home, the beautiful gift wrappings are demolished in record time each year. Before-and-after pictures are a definite necessity; otherwise nobody would believe I spent a full day adorning the gifts with handmade name tags and glittering and flocked Christmas paper that it takes the children only twenty minutes to destroy. No matter what part of the country it is in, a mess is a mess.

As at home, the opening of gifts is followed by a battle to convince the children they must get dressed for church and to give them the assurance that their toys will still be under the tree when we return. As at home, we struggle through the Christmas morning traffic, sit through a too-long sermon, concern ourselves more with keeping the children content than we do with concentrating on the minister's words, and struggle back through the traffic, just as we did up North. But, oh, the weather! The weather and the informal way of life make for important differences between Christmas in Olmsted Falls, Ohio, and Ft. Myers Beach, Florida.

At home in Olmsted Falls it is generally bleak and cold on December twenty-fifth. Granted, a snowfall of three inches or so can be a classic addition to this holiday, but more often than not, there are only dirty, gray slush and half-melted snowmen to greet me on Christmas Day. Instinctively, I take the warmest outfit I own out of the closet.

In Ft. Myers Beach there is the sound of the beckoning surf and the warmth of the golden morning sun to greet me. In front of the balcony some fluttering seagulls signal us with sharp, shrill tones in anticipation of their breakfast—scraps from our dinner of the previous evening. By the time the gifts are opened, the mess is cleared away, and a very simple breakfast is served, the temperature is just right for sunbathing. After church, I don my red and green bathing suit as the appropriate apparel for the rest of the day.

The Christmas tree we used to purchase in Olmsted Falls was always overpriced and misshapen. I had to place the daintily designed ornaments just so on the tree, and my husband cursed while he tried to string the lights. The children were yelled at for crinkling the tinsel and reprimanded unless each strand was placed perfectly on a branch.

One of the nicest experiences in Florida is the leisurely stroll that my husband and children take along the beach to search for the inimitable tree. When they spy a grove of Whispering Pines, my husband snaps off the plumpest branch. Upon their return, they place it in a milk carton now filled with wet sand. Each of us makes several ornaments with the stipulation that most materials must come from the beach, with the exception of thread, glue, glitter, and paint. To us the finished product is a marvelous Florida Christmas tree with color-coated shells chock-full of glitter dangling from the frail stems and a spiny, unbending starfish standing rigid at the top. We fondly dub our tree the "Charley Brown Christmas Tree."

At home, for several days before and on Christmas Day, I worked like a fool cleaning and cooking. I was compelled to invite my relatives for dinner. Every corner, drawer, and cupboard had to be immaculate. The turkey had to be stuffed and basted, the sweet potatoes candied, the gravy made as smooth as possible, and the pumpkin pie baked to perfection. The table had to be set elegantly with my best linen tablecloth and napkins, and the crystal and china had to be rewashed to sparkle. By the time we sat down to eat, I was too tired to lift my fork.

In Florida, it is every person for himself. It is my vacation, and my motto is, "God helps those who help themselves." Usually my husband will bring home some hamburgers after his golf game, or we may even splurge and purchase a bucket of Kentucky Fried Chicken. A real honest-to-goodness dish is a profane word to me, and a stiff penalty is invoked on anyone not using a paper plate. In the evening, I sip on something tropical and watch the sun set over Sanibel Island.

There is only one disadvantage to spending the Christmas season in Florida and that is the day I have to leave for home.

The comparison-contrast paper is especially effective as a means of writing about literature because when one literary work is compared with another, the comparison often provides fresh insights into both works. If, for example, you read the following two poems separately, you would probably not derive the same meaning from them as did the student who compared them in "Two Kinds of Love."

SONNET 29

When, in disgrace with Fortune and men's eyes,
I all alone beweep my outcast state,
And trouble deaf heaven with my bootless[1] cries,
And look upon myself and curse my fate,
Wishing me like to one more rich in hope,
Featured like him, like him with friends possessed,
Desiring this man's art, and that man's scope,
With what I most enjoy contented least;
Yet in these thoughts myself almost despising,
Haply I think on thee, and then my state,
Like to the lark at break of day arising
From sullen earth, sings hymns at heaven's gate;
   For thy sweet love remembered such wealth brings
   That then I scorn to change my state with kings.

—*William Shakespeare*

1. futile

SONNET 130

My mistress' eyes are nothing like the sun;
Coral is far more red than her lips' red;
If snow be white, why then her breasts are dun;
If hairs be wires, black wires grow on her head.

I have seen roses damasked, red and white,
But no such roses see I in her cheeks;
And in some perfumes is there more delight
Than in the breath that from my mistress reeks.
I love to hear her speak; yet well I know
That music hath a far more pleasing sound.
I grant I never saw a goddess go:
My mistress, when she walks, treads on the ground.
    And yet, by heaven, I think my love as rare
    As any she belied with false compare.

—*William Shakespeare*

Two Kinds of Love

JULIE OLIVERA

Shakespeare's Sonnet 29, "When, in disgrace with Fortune and men's eyes," and Sonnet 130, "My mistress' eyes are nothing like the sun," both strike me as very fine love poems. Both offer great tributes to the loved person. Love comes in all shapes and sizes, however, and I think the feelings expressed in "My mistress' eyes" are more realistic and more trustworthy. I'd rather be the woman that poem was written for than the other woman.

"When, in disgrace" begins by describing a situation in which the poet feels totally depressed. Totally is no exaggeration. He hasn't had any good "fortune," people look down on him, he is jealous of other people, heaven is "deaf" to his prayers. He has little or no hope. He has few, if any, friends. The things he enjoys most mean nothing to him. He even comes close to hating himself. The second part of the poem very beautifully says that even in a foul mood like that if he just happens to "think on thee," he cheers up. He realizes, in fact, that he is one of the luckiest men in the world. He has her love, and her love makes him richer than a king in all that really matters. "For thy sweet love remembered such wealth brings / That then I scorn to change my state with kings."

Well, I'd be flattered, of course, and I might even wipe away a tear, but I'm not sure how much I would trust him. Love is a great inspiration to fall back on if one's life starts going to pieces, but it also has to exist on a day-to-day basis, through all the normal wear and tear, through all the boredom and nothing-special times. If I save a drowning person, he might say with complete sincerity that he loves and adores me, but that is no real basis for a lifelong relationship. If it takes bad times to make the poet realize how much he loves his lady, what starts happening to the love when times aren't so bad?

In "My mistress' eyes," the poet is not depressed, but confident and cheerful. He is in love just as much, but this time with a real person, not a goddess or miracle worker. If anything bothers him, it is people who have to depend on illusions and lies to make their loves seem worthwhile. He still wouldn't trade places with a king, yet he knows and gladly accepts that other women are better-looking, and that they have nicer voices, and even that they have sweeter-smelling breath. He doesn't have to turn his lady into something she isn't in order to love her.

I think this expression of love is by far the more valid one. People want to be loved for what they are, imperfections and all. If someone says he loves me, I want to feel he loves *me* rather than an unrealistic mental image he has of me. If all he loves is the image, the love is an insult. In direct contrast, the poet in "When, in disgrace" seems to love the woman for what she does for him, while the poet in "My mistress' eyes" loves her simply for what she is.

Between the stickiness and sweetness of the first poem and the realism of the second, I have to choose the second. Both poems are fine, but one is written for rare moods, and the other is written for a lifetime.

Questions for Writing and Discussion

1. The writer depends on the poems to communicate her own feelings about love. Are her summaries of each poem accurate and complete?
2. What pattern of development does the writer use? Can you outline the paper?
3. Has the writer produced a unified comparison-and-contrast paper, or has she written two separate essays on two separate poems?
4. Do the poems strike you as presenting two opposing attitudes? The writer assumes they were written about two different women. Could they have been written about the same woman?

Readings

The groups of readings that follow were selected to provide you with subject matter for comparison and contrast papers of your own. Questions and possible writing assignments appear at the end of each group.

Two Detective Stories for Comparison and Contrast

Arthur Conan Doyle
THE ADVENTURE OF THE BLUE CARBUNCLE

I had called upon my friend Sherlock Holmes upon the second morning after Christmas, with the intention of wishing him the compliments of the season. He was lounging upon the sofa in a purple dressing-gown, a pipe-rack within his reach upon the right, and a pile of crumpled morning papers, evidently newly studied, near at hand. Beside the couch was a wooden chair, and on the angle of the back hung a very seedy and disreputable hard-felt hat, much the worse for wear, and cracked in several places. A lens and a forceps lying upon the seat of the chair suggested that the hat had been suspended in this manner for the purpose of examination.

"You are engaged," said I; "perhaps I interrupt you."

"Not at all. I am glad to have a friend with whom I can discuss my results. The matter is a perfectly trivial one"—he jerked his thumb in the direction of the old hat—"but there are points in connection with it which are not entirely devoid of interest and even of instruction."

I seated myself in his armchair and warmed my hands before his crackling fire, for a sharp frost had set in, and the windows were thick with the ice crystals. "I suppose," I remarked, "that, homely as it looks, this thing has some deadly story linked on to it—that it is the clue which will guide you in the solution of some mystery and the punishment of some crime."

"No, no. No crime," said Sherlock Holmes, laughing. "Only one of those whimsical little incidents which will happen when you have four million human beings all jostling each other within the space of a few square miles. Amid the action and reaction of so dense a swarm of humanity, every possible combination of events may be expected to take place, and many a little problem will be presented which may be striking and bizarre without being criminal. We have already had experience of such."

"So much so," I remarked, "that of the last six cases which I have added to my notes, three have been entirely free of any legal crime."

"Precisely. You allude to my attempt to recover the Irene Adler papers, to the singular case of Miss Mary Sutherland, and to the adventure of the man with the twisted lip. Well, I have no doubt that this small matter will fall into the same innocent category. You know Peterson, the commissionaire?"[1]

"Yes."

"It is to him that this trophy belongs."

"It is his hat."

"No, no; he found it. Its owner is unknown. I beg that you will look upon it not as a battered billycock but as an intellectual problem. And, first, as to how it came here. It arrived upon Christmas morning, in company with a good fat goose, which is, I have no doubt, roasting at this moment in front of Peterson's fire. The facts are these: about four o'clock on Christmas morning, Peterson, who, as you know, is a very honest fellow, was returning from some small jollification and was making his way homeward down Tottenham Court Road. In front of him he saw, in the gaslight, a tallish man, walking with a slight stagger, and carrying a white goose slung over his shoulder. As he reached the corner of Goodge Street, a row broke out between this stranger and a little knot of roughs. One of the latter knocked off the man's hat, on which he raised his stick to defend himself and, swinging it over his head, smashed the shop window behind him. Peterson had rushed forward to protect the stranger from his assailants; but the man, shocked at having broken the window, and seeing an official-looking person in uniform rushing towards him, dropped his goose, took to

---

1. doorman

his heels, and vanished amid the labyrinth of small streets which lie at the back of Tottenham Court Road. The roughs had also fled at the appearance of Peterson, so that he was left in possession of the field of battle, and also of the spoils of victory in the shape of this battered hat and a most unimpeachable Christmas goose."

"Which surely he restored to their owner?"

"My dear fellow, there lies the problem. It is true that 'For Mrs. Henry Baker' was printed upon a small card which was tied to the bird's left leg, and it is also true that the initials 'H. B.' are legible upon the lining of this hat; but as there are some thousands of Bakers, and some hundreds of Henry Bakers in this city of ours, it is not easy to restore lost property to any one of them."

"What, then, did Peterson do?"

"He brought round both hat and goose to me on Christmas morning, knowing that even the smallest problems are of interest to me. The goose we retained until this morning, when there were signs that, in spite of the slight frost, it would be well that it should be eaten without unnecessary delay. Its finder has carried it off, therefore, to fulfil the ultimate destiny of a goose, while I continue to retain the hat of the unknown gentleman who lost his Christmas dinner."

"Did he not advertise?"

"No."

"Then, what clue could you have as to his identity?"

"Only as much as we can deduce."

"From his hat?"

"Precisely."

"But you are joking. What can you gather from this old battered felt?"

"Here is my lens. You know my methods. What can you gather yourself as to the individuality of the man who has worn this article?"

I took the tattered object in my hands and turned it over rather ruefully. It was a very ordinary black hat of the usual round shape, hard and much the worse for wear. The lining had been of red silk, but was a good deal discoloured. There was no maker's name; but, as Holmes had remarked, the initials "H. B." were scrawled upon one side. It was pierced in the brim for a hat-securer, but the elastic was missing. For the rest, it was cracked, exceedingly dusty, and spotted in several places, although there seemed to have been some attempt to hide the discoloured patches by smearing them with ink.

"I can see nothing," said I, handing it back to my friend.

"On the contrary, Watson, you can see everything. You fail, however, to reason from what you see. You are too timid in drawing your inferences."

"Then, pray tell me what it is that you can infer from this hat?"

He picked it up and gazed at it in the peculiar introspective fashion which was characteristic of him. "It is perhaps less suggestive than it might have been," he remarked, "and yet there are a few inferences which are very distinct, and a few others which represent at least a strong balance of probability. That the man was highly intellectual is of course obvious upon the face of it, and also that he was fairly well-to-do within the last three years, although he has now fallen upon evil days. He had foresight, but has less now than formerly, pointing to a moral retrogression, which, when taken with the decline of his fortunes, seems to indicate some evil influence, probably drink, at work upon him. This may account also for the obvious fact that his wife has ceased to love him.''

''My dear Holmes!''

''He has, however, retained some degree of self-respect,'' he continued, disregarding my remonstrance. ''He is a man who leads a sedentary life, goes out little, is out of training entirely, is middle-aged, has grizzled hair which he has had cut within the last few days, and which he anoints with lime-cream. These are the more patent facts which are to be deduced from his hat. Also, by the way, that it is extremely improbable that he has gas laid on in his house.''

''You are certainly joking, Holmes.''

''Not in the least. Is it possible that even now, when I give you these results, you are unable to see how they are attained?''

''I have no doubt that I am very stupid, but I must confess that I am unable to follow you. For example, how did you deduce that this man was intellectual?''

For answer Holmes clapped the hat upon his head. It came right over the forehead and settled upon the bridge of his nose. ''It is a question of cubic capacity,'' said he; ''a man with so large a brain must have something in it.''

''The decline of his fortunes, then?''

''This hat is three years old. These flat brims curled at the edge came in then. It is a hat of the very best quality. Look at the band of ribbed silk and the excellent lining. If this man could afford to buy so expensive a hat three years ago, and has had no hat since, then he has assuredly gone down in the world.''

''Well, that is clear enough, certainly. But how about the foresight and the moral retrogression?''

Sherlock Holmes laughed. ''Here is the foresight,'' said he, putting his finger upon the little disc and loop of the hat-securer. ''They are never sold upon hats. If this man ordered one, it is a sign of a certain amount of foresight, since he went out of his way to take this precaution against the wind. But since we see that he has broken the elastic and has not troubled to replace it, it is obvious that he has less foresight now than formerly, which is a distinct proof of a weakening nature. On the other hand, he has endeavoured to conceal some of these stains upon the felt by daubing them with ink, which is a sign that he has not entirely lost his self-respect.''

''Your reasoning is certainly plausible.''

''The further points, that he is middle-aged, that his hair is grizzled, that it has been recently cut, and that he uses lime-cream, are all to be gathered from a close examination of the lower part of the lining. The lens discloses a large number of hair-ends, clean cut by the scissors of the barber. They all appear to be adhesive, and there is a distinct odour of lime-cream. This dust, you will observe, is not the gritty, gray dust of the street but the fluffy brown dust of the house, showing that it has been hung up indoors most of the time; while the marks of moisture upon the inside are proof positive that the wearer perspired very freely, and could, therefore, hardly be in the best of training.''

"But his wife—you said that she had ceased to love him."

"This hat has not been brushed for weeks. When I see you, my dear Watson, with a week's accumulation of dust upon your hat, and when your wife allows you to go out in such a state, I shall fear that you also have been unfortunate enough to lose your wife's affection."

"But he might be a bachelor."

"Nay, he was bringing home the goose as a peace-offering to his wife. Remember the card upon the bird's leg."

"You have an answer to everything. But how on earth do you deduce that the gas is not laid on in his house?"

"One tallow stain, or even two, might come by chance; but when I see no less than five, I think that there can be little doubt that the individual must be brought into frequent contact with burning tallow—walks upstairs at night probably with his hat in one hand and a guttering candle in the other. Anyhow, he never got tallow-stains from a gas-jet. Are you satisfied?"

"Well, it is very ingenious," said I, laughing; "but since, as you said just now, there has been no crime committed, and no harm done save the loss of a goose, all this seems to be rather a waste of energy."

Sherlock Holmes had opened his mouth to reply, when the door flew open, and Peterson, the commissionaire, rushed into the apartment with flushed cheeks and the face of a man who is dazed with astonishment.

"The goose, Mr. Holmes! The goose, sir!" he gasped.

"Eh? What of it, then? Has it returned to life and flapped off through the kitchen window?" Holmes twisted himself round upon the sofa to get a fairer view of the man's excited face.

"See here, sir! See what my wife found in its crop!" He held out his hand and displayed upon the centre of the palm a brilliantly scintillating blue stone, rather smaller than a bean in size, but of such purity and radiance that it twinkled like an electric point in the dark hollow of his hand.

Sherlock Holmes sat up with a whistle. "By Jove, Peterson!" said he, "this is treasure trove indeed. I suppose you know what you have got?"

"A diamond, sir? A precious stone. It cuts into glass as though it were putty."

"It's more than a precious stone. It is *the* precious stone."

"Not the Countess of Morcar's blue carbuncle!" I ejaculated.

"Precisely so. I ought to know its size and shape, seeing that I have read the advertisement about it in *The Times* every day lately. It is absolutely unique, and its value can only be conjectured, but the reward offered of £1000 is certainly not within a twentieth part of the market price."

"A thousand pounds! Great Lord of mercy!" The commissionaire plumped down into a chair and stared from one to the other of us.

"That is the reward, and I have reason to know that there are sentimental considerations in the background which would induce the Countess to part with half her fortune if she could but recover the gem."

"It was lost, if I remember aright, at the Hotel Cosmopolitan," I remarked.

"Precisely so, on December 22nd, just five days ago. John Horner, a plumber, was accused of having abstracted it from the lady's jewel-case. The evidence against him was so strong that the case has been referred to the Assizes. I have some account of the matter here, I believe." He rummaged amid his newspapers, glancing over the dates, until at last he smoothed one out, doubled it over, and read the following paragraph:

Hotel Cosmopolitan Jewel Robbery. John Horner, 26, plumber, was brought up upon the charge of having upon the 22d inst., abstracted from the jewel-case of the Countess of Morcar the valuable gem known as the blue carbuncle. James Ryder, upper-attendant at the hotel, gave his evidence to the effect that he had shown Horner up to the dressing-room of the Countess of Morcar upon the day of the robbery in order that he might solder the second bar of the grate, which was loose. He had remained with Horner some little time, but had finally been called away. On returning, he found that Horner had disappeared, that the bureau had been forced open, and that the small morocco casket in which, as it afterwards transpired, the Countess was accustomed to keep her jewel, was lying empty upon the dressing-table. Ryder instantly gave the alarm, and Horner was arrested the same evening; but the stone could not be found either upon his person or in his rooms. Catherine Cusack, maid to the Countess, deposed to having heard Ryder's cry of dismay on discovering the robbery, and to having rushed into the room, where she found matters as described by the last witness. Inspector Bradstreet, B division, gave evidence as to the arrest of Horner, who struggled frantically, and protested his innocence in the strongest terms. Evidence of a previous conviction for robbery having been given against the prisoner, the magistrate refused to deal summarily with the offence, but referred it to the Assizes. Horner, who had shown signs of intense emotion during the proceedings, fainted away at the conclusion and was carried out of court.

"Hum! so much for the police-court," said Holmes thoughtfully, tossing aside the paper. "The question for us now to solve is the sequence of events leading from a rifled jewel-case at one end to the crop of a goose in Tottenham Court Road at the other. You see, Watson, our little deductions have suddenly assumed a much more important and less innocent aspect. Here is the stone; the stone came from the goose, and the goose came from Mr. Henry Baker, the gentleman with the bad hat and all the other characteristics with which I have bored you. So now we must set ourselves very seriously to finding this gentleman and ascertaining what part he has played in this little mystery. To do this, we must try the simplest means first, and these lie undoubtedly in an advertisement in all the evening papers. If this fail, I shall have recourse to other methods."

"What will you say?"

"Give me a pencil and that slip of paper. Now, then:

Found at the corner of Goodge Street, a goose and a black felt hat. Mr. Henry Baker can have the same by applying at 6:30 this evening at 221B, Baker Street.

That is clear and concise."

"Very. But will he see it?"

"Well, he is sure to keep an eye on the papers, since, to a poor man, the loss was a heavy one. He was clearly so scared by his mischance in breaking the window and by the approach of Peterson that he thought of nothing but flight, but since then he must have bitterly regretted the impulse which caused him to drop his bird. Then, again, the introduction of his name will cause him to see it, for everyone who knows him will direct his attention to it. Here you are, Peterson, run down to the advertising agency and have this put in the evening papers."

"In which, sir?"

"Oh, in the *Globe, Star, Pall Mall, St. James's, Evening News Standard, Echo,* and any others that occur to you."

"Very well, sir. And this stone?"

"Ah, yes, I shall keep the stone. Thank you. And, I say, Peterson, just buy a goose on your way back and leave it here with me, for we must have one to give to this gentleman in place of the one which your family is now devouring."

When the commissionaire had gone, Holmes took up the stone and held it against the light. "It's a bonny thing," said he. "Just see how it glints and sparkles. Of course it is a nucleus and focus of crime. Every good stone is. They are the devil's pet baits. In the larger and older jewels every facet may stand for a bloody deed. This stone is not yet twenty years old. It was found in the banks of the Amoy river in southern China and is remarkable in having every characteristic of the carbuncle, save that it is blue in shade instead of ruby red. In spite of its youth, it has already a sinister history. There have been two murders, a vitriol-throwing, a suicide, and several robberies brought about for the sake of this forty-grain weight of crystallized charcoal. Who would think that so pretty a toy would be a purveyor to the gallows and the prison? I'll lock it up in my strong box now and drop a line to the Countess to say that we have it."

"Do you think that this man Horner is innocent?"

"I cannot tell."

"Well, then, do you imagine that this other one, Henry Baker, had anything to do with the matter?"

"It is, I think, much more likely that Henry Baker is an absolutely innocent man, who had no idea that the bird which he was carrying was of considerably more value than if it were made of solid gold. That, however, I shall determine by a very simple test if we have an answer to our advertisement."

"And you can do nothing until then?"

"Nothing."

"In that case I shall continue my professional round. But I shall come back in the evening at the hour you have mentioned, for I should like to see the solution of so tangled a business."

"Very glad to see you. I dine at seven. There is a woodcock, I believe. By the way, in view of recent occurrences, perhaps I ought to ask Mrs. Hudson to examine its crop."

I had been delayed at a case, and it was a little after half-past six when I found myself in Baker Street once more. As I approached the house I saw a tall man in a Scotch bonnet with a coat which was buttoned up to his chin waiting outside in the bright semicircle which was thrown from the fanlight. Just as I arrived the door was opened, and we were shown up together to Holmes's room.

"Mr. Henry Baker, I believe," said he, rising from his armchair and greeting his visitor with the easy air of geniality which he could so readily assume. "Pray take this chair by the fire, Mr. Baker. It is a cold night, and I observe that your circulation is more adapted for summer than for winter. Ah, Watson, you have just come at the right time. Is that your hat, Mr. Baker?"

"Yes, sir, that is undoubtedly my hat."

He was a large man with rounded shoulders, a massive head, and a broad, intelligent face, sloping down to a pointed beard of grizzled brown. A touch of red in nose and cheeks, with a slight tremor of his extended hand, recalled Holmes's surmise as to his habits. His rusty black frock-coat was buttoned right up in front, with the collar turned up, and his lank wrists protruded from his sleeves without a sign of cuff or shirt. He spoke in a slow staccato fashion, choosing his words with care, and gave the impression generally of a man of learning and letters who had had ill-usage at the hands of fortune.

"We have retained these things for some days," said Holmes, "because we expected to see an advertisement from you giving your address. I am at a loss to know now why you did not advertise."

Our visitor gave a rather shamefaced laugh. "Shillings have not been so plentiful with me as they once were," he remarked. "I had no doubt that the gang of roughs who assaulted me had carried off both my hat and the bird. I did not care to spend more money in a hopeless attempt at recovering them."

"Very naturally. By the way, about the bird, we were compelled to eat it."

"To eat it!" Our visitor half rose from his chair in his excitement.

"Yes, it would have been of no use to anyone had we not done so. But I presume that this other goose upon the sideboard, which is about the same weight and perfectly fresh, will answer your purpose equally well?"

"Oh, certainly, certainly," answered Mr. Baker with a sigh of relief.

"Of course, we still have the feathers, legs, crop, and so on of your own bird, so if you wish—"

The man burst into a hearty laugh. "They might be useful to me as relics of my adventure," said he, "but beyond that I can hardly see what use the *disjecta membra* of my late acquaintance are going to be to me. No, sir, I think that, with your permission, I will confine my attentions to the excellent bird which I perceive upon the sideboard."

Sherlock Holmes glanced sharply across at me with a slight shrug of his shoulders.

"There is your hat, then, and there your bird," said he. "By the way, would it bore you to tell me where you got the other one from? I am somewhat of a fowl fancier, and I have seldom seen a better grown goose."

"Certainly, sir," said Baker, who had risen and tucked his newly gained property under his arm. "There are a few of us who frequent the Alpha Inn, near the Museum—we are to be found in the Museum itself during the day, you understand. This year our good host, Windigate by name, instituted a goose club, by which, on consideration of some few pence every week, we were each to receive a bird at Christmas. My pence were duly paid, and the rest is familiar to you. I am much indebted to you, sir, for a Scotch bonnet is fitted neither to my years nor my gravity." With a comical pomposity of manner he bowed solemnly to both of us and strode off upon his way.

"So much for Mr. Henry Baker," said Holmes when he had closed the door behind him. "It is quite certain that he knows nothing whatever about the matter. Are you hungry, Watson?"

"Not particulary."

"Then I suggest that we turn our dinner into a supper and follow up this clue while it is still hot."

"By all means."

It was a bitter night, so we drew on our ulsters and wrapped cravats about our throats. Outside, the stars were shining coldly in a cloudless sky, and the breath of the passers-by blew out into smoke like so many pistol shots. Our footfalls rang out crisply and loudly as we swung through the doctors' quarter, Wimpole Street, Harley Street, and so through Wigmore Street into Oxford Street. In a quarter of an hour we were in Bloomsbury at the Alpha Inn, which is a small public-house at the corner of one of the streets which runs down into Holborn. Holmes pushed open the door of the private bar and ordered two glasses of beer from the ruddy-faced, white-aproned landlord.

"Your beer should be excellent if it is as good as your geese," said he.

"My geese!" The man seemed surprised.

"Yes. I was speaking only half an hour ago to Mr. Henry Baker, who was a member of your goose club."

"Ah! yes, I see. But you see, sir, them's not *our* geese."

"Indeed! Whose, then?"

"Well, I got the two dozen from a salesman in Covent Garden."

"Indeed? I know some of them. Which was it?"

"Breckinridge is his name."

"Ah! I don't know him. Well, here's your good health, landlord, and prosperity to your house. Good-night.

"Now for Mr. Breckinridge," he continued, buttoning up his coat as we came out into the frosty air. "Remember, Watson, that though we have so homely a thing as a goose at one end of this chain, we have at the other a man who will certainly get seven years' penal servitude unless we can establish his innocence. It is possible that our inquiry may but confirm his guilt; but, in any case, we have a line of investigation which has been missed by the police, and which a singular chance has placed in our hands. Let us follow it out to the bitter end. Faces to the south, then, and quick march!"

We passed across Holborn, down Endell Street, and so through a zigzag of slums to Covent Garden Market. One of the largest stalls bore the name of Breckinridge upon it, and the proprietor, a horsy-looking man, with a sharp face and trim side-whiskers, was helping a boy to put up the shutters.

"Good-evening. It's a cold night," said Holmes.

The salesman nodded and shot a questioning glance at my companion.

"Sold out of geese, I see," continued Holmes, pointing at the bare slabs of marble.

"Let you have five hundred to-morrow morning."

"That's no good."

"Well, there are some on the stall with the gas-flare."

"Ah, but I was recommended to you."

"Who by?"

"The landlord of the Alpha."

"Oh, yes; I sent him a couple of dozen."

"Fine birds they were, too. Now where did you get them from?"

To my surprise the question provoked a burst of anger from the salesman.

"Now, then, mister," said he, with his head cocked and his arms akimbo, "what are you driving at? Let's have it straight, now."

"It is straight enough. I should like to know who sold you the geese which you supplied to the Alpha."

"Well, then, I shan't tell you. So now!"

"Oh, it is a matter of no importance; but I don't know why you should be so warm over such a trifle."

"Warm! You'd be as warm, maybe, if you were as pestered as I am. When I pay good money for a good article there should be an end of the business; but it's 'Where are the geese?' and 'Who did you sell the geese to?' 'What will you take for the geese?' One would think they were the only geese in the world, to hear the fuss that is made over them."

"Well, I have no connection with any other people who have been making inquiries," said Holmes carelessly. "If you won't tell us the bet is off, that is all. But I'm always ready to back my opinion on a matter of fowls, and I have a fiver on it that the bird I ate is country bred."

"Well, then you've lost your fiver, for it's town bred," snapped the salesman.

"It's nothing of the kind."

"I say it is."

"I don't believe it."

"D'you think you know more about fowls than I, who have handled them ever since I was a nipper? I tell you, all those birds that went to the Alpha were town bred."

"You'll never persuade me to believe that."

"Will you bet, then?"

"It's merely taking your money, for I know that I am right. But I'll have a sovereign on with you, just to teach you not to be obstinate."

The salesman chuckled grimly. "Bring me the books, Bill," said he.

The small boy brought round a small thin volume and a great greasy-backed one, laying them out together beneath the hanging lamp.

"Now then, Mr. Cocksure," said the salesman, "I thought that I was out of geese, but before I finish you'll find that there is still one left in my shop. You see this little book?"

"Well?"

"That's the list of the folk from whom I buy. D'you see? Well, then, here on this page are the country folk, and the numbers after their names are where their accounts are in the big ledger. Now, then! You see this other page in red ink? Well, that is a list of my town suppliers. Now, look at that third name. Just read it out to me."

" 'Mrs. Oakshott, 117, Brixton Road—249,' " read Holmes.

"Quite so. Now turn that up in the ledger."

Holmes turned the page indicated. "Here you are, 'Mrs. Oakshott, 117, Brixton Road, egg and poultry supplier.' "

"Now, then, what's the last entry?"

" 'December 22d. Twenty-four geese at 7s. 6d.' "

"Quite so. There you are. And underneath?"

" 'Sold to Mr. Windigate of the Alpha, at 12s.' "

"What have you to say now?"

Sherlock Holmes looked deeply chagrined. He drew a sovereign from his pocket and threw it down upon the slab, turning away with the air of a man whose disgust is too deep for words. A few yards off he stopped under a lamp-post and laughed in the hearty, noiseless fashion which was peculiar to him.

"When you see a man with whiskers of that cut and the 'Pink 'un' protruding out of his pocket, you can always draw him by a bet," said he. "I daresay that if I had put £100 down in front of him, that man would not have given me such complete information as was drawn from him by the idea that he was doing me on a wager. Well, Watson, we are, I fancy, nearing the end of our quest, and the only point which remains to be determined is whether we should go on to this Mrs. Oakshott to-night, or whether we should reserve it for to-morrow. It is clear from what that surly fellow said that there are others besides ourselves who are anxious about the matter, and I should—"

His remarks were suddenly cut short by a loud hubbub which broke out from the stall which we had just left. Turning round we saw a little rat-faced fellow standing in the centre of the circle of yellow light which was thrown by the swinging lamp, while Breckinridge, the salesman, framed in the door of his stall, was shaking his fists fiercely at the cringing figure.

"I've had enough of you and your geese," he shouted. "I wish you were all at the devil together. If you come pestering me any more with your silly talk I'll set the dog at you. You bring Mrs. Oakshott here and I'll answer her, but what have you to do with it? Did I buy the geese off you?"

"No; but one of them was mine all the same," whined the little man.

"Well, then, ask Mrs. Oakshott for it."

"She told me to ask you."

"Well, you can ask the King of Proosia, for all I care. I've had enough of it. Get out of this!" He rushed fiercely forward, and the inquirer flitted away into the darkness.

"Ha! this may save us a visit to Brixton Road," whispered Holmes. "Come with me, and we will see what is to be made of this fellow." Striding through the scattered knots of people who lounged round the flaring stalls, my companion speedily overtook the little man and touched him upon the shoulder. He sprang round, and I could see in the gas-light that every vestige of colour had been driven from his face.

"Who are you, then? What do you want?" he asked in a quavering voice.

"You will excuse me," said Holmes blandly, "but I could not help overhearing the questions which you put to the salesman just now. I think that I could be of assistance to you."

"You? Who are you? How could you know anything of the matter?"

"My name is Sherlock Holmes. It is my business to know what other people don't know."

"But you can know nothing of this?"

"Excuse me, I know everything of it. You are endeavouring to trace some geese which were sold by Mrs. Oakshott, of Brixton Road, to a salesman named Breckinridge, by him in turn to Mr. Windigate, of the Alpha, and by him to his club, of which Mr. Henry Baker is a member."

"Oh, sir you are the very man whom I have longed to meet," cried the little fellow with outstretched hands and quivering fingers. "I can hardly explain to you how interested I am in this matter."

Sherlock Holmes hailed a four-wheeler which was passing. "In that case we had better discuss it in a cosy room rather than in this windswept market-place," said he. "But pray tell me, before we go farther, who it is that I have the pleasure of assisting."

The man hesitated for an instant. "My name is John Robinson," he answered with a sidelong glance.

"No, no; the real name," said Holmes sweetly. "It is always awkward doing business with an alias."

A flush sprang to the white cheeks of the stranger. "Well, then," said he, "my real name is James Ryder."

"Precisely so. Head attendant at the Hotel Cosmopolitan. Pray step into the cab, and I shall soon be able to tell you everything which you would wish to know."

The little man stood glancing from one to the other of us with half-frightened, half-hopeful eyes, as one who is not sure whether he is on the verge of a windfall or a catastrophe. Then he stepped into the cab, and in half an hour we were back in the sitting-room at Baker Street. Nothing had been said during our drive, but the high, thin breathing of our new companion, and the claspings and unclaspings of his hands, spoke of the nervous tension within him.

"Here we are!" said Holmes cheerily as we filed into the room. "The fire looks very seasonable in this weather. You look cold, Mr. Ryder. Pray take the basketchair. I will just put on my slippers before we settle this little matter of yours. Now, then! You want to know what became of those geese?"

"Yes, sir."

"Or rather, I fancy, of that goose. It was one bird, I imagine, in which you were interested—white, with a black bar across the tail."

Ryder quivered with emotion. "Oh, sir," he cried, "can you tell me where it went to?"

"It came here."

"Here?"

"Yes, and a most remarkable bird it proved. I don't wonder that you should take an interest in it. It laid an egg after it was dead—the bonniest, brightest little blue egg that ever was seen. I have it here in my museum."

Our visitor staggered to his feet and clutched the mantel-piece with his right hand. Holmes unlocked his strong-box and held up the blue carbuncle, which shone out like a star, with a cold, brilliant, many-pointed radiance. Ryder stood glaring with a drawn face, uncertain whether to claim or to disown it.

"The game's up, Ryder," said Holmes quietly. "Hold up, man, or you'll be into the fire! Give him an arm back into his chair, Watson. He's not got blood enough to go in for felony with impunity. Give him a dash of brandy. So! Now he looks a little more human. What a shrimp it is, to be sure!"

For a moment he had staggered and nearly fallen, but the brandy brought a tinge of colour into his cheeks, and he sat staring with frightened eyes at his accuser.

"I have almost every link in my hands, and all the proofs which I could possibly need, so there is little which you need tell me. Still, that little may as well be cleared up to make the case complete. You had heard, Ryder, of this blue stone of the Countess of Morcar's?"

"It was Catherine Cusack who told me of it," said he in a crackling voice.

"I see—her ladyship's waiting-maid. Well, the temptation of sudden wealth so easily acquired was too much for you, as it has been for better men before you; but you were not very scrupulous in the means you used. It seems to me, Ryder, that there is the making of a very pretty villain in you. You knew that this man Horner, the plumber, had been concerned in some such matter before, and that suspicion would rest the more readily upon him. What did you do, then? You made some small job in my lady's room—you and your confederate Cusack—and you managed that he should be the man sent for. Then, when he had left, you rifled the jewel-case, raised the alarm, and had this unfortunate man arrested. You then—"

Ryder threw himself down suddenly upon the rug and clutched at my companion's knees. "For God's sake, have mercy!" he shrieked. "Think of my father! of my mother! It would break their hearts. I never went wrong before! I never will again. I swear it. I'll swear it on a Bible. Oh, don't bring it into court! For Christ's sake, don't!"

"Get back into your chair!" said Holmes sternly. "It is very well to cringe and crawl now, but you thought little enough of this poor Horner in the dock for a crime of which he knew nothing."

"I will fly, Mr. Holmes. I will leave the country, sir. Then the charge against him will break down."

"Hum! We will talk about that. And now let us hear a true account of the next act. How came the stone into the goose, and how came the goose into the open market? Tell us the truth, for there lies your only hope of safety."

Ryder passed his tongue over his parched lips. "I will tell you it just as it happened, sir," said he. "When Horner had been arrested, it seemed to me that it would be best for me to get away with the stone at once, for I did not know at what moment the police might not take it into their heads to search me and my room. There was no place about the hotel where it would be safe. I went out, as if on some commission, and I made for my sister's house. She had married a man named Oakshott, and lived in Brixton Road, where she fattened fowls for the market. All the way there every man I met seemed to me to be a policeman or a detective; and, for all that it was a cold night, the sweat was pouring down my face before I came to the Brixton Road. My sister asked me what was the matter, and why I was so pale; but I told her that I had been upset by the jewel robbery at the hotel. Then I went into the back yard and smoked a pipe, and wondered what it would be best to do.

"I had a friend once called Maudsley, who went to the bad, and has just been serving his time in Pentonville. One day he had met me, and fell into talk about the ways of thieves, and how they could get rid of what they stole. I knew that he would be true to me, for I knew one or two things about him; so I made up my mind to go right on to Kilburn, where he lived, and take him into my confidence. He would show me how to turn the stone into money. But how to get to him in safety? I thought of the agonies I had gone through in coming from the hotel. I might at any moment be seized and searched, and there would be the stone in my waistcoat pocket. I was leaning against the wall at the time and looking at the geese which were waddling about round my feet, and suddenly an idea came into my head which showed me how I could beat the best detective that ever lived.

"My sister had told me some weeks before that I might have the pick of her geese for a Christmas present, and I knew that she was always as good as her word. I would take my goose now, and in it I would carry my stone to Kilburn. There was a little shed in the yard, and behind this I drove one of the birds—a fine big one, white, with a barred tail. I caught it, and, prying its bill open, I thrust the stone down its throat as far as my finger could reach. The bird gave a gulp, and I felt the stone pass along its gullet and down into its crop. But the creature flapped and struggled, and out came my sister to know what was the matter. As I turned to speak to her the brute broke loose and fluttered off among the others.

" 'Whatever were you doing with that bird, Jem?' says she.

" 'Well,' said I, 'you said you'd give me one for Christmas, and I was feeling which was the fattest.'

" 'Oh,' says she, 'we've set yours aside for you—Jem's bird, we call it. It's the big white one over yonder. There's twenty-six of them, which makes one for you, and one for us, and two dozen for the market.'

" 'Thank you, Maggie,' says I; 'but if it is all the same to you, I'd rather have that one I was handling just now.'

" 'The other is a good three pound heavier,' said she, 'and we fattened it expressly for you.'

" 'Never mind. I'll have the other, and I'll take it now,' said I.

" 'Oh, just as you like,' said she, a little huffed. 'Which is it you want, then?'

" 'That white one with the barred tail, right in the middle of the flock.'

" 'Oh, very well. Kill it and take it with you.'

"Well, I did what she said, Mr. Holmes, and I carried the bird all the way to Kilburn. I told my pal what I had done, for he was a man that it was easy to tell a thing like that to. He laughed until he choked, and we got a knife and opened the goose. My heart turned to water, for there was no sign of the stone, and I knew that some terrible mistake had occurred. I left the bird, rushed back to my sister's, and hurried into the back yard. There was not a bird to be seen there.

" 'Where are they all, Maggie?' I cried.

" 'Gone to the dealer's, Jem.'

" 'Which dealer's?'

" 'Breckinridge, of Covent Garden.'

" 'But was there another with a barred tail?' I asked, 'the same as the one I chose?'

" 'Yes, Jem; there were two barred-tailed ones, and I could never tell them apart.'

"Well, then, of course I saw it all, and I ran off as hard as my feet would carry me to this man Breckinridge; but he had sold the lot at once, and not one word would he tell me as to where they had gone. You heard him yourselves to-night. Well, he has always answered me like that. My sister thinks that I am going mad. Sometimes I think that I am myself. And now—and now I am myself a branded thief, without ever having touched the wealth for which I sold my character. God help me! God help me!" He burst into convulsive sobbing, with his face buried in his hands.

There was a long silence, broken only by his heavy breathing, and by the measured tapping of Sherlock Holmes's finger-tips upon the edge of the table. Then my friend rose and threw open the door.

"Get out!" said he.

"What, sir! Oh, Heaven bless you!"

"No more words. Get out!"

And no more words were needed. There was a rush, a clatter upon the stairs, the bang of a door, and the crisp rattle of running footfalls from the street.

"After all, Watson," said Holmes, reaching up his hand for his clay pipe, "I am not retained by the police to supply their deficiencies. If Horner were in danger it would be another thing; but this fellow will not appear against him, and the case must collapse. I suppose that I am commuting a felony, but it is just possible that I am saving a soul. This fellow will not go wrong again; he is too terribly frightened. Send him to jail now, and you make him a jail-bird for life. Besides, it is the season for forgiveness. Chance has put in our way a most singular and whimsical problem, and its solution is its own reward. If you will have the goodness to touch the bell, Doctor, we will begin another investigation, in which, also, a bird will be the chief feature."

Ellery Queen
OBJECT LESSON

Ellery hurried down West 92nd Street toward the main entrance of Henry Hudson High School stealing guilty glances at his watch. Miss Carpenter had been crisply specific about place, date, and time: her home room, 109; Friday morning, April 22nd; first period ("Bell *at 8:40,* Mr. Queen"). Miss Carpenter, who had come to him with an unusual request, had struck him as the sort of dedicated young person who would not take kindly to a hitch in her crusade.

Ellery broke into an undignified lope.

The project for which she had enlisted his aid was formidable even for a crusading young teacher of Social Studies on the 9th Grade Junior High level. For two months merchants of the neighborhood had been reporting stores broken into by a teen-age gang. Beyond establishing that the crimes were the work of the same boys, who were probably students at Henry Hudson High School, the police had got nowhere.

Miss Carpenter, walking home from a movie late the previous Monday night, had seen three boys dive out of a smashed bakery window and vanish into an alley. She had recognized them as Howard Ruffo, David

Strager, and Joey Buell, all 15-year-old home-room students of hers. The juvenile crime problem was solved.

But not for Miss Carpenter. Instead of going to the police, Miss Carpenter had gone to Ellery, who lived on West 87th Street and was a hero to the youth of the neighborhood. Howard, David, and Joey were *not* hardened delinquents, she had told him, and she could *not* see their arrest, trial, and imprisonment as the solution to anything. True, they had substituted gang loyalty for the love and security they were denied in their unhappy slum homes, but boys who worked at after-school jobs and turned every cent in at home were hardly beyond recall, were they? And she had told him just where each boy worked, and at what.

"They're only patterning their behavior after criminals because they think criminals are strong, successful, and glamorous," Miss Carpenter had said; and what she would like him to do was visit her class and, under the pretext of giving a talk on the subject of Notorious Criminals I Have Known, paint such a picture of weak, ratting, empty, and violently ending criminality that David and Joey and Howard would see the error of their ways.

It had seemed to Ellery that this placed a rather hefty burden on his oratorical powers. Did Miss Carpenter have her principal's permission for this project?

No, Miss Carpenter had replied bravely, she did *not* have Mr. Hinsdale's permission, and she might very well lose her job when he heard about it. "But I'm *not* going to be the one who gives those boys the first shove toward reform school and maybe eventually a life sentence!" And besides, what did Mr. Queen have to lose but an hour of his time?

So Mr. Queen had feebly said yes, he would come; and here he was, at the door of the determined young woman's classroom . . . seven minutes *late.*

Ellery braced himself and opened the door.

The moment he set foot in the room he knew he had walked in on a catastrophe.

Louise Carpenter stood tensely straight at her desk, her pretty face almost as white as the envelope she was clutching. And she was glaring at a mass of boy and girl faces so blankly, so furtively quiet that the silence sizzled.

The first thing she said to him was, "I've been robbed."

The terrible mass of boy and girl eyes followed him to her desk. In his nose was the pungent smell of ink, glue, paper, chalk, musty wardrobe closets; surrounding him were discolored walls, peeling paint, tarnished fixtures, warped window poles, and mutilated desks.

"Robbed in my own classroom," Miss Carpenter choked.

He laid his coat and hat gently on her desk. "A practical joke?" He smiled at the class.

"Hardly. They didn't know you were coming." They had betrayed her, the sick shock in her voice said. "Class, this is Ellery Queen. I don't have to tell you who Mr. Queen is, and how honored we are to have him visit us." There was a gasp, a buzz, a spatter of applause. "Mr. Queen was kind enough to come here today as a special treat to give us a talk on crime. I didn't know he was going to walk in on one."

The spatter stopped dead.

"You're sure there has been a crime, Miss Carpenter?"

"An envelope with seven one-dollar bills in it was stolen, and from the way it happened the thief can only be someone in this room."

"I'm sorry to hear that."

He deliberately looked them over, wondering which of the forty-one pairs of eyes staring back at his belonged to Joey Buell, Howard Ruffo, and David Strager. He should have asked Louise Carpenter to describe them. Now it was too late.

Or was it?

It seemed to Ellery that three of the twenty-odd boy faces were rather too elaborately blank. One of them was set on husky shoulders; this boy was blond, handsome, and dead-white about the nostrils. The second was a sharp-nosed, jet-haired boy with Mediterranean coloring who was perfectly still except for his fingers, and they kept turning a pencil over and over almost ritually. The third, thin and red-haired, showed no life anywhere except in a frightened artery in his temple.

Ellery made up his mind.

"Well, if it's a real live crime," he said, turning to Louise, "I don't imagine anyone wants to hear me ramble on about crimes that are dead and buried. In fact, I think it would be more interesting if I gave the class a demonstration of how a crime is actually solved. What do you think, Miss Carpenter?"

Understanding leaped into her eyes, along with hope.

"I think," she said grimly, "it would be *lots* more interesting."

"Suppose we begin by finding out about the seven dollars. They were yours, Miss Carpenter?"

"One dollar was mine. Miss McDoud, an English teacher, is being married next month. A group of us are chipping in to buy her a wedding present, with me as banker. All this week teachers have been dropping in to leave their dollars in an envelope I've had on my desk. This morning—"

"That's fine for background, Miss Carpenter. Suppose we hear testimony from the class." Ellery surveyed them, and there was a ripple of tittering. Suddenly he pointed to a little lipsticked girl with an Italian haircut. "Would you like to tell us what happened this morning?"

"I don't know anything about the money!"

"Chicken." A boy's jeering voice.

"The boy who said that." Ellery kept his tone friendly. It was one of the three he had spotted, the husky blond one. "What's your name?"

"David Strager." His sneer said, *You don't scare me.* But his nostrils remained dead-white. He was the boy Miss Carpenter had said worked after school as a stock boy at the Hi-Kwality Supermarket on Amsterdam Avenue.

"All right, Dave. You tell us about this morning."

The boy glanced scornfully at the girl with the Italian haircut. "We all knew the money was in the envelope. This morning before the bell rings Mrs. Morrell comes in with her buck and Miss Carpenter puts it with the other money and lays the envelope on her desk. So afterward the bell rings, Mrs. Morrell splits, Miss Carpenter picks up the envelope and takes a look inside, and she hollers, 'I been robbed.' "

The thin boy with the red hair called out, "So what are we supposed to do, drop dead?" and winked at David Strager, who had already sat down. The big blond boy winked back.

"And your name?" Ellery asked the redhead.

"Joseph Buell," the boy answered defiantly. He was the one who worked at Kaplan's, the big cigar, candy, and stationery store on 89th Street. "Who wants their old seven bucks?"

"Somebody not only wants it, Joey, somebody's got it."

"Aaa, for all we know she took it herself." And this was the third of the trio, the sharp-faced dark boy. If Ellery was right, he was the one who delivered part-time for O'Donnel's Dry Cleaning on Columbus Avenue.

"And you are—?"

"Howard Ruffo."

The Three Musketeers, rushing to one another's support.

"You mean, Howard, you're charging Miss Carpenter with having stolen the teachers' money?" Ellery asked with a smile.

The boy's dark glance wavered. "I mean maybe she took it like by mistake. Mislaid it or somepin.' "

"As a matter of fact," came Louise's quiet voice, "when I saw the money wasn't in the envelope, my first thought was exactly that, Mr. Queen. So I searched myself thoroughly."

"May I see the envelope?"

"This isn't the one I was keeping the seven dollars in"—she handed him the envelope—"though it looks the same. I have a box of them in my locker there. The lock hasn't worked for ages. This one must have been stolen from my locker yesterday, or earlier this week."

"It's a blank envelope, Miss Carpenter. How do you know it isn't the one that contained the money?"

"Because the original had a notation in ink on the flap—*Gift Fund for Helen McDoud.*" She looked about and glances fell in windrows. "So this theft was planned, Mr. Queen. Someone came to class this morning armed with this duplicate envelope, previously stolen and filled with worthless paper, prepared to make a quick exchange if the opportunity arose. And it did. The class was milling around while Mrs. Morrell and I chatted."

The paper in the substitute envelope consisted of a sheaf of rectangular strips cut to the size of dollar bills.

"At the time you placed Mrs. Morrell's dollar among the others in the original envelope, was everybody here?"

"Yes. The door opened and closed only once after that—when Mrs. Morrell left. I was facing the door the whole time."

"Could Mrs. Morrell, as a practical joke, have made the switch?"

"She wasn't anywhere near my desk after I laid the envelope on it."

"Then you're right, Miss Carpenter. The theft was planned in advance by one of the boys or girls in this room, and the thief—and money—are both still here."

The tension was building beautifully. The boy must be in a sweat. He hadn't expected his theft to be found out so soon, before he got a chance to sneak the money out of the room.

"What time does the first period end, Miss Carpenter?"

"At 9:35."

Every head turned toward the clock on the wall.

"And it's only 8:56." Ellery said cheerfully. "That gives us thirty-nine minutes—more than enough time. Unless the boy or girl who planned this crime wants to return the loot to Miss Carpenter here and now?"

This time he stared directly from David to Howard to Joey. His stare said, *I hate to do this, boys, but of course I'll have to if you think you can get away with it.*

The Strager boy's full lips were twisted. The skinny redhead, Joey Buell, stared back sullenly. Howard Ruffo's pencil twirled faster.

It's one of those three, all right.

"I see we'll have to do it the hard way," Ellery said. "Sorry I can't produce the thief with a flick of my wrist, the way it's done in books, but in real life detection—like crime—is pretty unexciting stuff. We'll begin with a body search. It's voluntary, by the way. Anybody rather not chance a search? Raise your hand."

Not a muscle moved.

"I'll search the boys, Miss Carpenter. You roll those two bulletin boards over to that corner and search the girls."

The next few minutes were noisy. As each boy was searched and released he was sent to the blackboard at the front of the room. The girls were sent to the rear.

"Find anything, Miss Carpenter?"

"Rose Perez has a single dollar bill. The other girls either have small change or no money at all."

"No sign of the original envelope?"

"No."

"I found two boys with bills—in each case a single, too. David Strager and Joey Buell. No envelope."

Louise's brows met.

Ellery glanced up at the clock. 9:07.

He strolled over to her. "Don't show them you're worried. There's nothing to worry about. We have twenty-eight minutes." He raised his voice, smiling. "Naturally the thief has ditched the money, hoping to recover it when the coast is clear. It's therefore hidden somewhere in the classroom. All right, Miss Carpenter, we'll take the desks and seats first. Look under them too—chewing gum makes a handy adhesive. Eh, class?"

Four minutes later they looked at each other, then up at the clock.

9:11.

Exactly twenty-four minutes remaining.

"Well," said Ellery.

He began to ransack the room. Books, radiators, closets, supplies, lunchbags, schoolbags. Bulletin boards, wall maps, the terrestrial globe. The UN poster, the steel engravings of Washington and Lincoln. He even emptied Louise's three pots of geraniums and sifted the earth.

His eyes kept returning to the clock more and more often.

Ellery searched everything in the room, from the socket of the American flag to the insect-filled bowls of the old light fixtures, reached by standing on desks.

Everything.

"It's not here!" whispered Louise in his ear.

The Buell, Ruffo, and Strager boys were nudging one another, grinning.

"Well, well," Ellery said.

Interesting. Something of a problem at that.

Of course! He got up and checked two things he had missed—the cup of the pencil sharpener and the grid covering the loudspeaker of the PA system. No envelope. No money.

He took out a handkerchief and wiped his neck.

Really it's a little silly. A schoolboy!

Ellery glanced at the clock.

9:29.

Six minutes left in which not only to find the money but identify the thief!

He leaned against Louise's desk, forcing himself to relax.

It was these "simple" problems. Nothing big and important, like murder, blackmail, bank robbery. A miserable seven dollars lifted by a teen-age delinquent in an overcrowded classroom . . .

He thought furiously.

Let the bell ring at 9:35 and the boy strut out of Miss Carpenter's room undetected, with his loot, and he would send up a howl like a wolf cub over his first kill. *Who says these big-shot law jerks ain't monkeys? The biggest! He's a lot of nothin'. Wind. See me stand him on his ear? And this is just for openers. Wait till I get goin' for real, not any of this kid stuff . . .*

No, nothing big and important like murder. Just seven dollars, and a big shot to laugh at. Not important? Ellery nibbled his lip. It was probably the most important case of his career.

9:30.

Only four and a half minutes left!

Louise Carpenter was gripping a desk, her knuckles white. Waiting to be let down.

Ellery pushed away from the desk and reached into the patch pocket of his tweed jacket for his pipe and tobacco, thinking harder about Helen McDoud's seven-dollar gift fund than he had ever thought about anything in his life.

And as he thought . . .

At 9:32 he was intently examining the rectangles of paper the thief had put into the substitute envelope. The paper was ordinary cheap newsprint, scissored to dollar-bill size out of a colored comics section. He shuffled through the dummy dollars one by one, hunting for something. Anything!

The forty-one boys and girls were buzzing and giggling now.

Ellery pounced. Clinging to one of the rectangles was a needle-thin sliver of paper about an inch long, a sort of paper shaving. He fingered it, held it up to the light. It was not newsprint. Too full-bodied, too tough-textured.

Then he knew what it must be.

Less than two minutes left.

Feverishly he went through the remaining dollar-sized strips of comic paper.

And there it was. There it was!

This strip had been cut from the top of the comic sheet. On the margin appeared the name of a New York newspaper and the date *April 24, 1955.*

Think it over. Take your time. Lots of seconds in a minute.

The buzzing and giggling had died. Louise Carpenter was on her feet, looking at him imploringly.

A bell began clanging in the corridor.

First period over.

9:35.

Ellery rose and said solemnly, "The case is solved."

With the room cleared and the door locked, the three boys stood backed against the blackboard as if facing a firing squad. The bloom was gone from David Strager's cheeks. The blood vessel in Joey Buell's temples was trying to wriggle into his red hair. And Howard Ruffo's eyes were liquid with panic.

It's hard to be fifteen years old and trapped.

But harder not to be.

"Wha'd I do?" whimpered Howard Ruffo. "I didn't do nothin'."

"We didn't take Miss Carpenter's seven dollars," said David Strager, stiff-lipped.

"Can you say the same about Mr. Mueller's baked goods last Monday night, Dave?" Ellery paused gently. "Or any of the other things you boys have been making love to in the past two months?"

He thought they were going to faint.

"But this morning's little job," Ellery turned suddenly to the red-haired boy, "you pulled by yourself, Joey."

The thin body quivered. "Who, me?"

"Yes, Joey, you."

"You got rocks in your skull," Joey whispered. "Not me!"

"I'll prove it, Joey. Hand me the dollar bill I found in your jeans when I searched you."

"That's my dollar!"

"I know it, Joey. I'll give you another for it. Hand it over . . . Miss Carpenter."

"Yes, Mr. Queen!"

"To cut these strips of newspaper to the same size as dollar bills, the thief must have used a real bill as a pattern. If he cut too close, the scissors would shave off a sliver of the bill." Ellery handed her Joey's dollar. "See if this bill shows a slight indentation along one edge."

"It does!"

"And I found this sliver clinging to one of the dummies. Fit the sliver to the indented edge of Joey's bill. If Joey is guilty, it should fit exactly. Does it?"

Louise looked at the boy. "Joey, it does fit."

David and Howard were gaping at Ellery.

"What a break," Joey choked.

"Criminals make their own bad breaks, Joey. The thing inside you that told you you were doing wrong made your hand shake as you cut. But even if your hand hadn't slipped, I'd have known you were the one who substituted the strips of paper for the money."

"How? How could you?" It was a cry of bewilderment.

Ellery showed him the rectangular strip with the white margin. "See this, Joey? Here's the name of the newspaper, and the date is *April 24, 1955*.

What date is today?"

"Friday the 22nd . . ."

"Friday, April 22nd. But these strips of colored comics come from the newspaper of April 24th, Joey—*this coming Sunday's paper.* Who gets advance copies of the Sunday comics? Stores that sell newspapers in quantity. Getting the bulldog editions in advance gives them a jump on the Sunday morning rush, when they have to insert the news sections.

"Nothing to it, Joey. Which of you three boys had access before this morning to next Sunday's bulldog editions? Not David—he works in a supermarket. Not Howard—he works for a dry cleaner. But you work in a big cigar and stationery store, Joey, where newspapers must be one of the stock items."

Joey Buell's eyes glassed over.

"We think we're strong, Joey, and then we run into somebody stronger," Ellery said. "We think we're the smartest, and someone comes along to outsmart us. We beat the rap a dozen times, but the thirteenth time the rap beats us. You can't win, Joey."

Joey burst into tears.

Louise Carpenter made an instinctive gesture toward him. Ellery's headshake warned her back. He went close to the boy and tousled the red head, murmuring something the others could not hear. And after a while Joey's tears sniffled to an end and he wiped his eyes on his sleeve in a puzzled way.

"Because I think this is going to work out all right, Joey," Ellery said, continuing their curious colloquy aloud. "We'll have a session with Mr. Hinsdale, and then with some . . . guys I happen to know at Police Headquarters. After that it will be up to you."

Joey Buell gulped. "Okay, Mr. Queen." He did not look at his two friends.

David and Howard communicated silently. Then David turned to Ellery. "Where do we stand, Mr. Queen?"

"You and Howard are coming along."

The blond boy bit his lip. Then he nodded, and after a moment the dark boy nodded, too.

"Oh, I almost forgot." Ellery dipped briskly into the jacket pocket that held his pipe and tobacco. His hand reappeared with a wrinkled envelope, its flap written over. From the envelope protruded the corners of some one-dollar bills. "Your Helen McDoud wedding gift fund, Miss Carpenter. With Joey's compliments."

"I did forget!" gasped Louise. "Where did you find it?"

"Where Joey in desperation slipped it as I was frisking the other boys. The only thing in the room I didn't think of searching—my own pocket." Ellery winked at the three boys. "Coming, fellas?"

Questions for Writing or Discussion

1. In which story is the detective's relationship with other characters more fully developed?

2. Which story presents the more fully developed portrait of the detective?
3. Which story makes better use of humor?
4. In which story is the detective's treatment of the criminal too moralistic?
5. Which story uses logic more effectively?
6. We believe that one of these stories is a minor literary gem, and the other is not. Keeping in mind your answers to the above questions, write a paper that uses comparison and contrast to show that one story is superior to the other.
7. Compare and contrast Queen or Holmes to a current TV detective.

Coming of Age:
Two Stories for Comparison and Contrast

Katherine Mansfield
HER FIRST BALL

Exactly when the ball began Leila would have found it hard to say. Perhaps her first real partner was the cab. It did not matter that she shared the cab with the Sheridan girls and their brother. She sat back in her own little corner of it, and the bolster on which her hand rested felt like the sleeve of an unknown young man's dress suit; and away they bowled, past waltzing lamp-posts and houses and fences and trees.

"Have you really never been to a ball before, Leila? But, my child, how too weird—" cried the Sheridan girls.

"Our nearest neighbour was fifteen miles," said Leila softly, gently opening and shutting her fan.

Oh, dear, how hard it was to be indifferent like the others! She tried not to smile too much; she tried not to care. But every single thing was so new and exciting . . . Meg's tuberoses, Jose's long loop of amber, Laura's little dark head, pushing above her white fur like a flower through snow. She would remember for ever. It even gave her a pang to see her cousin Laurie throw away the wisps of tissue paper he pulled from the fastenings of his new gloves. She would like to have kept those wisps as a keepsake, as a remembrance. Laurie leaned forward and put his hand on Laura's knee.

"Look here, darling," he said. "The third and the ninth as usual. Twig?"[1]

Oh, how marvellous to have a brother! In her excitement Leila felt that if there had been time, if it hadn't been impossible, she couldn't have helped crying because she was an only child, and no brother had ever said "Twig?"

---

1. Understand?

to her; no sister would ever say, as Meg said to Jose that moment, "I've never known your hair go up more successfully than it has to-night!"

But, of course, there was no time. They were at the drill hall already; there were cabs in front of them and cabs behind. The road was bright on either side with moving fan-like lights, and on the pavement gay couples seemed to float through the air; little satin shoes chased each other like birds.

"Hold on to me, Leila; you'll get lost," said Laura.

"Come on, girls, let's make a dash for it," said Laurie.

Leila put two fingers on Laura's pink velvet cloak, and they were somehow lifted past the big golden lantern, carried along the passage, and pushed into the little room marked "Ladies." Here the crowd was so great there was hardly space to take off their things; the noise was deafening. Two benches on either side were stacked high with wraps. Two old women in white aprons ran up and down tossing fresh armfuls. And everybody was pressing forward trying to get at the little dressing-table and mirror at the far end.

A great quivering jet of gas lighted the ladies' room. It couldn't wait; it was dancing already. When the door opened again and there came a burst of tuning from the drill hall, it leaped almost to the ceiling.

Dark girls, fair girls were patting their hair, tying ribbons again, tucking handkerchiefs down the fronts of their bodices, smoothing marble-white gloves. And because they were all laughing it seemed to Leila that they were all lovely.

"Aren't there any invisible hair-pins?" cried a voice. "How most extraordinary! I can't see a single invisible hair-pin."

"Powder my back, there's a darling," cried someone else.

"But I must have a needle and cotton. I've torn simply miles and miles of the frill," wailed a third.

Then "Pass them along, pass them along!" The straw basket of programmes was tossed from arm to arm. Darling little pink-and-silver programmes, with pink pencils and fluffy tassels. Leila's fingers shook as she took one out of the basket. She wanted to ask someone, "Am I meant to have one too?" but she had just time to read: "Waltz 3. *Two, Two, in a Canoe.* Polka 4. *Making the Feathers Fly,*" when Meg cried, "Ready, Leila?" and they pressed their way through the crush in the passage towards the big double doors of the drill hall.

Dancing had not begun yet, but the band had stopped tuning, and the noise was so great it seemed that when it did begin to play it would never be heard. Leila, pressing close to Meg, looking over Meg's shoulder, felt that even the little quivering coloured flags strung across the ceiling were talking. She quite forgot to be shy; she forgot how in the middle of dressing she had sat down on the bed with one shoe off and one shoe on and begged her mother to ring up her cousins and say she couldn't go after all. And the rush of longing she had had to be sitting on the veranda of their forsaken upcountry home, listening to the baby owls crying "More pork" in the moonlight, was changed to a rush of joy so sweet that it was hard to bear alone. She clutched her fan, and, gazing at the gleaming, golden floor, the azaleas, the lanterns, the stage at one end with its red carpet and gilt chairs and the band in a corner, she thought breathlessly, "How heavenly; how simply heavenly!"

All the girls stood grouped together at one side of the doors, the men at the other, and the chaperones in dark dresses, smiling rather foolishly, walked with little careful steps over the polished floor towards the stage.

"This is my country cousin Leila. Be nice to her. Find her partners; she's under my wing," said Meg, going up to one girl after another.

Strange faces smiled at Leila—sweetly, vaguely. Strange voices answered. "Of course, my dear." But Leila felt the girls didn't really see her. They were looking towards the men. Why didn't the men begin? What were they waiting for? There they stood, smoothing their gloves, patting their glossy hair and smiling among themselves. Then, quite suddenly, as if they had only just made up their minds that that was what they had to do, the men came gliding over the parquet. There was a joyful flutter among the girls. A tall, fair man flew up to Meg, seized her programme, scribbled something; Meg passed him on to Leila. "May I have the pleasure?" He ducked and smiled. There came a dark man wearing an eyeglass, then cousin Laurie with a friend, and Laura with a little freckled fellow whose tie was crooked. Then quite an old man—fat, with a big bald patch on his head—took her programme and murmured, "Let me see, let me see!" And he was a long time comparing his programme, which looked black with names, with hers. It seemed to give him so much trouble that Leila was ashamed. "Oh, please don't bother," she said eagerly. But instead of replying the fat man wrote something, glanced at her again. "Do I remember this bright little face?" he said softly. "Is it known to me of yore?" At that moment the band began playing; the fat man disappeared. He was tossed away on a great wave of music that came flying over the gleaming floor, breaking the groups up into couples, scattering them, sending them spinning. . . .

Leila had learned to dance at boarding school. Every Saturday afternoon the boarders were hurried off to a little corrugated iron mission hall where Miss Eccles (of London) held her "select" classes. But the difference between that dusty-smelling hall—with calico texts on the walls, the poor terrified little woman in a brown velvet toque with rabbit's ears thumping the cold piano, Miss Eccles poking the girls' feet with her long white wand—and this was so tremendous that Leila was sure if her partner didn't come and she had to listen to that marvellous music and to watch the others sliding, gliding over the golden floor, she would die at least, or faint, or lift her arms and fly out of one of those dark windows that showed the stars.

"Ours, I think—" Someone bowed, smiled, and offered her his arm; she hadn't to die after all. Someone's hand pressed her waist, and she floated away like a flower that is tossed into a pool.

"Quite a good floor, isn't it?" drawled a faint voice close to her ear.

"I think it's most beautifully slippery," said Leila.

"Pardon!" The faint voice sounded surprised. Leila said it again. And there was a tiny pause before the voice echoed. "Oh, quite!" and she was swung round again.

He steered so beautifully. That was the great difference between dancing with girls and men, Leila decided. Girls banged into each other, and stamped on each other's feet; the girl who was gentleman always clutched you so.

The azaleas were separate flowers no longer; they were pink and white flags streaming by.

"Were you at the Bell's last week?" the voice came again. It sounded tired. Leila wondered whether she ought to ask him if he would like to stop.

"No, this is my first dance," said she.

Her partner gave a little gasping laugh. "Oh, I say," he protested.

"Yes, it is really the first dance I've ever been to." Leila was most fervent. It was such a relief to be able to tell somebody. "You see, I've lived in the country all my life up until now. . . ."

At that moment the music stopped, and they went to sit on two chairs against the wall. Leila tucked her pink satin feet under and fanned herself, while she blissfully watched the other couples passing and disappearing through the swing doors.

"Enjoying yourself, Leila?" asked Jose, nodding her golden head.

Laura passed and gave her the faintest little wink; it made Leila wonder for a moment whether she was quite grown up after all. Certainly her partner did not say very much. He coughed, tucked his handkerchief away, pulled down his waistcoat, took a minute thread off his sleeve. But it didn't matter. Almost immediately the band started, and her second partner seemed to spring from the ceiling.

"Floor's not bad," said the new voice. Did one always begin with the floor? And then, "Were you at the Neaves' on Tuesday?" And again Leila explained. Perhaps it was a little strange that her partners were not more interested. For it was thrilling. Her first ball! She was only at the beginning of everything. It seemed to her that she had never known what the night was like before. Up till now it had been dark, silent, beautiful very often—oh, yes—but mournful somehow. Solemn. And now it would never be like that again—it had opened dazzling bright.

"Care for an ice?" said her partner. And they went through the swing doors, down the passage, to the supper room. Her cheeks burned, she was fearfully thirsty. How sweet the ices looked on little glass plates, and how cold the frosted spoon was, iced too! And when they came back to the hall there was the fat man waiting for her by the door. It gave her quite a shock again to see how old he was; he ought to have been on the stage with the fathers and mothers. And when Leila compared him with her other partners he looked shabby. His waistcoat was creased, there was a button off his glove, his coat looked as if it was dusty with French chalk.

"Come along, little lady," said the fat man. He scarcely troubled to clasp her, and they moved away so gently, it was more like walking than dancing. But he said not a word about the floor. "Your first dance, isn't it?" he murmured.

"How *did* you know?"

"Ah," said the fat man, "that's what it is to be old!" He wheezed faintly as he steered her past an awkward couple. "You see, I've been doing this kind of thing for the last thirty years."

"Thirty years?" cried Leila. Twelve years before she was born!

"It hardly bears thinking about, does it?" said the fat man gloomily. Leila looked at his bald head, and she felt quite sorry for him.

"I think it's marvellous to be still going on," she said kindly.

"Kind little lady," said the fat man, and he pressed her a little closer, and hummed a bar of the waltz. "Of course," he said, "you can't hope to last anything like as long as that. No-o," said the fat man, "long before that you'll be sitting up there on the stage, looking on, in your nice black velvet. And these pretty arms will have turned into little short fat ones, and you'll beat time with such a different kind of fan—a black bony one." The fat man seemed to shudder. "And you'll smile away like the poor old dears up there, and point to your daughter, and tell the elderly lady next to you how some dreadful man tried to kiss her at the club ball. And your heart will ache, ache"—the fat man squeezed her closer still, as if he really was sorry for that poor heart—"because no one wants to kiss you now. And you'll say how unpleasant these polished floors are to walk on, how dangerous they are. Eh, Mademoiselle Twinkletoes?" said the fat man softly.

Leila gave a light little laugh, but she did not feel like laughing. Was it—could it all be true? It sounded terribly true. Was this first ball only the beginning of her last ball after all? At that the music seemed to change; it sounded sad, sad; it rose upon a great sigh. Oh, how quickly things changed! Why didn't happiness last for ever? For ever wasn't a bit too long.

"I want to stop," she said in a breathless voice. The fat man led her to the door.

"No," she said, "I won't go outside. I won't sit down. I'll just stand here, thank you." She leaned against the wall, tapping with her foot, pulling up her gloves and trying to smile. But deep inside her a little girl threw her pinafore over her head and sobbed. Why had he spoiled it all?

"I say, you know," said the fat man, "you mustn't take me seriously, little lady."

"As if I should!" said Leila, tossing her small dark head and sucking her underlip. . . .

Again the couples paraded. The swing doors opened and shut. Now new music was given out by the bandmaster. But Leila didn't want to dance any more. She wanted to be home, or sitting on the veranda listening to those baby owls. When she looked through the dark windows at the stars, they had long beams like wings. . . .

But presently a soft, melting, ravishing tune began, and a young man with curly hair bowed before her. She would have to dance, out of politeness, until she could find Meg. Very stiffly she walked in the middle; very haughtily she put her hand on his sleeve. But in one minute, in one turn, her feet glided, glided. The lights, the azaleas, the dresses, the pink faces, the velvet chairs, all became one beautiful flying wheel. And when her next partner bumped into the fat man and he said, "Pardon," she smiled at him more radiantly than ever. She didn't even recognize him again.

Joyce Carol Oates
WHERE ARE YOU GOING, WHERE HAVE YOU BEEN?

To Bob Dylan

Her name was Connie. She was fifteen and she had a quick nervous giggling habit of craning her neck to glance into mirrors, or checking other people's faces to make sure her own was all right. Her mother, who noticed everything and knew everything and who hadn't much reason any longer to look at her own face, always scolded Connie about it. "Stop gawking at yourself, who are you? You think you're so pretty?" she would say. Connie would raise her eyebrows at these familiar complaints and look right through her mother, into a shadowy vision of herself as she was right at that moment: she knew she was pretty and that was everything. Her mother had been pretty once too, if you could believe those old snapshots in the album, but now her looks were gone and that was why she was always after Connie.

"Why don't you keep your room clean like your sister? How've you got your hair fixed—what the hell stinks? Hair spray? You don't see your sister using that junk."

Her sister June was twenty-four and still lived at home. She was a secretary in the high school Connie attended, and if that wasn't bad enough—with her in the same building—she was so plain and chunky and steady that Connie had to hear her praised all the time by her mother and her mother's sisters. June did this, June did that, she saved money and helped clean the house and cooked and Connie couldn't do a thing, her mind was all filled with trashy daydreams. Their father was away at work most of the time and when he came home he wanted supper and he read the newspaper at supper and after supper he went to bed. He didn't bother talking much to them, but around his bent head Connie's mother kept picking at her until Connie wished her mother were dead and she herself were dead and it were all over. "She makes me want to throw up sometimes," she complained to her friends. She had a high, breathless, amused voice which made everything she said sound a little forced, whether it was sincere or not.

There was one good thing: June went places with girlfriends of hers, girls who were just as plain and steady as she, and so when Connie wanted to do that her mother had no objections. The father of Connie's best girlfriend drove the girls the three miles to town and left them off at a shopping plaza, so that they could walk through the stores or go to a movie, and when he came to pick them up again at eleven he never bothered to ask what they had done.

They must have been familiar sights, walking around that shopping plaza in their shorts and flat ballerina slippers that always scuffed the sidewalk, with charm bracelets jingling on their thin wrists; they would lean together to whisper and laugh secretly if someone passed by who amused or interested them. Connie had long dark blond hair that drew anyone's eye to it, and she wore part of it pulled up on her head and puffed out and the rest of it she let fall down her back. She wore a pullover jersey blouse that looked one way when she was at home and another way when she was away from home. Everything about her had two sides to it, one for home and one for anywhere that was not home: her walk that could be childlike and bobbing, or languid enough to make anyone think she was hearing music in her head, her mouth which was pale and smirking most of the time, but bright and pink on these evenings out, her laugh which was cynical and drawling at home—"Ha, ha, very funny"—but high-pitched and nervous anywhere else, like the jingling of the charms on her bracelet.

Sometimes they did go shopping or to a movie, but sometimes they went across the highway, ducking fast across the busy road, to a drive-in restaurant where older kids hung out. The restaurant was shaped like a big bottle, though squatter than a real bottle, and on its cap was a revolving figure of a grinning boy who held a hamburger aloft. One night in midsummer they ran across, breathless with daring, and right away someone leaned out a car window and invited them over, but it was just a boy from high school they didn't like. It made them feel good to be able to ignore him. They went up through the maze of parked and cruising cars to the bright-lit, fly-infested restaurant, their faces pleased and expectant as if they were entering a sacred building that loomed out of the night to give them what haven and what blessing they yearned for. They sat at the counter and crossed their legs at the ankles, their thin shoulders rigid with excitement, and listened to the music that made everything so good: the music was always in the background like music at a church service, it was something to depend upon.

A boy named Eddie came in to talk with them. He sat backward on his stool, turning himself jerkily around in semicircles and then stopping and turning again, and after awhile he asked Connie if she would like something to eat. She said she did and so she tapped her friend's arm on her way out—her friend pulled her face up into a brave droll look—and Connie said she would meet her at eleven, across the way. "I just hate to leave her like that," Connie said earnestly, but the boy said that she wouldn't be alone for long. So they went out to his car and on the way Connie couldn't help but let her eyes wander over the windshields and faces all around her, her face gleaming with a joy that had nothing to do with Eddie or even this place; it might have been the music. She drew her shoulders up and sucked in her breath with the pure pleasure of being alive, and just at that moment she happened to glance at a face just a few feet from hers. It was a boy with shaggy black hair, in a convertible jalopy painted gold. He stared at her and then his lips widened into a grin. Connie slit her eyes at him and turned away, but she couldn't help glancing back and there he was still watching her. He wagged a finger and laughed and said, "Gonna get you, baby," and Connie turned away again without Eddie noticing anything.

She spent three hours with him, at the restaurant where they ate hamburgers and drank Cokes in wax cups that were always sweating, and then down an alley a mile or so away, and when he left her off at five to eleven only the movie house was still open at the plaza. Her girlfriend was there, talking with a boy. When Connie came up the two girls smiled at each other and Connie said, "How was the movie?" and the girl said, "You should know." They rode off with the girl's father, sleepy and pleased, and Connie couldn't help but look at the darkened shopping plaza with its big empty parking lot and its signs that were faded and ghostly now, and over at the drive-in restaurant where cars were still circling tirelessly. She couldn't hear the music at this distance.

Next morning June asked her how the movie was and Connie said, "So-so."

She and that girl and occasionally another girl went out several times a week that way, and the rest of the time Connie spent around the house—it was summer vacation—getting in her mother's way and thinking, dreaming, about the boys she met. But all the boys fell back and dissolved into a single face that was not even a face, but an idea, a feeling, mixed up with the urgent insistent pounding of the music and the humid night air of July. Connie's mother kept dragging her back to the daylight by finding things for her to do or saying, suddenly, "What's this about the Pettinger girl?"

And Connie would say nervously, "Oh, her. That dope." She always drew thick clear lines between herself and such girls, and her mother was simple and kindly enough to believe her. Her mother was so simple, Connie thought, that it was maybe cruel to fool her so much. Her mother went scuffling around the house in old bedroom slippers and complained over the telephone to one sister about the other, then the other called up and the two of them complained about the third one. If June's name was mentioned her mother's tone was approving, and if Connie's name was mentioned it was disapproving. This did not really mean she disliked Connie, and actually Connie thought that her mother preferred her to June because she was prettier, but the two of them kept up a pretense of exasperation, a sense that they were tugging and struggling over something of little value to either of them. Sometimes, over coffee, they were almost friends, but something would come up—some vexation that was like a fly buzzing suddenly around their heads—and their faces went hard with contempt.

One Sunday Connie got up at eleven—none of them bothered with church—and washed her hair so that it could dry all day long, in the sun. Her parents and sister were going to a barbecue at an aunt's house and Connie said no, she wasn't interested, rolling her eyes to let mother know just what she thought of it. "Stay home alone then," her mother said sharply. Connie sat out back in a lawn chair and watched them drive away, her father quiet and bald, hunched around so that he could back the car out, her mother with a look that was still angry and not at all softened through the windshield, and in the back seat poor old June all dressed up as if she didn't know what a barbecue was, with all the running yelling kids and the flies. Connie sat with her eyes closed in the sun, dreaming and dazed with the warmth about her as if this were a kind of love, the caresses of love, and her mind slipped over onto thoughts of the boy she had been with the night before and how nice he had been, how sweet it always was, not the way someone like June would suppose but sweet, gentle, the way it was in movies and promised in songs; and when she opened her eyes she hardly knew where she was, the back yard ran off into weeds and a fence-line of trees and behind it the sky was perfectly blue and still. The asbestos "ranch house" that was now three years old startled her—it looked small. She shook her head as if to get awake.

It was too hot. She went inside the house and turned on the radio to drown out the quiet. She sat on the edge of her bed, barefoot, and listened for an hour and a half to a program called XYZ Sunday Jamboree, record after record of hard, fast, shrieking songs she sang along with, interspersed by exclamations from "Bobby King": "An' look here you girls at Napoleon's—Son and Charley want you to pay real close attention to this song coming up!"

And Connie paid close attention herself, bathed in a glow of slow-pulsed joy that seemed to rise mysteriously out of the music itself and lay languidly about the airless little room, breathed in and breathed out with each gentle rise and fall of her chest.

After a while she heard a car coming up the drive. She sat up at once, startled, because it couldn't be her father so soon. The gravel kept crunching all the way in from the road—the driveway was long—and Connie ran to the window. It was a car she didn't know. It was an open jalopy, painted a bright gold that caught the sunlight opaquely. Her heart began to pound and her fingers snatched at her hair, checking it, and she whispered "Christ, Christ," wondering how bad she looked. The car came to a stop at the side door and the horn sounded four short taps as if this were a signal Connie knew.

She went into the kitchen and approached the door slowly, then hung out the screen door, her bare toes curling down off the step. There were two boys in the car and now she recognized the driver: he had shaggy, shabby black hair that looked crazy as a wig and he was grinning at her.

"I ain't late, am I?" he said.

"Who the hell do you think you are?" Connie said.

"Toldja I'd be out, didn't I?"

"I don't even know who you are."

She spoke sullenly, careful to show no interest or pleasure, and he spoke in a fast bright monotone. Connie looked past him to the other boy, taking her time. He had fair brown hair, with a lock that fell onto his forehead. His sideburns gave him a fierce, embarrassed look, but so far he hadn't even bothered to glance at her. Both boys wore sunglasses. The driver's glasses were metallic and mirrored everything in miniature.

"You wanta come for a ride?" he said.

Connie smirked and let her hair fall loose over one shoulder.

"Don'tcha like my car? New paint job," he said. "Hey."

"What?"

"You're cute."

She pretended to fidget, chasing flies away from the door.

"Don'tcha believe me, or what?" he said.

"Look, I don't even know who you are," Connie said in disgust.

"Hey, Ellie's got a radio, see. Mine's broke down." He lifted his friend's arm and showed her the little transistor the boy was holding, and now Connie began to hear the music. It was the same program that was playing inside the house.

"Bobby King?" she said.

"I listen to him all the time. I think he's great."

"He's kind of great," Connie said reluctantly.

"Listen, that guy's *great*. He knows where the action is."

Connie blushed a little, because the glasses made it impossible for her to see just what this boy was looking at. She couldn't decide if she liked him or if he was just a jerk, and so she dawdled in the doorway and wouldn't come down or go back inside. She said, "What's all that stuff painted on your car?"

"Can'tcha read it?" He opened the door very carefully, as if he was afraid it might fall off. He slid out just as carefully, planting his feet firmly on the ground, the tiny metallic world in his glasses slowing down like gelatine

.hardening and in the midst of it Connie's bright green blouse. "This here is my name, to begin with," he said. ARNOLD FRIEND was written in tarlike black letters on the side, with a drawing of a round grinning face that reminded Connie of a pumpkin, except it wore sunglasses. "I wanta introduce myself, I'm Arnold Friend and that's my real name and I'm gonna be your friend, honey, and inside the car's Ellie Oscar, he's kinda shy." Ellie brought his transistor radio up to his shoulder and balanced it there. "Now these numbers are a secret code, honey," Arnold Friend explained. He read off the numbers 33, 19, 17 and raised his eyebrows at her to see what she thought of that, but she didn't think much of it. The left rear fender had been smashed and around it was written, on the gleaming gold background: DONE BY CRAZY WOMAN DRIVER. Connie had to laugh at that. Arnold Friend was pleased at her laughter and looked up at her. "Around the other side's a lot more—you wanta come and see them?"

"No."

"Why not?"

"Why should I?"

"Don'tcha wanta see what's on the car? Don'tcha wanta go for a ride?"

"I don't know."

"Why not?"

"I got things to do."

"Like what?"

"Things."

He laughed as if she had said something funny. He slapped his thighs. He was standing in a strange way, leaning back against the car as if he were balancing himself. He wasn't tall, only an inch or so taller than she would be if she came down to him. Connie liked the way he was dressed, which was the way all of them dressed: tight faded jeans stuffed into black, scuffed boots, a belt that pulled his waist in and showed how lean he was, and a white pullover shirt that was a little soiled and showed the hard small muscles of his arms and shoulders. He looked as if he probably did hard work, lifting and carrying things. Even his neck looked muscular. And his face was a familiar face, somehow: the jaw and chin and cheeks slightly darkened, because he hadn't shaved for a day or two, and the nose long and hawklike, sniffing as if she were a treat he was going to gobble up and it was all a joke.

"Connie, you ain't telling the truth. This is your day set aside for a ride with me and you know it," he said, still laughing. The way he straightened and recovered from his fit of laughing showed that it had been all fake.

"How do you what my name is?" she said suspiciously.

"It's Connie."

"Maybe and maybe not."

"I know my Connie," he said, wagging his finger. Now she remembered him even better, back at the restaurant, and her cheeks warmed at the thought of how she sucked in her breath just at the moment she passed him—how she must have looked to him. And he had remembered her. "Ellie and I come out here especially for you," he said. "Ellie can sit in back. How about it?"

"Where?"

"Where what?"

"Where're we going?"

He looked at her. He took off the sunglasses and she saw how pale the skin around his eyes was, like holes that were not in shadow but instead in light. His eyes were like chips of broken glass that catch the light in an amiable way. He smiled. It was as if the idea of going for a ride somewhere, to some place, was a new idea to him.

"Just for a ride, Connie sweetheart."

"I never said my name was Connie," she said.

"But I know what it is. I know your name and all about you, lots of things," Arnold Friend said. He had not moved yet but stood still leaning back against the side of his jalopy. "I took a special interest in you, such a pretty girl, and found out all about you like I know your parents and sister are gone somewheres and I know where and how long they're going to be gone, and I know who you were with last night, and your best girlfriend's name is Betty. Right?"

He spoke in a simple lilting voice, exactly as if he were reciting the words to a song. His smile assured her that everything was fine. In the car Ellie turned up the volume on his radio and did not bother to look around at them.

"Ellie can sit in the back seat," Arnold Friend said. He indicated his friend with a casual jerk of his chin, as if Ellie did not count and she should not bother with him.

"How'd you find out all that stuff?" Connie said.

"Listen: Betty Schultz and Tony Fitch and Jimmy Pettinger and Nancy Pettinger," he said, in a chant. "Raymond Stanley and Bob Hutter—"

"Do you know all those kids?"

"I know everybody."

"Look, you're kidding. You're not from around here."

"Sure."

"But—how come we never saw you before?"

"Sure you saw me before," he said. He looked down at his boots, as if he were a little offended. "You just don't remember."

"I guess I'd remember you," Connie said.

"Yeah?" He looked up at this, beaming. He was pleased. He began to mark time with the music from Ellie's radio, tapping his fists lightly together. Connie looked away from his smile to the car, which was painted so bright it almost hurt her eyes to look at it. She looked at that name, ARNOLD FRIEND. And up at the front fender was an expression that was familiar—MAN THE FLYING SAUCERS. It was an expression kids had used the year before, but didn't use this year. She looked at it for a while as if the words meant something to her that she did not yet know.

"What're you thinking about? Huh?" Arnold Friend demanded. "Not worried about your hair blowing around in the car, are you?"

"No."

"Think I maybe can't drive good?"

"How do I know?"

"You're a hard girl to handle. How come?" he said. "Don't you know I'm your friend? Didn't you see me put my sign in the air when you walked by?"

"What sign?"

"My sign." And he drew an X in the air, leaning out toward her. They were maybe ten feet apart. After his hand fell back to his side the X was still in the air, almost visible. Connie let the screen door close and stood perfectly still inside it, listening to the music from her radio and the boy's blend together. She stared at Arnold Friend. He stood there so stiffly relaxed, pretending to be relaxed, with one hand idly on the door handle as if he were keeping himself up that way and had no intention of ever moving again. She recognized most things about him, the tight jeans that showed his thighs and buttocks and the greasy leather boots and the tight shirt, and even that slippery friendly smile of his, that sleepy dreamy smile that all the boys used to get across ideas they didn't want to put into words. She recognized all this and also the singsong way he talked, slightly mocking, kidding, but serious and a little melancholy, and she recognized the way he tapped one fist against the other in homage to the perpetual music behind him. But all these things did not come together.

She said suddenly, "Hey, how old are you?"

His smile faded. She could see then that he wasn't a kid, he was much older—thirty, maybe more. At this knowledge her heart began to pound faster.

"That's a crazy thing to ask. Can'tcha see I'm your own age?"

"Like hell you are."

"Or maybe a coupla years older. I'm eighteen."

"Eighteen?" she said doubtfully.

He grinned to reassure her and lines appeared at the corners of his mouth. His teeth were big and white. He grinned so broadly his eyes became slits and she saw how thick the lashes were, thick and black as if painted with a black tarlike material. Then he seemed to become embarrassed, abruptly, and looked over his shoulder at Ellie. *"Him, he's crazy,"* he said. "Ain't he a riot, he's a nut, a real character." Ellie was still listening to the music. His sunglasses told nothing about what he was thinking. He wore a bright orange shirt unbuttoned halfway to show his chest, which was a pale, bluish chest and not muscular like Arnold Friend's. His shirt collar was turned up all around and the very tips of the collar pointed out past his chin as if they were protecting him. He was pressing the transistor radio up against his ear and sat there in a kind of daze, right in the sun.

"He's kinda strange," Connie said.

"Hey, she says you're kinda strange! Kinda strange!" Arnold Friend cried. He pounded on the car to get Ellie's attention. Ellie turned for the first time and Connie saw with shock that he wasn't a kid either—he had a fair, hairless face, cheeks reddened slightly as if the veins grew too close to the surface of his skin, the face of a forty-year-old baby. Connie felt a wave of dizziness rise in her at this sight and she stared at him as if waiting for something to change the shock of the moment, make it all right again. Ellie's lips kept shaping words, mumbling along with the words blasting in his ear.

"Maybe you two better go away," Connie said faintly.

"What? How come?" Arnold Friend cried. "We come out here to take you for a ride. It's Sunday." He had the voice of the man on the radio now. It was the same voice, Connie thought. "Don'tcha know it's Sunday all day and honey, no matter who you were with last night today you're with Arnold Friend and don't you forget it!—Maybe you better step out here," he said, and this last was in a different voice. It was a little flatter, as if the heat was finally getting to him.

"No. I got things to do."

"Hey."

"You two better leave."

"We ain't leaving until you come with us."

"Like hell I am—"

"Connie, don't fool around with me. I mean, I mean, don't fool *around*," he said, shaking his head. He laughed incredulously. He placed his sunglasses on top of his head, carefully, as if he were indeed wearing a wig, and brought the stems down behind his ears. Connie stared at him, another wave of dizziness and fear rising in her so that for a moment he wasn't even in focus but was just a blur, standing there against his gold car, and she had the idea that he had driven up the driveway all right but had come from nowhere before that and belonged nowhere and that everything about him and even about the music that was so familiar to her was only half real.

"If my father comes and sees you—"

"He ain't coming. He's at a barbecue."

"How do you know that?"

"Aunt Tillie's. Right now they're—uh—they're drinking. Sitting around," he said vaguely, squinting as if he were staring all the way to town and over to Aunt Tillie's back yard. Then the vision seemed to get clear and he nodded energetically. "Yeah. Sitting around. There's your sister in a blue dress, huh? And high heels, the poor sad bitch—nothing like you, sweetheart! And your mother's helping some fat woman with the corn, they're cleaning the corn—husking the corn—"

"What fat woman?" Connie cried.

"How do I know what fat woman, I don't know every goddam fat woman in the world!" Arnold laughed.

"Oh, that's Mrs. Hornby . . . Who invited her?" Connie said. She felt a little light-headed. Her breath was coming quickly.

"She's too fat. I don't like them fat. I like them the way you are, honey," he said, smiling sleepily at her. They stared at each other for a while, through the screen door. He said softly, "Now what you're going to do is this: you're going to come out that door. You're going to sit up front with me and Ellie's going to sit in the back, the hell with Ellie, right? This isn't Ellie's date. You're my date. I'm your lover, honey."

"What? You're crazy—"

"Yes, I'm your lover. You don't know what that is but you will," he said. "I know that too. I know all about you. But look: it's real nice and you couldn't ask for nobody better than me, or more polite. I always keep my word. I'll tell you how it is, I'm always nice at first, the first time. I'll hold you so tight you won't think you have to try to get away or pretend anything because you'll know you can't. And I'll come inside you where it's all secret and you'll give in to me and you'll love me—"

"Shut up! You're crazy!" Connie said. She backed away from the door. She put her hands against her ears as if she'd heard something terrible, something not meant for her. "People don't talk like that, you're crazy," she muttered. Her heart was almost too big now for her chest and its pumping made sweat break out all over her. She looked out to see Arnold Friend pause and then take a step toward the porch lurching. He almost fell. But, like a clever drunken man, he managed to catch his balance. He wobbled in his high boots and grabbed hold of one of the porch posts.

"Honey?" he said. "You still listening?"

"Get the hell out of here!"

"Be nice, honey. Listen."

"I'm going to call the police—"

He wobbled again and out of the side of his mouth came a fast spat curse, an aside not meant for her to hear. But even this "Christ!" sounded forced. Then he began to smile again. She watched this smile come, awkward as if he were smiling from inside a mask. His whole face was a mask, she thought wildly, tanned down onto his throat but then running out as if he had plastered makeup on his face but had forgotten about his throat.

"Honey—? Listen, here's how it is. I always tell the truth and I promise you this: I ain't coming in that house after you."

"You better not! I'm going to call the police if you—if you don't—"

"Honey," he said, talking right through her voice, "honey, I'm not coming in there but you are coming out here. You know why?"

She was panting. The kitchen looked like a place she had never seen before, some room she had run inside but which wasn't good enough, wasn't going to help her. The kitchen window had never had a curtain, after three years, and there were dishes in the sink for her to do—probably—and if you ran your hand across the table you'd probably feel something sticky there.

"You listening, honey? Hey?"

"—going to call the police—"

"Soon as you touch the phone I don't need to keep my promise and can come inside. You don't want that."

She rushed forward and tried to lock the door. Her fingers were shaking. "But why lock it," Arnold Friend said gently, talking right into her face. "It's just a screen door. It's just nothing." One of his boots was at a strange angle, as if his foot wasn't in it. It pointed out to the left, bent at the ankle. "I mean, anybody can break through a screen door and glass and wood and iron or anything else if he needs to, anybody at all and specially Arnold Friend. If the place got lit up with a fire honey you'd come runnin' out into my arms, right into my arms an' safe at home—like you knew I was your lover and'd stopped fooling around. I don't mind a nice shy girl but I don't like no fooling around." Part of those words were spoken with a slight rhythmic lilt, and Connie somehow recognized them—the echo of a song from last year, about a girl rushing into her boyfriend's arms and coming home again—

Connie stood barefoot on the linoleum floor, staring at him. "What do you want?" she whispered.

"I want you," he said.

"What?"

"Seen you that night and thought, that's the one, yes sir. I never needed to look any more."

"But my father's coming back. He's coming to get me. I had to wash my hair first—" She spoke in a dry, rapid voice, hardly raising it for him to hear.

"No, your Daddy is not coming and yes, you had to wash your hair and you washed it for me. It's nice and shining and all for me, I thank you, sweetheart," he said, with a mock bow, but again he almost lost his balance. He had to bend and adjust his boots. Evidently his feet did not go all the way down; the boots must have been stuffed with something so that he would seem taller. Connie stared out at him and behind him Ellie in the car, who seemed to be looking off toward Connie's right into nothing. This Ellie said, pulling the words out of the air one after another as if he were just discovering them, "You want me to pull out the phone?"

"Shut your mouth and keep it shut," Arnold Friend said, his face red from bending over or maybe from embarrassment because Connie had seen his boots. "This ain't none of your business."

"What—what are you doing? What do you want?" Connie said. "If I call the police they'll get you, they'll arrest you—"

"Promise was not to come in unless you touch that phone, and I'll keep that promise," he said. He resumed his erect position and tried to force his shoulders back. He sounded like a hero in a movie, declaring something important. He spoke too loudly and it was as if he were speaking to someone behind Connie. "I ain't made plans for coming in that house where I don't belong but just for you to come out to me, the way you should. Don't you know who I am?"

"You're crazy," she whispered. She backed away from the door but did not want to go into another part of the house, as if this would give him permission to come through the door. "What do you . . . You're crazy, you . . ."

"Huh? What're you saying, honey?"

Her eyes darted everywhere in the kitchen. She could not remember what it was, this room.

"This is how it is, honey: you come out and we'll drive away, have a nice ride. But if you don't come out we're gonna wait till your people come home and then they're all going to get it."

"You want that telephone pulled out?" Ellie said. He held the radio away from his ear and grimaced, as if without the radio the air was too much for him.

"I toldja shut up, Ellie," Arnold Friend said, "you're deaf, get a hearing aid, right? Fix yourself up. This little girl's no trouble and's gonna be nice to me, so Ellie keep to yourself, this ain't your date—right? Don't hem in on me. Don't hog. Don't crush, Don't bird dog. Don't trail me," he said in a rapid meaningless voice, as if he were running through all the expressions he'd learned but was no longer sure which one of them was in style, then rushing on to new ones, making them up with his eyes closed, "Don't crawl under my fence, don't squeeze in my chipmunk hole, don't sniff my glue, suck my popsicle, keep your own greasy fingers on yourself!" He shaded his eyes and peered in at Connie, who was backed against the kitchen table. "Don't mind him honey he's just a creep. He's a dope. Right? I'm the boy for you and like I said you come out here nice like a lady and give me your hand, and nobody else gets hurt, I mean, your nice old bald-headed daddy and your mummy and your sister in her high heels. Because listen: why bring them in this?"

"Leave me alone," Connie whispered.

"Hey, you know that old woman down the road, the one with the chickens and stuff—you know her?"

"She's dead!"

"Dead? What? You know her?" Arnold Friend said.

"She's dead—"

"Don't you like her?"

"She's dead—she's—she isn't here any more—"

"But don't you like her, I mean, you got something against her? Some grudge or something?" Then his voice dipped as if he were conscious of a rudeness. He touched the sunglasses perched on top of his head as if to make sure they were still there. "Now you be a good girl."

"What are you going to do?"

"Just two things, or maybe three," Arnold Friend said. "But I promise it won't last long and you'll like me the way you get to like people you're close to. You will. It's all over for you here, so come on out. You don't want your people in any trouble, do you?"

She turned and bumped against a chair or something, hurting her leg, but she ran into the back room and picked up the telephone. Something roared in her ear, a tiny roaring, and she was so sick with fear that she could do nothing but listen to it—the telephone was clammy and very heavy and her fingers groped down to the dial but were too weak to touch it. She began to scream into the phone, into the roaring. She cried out, she cried for her mother, she felt her breath start jerking back and forth in her lungs as if it were something Arnold Friend were stabbing her with again and again with no tenderness. A noisy sorrowful wailing rose all about her and she was locked inside it the way she was locked inside this house.

After a while she could hear again. She was sitting on the floor with her wet back against the wall.

Arnold Friend was saying from the door. "That's a good girl. Put the phone back."

She kicked the phone away from her.

"No, honey. Pick it up. Put it back right."

She picked it up and put it back. The dial tone stopped.

"That's a good girl. Now you come outside."

She was hollow with what had been fear, but what was now just an emptiness. All that screaming had blasted it out of her. She sat, one leg cramped under her, and deep inside her brain was something like a pinpoint of light that kept going and would not let her relax. She thought, I'm not going to see my mother again. She thought, I'm not going to sleep in my bed again. Her bright green blouse was all wet.

Arnold Friend said, in a gentle-loud voice that was like a stage voice, "The place where you came from ain't there any more, and where you had in mind to go is canceled out. This place you are now—inside your daddy's house—is nothing but a cardboard box I can knock down any time. You know that and always did know it. You hear me?"

She thought, I have got to think. I have to know what to do.

"We'll go out to a nice field, out in the country here where it smells so nice and it's sunny," Arnold Friend said. "I'll have my arms tight around you so you won't need to try to get away and I'll show you what love is like, what it does. The hell with this house. It looks solid all right," he said. He ran a fingernail down the screen and the noise did not make Connie shiver, as it would have the day before. "Now put your hand on your heart, honey. Feel that? That feels solid too but we know better, be nice to me, be sweet like you can because what else is there for a girl like you but to be sweet and pretty and give in?—and get away before her people come back?"

She felt her pounding heart. Her hand seemed to enclose it. She thought for the first time in her life that it was nothing that was hers, that belonged to her, but just a pounding, living thing inside this body that wasn't really hers either.

"You don't want them to get hurt," Arnold Friend went on. "Now get up, honey. Get up all by yourself."

She stood.

"Now turn this way. That's right. Come over here to me—Ellie, put that away, didn't I tell you? You dope. You miserable creepy dope," Arnold Friend said. His words were not angry but only part of an incantation. The incantation was kindly. "Now come out through the kitchen to me honey, and let's see a smile, try it, you're a brave sweet little girl and now they're eating corn and hot dogs cooked to bursting over an outdoor fire, and they don't know one thing about you and never did and honey you're better than them because not a one of them would have done this for you."

Connie felt the linoleum under her feet; it was cool. She brushed her hair back out of her eyes. Arnold Friend let go of the post tentatively and opened his arms for her, his elbows pointing in toward each other and his wrists limp, to show that this was an embarrassed embrace and a little mocking, he didn't want to make her self-conscious.

She put out her hand against the screen. She watched herself push the door slowly open as if she were safe back somewhere in the other doorway, watching this body and this head of long hair moving out into the sunlight where Arnold Friend waited.

"My sweet little blue-eyed girl," he said, in a half-sung sigh that had nothing to do with her brown eyes but was taken up just the same by the vast sunlit reaches of the land behind him and on all sides of him, so much land that Connie had never seen before and did not recognize except to know that she was going to it.

Questions for Writing or Discussion

1. What effect does music have on both Connie and Leila?
2. In what ways are going to a ball and going to a hamburger stand similar?
3. In both stories, the young men sound bored when they talk. Why?

4. In each story, an older man awakens the girl to a truth about herself. What is the truth in each case? What do the truths have in common?
5. Connie has an older sister to whom she feels superior. Leila has cousins whom she admires for being more worldly than she. Is this difference between the two girls important?
6. Leila is eager to tell each of her partners that she has never been to a ball before. Connie "wore a pullover jersey blouse that looked one way when she was at home and another way when she was away from home." Does this difference between the two girls account for the difference in the endings of the two stories? What is the difference? Why is it significant?
7. Write a paper in which you use comparison-contrast techniques to discuss the two stories as "initiation" stories.

Two Approaches to Disciplining Children

Virginia E. Pomeranz with Dodi Schultz
From THE FIRST FIVE YEARS

It is important to realize that no punishment is effective unless the alternatives are understood clearly to start with. In other words, a choice must be presented: "Either you will do what I have asked you to do or you will be punished." And the consequences of the behavior in question must be understood as well.

You and I are well aware that if we toss a glass vase about on the patio it may fall on the flagstones and break; we know this because it's part of our past experience. But your three-year-old is not likely to really comprehend your warning, "Susie, don't play with that; it's breakable, and very valuable." Susie may actually be quite astonished when the vase falls from her fingers and shatters. Punishing her is not really appropriate. You simply have to explain that's what you meant, and clean it up, and say, "Next time, be careful."

When punishment *is* called for, the thing to do is administer it without delay. Small children have very short memories. "I'll tell your father when he comes home, and are you going to get it!"—when that event is six hours in the future—is ridiculous. By that time the child will have long since forgotten the exact nature of the transgression, and the punishment will be meaningless. Secondly, as they said in *The Mikado*, "let the punishment fit the crime"—at least as closely as possible.

Let us say that two-year-old Georgie is playing in the sandbox with a group of other children and he bites another child. This is a dangerous act and should be firmly discouraged. You dash right over there, grab Georgie, and get his attention; you tell him that he is not ever to do that again, and that if he disobeys you he *will be punished.* You return to the bench, keeping a keen eye on Georgie. He does it again. Lose no time: immediately remove him from the sandbox and take him home. This is an appropriate deprivation, since he probably likes to play in the sandbox. (And if the act is repeated on another occasion, you might keep him out of the sandbox for several days.) Refusing to let him watch television, or play with his crayons, would not be punishments that fit the crime.

If on the other hand, Georgie takes it into his head to scribble on the dining-room wall—again, if the subject has never come up before, you must make the alternatives clear. You might say, "You are not to do that again. You may draw on the special place on the wall in your own room, but you are not to use any other wall. If you do so again, your crayons will be taken away from you." Again, an appropriate punishment. And again, follow through if the act is repeated: take the crayons away, for at least a day or two—at which point Georgie will probably begin asking for them. He should be reminded, when the crayons are returned, of why they were taken away—and the specifics of where they may and may not be used should be repeated.

How about depriving a child of food? I don't think sending a child to bed without supper is ever a proper form of punishment. Nor do I think depriving a youngster of even a favorite food treat—e.g., ice cream for dessert—is appropriate, unless the crime itself is directly connected with food. (Desserts, in any case, should be nutritious and considered part of the meal.)

If he has deliberately, in defiance of your directives to use his spoon and eat neatly, dumped his spinach on the floor, a no-dessert punishment might be appropriate. Or if he has, earlier in the day, rammed an ice cream cone into his brother's face, you are justified in saying, "You obviously do not know how to handle ice cream properly, and you are not going to have ice cream for a few days." But I do not think it right to say, "Because you have not eaten your spinach you may not have your ice cream." Failure to ingest one food is no reason to be deprived of another.

It is, incidentally, possible in any of these situations that the error will never be repeated. Partly because the child wishes to avoid the announced punishment. But partly, too, in response to your initial displeasure. . . . Children do, basically, want to win their parents' approval. Sometimes—not always, by a long shot—the disappointment or displeasure in your voice when you indicate what has been done wrong will be sufficient deterrent.

Do not, in any event, make idle threats. We have all witnessed scenes in which an exasperated mother says irately, "Johnny, if you don't stop that this very minute, we are going right home." Johnny, giving no sign that he has heard, keeps right on doing what he is doing, and his mother's next statement is, "Now come on, Johnny, stop doing that." Now he knows that she is not going to follow through. Or rather, he does not know *what* to believe. She may pick him up and take him home within the next thirty seconds. On the other hand, she may not. She has become completely unpredictable. And she has placed the child in a dilemma. Can he rely on any threats she makes? Can he rely on any promises whatever? Johnny is going to be pretty confused, since he is left without clear cause-and-effect premises on which to operate.

There are two forms of punishment I urge you not to use.

One is yelling. Very few parents can avoid yelling entirely, and that's understandable; there will be times when your patience is exhausted, and you will find yourself instinctively raising your voice. If these occasions are rare, the child will respond immediately, because the new and different tone of voice will startle him. But if you get into the habit of screaming at your child constantly, he will totally tune you out. Which will have two results, neither one desirable.

You will be hoarse by the end of the day. And because the child will learn to scream back at you, you will no longer converse in normal, conversational tones but will be trying to outshout each other continuously. This will leave you both exhausted. And child care will become a horrible burden, instead of the pleasure it should be.

Further, since your screaming has lost all special significance, some day when you shout at him as he is starting to cross the street in front of an oncoming car, he is not going to hear you.

Secondly, physical punishment. I think hitting a child is a very poor practice, chiefly because you are, by this action, suggesting a new form of behavior that does not occur instinctively in children. If you watch a group of small children playing together—children who have neither been hit themselves nor observed older youngsters fighting—you'll find that those who behave aggressively will push, pull, and occasionally bite; but they won't hit. If *you* hit the child, you are in fact demonstrating a form of behavior to him. And if you are doing it, it must be acceptable, right? You've told him, in other connections, that you want him to act "grown up," haven't you?

You have also introduced a distinct conflict by such action. Chances are you have taken some prior opportunity to point out that bullying, whether of younger siblings or smaller playmates, is not an acceptable form of behavior. Now here you are, hitting a three-year-old. And he looks up at you and says, "If I can't hit Jimmy, because he's littler than me—then how come you, a big person, can hit little me?" There is no answer, and there is egg all over your face. If he doesn't say it, he is thinking it. He is likely to reach the conclusion that bullying is okay after all, and may turn into the terror of the neighborhood. He will of course no longer trust any pronouncements of high principle on your part.

What if the child has taken it into his head to attack *you* physically? You must not permit it; we know that it can result in deep residual feelings of guilt in the child. But don't descend to his level and hit (or scratch or bite) him back. Simply seize the child's wrist(s) firmly. Say in firm, measured tones, "You are not to do that—ever." Hang onto him for at least a full minute. The child will inevitably realize that you possess vastly superior strength. When you let him go, he will feel bad, and there will be marks on his wrists—but you will not have done him any lasting damage, either physically or psychologically.

Fitzhugh Dodson
From HOW TO PARENT

It would be nice if we could rely entirely on the natural consequences of inadequate behavior to discipline a child. Unfortunately, natural consequences are not always sufficient. Sometimes we must find artificial or arbitrary consequences to apply to the behavior of a child.

There are three main methods we can use:

1. *We can deprive the child of something important to him.*

Suppose your five-year-old scribbles on your living room walls with crayons. Such behavior is "normal" for a two-year-old. But it is an act of hostility for a five-year-old. Unfortunately for your discipline, there are no unpleasant natural consequences for the child as a result of scribbling on the walls of your house. You have to create some artificial and arbitrary consequences which will set firm limits to the child, and, in effect, say to him: "No more of this!"

If you feel sufficiently angered when you discover it, you may immediately spank him. That is one type of artificial but unpleasant consequence for him. Or you might deprive him of some privilege, perhaps saying, "Danny, you're old enough to know not to draw on walls with crayons, so I guess you won't be allowed to use your crayons for three days. That will help to remind you that crayons are to be used on paper, not on walls."

2. *We can use social isolation by sending the child out of his social group or to his room.*

Suppose your four-year-old is disrupting the play of a group of children in your back yard. You might say to him, "Charles, I see you are not able to play well with the other children right now. You keep hitting them and causing trouble. You'll have to go to your room and play by yourself until you tell me that you're able to control your actions."

Whenever you use social isolation as a means of discipline, it is important you make it an open-ended rather than a closed-ended affair. Don't just send the child to his room, as if he had to stay there forever. The purpose of sending him to his room is not to incarcerate him indefinitely, but to enable a change in his behavior to take place. Always let him know that when his behavior is able to change and he is able to play reasonably with the other children, he can come back and play.

3. *We can spank a child.*

I want to make it clear that there is a "right" kind of spanking and a "wrong" kind. By the wrong kind I mean a cruel and sadistic beating. This fills a child with hatred, and a deep desire for revenge. This is the kind that is administered with a strap or stick or some other type of parental "weapon." Or it could also mean a humiliating slap in the face.

The right kind of spanking needs no special paraphernalia. Just the hand of the parent administered a few times on the kid's bottom. The right kind of spanking is a *positive* thing. It clears the air, and is vastly to be preferred to moralistic and guilt-inducing parental lectures.

Some of you may have heard the old saying "Never strike a child in anger." I think that that is psychologically very poor advice, and I suggest the opposite: "Never strike a child *except* in anger."

A child can understand very well when you strike him in anger. He knows you are mad at him and he understands why. What a child cannot understand is when he disobeys mother at 10 A.M. and she tells him, "All right, young man—your father will deal with you when he gets home!" Then when Dad arrives home he is expected to administer a spanking which will "really teach the boy a lesson." That's the kind of cold-blooded spanking a child cannot either understand or forgive.

What I advocate is the "pow-wow" type of spanking: your "pow" followed by his "Wow!" Spank your child only when you are furious at him and feel like letting him have it right then. Too many mothers nowadays seem to be afraid to spank their children. They talk and nag a great deal as a substitute; they try to negotiate with a child. This is a huge mistake because it reduces their authority as parents.

What you should do is to tell your child once or perhaps twice what you want him to do or to stop doing. Then, if he refuses to obey your reasonable request, and you have become frustrated and angry, let him have it right then and there!

After spanking, your first immediate reaction may be frustration and guilt. It may bother you that you've blown your cool.

Courage, Mother, all is not lost!

You can always say to your child, in your own way: "Look Mommy goofed. I lost my temper, and I'm sorry I did." Then you can go on from there. You don't have to be "stuck" with the guilt and the frustration and the unhappy feelings.

Wait until you really feel better about the situation and about your child. It might be five minutes or five hours later. But if you feel you have blown your stack, *it's important to admit it to your child.* Above all, don't pretend to him that the sole reason you spanked him was for his benefit. That's as phony as a three-dollar bill, and he will know it.

The main purpose of spanking, although most parents don't like to admit it, is to relieve the parent's feelings of frustration. All of us need to do this from time to time when our kids get on our nerves.

If we were 100 percent perfect parents, we would all be so mature we would never need to spank our kids except in unusual or extreme situations (such as when a child runs out into the street). The point is, we are not such 100 percent perfect parents. We are not able to administer discipline calmly and serenely all the time. It would be nice if we could. But life doesn't seem to work out that way. We get fed up when our kids misbehave and we lose our cool and swat them. But that's nothing to feel guilty about. We feel better and they feel better, the air is cleared.

Both parent and child get a chance to begin again. Having gotten angry feelings out of your system, you can once more feel positive toward your child. You can then assume your rightful role of parental authority.

Some of you may feel uncomfortable with the notion I have just advanced that the main purpose of spanking is to relieve the frustrated feelings of the parent. You may still be under the illusion that the purpose of spanking is solely to influence your child in a better direction. In this case, I refer you to one of my favorite cartoons, which shows a father whaling the tar out of his little boy, saying as he whales him, "That'll teach you to hit people!" (He's right—it will!)

Nevertheless, we parents are human, and so I say "spank away" if you need to. But, hopefully, if you follow the constructive suggestions I have made on child discipline, you will find you need to spank far less frequently than you otherwise would. And as your child grows older and becomes increasingly capable of self-regulation, you should have to spank far less often.

If you are quite honest with yourself, you will find that there are times when you will lose your temper, fly off the handle at your child, and yell at him or spank him—only to realize afterwards that what he did actually should not have elicited such a violent outburst from you. You were really mad at your husband or your neighbor. Or just cranky for some unknown reason. And you took it out on your child.

What can you do in such a situation? Well, you could pretend you are a holy paragon of virtue and that your child fully deserved the scolding or spanking he got. Or you can have the courage to say something like this to your child: "Danny, mother got mad at you and scolded you. But I can see now that you didn't do anything that was really that bad. I think I was really mad at something else and I was sort of taking it out on you. So I'm sorry."

Your child will feel a wonderful warm feeling toward you for admitting you are human and fallible. This will do wonders for his self-concept—and yours!

Questions for Writing or Discussion

1. Each article has a clearly stated thesis. What is the thesis in each case? Where is it stated?
2. The authors, in each case, make assumptions about the character of parents. What are the assumptions? Which to you seems more realistic?
3. The authors, in each case, have strong views about spanking a child. What are their respective views? Which to you seems more reasonable?
4. Each article recommends specific punishments for specific offenses. What are the crimes and punishments discussed in each article?
5. Write a paper in which you show that one of these two approaches to discipline is better than the other.

CHAPTER 11

WRITING AN ARGUMENTATIVE PAPER

An argumentative paper attempts to strengthen or change an attitude of the reader, or to persuade the reader to a particular point of view by means of logic. (See pp. 29–38 for a discussion of logic.) Although writers of argumentative papers may employ emotional appeals, they place their principal faith in appealing to the understanding of their readers.

The subject matter for argumentative papers must be controversial; that is, there must be the possibility for a difference of opinion on the subject. Otherwise, there would be no need for persuasion. That does not mean, however, that the subject matter need be earthshaking. Writers differ on how poems should be interpreted or on how cakes should be baked. In the sense that the purpose of an argumentative paper is to persuade a reader to a point of view, you have been writing argumentative papers since you began your study of English composition. In every paper you have written, you have taken a position on a subject and have offered logical reasons for holding that position.

A formal argumentative paper, however, has its own very specific requirements:

1. The writer states the problem or issue, sometimes tracing its causes.
2. In some cases the writer states the possible positions to be taken on the problem.
3. The writer states the position that the paper will take.
4. The writer offers proof that the position is the reasonable one to hold.
5. The writer anticipates objections to the position and refutes them.
6. The writer affirms the position and makes a final appeal.

A formal argumentative paper, also, can combine two or more of the methods of development in its organization. A defense of free speech, for example, might begin with a *definition* of the term and then review the major crises that arose in the *process* of maintaining that right in this country.

Since the Declaration of Independence is often held up as a model of a perfect argument, an analysis of it might be helpful. It begins with a statement of the problem: the United States finds it necessary to dissolve its political connections with Great Britain and assert its independence. This is followed by a definition of good government and the assertion that King George has violated the requirements of good government. This is the reason for the break with Great Britain. But Jefferson does not expect the rest of mankind simply to take his word that King George is a dreadful ruler. He offers proof in the form of twenty-eight violations of basic human rights. Then he anticipates possible criticisms of his argument: some might insist that the United States does not need to take such drastic action, that she could settle her differences in the courts; some might say that although George III is tyrannical, the United States must have friends in Great Britain who would plead her case with him. Jefferson refutes these possible criticisms and, having made his case as airtight as possible, concludes with a declaration of the country's independence.

Thomas Jefferson was, of course, a master of argumentation. Here is a student's argumentative paper on an issue that has aroused heated controversy in recent years. Read it and see what you think of his efforts.

The Right to Assume Responsibility
HUGH NICHOLES

The stereotyped motorcyclist is usually visualized as a hulking brute who is generally complaining about something. With the increasing popularity of motorcycles this stereotype is changing, but motorcyclists are still complaining. Many states have dictated that a motorcyclist may not ride without a crash helmet. At first glance the helmet laws seem to be an insignificant issue, certainly not anything to enrage citizens; the government is merely trying to save lives. The wisdom of wearing crash helmets is not being debated. Motorcyclists maintain that the state has infringed upon their constitutional rights with this law. They are correct.

A government may restrict an individual's freedom of choice if that freedom may cause other members of the public harm. By passing the helmet laws, the government has implied that the wearing of helmets is necessary to protect the public. This implication is unsupportable. A crash helmet protects only the person wearing it; it does nothing to protect bystanders in any way. A crash helmet does not in any way lessen the chances of losing control of a motorcycle, which might cause damage to the general public. In fact, a heavy cumbersome helmet may make hearing difficult or irritate the driver, which could result in damage to the general public. The only way a helmet might be of public benefit is in the protection of the passengers who are riding with the driver. It must be assumed that any passengers are on a motorcycle of their own free will; motorcycles are most impractical kidnapping vehicles. As such, the passenger enjoys the same rights and responsibilities as any motorcyclist.

It has been argued that crash helmets benefit the public indirectly. A person without a helmet who has been killed or mangled in a cycle crash is a liability to society. While this is entirely true, it is also discriminatory when applied only to motorcyclists. Since there are proportionately more deaths caused by car crashes than are caused by motorcycle crashes, and since persons killed or mangled in car crashes are also a liability to society, and since motorcyclists must wear helmets to deter such liabilities, then car drivers should be forced to wear helmets if the law is truly just. The usual response to this idea is the claim that cars offer more protection than motorcycles; riding a motorcycle is a greater risk. This may be true, but amateur mountain climbers and scuba divers would be astonished to find that taking a risk is illegal. The risk must be assumed by the motorcyclist, and it is entirely his responsibility to deal with any potential hazards.

The penalties exacted for riding without a helmet make the law even more objectionable. Not only is the rider fined, but he is cited for a moving traffic violation. From a legal point of view, the refusal to wear a crash helmet places the rider in the same category as reckless drivers, speeders, and other truly dangerous drivers. Violaters of the more reasonable traffic laws endanger the general public, while offenders of helmet laws endanger only themselves; there is no valid parallel between the two types of offenses. In spite of this fact, a cyclist may lose his driver's license by repeatedly refusing to protect himself according to the state's standards, even though society does not benefit by the removal of such a person from the road. The punishment is inappropriate for what the state terms a crime.

The governments of many states have created a law which unfairly deprives motorcyclists of their right to be responsible for the safety of their own persons. Through the helmet law, citizens who ride motorcylces may be penalized. As legitimate grounds for the law do not exist, the penalties are unjust. The law should be removed from the books.

Questions for Writing or Discussion

1. Does the writer disapprove of safety helmets or only of laws that require them? Where does he make the distinction? Is the distinction important?

2. Does the writer show an awareness of the arguments that can be offered against his own position?

3. The writing throughout is fairly formal, perhaps because the

writer does not want to be mistaken for the "hulking brute" stereotype of motorcyclists. Where does he introduce a note of humor to lighten the tone?
4. How convincing is the author's argument that motorcyclists are the victims of discrimination? Would he be happy if automobile drivers and mountain climbers were required to wear helmets?
5. Should laws require automobile drivers to fasten their seat belts? Would that differ in any significant way from requiring all citizens to eat balanced diets and engage in daily exercises?

Readings

The reading selections that follow are examples of argumentative writing. The first is a short essay by a former major league pitcher. The last two are classic documents of American history. As you study them, see if you can identify the six parts of a good argumentative paper in each.

Robin Roberts
STRIKE OUT LITTLE LEAGUE

In 1939, Little League baseball was organized by Bert and George Bebble and Carl Stotz of Williamsport, Pa. What they had in mind in organizing this kids' baseball program, I'll never know. But I'm sure they never visualized the monster it would grow into.

At least 25,000 teams, in about 5,000 leagues, compete for a chance to go to the Little League World Series in Williamsport each summer. These leagues are in more than fifteen countries, although recently the Little League organization has voted to restrict the competition to teams in the United States. If you judge the success of a program by the number of participants, it would appear that Little League has been a tremendous success. More than 600,000 boys from 8 to 12 are involved. But I say Little League is wrong—and I'll try to explain why.

If I told you and your family that I want you to help me with a project from the middle of May until the end of July, one that would totally disrupt your dinner schedule and pay nothing, you would probably tell me to get lost. That's what Little League does. Mothers or fathers or both spend four or five nights a week taking children to Little League, watching the game, coming home around 8 or 8:30 and sitting down to a late dinner.

These games are played at this hour because the adults are running the programs and this is the only time they have available. These same adults are in most cases unqualified as instructors and do not have the emotional stability to work with children of this age. The dedication and sincerity of these instructors cannot be questioned, but the purpose of this dedication should be. Youngsters eligible for Little League are of the age when their concentration lasts, at most, for five seconds—and without sustained concentration organized athletic programs are a farce.

Most instructors will never understand this. As a result there is a lot of pressure on these young people to do something that is unnatural for their age—so there will always be hollering and tremendous disappointment for most of these players. For acting their age, they are made to feel incompetent. This is a basic fault of Little League.

If you watch a Little League game, in most cases the pitchers are the most mature. They throw harder, and if they throw strikes very few batters can hit the ball. Consequently, it makes good baseball sense for most hitters to take the pitch. Don't swing. Hope for a walk. That could be a player's instruction for four years. The fun is in hitting the ball; the coach says don't swing. That may be sound baseball, but it does nothing to help a young player develop his hitting. What would seem like a basic training ground for baseball often turns out to be a program of negative thoughts that only retards a young player.

I believe more good young athletes are turned off by the pressure of organized Little League than are helped. Little Leagues have no value as a training ground for baseball fundamentals. The instruction at that age, under the pressure of an organized league program, creates more doubt and eliminates the naturalness that is most important.

If I'm going to criticize such a popular program as Little League, I'd better have some thoughts on what changes I would like to see.

First of all, I wouldn't start any programs until the school year is over. Any young student has enough of a schedule during the school year to keep busy.

These programs should be played in the afternoon—with a softball. Kids have a natural fear of a baseball; it hurts when it hits you. A softball is bigger, easier to see and easier to hit. You get to run the bases more and there isn't as much danger of injury if one gets hit with the ball. Boys and girls could play together. Different teams would be chosen every day. The instructors would be young adults home from college, or high-school graduates. The instructor could be the pitcher and the umpire at the same time. These programs could be run on public playgrounds or in schoolyards.

I guarantee that their dinner would be at the same time every night. The fathers could come home after work and relax; most of all, the kids would have a good time playing ball in a program in which hitting the ball and running the bases are the big things.

When you start talking about young people playing baseball at 13 to 15, you may have something. Organize them a little, but be careful; they are still young. But from 16 and on, work them really hard. Discipline them, organize the leagues, strive to win championships, travel all over. Give this age all the time and attention you can.

I believe Little League has done just the opposite. We've worked hard with the 8- to 12-year-olds. We overorganize them, put them under pressure they can't handle and make playing baseball seem important. When our young people reach 16 they would appreciate the attention and help from the parents, and that's when our present programs almost stop.

The whole idea of Little League baseball is wrong. There are alternatives available for more sensible programs. With the same dedication that has made the Little League such a major part of many of our lives, I'm sure we'll find the answer.

I still don't know what those three gentlemen in Williamsport had in mind when they organized Little League baseball. I'm sure they didn't want parents arguing with their children about kids' games. I'm sure they didn't want to have family meals disrupted for three months every year. I'm sure they didn't want young athletes hurting their arms pitching under pressure at such a young age. I'm sure they didn't want young boys who don't have much athletic ability made to feel that something is wrong with them because they can't play baseball. I'm sure they didn't want a group of coaches drafting the players each year for different teams. I'm sure they didn't want unqualified men working with the young players. I'm sure they didn't realize how normal it is for an 8-year-old boy to be scared of a thrown or batted baseball.

For the life of me, I can't figure out what they had in mind.

Questions for Writing or Discussion

1. The author pitched for the Philadelphia Phillies from 1948 to 1962 and was elected to the Baseball Hall of Fame in 1976. Does this information make you take his arguments more seriously or does it make no difference? Where does the author reveal his special inside knowledge of and experience with baseball?
2. Does the author ignore any strong arguments that could be made in favor of Little League?
3. Does the author exaggerate the drawbacks of Little League?
4. Is the conclusion an effective wrap-up or does it introduce fresh points?
5. What is the function of the second paragraph, in which the author writes about the success of Little League?

DECLARATION OF INDEPENDENCE

In Congress, July 4, 1776
The unanimous Declaration of the thirteen
United States of America

When in the course of human events, it becomes necessary for one people to dissolve the political bands which have connected them with another, and to assume among the powers of the earth, the separate and equal station to which the Laws of Nature and of Nature's God entitle them, a decent respect to the opinions of mankind requires that they should declare the causes which impel them to the separation.

We hold these truths to be self-evident, that all men are created equal, that they are endowed by their Creator with certain unalienable rights, that among these are life, liberty and the pursuit of happiness. That to secure these rights, governments are instituted among men, deriving their just powers from the consent of the governed. That whenever any form of government becomes destructive of these ends, it is the right of the people to alter or to abolish it, and to institute new government, laying its foundation on such principles and organizing its powers in such form, as to them shall seem most likely to effect their safety and happiness. Prudence, indeed, will dictate that governments long established should not be changed for light and transient causes; and accordingly all experience hath shown, that mankind are more disposed to suffer, while evils are sufferable, than to right themselves by abolishing the forms to which they are accustomed. But when a long train of abuses and usurpations, pursuing invariably the same object evinces a design to reduce them under absolute despotism, it is their right, it is their duty, to throw off such government, and to provide new guards for their future security. Such has been the patient sufferance of these Colonies; and such is now the necessity which constrains them to alter their former systems of government. The history of the present King of Great Britain is a history of repeated injuries and usurpations, all having in direct object the establishment of an absolute tyranny over these States. To prove this, let facts be submitted to a candid world.

He has refused his assent to laws, the most wholesome and necessary for the public good.

He has forbidden his Governors to pass laws of immediate and pressing importance, unless suspended in their operation till his assent should be obtained; and when so suspended, he has utterly neglected to attend to them.

He has refused to pass other laws for the accommodation of large districts of people, unless those people would relinquish the right of representation in the Legislature, a right inestimable to them and formidable to tyrants only.

He has called together legislative bodies at places unusual, uncomfortable, and distant from the depository of their public records, for the sole purpose of fatiguing them into compliance with his measures.

He has dissolved representative houses repeatedly, for opposing with manly firmness his invasions on the rights of the people.

He has refused for a long time, after such dissolutions, to cause others to be elected; whereby the legislative powers, incapable of annihilation, have returned to the people at large for their exercise; the State remaining in the meantime exposed to all the dangers of invasion from without and convulsions within.

He has endeavoured to prevent the population of these states; for that purpose obstructing the laws of naturalization of foreigners; refusing to pass others to encourage their migration hither, and raising the conditions of new appropriations of lands.

He has obstructed the administration of justice, by refusing his assent to laws for establishing judiciary powers.

He has made judges dependent on his will alone, for the tenure of their offices, and the amount and payment of their salaries.

He has erected a multitude of new offices, and sent hither swarms of officers to harass our people, and eat out their substance.

He has kept among us, in times of peace, standing armies without the consent of our legislatures.

He has affected to render the military independent of and superior to the civil power.

He has combined with others to subject us to a jurisdiction foreign to our constitution, and unacknowledged by our laws; giving his assent to their acts of pretended legislation:

For quartering large bodies of armed troops among us:

For protecting them, by a mock trial, from punishment for any murders which they should commit on the inhabitants of these States:

For cutting off our trade with all parts of the world:

For imposing taxes on us without our consent:

For depriving us in many cases, of the benefits of trial by jury:

For transporting us beyond seas to be tried for pretended offences:

For abolishing the free system of English laws in a neighbouring Province, establishing therein an arbitrary government, and enlarging its boundaries so as to render it at once an example and fit instrument for introducing the same absolute rule into these Colonies:

For taking away our Charters, abolishing our most valuable laws, and altering fundamentally the forms of our governments:

For suspending our own Legislatures, and declaring themselves invested with power to legislate for us in all cases whatsoever.

He has abdicated government here, by declaring us out of his protection and waging war against us.

He has plundered our seas, ravaged our coasts, burnt our towns, and destroyed the lives of our people.

He is at this time transporting large armies of foreign mercenaries to complete the works of death, desolation and tyranny, already begun with circumstances of cruelty and perfidy scarcely paralleled in the most barbarous ages, and totally unworthy the head of a civilized nation.

He has constrained our fellow citizens taken captive on the high seas to bear arms against their country, to become the executioners of their friends and brethren, or to fall themselves by their hands.

He has excited domestic insurrections amongst us, and has endeavoured to bring on the inhabitants of our frontiers, the merciless Indian savages, whose known rule of warfare, is an undistinguished destruction of all ages, sexes, and conditions.

In every stage of these oppressions we have petitioned for redress in the most humble terms: our repeated petitions have been answered only by repeated injury. A prince whose character is thus marked by every act which may define a tyrant is unfit to be the ruler of a free people.

Nor have we been wanting in attention to our British brethren. We have warned them from time to time of attempts by their legislature to extend an unwarrantable jurisdiction over us. We have reminded them of the circumstances of our emigration and settlement here. We have appealed to their native justice and magnanimity, and we have conjured them by the ties of our common kindred to disavow these usurpations, which would inevitably interrupt our connections and correspondence. They too have been deaf to the voices of justice and of consanguinity. We must, therefore, acquiesce in the necessity, which denounces our separation, and hold them, as we hold the rest of mankind, enemies in war, in peace friends.

We, therefore, the Representatives of the United States of America, in General Congress assembled, appealing to the Supreme Judge of the world for the rectitude of our intentions, do, in the name, and by authority of the good people of these Colonies, solemnly publish and declare, That these United Colonies are, and of right ought to be Free and Independent States; that they are absolved from all allegiance to the British Crown, and that all political connection between them and the state of Great Britain, is and ought to be totally dissolved; and that as Free and Independent States, they have full power to levy war, conclude peace, contract alliances, establish commerce, and to do all other acts and things which Independent States may of right do. And for the support of this declaration, with a firm reliance on the protection of Divine Providence, we mutually pledge to each other our lives, our fortunes, and our sacred honor.

Questions for Writing or Discussion

1. What does the Declaration of Independence devote most of its efforts to proving?
2. What basic assumptions does it make that do not need to be proved?
3. How does the Declaration of Independence take special pains to show that it is the product of rational, responsible men rather than hotheads? This question should make a good subject for a paper.
4. Where does the language become most emotional? Is this emotion justified where it occurs, and, if so, why?

Martin Luther King, Jr.
From LETTER FROM BIRMINGHAM JAIL[1]

April 16, 1963

My Dear Fellow Clergymen:

While confined here in the Birmingham city jail, I came across your recent statement calling my present activities "unwise and untimely." Seldom do I pause to answer criticism of my work and ideas. If I sought to answer all the

1. *Author's Note:* This response to a published statement by eight fellow clergymen from Alabama (Bishop C. C. J. Carpenter, Bishop Joseph A. Durick, Rabbi Hilton L. Grafman, Bishop Paul Hardin, Bishop Holan B. Harmon, the Reverend George M. Murray, the Reverend Edward V. Ramage and the Reverend Earl Stallings) was composed under somewhat constricting circumstances. Begun on the margins of the newspaper in which the statement appeared while I was in jail, the letter was

criticisms that cross my desk, my secretaries would have little time for anything other than such correspondence in the course of the day, and I would have no time for constructive work. But since I feel that you are men of genuine good will and that your criticisms are sincerely set forth, I want to try to answer your statement in what I hope will be patient and reasonable terms.

I think I should indicate why I am here in Birmingham, since you have been influenced by the view which argues against "outsiders coming in." I have the honor of serving as president of the Southern Christian Leadership Conference, an organization operating in every southern state, with head-quarters in Atlanta, Georgia. We have some eighty-five affiliated organiza-tions across the South, and one of them is the Alabama Christian Movement for Human Rights. Frequently we share staff, educational and financial resources with our affiliates. Several months ago the affiliate here in Birming-ham asked us to be on call to engage in a nonviolent direct-action program if such were deemed necessary. We readily consented, and when the hour came we lived up to our promise. So I, along with several members of my staff, am here because I was invited here. I am here because I have organizational ties here.

But more basically, I am in Birmingham because injustice is here. Just as the prophets of the eighth century B.C. left their villages and carried their "thus saith the Lord" far beyond the boundaries of their home towns, and just as the Apostle Paul left his village of Tarsus and carried the gospel of Jesus Christ to the far corners of the Greco-Roman world, so am I compelled to carry the gospel of freedom beyond my own home town. Like Paul, I must constantly respond to the Macedonian call for aid.

Moreover, I am cognizant of the interrelatedness of all communities and states. I cannot sit idly by in Atlanta and not be concerned about what happens in Birmingham. Injustice anywhere is a threat to justice every-where. We are caught in an inescapable network of mutuality, tied in a single garment of destiny. Whatever affects one directly, affects all indi-rectly. Never again can we afford to live with the narrow, provincial "outside agitator" idea. Anyone who lives inside the United States can never be considered an outsider anywhere within its bounds.

You deplore the demonstrations taking place in Birmingham. But your statement, I am sorry to say, fails to express a similar concern for the conditions that brought about the demonstrations. I am sure that none of you would want to rest content with the superficial kind of social analysis that deals merely with effects and does not grapple with underlying causes. It is unfortunate that demonstrations are taking place in Birmingham, but it is even more unfortunate that the city's white power structure left the Negro community with no alternative.

In any nonviolent campaign there are four basic steps: collection of the facts to determine whether injustices exist; negotiation; self-purification; and direct action. We have gone through all these steps in Birmingham. There

---

continued on scraps of writing paper supplied by a friendly Negro trusty, and concluded on a pad my attorneys were eventually permitted to leave me. Although the text remains in substance unaltered, I have indulged in the author's prerogative of polishing it for publication.

can be no gainsaying the fact that racial injustice engulfs this community. Birmingham is probably the most thoroughly segregated city in the United States. Its ugly record of brutality is widely known. Negroes have experienced grossly unjust treatment in the courts. There have been more unsolved bombings of Negro homes and churches in Birmingham than in any other city in the nation. These are the hard, brutal facts of the case. On the basis of these conditions, Negro leaders sought to negotiate with the city fathers. But the latter consistently refused to engage in good-faith negotiation.

Then, last September, came the opportunity to talk with leaders of Birmingham's economic community. In the course of the negotiations, certain promises were made by the merchants—for example, to remove the stores' humiliating racial signs. On the basis of these promises, the Reverend Fred Shuttlesworth and the leaders of the Alabama Christian Movement for Human Rights agreed to a moratorium on all demonstrations. As the weeks and months went by, we realized that we were the victims of a broken promise. A few signs, briefly removed, returned; the others remained.

As in so many past experiences, our hopes had been blasted, and the shadow of deep disappointment settled upon us. We had no alternative except to prepare for direct action, whereby we would present our very bodies as a means of laying our case before the conscience of the local and the national community. Mindful of the difficulties involved, we decided to undertake a process of self-purification. We began a series of workshops on nonviolence, and we repeatedly asked ourselves: "Are you able to accept blows without retaliating?" "Are you able to endure the ordeal of jail?" We decided to schedule our direct-action program for the Easter season, realizing that except for Christmas, this is the main shopping period of the year. Knowing that a strong economic-withdrawal program would be the by-product of direct action, we felt that this would be the best time to bring pressure to bear on the merchants for the needed change.

Then it occurred to us that Birmingham's mayoral election was coming up in March, and we speedily decided to postpone action until after election day. When we discovered that the Commissioner of Public Safety, Eugene "Bull" Connor, had piled up enough votes to be in the runoff, we decided again to postpone action until the day after the run-off so that the demonstrations could not be used to cloud the issues. Like many others, we wanted to see Mr. Connor defeated, and to this end we endured postponement after postponement. Having aided in this community need, we felt that our direct-action program could be delayed no longer.

You may well ask: "Why direct action? Why sit-ins, marches and so forth? Isn't negotiation a better path?" You are quite right in calling for negotiation. Indeed, this is the very purpose of direct action. Nonviolent direct action seeks to create such a crisis and foster such a tension that a community which has constantly refused to negotiate is forced to confront the issue. It seeks so to dramatize the issue that it can no longer be ignored. My citing the creation of tension as part of the work of the nonviolent-resister may sound rather shocking. But I must confess that I am not afraid of the word "tension." I have earnestly opposed violent tension, but there is a type of constructive, nonviolent tension which is necessary for growth.

Just as Socrates felt that it was necessary to create a tension in the mind so that individuals could rise from the bondage of myths and half-truths to the unfettered realm of creative analysis and objective appraisal, so must we see the need for nonviolent gadflies to create the kind of tension in society that will help men rise from the dark depths of prejudice and racism to the majestic heights of understanding and brotherhood.

The purpose of our direct-action program is to create a situation so crisis-packed that it will inevitably open the door to negotiation. I therefore concur with you in your call for negotiation. Too long has our beloved Southland been bogged down in a tragic effort to live in monologue rather than dialogue.

One of the basic points in your statement is that the action that I and my associates have taken in Birmingham is untimely. Some have asked: "Why didn't you give the new city administration time to act?" The only answer that I can give to this query is that the new Birmingham administration must be prodded about as much as the outgoing one, before it will act. We are sadly mistaken if we feel that the election of Albert Boutwell as mayor will bring the millennium to Birmingham. While Mr. Boutwell is a much more gentle person than Mr. Connor, they are both segregationists, dedicated to maintenance of the status quo. I have hope that Mr. Boutwell will be reasonable enough to see the futility of massive resistance to desegregation. But he will not see this without pressure from devotees of civil rights. My friends, I must say to you that we have not made a single gain in civil rights without determined legal and nonviolent pressure. Lamentably, it is an historical fact that privileged groups seldom give up their privileges voluntarily. Individuals may see the moral light and voluntarily give up their unjust posture; but, as Reinhold Niebuhr has reminded us, groups tend to be more immoral than individuals.

We know through painful experience that freedom is never voluntarily given by the oppressor; it must be demanded by the oppressed. Frankly, I have yet to engage in a direct-action campaign that was "well timed" in the view of those who have not suffered unduly from the disease of segregation. For years now I have heard the word "Wait!" It rings in the ear of every Negro with piercing familiarity. This "Wait" has almost always meant "Never." We must come to see, with one of our distinguished jurists, that "justice too long delayed is justice denied."

We have waited for more than 340 years for our constitutional and God-given rights. The nations of Asia and Africa are moving with jetlike speed toward gaining political independence, but we still creep at horse-and-buggy pace toward gaining a cup of coffee at a lunch counter. Perhaps it is easy for those who have never felt the stinging darts of segregation to say, "Wait." But when you have seen vicious mobs lynch your mothers and fathers at will and drown your sisters and brothers at whim; when you have seen hate-filled policemen curse, kick and even kill your black brothers and sisters; when you see the vast majority of your twenty million Negro brothers smothering in an airtight cage of poverty in the midst of an affluent society; when you suddenly find your tongue twisted and your speech stammering as you seek to explain to your six-year-old daughter why she can't go to the public amusement park that has just been advertised on television, and see tears welling up in her eyes when she is told that

Funtown is closed to colored children, and see ominous clouds of inferiority beginning to form in her little mental sky, and see her beginning to distort her personality by developing an unconscious bitterness toward white people; when you have to concoct an answer for a five-year-old son who is asking: "Daddy, why do white people treat colored people so mean?"; when you take a cross-country drive and find it necessary to sleep night after night in the uncomfortable corners of your automobile because no motel will accept you; when you are humiliated day in and day out by nagging signs reading "white" and "colored"; when your first name becomes "nigger," your middle name becomes "boy" (however old you are) and your last name becomes "John," and your wife and mother are never given the respected title "Mrs."; when you are harried by day and haunted by night by the fact that you are a Negro, living constantly at tiptoe stance, never quite knowing what to expect next, and are plagued with inner fears and outer resentments; when you are forever fighting a degenerating sense of "nobodiness"—then you will understand why we find it difficult to wait. There comes a time when the cup of endurance runs over, and men are no longer willing to be plunged into the abyss of despair. I hope, sirs, you can understand our legitimate and unavoidable impatience.

You express a great deal of anxiety over our willingness to break laws. This is certainly a legitimate concern. Since we so diligently urge people to obey the Supreme Court's decision of 1954 outlawing segregation in the public schools, at first glance it may seem rather paradoxical for us consciously to break laws. One may well ask: "How can you advocate breaking some laws and obeying others?" The answer lies in the fact that there are two types of laws: just and unjust. I would be the first to advocate obeying just laws. One has not only a legal but a moral responsibility to obey just laws. Conversely, one has a moral responsibility to disobey unjust laws. I would agree with St. Augustine that "an unjust law is no law at all."

Now, what is the difference between the two? How does one determine whether a law is just or unjust? A just law is a man-made code that squares with the moral law or the law of God. An unjust law is a code that is out of harmony with the moral law. To put it in the terms of St. Thomas Aquinas: An unjust law is a human law that is not rooted in eternal law and natural law. Any law that uplifts human personality is just. Any law that degrades human personality is unjust. All segregation statutes are unjust because segregation distorts the soul and damages the personality. It gives the segregator a false sense of superiority and the segregated a false sense of inferiority. Segregation, to use the terminology of the Jewish philosopher Martin Buber, substitutes an "I-it" relationship for an "I-thou" relationship and ends up relegating persons to the status of things. Hence segregation is not only politically, economically and sociologically unsound, it is morally wrong and sinful. Paul Tillich has said that sin is separation. Is not segregation an existential expression of man's tragic separation, his awful estrangement, his terrible sinfulness? Thus it is that I can urge men to obey the 1954 decision of the Supreme Court, for it is morally right; and I can urge them to disobey segregation ordinances, for they are morally wrong.

Let us consider a more concrete example of just and unjust laws. An unjust law is a code that a numerical or power majority group compels a minority group to obey but does not make binding on itself. This is *difference* made legal. By the same token, a just law is a code that a majority compels a minority to follow and that it is willing to follow itself. This is *sameness* made legal.

Let me give another explanation. A law is unjust if it is inflicted on a minority that, as a result of being denied the right to vote, had no part in enacting or devising the law. Who can say that the legislature of Alabama which set up that state's segregation laws was democratically elected? Throughout Alabama all sorts of devious methods are used to prevent Negroes from becoming registered voters, and there are some counties in which, even though Negroes constitute a majority of the population, not a single Negro is registered. Can any law enacted under such circumstances be considered democratically structured?

Sometimes a law is just on its face and unjust in its application. For instance, I have been arrested on a charge of parading without a permit. Now, there is nothing wrong in having an ordinance which requires a permit for a parade. But such an ordinance becomes unjust when it is used to maintain segregation and to deny citizens the First-Amendment privilege of peaceful assembly and protest.

I hope you are able to see the distinction I am trying to point out. In no sense do I advocate evading or defying the law, as would the rabid segregationist. That would lead to anarchy. One who breaks an unjust law must do so openly, lovingly, and with a willingness to accept the penalty. I submit that an individual who breaks a law that conscience tells him is unjust, and who willingly accepts the penalty of imprisonment in order to arouse the conscience of the community over its injustice, is in reality expressing the highest respect for law.

Of course, there is nothing new about this kind of civil disobedience. It was evidenced sublimely in the refusal of Shadrach, Meshach and Abednego to obey the laws of Nebuchadnezzar, on the ground that a higher moral law was at stake. It was practiced superbly by the early Christians, who were willing to face hungry lions and the excruciating pain of chopping blocks rather than submit to certain unjust laws of the Roman Empire. To a degree, academic freedom is a reality today because Socrates practiced civil disobedience. In our own nation, the Boston Tea Party represented a massive act of civil disobedience.

We should never forget that everything Adolf Hitler did in Germany was "legal" and everything the Hungarian freedom fighters did in Hungary was "illegal." It was "illegal" to aid and comfort a Jew in Hitler's Germany. Even so, I am sure that, had I lived in Germany at the time, I would have aided and comforted my Jewish brothers. If today I lived in a Communist country where certain principles dear to the Christian faith are suppressed, I would openly advocate disobeying that country's antireligious laws. . . .

Before closing I feel impelled to mention one other point in your statement that has troubled me profoundly. You warmly commended the Birmingham police force for keeping "order" and "preventing violence." I doubt that you would have so warmly commended the police force if you had seen its dogs sinking their teeth into unarmed, nonviolent Negroes. I doubt that you would so quickly commend the policemen if you were to observe their ugly and inhumane treatment of Negroes here in the city jail;

if you were to watch them push and curse old Negro women and young Negro girls; if you were to see them slap and kick old Negro men and young boys; if you were to observe them, as they did on two occasions, refuse to give us food because we wanted to sing our grace together. I cannot join you in your praise of the Birmingham police department.

It is true that the police have exercised a degree of discipline in handling the demonstrators. In this sense they have conducted themselves rather "nonviolently" in public. But for what purpose? To preserve the evil system of segregation. Over the past few years I have consistently preached that nonviolence demands that the means we use must be as pure as the ends we seek. I have tried to make clear that it is wrong to use immoral means to attain moral ends. But now I must affirm that it is just as wrong, or perhaps even more so, to use moral means to preserve immoral ends. Perhaps Mr. Connor and his policemen have been rather nonviolent in public as was Chief Pritchett in Albany, Georgia, but they have used the moral means of nonviolence to maintain the immoral end of racial injustice. As T. S. Eliot has said: "The last temptation is the greatest treason: To do the right deed for the wrong reason."

I wish you had commended the Negro sit-inners and demonstrators of Birmingham for their sublime courage, their willingness to suffer and their amazing discipline in the midst of great provocation. One day the South will recognize its real heroes. They will be the James Merediths, with the noble sense of purpose that enables them to face jeering and hostile mobs, and with the agonizing loneliness that characterizes the life of the pioneer. They will be old, oppressed, battered Negro women, symbolized in a seventy-two-year-old woman in Montgomery, Alabama, who rose up with a sense of dignity and with her people decided not to ride segregated buses, and who responded with ungrammatical profundity to one who inquired about her weariness: "My feets is tired, but my soul is at rest." They will be the young high school and college students, the young ministers of the gospel and a host of their elders, courageously and nonviolently sitting in at lunch counters and willingly going to jail for conscience' sake. One day the South will know that when these disinherited children of God sat down at lunch counters, they were in reality standing up for what is best in the American dream and for the most sacred values in our Judaeo-Christian heritage, thereby bringing our nation back to those great wells of democracy which were dug deep by the founding fathers in their formulation of the Constitution and the Declaration of Independence.

Never before have I written so long a letter. I'm afraid it is much too long to take your precious time. I can assure you that it would have been much shorter if I had been writing from a comfortable desk, but what else can one do when he is alone in a narrow jail cell, other than write long letters, think long thoughts and pray long prayers?

If I have said anything in this letter that overstates the truth and indicates an unreasonable impatience, I beg you to forgive me. If I have said anything that understates the truth and indicates my having a patience that allows me to settle for anything less than brotherhood, I beg God to forgive me.

I hope this letter finds you strong in the faith. I also hope that circumstances will soon make it possible for me to meet each of you, not as an integrationist or a civil-rights leader but as a fellow clergyman and a Christian brother. Let us all hope that the dark clouds of racial prejudice will soon pass away and the deep fog of misunderstanding will be lifted from our fear-drenched communities, and in some not too distant tomorrow the radiant stars of love and brotherhood will shine over our great nation with all their scintillating beauty.

Yours for the cause of Peace and Brotherhood,

Martin Luther King, Jr.

Questions for Writing and Discussion

1. What difference does the author draw between violent tension and "creative tension"?
2. What is the immediate aim of the protest demonstrations? What is the long-range aim?
3. How does the author distinguish between just laws and unjust laws? Does he believe that people have the right to disobey any law with which they disagree?
4. What section of the "Letter" relies primarily on an appeal to emotion rather than on logical argument? Is the emotional appeal out of place?
5. The direct audience for the letter is a group of clergymen who had previously been sympathetic to King's cause. What elements in the "Letter" show King's awareness of this special audience?

CHAPTER 12

WRITING A DESCRIPTIVE PAPER

"Write a description of a person or place that you know about from your own experience." An assignment of this sort may come as a welcome change of pace for you. Many English teachers give the assignment for precisely that reason. At last, you won't be writing about someone else's work. You may be asked to read some material to get an idea of how other writers have handled descriptions, but your subject will be your own. You will be comparatively free, if you wish, to let yourself go, to express yourself, and to be creative in a way most of your previous assignments have not allowed. Of course, all good writing is creative, but a descriptive theme enables you to express your emotions more directly and dramatically than elsewhere, and to use vivid, colorful language that might be inappropriate in an impersonal theme. Approached in the proper frame of mind, writing a descriptive theme is almost fun.

How do we apply the principles of good writing that this book has been hammering away at to a descriptive theme? The principles still exist, of course, despite the juicy sound of words like "creativity." Creativity does not mean formlessness, after all, and self-expression does not mean slop. What are the special elements that characterize a well-written descriptive theme? What are the special difficulties and temptations that we need to avoid? Writing will always be an elusive process, but the following comments should come in handy.

1. *Don't take inventory. You must have a thesis.* Periodically, shopkeepers need to take inventory. They itemize every single article in their store so that they will know which have sold well or poorly and will be able to order future goods intelligently. This procedure is vital to business survival, but if you try to include every piece of information you have on your subject in a descriptive theme, you are inviting disaster.

The writer who takes inventory may begin a theme this way:

> My friend Judy is twenty years old. She is a solid C student. She has black hair, brown eyes, and weighs 115 pounds. Her family is comfortably middle-class. Judy is very nearsighted, but is vain about her appearance and often does not wear her glasses. She's been my friend for many years, and I like her a lot.

This paragraph is simply a random collection of stray facts. No logic, no principle seems to be at work here except the desire to get everything in, to take inventory. But getting everything in is a task that has no end; if the writer feels Judy's grades are worth mentioning, what made him decide not to mention the titles of the books she has read over the past year? What made him decide that her grades were worth mentioning in the first place—or her weight, or her eyesight, or her family? Why are twenty thousand other facts about Judy not in the paper—the presents she received on her last birthday, her height, the name of her optometrist? If the writer is only taking inventory, all facts are of equal importance, which means in effect that no facts are of any importance.

A descriptive theme needs a thesis. This statement will come as no surprise to you, but it has a number of very specific consequences. It means that you must give up the effort to tell your reader everything. It means that you must think of your paper not as "A Description of Judy," but as an attempt to prove that "Judy is terribly vain," or "Many people think that Judy is a real grind, but she has a lot of fine qualities," or "Judy has no remarkable traits of any kind, and I wonder why she has been my best friend for so many years." It means that you must choose only descriptive details that are connected to your thesis, and that if it will break your heart to omit a colorful but irrelevant detail, you must change your thesis to make the detail relevant. Sometimes, of course, a simple change in phrasing can turn a seemingly irrelevant detail into something significant, and your thesis can remain unchanged. Notice how a thesis and a few additional phrases can transform the mess about Judy into a coherent start for a potentially effective paper.

> There is nothing at all special about my friend Judy. Judy is such a completely ordinary twenty-year-old woman that I often wonder how our friendship has lasted so long and stayed so warm.
>
> Just for starters, consider these totally ordinary facts about her. Physically, she has absolutely undistinguished black hair and brown eyes, stands a normal 5 feet 4 inches, and weighs a normal 115 pounds. Scholastically, she is a solid C student. By solid, I *mean* solid. In two

years at college, I can't recall her once getting a daring C− or an exciting C+. Her family—you guessed it—is comfortably middle-class, not too rich and not too poor. Even in her little flaws, Judy is just what you'd expect. Like so many people of her age, she tends to be vain about personal appearance and all too frequently tries to get by without her glasses, even though she's very nearsighted.

2. *Use lively specific details.* The most effective way of communicating an immediate sense of your subject is to use specific details—a lot of them. Don't spend as much time telling your reader that a room is old and neglected as you do telling about the squeaky floorboard right by the door, the lint collected in the coils of the radiator, the window that needs to be propped up with a sooty stick of wood. If you do the job with details, the sense of age and neglect will come through loud and clear. In many ways, the more precise the detail, the greater is its potential for arousing the attention of your reader. Nothing should be beneath your notice. The condition of a man's fingernails, the name of the store where a woman buys her clothes, or a broken traffic light on a street corner can convey as much information about a man, a woman, or a neighborhood—and convey it more interestingly—than any number of generalized comments.

3. *Choose a principle of organization that will present the descriptive details in a logical sequence.* All this suggestion means is that you should have some way of determining what comes first and what comes next. The particular organizing principle you select makes little difference as long as it helps create a coherent paper. In describing a snowstorm, for instance, you might organize by *time*, presenting the storm from the first hesitant flakes, through the massive downfall, to the Christmas-card quietness at the end of the storm. In describing a landscape, you might organize by *space*, beginning with the objects farthest from the observer and working your way closer. A physical description of a person could go from top to bottom or bottom to top.

Not all principles of organization have to be anything close to this rigid. A landscape description could be built by progressing from the most ordinary details to the least ordinary details. If the top-to-bottom approach to a description of a person strikes you as dull, you might organize the paper by unattractive features and attractive features or first impressions and second impressions. The important consideration is that some clear principle is needed to give structure to the paper.

Rules mean nothing, of course, until they are applied. What do you think of this student's effort at a descriptive theme?

Thunderstorms
ELLEN REPICKY

There is something about a thunderstorm that always seems to bring out the child in me. I don't know whether it is the enormous amount of water being poured down from the heavens or the powerful thunder and lightning tearing at the skies that make me act as though the world is coming to an end, but I do know that I feel uncontrollable fear and insecurity during thunderstorms.

Usually more of a happy-go-lucky person than anything else, when I hear that a thunderstorm is heading my way, I quickly change to a timid little girl. I run to my room, shut my door, and draw the blinds. By doing this, I pretend that nothing scary is going on outside, and everything is cool. But in my mind I can picture what is happening with complete clarity. The birds have flown to a safe place of refuge. The streets look like those in a ghost town. Even the sun has managed to hide herself from this ugliness. Just about now, the air is drenched with a foul, fishy odor. The darkening gray skies are traveling at a rapid pace, and the trees are bending backwards, yielding to the almighty wind. In the distance, a faint rumbling can be heard.

Crash! The thunder roars, and to my dismay the storm has begun. By this time, I am in sheer agony. Nothing can calm me down. My whole body is shaking incessantly, and I jump with each crash of thunder. The rain is beating fiercely on my window. I try not to let it intimidate me, but it does. Within my body, my stomach is doing somersaults. My head feels as light and vulnerable as a balloon. Outside, the wind is banging the shutters in tempo with the thunder and the raindrops. Some might think that this chorus is beautiful music, but I don't. Suddenly I notice the frightening sounds have diminished, and I feel my heartbeat slow, for I know that the worst is over. And I have lived through one more thunderstorm.

I know that my actions are immature, but there is nothing I can do about them. Every time there is a thunderstorm I revert to being a helpless, hysterical child. When the sun comes back out, I laugh at myself, of course, but that lasts only until the next time. And the next time always comes.

Questions for Writing or Discussion

1. What is the thesis? Does the writer keep her thesis in mind through the body of the paper?
2. Should the writer have devoted more attention to the storm itself? Should she have devoted more attention to her feelings? Or is the proportion just about right?
3. A curious element in this paper is that the writer, particularly in paragraph two, presents a picture of what she did not see (she is hiding in her room). Why is this technique so effective?
4. What phase of the storm does the writer concentrate on most? Why?

5. In paragraph two, "The darkening gray skies are traveling at a rapid pace" seems dull and abstract. How could the phrase be enlivened?

6. Almost everyone has deep-seated fears, and the objects of those fears offer excellent topics for descriptive papers. Write a short descriptive paper about your fear of one of the following: darkness, insects, rats, dogs, heights, fires, getting lost, failing a course, contracting a particular illness, drowning, driving on snowy roads, flying.

Readings

The examples of description that follow show seasoned professional writers at work. Note how description is never allowed to become merely a piece of pretty writing but is used to communicate insights into people and society.

Charles Dickens
MISS MURDSTONE from "David Copperfield"

It was Miss Murdstone who was arrived, and a gloomy-looking lady she was; dark, like her brother, whom she greatly resembled in face and voice, and with very heavy eyebrows, nearly meeting over her large nose, as if, being disabled by the wrongs of her sex from wearing whiskers, she had carried them to that account. She brought with her two uncompromising hard black boxes, with her initials on the lids in hard brass nails. When she paid the coachman she took her money out of a hard steel purse, and she kept the purse in a very jail of a bag which hung upon her arm by a heavy chain, and shut up like a bite. I had never, at that time, seen such a metallic lady altogether as Miss Murdstone was.

Wilkie Collins
MARIAN HALCOMBE from "The Woman in White"

My first glance round me, as the man opened the door, disclosed a well-furnished breakfast-table, standing in the middle of a long room, with many windows in it. I looked from the table to the window farthest from me, and saw a lady standing at it, with her back turned towards me. The instant my eyes rested on her, I was struck by the rare beauty of her form, and by the unaffected grace of her attitude. Her figure was tall, yet not too tall; comely and well-developed, yet not fat; her head set on her shoulders with an easy, pliant firmness; her waist, perfection in the eyes of a man, for it occupied its natural place, it filled out its natural circle, it was visibly and delightfully undeformed by stays. She had not heard my entrance into the room; and I allowed myself the luxury of admiring her for a few moments, before I moved one of the chairs near me, as the least embarrassing means of attracting her attention. She turned towards me immediately. The easy elegance of every movement of her limbs and body as soon as she began to advance from the far end of the room, set me in a flutter of expectation to see her face clearly. She left the window—and I said to myself, The lady is dark. She moved forward a few steps—and I said to myself, The lady is young. She approached nearer—and I said to myself (with a sense of surprise which words fail me to express), The lady is ugly!

Never was the old conventional maxim, that Nature cannot err, more flatly contradicted—never was the fair promise of a lovely figure more strangely and startlingly belied by the face and head that crowned it. The lady's complexion was almost swarthy, and the dark down on her upper lip was almost a moustache. She had a large, firm, masculine mouth and jaw; prominent, piercing, resolute brown eyes; and thick, coal-black hair, growing unusually low down on her forehead. Her expression—bright, frank, and intelligent—appeared, while she was silent, to be altogether wanting in those feminine attractions of gentleness and pliability, without which the beauty of the handsomest woman alive is beauty incomplete. To see such a face as this set on shoulders that a sculptor would have longed to model—to be charmed by the modest graces of action through which the symmetrical limbs betrayed their beauty when they moved, and then to be almost repelled by the masculine form and masculine look of the features in which the perfectly shaped figure ended—was to feel a sensation oddly akin to the helpless discomfort familiar to us all in sleep, when we recognise yet cannot reconcile the anomalies and contradictions of a dream.

Questions for Writing or Discussion

1. Who makes better use of specific details, Dickens or Collins?
2. Does Collins ever "take inventory," or are all his comments related to a main idea?
3. Identify the topic sentences in the Dickens and Collins passages.
4. Write a description of an unusually good-looking or unusually ugly man or woman.

Donald E. Westlake
JERRY MANELLI'S FATHER

Jerry's father had retired two years ago from his job in a department store's warehouse out on Long Island, and as soon as he became a senior citizen his name got onto more rotten mailing lists than you could shake your fist at. Everybody wants to hustle the old folks. A running theme in all this junk mail was that retired people ought to have a hobby, take up the slack from no longer having a job. The old man had never *worked* a day in his life—he'd spent most of his laboring years trying to figure a way to slip unnoticed out of the warehouse with a sofa—but he believed this hobby thing as though the Virgin herself had come down on a cloud to give him his instructions. "Man without a hobby shrivels up and dies," he'd say. "A hobby keeps your mind active, your blood circulating, keeps you young. They've done studies, they got statistics, it's a proven thing."

Unfortunately, though, the old man had never had a hobby in his life, didn't really know what the hell a hobby was, and couldn't keep up his interest in any hobby he tried. He'd been through stamp collecting, coin collecting, matchbook collecting. He'd paid good money for a ham radio but he never used it, because, "I don't have anything to say. I don't even know those people." He'd tried making a ship in a bottle, and within half an hour he'd busted the bottle on the radiator and stalked out of the house. He was going to build a St. Patrick's Cathedral out of toothpicks, and got as far as the first step. He figured he'd become an expert on baseball statistics, but the last time he'd looked at baseball there were sixteen teams in the two major leagues and now there were hundreds. He started clipping things out of the newspapers—disaster stories or funny headlines ("Action on Building Bribes Delayed by Lack of Funds," for instance, from the *New York Times*)—and all he managed to do was cut the dining room tablecloth with the scissors, and glue his fingers together.

The old man didn't know it, and nobody would tell him, but it turned out his hobby was looking for hobbies. It was certainly keeping his mind active and his blood circulating, and if he was actually out in the park now with a homemade kite then maybe it was also keeping him young.

Questions for Writing or Discussion

1. Which sentence serves as the thesis statement?
2. How has "the old man" turned failure into success?
3. What was the intended meaning of the newspaper headline? What meaning does it seem to have in print?
4. Write a description of a relative that focuses on only one outstanding personality trait.

Mark Twain (Samuel L. Clemens)
THE PROFESSIONAL

The face of the water [of the Mississippi River where the author was a steamboat pilot] in time became a wonderful book—a book that was a dead language to the uneducated passenger but which told its mind to me without reserve, delivering its most cherished secrets as clearly as if it uttered them with a voice. And it was not a book to be read once and thrown aside, for it had a new story to tell every day. Throughout the long twelve hundred miles there was never a page that was void of interest, never one that you could leave unread without loss, never one that you would want to skip, thinking you could find higher enjoyment in some other thing. There never was so wonderful a book written by man, never one whose interest was so absorbing, so unflagging, so sparklingly renewed with every reperusal. The passenger who could not read it was charmed with a peculiar sort of faint dimple on its surface (on the rare occasions when he did not overlook it altogether) but to the pilot that was an *italicized* passage; indeed it was more than that, it was a legend of the largest capitals with a string of shouting exclamation-points at the end of it, for it meant that a wreck or a rock was buried there that could tear the life out of the strongest vessel that ever floated. It is the faintest and simplest expression the water ever makes, and the most hideous to a pilot's eye. In truth, the passenger who could not read this book saw nothing but all manner of pretty pictures in it, painted by the sun and shaded by the clouds, whereas to the trained eye these were not pictures at all, but the grimmest and most dead-earnest of reading matter.

Now when I had mastered the language of this water, and had come to know every trifling feature that bordered the great river as familiarly as I knew the letters of the alphabet, I had made a valuable acquisition. But I had lost something, too. I had lost something which could never be restored to me while I lived. All the grace, the beauty, the poetry, had gone out of the majestic river! I still kept in mind a certain wonderful sunset which I witnessed when steamboating was new to me. A broad expanse of the river was turned to blood; in the middle distance the red hue brightened into gold, through which a solitary log came floating, black and conspicuous; in one place a long, slanting mark lay sparkling upon the water; in another the surface was broken by boiling, tumbling rings, that were as many-tinted as an opal; where the ruddy flush was faintest, was a smooth spot that was covered with graceful circles and radiating lines, ever so delicately traced; the shore on our left was densely wooded, and the somber shadow that fell from this forest was broken in one place by a long, ruffled trail that shone like silver; and high above the forest wall a clean-stemmed dead tree waved a single leafy bough that glowed like a flame in the unobstructed splendor that was flowing from the sun. There were graceful curves, reflected images, woody heights, soft distances; and over the whole scene, far and near, the dissolving lights drifted steadily, enriching it every passing moment with new marvels of coloring.

I stood like one bewitched. I drank it in, in a speechless rapture. The world was new to me, and I had never seen anything like this at home. But as I have said, a day came when I began to cease from noting the glories and the charms which the moon and the sun and the twilight wrought upon the river's face; another day came when I ceased altogether to note them. Then, if that sunset scene had been repeated, I should have looked upon it without rapture, and should have commented upon it, inwardly, after this fashion: "This sun means that we are going to have wind to-morrow; that floating log means that the river is rising, small thanks to it; that slanting mark on the water refers to a bluff reef which is going to kill somebody's steamboat one of these nights, if it keeps on stretching out like that; those tumbling 'boils' show a dissolving bar and a changing channel there; the lines and circles in the slick water over yonder are a warning that that troublesome place is shoaling up dangerously; that silver streak in the shadow of the forest is the 'break' from a new snag, and he has located himself in the very best place he could have found to fish for steamboats; that tall dead tree, with a single living branch, is not going to last long, and then how is a body ever going to get through this blind place at night without the friendly old landmark?"

No, the romance and beauty were all gone from the river. All the value any feature of it had for me now was the amount of usefulness it could furnish toward compassing the safe piloting of a steamboat. Since those days, I have pitied doctors from my heart. What does the lovely flush in a beauty's cheek mean to a doctor but a "break" that ripples above some deadly disease? Are not all her visible charms sown thick with what are to him the signs and symbols of hidden decay? Does he ever see her beauty at all, or doesn't he simply view her professionally and comment upon her unwholesome condition all to himself? And doesn't he sometimes wonder whether he has gained most or lost most by learning his trade?

Questions for Writing or Discussion

1. Identify all the words and phrases in paragraph one that describe the river as being a book.
2. After paragraph one, does the author ever repeat the idea of the river's being a book?
3. Which sentence or sentences first state the thesis? Where is the thesis restated?
4. In paragraph two's description of the sunset, what principle of organization determines the order in which the details are presented?
5. Do you agree with the author that increased knowledge interferes with simple emotional pleasure?
6. Write a description of a person or place emphasizing the contrast between past and present.

John Steinbeck
THE USED CAR LOT from "The Grapes of Wrath"

In the towns, on the edges of the towns, in fields, in vacant lots, the used-car yards, the wreckers' yards, the garages with blazoned signs—Used Cars, Good Used Cars. Cheap transportation, three trailers. '27 Ford, clean.

Published in 1939, John Steinbeck's *The Grapes of Wrath* deals with the hardships of the "Okies," dispossessed farmers of Oklahoma and neighboring states who fled from the drought-created "Dust Bowl" to become migrant farm workers in California. "The Used Car Lot," Chapter 7 of the novel, presents a vivid picture of the hopeless battle to find cheap, reliable transportation for the thousand-mile trip west.

Checked cars, guaranteed cars. Free radio. Car with 100 gallons of gas free. Come in and look. Used Cars. No overhead.

A lot and a house large enough for a desk and chair and a blue book. Sheaf of contracts, dog-eared, held with paper clips, and a neat pile of unused contracts. Pen—keep it full, keep it working. A sale's been lost 'cause a pen didn't work.

Those sons-of-bitches over there ain't buying. Every yard gets 'em. They're lookers. Spend all their time looking. Don't want to buy no cars; take up your time. Don't give a damn for your time. Over there, them two people—no, with the kids. Get 'em in a car. Start 'em at two hundred and work down. They look good for one and a quarter. Get 'em rolling. Get 'em out in a jalopy. Sock it to 'em! They took our time.

Owners with rolled-up sleeves. Salesmen, neat, deadly, small intent eyes watching for weaknesses.

Watch the woman's face. If the woman likes it we can screw the old man. Start 'em on that Cad'. Then you can work 'em down to that '26 Buick. 'F you start on the Buick, they'll go for a Ford. Roll up your sleeves an' get to work. This ain't gonna last forever. Show 'em that Nash while I get the slow leak pumped up on that '25 Dodge. I'll give you a Hymie when I'm ready.

What you want is transportation, ain't it? No baloney for you. Sure the upholstery is shot. Seat cushions ain't turning no wheels over.

Cars lined up, noses forward, rusty noses, flat tires. Parked close together.

Like to get in to see that one? Sure, no trouble. I'll pull her out of the line.

Get 'em under obligation. Make 'em take up your time. Don't let 'em forget they're takin' your time. People are nice, mostly. They hate to put you out. Make 'em put you out, an' then sock it to 'em.

Cars lined up, Model T's, high and snotty, creaking wheel, worn bands. Buicks, Nashes, De Sotos.

Yes, sir. '22 Dodge. Best goddamn car Dodge ever made. Never wear out. Low compression. High compression got lots a sap for a while, but the metal ain't made that'll hold it for long. Plymouths, Rocknes, Stars.

Jesus, where'd that Apperson come from, the Ark? And a Chalmers and a Chandler—ain't made 'em for years. We ain't sellin' cars—rolling junk. Goddamn it, I got to get jalopies. I don't want nothing for more'n twenty-five, thirty bucks. Sell 'em for fifty, seventy-five. That's a good profit. Christ, what cut do you make on a new car? Get jalopies. I can sell 'em fast as I get 'em. Nothing over two hundred fifty. Jim, corral that old bastard on the sidewalk. Don't know his ass from a hole in the ground. Try him on that Apperson. Say, where is that Apperson? Sold? If we don't get some jalopies we got nothing to sell.

Flags, red and white, white and blue—all along the curb. Used Cars. Good Used Cars.

Today's bargain—up on the platform. Never sell it. Makes folks come in, though. If we sold that bargain at that price we'd hardly make a dime. Tell 'em it's jus' sold. Take out that yard battery before you make delivery. Put in that dumb cell. Christ, what they want for six bits? Roll up your sleeves—pitch in. This ain't gonna last. If I had enough jalopies I'd retire in six months.

Listen, Jim, I heard that Chevvy's rear end. Sounds like bustin' bottles. Squirt in a couple quarts of sawdust. Put some in the gears, too. We got to move that lemon for thirty-five dollars. Bastard cheated me on that one. I offer ten an' he jerks me to fifteen, an' then the son-of-a-bitch took the tools out. God Almighty! I wisht I had five hundred jalopies. This ain't gonna last. He don't like the tires? Tell 'im they got ten thousand in 'em, knock off a buck an' a half.

Piles of rusty ruins against the fence, rows of wrecks in back, fenders, grease-black wrecks, blocks lying on the ground and a pig weed growing up through the cylinders. Brake rods, exhausts, piled like snakes. Grease, gasoline.

See if you can't find a spark plug that ain't cracked. Christ, if I had fifty trailers at under a hundred I'd clean up. What the hell is he kickin' about? We sell 'em, but we don't push 'em home for him. That's good! Don't push 'em home. Get that one in the Monthly, I bet. You don't think he's a prospect? Well, kick 'im out. We got too much to do to bother with a guy that can't make up his mind. Take the right front tire off the Graham. Turn that mended side down. The rest looks swell. Got tread an' everything.

Sure! There's fifty thousan' in that ol' heap yet. Keep plenty oil in. So long. Good luck.

Lookin' for a car? What did you have in mind? See anything attracts you? I'm dry. How about a little snort a good stuff? Come on, while your wife's lookin' at that La Salle. You don't want no La Salle. Bearings shot. Uses too much oil. Got a Lincoln '24. There's a car. Run forever. Make her into a truck.

Hot sun on rusted metal. Oil on the ground. People are wandering in, bewildered, needing a car.

Wipe your feet. Don't lean on that car, it's dirty. How do you buy a car? What does it cost? Watch the children, now. I wonder how much for this one? We'll ask. It don't cost money to ask. We can ask, can't we? Can't pay a nickel over seventy-five, or there won't be enough to get to California.

God, if I could only get a hundred jalopies. I don't care if they run or not.

Tires, used, bruised tires, stacked in tall cylinders; tubes, red, gray, hanging like sausages.

Tire patch? Radiator cleaner? Spark intensifier? Drop this little pill in your gas tank and get ten extra miles to the gallon. Just paint it on—you got a new surface for fifty cents. Wipers, fan belts, gaskets? Maybe it's the valve. Get a new valve stem. What can you lose for a nickel?

All right, Joe. You soften 'em up an' shoot 'em in here. I'll close 'em, I'll deal 'em or I'll kill 'em. Don't send in no bums. I want deals.

Yes, sir, step in. You got a buy there. Yes, sir! At eighty bucks you got a buy.

I can't go no higher than fifty. The fella outside says fifty.

Fifty. Fifty? He's nuts. Paid seventy-eight fifty for that little number. Joe, you crazy fool, you tryin' to bust us? Have to can that guy. I might take sixty. Now look here, mister, I ain't got all day. I'm a business man but I ain't out to stick nobody. Got anything to trade?

Got a pair of mules I'll trade.

Mules! Hey, Joe, hear this? This guy wants to trade mules. Didn't nobody tell you this is the machine age? They don't use mules for nothing but glue no more.

Fine big mules—five and seven years old. Maybe we better look around.

Look around! You come in when we're busy, an' take up our time an' then walk out! Joe, did you know you was talkin' to pikers?

I ain't a piker. I got to get a car. We're goin' to California. I got to get a car.

Well, I'm a sucker. Joe says I'm a sucker. Says if I don't quit givin' my shirt away I'll starve to death. Tell you what I'll do—I can get five bucks apiece for them mules for dog feed.

I wouldn't want them to go for dog feed.

Well, maybe I can get ten or seven maybe. Tell you what we'll do. We'll take your mules for twenty. Wagon goes with 'em, don't it? An' you put up fifty, an' you can sign a contract to send the rest at ten dollars a month.

But you said eighty.

Didn't you never hear about carrying charges and insurance? That just boosts her a little. You'll get her all paid up in four-five months. Sign your name right here. We'll take care of ever'thing.

Well, I don't know—

Now, look here. I'm givin' you my shirt, an' you took all this time. I might a made three sales while I been talkin' to you. I'm disgusted. Yeah, sign right there. All right, sir. Joe, fill up the tank for this gentleman. We'll give him gas.

Jesus, Joe, that was a hot one! What'd we give for that jalopy? Thirty bucks—thirty-five wasn't it? I got that team, an' if I can't get seventy-five for that team, I ain't a business man. An' I got fifty cash an' a contract for forty more. Oh, I know they're not all honest, but it'll surprise you how many kick through with the rest. One guy come through with a hundred two years after I wrote him off. I bet you this guy sends the money. Christ, if I could only get five hundred jalopies! Roll up your sleeves, Joe. Go out an' soften 'em, an' send 'em in to me. You get twenty on that last deal. You ain't doing bad.

Limp flags in the afternoon sun. Today's Bargain. '29 Ford pickup, runs good.

What do you want for fifty bucks—a Zephyr?

Horsehair curling out of seat cushions, fenders battered and hammered back. Bumpers torn loose and hanging. Fancy Ford roadster with little colored lights at fender guide, at radiator cap, and three behind. Mud aprons, and a big die on the gear-shift lever. Pretty girl on tire cover, painted in color and named Cora. Afternoon sun on the dusty windshields.

Christ, I ain't had time to go out an' eat! Joe, send a kid for a hamburger.

Spattering roar of ancient engines.

There's a dumb-bunny lookin' at that Chrysler. Find out if he got any jack in his jeans. Some a these farm boys is sneaky. Soften 'em up an' roll 'em in to me, Joe. You're doin' good.

Sure, we sold it. Guarantee? We guaranteed it to be an automobile. We didn't guarantee to wet-nurse it. Now listen here, you—you bought a car, an' now you're squawkin'. I don't give a damn if you don't make payments. We ain't got your paper. We turn that over to the finance company. They'll get after you, not us. We don't hold no paper. Yeah? Well you jus' get tough an' I'll call a cop. No, we did not switch the tires. Run 'im outa here, Joe. He bought a car, an' now he ain't satisfied. How'd you think if I bought a steak an' et half an' try to bring it back? We're runnin' a business, not a charity ward. Can ya imagine that guy, Joe? Say—looka there! Got a Elk's tooth! Run over there. Let 'em glance over that '36 Pontiac. Yeah.

Square noses, round noses, rusty noses, shovel noses, and the long curves of streamlines, and the flat surfaces before streamlining. Bargains Today. Old monsters with deep upholstery—you can cut her into a truck easy. Two-wheel trailers, axles rusty in the hard afternoon sun. Used Cars. Good Used Cars. Clean, runs good. Don't pump oil.

Christ, look at 'er! Somebody took nice care of 'er.

Cadillacs, La Salles, Buicks, Plymouths, Packards, Chevvies, Fords, Pontiacs. Row on row, headlights glinting in the afternoon sun. Good Used Cars.

Soften 'em up, Joe. Jesus, I wisht I had a thousand jalopies! Get 'em ready to deal, an' I'll close 'em.

Goin' to California? Here's jus' what you need. Looks shot, but they's thousan's of miles in her.

Lined up side by side. Good Used Cars. Bargains. Clean, runs good.

Questions for Writing or Discussion

1. Steinbeck's thesis is never stated directly but is strongly felt in almost every word. What is the thesis?
2. Does the author go to unconvincing extremes? Are the buyers too innocent to believe, the dealers too evil?
3. What repeated wish is expressed by the owner of the used car lot? Where else does the author use repetition to heighten the effect of his writing?
4. Why does the author make such frequent use of sentence fragments?
5. Is the author describing one used car lot or many?
6. Using Steinbeck's impressionistic or stream-of-consciousness approach, write a description of one of the following: Christmas shopping, rush hour, a traffic jam, a crowded beach or swimming pool, an airport, an amusement park, spectators at a sporting event. Remember the need for a clear thesis.

CHAPTER 13

WRITING
AN ANALYSIS
OF LITERATURE

To analyze is to study a complex substance by examining one or more of its parts and then to show the relationship of each part to the whole. When you are given an assignment such as "Describe the unpleasant new insight into his own character that the doctor discovers in 'The Use of Force' " or "Explain the direct and indirect reasons for the disruption of the play in 'The Revolt of the Evil Fairies,' " you are being asked to write a literary analysis. Sometimes teachers like to assign a special form of literary analysis called "explication," in which a poem or short story is examined pretty much word by word or paragraph by paragraph to show how each element fits into the general pattern and purpose of the entire work.

We are convinced that nobody ever learned how to write a good literary analysis from reading instructions in a textbook. Your instructor has undoubtedly devoted a large portion of his or her professional life to analyzing literature. A few classroom sessions with your instructor, digging into specific works without worrying too much about preestablished methods and rules, will probably teach you far more than we can. In addition, most composition courses devote at least one quarter to the systematic study of literature, and you will very likely be using an anthology with a full discussion of the technical terms you need to know and a vast selection of different types of literature.

All we would like to do in this chapter is to suggest a few guidelines that should make your life easier when you have to write an analysis. We can't tell you *what* to say—that will vary with each assignment, depending on the material you are analyzing, and some subjects offer a good deal of leeway for individual interpretations and insights. In addition, whatever you say, we can't tell you very much new about *how* to say it—by this time, you should have a reasonable knowledge of the requirements for any piece of good writing. Still, we believe that the following common sense suggestions will be helpful.

1. *Read the material slowly.* When you need to wade through a pile of junk, fast reading is fine. When you are reading good or great literature, much of which treats complex ideas and emotions, often with complex means of expression, the intelligent approach is to read slowly. Moreover, any analysis involves the close examination of details. Fast reading can give you a general sense of the main points, but it can't prepare you to deal competently with all the concerns of a full-fledged analysis.

2. *Reread.* When you read a story or poem for the first time, you can't possibly have any valid notion of what the author is up to. The author knows how the story is going to end, but you don't. That's why you're reading it—to find out. And since the author does know in advance what is going to happen on that last page, he or she has been making all sorts of crucial preparations earlier in the story to lead into the ending. On a first reading, those earlier pages cannot mean much to you. They can create interest or suspense, but that's about all, since you don't yet know anything of the author's purpose. Once you do understand what the author has been trying to do, and then *read the story again,* all the ingredients will begin to register in a different way, a way that is emotionally and intellectually impossible to achieve in a first reading. The seemingly separate parts of the story can now come through to you as pieces within a logical pattern. Without a sense of that logical pattern and of how all elements are related to it, your analysis will be weak and incomplete.

3. *Assume that everything is significant.* In good literature, nothing should be an accident. Each word, each character, each thought, each incident should make a contribution to the total effect the author is trying for. The contribution is sometimes obvious and direct: the author casually mentions that a car is nine years old because later on the car will break down. At other times, the contribution is indirect: the author spends a paragraph describing a glowing fireplace in order to establish a homey mood that fits in with the story's central idea—the joys of family life. As you think about the material you are going to analyze, as you brood about what you are going to say and how you are going to say it, keep in mind that *nothing is beneath your notice.* Assume that everything serves a purpose and that you have not reached a full understanding of the story, poem, or play until you clearly see the purpose that everything serves. When you come up against elements that serve no purpose, you can safely conclude that the work is imperfect. Read closely, and give serious attention to details. When you get to

the writing stage, make liberal use of the details to support your comments. No matter how much actual work you have done, if you do not rely heavily on references to details, your analysis will seem to be based on vague impressions and snap judgments.

4. *Do not study details out of context.* Your response to the details of a work—a word, a phrase, a character, an incident—depends upon the work as a whole. A sentence like "Mrs. Smythe spent twenty minutes arranging the flowers in the vase" could appear in a satire of a fussy little old lady or a moving sketch of a mother preparing the house for her son's return from the army. A diploma may appear in one place as a symbol of hope and in another as a symbol of despair. Your analysis or interpretation of the flower arranging or the diploma must obviously be in harmony with the rest of the work. If an analysis presents the diploma as a symbol of hope in a story which insists that education is meaningless and useless, the analysis is probably wrong. Make sure that your "reading" of a detail helps to make sense of the whole work. Keep the intentions of the whole work in mind as you consider the proper approach to take toward one of its parts.

One more observation: try not to let your purely personal tastes or prejudices interfere with your responses. If a writer in the context of a short story has a character light a cigarette to show nervousness, fight off the temptation to analyze the character as a stupid person who doesn't know that cigarettes are hazardous to health. If another writer presents a sympathetic and approving study of a couple who decide to stay married for the sake of the children, don't analyze the couple as victims of outmoded bourgeois morality and a repressive society. An analysis explains what is going on in a piece of literature, not what your own philosophy of life may happen to be.

Now read the following poem.

OZYMANDIAS

I met a traveller from an antique land
Who said: Two vast and trunkless legs of stone
Stand in the desert. Near them, on the sand,
Half sunk, a shattered visage lies, whose frown,
And wrinkled lip, and sneer of cold command,
Tell that its sculptor well those passions read
Which yet survive, stamped on these lifeless things,
The hand that mocked them, and the heart that fed:[1]
And on the pedestal these words appear:

1. The passions stamped on the broken face of the statue survive the hand (of the sculptor) that mocked them and the heart (of Ozymandias) that fed them.

"My name is Ozymandias, king of kings:
Look on my works, ye Mighty, and despair!"
Nothing beside remains. Round the decay
Of that colossal wreck, boundless and bare
The lone and level sands stretch far away.

—*Percy Bysshe Shelley*

The assignment given to students was "Discuss the implications of the inscription on the pedestal of the statue in Shelley's 'Ozymandias.' " What do you think of this effort?

Enough Despair to Go Around
ALAN BENJAMIN

In Percy Bysshe Shelley's "Ozymandias," we are told that the following words are inscribed on the pedestal of a broken statue in the desert: "My name is Ozymandias, king of kings:/ Look on my works, ye Mighty, and despair!" What King Ozymandias had in mind when he chose those words is dramatically different from the meaning they have now. The new meaning comes not from Ozymandias but from the passage of time.

The still visible "wrinkled lip and sneer of cold command" suggest the vanity and arrogance that motivated Ozymandias to have his statue built in the first place. The "colossal" size of the statue and Ozymandias's description of himself as "king of kings" add to the impression that he thought a great deal of himself and wanted others to do the same. We can imagine the statue being erected at the gates or in the central square of King Ozymandias's great capital city. Marble buildings gleam in the sunlight: the palace, the treasury, the temples, the monuments to military victories. Powerful and "mighty" people from all over the known world come to see the wonders of Ozymandias's kingdom. "Look on my works, ye Mighty, and despair," sneers Ozymandias. Despair because your creations, your works, will never be able to equal the magnificence of mine. Despair because when you look at my works you can only feel a sense of the pitiful insignificance of your own.

Time passes. Time eats away marble. Buildings and statues crumble. The glorious, thriving kingdom of Ozymandias is now a desert. Two grotesque stone legs stick up in the air, and together with a "shattered visage" they are all that is left of the statue. Everything else is sand and desolation. In one sense, the inscription on the pedestal has now become meaningless, for there are no more "works" left to look on, and we can think only of how silly Ozymandias must have been. In another sense, the words are filled with a strong new meaning, stronger and far more true than Ozymandias ever dreamed. Powerful and mighty people today can look at Ozymandias's works and still despair. This time, however, they will despair not because of envy, but because they can see the eventual fate of all their own works. They will despair because, even if their own works surpass those of Ozymandias, it won't make any difference. They will despair now because they can see that all material things crumble to dust and that people who put their faith in such things are doomed to futility and disappointment.

Ozymandias originally hoped that the despair would come from petty and foolish reasons. Today it can come from more intelligent and realistic reasons. But there is still more than enough despair to go around as "the lone and level sands stretch far away."

Questions for Writing or Discussion

1. Is there a clear thesis? If so, where is it first presented?
2. Does paragraph two have a topic sentence? If not, does it need one?
3. In the next-to-last sentence of paragraph three, what does "it" refer to? Should the sentence be revised?
4. Is the writing, particularly in paragraph three, too emotional for an analysis, or does the emotional writing make the paper more interesting to read?
5. Does the last paragraph effectively summarize the writer's main points? Is the last sentence too dramatic?

SOME NOTES ON A FEW LITERARY TERMS

A number of fairly specialized words get flung about a great deal in discussing literature. Most of them have meaning and can be valuable—even indispensable—when used wisely, but sometimes they serve to show off or dress up a perfectly simple point in an atmosphere of obscurity and fraudulent importance. What follows is not intended to be a dictionary of literary terms, but rather some helpful comments on a few of the most troublesome and frequently abused terms.

Hidden meanings

A number of students are fond of using this phrase when they discuss or write about literature—and it means nothing. No writer who is any good goes around hiding meanings. Writers have enough trouble expressing them openly. The few writers who do play hide-and-seek with their readers are generally pretentious fakes. At any rate, avoid the "hidden meanings" approach to literature. Never use the phrase, as many people do, to refer to an idea or emotion that the author had no intention of concealing, but that you just didn't happen to notice on a first reading.

Moral and theme

Good literature, in general, is not pure art in the sense that a painting of a pretty landscape is pure art. Most literature attempts far more directly than such paintings to make a comment on life. In considering a story like William Carlos Williams's "The Use of Force" (p. 151), we can and should discuss artistic elements such as plot construction and dialogue, but the story is also a comment on violence and human nature. The author has "something to say." Our response to the story depends largely on how well that "something" comes through to us. Without artistry, of course, the author's comment has no chance of coming through, but the author obviously has more than artistry alone on his mind. If literature attempts to be a comment on life, the critic needs to understand that comment fully. If a work has something to say, we must ask ourselves *what* it is saying as well as how it is saying it.

A comment on life, however, is not necessarily a *moral*. In good literature, especially modern literature, it is almost never a moral. This fact confuses many inexperienced readers. For them the question of "what does it mean" or "what does it say" usually implies "what is the moral"—the direct, simple, short statement of a lesson or message to be drawn from the work. When they find no clear moral, they tend to feel cheated or frustrated. Why can't writers just come right out with it and say what they mean? Why are they so fond of hidden meanings (even if the authors of this book state that they're not supposed to be)? Why do they indulge in these mystifying literary games?

There are two ways of answering these questions, one simple and one not so simple. First, morals have a way of being tidy, catchy, and dangerously superficial. They are fine in proverbs. They are fine in children's stories and five-minute sermons. An adult mind, however, can't help being suspicious of truths that are so conveniently packaged. Life is too complicated to be handled with the complacent certainties of Aesop's *Fables* or *Poor Richard's Almanac*. Literature produced by a thoughtful writer attempts to capture some of the quality of life itself, and the preachy oversimplications inherent in moralizing spring from distortions of life. *He who hesitates is lost; life begins at forty; it's no use crying over spilt milk*—this stuff sounds good enough, but we all know that sometimes hesitation is advisable, that a significant life can begin at any age, and that crying over spilt milk has inspired, among many other things, some immortal poetry. When you look for neat little morals in literature, you cheat yourself and you are unfair to the writer. If a writer's comment on life can be summed up in a moral, the odds are that you have wasted your time reading the entire work.

The second reason that people have trouble when they set out to find morals is that a good writer *dramatizes* ideas. The ideas, in other words, are rarely expressed directly, as they would be in a sermon or a philosophy or sociology textbook. Insofar as the writer has any ideas, they grow out of the characters the writer creates and their response to the situations the writer devises for them. Thus, because we care about the characters, the ideas register on our emotions as well as our intellects. Writers try to convey life, not merely ideas *about* life—for if the ideas are all that matter, their works are elaborate shams that should have been sermons, textbooks, or letters to the editor of their local newspapers. The good writer does not *tell* us, "Young love can be beautiful, but can create a lot of problems, too"; he writes *Romeo and Juliet*. Granted, we may get this abstract idea about love from the play, along with many other ideas just as significant, but primarily we get a far richer sense of profound concern for two human beings. William Carlos Williams does not *tell* us "The use of violence, even in the best causes, is always dangerous" or "All people have violent tendencies buried within them" or any number of other morals that can be squeezed out of the story; he writes "The Use of Force" and shows us violence in action. He dramatizes. Those who read the story as it was meant to be read do not simply wind up feeling abstractly afraid of violence—who needs a story for that?—but cringing with shock and perhaps self-knowledge at a good man's unleashing of the terrifying urges locked inside each of us. How do you put that into a moral?

As readers and critics we are much better off in dealing with a writer's something-to-say if we think not of the moral, but of the *theme*. Life, as we have stated, is too complex to be reduced to morals, and writers attempt to dramatize life in all its depth and complexity. A theme in literature is not a moral, a message, or a piece of advice; rather, it is *the underlying issue, the basic area of permanent human experience treated by the author*. A theme does not make a statement; it names a subject. We can say that the theme or themes of *Romeo and Juliet* are love, and family, and fate, and conflicting loyalties, and reason vs. passion. We could add to the list, and a good critic could probably then find a way of linking all the separate themes into one theme that covers them all. The author offers comments on these separate themes by creating certain characters who act in certain ways. Are we really entitled to draw general morals from these themes? Almost certainly not. Romeo and Juliet are individuals, not representatives of all young lovers. Their families are feuding, as most families are not. The characters in the play face issues that are permanent ingredients of human life and respond to these issues in their own way—and *that* is why the play has something to say, not because it gives us handy hints on how to live our own lives. Discussing the ideas in literature through the concept of theme enables us to escape from the tyranny of moralizing. It enables writers to be what they are best at being: writers, not philosophers, prophets, reformers, or know-it-alls.

Symbols

A symbol is a person, place, or thing that stands for or strongly suggests something in addition to itself, generally an abstract idea more important than itself. Don't let this definition intimidate you. Symbols are not fancy literary devices that readers have to wrestle with. In fact, the daily, nonliterary lives of readers are filled, quite comfortably and naturally, with more symbols than exist in any book ever written.

A mink coat, for example, is a piece of clothing made from the pelt of an animal in the weasel family, but for many people it stands for something else: it is a symbol of success or status or good taste. People do not make sacrifices and sounds of ecstasy over the pelt of a weasel, but over a symbol. A beard, to cite another example, is a hairy growth on a man's face, but a person would have to be a recent arrival from another planet not to realize that a beard is often viewed as a symbol of anything from youthful self-assertion to political radicalism. Our lives are pervaded, perhaps dominated, by symbols. Think about the different symbolic meanings everyone gives to the following: a Cadillac, a new house, money, rats, a college diploma, a trip to Europe, a crucifix, a date with a popular and good-looking girl, the American flag, a blind date, Lawrence Welk, the F.B.I., Niagara Falls, Valley Forge, a fireplace.

Making symbols and reacting to symbols seem such basic ingredients of the human mind that we should hardly be astonished to find symbols in literature. Symbols have an extremely practical value to a writer, however. They enable the writer to communicate abstract concepts with the energy and vitality that can come only from specific details. Just as some people may be indifferent to abstract oratory about freedom's being a good thing but deeply moved by a visit to the Statute of Liberty, a reader may be bored or antagonistic to philosophical assertions about the passing of time but intensely impressed by the specific symbol—from a novel by Arnold Bennett—of a wedding ring almost totally embedded in the fat flesh on the finger of an old woman. Symbols of abstract ideas can often have a dramatic impact that the ideas themselves cannot, and sometimes in the hands of a master, symbols can express what might otherwise be almost inexpressible.

Our comments so far have stressed that symbols in literature are not as difficult and mysterious as they are sometimes imagined to be. Dealing with symbols is nevertheless not child's play, and four major traps lie in wait for critics—professionals no less than amateurs.

First, the symbol stands for or suggests something *in addition to* itself, *not instead of* itself. The symbolic level of a story or poem should never be allowed to dwarf the other levels—especially the basic level of people and plot. The wedding ring on the fat finger beautifully suggests the sadness of the passing of time, but it also tells us in a straightforward, down-to-earth, nonsymbolic fashion that the woman eats too much and hasn't taken very good care of herself.

Second, symbols are usually obvious. If a critic has to struggle to establish that something functions as a symbol, it probably was not meant to be one. Excessive ingenuity in symbol hunting is one of the worst of all critical sins. Stick to what the author clearly intends. In Hemingway's *A Farewell to Arms,* one of the lovers says that she is afraid of the rain because she dreams that it means her death. Then, when she does die and it is indeed raining, we can say that the rain is a symbol of death. This is a deliberately simple example, of course, but the principle is perfectly valid: real symbols are usually obvious because writers tend to make big productions of them.

Third, symbols should not be confused with ordinary significant details. This confusion can be the main reason a symbol hunter pounces on a nonsymbol. A symbol stands for or suggests something substantially different from itself. Rain may symbolize death. A veil may symbolize isolation. Springtime may symbolize youth, rebirth, longing, hope. If a character in a story, however, wipes his running nose with the back of his hand and doesn't cover his mouth when he coughs, we simply know that he has bad manners (in addition to a cold). The way he wipes his nose is not a symbol of bad manners, nor is the way he coughs; they *are* bad manners, details about the character that reveal something about him. A symbol is a person, place, or thing that bears little concrete resemblance to whatever it stands for or suggests; the reader must make a major mental leap to identify the symbol with its meaning. A significant detail about a person, place, or thing, on the other hand, merely conveys more information about or insight into its subject.

Fourth, nobody who writes about literature should be too eager to make a symbol stand for any one thing in particular. The most effective symbols often are not meant to work that way at all. They *stand for* nothing. They are meant to *suggest*—on an emotional level, at times a virtually subconscious level—a number of different and elusive concepts. That is precisely why symbols can be so valuable. Herman Melville's white whale in *Moby-Dick*, to mention a single example, is surely not meant to symbolize any one idea. The whale becomes such a powerful symbol because it suggests so many ideas: evil, man's insignificance, the unchanging order of the universe, nature, God's will, and so on. Symbols are often a great writer's imaginative shortcuts for dealing with the imposing and frightening complexity of life as we know it.

Metaphors and similes

Metaphors and similes are the two most common kinds of figurative language or figures of speech. A working definition of figurative language might be language that cannot be taken literally. In one way or another, figurative language departs from the conventional meaning and expression of words to bring about special effects, usually emotional. Figurative language is a common ingredient of our speech and writing; it is basic to almost all poetry, far more so than rhyme or meter.

A simile is a comparison using *like* or *as.*

The lecture was as dry as the Sahara Desert.

The nonsmokers at the cocktail party drew themselves into a small circle, like a wagon train surrounded by Indians.

All through that dreary summer weekend, we felt as if life had turned into a slow-motion movie.

A metaphor is often defined as a comparison that does without the *like* or *as,* thus establishing a closer connection between the items compared. It is also helpful, however, to think of a metaphor as a word or phrase generally used in one frame of reference that is shifted to another frame of reference.

The lecture was a Sahara Desert of dryness.

Our lives that dreary summer weekend had turned into a slow-motion movie.

She had ice-water in her veins.

Life is a cabaret.

The president told his administrators to stonewall the opposition.

Bill is the sparkplug of his team.

We thought the new boss was going to be a tiger, but he turned out to be a pussycat.

As indicated by many of the previous examples, our daily language is filled with metaphors. A number of them are so familiar that we have to struggle to recognize their metaphorical nature.

the arms of a chair	a wallflower
a clean sweep	the legs of a table
the traffic crawled	the heart of the matter
a green rookie	it's all a whitewash
a poker face	peaches-and-cream complexion

Effective metaphors and similes enable writers to stimulate and direct the emotions of their readers, to communicate their own emotions with concrete images rather than flat, abstract statements, and thus to develop stylistic color and excitement. Readers and critics should pay particular attention to metaphorical *patterns*—metaphors sustained and developed through a whole work rather than dropped after one sentence. Many writers consciously use such patterns to achieve greater unity, consistency, and dramatic power.

Exercise

Look over the following poems. First, identify each metaphor and simile. Second, try to find any patterns running through the entire poem. Third, consider whether the metaphors and similes are effective, and why.

PLAYS

Alas, how soon the hours are over,
Counted us out to play the lover!
And how much narrower is the stage,
Allotted us to play the sage!

But when we play the fool, how wide
The theater expands; beside,
How long the audience sits before us!
How many prompters! what a chorus!

—*Walter Savage Landor*

NOT WAVING BUT DROWNING

Nobody heard him, the dead man,
But still he lay moaning:
I was much further out than you thought
And not waving but drowning.

Poor chap, he always loved larking[1]
And now he's dead
It must have been too cold for him his heart gave way,
They said.

Oh, no no no, it was too cold always
(Still the dead one lay moaning)
I was much too far out all my life
And not waving but drowning.

—Stevie Smith

1. Having fun.

IF WE MUST DIE

If we must die, let it not be like hogs
Hunted and penned in an inglorious spot,
While round us bark the mad and hungry dogs,
Making their mock at our accursèd lot.
If we must die, O let us nobly die,
So that our precious blood may not be shed
In vain; then even the monsters we defy
Shall be constrained to honor us though dead!
O kinsmen we must meet the common foe!
Though far outnumbered let us show us brave,
And for their thousand blows deal one deathblow!
What though before us lies the open grave?
Like men we'll face the murderous, cowardly pack,
Pressed to the wall, dying, but fighting back!

—Claude McKay

BRIDAL COUCH

Follows this a narrower bed,
Wood at feet, wood at head;
Follows this a sounder sleep,
Somewhat longer and too deep.

All too meanly and too soon
Waxes once and wanes our moon;
All too swiftly for each one
Falls to dark our winter sun.

Let us here then wrestle death,
Intermingled limb and breath,
Conscious both that we beget
End of rest, endless fret,

And come at last to permanence,
Tired dancers from a dance,
Yawning, and content to fall
Into any bed at all.

—*Donald J. Lloyd*

Tone

In speaking and in writing, tone is not only an inseparable part of meaning, but also helps to create meaning. It is one of the ways by which speakers and writers convey their attitudes toward their subjects. When people exclaim to us, "Don't use that tone of voice with me," or "I don't like your tone," they may have nothing against the literal meaning of the words we have used, but may still have perfectly valid grounds for objecting to what we have said. Depending on what we do with our voices, our silences and pauses, and the words we choose to stress, we can make our attitude (our tone) angry, impatient, amused, contemptuous, appreciative, sarcastic, and so on. Notice how each of the following can change drastically in meaning as the tone varies:

> Waiter!
>
> I'm going to the opera next week.
>
> Yes, dear, I think you drive very, very well.
>
> My wife just had triplets.
>
> Late papers, as usual, will not be accepted.

It's easy enough to recognize tone in speech, but what about writing? Writers can't raise and lower their voices, at least not in the usual sense. They may underline or capitalize an occasional word for emphasis, but they can hardly express through these means the hundred shades of emphasis that human speech can. Moreover, speakers can use gestures and facial expressions to help establish tone, and these conveniences are obviously unavailable to a writer. To compensate, writers must carefully use all the resources that *are* at their command; they must manage to choose appropriate words, word order, contexts, connotations, figurative language, sounds, and rhythms. All these elements and more add up to tone. Somehow or other, as we know, writers do successfully create tone, for we feel it in everything we read. Primarily through our awareness of and response to tone, we discover if a writer wants us to feel pity or scorn—or both—for a character, hatred or fear of an idea, passionate involvement or sophisticated detachment toward a plot. Consider the differences in the poems in the last exercise: the witty elegance of "Plays," the rage and bitterness of "If We Must Die," the restrained pathos of "Not Waving but Drowning."

Readings

This chapter ends with a group of four short stories. The first is accompanied by a student paper which should stimulate further thought about the story and about the writing of literary analysis in general. The remaining stories present additional opportunities for writing your own papers, this time without the inspiration of the efforts of other students.

Shirley Jackson
CHARLES

The day my son Laurie started kindergarten he renounced corduroy overalls with bibs and began wearing blue jeans with a belt; I watched him go off the first morning with the older girl next door, seeing clearly that an era of my life was ended, my sweet-voiced nursery-school tot replaced by a long-trousered, swaggering character who forgot to stop at the corner and wave good-bye to me.

He came home the same way, the front door slamming open, his cap on the floor, and the voice suddenly become raucous shouting, "Isn't anybody *here?*"

At lunch he spoke insolently to his father, spilled his baby sister's milk, and remarked that his teacher said we were not to take the name of the Lord in vain.

"How *was* school today?" I asked, elaborately casual.

"All right," he said.

"Did you learn anything?" his father asked.

Laurie regarded his father coldly. "I didn't learn nothing," he said.

"Anything," I said. "Didn't learn anything."

"The teacher spanked a boy, though," Laurie said, addressing his bread and butter. "For being fresh," he added, with his mouth full.

"What did he do?" I asked. "Who was it?"

Laurie thought. "It was Charles," he said. "He was fresh. The teacher spanked him and made him stand in a corner. He was awfully fresh."

"What did he do?" I asked again, but Laurie slid off his chair, took a cookie, and left, while his father was still saying, "See here, young man."

The next day Laurie remarked at lunch, as soon as he sat down, "Well, Charles was bad again today." He grinned enormously and said, "Today Charles hit the teacher."

"Good heavens," I said, mindful of the Lord's name, "I suppose he got spanked again?"

"He sure did," Laurie said. "Look up," he said to his father.

"What?" his father said, looking up.

"Look down," Laurie said. "Look at my thumb. Gee, you're dumb." He began to laugh insanely.

"Why did Charles hit the teacher?" I asked quickly.

"Because she tried to make him color with red crayons," Laurie said. "Charles wanted to color with green crayons so he hit the teacher and she spanked him and said nobody play with Charles but everybody did."

The third day—it was Wednesday of the first week—Charles bounced a see-saw on to the head of a little girl and made her bleed, and the teacher made him stay inside all during recess. Thursday Charles had to stand in a corner during story-time because he kept pounding his feet on the floor. Friday Charles was deprived of blackboard privileges because he threw chalk.

On Saturday I remarked to my husband, "Do you think kindergarten is too unsettling for Laurie? All this toughness, and bad grammar, and this Charles boy sounds like such a bad influence."

"It'll be all right," my husband said reassuringly. "Bound to be people like Charles in the world. Might as well meet them now as later."

On Monday Laurie came home late, full of news. "Charles," he shouted as he came up the hill; I was waiting anxiously on the front steps. "Charles," Laurie yelled all the way up the hill, "Charles was bad again."

"Come right in," I said, as soon as he came close enough. "Lunch is waiting."

"You know what Charles did?" he demanded, following me through the door. "Charles yelled so in school they sent a boy in from first grade to tell the teacher she had to make Charles keep quiet, and so Charles had to stay after school. And so all the children stayed to watch him."

"What did he do?" I asked.

"He just sat there," Laurie said, climbing into his chair at the table. "Hi, Pop, y'old dust mop."

"Charles had to stay after school today," I told my husband. "Everyone stayed with him."

"What does this Charles look like?" my husband asked Laurie. "What's his other name?"

"He's bigger than me," Laurie said. "And he doesn't have any rubbers and he doesn't ever wear a jacket."

Monday night was the first Parent-Teachers meeting, and only the fact that the baby had a cold kept me from going; I wanted passionately to meet Charles's mother. On Tuesday Laurie remarked suddenly, "Our teacher had a friend come to see her in school today."

"Charles's mother?" my husband and I asked simultaneously.

"Naaah," Laurie said scornfully. "It was a man who came and made us do exercises, we had to touch our toes. Look." He climbed down from his chair and squatted down and touched his toes. "Like this," he said. He got solemnly back into his chair and said, picking up his fork, "Charles didn't even *do* exercises."

"That's fine," I said heartily. "Didn't Charles want to do exercises?"

"Naaah," Laurie said. "Charles was so fresh to the teacher's friend he wasn't *let* do exercises."

"Fresh again?" I said.

"He kicked the teacher's friend," Laurie said. "The teacher's friend told Charles to touch his toes like I just did and Charles kicked him."

"What are they going to do about Charles, do you suppose?" Laurie's father asked him.

Laurie shrugged elaborately. "Throw him out of school, I guess," he said.

Wednesday and Thursday were routine; Charles yelled during story hour and hit a boy in the stomach and made him cry. On Friday Charles stayed after school again and so did all the other children.

With the third week of kindergarten Charles was an institution in our family; the baby was being a Charles when she cried all afternoon; Laurie did a Charles when he filled his wagon full of mud and pulled it through the kitchen; even my husband, when he caught his elbow in the telephone cord and pulled telephone, ashtray, and a bowl of flowers off the table, said, after the first minute, "Looks like Charles."

During the third and fourth weeks it looked like a reformation in Charles; Laurie reported grimly at lunch on Thursday of the third week, "Charles was so good today the teacher gave him an apple."

"What?" I said, and my husband added warily, "You mean Charles?"

"Charles," Laurie said. "He gave the crayons around and he picked up the books afterward and the teacher said he was her helper."

"What happened?" I asked incredulously.

"He was her helper, that's all," Laurie said, and shrugged.

"Can this be true, about Charles?" I asked my husband that night. "Can something like this happen?"

"Wait and see," my husband said cynically. "When you've got a Charles to deal with, this may mean he's only plotting."

He seemed to be wrong. For over a week Charles was the teacher's helper; each day he handed things out and he picked things up; no one had to stay after school.

"The P.T.A. meeting's next week again," I told my husband one evening. "I'm going to find Charles's mother there."

"Ask her what happened to Charles," my husband said. "I'd like to know."

"I'd like to know myself," I said.

On Friday of that week things were back to normal. "You know what Charles did today?" Laurie demanded at the lunch table, in a voice slightly awed. "He told a little girl to say a word and she said it and the teacher washed her mouth out with soap and Charles laughed."

"What word?" his father asked unwisely, and Laurie said, "I'll have to whisper it to you, it's so bad." He got down off his chair and went around to his father. His father bent his head down and Laurie whispered joyfully. His father's eyes widened.

"Did Charles tell the little girl to say *that?*" he asked respectfully.

"She said it *twice,*" Laurie said. "Charles told her to say it *twice.*"

"What happened to Charles?" my husband asked.

"Nothing," Laurie said. "He was passing out the crayons."

Monday morning Charles abandoned the little girl and said the evil word himself three or four times, getting his mouth washed out with soap each time. He also threw chalk.

My husband came to the door with me that evening as I set out for the P.T.A. meeting. "Invite her over for a cup of tea after the meeting," he said. "I want to get a look at her."

"If only she's there," I said prayerfully.

"She'll be there," my husband said. "I don't see how they could hold a P.T.A. meeting without Charles's mother."

At the meeting I sat restlessly, scanning each comfortable matronly face, trying to determine which one hid the secret of Charles. None of them looked to me haggard enough. No one stood up in the meeting and apoligized for the way her son had been acting. No one mentioned Charles.

After the meeting I identified and sought out Laurie's kindergarten teacher. She had a plate with a cup of tea and a piece of chocolate cake; I had a plate with a cup of tea and a piece of marshmallow cake. We maneuvered up to one another cautiously, and smiled.

"I've been so anxious to meet you," I said. "I'm Laurie's mother."

"We're all so interested in Laurie," she said.

"Well, he certainly likes kindergarten," I said. "He talks about it all the time."

"We had a little trouble adjusting, the first week or so," she said primly, "but now he's a fine little helper. With occasional lapses, of course."

"Laurie usually adjusts very quickly," I said. "I suppose this time it's Charles's influence."

"Charles?"

"Yes," I said, laughing, "you must have your hands full in that kindergarten, with Charles."

"Charles?" she said. "We don't have any Charles in the kindergarten."

Questions for Writing or Discussion

1. Does the story provide any indications of why Laurie invents the character of Charles?
2. How are Laurie's parents supposed to strike the reader? Are they good, bad, or in-between? Are they too permissive?

3. How does the response of Laurie's parents help perpetuate the existence of Charles?
4. Did you suspect the truth about Charles before the end of the story? If so, what started your suspicion?
5. Is there cause for serious concern about the future mental health of Laurie?

The Beginning of the End

HARRIET McKAY

Until the last sentence of Shirley Jackson's "Charles," I had no idea that Charles, the terror of kindergarten, was an imaginary person created by Laurie and that Charles's little monster antics were really Laurie's own antics. The author fooled me completely, but I have to admit that she played fair. She gave her readers all the clues they needed to make a sensible guess about how the story would end.

Laurie's own personality offers one set of clues. Even before classes start, Jackson lets us know that Laurie might have a lot to overcompensate for. His mother has been dressing him in cute little boy clothes and thinking of him as a "sweet-voiced nursery-school tot." It is at Laurie's own insistence that he begins wearing tough-kid blue jeans. In addition, any boy nicknamed "Laurie" is due for some problems; one doesn't need to be a sexist pig to say that boys named "Laurence" ought to be called "Larry" and that "Laurie," to put it bluntly, is a sissy name. No wonder Laurie goes overboard. He's not a little boy anymore. He has hit the big time in kindergarten, and he begins "swaggering" even before his first class.

Laurie's behavior at home after school starts is another giveaway. Charles may be a monster at school, but Laurie isn't that much better at lunchtime. After only one class, he slams the door, throws his hat on the floor, shouts, speaks "insolently," makes deliberate mistakes in grammar, doesn't look at people when he talks to them but talks to the bread and butter instead, speaks with his mouth full, leaves the table without asking permission and while his father is still talking to him. This is no sweet little tot. His doting parents might try to pin Laurie's behavior on the bad influence of Charles, but that's certainly not the only possible explanation, and that's what doting parents have always tried to do. Besides, it would be stretching things to the limit to imagine that even Charles could have that great an influence after only one morning in the same classroom with him.

Still another giveaway is Laurie's explanation for being late. It's impossible to believe that a group of kindergarten kids would voluntarily stay after school to watch a child being punished. Laurie's parents swallow this story so easily that many readers probably don't notice how fantastic the story really is—but an alert reader would have noticed.

Finally, all through the story Laurie's parents are being so poised and cool about everything that I really wonder why I did not realize that they would have to be brought down a few pegs at the end of the story. Do they ever make a serious effort to correct their son's bad manners? Do they ever tell him to stay away from a rotten kid like Charles? Heavens no, they're much too enlightened. The parents think Charles is amusing, and they can't wait to meet Charles's mother so that they can feel superior to her. In simple justice they deserve what they get, and I should have seen it coming.

Laurie's personality and behavior, his unbelievable explanation for being late, and his parents' complacency all give readers the clues they need to predict the surprise ending.

Questions for Writing or Discussion

1. Is the writer's frequent mention of herself inappropriate for literary analysis?
2. Is the frequent use of slang and other extremely informal language (*rotten kid, sissy, hit the big time, little monster, Heavens no*) inappropriate for literary analysis?
3. Should a separate paragraph have been devoted to the issue of Laurie's lateness? If not, how could the issue have been treated more effectively?
4. What details from the story does the writer omit that could have strengthened her case?
5. Is the last paragraph too short? too abrupt? too dull?

Roald Dahl
THE LANDLADY

Billy Weaver had travelled down from London on the slow afternoon train, with a change at Reading on the way, and by the time he got to Bath it was about nine o'clock in the evening and the moon was coming up out of a clear, starry sky over the houses opposite the station entrance. But the air was deadly cold and the wind was like a flat blade of ice on his cheeks.

"Excuse me," he said to a porter, "but is there a fairly cheap hotel not too far away from here?"

"Try the Bell and Dragon," the porter answered, pointing down the road. "They might take you in. It's about a quarter of a mile along on the other side."

Billy thanked him and picked up his suitcase and set out to walk the quarter mile to the Bell and Dragon. He had never been to Bath before. He didn't know anyone who lived there. But Mr. Greenslade at the Head Office in London had told him it was a splendid town. "Find your own lodgings," he said, "and then go along and report to the branch manager as soon as you've got yourself settled."

Billy was seventeen years old. He was wearing a new navy-blue overcoat, a new brown trilby hat, and a new brown suit, and he was feeling fine. He walked briskly down the street. He was trying to do everything briskly these days. Briskness, he had decided, was *the* one common characteristic of all successful businessmen. The big shots up at Head Office were absolutely fantastically brisk all the time. They were amazing.

There were no shops on this wide street that he was walking along, only a line of tall houses on each side, all of them identical. They had porches and pillars and four or five steps going up to their front doors, and it was obvious that once upon a time they had been very swanky residences. But now, even in the darkness, he could see that the paint was peeling from the woodwork on their doors and windows, and that the handsome white façades were cracked and blotchy from neglect.

Suddenly, not six yards away, in a downstairs window that was brilliantly illuminated by a street lamp, Billy caught sight of a printed notice propped up against the glass in one of the upper panes. It said, "BED AND BREAKFAST." There was a vase of yellow chrysanthemums, tall and beautiful, standing just underneath the notice.

He stopped walking. He moved a bit closer. Green curtains (some sort of velvety material) were hanging down on either side of the window. The chrysanthemums looked wonderful beside them. He went right up and peered through the glass into the room, and the first thing he saw was a bright fire burning on the hearth. On the carpet in front of the fire, a pretty little dachshund was curled up asleep, with its nose tucked into its belly. The room itself, as far as he could see in the half darkness, was filled with pleasant furniture. There was a baby-grand piano and a big sofa and several plump armchairs, and in one corner he spotted a large parrot in a cage. Animals were usually a good sign in a place like this, Billy told himself, and all in all, it looked as though it would be a pretty decent house to stay in. Certainly it would be more comfortable than the Bell and Dragon.

On the other hand, a pub would be more congenial than a boarding house. There would be beer and darts in the evenings, and lots of people to talk to, and it would probably be a good bit cheaper, too. He had stayed a couple of nights in a pub once before, and he had liked it. He had never stayed in any boarding houses, and to be perfectly honest, he was a tiny bit frightened of them. The name itself conjured up images of watery cabbage, rapacious landladies, and a powerful smell of kippers in the living room. After dithering about like this in the cold for two or three minutes, Billy decided that he would walk on and take a look at the Bell and Dragon before making up his mind. He turned to go.

And now a queer thing happened to him. He was in the act of stepping back and turning away from the window when all at once his eye was caught again and held in the most peculiar manner by the small notice that was there. "BED AND BREAKFAST," it said. "Bed and Breakfast, bed and breakfast, bed and breakfast." Each word was like a large black eye staring at him through the glass, holding him, compelling him, forcing him to stay where he was and not walk away from that house, and the next thing he knew he was actually moving across from the window to the front door, climbing the steps that led up to it, and reaching for the bell.

He pressed the bell. Far away in a back room, he heard it ringing, and then *at once*—it must have been at once, because he hadn't even had time to take his finger from the bell button—the door swung open and a woman was standing there. Normally, you ring a bell and you have at least a half-minute wait before the door opens. But this person was like a jack-in-the-box. He pressed the bell—and out she popped! It made him jump.

She was about forty-five or fifty years old, and the moment she saw him she gave him a warm, welcoming smile. *"Please* come in," she said pleasantly. She stepped aside, holding the door wide open, and Billy found himself automatically starting forward. The compulsion, or, more accurately, the desire to follow after her into that house was extraordinarily strong, but he held himself back.

"I saw the notice in the window," he said.

"Yes, I know."

"I was wondering about a room."

"It's *all* ready for you, my dear," she said. She had a round pink face and very gentle blue eyes.

"I was on my way to the Bell and Dragon," Billy told her. "But the notice in your window just happened to catch my eye."

"My dear boy," she said, "why don't you come in out of the cold?"

"How much do you charge?"

"Five and sixpence a night, including breakfast."

It was fantastically cheap. It was less than half of what he had been willing to pay.

"If that is too much," she added, "then perhaps I can reduce it just a tiny bit. Do you desire an egg for breakfast? Eggs are expensive at the moment. It would be sixpence less without the egg."

"Five and sixpence is fine," he answered. "I should like very much to stay here."

"I knew you would. Do come in."

She seemed terribly nice. She looked exactly like the mother of one's best school friend welcoming one into the house to stay for the Christmas holidays. Billy took off his hat and stepped over the threshold.

"Just hang it there," she said, "and let me help you with your coat."

There were no other hats or coats in the hall. There were no umbrellas, no walking sticks—nothing.

"We have it *all* to ourselves," she said, smiling at him over her shoulder as she led the way upstairs. "You see, it isn't very often I have the pleasure of taking a visitor into my little nest."

The old girl is slightly dotty, Billy told himself. But at five and sixpence a night, who gives a damn about that? "I should've thought you'd be simply swamped with applicants," he said politely.

"Oh, I am, my dear, I am. Of course I am. But the trouble is that I'm inclined to be just a teeny-weeny bit choosy and particular—if you see what I mean."

"Ah, yes."

"But I'm always ready. Everything is always ready day and night in this house, just on the off chance that an acceptable young gentleman will come along. And it is such a pleasure, my dear, such a very great pleasure when now and again I open the door and I see someone standing there who is just *exactly* right." She was halfway up the stairs, and she paused with one hand on the stair rail, turning her head and smiling down at him with pale lips. "Like you," she added, and her blue eyes travelled slowly all the way down the length of Billy's body to his feet and then up again.

On the second-floor landing, she said to him, "This floor is mine."

They climbed up another flight. "And this one is *all* yours," she said.

"Here's your room. I do hope you'll like it." She took him into a small but charming front bedroom, switching on the light as she went in.

"The morning sun comes right in the window, Mr. Perkins. It is Mr. Perkins, isn't it?"

"No," he said. "It's Weaver."

"Mr. Weaver. How nice. I've put a water bottle between the sheets, to warm them up, Mr. Weaver. It's such a comfort to have a hot-water bottle in a strange bed with clean sheets, don't you agree? And you may light the gas fire at any time, if you feel chilly."

"Thank you," Billy said. "Thank you ever so much." He noticed that the bedspread had been taken off the bed and that the bedclothes had been neatly turned back on one side, all ready for someone to get in.

"I'm so glad you appeared," she said, looking earnestly into his face. "I was beginning to get worried."

"That's all right," Billy answered brightly. "You mustn't worry about me." He put his suitcase on the chair and started to open it.

"And what about supper, my dear? Did you manage to get anything to eat before you came here?"

"I'm not a bit hungry, thank you," he said. "I think I'll just go to bed as soon as possible, because tomorrow I've got to get up rather early and report to the office."

"Very well, then. I'll leave you now so that you can unpack. But before you go to bed, would you be kind enough to pop into the sitting room on the ground floor and sign the book? Everyone has to do that, because it's the law of the land, and we don't want to go breaking any laws at *this* stage in the proceedings, do we?" She gave him a little wave of the hand and went quickly out of the room and closed the door.

Now the fact that his landlady appeared to be slightly off her rocker didn't worry Billy in the least. After all, she not only was harmless—there was no question about that—but she was also quite obviously a kind and generous soul. He guessed that she had probably lost a son in the war, or something like that, and had never got over it. So a few minutes later, after unpacking his suitcase and washing his hands, he trotted downstairs to the ground floor and entered the living room. His landlady wasn't there, but the fire was glowing on the hearth, and the little dachshund was still sleeping soundly in front of it. The room was wonderfully warm and cozy. I'm a lucky fellow, he thought, rubbing his hands. This is a bit of all right.

He found the guestbook lying open on the piano, so he took out his pen and wrote down his name and address. There were only two other entries above his on the page, and as one always does with guestbooks, he started to read them. One was a Christopher Mulholland, from Cardiff. The other was Gregory W. Temple, from Bristol.

That's funny, he thought suddenly. Christopher Mulholland. It rings a bell. Now where on earth had he heard that rather unusual name before? Was it a boy at school? No. Was it one of his sister's numerous young men, perhaps, or a friend of his father's? No, no, it wasn't any of those. He glanced down again at the book.

Christopher Mulholland, 231 Cathedral Road, Cardiff
Gregory W. Temple, 27 Sycamore Drive, Bristol

As a matter of fact, now he came to think of it, he wasn't at all sure that the second name didn't have almost as much of a familiar ring about it as the first.

"Gregory Temple?" he said aloud, searching his memory. "Christopher Mulholland? . . ."

"Such charming boys," a voice behind him answered, and he turned and saw his landlady sailing into the room with a large silver tea tray in her hands. She was holding it well out in front of her and rather high up, as though the tray were a pair of reins on a frisky horse.

"They sound somehow familiar," he said.

"They do? How interesting."

"I'm almost positive I've heard those names before somewhere. Isn't that odd? Maybe it was in the newspapers. They weren't famous in any way, were they? I mean, famous cricketers or footballers or something like that?"

"Famous?" she said, setting the tea tray down on the low table in front of the sofa. "Oh, no, I don't think they were famous. But they were incredibly handsome, both of them, I can promise you that. They were tall and young and handsome, my dear, just exactly like you."

Once more, Billy glanced down at the book. "Look here," he said, noticing the dates. "This last entry is over two years old."

"It is?"

"Yes indeed. And Christopher Mulholland's is nearly a year before that—more than *three* years ago."

"Dear me," she said, shaking her head and heaving a dainty little sigh. "I would never have thought it. How time does fly away from us all, doesn't it, Mr. Wilkins?"

"It's Weaver," Billy said. "W-e-a-v-e-r."

"Oh, of course it is!" she cried, sitting down on the sofa. "How silly of me. I do apologize. In one ear and out the other, that's me, Mr. Weaver."

"You know something?" Billy said. "Something that's really quite extraordinary about all this?"

"No, dear, I don't."

"Well, you see, both of these names—Mulholland and Temple—I not only seem to remember each one of them separately, so to speak, but somehow or other, in some peculiar way, they both appear to be sort of connected together as well. As though they were both famous for the same sort of thing, if you see what I mean—like . . . well . . . like Dempsey and Tunney, for example, or Churchill and Roosevelt."

"How amusing," she said. "But come over here now dear, and sit down beside me on the sofa and I'll give you a nice cup of tea and a ginger biscuit before you go to bed."

"You really shouldn't bother," Billy said. "I didn't mean you to do anything like that." He stood by the piano, watching her as she fussed about with the cups and saucers. He noticed that she had small, white, quickly moving hands and red fingernails.

"I'm almost positive it was in the newspapers I saw them," Billy said. "I'll think of it in a second. I'm sure I will."

There is nothing more tantalizing than a thing like this that lingers just outside the borders of one's memory. He hated to give up. "Now wait a minute," he said. "Wait just a minute. Mulholland . . . Christopher Mulholland . . . wasn't *that* the name of the Eton schoolboy who was on a walking tour through the West Country and then all of a sudden—"

"Milk?" she said. "And sugar?"

"Yes, please. And then all of a sudden—"

"Eton schoolboy?" she said. "Oh, no, my dear, that can't possibly be right because *my* Mr. Mulholland was certainly not an Eton schoolboy when he came to me. He was a Cambridge undergraduate. Come over here now and sit next to me and warm yourself in front of this lovely fire. Come on. Your tea's all ready for you." She patted the empty place beside her on the sofa and sat there smiling at Billy and waiting for him to come over.

He crossed the room slowly and sat down on the edge of the sofa. She placed his teacup on the table in front of him.

"*There* we are," she said. "How nice and cozy this is, isn't it?"

Billy started sipping his tea. She did the same. For half a minute or so, neither of them spoke. But Billy knew that she was looking at him. Her body was half turned toward him, and he could feel her eyes resting on his face, watching him over the rim of her teacup. Now and again, he caught a whiff of a peculiar smell that seemed to emanate directly from her person. It was not in the least unpleasant, and it reminded him—well, he wasn't quite sure what it reminded him of. Pickled walnuts? New leather? Or was it the corridors of a hospital?

At length she said, "Mr. Mulholland was a great one for his tea. Never in my life have I seen anyone drink as much tea as dear, sweet Mr. Mulholland."

"I suppose he left fairly recently," Billy said. He was still puzzling his head about the two names. He was positive now that he had seen them in the newspapers—in the headlines.

"Left?" she said, arching her brows. "But my dear boy, he never left. He's still here. Mr. Temple is also here. They're on the fourth floor, both of them together."

Billy set his cup down slowly on the table and stared at his landlady. She smiled back at him, and then she put out one of her white hands and patted him comfortingly on the knee.

"How old are you, my dear?" she asked.

"Seventeen."

"Seventeen!" she cried. "Oh, it's the perfect age! Mr. Mulholland was also seventeen. But I think he was a trifle shorter than you are; in fact, I'm sure he was and his teeth weren't *quite* so white. You have the most beautiful teeth, Mr. Weaver, did you know that?"

"They're not as good as they look," Billy said. "They've got simply masses of fillings in them at the back."

"Mr. Temple, of course, was a little older," she said, ignoring his remark. "He was actually twenty-eight. And yet I never would have guessed it if he hadn't told me—never in my whole life. There wasn't a *blemish* on his body."

"A what?" Billy said.

"His skin was *just* like a baby's."

There was a pause. Billy picked up his teacup and took another sip of his tea, then he set it down gently in its saucer. He waited for her to say something else, but she seemed to have lapsed into another of her silences.

He sat there staring straight ahead of him into the far corner of the room, biting his lower lip.

"That parrot," he said at last. "You know something? It had me completely fooled when I first saw it through the window. I could have sworn it was alive."

"Alas, no longer."

"It's most terribly clever the way it's been done," he said. "It doesn't look in the least bit dead. Who did it?"

"I did."

"You did?"

"Of course," she said. "And have you met my little Basil as well?" She nodded toward the dachshund curled up so comfortably in front of the fire, and Billy looked at it, and as he did so he suddenly realized that this animal all the time had been just as silent and motionless as the parrot. He put out a hand and touched it gently on the top of its back. The back was hard and cold, and when he pushed the hair to one side with his fingers, he could see the skin underneath, grayish-black and dry and perfectly preserved.

"Good gracious me," he said. "How absolutely fascinating." He turned away from the dog and stared with deep admiration at the little woman beside him on the sofa. "It must be most awfully difficult to do a thing like that."

"Not in the least," she said. "I stuff *all* my little pets myself when they pass away. Will you have another cup of tea?"

"No thank you," Billy said. The tea tasted faintly of bitter almonds, and he didn't care much for it.

"You did sign the book, didn't you?"

"Oh, yes."

"That's good. Because later on, if I happened to forget what you were called, then I could always come down here and look it up. I still do that almost every day with Mr. Mulholland and Mr. . . . Mr. . . . ."

"Temple," Billy said. "Gregory Temple. Excuse my asking, but haven't there been *any* other guests here except them in the last two or three years?"

Holding her teacup high in one hand, inclining her head slightly to the left, she looked up at him out of the corners of her eyes and gave him another gentle little smile.

"No, my dear," she said. "Only you."

Questions for Writing and Discussion

1. Does Billy's own character contribute in part to his destruction? Would you yourself have left the landlady's house before teatime? Explain.
2. At the start of the story, why does the author bother telling us about the weather, Billy's method of transportation, Billy's clothing, and his attitudes toward business?
3. Does the hypnotic power of the "Bed and breakfast" sign introduce a supernatural element out of keeping with the rest of the story?

4. Does the author "play fair" in preparing us for the surprise ending? (See the student paper on "Charles," p. 263.) This question is a good topic for a paper and could lead to an interesting comparison-and-contrast paper on "The Landlady" and "Charles."

Dorothy Parker
YOU WERE PERFECTLY FINE

The pale young man eased himself carefully into the low chair, and rolled his head to the side, so that the cool chintz comforted his cheek and temple.

"Oh, dear," he said. "Oh, dear, oh, dear, oh, dear. Oh."

The clear-eyed girl, sitting light and erect on the couch, smiled brightly at him.

"Not feeling so well today?" she said.

"Oh, I'm great," he said. "Corking, I am. Know what time I got up? Four o'clock this afternoon, sharp. I kept trying to make it, and every time I took my head off the pillow, it would roll under the bed. This isn't my head I've got on now. I think this is something that used to belong to Walt Whitman. Oh, dear, oh, dear, oh, dear."

"Do you think maybe a drink would make you feel better?" she said.

"The hair of the mastiff that bit me?" he said. "Oh, no, thank you. Please never speak of anything like that again. I'm through. I'm all, all through. Look at that hand; steady as a humming-bird. Tell me, was I very terrible last night?"

"Oh, goodness," she said, "everybody was feeling pretty high. You were all right."

"Yeah," he said. "I must have been dandy. Is everybody sore at me?"

"Good heavens, no," she said. "Everyone thought you were terribly funny. Of course, Jim Pierson was a little stuffy, there, for a minute at dinner. But people sort of held him back in his chair, and got him calmed down. I don't think anybody at the other tables noticed it at all. Hardly anybody."

"He was going to sock me?" he said. "Oh, Lord. What did I do to him?"

"Why, you didn't do a thing," she said. "You were perfectly fine. But you know how silly Jim gets, when he thinks anybody is making too much fuss over Elinor."

"Was I making a pass at Elinor?" he said. "Did I do that?"

"Of course you didn't," she said. "You were only fooling, that's all. She thought you were awfully amusing. She was having a marvelous time. She only got a little tiny bit annoyed just once, when you poured the clam-juice down her back."

"My God," he said. "Clam-juice down that back. And every vertebra a little Cabot. Dear God. What'll I ever do?"

"Oh, she'll be all right," she said. "Just send her some flowers, or something. Don't worry about it. It isn't anything."

"No, I won't worry," he said. "I haven't got a care in the world. I'm sitting pretty. Oh, dear, oh, dear. Did I do any other fascinating tricks at dinner?"

"You were fine," she said. "Don't be so foolish about it. Everybody was crazy about you. The maître d'hôtel was a little worried because you wouldn't stop singing, but he really didn't mind. All he said was, he was afraid they'd close the place again, if there was so much noise. But he didn't care a bit, himself. I think he loved seeing you have such a good time. Oh, you were just singing away, there, for about an hour. It wasn't so terribly loud, at all."

"So I sang," he said. "That must have been a treat. I sang."

"Don't you remember?" she said. "You just sang one song after another. Everybody in the place was listening. They loved it. Only you kept insisting that you wanted to sing some song about some kind of fusiliers or other, and everybody kept shushing you, and you'd keep trying to start it again. You were wonderful. We were all trying to make you stop singing for a minute, and eat something, but you wouldn't hear of it. My, you were funny."

"Didn't I eat any dinner?" he said.

"Oh, not a thing," she said. "Every time the waiter would offer you something, you'd give it right back to him, because you said that he was your long-lost brother, changed in the cradle by a gypsy band, and that anything you had was his. You had him simply roaring at you."

"I bet I did," he said. "I bet I was comical. Society's Pet, I must have been. And what happened then, after my overwhelming success with the waiter?"

"Why nothing much," she said. "You took a sort of dislike to some old man with white hair, sitting across the room, because you didn't like his necktie and you wanted to tell him about it. But we got you out, before he got really mad."

"Oh, we got out," he said. "Did I walk?"

"Walk! Of course you did," she said. "You were absolutely all right. There was that nasty stretch of ice on the sidewalk, and you did sit down awfully hard, you poor dear. But good heavens, that might have happened to anybody."

"Oh, sure," he said. "Louisa Alcott or anybody. So I fell down on the sidewalk. That would explain what's the matter with my—Yes. I see. And then what, if you don't mind?"

"Ah, now, Peter!" she said. "You can't sit there and say you don't remember what happened after that! I did think that maybe you were just a little tight at dinner—oh, you were perfectly all right, and all that, but I did know you were feeling pretty gay. But you were so serious, from the time you fell down—I never knew you to be that way. Don't you know, how you told me I had never seen your real self before? Oh, Peter, I just couldn't bear it, if you didn't remember that lovely long ride we took together in the taxi! Please, you do remember that, don't you? I think it would simply kill me, if you didn't."

"Oh, yes," he said. "Riding in the taxi. Oh, yes, sure. Pretty long ride, hmm?"

"Round and round and round the park," she said. "Oh, and the trees were shining so in the moonlight. And you said you never knew before that you really had a soul."

"Yes," he said. "I said that. That was me."

"You said such lovely, lovely things," she said. "And I'd never known, all this time, how you had been feeling about me, and I'd never dared to let you see how I felt about you. And then last night—oh, Peter dear, I think that taxi ride was the most important thing that ever happened to us in our lives."

"Yes," he said. "I guess it must have been."

"And we're going to be so happy," she said. "Oh, I just want to tell everybody! But I don't know—I think maybe it would be sweeter to keep it all to ourselves."

"I think it would be," he said.

"Isn't it lovely?" she said.

"Yes," he said. "Great."

"Lovely!" she said.

"Look here," he said, "do you mind if I have a drink? I mean, just medicinally, you know. I'm off the stuff for life, so help me. But I think I feel a collapse coming on."

"Oh, I think it would do you good," she said. "You poor boy, it's a shame you feel so awful. I'll go make you a whisky and soda."

"Honestly," he said, "I don't see how you could ever want to speak to me again, after I made such a fool of myself, last night. I think I'd better go join a monastery in Tibet."

"You crazy idiot!" she said. "As if I could ever let you go away now! Stop talking like that. You were perfectly fine."

She jumped up from the couch, kissed him quickly on the forehead, and ran out of the room.

The pale young man looked after her and shook his head long and slowly, then dropped it in his damp and trembling hands.

"Oh, dear," he said. "Oh, dear, oh, dear, oh, dear."

Questions for Writing or Discussion

1. Why does the woman keep telling Peter that he was perfectly fine when he most certainly was not? Is she simply trying to cheer him up, or are her motives more complex?

2. What does the story reveal about the social set in which the characters circulate?

3. The story is written almost entirely in dialogue. Are the few observations made directly by the author merely objectively described facts, or do they help shape our responses to the story?

4. Which character is in a worse situation? Which character do we feel sorrier for?

5. Assuming we do feel sorry for the characters, how does the story manage to be so successful as comedy?

Nathaniel Hawthorne
THE BIRTHMARK

In the latter part of the last century[1] there lived a man of science—an eminent proficient in every branch of natural philosophy—who not long before our story opens had made experience of a spiritual affinity more attractive than any chemical one. He had left his laboratory to the care of an assistant, cleared his fine countenance from the furnace-smoke, washed the stain of acids from his fingers, and persuaded a beautiful woman to become his wife. In those days, when the comparatively recent discovery of electricity, and other kindred mysteries of nature, seemed to open paths into the region of miracle, it was not unusual for the love of science to rival the love of woman in its depth and absorbing energy. The higher intellect, the imagination, the spirit, and even the heart, might all find their congenial aliment[2] in pursuits which, as some of their ardent votaries[3] believed, would ascend from one step of powerful intelligence to another until the philosopher should lay his hand on the secret of creative force, and perhaps make new worlds for himself. We know not whether Aylmer possessed this degree of faith in man's ultimate control over nature. He had devoted himself, however, too unreservedly to scientific studies ever to be weaned from them by any second passion. His love for his young wife might prove the stronger of the two, but it could only be by intertwining itself with his love of science and uniting the strength of the latter to its own.

Such a union accordingly took place, and was attended with truly remarkable consequences and a deeply impressive moral. One day, very soon after their marriage, Aylmer sat gazing at his wife with a trouble in his countenance that grew stronger, until he spoke.

"Georgiana," said he, "has it never occurred to you that the mark upon your cheek might be removed?"

"No, indeed," said she smiling; but, perceiving the seriousness of his manner, she blushed deeply. "To tell you the truth, it has been so often called a charm that I was simple enough to imagine it might be so."

"Ah! upon another face perhaps it might," replied her husband, "but never on yours. No, dearest Georgiana; you came so nearly perfect from the hand of Nature that this slightest possible defect—which we hesitate whether to term a defect or a beauty—shocks me as being the visible mark of earthly imperfection."

"Shocks you, my husband!" cried Georgiana, deeply hurt, at first reddening with momentary anger, but then bursting into tears. "Then why did you take me from my mother's side? You cannot love what shocks you."

To explain this conversation it must be mentioned that in the centre of Georgiana's left cheek there was a singular mark deeply interwoven, as it were, with the texture and substance of her face. In the usual state of her complexion—a healthy though delicate bloom—the mark wore a tint of deeper crimson which imperfectly defined its shape amid the surrounding rosiness. When she blushed, it gradually became more indistinct, and finally vanished amid the triumphant rush of blood that bathed the whole cheek

1. the eighteenth century
2. nourishment
3. worshippers

with its brilliant glow. But if any shifting emotion caused her to turn pale, there was the mark again, a crimson stain upon the snow, in what Aylmer sometimes deemed an almost fearful distinctness. Its shape bore not a little similarity to the human hand, though of the smallest pigmy size. Georgiana's lovers were wont to say that some fairy at her birth-hour had laid her tiny hand upon the infant's cheek, and left this impress there in token of the magic endowments that were to give her such sway over all hearts. Many a desperate swain[4] would have risked life for the privilege of pressing his lips to the mysterious hand. It must not be concealed, however, that the impression wrought by this fairy sign-manual varied exceedingly according to the difference of temperament in the beholders. Some fastidious persons—but they were exclusively of her own sex—affirmed that the bloody hand, as they chose to call it, quite destroyed the effect of Georgiana's beauty, and rendered her countenance even hideous. But it would be as reasonable to say that one of those small blue stains which sometimes occur in the purest statuary marble would convert the Eve of Powers[5] to a monster. Masculine observers, if the birthmark did not heighten their admiration, contented themselves with wishing it away that the world might possess one living specimen of ideal loveliness without the semblance of a flaw.

After his marriage—for he thought little or nothing of the matter before—Aylmer discovered that this was the case with himself. Had she been less beautiful—if Envy's self could have found aught else to sneer at—he might have felt his affection heightened by the prettiness of this mimic hand, now vaguely portrayed, now lost, now stealing forth again, and glimmering to and fro with every pulse of emotion that throbbed within her heart. But, seeing her otherwise so perfect, he found this one defect grow more and more intolerable with every moment of their united lives. It was the fatal flaw of humanity which Nature in one shape or another stamps ineffaceably on all her productions, either to imply that they are temporary and finite, or that their perfection must be wrought by toil and pain. The crimson hand expressed the ineludible grip in which mortality clutches the highest and purest of earthly mold, degrading them into kindred with the lowest, and even with the very brutes, like whom their visible frames return to dust. In this manner, selecting it as the symbol of his wife's liability to sin, sorrow, decay and death, Aylmer's sombre imagination was not long in rendering the birthmark a frightful object, causing him more trouble and horror than ever Georgiana's beauty, whether of soul or sense, had given him delight.

At all the seasons which should have been their happiest he invariably, and without intending it—nay, in spite of a purpose to the contrary—reverted to this one disastrous topic. Trifling as it at first appeared, it so connected itself with innumerable trains of thought and moods of feeling that it became the central point of all. With the morning twilight Aylmer opened his eyes upon his wife's face and recognized the symbol of imperfection; and when they sat together at the evening hearth, his eyes wandered stealthily to her cheek, and beheld, flickering with the blaze of the

---

4. male admirer
5. statue by the American sculptor, Hiram Powers (1805–1873)

woodfire, the spectral hand that wrote mortality where he would fain have worshipped. Georgiana soon learned to shudder at his gaze. It needed but a glance, with the peculiar expression that his face often wore, to change the roses of her cheek into a deathlike paleness, amid which the crimson hand was brought strongly out like a bas-relief[6] of ruby on the whitest marble.

Late one night, when the lights were growing dim, so as hardly to betray the stain on the poor wife's cheek, she herself for the first time voluntarily took up the subject.

"Do you remember, my dear Aylmer," said she, with a feeble attempt at a smile—"have you any recollection of a dream last night about this odious hand?"

"None—none whatever," replied Aylmer, starting; but then he added in a dry, cold tone, affected for the sake of concealing the real depth of his emotion, "I might well dream of it, for before I fell asleep it had taken a pretty firm hold of my fancy."

"And you did dream of it," continued Georgiana, hastily; for she dreaded lest a gush of tears should interrupt what she had to say—"a terrible dream. I wonder that you can forget it. Is it possible to forget this one expression?—'It is in her heart now: we must have it out.' Reflect, my husband; for by all means I would have you recall that dream."

The mind is in a sad state when Sleep the all-involving cannot confine her spectres within the dim region of her sway, but suffers them to break forth, affrighting this actual life with secrets that perchance belong to a deeper one. Aylmer now remembered his dream. He had fancied himself with his servant Aminadab, attempting an operation for the removal of the birthmark. But the deeper went the knife, the deeper sank the hand, until at length its tiny grasp appeared to have caught hold of Georgiana's heart, whence, however, her husband was inexorably resolved to cut or wrench it away.

When the dream had shaped itself perfectly in his memory, Aylmer sat in his wife's presence with a guilty feeling. Truth often finds its way to the mind close-muffled in robes of sleep, and then speaks with uncompromising directness of matters in regard to which we practice an unconscious self-deception during our waking moments. Until now he had not been aware of the tyrannizing influence acquired by one idea over his mind, and of the lengths which he might find in his heart to go for the sake of giving himself peace.

"Aylmer," resumed Georgiana, solemnly, "I know not what may be the cost to both of us to rid me of this fatal birthmark. Perhaps its removal may cause cureless deformity. Or, it may be, the stain goes as deep as life itself. Again, do we know that there is a possibility, on any terms, of unclasping the firm grip of this little hand which was laid upon me before I came into the world?"

"Dearest Georgiana, I have spent much thought upon the subject," hastily interrupted Aylmer; "I am convinced of the perfect practicability of its removal."

"If there be the remotest possibility of it," continued Georgiana, "let the attempt be made, at whatever risk. Danger is nothing to me, for life, while

---

6. flat piece of sculpture with figures raised slightly from the surface

this hateful mark makes me the object of your horror and disgust—life is a burden which I would fling down with joy. Either remove this dreadful hand or take my wretched life. You have deep science; all the world bears witness of it. You have achieved great wonders; cannot you remove this little, little mark which I cover with the tips of two small fingers? Is this beyond your power, for the sake of your own peace and to save your poor wife from madness?"

"Noblest, dearest, tenderest wife!" cried Aylmer, rapturously. "Doubt not my power. I have already given this matter the deepest thought—thought which might almost have enlightened me to create a being less perfect than yourself. Georgiana, you have led me deeper than ever into the heart of Science. I feel myself fully competent to render this dear cheek as faultless as its fellow, and then, most beloved, what will be my triumph when I shall have corrected what Nature left imperfect in her fairest work! Even Pygmalion, when his sculptured woman assumed life, felt not greater ecstasy than mine will be."

"It is resolved, then," said Georgiana, faintly smiling. "And, Aylmer, spare me not, though you should find the birthmark take refuge in my heart at last."

Her husband tenderly kissed her cheek—her right cheek, not that which bore the impress of the crimson hand.

The next day Aylmer apprised his wife of a plan that he had formed whereby he might have opportunity for the intense thought and constant watchfulness which the proposed operation would require, while Georgiana, likewise, would enjoy the perfect repose essential to its success. They were to seclude themselves in the extensive apartments occupied by Aylmer as a laboratory, and where during his toilsome youth he had made discoveries in the elemental powers of nature that had roused the admiration of all the learned societies in Europe. Seated calmly in this laboratory, the pale philosopher had investigated the secrets of the highest cloud-region and of the profoundest minds; he had satisfied himself of the causes that kindled and kept alive the fires of the volcano, and had explained the mystery of fountains and how it is that they gush forth, some so bright and pure and others with such rich medicinal virtues, from the dark bosom of the earth. Here, too, at an earlier period, he had studied the wonders of the human frame, and attempted to fathom the very process by which Nature assimilates all her precious influences from earth and air and from the spiritual world to create and foster man, her masterpiece. The latter pursuit, however, Aylmer had long laid aside in unwilling recognition of the truth against which all seekers sooner or later stumble—that our great creative mother, while she amuses us with apparently working in the broadest sunshine, is yet severely careful to keep her own secrets, and in spite of her pretended openness shows us nothing but results. She permits us, indeed, to mar, but seldom to mend, and, like a jealous patentee, on no account to make. Now, however, Aylmer resumed these half-forgotten investigations—not, of course, with such hopes or wishes as first suggested them, but because they involved much physiological truth and lay in the path of his proposed scheme for the treatment of Georgiana.

As he led her over the threshold of the laboratory Georgiana was cold and tremulous. Aylmer looked cheerfully into her face with intent to reassure her, but was so startled with the intense glow of the birthmark upon the whiteness of her cheek that he could not restrain a strong convulsive shudder. His wife fainted.

"Aminadab! Aminadab!" shouted Aylmer, stamping violently on the floor.

Forthwith there issued from an inner apartment a man of low stature but bulky frame, with shaggy hair hanging about his visage, which was grimed with the vapors of the furnace. This personage had been Aylmer's under-worker during his whole scientific career, and was admirably fitted for that office by his great mechanical readiness and the skill with which, while incapable of comprehending a single principle, he executed all the practical details of his master's experiments. With his vast strength, his shaggy hair, his smoky aspect, and the indescribable earthiness that incrusted him, he seemed to represent man's physical nature, while Aylmer's slender figure and pale, intellectual face were no less apt a type[7] of the spiritual element.

"Throw open the door of the boudoir, Aminadab," said Aylmer, "and burn a pastille."[8]

"Yes, master," answered Aminadab, looking intently at the lifeless form of Georgiana; and then he muttered to himself, "if she were my wife, I'd never part with that birthmark."

When Georgiana recovered consciousness, she found herself breathing an atmosphere of penetrating fragrance, the gentle potency of which had recalled her from her death-like faintness. The scene around her looked like enchantment. Aylmer had converted those smoky, dingy, sombre rooms where he had spent his brightest years in recondite pursuits into a series of beautiful apartments not unfit to be the secluded abode of a lovely woman. The walls were hung with gorgeous curtains which imparted the combina-tion of grandeur and grace that no other species of adornment can achieve, and as they fell from the ceiling to the floor their rich and ponderous folds, concealing all angles and straight lines, appeared to shut in the scene from infinite space. For aught Georgiana knew, it might be a pavilion among the clouds. And Aylmer, excluding the sunshine, which would have interfered with his chemical processes, had supplied its place with perfumed lamps emitting flames of various hue, but all uniting in a soft, empurpled radiance. He now knelt by his wife's side, watching her earnestly, but without alarm, for he was confident in his science, and felt that he could draw a magic circle round her within which no evil might intrude.

"Where am I? Ah! I remember," said Georgiana, faintly; and she placed her hand over her cheek to hide the terrible mark from her husband's eyes.

"Fear not, dearest," exclaimed he. "Do not shrink from me. Believe me, Georgiana, I even rejoice in this single imperfection, since it will be such a rapture to remove it."

"Oh, spare me!" sadly replied his wife. "Pray, do not look at it again. I never can forget that convulsive shudder."

In order to soothe Georgiana, and, as it were, to release her mind from the burden of actual things, Aylmer now put in practice some of the light

---

7. symbol
8. a medicinal tablet or mixture

and playful secrets which science had taught him among its profounder lore. Airy figures, absolutely bodiless ideas and forms of unsubstantial beauty, came and danced before her, imprinting their momentary footsteps on beams of light. Though she had some indistinct idea of the method of these optical phenomena, still the illusion was almost perfect enough to warrant the belief that her husband possessed sway over the spiritual world. Then, again, when she felt a wish to look forth from her seclusion, immediately, as if her thoughts were answered, the procession of external existence flitted across a screen. The scenery and the figures of actual life were perfectly represented, but with that bewitching yet indescribable difference which always makes a picture, an image or a shadow, so much more attractive than the original. When wearied of this, Aylmer bade her cast her eyes upon a vessel containing a quantity of earth. She did so, with little interest at first, but was soon startled to perceive the germ of a plant shooting upward from the soil. Then came the slender stalk; the leaves gradually unfolded themselves, and amid them was a perfect and lovely flower.

"It is magical," cried Georgiana; "I dare not touch it."

"Nay, pluck it," answered Aylmer—"pluck it and inhale its brief perfume while you may. The flower will wither in a few moments, and leave nothing save its brown seed-vessels; but thence may be perpetuated a race as ephemeral as itself."

But Georgiana had no sooner touched the flower than the whole plant suffered a blight, its leaves turning coal-black, as if by the agency of fire.

"There was too powerful a stimulus," said Aylmer, thoughtfully.

To make up for this abortive experiment, he proposed to take her portrait by a scientific process of his own invention. It was to be effected by rays of light striking upon a polished plate of metal. Georgiana assented, but on looking at the result was affrighted to find the features of the portrait blurred and indefinable, while the minute figure of a hand appeared where the cheek should have been. Aylmer snatched the metallic plate and threw it into a jar of corrosive acid.

Soon, however, he forgot these mortifying failures. In the intervals of study and chemical experiment he came to her flushed and exhausted, but seemed invigorated by her presence, and spoke in glowing language of the resources of his art. He gave a history of the long dynasty of the alchemists, who spent so many ages in quest of the universal solvent by which the golden principle might be elicited from all things vile and base. Aylmer appeared to believe that by the plainest scientific logic it was altogether within the limits of possibility to discover this long-sought medium; but, he added, a philosopher who should go deep enough to acquire the power would attain too lofty a wisdom to stoop to the exercise of it. Not less singular were his opinions in regard to the Elixir Vitae. He more than intimated that it was at his option to concoct a liquid that should prolong life for years—perhaps interminably—but that it would produce a discord in nature which all the world, and chiefly the quaffer of the immortal nostrum,[9] would find cause to curse.

---

9. medicine

"Aylmer, are you in earnest?" asked Georgiana, looking at him with amazement and fear. "It is terrible to possess such power, or even to dream of possessing it."

"Oh, do not tremble, my love," said her husband; "I would not wrong either you or myself by working such inharmonious effects upon our lives. But I would have you consider how trifling, in comparison, is the skill requisite to remove this little hand."

At the mention of the birthmark, Georgiana, as usual, shrank as if a red-hot iron had touched her cheek.

Again Aylmer applied himself to his labors. She could hear his voice in the distant furnace-room giving directions to Aminadab, whose harsh, uncouth, misshapen tones were audible in response, more like the grunt or growl of a brute than human speech. After hours of absence Aylmer reappeared, and proposed that she should now examine his cabinet of chemical products and natural treasures of the earth. Among the former he showed her a small vial in which, he remarked, was contained a gentle yet most powerful fragrance capable of impregnating all the breezes that blow across a kingdom. They were of inestimable value, the contents of that little vial; and as he said so he threw some of the perfume into the air and filled the room with piercing and invigorating delight.

"And what is this?" asked Georgiana, pointing to a small crystal globe containing a gold-colored liquid. "It is so beautiful to the eye that I could imagine it the Elixir of Life."

"In one sense it is," replied Aylmer—"or, rather, the Elixir of Immortality. It is the most precious poison that ever was concocted in this world. By its aid I could apportion the lifetime of any mortal at whom you might point your finger. The strength of the dose would determine whether he were to linger out years or drop dead in the midst of a breath. No king on his guarded throne could keep his life, if I, in my private station, should deem that the welfare of millions justified me in depriving him of it."

"Why do you keep such a terrific drug?" inquired Georgiana, in horror.

"Do not mistrust me, dearest," said her husband, smiling; "its virtuous potency is yet greater than its harmful one. But see! here is a powerful cosmetic. With a few drops of this in a vase of water freckles may be washed away as easily as the hands are cleansed. A stronger infusion would take the blood out of the cheek and leave the rosiest beauty a pale ghost."

"It is with this lotion that you intend to bathe my cheek?" asked Georgiana, anxiously.

"Oh, no!" hastily replied her husband; "this is merely superficial. Your case demands a remedy that shall go deeper."

In his interviews with Georgiana, Aylmer generally made minute in-quiries as to her sensations, and whether the confinement of the rooms and the temperature of the atmosphere agreed with her. These questions had such a particular drift that Georgiana began to conjecture that she was already subjected to certain physical influences, either breathed in with the fragrant air or taken with her food. She fancied, likewise—but it might be altogether fancy—that there was a stirring up of her system, a strange, indefinite sensation creeping through her veins and tingling, half painfully, half pleasurably, at her heart. Still, whenever she dared to look into the mirror, there she beheld herself pale as a white rose and with the crimson birthmark stamped upon her cheek. Not even Aylmer now hated it so much as she.

To dispel the tedium of the hours which her husband found it necessary to devote to the processes of combination and analysis, Georgiana turned over the volumes of his scientific library. In many dark old tomes she met with chapters full of romance and poetry. They were the works of the philosophers of the Middle Ages, such as Albertus Magnus, Cornelius Agrippa, Paracelsus, and the famous friar who created the prophetic Brazen Head. All these antique naturalists stood in advance of their centuries, yet were imbued with some of their credulity, and therefore were believed, and perhaps imagined themselves, to have acquired from the investigation of nature a power above nature, and from physics a sway over the spiritual world. Hardly less curious and imaginative were the early volumes of the *Transactions* of the Royal Society, in which the members, knowing little of the limits of natural possibility, were continually recording wonders or proposing methods whereby wonders might be wrought.

But to Georgiana the most engrossing volume was a large folio from her husband's own hand in which he had recorded every experiment of his scientific career, with its original aim, the methods adopted for its development and its final success or failure, with the circumstances to which either event was attributable. The book, in truth, was both the history and emblem of his ardent, ambitious, imaginative, yet practical and laborious life. He handled physical details as if there were nothing beyond them, yet spiritualized them all, and redeemed himself from materialism by his strong and eager aspiration toward the infinite. In his grasp the veriest clod of earth assumed a soul. Georgiana, as she read, reverenced Aylmer, and loved him more profoundly than ever, but with less entire dependence on his judgment than heretofore. Much as he had accomplished, she could not but observe that his most splendid successes were almost invariably failures, if compared with the ideal at which he aimed. His brightest diamonds were the merest pebbles, and felt to be so by himself, in comparison with the inestimable gems which lay hidden beyond his reach. The volume rich with achievements that had won renown for its author was yet as melancholy a record as ever mortal hand had penned. It was the sad confession and continued exemplification of the shortcomings of the composite man, the spirit burdened with clay and working in matter, and of the despair that assails the higher nature at finding itself so miserably thwarted by the earthly part. Perhaps every man of genius, in whatever sphere, might recognize the image of his own experience in Aylmer's journal.

So deeply did these reflections affect Georgiana that she laid her face upon the open volume and burst into tears. In this situation she was found by her husband.

"It is dangerous to read in a sorcerer's book," said he, with a smile, though his countenance was uneasy and displeased. "Georgiana, there are pages in that volume which I can scarcely glance over and keep my senses. Take heed lest it prove as detrimental to you."

"It has made me worship you more than ever," said she.

"Ah! wait for this one success," rejoined he, "then worship me if you will. I shall deem myself hardly unworthy of it. But come! I have sought you for the luxury of your voice; sing to me, dearest."

So she poured out the liquid music of her voice to quench the thirst of his spirit. He then took his leave with a boyish exuberance of gayety, assuring her that her seclusion would endure but a little longer, and that the result was already certain. Scarcely had he departed, when Georgiana felt irresistibly impelled to follow him. She had forgotten to inform Aylmer of a symptom which for two or three hours past had begun to excite her attention. It was a sensation in the fatal birthmark—not painful, but which induced a restlessness throughout her system. Hastening after her husband, she intruded for the first time into the laboratory.

The first thing that struck her eye was the furnace, that hot and feverish worker, with the intense glow of its fire, which by the quantities of soot clustered above it seemed to have been burning for ages. There was a distilling apparatus in full operation. Around the room were retorts, tubes, cylinders, crucibles and other apparatus of chemical research. An electrical machine stood ready for immediate use. The atmosphere felt oppresively close, and was tainted with gaseous odors which had been tormented forth by the processes of Science. The severe and homely simplicity of the apartment, with its naked walls and brick pavement, looked strange, accustomed as Georgiana had become to the fantastic elegance of her boudoir. But what chiefly—indeed, almost solely—drew her attention was the aspect of Aylmer himself.

He was pale as death, anxious and absorbed, and hung over the furnace as if it depended upon his utmost watchfulness whether the liquid which it was distilling should be the draught of immortal happiness or misery. How different from the sanguine and joyous mien that he had assumed for Georgiana's encouragement!

"Carefully now, Aminadab! Carefully, thou human machine! Carefully, thou man of clay!" muttered Aylmer, more to himself than his assistant. "Now, if there be a thought too much or too little it is all over."

"Hoh! hoh!" mumbled Aminadab. "Look, master, look!"

Aylmer raised his eyes hastily, and at first reddened, then grew paler than ever, on beholding Georgiana. He rushed toward her and seized her arm with a grip that left the print of his fingers upon it.

"Why do you come hither? Have you no trust in your husband?" cried he, impetuously. "Would you throw the blight of that fatal birthmark over my labors? It is not well done. Go, prying woman, go!"

"Nay, Aylmer," said Georgiana, with a firmness of which she possessed no stinted endowment, "it is not you that have a right to complain. You mistrust your wife. You have concealed the anxiety with which you watch the development of this experiment. Think not so unworthily of me, my husband. Tell me all the risk we run, and fear not that I shall shrink, for my share in it is far less than your own!"

"No, no, Georgiana!" said Aylmer, impatiently; "it must not be."

"I submit," replied she, calmly. "And, Aylmer, I shall quaff whatever draught you bring me, but it will be on the same principle that would induce me to take a dose of poison if offered by your hand."

"My noble wife!" said Aylmer, deeply moved; "I knew not the height and depth of your nature until now. Nothing shall be concealed. Know, then, that this crimson hand, superficial as it seems, has clutched its grasp into your being with a strength of which I had no previous conception. I have already administered agents powerful enough to do aught except to change your entire physical system. Only one thing remains to be tried; if that fails us, we are ruined!"

"Why did you hesitate to tell me this?" asked she.

"Because, Georgiana," said Aylmer, in a low voice, "there is danger."

" 'Danger'! There is but one danger—that this horrible stigma shall be left upon my cheek," cried Georgiana. "Remove it, remove it, whatever be the cost, or we shall both go mad."

"Heaven knows your words are too true," said Aylmer, sadly. "And now, dearest, return to your boudoir. In a little while all will be tested."

He conducted her back, and took leave of her with a solemn tenderness which spoke far more than his words how much was now at stake.

After his departure Georgiana became wrapped in musings. She considered the character of Aylmer, and did it completer justice than at any previous moment. Her heart exulted while it trembled at his honorable love, so pure and lofty that it would accept nothing less than perfection, nor miserably make itself contented with an earthlier nature than he had dreamed of. She felt how much more precious was such a sentiment than that meaner kind which would have borne with the imperfection for her sake, and have been guilty of treason to holy love by degrading its perfect idea to the level of the actual. And with her whole spirit she prayed that for a single moment she might satisfy his highest and deepest conception. Longer than one moment, she well knew, it could not be, for his spirit was ever on the march, ever ascending, and each instant required something that was beyond the scope of the instant before.

The sound of her husband's footsteps aroused her. He bore a crystal goblet containing a liquor colorless as water, but bright enough to be the draught of immortality. Aylmer was pale, but it seemed rather the consequence of a highly-wrought state of mind and tension of spirit than of fear or doubt.

"The concoction of the draught has been perfect," said he in answer to Georgiana's look. "Unless all my science have deceived me, it cannot fail."

"Save on your account, my dearest Aylmer," observed his wife, "I might wish to put off this birthmark of mortality by relinquishing mortality itself, in preference to any other mode. Life is but a sad possession to those who have attained precisely the degree of moral advancement at which I stand. Were I weaker and blinder, it might be happiness; were I stronger, it might be endured hopefully; but, being what I find myself, methinks I am of all mortals the most fit to die."

"You are fit for heaven without tasting death," replied her husband. "But why do you speak of dying? The draught cannot fail. Behold its effect upon this plant."

On the window-seat there stood a geranium diseased with yellow blotches, which had overspread all its leaves. Aylmer poured a small quantity of the liquid upon the soil in which it grew. In a little time, when the roots of the plant had taken up the moisture, the unsightly blotches began to be extinguished in a living verdure.

"There needed no proof," said Georgiana quietly. "Give me the goblet; I joyfully stake all upon your word."

"Drink, then, thou lofty creature!" exclaimed Aylmer, with fervid admiration. "There is no taint of imperfection on thy spirit. Thy sensible[10] frame, too, shall soon be all perfect."

She quaffed the liquid, and returned the goblet to his hand.

"It is grateful,"[11] said she, with a placid smile. "Methinks it is like water from a heavenly fountain, for it contains I know not what of unobtrusive fragrance and deliciousness. It allays a feverish thirst that had parched me for many days. Now, dearest, let me sleep. My earthly senses are closing over my spirit like the leaves around the heart of a rose at sunset."

She spoke the last words with a gentle reluctance, as if it required almost more energy than she could command to pronounce the faint and lingering syllables. Scarcely had they loitered through her lips ere she was lost in slumber. Aylmer sat by her side, watching her aspect with the emotions proper to a man the whole value of whose existence was involved in the process now to be tested. Mingled with this mood, however, was the philosophic investigation characteristic of the man of science. Not the minutest symptom escaped him. A heightened flush of the cheek, a slight irregularity of breath, a quiver of the eyelid, a hardly perceptible tremor through the frame—such were the details which as the moments passed he wrote down in his folio volume. Intense thought had set its stamp upon every previous page of that volume, but the thoughts of years were all concentrated upon the last.

While thus employed he failed not to gaze often at the fatal hand, and not without a shudder. Yet once, by a strange and unaccountable impulse, he pressed it with his lips. His spirit recoiled, however, in the very act, and Georgiana, out of the midst of her deep sleep, moved uneasily and murmured, as if in remonstrance. Again Aylmer resumed his watch. Nor was it without avail. The crimson hand, which at first had been strongly visible upon the marble paleness of Georgiana's cheek, now grew more faintly outlined. She remained not less pale than ever, but the birthmark with every breath that came and went lost somewhat of its former distinctness. Its presence had been awful; its departure was more awful still. Watch the stain of the rainbow fading out of the sky, and you will know how that mysterious symbol passed away.

"By Heaven, it is wellnigh gone!" said Aylmer to himself, in almost irrepressible ecstasy. "I can scarcely trace it now. Success! Success! And now it is like the faintest rose-color; the slightest flush of blood across her cheek would overcome it. But she is so pale!"

He drew aside the window-curtain and suffered the light of natural day to fall into the room and rest upon her cheek. At the same time he heard a gross, hoarse chuckle which he had long known as his servant Aminadab's expression of delight.

"Ah, clod! Ah, earthly mass!" cried Aylmer, laughing in a sort of frenzy. "You have served me well! Matter and spirit—earth and heaven—have both done their part in this. Laugh, thing of the senses! You have earned the right to laugh."

---

10. physical
11. pleasing

These exclamations broke Georgiana's sleep. She slowly unclosed her eyes and gazed into the mirror which her husband had arranged for that purpose. A faint smile flitted over her lips when she recognized how barely perceptible was now that crimson hand which had once blazed forth with such disastrous brilliancy as to scare away all their happiness. But then her eyes sought Aylmer's face with a trouble and anxiety that he could by no means account for.

"My poor Aylmer!" murmured she.

"Poor? Nay—richest, happiest, most favored!" exclaimed he. "My peerless bride, it is successful. You are perfect!"

"My poor Aylmer!" she repeated with a more than human tenderness. "You have aimed loftily; you have done nobly. Do not repent that with so high and pure a feeling you have rejected the best the earth could offer. Aylmer, dearest Aylmer, I am dying."

Alas, it was too true! The fatal hand had grappled with the mystery of life, and was the bond by which an angelic spirit kept itself in union with a mortal frame. As the last crimson tint of the birthmark—that sole token of human imperfection—faded from her cheek, the parting breath of the now perfect woman passed into the atmosphere, and her soul, lingering a moment near her husband, took its heavenward flight. Then a hoarse, chuckling laugh was heard again. Thus ever does the gross fatality of earth exult in its invariable triumph over the immortal essence which in this dim sphere of half development demands the completeness of a higher state. Yet, had Aylmer reached a profounder wisdom, he need not thus have flung away the happiness which would have woven his mortal life of the selfsame texture with the celestial. The momentary circumstance was too strong for him: he failed to look beyond the shadowy scope of time, and, living once for all in eternity, to find the perfect future in the present.

Questions for Writing or Discussion

1. What does the birthmark represent? Does the author tell us directly, or is his meaning obscure? What does Aminadab represent? What does the failure of the experiment represent?
2. Does the philosophy in the story overwhelm the human interest? Do we care about Aylmer and Georgiana as man and woman, as husband and wife, or are we interested in them only as symbols?
3. What elements of conventional science fiction and horror stories does the author incorporate into his work?
4. Apart from the author's language, what strikes you as being particularly old-fashioned about the story?
5. What does the author respect about science and scientists? What does he fear? Do you feel his fears have become more relevant or less relevant with the passage of time?
6. Aylmer's attitudes need not be restricted to scientists. Where else can the refusal to accept anything less than perfection lead to disaster?

❧ Careful attention to details is necessary for ❧
the success of your research project.

PART 3

RESEARCH

14
WRITING A RESEARCH PAPER

CHAPTER 14

WRITING
A RESEARCH
PAPER

Not much is certain in this world—and that familiar truth includes Freshman English. When you begin Freshman English, you can't be certain if your instructor will be casual about grammar and spelling or care about nothing *but* grammar and spelling. Depending on which instructor you have, most of your papers may be essays based on personal experiences or formal analyses of class readings. Some instructors seem to show movies at every meeting; others seem to think they are making an audiovisual breakthrough when they write two words on the blackboard. At least one certainty does exist, however. Sometime during your year of Freshman English, you are going to be assigned a research paper.

A research paper (or "library paper" or "term paper") is a nearly universal assignment not merely because it's an academic tradition, but also because it serves a number of worthwhile, practical purposes:

1. The research paper teaches you how to handle substantially longer pieces of writing than does the normal classroom theme. At a bare minimum, the research paper will be five or six typed pages; most papers will probably be two or three times as long.
2. The research paper teaches you how to use the library. It's probably only a slight exaggeration to state that any adequate library contains most of the information in the world, all accessible and all free. You may not want to know everything, but when you want to know *something*, it's important to be able to find it.
3. The research paper makes you an expert. Whatever your subject, by the time you have completed your paper, you

know more about that subject than at least 99 percent of the
rest of the people on the planet. The satisfactions are deep
and lasting. Few differences are greater than the difference
between the dabbler and the authority.

4. The research paper prepares you for success in your other
   courses. To some extent, teaching how to write research
   papers is a service the English department performs for other
   departments. As you go through college, particularly as you
   take more and more upper-level courses, you will find increasing stress being placed on research papers. At the upper
   levels, instructors tend to want students to demonstrate real
   mastery of the course materials—mastery that can come only
   through intense exploration of a subject rather than the dash-
   ing off of a fifteen- or thirty-minute essay during a mid-term
   or final exam.

THE REPORT AND THE THESIS PAPER

Virtually every research paper requires that you gather facts, alleged
facts, and opinions (sometimes conflicting opinions) from a variety
of sources and that you organize and present those facts and
opinions in your own way through your own hard work. Every
research paper requires that you *document* in footnotes and a bibliography whatever sources you have used. Still, there are two distinct
kinds of research paper. The first is the *report*. In the report, you
present objectively the information available about your subject; you
are not concerned with expressing your own point of view. A paper
titled *Recent Advances in Treating Leukemia* or *The World Series Scandal
of 1919* might be a report: in such a paper you would present all the
known facts, including impartial accounts of any differing opinions,
but you would have no particular opinion of your own to offer to the
reader. The second kind of research paper is one with a *thesis*. In a
thesis paper, you do just as much research as for the straight report,
but you feel that the facts about your chosen subject call for interpretation, and you try to persuade the reader that your interpretation or
opinion is correct. Rather than merely stating the facts, you use
them to back up your opinion. For example, on pp. 324–337, a
student thesis paper strongly advocates going ahead with the building of nuclear power plants.

Many subjects, of course, can be dealt with either as a report *or*
as a thesis paper. Reports titled *Custer's Last Stand* and *The Lizzie
Borden Murder Case*[1] would give the reader information about two

---

1. "Lizzie Borden took an ax/And gave her mother forty whacks./When she saw what
she had done,/She gave her father forty-one."

colorful episodes of the American past. Thesis papers on the same subjects would give the reader all or most of the same information, but the main purpose would be to argue, for example, that the battle of the Little Big Horn would never have taken place if it had not been for Custer's foolishness and vanity or that Lizzie Borden was really innocent of the murder charge brought against her.

Before you get deeply involved in your research project, make sure you know whether your instructor wants a report or a thesis paper, or if either will be acceptable.

CHOOSING A SUBJECT

The best subject for your research paper is often one that you are generally interested in and curious about. If you start out knowing everything or thinking that you know everything about your subject, all your research may be boring repetition of the familiar, and, if you are writing a thesis paper, you may not be sufficiently open-minded to evaluate fairly any views that conflict with your own. On the other hand, you'll naturally want to avoid subjects that may demand technical knowledge you do not possess. You may be vaguely interested in Einstein's theory of relativity, but that topic would surely be a poor choice for most students.

As you begin to formulate a subject, remember the importance of limiting it. *Custer's Last Stand* and *The Lizzie Borden Murder Case* might make good papers. No good paper of reasonable length could be written, however, on such topics as *Famous Battles* or *Great Trials*.

One final suggestion: Don't be too eager to settle on any single topic immediately. If you have two or three possibilities in mind, so much the better. There may not be as much information available on your first choice as you had hoped, and it's comforting to have something ready to fall back on.

PRELIMINARY READING AND THE PRELIMINARY OUTLINE

Once you have an idea of the topic or topics you might be interested in, it's time for a trip to the library. Your purpose is to do some fairly easygoing "reading around." You want to make sure that the subject that seemed so interesting when you were thinking about it is still interesting when you are reading about it. You want to acquire enough of a general perspective on your subject to be able to respond effectively when you begin more serious and detailed reading.

Usually, the most sensible place in which to begin reading around is a recent edition of a general adult encyclopedia such as the

Encyclopaedia Britannica or the *Encyclopedia Americana*. No significant research paper is going to use an encyclopedia article as a major source; the article contains only a broad survey of its subject, whereas a research paper explores its subject in depth. At this stage, however, a broad survey is all you want.

In fairness, some encyclopedia articles, especially the longer ones, may be written by leading authorities and contain much useful information. In such cases, you needn't be shy about using the articles as *minor* sources. If you come across an article that strikes you as potentially usable in your paper, make out a bibliography card for it (see pp. 298–303) and take notes (see pp. 303–308).

Some encyclopedia articles may also be valuable because they conclude with a brief list of outstanding books and articles on their subject. These references can help you to determine whether enough material is available for your paper, and they can give you some specific titles to look for immediately.

As good as or better than general encyclopedias for preliminary reading may be a number of specialized encyclopedias, dictionaries, and other reference works. For example, if you are writing about an American who is *no longer living,* the *Dictionary of American Biography* may have an excellent article. The *Dictionary of National Biography* supplies similar information about *English* figures who are no longer living. A brief list of some other specialized reference works follows:

ART

Britannica Encyclopaedia of American Art (1973)

Encyclopedia of World Art, 15 vols. (1959–69)

Bernard S. Myers, ed., *Encyclopedia of Painting,* 3rd ed. (1970)

BUSINESS

Douglas Greenwald, *The McGraw-Hill Dictionary of Modern Economics,* 2nd ed. (1973)

Glen G. Munn, *Encyclopedia of Banking and Finance,* 7th ed. (1973)

Harold S. Sloan and Arnold J. Zurcher, *A Dictionary of Economics,* 5th ed. (1970)

EDUCATION

Encyclopedia of Education, 10 vols. (1971)

Encyclopedia of Educational Research, 4th ed. (1969)

HISTORY

James Truslow Adams, ed., *Dictionary of American History,* 2nd ed., 6 vols. (1942–1963)

The Cambridge Ancient History, 3rd ed., 12 vols. (1970–75)

The Cambridge Medieval History, 8 vols. (1911–36)

The Cambridge Modern History, 14 vols. (1902–26)

William L. Langer, *An Encyclopedia of World History*, 5th ed. (1972)

LITERATURE

Albert C. Baugh, *A Literary History of England*, 2nd ed. (1967)

John Buchanan-Brown, ed., *Cassell's Encyclopedia of World Literature*, rev. ed. (1973)

James D. Hart, *The Oxford Companion to American Literature*, 4th ed. (1965)

Phyllis Hartnoll, *The Oxford Companion to the Theatre*, 3rd ed. (1967)

Paul Harvey, *The Oxford Companion to English Literature*, 4th ed. (1967)

Robert Spiller and others, *Literary History of the United States*, 4th ed., 2 vols. (1974)

Roger Whitlow, *Black American Literature* (1973)

Percy Wilson and Bonamy Dobree, *The Oxford History of English Literature*, 12 vols. (1945–63)

MUSIC

Sir George Grove, *Dictionary of Music and Musicians*, ed. Eric Blom, 5th ed., 10 vols. (1955; supplement 1961)

The New Oxford History of Music, 10 vols. (1954–74)

Percy A. Scholes, *The Oxford Companion to Music*, 10th ed. (1970)

PHILOSOPHY

Frederick C. Copleston, *A History of Philosophy*, 8 vols. (1947–66)

Paul Edwards, ed., *The Encyclopedia of Philosophy*, 4 vols. (1973)

PSYCHOLOGY

H. J. Eysenck and others, *Encyclopedia of Psychology*, 3 vols. (1972)

Robert M. Goldenson, *The Encyclopedia of Human Behavior*, 2 vols. (1970)

RELIGION

F. L. Cross and Elizabeth A. Livingstone, *The Oxford Dictionary of the Christian Church* (1974)

The New Catholic Encyclopedia, 15 vols. (1967)

Geoffrey Parrinder, *A Dictionary of Non-Christian Religions* (1973)

Cecil Roth, ed., *The Standard Jewish Encyclopedia*, rev. ed. (1962)

SCIENCE

McGraw-Hill Encyclopedia of Science and Technology, 3rd ed., 15 vols. (1971)

Van Nostrand's Scientific Encyclopedia, 4th ed. (1968)

SOCIAL SCIENCE AND POLITICS

John P. Davis, ed., *The American Negro Reference Book* (1966)

Bert F. Hoselitz, ed., *A Reader's Guide to the Social Sciences*, rev. ed. (1972)

Barry T. Klein, ed., *Reference Encyclopedia of the American Indian*, 2nd ed. (1973–74)

E. R. A. Seligman and Alvin Johnson, eds., *Encyclopedia of the Social Sciences,* 15 vols. (1930–34)

David L. Sills, ed., *International Encyclopedia of the Social Sciences,* 17 vols. (1968)

Edward C. Smith and Arnold J. Zurcher, eds., *Dictionary of American Politics,* 2nd ed. (1968)

If all goes well in your preliminary reading, you should know enough to feel confident about your choice of subject and perhaps enough to be able to limit your subject further than you originally intended. Best of all, you should be in a position to draw up a *preliminary outline* or scratch outline indicating what the major divisions of your paper are likely to be. For a paper on the Lizzie Borden murder case, to mention one example, you might construct the following headings: The Crime, The Trial, The Controversy. Nothing elaborate is needed; the outline will be revised and expanded as you go along. In the meantime, the preliminary outline enables you to read and take notes as part of a systematic plan. You'll know what information is relevant and irrelevant, what divisions of the paper you need to work on more thoroughly, and so on.

When your preliminary outline is completed, it's time for some serious reading, and that brings us to the subject of *bibliography.*

A WORKING BIBLIOGRAPHY

A bibliography, in the sense that you will be using the term, is a list of books, articles, and other publications which serve as the sources of information for your paper. There are two kinds of bibliographies: the *working* bibliography and the *final* bibliography. The working bibliography is a set of cards listing any sources which might be useful to you. The final bibliography, which you will prepare after you complete your paper, is the list of sources you actually use in writing the paper. Since you cannot know in advance which books or articles will contain useful information, you will have to prepare *bibliography cards* for every source that looks useful. As you read, you will eliminate cards for those sources which turn out not to be helpful.

Finding Sources

The two best places to look for names of books and articles are the book index and the periodical indexes. These, like the encyclopedias you have already consulted, are located in the reference room of the library.

THE BOOK CATALOGUE

The forms of book catalogues differ from library to library. Some libraries use computer printouts, bound into books, to list their holdings. Some libraries list their holdings on microfiche cards, sheets of microfilm about the size of filing cards. Since one microfiche card can list approximately a hundred titles, its use saves a great deal of library space. Its drawback to you as a researcher is that, to find the titles you want, you will have to learn to use the reading machine which will be located near the files of cards. Using the machine is not difficult, but you should probably get help from the librarian the first time you try it.

The most common method of listing books is by means of a *card catalogue,* an alphabetical filing system in which a separate card is used to index every book in the library. If you can use the card catalogue, you can use the other kinds of catalogues, since all provide essentially the same information. For this reason, we will limit our discussion of book catalogues to the *card catalogue.*

The library will list every book it holds three times: one card will list the book by its *subject,* one will list it by *author,* and the third will list the book by *title. A Swinger of Birches: A Portrait of Robert Frost* by Sidney Cox, for example, would be listed among the S's (for *Swinger*) in the title file—*A, an,* and *the* are not used in alphabetizing. The book would also be listed among the F's (for *Frost, Robert*) in the subject file, and among the C's (for *Cox, Sidney*) in the author file. A set of catalogue cards is shown on p. 296.

In addition to listing books by author, title, and subject, most card catalogues usually also contain *cross-reference cards* which suggest other subject headings. If, for example, you looked up *newspapers,* a cross-reference card might tell you to "see *journalism.*"

PERIODICAL INDEXES

To find magazine or journal articles, you will need to consult the *periodical indexes.* The most frequently used index is *The Readers' Guide to Periodical Literature,* an index of articles which have appeared in popular magazines during any given year since 1906. *The Readers' Guide* appears monthly in pamphlet form and is permanently bound every two years. If your subject is very current, you would, of course, use the most recent *Readers' Guide.* If, however, your subject deals with a particular period in the past, you would want to consult *The Readers' Guide* for the year or years that are appropriate for your subject. If, for instance, your subject is the presidency of Franklin Roosevelt, you would surely want to consult *The Readers' Guide* for the years 1933–1945, in addition to consulting guides of later years to see how Roosevelt's administration was evaluated after his death.

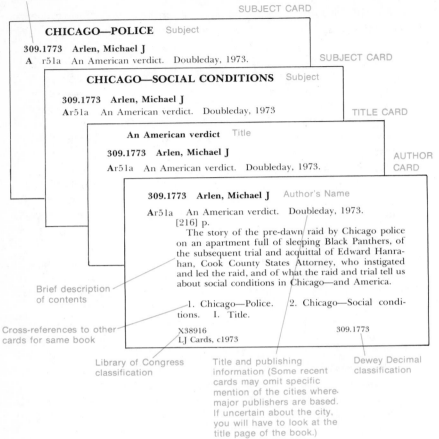

Call Number

SUBJECT CARD

CHICAGO—POLICE   Subject

309.1773   Arlen, Michael J
A   r51a   An American verdict. Doubleday, 1973.

SUBJECT CARD

CHICAGO—SOCIAL CONDITIONS   Subject

309.1773   Arlen, Michael J
Ar51a   An American verdict.   Doubleday, 1973

TITLE CARD

An American verdict   Title

309.1773   Arlen, Michael J
Ar51a   An American verdict.   Doubleday, 1973.

AUTHOR
CARD

309.1773   Arlen, Michael J   Author's Name

Ar51a   An American verdict.   Doubleday, 1973.
[216] p.
     The story of the pre-dawn raid by Chicago police
on an apartment full of sleeping Black Panthers, of
the subsequent trial and acquittal of Edward Hanra-
han, Cook County States Attorney, who instigated
and led the raid, and of what the raid and trial tell us
about social conditions in Chicago—and America.

1. Chicago—Police. 2. Chicago—Social conditions.   I. Title.

X38916
LJ Cards, c1973

309.1773

Brief description
of contents

Cross-references to other
cards for same book

Library of Congress
classification

Title and publishing
information (Some recent
cards may omit specific
mention of the cities where
major publishers are based.
If uncertain about the city,
you will have to look at the
title page of the book.)

Dewey Decimal
classification

Sample Catalogue Cards

Although the guide does index authors, you will probably find it easier to look for subject headings. When you have located the heading or headings you need, you will find listed under the headings all the articles on that subject which have appeared in popular American magazines for the period covered by the particular guide.

Because *The Readers' Guide* indexes so much material, the entries must be printed in as little space as possible. That means, for one thing, that a number of abbreviations are used. If you do not understand an abbreviation, you will find keys and explanations of all abbreviations at the beginning of each issue. The need to conserve space also means that the editors will not punctuate titles, dates, and pages as you will in your paper. Here is an example of a *Readers' Guide* entry:

RESEARCH institutions
   Thumbs down on think tanks. N. Walsh. Science
   174:1008 D 3 '71

The first line (RESEARCH institutions) is the subject heading under which the index classifies articles dealing with this topic. The next line begins the entry for one magazine article on that subject. "Thumbs down on Think Tanks" is the title of an article written by N. Walsh. The article appeared in *Science,* volume 174, page 1008, in the issue dated December 3, 1971.

The Readers' Guide is a good place to start, but it does, after all, index only popular American magazines. For most subjects, you will also want to read articles written by scholars in the field in order to get more specialized information. Almost every academic discipline has one or more journals to which specialists in the field contribute, and you would certainly want to look at their articles. To find them, you would consult the special index covering your subject. Most indexes are arranged in the same way as *The Readers' Guide,* so you will have no difficulty using the special indexes if you have mastered the use of *The Readers' Guide.*

Following is a list of some of the special indexes you might want to consult. It is by no means complete, but it will give you some idea of the kinds of indexes available. Should you want these or other special indexes, you will find them in the same area of the reference room that contains *The Readers' Guide.*

Agriculture Index
Applied Science and Technology Index
Art Index
Biological Abstracts
Business Periodicals Index
Chemical Abstracts
Educational Index
Engineering Index
Index of Economic Journals
Index to Legal Periodicals
Music Index
Social Sciences and Humanities Index

NEWSPAPER INDEXES

Unfortunately, few newspapers are indexed. Some public libraries are now making the effort to index articles on local subjects which appear in their cities' major papers, but such indexes are far from complete. The only newspaper index which gives a complete listing of every article that has appeared in its newspaper during a given year is *The New York Times Index*, which has been published since 1913. If your subject concerns a locality other than New York and you need newspaper articles from local papers, you must be prepared to page through or scan on microfilm the newspapers issued during the period your subject covers.

Making Bibliography Cards

In preparing your working bibliography, the most efficient method is to make out one three-by-five-inch card for each promising title you find. Obviously, you will not use all the sources for which you make cards, but it saves time to make cards for any title that might be useful before you begin your reading. Cards are easy to handle, and they permit you to add new sources or delete sources which turn out to be useless. Cards can also be alphabetized easily, and that will save you time when you make up your final bibliography, which must be alphabetized.

BIBLIOGRAPHY CARDS FOR BOOKS

It is important that you make proper bibliography cards as you go along because, again, following the correct procedure now will save you time and frustration when you begin to write footnotes and bibliography entries for your paper. Make certain, then, that each of your book cards includes the following information and adheres to all the given instructions on matters of form:

1. The complete call number of the book. (See sample catalogue cards on p. 296.) If you do not copy the complete call number correctly, you cannot get the book.
2. The author's name (last name first), followed by a period.
3. For an essay, a poem, a short story, or a play in a collection, the title of the relevant selection, followed by a period and enclosed in quotation marks.
4. The title of the book, underlined and followed by a period.
5. The city in which the book was published, followed by a colon.
6. The name of the publishing company, followed by a comma.
7. The copyright date, followed by a period.

Some books will require even more information. If the book is edited, the editor's name must also appear on the card, and if the book is translated, the translator's name must be given. If the book has more than one edition or has been revised, that information should appear on your card. Finally, if the work contains more than one volume, the number of volumes and the volume number you want should be indicated. (See p. 302 for sample bibliography cards.)

OTHER BIBLIOGRAPHY FORMS FOR BOOKS

A Book by Two Authors

Danziger, Marlies K., and W. Stacy Johnson. *An Introduction to Literary Criticism.* Boston: D. C. Heath and Company, 1961.

> Only the name of the first author is inverted. The order of the names is the same as that on the title page.

A Book with Three or More Authors

Watkins, Fred C., and others. *Practical English Handbook,* 4th ed. Boston: Houghton Mifflin Company, 1970.

> Only the name of the first author is given, and it is followed by the notation *and others.* The name given is the first name that appears on the title page.

A Book with an Editor

Kallsen, Loren J., ed. *The Kentucky Tragedy: A Problem in Romantic Attitudes.* Indianapolis: The Bobbs-Merrill Company, Inc., 1963.

> The editor collected several documents about a famous murder case. No authors are given, and the editor's name is listed before the title.

An Edition of an Author's Work

Thoreau, Henry David. *Collected Poems.* Ed. Carl Bode. Chicago: Packard and Co., 1943.

> However, if the editor's work rather than the text is under discussion, place the editor's name first, followed by a comma, followed by "ed." or "eds."

Stauffer, Donald A., ed. *Selected Poetry and Prose of Coleridge.* New York: The Modern Library, 1951.

Editions Other Than the First

Decker, Randall E. *Patterns of Exposition.* 5th ed. Boston: Little, Brown and Company, 1976.

> If the edition were a revised edition rather than a numbered edition, the abbreviation "rev. ed." would appear after the title.

An Edited Collection or Anthology

Schlesinger, Arthur, Jr., and Morton White, eds. *Paths of American Thought.*
Boston: Houghton Mifflin Company, 1970.

Schlesinger and White collected essays written by several
different authors.

A Translated Work

Böll, Heinrich. *End of a Mission.* Trans. Leila Vennewitz. New York:
McGraw-Hill Book Company, 1974.

A Work of More Than One Volume

Adams, Wallace E., and others, eds. *The Western World: To 1770.* 2 vols. New
York: Dodd, Mead & Company, 1968.

A Pamphlet

Treat a pamphlet as if it were a book, using the name of the
committee or organization that put the pamphlet together as
the author if no author's name is provided.

One Section of a Book Written by Several Authors

Mizener, Arthur. "To Meet Mr. Eliot." In *T. S. Eliot: A Collection of Critical
Essays.* Ed. Hugh Kenner. Englewood Cliffs, N.J.: Prentice-Hall, Inc.,
1962.

BIBLIOGRAPHY CARDS FOR MAGAZINE ARTICLES

A card for a magazine article should give the name of the
author—if an author is listed—last name first and first name followed by a period; the title of the article in quotation marks with a
period before the closing quotation marks; the name of the magazine
underlined and followed by a comma; the volume and issue
number; the date in parentheses, followed by a comma; and the
page numbers followed by a period. (See the sample bibliography
card for magazine articles on p. 302.)

OTHER BIBLIOGRAPHY FORMS FOR MAGAZINES

Lewis, Bernard. "The Return of Islam." *Commentary,* 61, No. 1 (January
1976), 39–49.

Both the volume and the issue number within that volume are
given. The figures "61, No. 1" stand for "volume 61, issue
number one."

Lamborn, R. L. "Must They Be Crazy, Mixed-up Kids?" *The New York Times
Magazine,* June 26, 1955, pp. 20–21.

The sample card (p. 302) shows the standard form for a
magazine article. The volume number appears before the date,

which is placed in parentheses, and the page numbers follow. The words "volume" and "page" or "pages" (or their abbreviations, "vol.," "p.," "pp.") are not given when both volume and page numbers appear. In the entry above, however, no volume number is given. In this case, the date does not appear in parentheses, and the abbreviation "pp." is used.

"Thoughts from the Lone Cowboy." *Time,* 109, No. 9 (February 28, 1977), 20.

No author is given. In such a case, the first part of the entry is the title of the article. The word "anonymous" (or its abbreviation, "anon.") should not be used.

BIBLIOGRAPHY CARDS FOR NEWSPAPER ARTICLES

A card for a newspaper article should give the name of the author—if an author is listed—last name first and first name followed by a period; the title of the article in quotation marks with a period before the closing quotation marks; the name of the newspaper underlined and followed by a comma; the date followed by a comma; and the page numbers, followed by a period. (See the sample bibliography card for a newspaper article on p. 302.)

If the article is unsigned, the first part of the bibliography entry is the title of the article. If a newspaper has labeled sections, the section number in which the article appeared should also be given. When a section number is given, a period follows the date.

ANOTHER BIBLIOGRAPHY FORM FOR NEWSPAPERS

"Trudeau on Separatism." *The* [Cleveland] *Plain Dealer,* February 24, 1977. Sec. A, p. 22.

If the name of the city is part of the title of the newspaper, as in *The New York Times,* it is underlined. If the name of the city is not a part of the title, the city is inserted in brackets and is not underlined. If the city is not well known, the name of the state is also included in brackets.

BIBLIOGRAPHY CARDS FOR ENCYCLOPEDIA ARTICLES

Kealunohonoku, Joan W. "Hula." *Encyclopedia Americana,* 1971, 14, 542.

The above sample shows the standard form for a signed encyclopedia article. In many encyclopedias, the author's initials are given at the end of the article. You will have to check the list of abbreviations at the beginning of the volume to find the author's name.

A card for an encyclopedia article should give the name of the author, last name first and first name followed by a period; the title of the article in quotation marks, with a period before the closing quotation marks; the name of the encyclopedia, underlined and

809.892   Call Number
M694L

Moers, Ellen!   Author
<u>Literary Women</u>!   Title
Garden City, New York: City of Publication
Publishing
Company   Doubleday & Company. Inc.,
1976   Copyright Date

BOOK WITH ONE AUTHOR

Arvin, Newton.   Author
"Homage to Robert Herrick."   Title of Article
<u>New Republic</u>,   Name of Magazine
LXXXII   Volume Number
(March 6, 1935),   Date
93 - 95.   Pages

MAGAZINE ARTICLE

Hess, John L.   Author
"A Sizzling Battle in the   Title of Article
Burger Business."
The <u>New York Times</u>,   Name of Newspaper
March 13, 1977,   Date
Sec. 3, pp. 1, 9.   Section and Pages

NEWSPAPER ARTICLE

Sample Bibliography Cards

followed by a comma; the date, followed by a comma; the volume number, followed by a comma; and the page numbers, followed by a period.

ANOTHER BIBLIOGRAPHY FORM FOR ENCYCLOPEDIAS

"Massachusetts Bay Company." *The Columbia Encyclopedia,* 1963, p. 1317.

This encyclopedia has only one volume. When no volume number is given, use the abbreviation "p." or "pp." before the page numbers.

BIBLIOGRAPHY CARDS FOR OTHER KINDS OF SOURCES

Book Review. If the book review has a title, treat the review as you would any other magazine article. If the review is untitled, treat it as follows:

Adams, Phoebe-Lou. Review of *Black Sun,* by Geoffrey Wolff. *Atlantic,* 238, No. 3 (September 1976), 99.

Interview. The title or some indication of the authority of the person interviewed is given. It is also good to include the topic of the interview as well as the place and date:

Guhde, Barbara, Associate Professor of Modern British Literature, State University College at Brockport, New York, interview in Brockport, April 26, 1977, concerning Blake's influence on the works of Joyce Cary.

Letter. Give the author, the recipient, the place and date the letter was written, and the present location of the letter.

Bohi, John. A letter in my possession to Arthur H. Adams, dated at Hamburg, Germany, September 30, 1971.

Selection from a Casebook. Give the bibliography for the original printing and follow it with the documentation for the reprint.

Maclean, Hugh N. "Conservatism in Modern American Fiction." *College English,* XV (March 1954), 315–325. Reprinted in *J. D. Salinger and the Critics.* Eds. William F. Belcher and James W. Lee. Belmont, California: Wadsworth Publishing Company, Inc., 1962.

TAKING NOTES

When you have completed your bibliography cards, you are ready to begin taking the notes which will provide the evidence for your paper. Without good notes, you cannot hope to write a good paper. What, then, are the requirements for taking good notes?

Cards for Notes

To begin with, you should take your notes on cards. Opinions vary about the size of the cards that should be used. Some researchers prefer three-by-five-inch cards, believing that a note which requires more space is probably too long. Others prefer four-by-six-inch cards, believing that some notes must be long. In addition to extra space, the four-by-six-inch card offers the advantage of being obviously distinct from your bibliography cards. But size is a matter of personal choice. Taking notes any way other than on cards is not. Taking your notes in a notebook is simply not efficient. The idea is to be able to organize and reorganize your notes according to the facts and opinions they contain, not according to the books or magazines the material came from. You can shuffle cards, but you can't reorganize material in a notebook without a lot of cutting and pasting. Rule number one, then, is *take your notes on cards.*

Scope of Notes

Rule number two is *place only one note on a card.* One note is *one* fact, *one* idea, *one* opinion. If you put two facts or ideas or opinions on one note card, one of them is likely to get buried or lost among your accumulated notes. Either that, or as you organize and reorganize your notes, you may find that you will have to recopy that second fact, idea, or opinion, or take the time to cut notes into smaller units—all very inefficient. So put *one* fact, *one* idea, or *one* opinion on a card. Of course, you should not waste time making notes of facts or opinions on information you and your reader should already know. It isn't necessary, for example, to note that George Washington was the first American president.

Content of Notes

What do you look for when taking notes? You should look for any fact, idea, or opinion not generally known which appears to relate to your topic. You will, of course, take far more notes than you need for your final paper, but if you plan to do an honest job of research, you should investigate your subject as thoroughly as you can and wait until later to start weeding out notes you don't actually need. It's easier to take a few extra notes than it is to go back to the library and reread a book or article when you discover, after you start writing the paper, that you don't have enough evidence to make a point.

Nevertheless, you should not simply take notes at random. You have begun your research with at least a vague idea of what you want to prove or report. The sooner the idea becomes definite, the more directed and less time-consuming your note taking will become. But don't worry if you find yourself taking many notes from the first sources you read. After all, the subject is fairly new to you, and everything seems important. You should soon get a focus on the material, and then you can become more selective in the notes you take.

Consider that example about the Lizzie Borden case. If you choose such a topic, you might, at first, be so fascinated by the story that you take notes on every aspect of the accused's life that could possibly have led to the crime: Her mother made her stand in the corner for hours when she was only three; her father made cutting remarks about her appearance, etc. But soon you may decide that you will not try to provide Lizzie Borden with a motive; you will begin by simply describing the crime: what happened. Once you have made that decision, your reading will be focused. You will look specifically for information about what happened at the scene of the crime.

Similarly, you can restrict the other major topics of the tentative outline. A complete description of the trial could fill a book, as you soon learn when you begin reading the evidence. You could decide, after a little reading, that you will not try to handle the testimony of character witnesses, that you will concentrate solely on physical evidence presented by the prosecution and its rebuttal by the defense. And you may decide to describe the controversy only in terms of Lizzie Borden's legal guilt or innocence, thus eliminating the need to deal with the sociological or psychological arguments that are sometimes raised in discussions of the case. Again, this kind of limiting of your topic will direct your note taking and save you a great deal of time because you will know exactly what kind of information you are looking for.

Limit your subject and your approach to it, then, just as soon as you can, so you can perform the job of note taking efficiently.

Documentation of Notes

Every note card should contain two kinds of information: the fact, idea or opinion and the exact source from which you get the information. (See the sample note cards on p. 306.) Since you have the complete data for the source on your bibliography card, you need to give yourself just enough information on the note card to refer you to the proper bibliographical reference. Usually, the author's last name and the page number from which you take the information will be sufficient. Occasionally, you will have two works by the same author. In that case, use the author's last name and an

Melville, Moby-Dick, p 165

" So that by no possibility could [Samuel Taylor] Coleridge's wild Rhyme ['The Rime of the Ancient Mariner'] have had ought to do with those mystical impressions which were mine, when I saw the bird upon our deck. For neither had I then read the Rhyme nor knew the bird to be an 'albatross.' "

A note containing a direct quotation and an insertion in brackets.

Melville, Moby-Dick, p. 165

Ishmael describes the first time he ever saw an albatross. He recounts that in "Antarctic seas," he found the bird "dashed upon the main hatches." The appearance of the bird, with its vast wings and its utter whiteness, caused him to believe he had "peeped to secrets which took hold of God" and made such an impression on him that, he says, "I bowed myself."

A note combining a paraphrase of the original and some direct quotation.

Melville, Moby-Dick, p. 165

Ishmael, while describing his feelings on first seeing an albatross, denies having read Coleridge's " The Rime of the Ancient Mariner " or even knowing the name of the bird he saw.

A note containing a paraphrase of the original material.

Melville, Letter to Hawthorne, pp. 557-559

" Let any clergyman try to preach the Truth from its very stronghold, the pulpit, and they [the mass of men] would ride him out of his church on his own pulpit bannister.... Why so? Truth is ridiculous to men [because they do not understand that Truth involves both heart and mind]. (557)
. . . .
The reason the mass of men fear God, and at bottom dislike Him, is because they rather distrust His heart, and fancy Him all brain like a watch." (559)

A note containing a direct quotation from which several paragraphs have been omitted.

Sample Note Cards

abbreviated form of the work's title to distinguish one source from another. If no author is given, use an abbreviation of the title of the book or article. Do not, however, use simply the name of a magazine. You could, for example, be using several articles from various issues of *Time*. If you simply write *"Time,* p. 118" on your note card, you won't have enough information to refer you to the bibliography card which lists the particular article from which you are taking notes.

Quotation of Sources

You may quote the actual wording used in your source, or you may *paraphrase*—that is, put in your own words—the facts or ideas contained in the original. But if you do quote your source, you must be certain that you put quotation marks around the material you take. It may be a month or more between the time you take the note and the time you write your paper, and you don't want any uncertainty about which words are yours and which are those of the original author. You must also be certain that you copy the quotation exactly as it appears in the original. If the original has an obvious error, copy the error and follow it in brackets with [*sic*], the Latin word for "thus." Underline *sic* when you type or write the word. In print, the word would be italicized.

Occasionally, you may want to quote only parts of an entire passage. If you leave out a whole paragraph or two, indicate the omission by placing spaced dots all the way across the card. If you leave out a part of a sentence or one or two sentences, indicate the omission by placing three spaced dots (an ellipsis) where the sentence or part of the sentence has been left out. If you omit the beginning of a sentence, place the quotation marks *before* the ellipsis. If you omit the end of a sentence, place the quotation marks *after* the ellipsis and the end punctuation (period, question mark, or exclamation point).

A word or two of caution about using the ellipsis: Never alter the meaning of the original by using an ellipsis. If the original statement reads, "This is not the most exciting movie of the year," using an ellipsis to omit the word *not* would be dishonest. Secondly, be sure that you still have a complete sentence when you use the ellipsis. Don't omit from the sentence important elements such as subjects and verbs.

When quoting, you will sometimes find it necessary to clarify a word or date in the original quotation because you are taking the words out of context. Pronouns, for example, may need clarification. In context, "He suffered extreme hardships" may be perfectly clear.

Isolated on a note card, however, the pronoun *he* may need to be explained. If you want to insert a word, phrase, or figure into the quotation, do so by putting the information in *brackets,* not parentheses: "He [Lincoln] suffered extreme hardships." Or the original might read, "In that year, he faced the greatest crisis of his life." The sentence, taken out of context, does not identify the year. You would want to insert it: "In that year [1839], he faced the greatest crisis of his life."

Paraphrase of Sources

Despite our lengthy advice on how to handle quotations, we urge you to quote sparingly. Most of your notes should be paraphrases—that is, summaries of the original material. Of course, if you are in a hurry and don't have time to think about the best way to paraphrase a note, rather than risk plagiarism (see "Plagiarism," p. 316), do quote the material and later decide how best to put it in your own words.

Disagreements: Facts and Opinions

One final warning on note taking: As you take notes, don't assume that just because something is in print, it must be true. Be careful to distinguish between a writer's statement of fact and expression of opinion. There is a world of difference between saying that Aaron Burr was the vice-president of the United States and saying that Aaron Burr was a scoundrel. In rare cases in which there appears to be an outright disagreement between authors on matters of fact, slam on your mental brakes and do some fast checking. One of the standard reference works or encyclopedias might be a good source for resolving such disagreements or disputes. When you don't feel you have sufficient basis for deciding which opinion is correct, it seems simple common sense to acknowledge frankly the difference of opinion and to present both opinions as honestly as possible.

OUTLINING

The research paper must meet the same requirements of good writing as any other paper you have written in your English course. It must have a thesis or purpose. It must support the thesis or purpose by using specific facts presented in specific language. And it must be organized; therefore, you must prepare a formal, written outline. The mental outline that may have been enough for a short theme will not be of any use for a research paper.

Although you may already have written outlines for many papers, we urge you, in case you have forgotten any important rules about outlining, to reread Chapter 3 of the text. A good outline is a good outline—whether it is for a four-paragraph essay or for a ten-page research paper. But we won't try to convince you that writing a good outline for a research paper is as easy as writing one for a four-paragraph paper. The research paper is certainly the longest and most complex paper you will write in your freshman English course, and it requires careful planning.

Making a Slug Outline

Start by reading and rereading all your notes very carefully. You have accumulated the notes over a period of weeks, and you may not have a precise picture of just what material you have gathered. Read the notes carefully, then. Some notes will have to be set aside. But in the others, you will begin to see a pattern. You will find that you have several groups of notes, each group relating to a single subject. If you took notes on the Lizzie Borden case, for example, you would probably have several notes which could be headed *reporting the crime,* let's say, or others which could be headed *clues at scene.* When you are familiar enough with your notes that you can arrange them in piles according to single headings, you are ready to write a *slug*—that is, a brief heading which indicates the content of the note—on each card. Don't try to be creative here and write a different heading for each card; you *should* have several cards with the same slug.

Because you may change your mind about the point that a particular note should support, it would be a good idea to write the slugs in pencil at first. That way you can easily change the slugs until you feel secure about the way the notes should be used. Once you have made a final decision, write a slug in ink in the upper right-hand corner of each card so that it can be seen quickly as you shuffle through your cards.

Writing a Formal Outline

If you have succeeded in writing slugs on each card, the outline will almost write itself. Either a topic outline or a sentence outline is acceptable, although if you plan to prove a thesis, it is probably wise to make a sentence outline; doing so will force you to state in a complete thought how each section of your paper contributes to the thesis. Observe all the conventions of good outlining as you write, using the slugs on your note cards as guides for topics and sub-topics. (See the outline for the sample paper on p. 325–326.)

WRITING THE PAPER

All the rules of good writing that you have learned so far apply to the research paper. But the research paper presents a special problem: you must make borrowed material a part of your own statement. You have spent several weeks now taking notes; you have studied them and have decided how they can be organized, and that is half the battle. If, however, you simply string your notes together, you will not be writing a research paper; you will merely be transcribing your notes. The paper must be yours—your idea, your organization, and, for the most part, your words. The notes should be used to back up your ideas, and they should be integrated into your statement. Otherwise, you do not have an honest research paper.

In the following excerpt from a student paper, the writer merely strings notes together.

W. E. B. DuBois believed that "the problem of the twentieth century is the problem of the color line."[4]

DuBois became aware of racial differences at an early age. He related this experience vividly:

> The exchange [of children's calling cards] was merry, till one girl, a tall new comer, refused my card—refused it peremptorily, with a glance. Then it dawned on me with a certain suddenness that I was different from the others; or like, mayhap, in heart and life and longing, but shut out from this world by a vast veil.[5]

DuBois felt that dreams of opportunities and fulfillment were reserved solely for whites.

> The shades of the prison-house closed around about us all: walls strait and stubborn to the whitest, but relentlessly narrow, tall, and unscalable to sons of night who must plod darkly on in resignation, or beat unavailing palms against the stone, or steadily, half hopelessly, watch the streak of blue above.[6]

When his infant son died, DuBois was depressed, but yet he rejoiced because his son would not have to endure life "behind the veil."[7]

> All that day and all that night there sat an awful gladness in my heart—nay blame me not if I see the world thus darkly through the veil, and my soul whispers ever to me, saying, "not dead, not dead,

but escaped, not bound, but free." No bitter meanness now shall sicken his baby heart till it die a living death, no taunt shall madden his happy boyhood. Fool that I was to think or wish that this little soul should grow choked and deformed within the veil! . . . Well sped, my boy, before the world had dubbed your ambition insolence, had held your ideals unattainable, and taught you to cringe and bow. Better for this nameless void that stops my life than a sea of sorrow for you.[8]

---

[4]W. E. B. DuBois, *The Souls of Black Folk* (New York: Dodd, Mead, 1961), p. xiv.
[5]DuBois, p. 16.
[6]DuBois, p. 16.
[7]DuBois, p. 155.
[8]DuBois, pp. 155–56.

The student has simply copied his notes into his paper. Since the purpose of the paper is not to reveal DuBois's style, but to compare his attitude toward being black with that of Booker T. Washington, the lengthy quotations from DuBois's autobiography serve little purpose in advancing the student's idea. They simply take up space. The point could be made more clearly if it were phrased largely in the student's own words:

W. E. B. DuBois, who believed that "the problem of the twentieth century is the problem of the color line,"[4] learned as a child that he could be rejected simply because of the color of his skin. Later, he came to believe that dreams of opportunities and fulfillment were reserved solely for whites, and he compared the life of blacks in America with that of prison inmates. Indeed, he grew so bitter about the plight of blacks that he rejoiced when his infant son died because the child would never have to experience the prejudice that he had felt.[5]

---

[4]W. E. B. DuBois, *The Souls of Black Folk* (New York: Dodd, Mead, 1961), p. xiv.
[5]DuBois, p. 16 and pp. 155–56.

In this version, the writer has composed a unified paragraph which makes his point clearly without the use of so many quotations. (A good, safe rule of thumb is, unless the subject of your **paper is an author's style, quote no more than ten percent of your paper.**) The second paragraph also avoids the sin of overdocumentation. Five footnotes have been replaced by only two. This version shows a much greater mastery of the material than does the first version.

First Rough Draft

To remove the temptation of simply stringing notes together, you might try our method of writing a first rough draft. We suggest that you set your notes aside, put your outline in front of you, and start writing. In this draft, the point is to get your ideas down on paper. Don't worry about grammar or punctuation. Don't try to work in quotations. You should be familiar enough with the contents of your notes by now to remember the general ideas they contain. Just write, perhaps on every third line of a legal pad, until you have developed every point in your outline.

If you have really studied your notes, and if you have constructed a reasonable outline, following this procedure should assure that you will develop your own ideas in your own way.

Second Rough Draft

Now, write the paper again. This time you will consult your notes to add quotations where they seem appropriate and to fill in specific facts you might not have remembered in writing the first rough draft. You will check your notes, too, to be sure that the facts, ideas, or opinions you have reported are accurate. And in this second effort, you will make some attempt to correct any grammar or punctuation errors you made in the first draft and to rephrase awkward sentences. Then you will add footnotes. (See "Footnote Forms," pp. 318–322.)

Once you have completed this draft, go back through it several times to make certain that you have quoted accurately, that you have documented every source properly, and that you have polished your language as well as you can. Don't hesitate during this process to use scissors and scotch tape to add, delete, or shift passages as you go along.

Third Rough Draft

If you think you have polished the paper as much as you can, make a third copy, complete with quotations and footnotes. Many instructors will not accept a final copy of a paper unless they have seen and approved the rough draft. If your instructor falls into this category, this is the rough draft you should submit. Your instructor will make suggestions, point out stylistic problems, and indicate the parts of your paper that are not developed as fully as they might be. Conscientious students heed their instructors' suggestions and make the appropriate changes on the third rough draft before typing the final paper.

Use of Quotations

The first rule regarding the use of direct quotations is use as few as you can. It is possible, in fact, to write an entire paper without using any direct quotations. There are, however, some cases in which direct quotations are called for:

1. If your subject is a literary one, you would, of course, want to represent the style of the author. Indeed, your purpose might demand an analysis of certain passages in the work. In that case, you certainly must quote the passages that you intend to discuss in detail.

Following is a section of a paper in which the writer argues that Herman Melville, in composing *Moby-Dick*, was influenced by Samuel Taylor Coleridge's "The Rime of the Ancient Mariner":

One other image in Chapters 51 and 52 of *Moby-Dick* illustrates a slightly different aspect of the process of adapting Coleridge's images. In this image, Melville incorporates both the image and the mood of the source in Coleridge's work. It occurs while the *Pequod* is still at the Cape of Good Hope:

Few or no words were spoken, and the silent ship, as if manned by painted sailors in wax, day after day tore on through the swift madness and gladness of the demoniac waves.

Except that the ship is given motion, it is surely the Ancient Mariner's ship on which

Day after day, day after day
We stuck, nor breath nor motion;
As idle as a painted ship
Upon a painted ocean.

Clearly, the quotations are necessary to show Coleridge's influence on Melville's work.

2. If the original is so perfectly stated that much of its value is in the way it is worded, you may want to quote the original. The conclusion of Lincoln's second inaugural address might be such a quotation:

With malice toward none; with charity for all; with firmness in the right, as God gives us to see the right, let us strive on to finish the work we are in; to bind up the nation's wounds; to care for him who shall have borne the battle, and for his widow, and his orphan—to do all which may achieve and cherish a just and lasting peace among ourselves, and with all nations.

3. If your source has made a statement which is so outrageous or controversial that readers of your paper might question whether you have represented the idea correctly, quote the original statement.

Aside from the statistics, there are those in the nuclear field who make some rather strong accusations about the expertise of nuclear energy's critics. According to W. E. Cooper, the motives of the critics and the expertise of the technicians are "grossly unbalanced." Cooper states,

We are trying to balance the opposing motivations with groups which are grossly unbalanced in expertise. Here is the source of our present difficulties. We are trying to find the answers to difficult technical questions by using the adversary principle instead of impartial evaluations by experts, and the conflicts end up in the courts where decisions are made by people who have no technical competence at all!

When you do quote, make every effort you can to work the quotation into your own statement. It will be obvious, of course, that you are quoting, but the flow of your sentence should not be affected by the quotation:

Forster points directly to the need for myth: "Why has not England a great mythology?" he asks, and suggests that England's mythology "has not advanced beyond daintiness" because, unlike Greek mythology, it has not derived from the earth.

Because the quotations are worked into the writer's own sentence, they require no special punctuation other than the quotation marks. If you want to introduce a longer quotation, punctuation depends on the words that precede the quote.
If the introductory words form a complete sentence, use a colon:

That Forster intended to establish man's need for connection with the earth is evident in his statement about London:

London was but a foretaste of this nomadic civilization which is altering human nature so profoundly, and throws upon personal relations a stress greater than they have ever borne before. Under cosmopolitanism, if it comes, we shall receive no help from the earth. Trees and meadows and mountains will only be a spectacle, and the binding force that they once exercised on character must be entrusted to Love alone. May Love be equal to the task!

If the introductory words do not form a complete sentence, imagine that the quote itself is the rest of the sentence and punctuate accordingly:

According to Forster,

London was but a foretaste of this nomadic civilization which is altering human nature so profoundly, and throws upon personal relations a stress greater than they have ever borne before. Under cosmopolitanism, if it comes, we shall receive no help from the earth. Trees and meadows and mountains will only be a spectacle, and the binding force that they once exercised on character must be entrusted to Love alone. May Love be equal to the task!

or

Forster writes that

> London was but a foretaste of this nomadic civilization which is altering human nature so profoundly, and throws upon personal relations a stress greater than they have ever borne before. Under cosmopolitanism, if it comes, we shall receive no help from the earth. Trees and meadows and mountains will only be a spectacle, and the binding force that they once exercised on character must be entrusted to Love alone. May Love be equal to the task!

As all the above examples of quotations illustrate, you should put a *short quotation* into your own paragraph or sentence, indicating that the material is quoted by placing quotation marks around the quoted passage. Set *long quotations* off by themselves. The quoted matter should be blocked and single-spaced, as in the immediately preceding examples. When you block a quotation, *do not use quotation marks*. (See "Quotation Marks" in the "Handbook," pp. 424–425.) That the material is blocked and single-spaced *means* that it is quoted.

Use of Footnotes

Unless the material is something as well known as the Gettysburg Address, when you take facts or ideas from someone else, you must credit the source by footnoting the material. Such a statement often frightens students because their first assumption is that they will have to footnote almost every sentence in their papers. That is not the case.

You should, of course, footnote all direct quotations which are not well known. You should also footnote all facts and opinions which are not common knowledge—*even when you have put the facts or opinions into your own words.* Two kinds of facts or opinions come under the heading *common knowledge:* those facts which everyone in our culture should know (George Washington was the first president of the United States, for example), and those facts which are common knowledge in the field you are investigating. Suppose you are writing a paper on Custer's last stand. You might not have known, when you began reading, the name of the Indian tribe that fought Custer and his men. If every source you read, however, says that it was the Sioux tribe, you would not need to make a footnote for that fact. Your wide reading lets you know that the fact is commonly known to historians. Nor would it be necessary to footnote the opinion that Custer blundered; most historians agree that he did. But any theories about why Custer led his men into such a trap should be footnoted.

At this point you may be feeling vaguely disturbed by the fuss being made about apparent trivialities of quoting and footnoting.

Unfortunately, these are the only devices by which your reader will be able to distinguish between the material drawn from other sources and the material that is your own. If you do not pay the most careful attention to the techniques of quoting and footnoting, you run the risk of being accused of plagiarism.

PLAGIARISM

Plagiarism is the use of facts, opinions, and language taken from another writer without acknowledgment. In its most sordid form, plagiarism is outright theft or cheating: a person has another person write the paper or simply steals a magazine article or section of a book and pretends to have produced a piece of original writing. Far more common is plagiarism in dribs and drabs: a sentence here and there, a paragraph here and there. Unfortunately, small-time theft is still theft, and small-time plagiarism is still plagiarism. For your own safety and self-respect, remember the following rules—not guidelines, *rules:*

1. The language in your paper must either be your own or a direct quote from the original author.
2. Changing a few words or phrases from another writer's work is not enough to make the writing "your own." Remember Rule 1. The writing is either your own or the other person's; there are no in-betweens.
3. Footnotes acknowledge that the fact or opinion expressed comes from another writer. If the *language* comes from another writer, quotation marks are necessary *in addition* to a footnote.

Now for a detailed example.

ORIGINAL PASSAGE

In 1925 Dreiser produced his masterpiece, the massively impressive *An American Tragedy.* By this time—thanks largely to the tireless propagandizing on his behalf by the influential maverick critic H. L. Mencken and by others concerned with a realistic approach to the problems of American life—Dreiser's fame had become secure. He was seen as the most powerful and effective destroyer of the genteel tradition that had dominated popular American fiction in the post-Civil War period, spreading its soft blanket of provincial, sentimental romance over the often ugly realities of life in modern, industrialized, urban America. Certainly there was nothing genteel about Dreiser, either as man or novelist. He was the supreme poet of the squalid, a man who felt the terror, the pity, and the beauty underlying the American dream. With an eye at once ruthless and compassionate, he saw the tragedy inherent in the American success ethic; the soft underbelly, as it were, of the Horatio Alger rags-to-riches myth so appealing to the optimistic

American imagination. [Richard Freedman, *The Novel* (New York: News-week Books, 1975), pp. 104–105]

Student Version	Comment
There was nothing genteel about Dreiser, either as man or novelist. He was the supreme poet of the squalid, a man who felt the terror, the pity, and the beauty underlying the American dream.	Obvious plagiarism: word-for-word repetition without acknowledgement.
There was nothing genteel about Dreiser, either as man or novelist. He was the supreme poet of the squalid, a man who felt the terror, the pity, and the beauty underlying the American dream.[1] [1]Richard Freedman, *The Novel* (New York: Newsweek Books, 1975), p. 104.	Still plagiarism. *The footnote alone does not help.* The language is the original author's, and only quotation marks around the whole passage *plus* a footnote would be correct.
Nothing was genteel about Dreiser as a man or as a novelist. He was the poet of the squalid and felt that terror, pity, and beauty lurked under the American dream.	Still plagiarism. A few words have been changed or omitted, but by no stretch of the imagination is the student writer using his own language.
"Nothing was genteel about Dreiser as a man or as a novelist. He was the poet of the squalid and felt that terror, pity, and beauty lurked under the American dream."[1] [1]Richard Freedman, *The Novel* (New York: Newsweek Books, 1975), p. 104.	Not quite plagiarism, but incorrect and inaccurate. Quotation marks indicate exact repetition of what was originally written. The student writer, however, has changed some of the original and is not entitled to use quotation marks.
"Certainly there was nothing genteel about Dreiser, either as man or novelist. He was the supreme poet of the squalid, a man who felt the terror, the pity, and the beauty underlying the American dream."[1] [1]Richard Freedman, *The Novel* (New York: Newsweek Books, 1975), p. 104.	Correct. The quotation marks acknowledge the words of the original writer. The footnote is also needed, of course, to give the reader specific information about the source of the quote.

By 1925 Dreiser's reputation was firmly established. The reading public viewed Dreiser as one of the main contributors to the downfall of the "genteel tradition" in American literature. Dreiser, "the supreme poet of the squalid," looked beneath the bright surface of American life and values and described the frightening and tragic elements, the "ugly realities," so often overlooked by other writers.[1]

Correct. The student writer uses his own words to summarize most of the original passage. The footnote shows that the ideas expressed come from the original writer, not from the student. The few phrases kept from the original passage are carefully enclosed in quotation marks.

---

[1]Richard Freedman, *The Novel* (New York: Newsweek Books, 1975), pp. 104–105.

FOOTNOTE FORMS

When you are ready to add footnotes to your rough draft, you will have to consult your bibliography cards in order to change the brief notations which you made on your note cards into proper footnote entries. As you will see by studying the examples of various kinds of footnotes below, footnotes contain essentially the same information as do bibliography entries, but the arrangement and punctuation of that information are a little different.

FIRST REFERENCES

A *first* footnote reference to a book should include the author, the title, the facts of publication, and the page or pages referred to. The author's name is not inverted in the footnote since you will not, of course, place footnotes in alphabetical order. Below are samples of *first* footnotes for the sources cited in the discussion of bibliography (pp. 298–303). Notice the differences in punctuation between a bibliography entry and a footnote entry.

A Book with One Author

[1]Ellen Moers, *Literary Women* (Garden City, New York: Doubleday & Company, Inc., 1976), p. 198.

A Book with Two Authors

[2]Marlies K. Danziger and W. Stacy Johnson, *An Introduction to Literary Criticism* (Boston: D. C. Heath and Company, 1961), p. 324.

A Book with Three or More Authors

[3]Fred C. Watkins and others, *Practical English Handbook,* 4th ed. (Boston: Houghton Mifflin Company, 1970), p. 73.

A Book with an Editor

[4]Loren J. Kallsen, ed., *The Kentucky Tragedy: A Problem in Romantic Attitudes* (Indianapolis: The Bobbs-Merrill Company, Inc., 1963), pp. 371–72.

An Edition of an Author's Work

[5]Henry David Thoreau, *Collected Poems,* ed. Carl Bode (Chicago: Packard and Co., 1943), p. 189.

If the editor's work, not the author's, is under discussion, use the following form:

[6]Donald A. Stauffer, ed., *Selected Poetry and Prose of Coleridge* (New York: The Modern Library, 1951), p. xii.

An Edition Other Than the First

[7]Randall E. Decker, *Patterns of Exposition,* 5th ed. (Boston: Little, Brown and Company, 1976), p. 87.

If the edition were a revised edition rather than a numbered edition, the abbreviation "rev. ed." would appear after the title.

An Edited Collection or Anthology

[8]Arthur Schlesinger, Jr. and Morton White, eds., *Paths of American Thought* (Boston: Houghton Mifflin Company, 1970), p. 23.

A Translated Work

[9]Heinrich Böll, *End of a Mission,* trans. Leila Vennewitz (New York: McGraw-Hill Book Company, 1974), p. 345.

A Work of More Than One Volume

[10]Wallace E. Adams and others, eds., *The Western World: To 1770,* I (New York: Dodd, Mead & Company, 1968), p. 548.

Notice that although the bibliography entry refers to a two-volume work, the writer has referred only to the first volume.

One Section of a Book Written by Several Authors

[11]Arthur Mizener, "To Meet Mr. Eliot," in *T. S. Eliot: A Collection of Critical Essays,* ed. Hugh Kenner (Englewood Cliffs, N.J.: Prentice-Hall, Inc. 1962), p. 20.

A footnote reference to a magazine should include the author, the title of the article, the name of the magazine, the volume and issue number, the date, and the page or pages referred to. A footnote to a magazine is almost identical to the bibliography entry except that the author's name is not inverted and, instead of giving all the pages of the article—as in a bibliography—you indicate only the specific page or pages referred to in your text.

[12]Newton Arvin, "Homage to Robert Herrick," *New Republic,* LXXXII (March 6, 1935), 94.

[13]Bernard Lewis, "The Return of Islam," *Commentary,* 61, No. 1 (January, 1976), 41.

Both the volume and the number within that volume are given. The figures "61, No. 1" stand for "volume 61, number one."

[14]R. L. Lamborn, "Must They Be Crazy, Mixed-up Kids?" *The New*

Because no volume number is given, the abbreviation "p." is used before the page number and the date is not placed in ( ).

[15]"Thoughts from the Lone Cowboy," *Time,* 109, No. 9 (February 28, 1977), 20.

A footnote for a newspaper article should give the name of the author (if an author is listed), the title of the article, the name of the newspaper, the date, and the page. If the newspaper is divided into sections, the section number will also be given.

[16]John L. Hess, "A Sizzling Battle in the Burger Business," *The New York Times,* March 13, 1977, sec. 3, p. 1.

[17]"Trudeau on Separatism," *The* [Cleveland] *Plain Dealer,* February 24, 1977, sec. A, p. 22.

The name of the city is not part of the title of this newspaper and is indicated in brackets.

A footnote reference to an encyclopedia article is almost identical to the bibliography entry except that the author's name (if given) is not inverted and a comma rather than a period follows the title of the article.

[18]Joan W. Kealunohonoku, "Hula," *Encyclopedia Americana,* 1971, 14, 542.

[19]"Massachusetts Bay Company," *The Columbia Encyclopedia,* 1963, p. 1317.

Since this is a one-volume encyclopedia and no volume number is given, the abbreviation "p." appears before the page number.

OTHER FOOTNOTE FORMS

An Untitled Book Review

[20]Phoebe-Lou Adams, Review of *Black Sun,* by Geoffrey Wolff, *Atlantic,* 238, No. 3 (September 1976), p. 99.

Interview

²¹Barbara Guhde, Associate Professor of Modern British Literature, State University College at Brockport, New York, interview in Brockport, April 26, 1977, concerning Blake's influence on the works of Joyce Cary.

Letter

²²John Bohi, a letter in my possession to Arthur H. Adams, dated at Hamburg, Germany, September 30, 1971.

Selection from a Casebook

²³Hugh N. Maclean, "Conservatism in Modern American Fiction," *College English,* XV (March 1954), 315–325. Reprinted in *J. D. Salinger and the Critics,* eds. William F. Belcher and James W. Lee (Belmont, California: Wadsworth Publishing Company, Inc., 1962), p. 13.

SUBSEQUENT REFERENCES

Thus far we have been dealing with the detailed first reference to any source. Subsequent references to the same source are much shorter and much simpler. For almost any material, the author's last name and a page number will be sufficient:

⁴Moers, p. 199.

⁸Mizener, p. 21.

¹⁰Lewis, p. 41.

¹⁵Hess, p. 1.

¹⁶Kealunohonoku, p. 542.

If your reference is to one volume of a multi-volume work, your footnote will need to include the volume number:

⁶Adams and others, II, 78.

If you have used more than one work by the same author, the page number and author's name will not give the reader enough information. Write the title of the work after the author's last name. If the title is long, you may use a shortened form. After first references, for example, to Ernest Hemingway's *For Whom the Bell Tolls* and *Across the River and into the Trees,* subsequent references may look like this:

⁷Hemingway, *Bell,* p. 30.

⁹Hemingway, *Across the River,* p. 127.

When the author is unknown or unnamed, subsequent references consist of the title and page number:

¹³"Thoughts from the Lone Cowboy," p. 20.

¹⁷"Trudeau on Separatism," p. 22.

¹⁹"Massachusetts Bay Company," p. 1317.

Two concluding comments: *first,* forget about the Latin abbreviations formerly common in footnotes, particularly in subsequent references—*Ibid., op. cit.,* etc. Such usages have largely become things of the past. *Second,* footnotes may appear at the bottom of each page of the text of your paper *or* in one long list on a separate page or pages immediately after the text. If the footnotes are on the bottom of each page, be sure to keep numerical sequence throughout the paper: *do not* begin with a new footnote number 1 on each page. Check with your instructor about the footnoting method you should use. If your instructor has no preference, you will probably find it easier to type all footnotes on a separate page.

FINAL BIBLIOGRAPHY

The final bibliography lists sources actually referred to in your paper. It may also include material that was of genuine value in adding to your insights and perspectives on the subject but which you did not have occasion to refer to specifically. (Such sources are sometimes listed separately under the heading "Supplementary Bibliography.") The final bibliography should not include titles you consulted that turned out to be of little or no value in your paper.

For a typed sample of a final bibliography, see the student paper, p. 337. Note in particular the following points:

1. Bibliography entries are arranged in alphabetical order according to the last name of the author.
2. For entries where the author is unknown or unlisted, alphabetical order is determined by the first important word of the title.
3. The first line of each entry begins at the lefthand margin. All other lines of each entry are indented five spaces.
4. The following form should be used in cases where more than one title by the same author is being used:

Melville, Herman. *Moby-Dick* in *Moby-Dick: An Authoritative Text, Reviews and Letters by Melville, Analogues and Sources, Criticism.* Eds. Harrison Hayford and Hershel Parker. New York: W. W. Norton & Company, Inc., 1967.

————. *White Jacket or The World in a Man-of-War.* Ed. Hennig Cohen. New York: Holt, Rinehart and Winston, 1967.

SAMPLE PAPER

Our discussion of research papers concludes with a paper on a topic of current controversy. While by no means perfect, the paper represents a serious effort by a serious student to apply the lessons of this chapter. Whatever the final merits of the stand the author takes, the paper can serve as a ready reference for most matters of form.

When you write your own research papers, you may find the following checklist a handy guide to some easily forgotten fine points:

Title Page

Is your title in capital letters?

Have you included your name?

Outline

Is the title of your paper repeated at the top of your outline?

Have you included your thesis statement after the paper's title?

Have you used a consistent pattern of numbering and lettering?

Body

Are the pages correctly numbered?

Are all the footnotes included either at the bottom of each page or at the end of the paper? (Check with your instructor before deciding which form to use.)

Is the number of each footnote raised half a line?

Have you used the blocked form for long quotations?

Footnotes

Have you placed the author's first name first?

Have you indented the first line of each footnote, and is the second line of each at the left-hand margin?

Is the title of each work correctly marked with quotation marks or underlining?

Does each footnote end with a period?

Are the footnotes correctly numbered, with no numbers repeated or omitted?

Bibliography

Have you placed the author's last name first?

Are all the entries in alphabetical order?

Is the first line of each entry at the left-hand margin, and is the second line of each indented?

Does each entry end with a period?

THE RELIABILITY OF NUCLEAR POWER PLANTS

by

F. L. Fende

English 103

June 4, 1976

for

Professor Norlin

OUTLINE

THE RELIABILITY OF NUCLEAR POWER PLANTS

THESIS: Nuclear power plants are a safe and reliable source of energy
          and their further development should be continued in order to
          satisfy mankind's never-ending need for energy.

I.   Today's critics of nuclear energy question the need for nuclear
     power and would lead us to believe nuclear power can have a
     devastating effect on mankind.

     A.   Atomic energy is compared with the atomic bomb.

     B.   Atomic energy is seen as a poisoned power and is compared
          with toxic industrial agents.

          1.   Fission by-products released into the atmosphere are
               said to be the greatest danger to mankind.

          2.   Nuclear power plants are said to be defenseless against
               enemy attack.

     C.   Some critics feel we do not need the additional energy supplied
          by nuclear power.

II. The proponents of nuclear energy have strong arguments in favor of
     nuclear power plants.

     A.   Scientists have proven that it would be impossible for a
          nuclear power plant to explode like an atomic bomb.

     B.   The experts in nuclear energy say that radiation is a normal
          part of life.

          1.   They contend radiation is not new to us, and it has
               always been present in natural sources.

          2.   They feel that radiation released from nuclear power
               plants is negligible.

     C.   The overwhelming pressure from the critics has caused the A.E.C.
          to finance and study the reliability of nuclear power plants.

          1.   An excellent history of safety has supported the cause of
               nuclear energy.

          2.   Nuclear power is compared with other sources of energy.

i

ii

D. Those in support of the cause of nuclear energy question the expertise and motives of the critics.

E. Simple economics point to a need for nuclear energy.

In 1957 the United States reached a new threshold in nuclear technology. The first commercial nuclear power plant went into operation in
Shippingport, Pennsylvania. Since that time, the number of operable
nuclear power plants has increased to forty-seven, and it is projected
that by the year 1986 there will be 206 commercially operated nuclear
power plants.[1] Along with this increase in nuclear energy, the magnitude
of the controversy dealing with the safety of nuclear power has increased.
The opponents of nuclear power contend that it is dangerous to mankind.
Some opponents question the need for nuclear energy on the basis that we
can live without it and its pitfalls. On the other hand, the proponents
of nuclear power argue that it is a safe form of energy, and they contend
that the additional nuclear energy is necessary in order to supplement
this country's never-ending need for energy. Each side in this controversy takes a firm stand on its beliefs; however, the facts, based on
the expertise of those in the nuclear field and on the safe history of
nuclear power, indicate that nuclear power plants are a reliable source
of energy, and that further development of nuclear power should be
continued.

Today's critics of nuclear power would lead us to believe that
nuclear power can have a devastating effect on mankind. Richard Curtis,
author of Perils of the Peaceful Atom, reports that Supreme Court
Justices William Douglas and Hugo Black consider nuclear power "the most
deadly, the most dangerous process man has ever conceived."[2] This sort
of attitude is not only conveyed by our high officials, but also carries
on down the ranks. There are those who have written extensive works

1

2

pertaining to the pitfalls of nuclear power, and it is not difficult to
understand how the attitudes of today's critics have developed. The
most common denominator associated with nuclear energy is the emotional
reaction most people have to the past history of devastation caused by
the atomic bomb. Richard Curtis displays this attitude when he states
that "each [nuclear power plant] will be fueled with a great many times
the amount of uranium required to destroy Hiroshima."[3] The reference to
the bomb is enough to place some doubt in the minds of most people, and
it seems to have become a tool used by critics in their fight against
nuclear power. One such critic, John Gofman, argues that "one per cent
of the inner radioactivity . . . from one plant could put as much harmful
contamination . . . into the environment as 10 bombs."[4]

Gofman's claim highlights another issue. There are those who feel
that radioactivity may be the most critical pitfall of nuclear power.
Curtis suggests that "the greatest potential hazard" in nuclear power
plants is the radioactive by-products produced by fission and the
possibility that these products can be released over the general populace.
He also goes on to say that these by-products are more toxic than any
known chemical agent used in industry.[5] Although Curtis does not state
any exact agent, one may assume he is referring to toxic agents such as
chlorine used in our water systems or mercury, which has been cited for
its toxic qualities.

Comparing these agents with the radioactivity of fission products
is probably a fair comparison, although there are no facts which sub-
stantiate these allegations. On the other hand, Gofman contends that
"no one has ever produced evidence that any specific amount of radiation
will be without harm."[6] The critic's concern for the potential dangers
of radioactive fission by-products is well taken, and no one will disagree

that excessive doses of radioactivity are deadly. Then again, one cannot
help but feel that most fears are based on past experience with atomic
bomb tests and the devastation of Hiroshima.

Some of those who argue against nuclear energy take a more practical
stand in their fight against nuclear power. Their concern is with the
vulnerability of nuclear plants at the time of enemy attacks or the
plants' exposure to natural catastrophe. Gofman states that "unprotected,
above ground nuclear power plants . . . would certainly be large
liabilities . . . under attack."[7] Gofman's approach is sensible, and
his obvious concern is that the internal radiation present in a nuclear
plant would be exposed to the public, although one may ask which would
be of more concern, the nuclear plant radiation due to enemy attack or
the overall consequences of the enemy attack.

There are some critics who feel that the world should cut back on
its energy consumption rather than risk the perils of nuclear energy.
This has led one critic, Ralph Nader, a man who carries a great deal of
weight in the consumer market, to suggest that "Americans could willingly
accept a 40% reduction in energy consumption."[8] Nader has also suggested
that if the public had a choice between candles and nuclear power, the
public would be wise to choose the candles.[9] This seems like quite a
drastic measure. It would be interesting to see how many people would
be willing to burn wood in their stoves or go back to using the old-style
icebox.

The proponents of nuclear power have strong arguments in favor of
nuclear energy, and they present their case for nuclear energy in a
realistic and practical manner. The accusations of those who compare
nuclear power plants with the atomic bomb are countered with sound fact.
James Stokley, author of The New World of the Atom, has argued this point

4

about nuclear power and put his views in a form that the ordinary layman

can understand. Stokley states,

> Since the most peaceful application of nuclear energy has
> been in the production and distribution of electrical power
> from nuclear sources, let us consider the possible hazards.
> First of all the nuclear reactor cannot explode like a bomb.
> In the bomb pieces of essentially pure uranium 235, or some
> other fissile material must be brought together and held for
> an instant in one compact mass. But the power reactor, even
> with highly enriched uranium, has fuel elements that are
> small and scattered. Even an accident could not bring them
> together to form a critical mass . . . .[10]

Aside from Stokley's understanding of nuclear energy, he has a good

feel for the cause of the controversies regarding nuclear power. Stokley

points out that "we cannot forget the hundreds of thousands killed at

Hiroshima and Nagasaki . . . . The tendency of many to identify atomic

power plants . . . with the bomb has made people fear and oppose them."[11]

In answer to the critics' concern for the radiation emitted from

nuclear plants, the experts in nuclear energy say that radiation is a

normal part of life. They contend that radiation is not new to us, and

they explain that "it has always come from natural sources. Living

organisms on earth have always been exposed to it, even long before man

evolved."[12] Certain facts have been established by the Atomic Energy

Commission and other scientific institutes and used as a comparison to

evaluate the radiation emitted by nuclear power plants. It has been

established that the average dose of natural radiation from cosmic rays

and other natural sources is 125 millirems a year; however, airline

pilots receive an additional 5 millirems of natural radiation annually

because there is less resistance to cosmic radiation at high altitudes.

For the same reason, people in Denver, Colorado, receive an additional

75 millirems of natural radiation a year.[13] Any viewer of television

receives additional radiation from a television set; radiation is also

transmitted by a radium dial on a wristwatch and by medical X-rays.

5

After all is said about natural radiation, the answer to one question remains: How dangerous is the radiation in nuclear power plants? In Stokley's research, he found that the radiation emitted from nuclear power plants is negligible. Stokley admits to the large amount of fissionable products present in nuclear power plants; however, he discloses that "more than 99.999 per cent are held in the fuel elements,..." and he claims that the prime goal in the construction of nuclear plants is to build them so they retain as much of the ten thousandth of a percent of potentially harmful radiation as possible.[14]

Aside from Stokley's findings, the Toledo Edison Company has gone one step further in answering the questions about the dangers of radioactivity. Using previous operating experience as a gauge, the Toledo Edison Company insists that "if a person were to remain at the edge of the Davis-Besse plant site for 24 hours a day for an entire year, he would receive a maximum of five millirems a year of radiation."[15] This is the same dose a pilot receives making coast to coast flights. Since the National Committee on Radiation Protection has set 170 millirems per year above natural radiation as the maximum amount of radiation to which the general public should be exposed,[16] one can conclude that 5 millirems does seem insignificant and surely will not exhaust man's bank of 170 millirems a year.

The overwhelming pressure by the critics of nuclear energy has caused the Atomic Energy Commission to finance studies of the reliability of nuclear power plants. One such report, directed by Norman C. Rasmussen, professor of nuclear engineering at M.I.T., has stirred quite a bit of enthusiasm among the proponents of nuclear power. W. E. Cooper has concluded, on the basis of Rasmussen's report, that "the consequences of potential reactor accidents are no larger, and in many cases, are much

6

smaller than those of non-nuclear accidents having similar consequences."

Cooper went on to explain that the non-nuclear accidents compared were

fires, explosions, toxic chemical releases, dam failures, airplane

crashes and earthquakes.[17]

Other experts in the nuclear field have come to similar conclusions

based on Rasmussen's report. E. Gellatte feels that a loss-of-reactor-

coolant accident would probably be one of the worst consequences and

that it would be considered a severe catastrophe. However, he concluded

that the possibility of such an accident would be one chance in ten

billion.[18] Rasmussen's report and the conclusions reached by its

interpreters surely make a case in favor of nuclear power.

Even though Rasmussen's report and the conclusions of its interpreters

add to the case for nuclear power, they lead us to another area which shows

even more evidence that favors nuclear power. The historical safety record

of nuclear power plants is impeccable. In fact, most of the studies of

nuclear power plant reliability were based on their unmarred past. Con-

firming this point of view, one proponent of nuclear power declares,

"Counting commercial and military power reactors, there have been almost

2,000 reactor-years of experience with no nuclear accidents."[19] Then

again, there are those who feel that there are risks involved in any new

technology. J. J. O'Connor feels exactly this way; however, he has

observed that, to date, there have been no "appreciable uncontrolled"

radiation releases from commercial nuclear plants.[20]

Whether these statistics have any bearing on the case for nuclear

energy or not, there are those who rightly question the safety of nuclear

power plants as compared to other sources of energy. Statistics regarding

the safety of fossil-fired plants have been recorded long before the

nuclear age. As far back as 1890, records of boiler explosions have been recorded with as many as 20 deaths attributed to these explosions.[21] In

a recent four-year study, using an evenly distributed sample of nuclear,

fossil and hydro-electric power plants, it was disclosed that there were

no fatal or permanently disabling accidents in nuclear power plants. On

the other hand, there were six fatal or permanently disabling accidents

recorded for the non-nuclear plants in this four-year period.[22] After

reviewing the most recent statistics, one might question the safety of

fossil-fired power plants rather than the safety of nuclear power.

Aside from the statistics, there are those in the nuclear field who

make some rather strong accusations about the expertise of nuclear

energy's critics. According to W. E. Cooper, the motives of the critics

and the expertise of the technicians are "grossly unbalanced." Cooper

states,

> We are trying to balance the opposing motivations with
> groups which are grossly unbalanced in expertise. Here
> is the source of our present difficulties. We are trying
> to find the answers to difficult technical questions by
> using the adversary principle instead of impartial
> evaluations by experts, and the conflicts end up in the
> courts where decisions are made by people who have no
> technical competence at all![23]

Although Cooper's analogy seems harsh, he does point out a glimmer

of hope. He feels that the production of voluntary standards such as

the ASME Boiler and Pressure Vessel Code Nuclear Rules will help balance

this communication gap between the experts and non-experts.[24] Indeed,

this sort of a system would surely answer the questions asked about

nuclear power and it certainly stands to reason that there is a need to

bridge the communication gap.

The facts outlined thus far certainly make a case for nuclear power,

but one question remains unanswered. Is there a need for nuclear power

plants? The proponents of nuclear energy use basic economics to show a

need for nuclear energy. The current energy crisis and predictions of

8

future energy demand would lead us to believe that there is a definite

need for nuclear power.   John N. Nissikas suggests that 70 percent of our

energy demand in 1990 will be supplemented by fossil fuel, and by the

year 1980 "half of our oil consumption will be imported if foreign

supplies are available . . . ."[25]

With this large demand for fossil fuels and our dependence on foreign

oil, a good portion of the energy demand is left to be supplemented by

other sources such as nuclear, hydroelectric, or possibly solar power.

Certainly the dependence on foreign oil alone shows a need for a supplemen-

tal energy source.   One observer has concluded that "competition from nuclear

power plants will eventually have a stabilizing effect on world oil

prices" and that nuclear energy will be one-half as costly as other sources

by 1980.[26]

The projected energy demands and the dependence on foreign oil do

show a need for supplemental energy of some kind.   Solar energy and wind

energy are certainly possibilities, but they are fairly new and untested.

Nuclear power has proved to be a safe and reliable source of energy and

should be slated to supplement our future energy demands.

9

FOOTNOTES

[1]James Stokley, <u>The New World of the Atom</u> (New York: Ires Washburn, 1970), p. 5.

[2]Quoted by Richard Curtis and others, <u>Perils of the Peaceful Atom: The Myth of Safe Nuclear Power Plants</u> (New York: Doubleday, 1969), p. ix.

[3]Curtis, p. ix.

[4]John William Gofman, <u>Poisoned Power: The Case Against Nuclear Power Plants</u> (Emmaus, Pennsylvania: Rodale Press, 1971), p. 8.

[5]Curtis, p. 11.

[6]Gofman, p. 92.

[7]Gofman, p. 8.

[8]Quoted by S. Rippon, "Making the Case for Nuclear Power," <u>Nuclear Engineering International</u>, 19 (September 1974), 741.

[9]Quoted by Stanley C. Gualt, "Appliances and Energy: One Expert's Outlook," <u>The</u> [Cleveland] <u>Plain Dealer</u>, April 22, 1975, Energy Supplement, p. 2.

[10]Stokley, p. 169.

[11]Stokley, p. 169.

[12]Stokley, p. 171.

[13]<u>Facts About Radiation</u> (Toledo, Ohio: The Toledo Edison Company, 1968), p. 5.

[14]Stokley, p. 170.

[15]<u>Facts About Radiation</u>, p. 5.

[16]Curtis, p. 151.

[17]W. E. Cooper and others, "Nuclear Vessels are Safe," <u>Mechanical Engineering</u>, 97 (April 1975), 19.

[18]Quoted by J. Anderson, "J.C.A.E. Recommends 20 More Years for Price," <u>Electrical World</u>, 182 (September 15, 1974), 26.

[19]R. Gillette, "Nuclear Safety: Calculating The Odds of Disaster," <u>Science</u>, 185 (September 6, 1974), 839.

[20]J. J. O'Connor, "Boiler Explosions Last Month--A Historical Perspective," <u>Power</u>, 119 (May 1975), 9.

10

^{21} O'Connor, p. 9.

^{22} A. D. Bertolett, "Accident-rate Sample Favors Nuclear," _Electrical World_, 182 (July 15, 1974), 41.

^{23} Cooper, p. 21.

^{24} Cooper, p. 21.

^{25} John N. Nassikas, "National Energy Policy: Directions and Developments," _Proceedings of The American Power Conference_, ed. Betty Haigh (Chicago: Institute of Technology, 1973), pp. 4-8.

^{26} Rippon, p. 742.

11

BIBLIOGRAPHY

Anderson, J. "JCAE Recommends 20 More Years for Price."
    Electrical World, 182 (September 15, 1974), 26.

Bertolett, A. D., and others. "Accident-rate Sample Favors Nuclear."
    Electrical World, 182 (July 15, 1974), 40-41.

Cooper, W. E., and others. "Nuclear Vessels are Safe."
    Mechanical Engineering, 97 (April 1975), 18-23.

Curtis, Richard, and others. Perils of the Peaceful Atom: The Myth
    of Safe Nuclear Power Plants. New York: Doubleday, 1969.

Facts About Radiation. Toledo, Ohio: The Toledo Edison Company, 1968.

Gillette, R. "Nuclear Safety: Calculating the Odds of Disaster."
    Science, 185 (September 6, 1974), 838-39.

Gofman, John William. Poisoned Power: The Case Against Nuclear Power
    Plants. Emmaus, Pennsylvania: Rodale Press, 1971.

Gualt, Stanley C. "Appliances and Energy: One Expert's Outlook."
    The [Cleveland] Plain Dealer, April 22, 1975, Energy Supplement,
    p. 2.

Hauster, R. L. "Nuclear Power Plant Reliability." Combustion, 46
    (August 1974), 28-29.

Nassikas, John N. "National Energy Policy: Directions and Developments."
    Proceedings Of The American Power Conference. Ed. Betty Haigh.
    Chicago: Institute of Technology, 1973, pp. 4-17.

O'Connor, J. J. "Boiler Explosions Last Month--A Historical Perspective."
    Power, 119 (May 1975), 9.

"Purdue's Expert Looks at U. S. Energy Options Today."
    The [Cleveland] Plain Dealer, April 22, 1975, Energy Supplement,
    p. 10.

Rippon, S. "Making the Case for Nuclear Power." Nuclear Engineering
    International, 19 (September 1974), 741-43.

Stokley, James. The New World of the Atom. New York: Ires Washburn,
    1970.

Be fussy. Good style is the product of
thoughtful revision.

PART 4
STYLE

INTRODUCTORY NOTE
Refining Your Use of Language

Writing a well-organized theme is one thing. Writing a well-organized *good* theme is another, more complicated thing. Thousands of rusty filing cabinets and dusty shelves are filled with perfectly well-organized writings that got their authors nothing but bored and irritated readers—not to mention poor grades. These writings all had a thesis; they all attempted to prove the thesis; they all had an introduction, a body, and a conclusion. The paragraphs in these writings all had topic sentences, and the topic sentences were all connected to the thesis. In short, these writings followed all the directions and advice that this book has given so far. What went wrong?

The answer to that begins with another question. Do we waste time praising a relative's remodeled home because the sofa is in the living room, the stove in the kitchen, and the carpeting on the floors? We all know that if the sofa had been crammed into the bathroom and the stove dumped on top of the coffee table, we'd be faced with a disaster, but we generally take logical organization for granted. Like a home without this organization, an unorganized piece of writing is an obvious disaster. In a reasonably well-organized work, however, the reader simply assumes the structure is satisfactory and turns his or her attention to other matters. The reader is right, too. Few homeowners have ever received compliments for their good sense in putting the bed in the bedroom, and few writers have ever been praised for their superb mastery of topic sentences.

When we do praise writers, we generally praise them because they use language well, because they know how to work with words. We may think we liked a particular story or article because its ideas were powerful and interesting, but it was the words that *made* the ideas powerful and interesting. The same ideas expressed by a less skillful writer would appear flat and boring. Compare, for instance, the simple strength of the Christmas wish, "Peace on earth, good will to men," to this grotesque version of the same idea:

> All concerned and involved individuals at this point in time aspire to and wish for universal nonbelligerency militarywise and benevolence-orientated interpersonal relationships between persons.

A good writer knows how to handle language and can fascinate us with instructions on how to use automobile directional signals; a poor writer does not know how to handle language and can bore us with a passionate love letter.

This section of the book, then, discusses ways of "refining your use of language." We can assume that grammar and organization are no longer major problems and start to concentrate on style—how to write not only correctly, but *well*.

CHAPTER 15

"PROPER WORDS IN PROPER PLACES"

Jonathan Swift once defined good style as "proper words in proper places." Gustave Flaubert, the great French novelist, felt that the writer's craft was embodied in the quest for *le mot juste,* the right word. On one level or another, everyone who writes is involved in the same quest. Total success, if it has ever been achieved, probably depends on such vital but indefinable qualities as sensitivity, perceptiveness, creativity, and dozens of others. Fortunately, few people expect or demand total success. Nearly all writers can learn to hit the right word more often than they used to simply by becoming more alert to the possibilities of language.

DENOTATION AND CONNOTATION

Traditionally, the most logical place to begin thinking about right and wrong words is in the distinction between *denotation* and *connotation.* A few examples will help to clarify that distinction.

Let's assume that you have finished with the drudgery of getting a diploma and are now the head of a successful advertising agency. A major motor corporation wants you to handle the campaign introducing a new intermediate-size automobile. Would you recommend calling the car the Giraffe, the Porcupine, or the Eagle?

Let's assume now that instead of becoming a big shot in an advertising agency, you've become a humble schoolteacher. You have almost finished writing reports to the parents of your fourth graders. You've saved the most difficult for last: what can you put down about your big problem, Suzy Mae? Do you write, "Suzy Mae has not done a single bit of honest-to-goodness work all year," or "Suzy Mae has not been working up to her full capacity"?

Now let's assume that, big shot or schoolteacher, you wound up making the wrong decision. You're depressed and annoyed. All you want to do is forget your problems. At a weekend party, you have too much to drink. "Oh, brother!" says your loyal spouse, "did you ever get looped last night!"

"Looped?" you answer. "Nonsense! I just got a little high!"

What do all these stories have in common? Just this: meaning comes as much or more from the *connotations* of words as from their *denotations*. The denotation of a word is its explicit, surface meaning, its bare "dictionary meaning." Call the new car anything at all; whatever name you come up with will *denote* a certain mechanical device with set wheelbase and rear headroom measurements, fuel tank capacity, engine size, and so on. Describe Suzy Mae harshly or kindly; your comments will denote that she does not do enough work. Think of yourself as "high" or "looped"; both words denote the condition of having had too much to drink.

But an advertising agency that thinks only of the denotations of words will soon go broke. A teacher who thinks it doesn't matter how Suzy Mae is described as long as the message comes through that she is lazy will soon be in serious trouble with the girl's parents. Married couples who don't realize that words like *looped* and *nag* and *scold* and *love* have meanings far beyond their denotations will probably find their lives turning into one long quarrel. Most words have connotations as well as denotations. The *connotation* of a word is its implicit meaning, the meaning derived from the atmosphere, the vibrations, the emotions that we associate with the word. The connotations are not always entered next to a word in the dictionary, but they are associated with the word in people's minds. Words such as *Las Vegas* or *South Africa*, for example, simply denote a particular city or country—a mere geographical location; but they also have an emotional significance for most people that has nothing to do with geography or dictionaries. Again, consider a word like *marijuana*. Its denotation is perfectly straightforward—a species of plant that can be used as a narcotic—but its connotations are endless, ranging from relaxation and self-expression on one side to crime and decadence on the other. Moreover, no one could have a valid idea of the full meaning of the word without being aware of these connotations.

Let's look more closely at how connotations work to determine our responses. We all probably agree that among Giraffe, Porcupine, and Eagle, the last name is the only reasonable choice for the new car. It may be no stroke of genius, as names go, but it wins easily against the competition. For most people, the idea of an eagle carries with it connotations of power, speed, and perhaps freedom and beauty as well. These are concepts that motivate people who buy cars, no matter how loudly they may proclaim that their sole interest is "just transportation." Consider the animal names in recent use for car models and notice how many connote power or speed, or both: Cougar, Mustang, Impala, Bobcat, Skylark, Bronco, Colt, Rabbit, Thunderbird, Firebird, Roadrunner. The name Eagle, then, has certain connotations that might be helpful in marketing the car.

What are the connotations of Giraffe? We think of tremendous—even absurd—size, of something that basically looks funny. Zoologists may tell us that giraffes are actually capable of running extremely fast, but the average person associates the animals far more with awkwardness than with speed. What about Porcupine? When the average person bothers to think about porcupines at all, the connotations are likely to be of pesky creatures that sensible folks try to stay away from.

Giraffe, Porcupine, and Eagle denote the same product, to be sure. We can assume that whatever name is given to the new car, the car's performance will be the same. But people respond to the connotations of words, and it is hard to conceive of finding many buyers for the Giraffe or the Porcupine. One of Shakespeare's most famous lines is, "A rose by any other name would smell as sweet." From a strictly scientific point of view he was undoubtedly correct. In all other respects, he was dead wrong.

Developing a sensitivity to the connotations of words is a valuable asset for any writer. Was the person who had too much to drink *inebriated, intoxicated, drunk, looped, smashed, tipsy, high, crocked, pickled, loaded,* or *blotto?* You have all these words to choose from, and many more besides. Is an overweight person *plump, fat, pudgy, obese, chubby, portly, chunky, corpulent, stout,* or *stocky?* Few greater compliments can be paid to writers than to say that they have a knack for choosing the right word. That knack does not come simply from having a large vocabulary, but from sensing the fine distinctions in connotation that separate two words with similar denotations.

A well-developed sense of the importance of connotations is also a valuable asset for any reader, especially any reader who happens to be taking an English course. Most English instructors, after all, ask you to write about the material you have read; you are probably licked before you start unless you have read that material alertly. We have seen how connotations determine meaning, and if you miss the connotations of many words, the basic meaning of a selection may easily elude you. Beyond this, once you begin discussing a writer's style, you are bound to feel rather helpless unless you know something about connotations. "Compare the tone in Love Poem A to the tone in Love Poem B." "How does the author's use of irony add to the effect of the story?" "Why does the author use the word 'drowsy' instead of 'sleepy' in line 7?" These may or may not be tough questions. Remember, though, that style gives life to language and that the fundamental element of style is the writer's choice of words.

Exercise A

Rearrange each group of words by connotation, from the least favorable term to the most favorable. In many cases opinions will differ; there are few purely right and purely wrong answers.

 1. police officer, cop, fuzz, pig, smokey
 2. stupid, retarded, slow, dumb, moronic
 3. gaudy, loud, colorful, flashy, vulgar
 4. unusual, crazy, weird, eccentric, odd
 5. drink, cocktail, booze, rotgut, alcoholic beverage
 6. lean, thin, slender, skinny, undernourished
 7. cheap, thrifty, stingy, miserly, frugal
 8. uptight, nervous, edgy, apprehensive, anxiety-ridden
 9. pretty, gorgeous, lovely, good-looking, cute
10. laugh, chuckle, giggle, guffaw, snicker

Exercise B

All the words in the parentheses can be used in the sentences in which they appear. Discuss how the meaning of the sentence changes, depending on which word is used.

 1. The professor's solution to the dilemma was (clever, wise).
 2. The football team needs a more (enthusiastic, strongly-motivated) quarterback.
 3. My father says that as a young man he (loved, adored) Marilyn Monroe.
 4. This satire of American politics is unusually (funny, entertaining).
 5. Investments in municipal bonds are likely to be more (dangerous, risky, insecure) than many people think.
 6. Sometimes (solitude, loneliness, isolation) can be good for the soul.
 7. My mother's gossip made me feel (embarrassed, awkward, ashamed).
 8. He was as smart as (a fox, a trained dog in a circus, Albert Einstein).
 9. Congresswoman Saunders is a gifted (speaker, talker, orator).
10. Her excuse for being late was completely (unbelievable, fantastic).

ABSTRACT WRITING AND CONCRETE WRITING

The distinction between denotation and connotation, while valuable to a writer, can sometimes seem a bit remote and philosophical. It's easier to see the immediate, practical consequences to a writer's quest for the right word in the distinction between abstract writing and concrete writing.

Abstract writing is writing that lacks specific details and is filled with vague, indefinite words and broad, general statements. Every piece of writing needs generalizations, of course, and vague words such as *nice* and *interesting* can be useful. But writing that is dominated by such words is abstract writing, and abstract writing is the main cause of bored readers. It is often a reflection of lazy or careless thinking. It can interfere with full communication of meaning. It prevents many students from developing their themes adequately ("I've already said all I have to say. How am I supposed to get 300 more words on this subject?")

Abstract writing occurs when someone writes:

Too much poverty exists in this country.
INSTEAD OF
I see one-third of a nation ill-housed, ill-clad, ill-nourished.

Mr. Jones is a tough grader.
INSTEAD OF
Mr. Jones flunked 75% of his class and gave no higher than a C to the students who passed.

Don't fire until they're extremely close.
INSTEAD OF
Don't fire until you see the whites of their eyes.

The story is quite amusing in places, but basically is very serious.
INSTEAD OF
Underneath the slapstick humor, the story presents a bitter attack on materialism and snobbishness.

Religious faith is important, but practical considerations are also important.
INSTEAD OF
Trust in God, and keep your powder dry.

Nothing is technically wrong with the above examples of abstract writing, but we need only compare them to the rewritten concrete versions to see their basic inadequacy. They convey less information. They are less interesting. They have less impact. There is nothing wrong with them except that they are no good.

Specific Details

The use of specific details is the most direct way to avoid abstract writing. We tend to get irritated with a politician—or college dean—who, when confronted by a crucial issue, releases a press statement declaring, "We will give this matter our careful consideration." We get irritated not because the matter doesn't require careful consideration, but because the abstractness of the statement makes us suspect that we have just received a strong whiff of hot air. That suspicion will probably decrease significantly if the statement goes on to tell us the names of the people who will confer on this issue next Monday under orders to present recommendations within two weeks, those recommendations to be acted on inside of forty-eight hours. In this case, the specific details have served to support the generalization, have given us a clear notion of what the generalization means, and have helped create an impression of seriousness and sincerity.

Politicians and college deans are not the only people who sometimes seem too fond of hot air. Much of the material we read every day is abstract: flabby, dull, vague, and essentially meaningless. Like hot air, it lacks real body, real substance. The sports columnist writes, "The team should do better this year," and leaves it at that, instead of adding, "It should finish in third or fourth place and even has a fighting chance for the pennant." The teacher writes an angry letter saying, "This school ignores all vital needs of the faculty," and sounds like just another crank unless the letter goes on and points to *specific* needs that have in fact been ignored.

Student writing, from essay exams to themes in composition courses, could be vastly improved if more attention were paid to eliminating excessive abstraction and adding specific details. The more specific details, the less chance of hot air. Students should not tolerate the same things in their own writing that antagonize them in someone else's. Our use of language, not to mention our level of thought, would probably improve a hundredfold if we established an informal rule *never* to make an unsupported general statement, a general statement not backed up by specific details.

This rule sounds easy enough, but it means what it says. It means a writer should never try to get by with sentences such as, "The day was too hot"; "The hero of the story was very ambitious"; "The establishment is corrupt"; "The Industrial Revolution brought about many changes." These sentences are neither ungrammatical nor necessarily incorrect, but if they are not backed up by specific details they are worthless. "The day was too hot" is uninteresting and unpersuasive. *Back it up.* The reader should know that the temperature was 93 degrees, that Bill's sweaty glasses kept slipping off his nose, that even the little kids who usually filled the street were inside trying to keep cool, that a cocker spaniel who had managed to find a spot of shade was too exhausted and miserable to bother brushing away the flies. Whatever the piece of writing—a letter of application for a job, an analysis of a short story, a final exam in history—specific details give the writing life and conviction that abstractions alone can never achieve.

One more point about specific details: within reason, *the more specific the better.* As long as the detail is relevant—as long, that is, as it backs up the generalization and is not instantly obvious as too trivial for consideration—the writer is unlikely to go wrong by being too specific. On a history exam, a student may generalize, "In the Revolutionary War, the Americans had many difficulties." As specific support for that statement, the student may go on to write, "The number of Tories was quite large." But better in all respects would be, "Tories numbered as much as 30% of the population." The more specific the better, and one can almost always be more specific. Eventually, it is true, one can defeat one's purpose; it would be a mistake to give the reader the names and addresses of all the Tories during the Revolutionary War. The writing would then become so overwhelmed by specifics that the major point would be lost. Elementary common sense is usually the best guide in preventing that kind of mistake, and in actual practice few student writers run up against the problem of being too specific.

To summarize: support all your generalizations with relevant specific details. Remember that, within reason, the more specific the details, the better the writing.

Abstract (weak)

The telephone is a great scientific achievement, but it can also be a great inconvenience. Who could begin to count the number of times that phone calls have come from unwelcome people or on unwelcome occasions? Telephones make me nervous.

More Specific (better)

The telephone is a great scientific achievement, but it can also be a great pain. I get calls from bill collectors, hurt relatives, salespeople, charities, and angry neighbors. The calls always seem to come at the worst times, too. They've interrupted my meals, my baths, my parties, my sleep. I couldn't get along without telephones, but sometimes they make me a nervous wreck.

Still More Specific (much better)

The telephone is a great scientific achievement, but it can also be a great big headache. More often than not, that cheery ringing in my ears brings messages from the Ace Bill Collecting Agency, my mother (who is feeling snubbed for the fourth time that week), salesmen of encyclopedias and magazines, solicitors for the Policeman's Ball and Disease of the Month Foundation, and neighbors complaining about my dog. That's not to mention frequent wrong numbers—usually for someone named "Arnie." The calls always seem to come at the worst times, too. They've interrupted steak dinners, hot tubs, Friday night parties, and Saturday morning sleep-ins. There's no escape. Sometimes I wonder if there are any telephones in padded cells.

Exercise

Invent two or three specific details to back up each of the following generalizations. Use some imagination. Remember, the more specific the better. Don't settle for a detail like "He reads many books" to support the statement, "My teacher is very intellectual."

1. Local television news programs stress whatever is trivial or violent.
2. I have a terrible memory.
3. It's possible to tell a great deal about people from the way they shake hands.
4. The importance of a college education has been exaggerated.
5. The 55 mile per hour speed limit has added in some ways to the dangers of driving.
6. Our society systematically discriminates against left-handed people.
7. Essay examinations cannot be evaluated fairly.
8. My father has horrible taste in neckties.
9. Suburban life stifles individuality.
10. Bill is a sloppy eater.

Specific Words and Phrases

Writers who take seriously our "the-more-specific-the-better" rule will find not only that their writing has more impact and meaning, but also that their style as a whole, their use of language, has started to change significantly. Specific details in themselves are not a guarantee of good writing. Something has to happen to the language, too. The words with which a specific detail is presented must *themselves* be specific. In fact, through using specific words, a good writer can make even the most tiresomely familiar abstractions take on new life.

For most writers, the biggest challenge is learning to recognize when a particular word or phrase is not specific enough, and why. Often the first word that pops into our heads doesn't really work as effectively as it should. "He smiled," for example, may seem the natural way to describe a common facial expression. What rational person could complain about such a straightforward phrase? But have we truly conveyed the exact expression we are trying to write about or have we just settled for a fuzzy approximation? Wouldn't our readers get a clearer picture of the face we have in mind if we tried to pin down the word that best describes *this* smile: He grinned? smirked? sneered? leered? simpered? turned up the corners of his mouth? smiled half-heartedly? smiled broadly? Once we develop the habit of checking our original word choices carefully, making sure we've come as close to our precise meaning as possible, our style will become at once more specific and more colorful.

Nobody, it is true, will ever be ridiculed or exposed to public disgrace for writing, "She went to the door." But surely our readers deserve to be told, and surely we should want them to know, if she ran or walked or strolled or strutted or shuffled or limped or stumbled or sauntered or trotted or tiptoed to that door. Only one abstract word needs to be changed here, but the person who habitually recognizes that abstract word, refuses to let it pass, and selects a specific word to replace it is no longer just someone who writes, but a *writer*.

Using specific words is a different matter from supporting generalizations with details, though specific words may sometimes help give us a more detailed picture. Selecting specific words is primarily a means of expression, a way of putting things, a style. "He wore a hat" becomes, "His top hat was tilted jauntily over one eyebrow." We are not backing up a previous statement about someone's clothing preferences here—we are making a statement that has a specific meaning in and of itself. Together, specific details and specific words are the primary means of eliminating boring and dreary abstractions from our writing.

Exercise

In the sentences below, the *italicized* words or phrases are abstract and dull. Find a specific word or short phrase that can substitute for the abstract one and will fit the meaning of the rest of the sentence.

1. The *official* said that *services* would be *reduced*.
2. My friend sought out *her spiritual advisor* at *the church of her choice*.
3. The *small vehicle* crashed into the *big vehicle* at the *intersection*.
4. My parents gave me a *nice watch* for the *great event*.
5. X-rays revealed that the *football player* had a *serious injury*.

6. Since *the weather was good,* they decided on an *outing.*
7. Bill had been *in a low-income bracket* for *a long time.*
8. The *parent punished* the *child.*
9. Susan *acted wildly* and *talked strangely.*
10. *The local savings institution* has just *readjusted its interest rates.*

Comparisons

Another way of relieving the tedium of abstract writing and increasing the liveliness of concrete writing is to use effective figures of speech, particularly comparisons (see pp. 255–256 for a discussion of metaphors and similes). Sometimes a writer may have a hard time coming up with a forceful substitute for a humdrum expression like "it was very easy." There are plenty of synonyms for "very easy," of course, but the writer's best bet might be a comparison: *It was as easy as* (or *It was so easy it was like . . .) drinking a second glass of beer,* or *splattering toothpaste on the bathroom mirror,* or *forgetting the car keys.* Good comparisons are attention-getters. They provide a legitimate opportunity to show off a bit. They can demonstrate a writer's imagination or sense of humor. They can add a helpful spark to otherwise pedestrian writing.

Two cautions are in order. First, use comparisons in moderation. The more comparisons a piece of writing contains, the less impact each one is likely to have. Second, and more important, avoid the routine, trite comparisons with which our language is filled. Don't write "It was as easy as pie" or "It was as easy as taking candy from a baby." Try to be fresh and different. Rather than be trite, avoid comparisons altogether.

Make sure, by the way, that you phrase your comparisons correctly, whether you are using them for lively specific detail or as a simple means of making a point—"Alice is smarter than Sally," for example. Often, there is no problem, and we can do what comes naturally. But sometimes, through careless phrasing, we can appear to be comparing things that we had no intention of comparing, things that can't be compared because no relationship exists between them. None of us would think of writing "Eyebrows are better than hubcaps," but many of us have probably tossed off illogical sentences like the following:

INCORRECT	IMPROVED
Some of these horror stories are very similar to Edgar Allan Poe.	*Not what the writer meant.* He intended to compare the horror stories of one writer to the horror stories of another writer; instead, he

pointlessly compared the horror stories of one writer to another writer—period. He should have written:

Some of these horror stories are very similar to Edgar Allan Poe's.

OR

Some of these horror stories are very similar to those of Edgar Allan Poe.

His appetite was as huge as a pig.	His appetite was as huge as a pig's.
	OR
	His appetite was as huge as that of a pig.
	OR
	His appetite was as huge as a pig's appetite.
The new supermarket's prices are higher than the competition.	The new supermarket's prices are higher than the competition's.
	OR
	The new supermarket's prices are higher than those of the competition.

Another kind of illogical comparison unintentionally excludes an item of comparison from the group that it belongs to through the omission of the word *other:*

INCORRECT	IMPROVED
Lincoln had more detailed knowledge of the Bible than any American president.	Lincoln had more detailed knowledge of the Bible than any *other* American president.
My high school paid less attention to sports than any school in the city.	My high school paid less attention to sports than any *other* school in the city.

Sometimes, too, improper phrasing can result in confusion. What did the writer of these sentences want to say?

I like him more than you.	Did the writer mean *I like him more than you like him* or *I like him more than I like you?*
Hemingway is more indebted to Mark Twain than anyone else.	Did the writer mean *Hemingway is more indebted to Mark Twain than to anyone else* or *Hemingway is more indebted to Mark Twain than anyone else is?*

Exercise A

Make up *two* phrases to complete each of the following comparisons. Be prepared to tell which of your phrases is better and why.

1. My older brother is as bossy as . . .
2. The long wait was as nervewracking as . . .
3. The dentist looked at me like . . .
4. The drunk staggered as unsteadily as . . .
5. Expecting common courtesy from him is like . . .
6. Her hair was such a mess that I was reminded of . . .
7. The Congressman's explanation was as plausible as . . .
8. A tender glance from my sweetheart is more precious to me than . . .
9. If you'd buy an insurance policy from him, you're the kind of person who . . .
10. The prospect of a career in the army has all the appeal of . . .

Exercise B

Rephrase the sentences below where necessary.

1. My mother loves me more than my father.
2. Van Gogh's technique is not as skillful as Cezanne.
3. The use of nuclear energy arouses more emotions than any controversial issue.
4. I owe the bank less than you.
5. His unearthly paleness was like a ghost.
6. He was as busy as a bee.
7. All things considered, Jane's bad luck has been worse than anyone's.
8. *Fiddler on the Roof* had a longer run than any Broadway musical.
9. Our gross national product is substantially larger than the Soviet Union.
10. She enjoys Flip Wilson more than Bill Cosby.

WORDINESS AND ECONOMY

Many human individuals use more words than are absolutely necessary and essential to express the thoughts and ideas which they (the human individuals) are attempting to communicate. They repeat the same thing constantly and say the same thing over and over again. Sometimes instead of actually repeating themselves they merely substitute various and sundry long phrases for a simple word due to the fact that it is their opinion that readers will be impressed by this writing method of procedure. But in the modern contemporary world of today, good writing should never be wordy. It should be economical; that is, it should say what it has to say, and then stop, cease, and desist.

In case you haven't noticed, the paragraph you just read violates all of its own good advice. You can find examples of wordiness everywhere: "human individuals" instead of "people," "thoughts and ideas" instead of "thoughts" *or* "ideas," "due to the fact that" instead of "because," "it is their opinion" instead of "they think." The whole paragraph could be cut to half its length without losing anything but a mass of nonfunctioning words:

> Many people use more words than are necessary to express their thoughts. They repeat the same things constantly or substitute long phrases for a simple word because they want to impress their readers. **But good writing should never be wordy: it should say what it has to say, and then stop.**

Wordiness is a major writing problem. It is hard to avoid because it can turn up for any number of reasons, and writers usually don't realize that they are being wordy. Nobody wants to be a windbag, yet unneeded words sneak into nearly everyone's writing.

Before discussing the different kinds of wordiness, we should clear up one point. Wordiness results from words that don't do anything—it has no direct connection to mere number of words. A poor writer can produce a wordy paragraph on the meaning of freedom; a good writer can produce a whole book on the same subject that is not wordy. If the words contribute to the effect the author wants, if eliminating any of them would sacrifice something valuable, then the author is *not* being wordy. Many pieces of writing with lots of specific details are longer than abstract versions of the same pieces would be, but getting rid of the details would mean a loss of interest and clarity. Only when words can be eliminated without any harm being done do we find real wordiness.

Deadwood

Some words are like "dead wood" on a tree or bush. Unless these words are removed, they sap the strength of the healthy words around them. Moreover, being dead, they can be removed with little or no tampering with the rest of the sentence, as in the examples that follow.

DEADWOOD	IMPROVED
His hair was red in color.	His hair was red.
Pollution conditions that exist in our cities are disgraceful.	Pollution in our cities is disgraceful.
The building has a height of 934 feet.	The building rises 934 feet.
She was in a depressed state of mind.	She was depressed.
Disneyland struck us as a fascinating kind of place.	Disneyland struck us as fascinating.
In this day and age we live in, people seem totally apathetic about everything.	People today seem totally apathetic.
The hero of the story was an individual in the high-income bracket.	The hero of the story was wealthy.
The validity of such statements should not be adhered to.	Such statements are invalid.
He spoke to her in a harsh manner.	He spoke to her harshly.
I am going to major in the field of sociology.	I am going to major in sociology.
The character had a hard type of decision to make.	The character had a hard decision to make.
Because of the fact that my teacher disliked me, he gave me a bad grade.	Because my teacher disliked me, he gave me a bad grade.
Sometimes the moral of a story is a very important factor.	Sometimes the moral of a story is very important.
The story "Quality," written by the author John Galsworthy, is a story with an unhappy ending.	"Quality" by John Galsworthy is a story with an unhappy ending.

The wise writer is always on the lookout for deadwood, especially in revision. Deadwood infiltrates nearly everyone's first draft, but there is no room for these tiresome words-without-purpose in a finished composition. As a general rule, it is safe to assume that if words can be removed without harming anything—as in the examples above—they should be removed.

Pointless Repetition of Meaning

Pointless repetition of meaning is a special kind of deadwood. Aside from adding useless words, such repetition reflects writers' lack of confidence in themselves—their fear that their point will not be clear unless they make it twice. Unfortunately, this overemphasis usually suggests sloppy thinking to the reader, rather than a desire for accuracy.

POINTLESS REPETITION	IMPROVED
The film was very interesting and fascinating.	The film was fascinating.
Our streams are filthy and dirty.	Our streams are filthy.
This approach could end in a catastrophic conclusion.	This approach could end catastrophically.
The author gives examples of different and varied criticisms of the novel.	The author gives examples of different criticisms of the novel.
To begin with, in the first place, the story has terrific suspense.	In the first place, the story has terrific suspense.
Some early critics of Jonathan Swift called him an insane madman suffering from the symptoms of mental disease.	Some early critics of Jonathan Swift called him insane.
There is no question about the worth and value of obtaining an education.	There is no question about the value of obtaining an education.
He has no emotional feelings.	He has no feelings.
Each and every person ought to read a newspaper.	Everyone ought to read a newspaper.
The new administration will make the exact same mistake as the old one.	The new administration will make the same mistake as the old one.

Exercise

Point out any instances of deadwood and pointless repetition in the following sentences.

1. The color of her hair was black, and the color of her eyes was brown.
2. Gun-control legislation is a controversial kind of issue.
3. We need to get back to the basic fundamentals.
4. At the end of the program, the two competing contestants were tied.
5. The area of heredity still has many uncertain aspects to it.
6. The beginning of the play starts out in a very impressive manner.

7. Men and women of both sexes must join the combat to fight for a better world.
8. His race, color, and creed mean nothing to me.
9. This country has ignored the problems and difficulties of its elderly senior citizens.
10. I pledge to oppose the forces of godless atheism and disloyal treason.
11. He gave a forceful, energetic, and dynamic type of presentation of his opinion and point of view.
12. All day long, he took forever to make up his mind.
13. We would welcome hearing your comments and reactions.
14. She responded with a favorable attitude to the social life environment at the singles apartment facility.
15. A slow student who does not learn as quickly as other students needs to be singled out for special attention by the individual responsible for teaching.
16. The man her mother married was a cruel and unkind stepfather to her.
17. He disliked me due to the fact that I spoke to him in a sarcastic way.
18. Teenage young people can benefit from travel experiences.
19. Your car or automobile needs service and maintenance at regularly spaced intervals.
20. The class situation stimulates interpersonal communication between students.

Delay of Subject

There is, there has, it is, and *it has*—in all tenses—are frequent causes of wordiness. Nothing is wrong with these phrases in themselves; they are necessary parts of the language, and some thoughts might be inexpressible without them. Too often, however, they are used carelessly and delay a sentence or clause from getting down to business. In the following examples, the original sentences begin with words that have no more purpose than the throat-clearing noises made by a speaker before a talk. The revised sentences begin with important words, words that communicate the central concern of each sentence.

WORD DELAY	IMPROVED
There are too many people who care only for themselves.	Too many people care only for themselves.
It has often been commented on by great philosophers that philosophy solves nothing.	Great philosophers have often commented that philosophy solves nothing.

There have been a number of conflicting studies made of urban problems.	A number of conflicting studies have been made of urban problems.
It was on December 7, 1941, that the Japanese attacked the U.S. fleet at Pearl Harbor.	On December 7, 1941, the Japanese attacked the U.S. fleet at Pearl Harbor.
It is a fact that there has been a great increase in sensationalism in the theater.	Sensationalism in the theater has greatly increased.

Inadequate Clause-cutting

One of the most effective ways of reducing wordiness is to cut a cumbersome dependent or independent clause into a shorter phrase or, if possible, a single word. This clause-cutting can result in a tighter, more economical structure, with the phrase or word more firmly incorporated into the sentence than the original clause ever was. Sometimes, of course, a writer may choose to leave the clause alone for a perfectly valid reason, such as emphasis. But more often than not, such clauses are tacked on awkwardly and add unnecessary words; they should always be examined with a critical eye.

WORDY CLAUSE	IMPROVED
The girl who had red hair was a flirt.	The red-haired girl was a flirt.
Some of the students who were more enthusiastic wrote an extra paper.	Some of the more enthusiastic students wrote an extra paper.
The story was very exciting. It was all about ghosts.	The ghost story was very exciting.
Alexander the Great was a man who tried to conquer the world.	Alexander the Great tried to conquer the world.
The applause, which sounded like a thunderclap, shook the auditorium.	The applause shook the auditorium like a thunderclap.
No one who has a child of his or her own can fail to appreciate the charm of this poem.	No parent can fail to appreciate the charm of this poem.
Passionate love is a feeling that has inspired many great writers and artists.	Passionate love has inspired many great writers and artists.
He is an extremely ambitious man; he is scheming to replace his boss.	Extremely ambitious, he is scheming to replace his boss.
The two main characters in the play have similar attitudes toward other people and the way in which each feels about the conventions of society.	The two main characters in the play have similar attitudes toward other people and social conventions.

Exercise

Rewrite these sentences to make them more economical, cutting clauses and eliminating wordy delay of subject wherever possible.

1. The dream that I have been experiencing every night probably has deep psychological significance.
2. People who drive while they are drunk should be given mandatory prison sentences.
3. There is no newspaper that has a better international reputation than the *New York Times*.
4. She is a woman who has always valued her career above her family.
5. It is no disgrace to apologize when you have done something wrong.
6. There are two kinds of people I hate.
7. The idea of a guaranteed annual wage is a notion that conflicts with many traditional middle-class values.
8. Emerson had an extremely optimistic philosophy. It probably reflected the spirit of mid-nineteenth century America.
9. There was nothing in the old house that seemed familiar to me.
10. Many nonconformists who are so proud of themselves are the worst conformists of all.
11. Cars that are made in Germany do not have the reputation for good workmanship that they used to have.
12. Roger Staubach, who plays for the Dallas Cowboys, has a nickname which is "Roger the Dodger."
13. There have been many complicated plans that have been proposed to help New York City regain financial stability.
14. People who play practical jokes are people who are basically insecure.
15. A movie that was about a big shark and a movie that was about a big gorilla contained more human interest than many movies that had greater artistic pretensions.
16. There are many professors who really are absentminded—except when it comes to due-dates for term papers.
17. In the elections that took place in 1976, President Ford carried almost every state that was west of the Mississippi.
18. When he was threatened with blackmail over letters he had written to the woman who had been his mistress, the Duke of Wellington replied, "Publish and be damned!"
19. The old show "Star Trek" still has thousands of loyal fans. They are affectionately known as "Trekkies."
20. On "Star Trek" Mr. Spock was played by an actor whose name was Leonard Nimoy. Mr. Spock was characterized as a completely rational being.

CHAPTER 16

STYLISTIC PROBLEMS AND THEIR SOLUTIONS

We have already outlined the general principles that writers should put into practice in developing their styles: choosing the word with the proper connotations, keeping the writing specific, and eliminating wordiness. But even writers who have mastered these ideas can still run into difficulty with particular stylistic problems. Often without realizing it, they may toss in a handy cliché, ignore a string of phrases that aren't parallel, repeat a word monotonously, or pass over an awkward passive verb. For such problems general principles are sometimes *too* general.

In this chapter, we define and discuss those problems that are most likely to arise so that you can either avoid them entirely or recognize and correct them if they do appear in your writing. We also explain which of these stylistic elements can serve a valid purpose when used consciously and carefully.

TRITENESS

A trite expression or *cliché*, is a word or phrase that has become worn out through overuse. Many trite expressions may once have been original and even brilliant, but through constant repetition they have lost whatever impact they once had. If a writer uses many trite expressions, a reader may be tempted to assume that the thoughts are as secondhand as the language.

Triteness generally calls attention to itself in some way. Words like *the, a, man, come, go* are not trite even though they are used all the time, because they are simple, direct, and unself-conscious. Trite expressions are pretentious. They seem, on the surface, to convey a thought or feeling particularly well, and people who haven't read enough to recognize them sometimes think them clever, or elegant, or lively. Experienced readers, however, interpret them for what they usually are: evidence of a writer's laziness and lack of imagination.

The only way to handle triteness is to eliminate it. Apologetic little quotation marks do not help. If the writer has been trite, quotation marks call more attention to the fault and let the reader know that the triteness was no accident.

The list below contains a number of trite expressions. Avoid them. Choose fifteen from the list and try to think of original and effective ways to express the same ideas.

more fun than a barrel of monkeys	imperialist lackey
worth its weight in gold	Iron Curtain
over the hill	do unto others
stop on a dime	flat as a pancake
fresh as a daisy	dumb as an ox
happy as a lark	meaningful dialogue
hard as nails	turned on
have someone in a corner	red as a rose
make a long story short	tired but happy
no use crying over spilled milk	a good time was had by all
a penny saved is a penny earned	white as snow
cool as a cucumber	black as pitch
pretty as a picture	put it in a nutshell
in the pink	Mother Nature
hale and hearty	Father Time
apple-pie order	spread like wildfire
under the weather	the crack of dawn
devil-may-care attitude	spring chicken
go at it tooth and nail	dog-eat-dog
generation gap	survival of the fittest
every cloud has a silver lining	south of the border
sick as a dog	armed to the teeth
work like a dog	lean and lanky
easy as pie	flattery will get you nowhere
sweet as sugar	a matter of life and death
quick as a wink	male chauvinist pig
quick as a flash	a bolt from the blue
greased lightning	father of his country
tender loving care	signed, sealed, and delivered

sly as a fox	open-and-shut case
stubborn as a mule	flash in the pan
rat race	babe in the woods
Old Glory	not a cloud in the sky
trial and error	feathered friends
struggle for existence	slow as molasses
the bigger they are the harder they fall	do your own thing
sad but true	last but not least

In addition to the kind of phrases listed above, some familiar—and important—ideas have been expressed in the same language so often that the ideas themselves seem trite unless they are worded differently. No matter how much we believe in the need for stable human relationships, we are not going to get very excited when someone tells us "People must learn to get along with one another." If we are presenting one of these ideas, we must express it in a dramatic, forceful way, or at least show that we do not regard it as a profound new insight. Here is a partial list of such potentially trite ideas:

The older generation has made a mess of things.
A good marriage involves more than sex.
Getting to know people of different backgrounds is a good thing.
College is more difficult than high school.
Pollution is a major problem in the United States.
Education is necessary for many jobs.
We live in a technological society.
This problem could have been avoided by better communication.
This problem will be solved by better communication.
We need to think more about people who are less fortunate.
It is possible to have different opinions about a poem.
Nature is beautiful.
Adults have more responsibilities than children.
This issue is very complicated.

EUPHEMISMS

A euphemism is a word or phrase used as a polite substitute for a more natural but less refined word or phrase. Euphemisms can be handy to have around, especially in social situations. Chances are that clergymen and grandmothers will be happier and more comfortable to hear us react to a stubbed toe with "Oh dear" for "Oh damn" or "Good gracious" for "Good God." Chances are that the widow with two children will find her grief easier to bear if we say, "I was so sorry to hear about Fred," and thoughtfully omit the unpleasant medical details. As a rule, though, euphemisms should be avoided, especially in writing. They generally seem pretentious, fussy, and old-fashioned. They can make writers appear afraid to face facts and say what they mean. The natural, honest word is usually the best one, so long as honesty is not confused with exhibitionistic crudeness or vulgarity. In most cases, then, avoid writing both "He passed on to a better world" and "He croaked." Try "He died."

EUPHEMISMS	HONEST TERMS
low-income individual	poor person
urban poverty area	slum
sanitation worker	garbage collector
custodian *or* superintendent	janitor
mortician *or* funeral director	undertaker
conflict	war
distortion of the facts	lie
casualties	dead and wounded
senior citizen	old person
powder one's nose	go to the bathroom
financially embarrassed	in debt
reconditioned	used
to pass on	to die

Exercise _____

Locate trite expressions and euphemisms in the sentences below and suggest good alternatives.

1. Consumption of unwise amounts of intoxicating beverages left him in less than full possession of all his faculties.
2. I told him to look before he leaped, but he insisted on doing his own thing.
3. Carol kept arguing like a dumb bunny even though she didn't have a leg to stand on.
4. As the sun sank slowly in the west, we bade a fond farewell to the Emerald Isle.
5. Institutions of higher learning should offer their students viable alternatives careerwise.

6. The casket for the dear departed cost a pretty penny.
7. The army executed a strategic withdrawal.
8. Mr. Smith's immediate superior told him that his services would no longer be required.
9. After a long drive, the powder room at the gas station was a sight for sore eyes.
10. Our feathered friends sang their hearts out for us.

USE OF PASSIVE VERBS

In most English sentences, the subject performs an action.

> John likes this poem.
>
> The critic saw the movie.
>
> The senator is going to vote for the bill.

The verb in such sentences is said to be in the *active voice.* The active voice is direct, clear, and concise; in most sentences, it is what we expect.

Too often, however, instead of using the natural active voice, writers substitute the more stilted *passive voice.* A verb in the passive voice combines a form of *to be* with the past participle of the verb: *is given, has been delivered, was mailed.* Thus, instead of *acting,* the subject of the sentence is *acted upon.*

> This poem is liked by John.
>
> The movie was seen by the critic.
>
> The bill is going to be voted for by the senator.

Compared to the active voice, the passive is generally awkward, exceedingly formal, and wordy. It is better to write "This theme will analyze the story" than "The story will be analyzed in this theme." It is better to write "My sociology teacher offered some challenging insights into contemporary problems" than "Some challenging insights into contemporary problems were offered by my sociology teacher."

On occasion, the passive voice doesn't sound bad, of course. Such occasions may arise when the actor is unknown, insignificant, or nonexistent, or when a deliberately impersonal tone is required. Don't be afraid of the passive when it seems normal and unforced—as in the last part of the preceding sentence—but always be alert to its dangers. Here are a few examples of perfectly acceptable passives:

The game was delayed because of rain.

The eighteenth century has been called the Age of Enlightenment.

Your prompt attention to this request for payment will be appreciated.

The building will be finished in a few months.

We have been victimized time after time.

Exercise

In the sentences below, change the passive voice to the active voice wherever appropriate.

1. This paper was graded by the teacher last night.
2. The forms must be returned before April 15 by you.
3. No one is more respected than Dr. Wells.
4. Another perfect pass was dropped by the wide receiver.
5. The embezzler was imprisoned for his crimes.
6. The embezzler was imprisoned for his crimes by the court.
7. Don't believe everything that you are told.
8. The victim was pronounced dead on arrival.
9. The victim was pronounced dead on arrival by the coroner.
10. The exam was passed by me but failed by my best friend.

PARALLELISM

Essentially, parallelism means expressing ideas and facts of equal (or coordinate or "parallel") importance in the same grammatical form. We do it all the time, almost unconsciously.

The store was filled with *chairs, tables, sofas,* and *lamps.*	*a group of four nouns*
He *came home, ate dinner,* and *went to bed.*	*three verb phrases*
You can get there by *car, bus,* or *plane.*	*three nouns*
I thought the climactic episode in the story was *shocking, offbeat,* and *amusing.*	*three adjectives*

Parallel grammatical structure reinforces the writer's thought by stressing the parallel importance of the various sentence elements, and so makes life easier for the reader. Many of the most famous phrases in our language draw strength in part from effective use of parallelism:

. . . *life, liberty,* and the *pursuit* of happiness — *group of three nouns*

. . . *of the people, by the people,* and *for the people* — *three prepositional phrases*

love me or *leave me* — *two imperatives*

Early *to bed* and early *to rise*/Makes a man healthy, and *wealthy* and *wise* — *two infinitives/three adjectives*

To *be* or not to *be* — *two infinitives*

Friends, Romans, countrymen . . . — *three nouns*

I come *to bury Caesar,* not *to praise him* — *two infinitives with objects*

I came, I saw, I conquered — *three independent clauses*

Peace on earth, good will toward men — *two nouns, each with prepositional phrase*

Better be *safe* than *sorry* — *two adjectives*

. . . *the land of the free* and *the home of the brave* — *two nouns, each with a prepositional phrase*

Now notice how faulty parallelism or lack of parallelism can sabotage a sentence.

You can get there by *car, bus,* or *fly.* — *two nouns, and all of a sudden a verb*

I thought the climactic episode in the story was *shocking, offbeat,* and *I found it very amusing.* — *two adjectives, coupled with an independent clause*

The teacher told us *to work fast* and *that we should write on only one side of the paper.* — *shift from infinitive to clause*

She *liked* people and *was liked* by people. — *shift from active to passive voice*

Bill was a *good husband,* a *loving father,* and *worked hard.* — *adjective-noun, adjective-noun, verb-adverb*

Descriptive words added to some of the parallel elements do not break the basic parallelism and can be valuable in avoiding monotony.

Judith had *brains, talent,* and an extremely charming *personality.* — *still parallel: a group of three nouns, even though one is modified by an adjective, and the adjective is modified by an adverb*

The man owned a *mansion* and a fine *collection* of modern etchings. — *still parallel: two nouns, even though one of them is modified by an adjective and followed by a prepositional phrase*

The baby has now learned how to *whimper, shriek, yell* loudly, and *cry* its head off.   *still parallel: four infinitives, even though one is modified by an adverb and one is followed by an object*

Parallelism, then, is an indispensable aid to style and meaning, but keep in mind that its value is limited to cases in which the various elements are of equal importance. If we try to parallel unequal elements, we can wind up with startling calamities, unless we are being intentionally humorous:

He had wealth, vitality, sophistication, and a short nose.

The story offers a profound message of inspiration and hope to mankind and occupies pages 152 to 170 of our textbook.

My friend John is a revolutionary activist and a former cub scout.

We must all work together to eliminate war, disease, hunger, and dirty movies.

Exercise

Which of the following sentences use faulty parallelism? Which use parallelism correctly? Which use inappropriate parallelism? Make corrections in the sentences that need them.

1. In "The Use of Force," the child is foolish, stubborn, and a girl who fears she may die.
2. I am thinking of a career in law, medicine, or doing chemical research.
3. Percy Bysshe Shelley wrote some of the greatest poems in the English language, lived a spectacularly scandalous private life, and had a weird middle name.
4. A healthy family life can give a young person a feeling of security, a desire for excellence, and that most important of all qualities, a strong sense of identity.
5. Farrah Fawcett-Majors helped make "Charlie's Angels" a show that was sexy, funny, and a success.
6. Three kinds of weeds grow on people's lawns: weeds, more weeds, and nothing but weeds.
7. Food in the school cafeteria is tasteless and a ridiculous expense.
8. He was a snob about wine, food, clothing, and seeing people make grammatical mistakes.
9. Sister Philomena told us we were noisy, spiteful, and to pay more attention.
10. The repairman worked steadily, fixed the washer, charged a reasonable price, and was respected by Mrs. Clark.

SUBORDINATION

Which of these observations on that great new epic, *The Return of the Hideous Vampire,* is likely to be most significant?

> It was produced by Paramount Brothers.
> It is one of the best horror movies of the last ten years.
> It was filmed in technicolor.

Which of these facts about Earnest N. Dogood deserves the most emphasis?

> He is a Republican.
> He has announced his candidacy for President of the United States.
> He is a senator.

The answers are obvious; in both cases, the second item is the one you should have chosen. Neither set of statements would be appropriate as a list of parallel thoughts—because ideas and facts are not all created equal. This simple truth has tremendous consequences for our writing.

If we tried to present all the information we have as if it really were of equal, parallel importance, we would probably wind up with a form of baby talk. At one time or another, many of us have probably had to suffer through a young child's account of a movie or television show. To the child, everything is supremely fascinating. Distinctions between major and minor episodes mean nothing, and the child can easily make a plot summary seem to last as long as the show itself:

> First the cowboy woke up and he got dressed and then he went downstairs and he got on his horse and his horse's name was Big Boy and then he rode off on his horse to fight the bad guy.

Note that the child gives equal emphasis to all the facts by expressing each one as an independent clause, a unit that can stand alone as a separate sentence: *the cowboy woke up, he got dressed, he ate,* etc. This equality is further stressed by the use of *and* to tie the clauses together. *And* simply links new ingredients to a sentence or phrase—it doesn't help the reader decide which ingredient is more significant (*ham and eggs, boys and girls, war and peace,* for example). Essentially, the problem with the cowboy story is that important facts are forced to compete for our attention with relatively trivial ones.

Instead of giving equal weight to each fact, then, and creating a monotonous stream of unfiltered data, a skillful writer will *subordi-*

nate some of those facts, arranging the sentence or paragraph so that some parts are clearly secondary to others.

> After waking up, eating, going downstairs, and getting on his horse, Big Boy, the cowboy rode off to fight with the bad guy.

We certainly have no specimen of prize-winning prose here, but we don't have the total mess we started out with either. This revision contains only one independent clause—*the cowboy rode off to fight with the bad guy*—and that clause contains the most important fact. None of the other independent clauses in the original sentence survives. They have all been subordinated grammatically and no longer clamor for the reader's primary attention.

Look again at the beginning of this section on subordination. We have three pieces of information about a movie. The writer with no sense of subordination merely smacks down each point as it comes to mind without attempting to differentiate between major and minor items but, instead, giving each item a sentence to itself.

> *The Return of the Hideous Vampire* was produced by Paramount Brothers. It is one of the best horror movies of the last ten years. It was filmed in technicolor.

By contrast, with proper subordination the writer collects the three related observations, reserves the independent clause for the most important one, and tucks away the rest in a less conspicuous place.

> *The Return of the Hideous Vampire,* a technicolor film produced by Paramount Brothers, is one of the best horror movies of the last ten years.

We can see the same principle at work with Earnest N. Dogood.

UNSUBORDINATED	SUBORDINATED
Earnest N. Dogood is a Republican. He has announced his candidacy for President of the United States. He is a senator.	Senator Earnest N. Dogood, a Republican, has announced his candidacy for President of the United States.

Remember that related ideas can often be tied together in a way that shows their relationships more clearly. Remember that an independent clause, whether it stands alone as a single sentence or is incorporated into a complex sentence, is a loud cry for attention and should generally be saved for matters of importance.

Here are a few more examples of how subordination can improve your writing:

UNSUBORDINATED	SUBORDINATED
John is a wonderful person. He is very shy. He is extremely kind to everybody.	Although very shy, John is a wonderful person who is extremely kind to everybody.
	OR, IF YOU WANT TO EMPHASIZE THE SHYNESS
	Although he is a wonderful person who is extremely kind to everybody, John is very shy.
This play explores the fate of love in a mechanized society. It is highly symbolic, and it has two acts.	This highly symbolic play of two acts explores the fate of love in a mechanized society.
Professor Jones is terribly sarcastic. He is also a tough grader. It is true that he knows his subject. Most students dislike him, however.	Despite Professor Jones's knowledge of his subject, most students dislike him because of his terrible sarcasm and tough grading.

Exercise

Rewrite the following sentences, making effective use of subordination.

1. Romantic love is not enough to make a marriage succeed if intelligence is not also present.
2. Shy people create many problems for themselves. I know this from experience. I am shy myself.
3. This film may be the worst one that has ever been made. The acting is bad. The humor is cheap. The exploitation of sex is disgusting.
4. It was sad to hear him say such harsh things about poor people. He had once been poor himself.
5. Terry's mother was washing the dishes, and Terry was helping her. Then Terry heard a scream outside that was very frightening.
6. I am rarely confident about my work, but I thought I had done well on the exam.
7. The novel leaves its readers deeply shaken, and it is also very well written.
8. Scientists tend to laugh at voodoo as superstition. It is still a real religion, and it is taken seriously by many thousands of people.
9. Professor Fosdick spent a year in England. It was extremely busy, and it could also turn out to be profitable.
10. My uncle will never give up his dream of making a killing on the stock market. All his investments have been bad so far, and people laugh at him constantly.

SENTENCE MONOTONY AND VARIETY

Readers frequently find themselves struggling to concentrate on a string of sentences even though nothing obvious seems to be wrong. Sentence by sentence, in fact, the author may be writing perfectly well. Put the sentences together, though, and monotony sets in. The monotony can usually be attributed either to a series of sentences that are all, or nearly all, of the same *length* or the same *structure.*

Sentence Length

Sentences come short, medium, and long—and the simple principle for effective writing is to *try for variety.* Don't take this principle more rigidly than it's intended. Don't assume, for instance, that every single short sentence must be followed by a long one, and vice versa. A string of short or long sentences can sometimes be effective, providing that it is eventually followed by a sentence that varies the pattern. Common sense and alertness will tell you when variety is needed. Just remember that too many sentences of the same length bunched together can create a monotonous style and a restless reader.

MONOTONOUS	IMPROVED
He told us the car got good mileage. He said the tires were excellent. The engine was supposed to be quiet. The transmission was supposed to be smooth. He stressed that the brake linings still had plenty of wear. Everything he said was a lie.	He told us the car got good mileage and that it had excellent tires, a quiet engine, a smooth transmission, and sound brake linings. In other words, he lied.
I thought the course was going to be easy, but I was wrong, because after a two-week sickness early in the term I could never find the time to catch up with the assignments, and I kept getting poor grades. I wish I had had the foresight to see what was coming and had taken the initiative either to drop the course or to ask the teacher for an incomplete, but pride or vanity kept me plugging away, and nothing did any good.	I thought the course was going to be easy, but I was wrong. After a two-week sickness early in the term, I could never find the time to catch up with the assignments, and I kept getting poor grades. Why didn't I drop? Why didn't I ask for an incomplete? If I'd known for sure what was coming, I probably would have done one or the other. Pride or vanity kept me plugging away, however, and nothing did any good.

Sentence Structure

Regardless of sentence length, a group of sentences can become monotonous because each sentence uses the same basic structure.

All the sentences begin with a present participle (-*ing* endings), for example, or the first word of each sentence is automatically the subject of that sentence, or the first word is *never* the subject. Perhaps every sentence turns out to be a compound sentence (two or more independent clauses) or a complex sentence (one independent clause and one or more dependent clauses). Now forget about the grammatical terms. Remember only that there are many different ways of structuring a sentence, and wise writers never limit themselves to one. Variety is again the key.

MONOTONOUS

Entering the personnel manager's office, Bill wanted to make a good impression. Smiling, he shook hands. Sitting down, he tried not to fidget. Answering the questions politely, he kept his voice low and forced himself not to say "uh." Being desperate for a job, he had to be at his best. Wondering if his desperation showed, he decided to risk a little joke.

Red wine goes best with meat, and white wine goes best with fish. Red wine should be served at room temperature, and white wine should be chilled. Red wine should usually be opened about a half hour before serving, and the accumulated gasses should be allowed to escape from the bottle. These rules are not meaningless customs, but they are proven by centuries of experience, and they improve the taste of the food as well as the wine.

IMPROVED

Entering the personnel manager's office, Bill wanted to make a good impression. He smiled, shook hands, and tried not to fidget when he sat down. He answered questions politely, keeping his voice low and forcing himself not to say "uh." Bill was desperate for a job. He had to be at his best. Wondering if his desperation showed, he decided to risk a little joke.

Red wine goes best with meat, and white wine goes best with fish. Unlike white wine, which should be served chilled, red wine should be served at room temperature. Red wine also benefits from being opened about a half hour before serving to allow the accumulated gasses to escape from the bottle. Proven by experience, these rules improve the taste of the food as well as the wine. They are not meaningless customs.

REPETITION, GOOD AND BAD

Repetition for Clarity

Repetition can help to clarify meaning and get the writer and reader from one sentence or clause to another. One of the simplest and most valuable transitional devices for a writer is the repetition of a key word or phrase, sometimes in slightly altered form, from a preceding sentence or clause:

> Five drug *companies* have been accused of misleading advertising. The first of these *companies* is . . .

Critics tend to make too much of a fuss about *symbols*. *Symbols* are not obscure artistic tricks. Our own daily lives are filled with *symbols*.

Few people want to be thought of as extremely *conventional*, but respect for *conventions* of some sort is necessary for any society to function adequately.

Repetition for Impact

Repetition can often add effective emotional impact:

> We've shrugged at scandals. We've shrugged at violence. We've shrugged at overpopulation and pollution and discrimination. Now it's time to stop shrugging.

> When she lost her husband, she lost her friend, lost her lover, lost her confidant. She lost everything that gave meaning to her life.

> The decision must be made this week—not this year, not this month, not early next week, but this week.

If not handled skillfully and tastefully, repetition for impact can also lead to foolish emotionalism or unnecessary stress on the obvious:

> It's important to plan ahead in writing. It's really, really important.

> Must cruel developers have their way forever? What of the flowers? What of the trees? What of the grass? What of the homeless birds and squirrels and bunnies?

> There is too much violence on television. Bang, bang, bang, bang, bang—that's all we ever hear. Bang, bang, bang.

Undesirable Repetition of Meaning

This kind of repetition (already discussed under "Wordiness," pp. 353–358) involves stating a point that is already sufficiently clear:

> The American flag is red, white, and blue *in color.*

> She was remarkably beautiful. *She was, in fact, quite exceptionally good-looking.*

> The effect *and outcome* of all this was most unfortunate.

> In today's *modern contemporary* world . . .

Undesirable Repetition of the Same Word

We have noted that repetition of a word (either the same word or a different form of that word, as in *conventional/conventions*) can be helpful. It can also be monotonous and irritating, however, especially when the word itself is not crucial to the meaning of the passage; words such as *very, really,* and *interesting* are major offenders.

I am *very* pleased to be here on this *very* distinguished occasion. Your *very* kind remarks and your *very* generous gift have left me *very* much at a loss for words, but *very* deeply appreciative.

I *really* enjoyed reading this story. It was a *really* exciting story with *real* people in *real* situations. The suspense was *really* terrific.

We had a *wonderful* time in Florida. During the day we went swimming, and at night we saw some *really interesting* shows. The weather was great, the food was *really* just *wonderful,* and the sights were *very interesting.*

Beware of using different forms of the same word *through carelessness.* You can create an awkward and confusing sentence before you know it.

We had a *wonderful* time seeing the *wonders* of Florida.

The *beauties* of Shakespeare's sonnets are outstandingly *beautiful.*

People must be made more *aware* of the need for increased *awareness* of our environment.

One more menace to watch out for is repetition of words in the same sentence, or otherwise close together, *if there is a change in the meaning of the word.* Never commit this particular crime unless you are trying to be intentionally humorous.

Only a perfect *dope* would experiment with *dope.*

Gary *Player* is an excellent golf *player.*

If I *run* hard, my nose will *run.*

Our weekly games of *bridge* have helped build a friendly *bridge* of understanding between our two families.

Undesirable Repetition of Sounds

Save rhymes for poetry. Avoid horrors like these:

The condemnation of the administration was brought about by its own lack of ability and student hostility.

The church is reexamining its position on the condition of the mission.

The Allied troops' defensive stance stopped the German advance into France.

Go easy on alliteration, the repetition of sounds at the beginning of words. Every once in a while, alliteration can be effective, but when a writer is obviously pouring it on, the results are silly at best.

We must toss these sneering, snickering, swindling swine out of office.

The orchestra's bold blowing of the brasses thrilled me to the bottom of my being.

The main piece of furniture in the room was a dirty, damaged, dilapidated, and dreary old desk.

Exercise

Point out any undesirable repetition in the sentences below and make the necessary corrections.

1. I no longer desire to read novels concerned solely with bestial passion and illicit desire.
2. This was a memorable short story; it will truly be hard to forget.
3. I was deeply moved by the singer's rendition of that moving old ballad.
4. It's simply marvelous the way you can stand on the corner and simply pass out leaflets to hundreds of people who are simply passing by.
5. The supervisor's role is to train the applicant's brain to attain higher skills.
6. The bulging belly of this butterball becomes more than I can bear.
7. A burglar stole Mrs. Plutocratz's jewelry and mink stole.
8. I asked her to marry me, and she said yes. She said yes!
9. The carpenter has such energy and drive that it's a pleasure just to watch him drive a nail into a piece of wood.
10. The really hard, really difficult goal is the one that is really most worth attaining and achieving.

SLANG

A carefully chosen, appropriate slang expression can sometimes add interest and liveliness to writing. It can be helpful in establishing a humorous or casual tone. More significantly, in a few cases, it can suggest an attitude or a shade of meaning that a more conventional expression could not. By and large, slang is inappropriate for the comparatively formal, analytical writing that college courses demand. But when you feel sure that a slang expression can genuinely communicate something you would not otherwise be able to get across, don't be afraid to use it. Incidentally, forget about the coy little quotation marks that many writers put around slang expressions to show that they are really sophisticated people who could use better language if they wanted to. Good slang should seem natural, and if it is natural, it doesn't need quotes.

> After spending their teens dreaming of chicks, broads, dames, dolls, and assorted foxy ladies, many young men are at a loss when they finally meet a real woman.

Billed as a luxury resort, the hotel was just a high-priced dump.

I don't think I'll ever be able to forget the creepy old busybody who used to live next door to us.

Be careful about using slang, however. Don't use it to show how up-to-date you are; slang changes so fast that what seemed current yesterday is often embarrassingly old-fashioned tomorrow. Don't use slang to show your reader what a folksy person you are; that technique almost always falls flat. Avoid crude sentences like these:

In *Hamlet,* Hamlet's girl friend, Ophelia, goes nuts.

This profound political allegory really turned me on.

A good college devotes itself to academic excellence, social service, and intellectual stimulation. It can be a real hip place.

Albert Einstein was one of the big brains of the twentieth century.

FANCY WRITING

For every writer who uses slang to show off, there are probably a dozen who show off by habitually using big or unfamiliar words. A large vocabulary is a splendid tool for any writer, of course, but that fancy word or phrase should be used only when it adds something valuable to tone or meaning that a more familiar word or phrase could not add. If the familiar word will do the job as well, use it; the unfamiliar word will seem stilted and pretentious.

FANCY	IMPROVED
Many of our new buildings suffer from inadequate fenestration.	Many of our new buildings have too few windows.
Some of the water we drink is insalubrious.	Some of the water we drink is unhealthy.
They raised their hands in the time-honored gesture of respect to the emblem of their nation's sovereignty.	They saluted their country's flag.
Human individuals who reside in abodes of glass should not hurl objects of masonry.	People who live in glass houses shouldn't throw bricks.
Charles Dickens's novelistic achievements are veritably unrivaled in English letters.	Charles Dickens wrote better novels than any other English writer.
We require an augmentation of interpersonal communications on substantive issues.	We need to talk more to each other about important issues.

MISCELLANEOUS DO'S AND DON'TS

Some special stylistic problems common to classroom writing don't fit conveniently under any of the big labels, so we've included brief comments about them here. Our comments are based on the assumption that you are writing for an audience of intelligent nonspecialists who have not yet made up their minds about your subject. You may argue that you're really writing for your instructor alone, but most English instructors have worked hard at training themselves to dismiss purely personal quirks and preferences from their reading of student themes. Despite the red pens or pencils in their hands, when they look at themes, they mentally turn themselves into an imaginary general reader—the intelligent, uncommitted nonspecialist just mentioned.

1. *Don't write a personal letter to your instructor.*

This assignment at first confused me, but after several cups of coffee and too many cigarettes, I began to get an idea: I remembered that last week you said something about certain kinds of literature depending on formal patterns, and I think I've come up with an interesting notion about the two stories we just read. See what you think.

If that paragraph were read by anyone other than the teacher or the members of the class in which the stories were discussed, it would make almost no sense. What difference does it make to a general reader how much coffee the student drank? What assignment does the student refer to? What stories did the class just read?

2. *Don't make formal announcements of what you are going to do.*

In this paper I am going to prove that Langston Hughes was attacking slum landlords.

The thesis which I shall attempt to prove in this paper is that the energy crisis is an invention of the large oil companies.

It's distracting and unnecessary to begin a paper with a trumpet fanfare. Don't tell the reader what you are going to do. Get down to business and do it.

In "The Ballad of the Landlord," Langston Hughes attacks slum landlords.

The energy crisis is an invention of the large oil companies.

3. *Avoid a speechmaking tone.*

In conclusion, let me simply say that . . .

With your permission, I'd like to make a few observations on that point.

Such sentences introduce an irritating artificial quality into written English.

4. Don't hedge.

> In my opinion, the Industrial Revolution was a major chapter in the history of civilization.

> I think that Dr. Watson is childishly impressed by Sherlock Holmes.

Go easy on terms such as *in my opinion, I think,* etc. Of course you think, and the paper *is* your opinion, your interpretation of the material—backed up by all the facts necessary to support it. An apologetic or uncertain tone suggests that you do not have faith in your ideas, and if you do not believe in what you say, your audience probably won't either. Of course, you would not state a personal theory as a universal truth; but don't weaken solid ideas by hedging, and don't expect an *in my opinion* to make a shaky idea more acceptable.

5. Don't bluster.

> Anyone but an idiot can see that Hughes's poem protests against the treatment of blacks.

> Legalized prostitution is opposed mainly by neurotic hypocrites and religious nuts.

Blustering is the opposite of hedging. Its effect on an intelligent audience is just as negative.

6. Be careful about using "you" as an indefinite pronoun.

> Even though you are a drug addict, you are not necessarily an evil person.

> Your constant arguments with your parents are part of the process of growing up.

You is the pronoun of direct address. In this book, for example, we, the authors, write to you, the students in a composition course, and thus address you directly. But in writing aimed at a general audience, it is preferable to use the indefinite pronouns: *anyone, one, each, either, neither, another, anybody, someone, somebody, everyone, everybody,* and *nobody.* And *you* cannot be substituted for *the speaker, the character, the average citizen, people, the student, the author, the reader,* and so on. Since you cannot be sure of the age, class, sex, or living conditions of your readers, you will not want to chance offending or unintentionally amusing them by attributing to them attitudes, strengths, vices, or talents they may not possess.

> Drug addicts are not necessarily evil.

> Constant arguments with parents are part of the process of growing up.

7. Define unfamiliar terms. This advice is especially important in any paper on technical subjects. An audience of nonspecialists can be expected to have the general knowledge of educated citizens, nothing more. Avoid jargon—the special language of particular professions and activities—whenever you can. When you can't, see to it that your reader understands you. A paper on automobile repairs, for instance, would need to define terms such as *universal joint* and *differential*. A paper on legal problems would need to define *tort* and *writ of mandamus*. A paper on finance would need to define *cash flow* and *price-earnings ratio*.

Exercise

Comment on the stylistic problems in each of the sentences below.

1. From time to time, sentimental fools have urged abolition of the death penalty.
3. Thus the poem clearly shows, I believe, that all earthly power is only temporary.
3. I've really tried to do better in this paper, but I just can't seem to get the hang of it.
4. Cobalt treatment engendered remission.
5. This theme will demonstrate that housework can be fun.
6. Recent government programs mean that you will no longer have to neglect your illegitimate children.
7. God is not dead. The rest of my paper will make an effort to establish a logical proof for this statement.
8. Let me add one further comment, if I may.
9. Roberts got bored with clipping coupons and went into commodities and convertibles.
10. It seems to me that our country's balance of payments problem has been grossly neglected.
11. Writing this comparison-and-contrast paper involved less drudgery than I first thought it would.
12. It is my intention, then, to provide my readers with the information they will need to make up their own minds.
13. Being happy at one's job, to my way of thinking, is a truly important ingredient of a full life.
14. Your career as a ballerina demands that you practice every day no matter how tired you are.
15. The morons and crooks who oppose federal funding of research on solar energy ought to be exposed once and for all.

Repeated errors in grammar and mechanics
are often severely penalized.

PART 5

HANDBOOK
AND GLOSSARY

USING THE HANDBOOK
AND GLOSSARY

DEFINITIONS OF USEFUL
GRAMMATICAL TERMS

HANDBOOK

GLOSSARY OF PROBLEM WORDS

USING THE HANDBOOK
AND GLOSSARY

This part of the book is intended as a quick guide to basic writing skills. Use it to check up on grammatical points that have become vague in your mind, to answer simple questions that may occur to you while writing, and to correct any mechanical errors that your instructor finds in your work. Most first-year English courses assume that you have already mastered grammar, punctuation, standard word usage, and the other basics. For the most part, you probably have—but even skilled professional writers sometimes need to use a reference book. Your instructor, at any rate, will probably devote little classroom time to mechanics; it is your responsibility to see that your papers are grammatically correct, and this Handbook and Glossary should help you do just that.

Both Handbook and Glossary are arranged alphabetically. The Handbook (pp. 388–441) discusses the most common areas of trouble: commas, fragmentary sentences, etc. Consult the relevant listing whenever your instructor calls attention to a writing mistake. A number of exercises on more difficult points have been provided so that you can test your understanding of these points. The Glossary (pp. 442–468) explains specific words and phrases that are a frequent source of confusion.

We have tried to keep this material as straightforward as possible. Our main assumption is that standard written English is an essential tool for educated people. In general, we have taken a direct yes-or-no, right-or-wrong approach, even though that approach may sometimes oversimplify complex and controversial issues. Our purpose is to give reasonable answers to common questions—not to write a dissertation on obscure grammatical details.

Immediately following is a special group of definitions of important grammatical terms. Some of these terms will turn up from time to time in the Handbook and Glossary, and if they are unfamiliar to you, this list may prove useful.

DEFINITIONS
OF USEFUL
GRAMMATICAL
TERMS

Active voice. See *Voice*.

Adjective. A word that modifies or limits a noun or pronoun: the *tall* man, he is *tall*, the man with *green* eyes. Most adjectives have three forms: the basic form (*tall*); the comparative form, usually indicated by an *-er* ending (*taller*); and the superlative form, usually indicated by an *-est* ending (*tallest*). The comparative form is used for comparing groups of two, and the superlative form for comparing groups of three or more.

> A basketball center is taller than a guard.
>
> A basketball center is ordinarily the tallest person on the team.
>
> Sue is smarter than I.
>
> Ellen is smarter than she used to be.
>
> Sarah is the smartest person in the class.

Instead of having *-er* and *-est* endings for comparative and superlative forms, some adjectives—generally those of three or more syllables—are preceded by *more* and *most*. Still other adjectives have highly irregular forms.

> *Examples:* forgetful, more forgetful, most forgetful; perilous, more perilous, most perilous; good, better, best; bad, worse, worst; etc.

Adjective clause. A dependent clause that modifies a noun or pronoun. Adjective clauses are introduced by *who, which, that, whose,* and *whom.*

> The man *who lives next door* is my friend.
>
> The Titanic, *which was considered unsinkable*, went to the bottom of the sea on its maiden voyage.
>
> The car *that was stolen yesterday* was recovered by the police.
>
> The man *whom you addressed* is my father.

Adverb. A word that modifies a verb, an adjective, or another adverb.

John walked *slowly*.

The man had *very* green eyes.

She spoke *rather loudly*.

Most adverbs are formed by adding *-ly* to an adjective.

Adjective	*Adverb*
The sun was *bright*.	The sun shone *brightly*.
The *furious* lion roared.	*Furiously*, the lion roared.
The teacher told the class to be *more quiet*.	The teacher told the class to behave *more quietly*.

Adverbial clause. A dependent clause that functions as an adverb.

He was late for school *because he missed the bus*.

When he arrived, class had already begun.

Antecedent. The noun or pronoun to which a pronoun refers.

John left *his* lunch at home.

Here, the pronoun *his* refers to its noun antecedent, John.

Appositive. A noun or noun equivalent usually following another noun and further identifying it.

Napoleon, *the great French general*, was defeated by Wellington.

The first Chief Justice, *John Marshall*, is a towering figure in American history.

Auxiliary verb. A "helping verb," a verb used before another to form a verb phrase: forms of *to be* (*am* going, *were* going); modals (*can* go, *might* go, *will* go); forms of *have* (*have* gone, *had* gone); forms of *do* (*does* go, *did* go).

Clause. A group of words with a subject and predicate. A clause can be *independent;* that is, it can stand alone as a separate sentence.

John went home.

A clause can also be *dependent;* that is, it cannot stand alone, but must depend on an independent clause to complete its meaning.

After I came home, I took a nap.

The man *who lived next door* died.

Complement. Usually a noun, pronoun, or adjective that follows a linking verb and is necessary for logical completion of the predicate.

Marilyn Monroe was an *actress*.

Who are *you?*

That proposal seems *sensible*.

Conjunction. A word used to join parts of sentences or clauses. *Coordinating conjunctions* (joining words or clauses of equal importance) are *and, or, but, for, nor, yet, so; subordinating conjunctions* (linking **dependent and independent clauses**) are *because, while, when, although, until, after.* etc.

Coordinating conjunction. See *Conjunction.*

Dependent clause. See *Clause, Adjective Clause, Adverbial Clause, Noun Clause.*

Direct object. See *Object.*

Expletive. A word that does not contribute directly to meaning but merely introduces a sentence or clause: *it, there.*

> *It* is raining.
> *There* are five boys here.

Independent clause. See *Clause.*

Infinitive. Simple form of a verb preceded by *to: to come, to go.*

Intransitive verb. See *Verb.*

Linking verb. See *Verb.*

Noun. Traditionally defined as the name of a person, place, thing, or concept, nouns are generally used as the subject, object, or complement of a sentence: *Roosevelt, Bill, accountant, California, Lake Ontario, Boulder Dam, desk, car, freedom, love.*

Noun clause. A dependent clause that performs the function of a noun.

> *That she works hard* is beyond doubt.
> He said *that he would go.*

See *Clause.*

Object. The person, place, or thing that receives the action of a verb, or the noun or pronoun after a preposition.

> John shot *Joe.*
> Florence kissed *him.*
> All motives are suspect to *them.*
> You'll find your *gloves* in the *car.*

Passive voice. See *Voice.*

Person. The form of pronouns and verbs that indicates the speaker (*first person*), the person or thing spoken to (*second person*), or the person or thing spoken about (*third person*).

	Pronoun	*Verb*
First person	I, we	go
Second person	you	go
Third person	he, she, it	goes
	they	go

Predicate. The part of a clause that tells what the subject does, or what is being done to the subject.

> John *went home.*

See *Subject.*

Preposition. A connecting word such as *in, by, from, on, to, with,* etc., that shows the relation of a noun or a pronoun to another element in a sentence.

> The man *with* the gun shot the deer.

Pronoun. A word which takes the place of a noun. It may be personal (*I, you, he, she, it, we, they, me, him, her,* etc.), possessive (*my, mine, your, yours, his,* etc.), reflexive or intensive (*myself, yourself, himself,* etc.), relative (*who, which, that*), interrogative (*who, which, what*), or indefinite (*anyone, somebody, nothing,* etc.).

Sentence. A group of words beginning with a capital letter and ending with a period, question mark, or exclamation point that contains at least one independent clause.

> Birds sing.
>
> Do birds sing?
>
> Shut up, all you birds!

See *Clause, Subject, Predicate.*

Subject. A word, phrase, or clause that names the person, place, thing, or idea which the sentence is about.

> *John* went home.
>
> The president's *speech* was heard by 100,000 people.

See *Predicate.*

Subordinating conjunction. See *Conjunction.*

Transitive verb. See *Verb.*

Verb. A word that expresses an action, an occurrence, or a state of being. Verbs may be divided into three classes: *transitive* verbs, which require objects to complete their meaning (Mary *admires* him); *intransitive* verbs, which are complete in themselves (John *trembled*); and *linking* verbs, which join a subject to its complement (Phyllis *is* a beauty; Their actions *were* cowardly).

Voice. The quality of a verb that tells whether the subject *acts* or is *acted upon.* A verb is in the *active* voice when its subject does the acting, and in the *passive* when its subject is acted upon.

> *Active:* The Senate passed the new law.
>
> *Passive:* The new law was passed by the Senate.

HANDBOOK

Abbreviations. As a rule, avoid abbreviations.

WRONG	RIGHT
The financial ills of N.Y.C. and other municipalities can be cured only by aid from the federal gov't.	The financial ills of New York City and other municipalities can be cured only by aid from the federal government.
Thanksgiving comes on the fourth Thurs. of Nov.	Thanksgiving comes on the fourth Thursday of November.
I had trouble finding the proper st. & had to ask a taxi driver for directions.	I had trouble finding the proper street and had to ask a taxi driver for directions.

Even when abbreviations are permissible, it is nearly always acceptable in standard English to spell a word in its entirety; therefore, when in doubt, spell it out.

There are only a few cases in which abbreviations are required or preferable.

A. *Standard forms of address.* Before a person's name, it is standard usage to write *Mr., Mrs., Ms., Dr.,* or *St.* (for Saint, not street).

B. *Titles.* If both a person's surname (last) and given name (first) or initials are used, then it is acceptable to write *Rev., Hon., Prof., Sen.*

Rev. John Rice, Prof. A. J. Carr (but not Rev. Rice or Prof. Carr)

C. *Degrees.* After a name, abbreviate academic degrees, *Jr.,* and *Sr.* Academic degrees may also be abbreviated when used by themselves.

Thomas Jones, M.D.

He is now studying for a B.A.

D. *Organizations.* The names of many organizations and some countries are commonly abbreviated, often without periods.

NATO   NAACP   USSR   UN   USA   AFL-CIO

E. *Other.* Footnote references and bibliographical terms are nearly always abbreviated, as are a few common words.

etc.	*pp. 137–140*
ibid.	vol.
et al	LSD
p. 23	DDT

Adjective-Adverb Confusion. Adjectives modify nouns.

> Getting a diploma takes *hard* work.
>
> The boxer's *left* jab is his *strongest* weapon.
>
> The *better* team won.
>
> The porridge was *hot*.

Adverbs modify verbs, adjectives, or other adverbs.

> We walked *carefully*.
>
> *Foolishly*, we kept arguing until midnight.
>
> The porridge was *very* hot.
>
> The doctor had to cut *quite* deeply.

Most adverbs are formed by adding *-ly* to adjectives:

ADJECTIVE:	nice	strong	poor
ADVERB:	nicely	strongly	poorly

When an adjective already ends in *y* or *ly*, the *y* may sometimes have to be changed to an *i* before the adverbial *-ly* ending is added. A few of the resulting adverbs may sound so awkward that an adverbial phrase is the preferred form:

ADJECTIVE:	pretty	messy	nasty
ADVERB:	prettily	messily	nastily

BUT

ADJECTIVE:	friendly	lovely	heavenly
ADVERB:	in a friendly way	in a lovely way	in a heavenly way

A few adjectives and adverbs are identical in form:

> ADJECTIVE: He is a *better* person for the experience.
>
>   *Fast* drivers are dangerous drivers.
>
> ADVERB: He did *better* than I.
>
>   I can type *fast*.

Some words are adverbs in themselves—adverbs to start with—and do not spring from adjectives: *very, quite, rather, somewhat,* etc. Other adverbs are irregular: the adjective *good*, for example, is expressed as an adverb by the word *well*.

> ADJECTIVE: He was a *good* worker.
>
> ADVERB: He did the work *well*.

Confusion of adjectives and adverbs is among the most common grammatical errors and is likely to turn up from one of the following causes.

A. *Misuse of an adjective to modify a verb.*

> WRONG: I wish she acted *different*.
>
>   He answered *rude*.

Bill did *good* on his examination.

Let's speak *direct* to each other.

RIGHT: I wish she acted *differently*.

He answered *rudely*.

Bill did *well* on his examination.

Let's speak *directly* to each other.

B. *Misuse of an adjective to modify an adverb or other adjective.*

WRONG: The price was *sure* very expensive.

The patient is *considerable* worse today.

My teacher is *real* strict.

RIGHT: The price was *surely* very expensive.

The patient is *considerably* worse today.

My teacher is *really* strict.

C. *Misuse of an adverb after a linking verb.* The correct modifier after a linking verb is an adjective. The single most common linking verb is *to be* (*am, is, are, was, were, will be,* etc.). Verbs dealing with the senses—sight, touch, taste, smell, hearing—are often used as linking verbs: *feel, look, sound, taste, appear.* Other verbs frequently serving as linking verbs are *get, seem, remain, become.*

WRONG: I feel *prettily.*

The music sounds *beautifully.*

The food tastes *badly.*

He seems *cheerfully.*

RIGHT: I feel *pretty.*

The music sounds *beautiful.*

The food tastes *bad.*

He seems *cheerful.*

Some verbs, including many of those just listed, may be used as transitive or intransitive verbs, as well as linking verbs. In such cases, note how an adjective or adverb determines meaning.

I smell bad. (I need to buy deodorant.)

I smell badly. (My sinuses are stuffed up.)

He looks evil. (He looks like a wicked person.)

He looks evilly. (When he stares at me, I get frightened.)

I feel terrible. (I am depressed or in ill health.)

I feel terribly. (My sense of touch has deserted me.)

Exercise

Choose the right adjective or adverb.

1. My employer has treated me very (shabby, shabbily).

2. My health is (good, well).

3. The teacher talked (rough, roughly) to the student.   *adverb talked*

4. The student's answer came back (furious, furiously).   *adverb*

5. The pathetic old man breathed (painful, painfully).   *adverb*

6. As (near, nearly) as I can determine, the first job offer seems the best.   *adverb*

7. All our products are (fresh, freshly) baked each day.   *mod*

8. Speaking (personal, personally), I think the coach is the only real problem the team has.   *mod*

9. My deep love for you becomes more (deep, deeply) each day.   *adv, L√*

10. If you act (bad, badly), you will be treated (bad, badly).   *mod adv.*

11. Please keep (calm, calmly).   *ag.*

12. Far from being a snob, Frank is a (real, really) fine person once you get to know him.

13. The potato salad tasted (unpleasant, unpleasantly).   *a Lc*

14. My sister looks (splendid, splendidly) in her new pants suit.   *ag. L√*

15. When my candidate lost, I felt as (unhappy, unhappily) as could be.   *ag m-c lost*   *L√*

Adjectives, coordinate. See *Comma, E.*

Adverbs. See *Adjective-Adverb Confusion*

Agreement. See *Pronouns: agreement* or *Subject-verb agreement.*

Apostrophe. The apostrophe is used in forming contractions, plurals, and possessives.

A. *Contractions.* In contractions, the apostrophe indicates that a letter has been left out.

it is = it's	she is = she's	who is = who's
let us = let's	you are = you're	do not = don't

B. *Plurals.* The 's is used to form the plural of lower-case letters and of abbreviations followed by periods: a's, x's, B.A.'s, Ph.D.'s, P.O.W.'s. Either 's or s may be used to form such plurals as the following, though 's is becoming less common:

the 1930s *or* the 1930's	the &s *or* the &'s
the three Rs *or* the three R's	several YMCAs *or* several YMCA's

C. *Possessives.* An apostrophe is used to form the possessive of nouns and indefinite pronouns. The first task is to determine whether a possessive apostrophe is needed. If one is needed, the second task is to use it correctly.

Difficulties for many people begin with the confusion of speaking with writing. In speech, *cats, cat's,* and *cats'* all sound identical. The meanings are all different, however, and in writing, those differences show up immediately. *Cats* is a simple plural—s is added to the singular and no apostrophe is used.

The cats howled all night.

Purring is a way cats have of showing affection.

Liver is a favorite food for many cats.

Cat's is a possessive singular, another way of expressing the thought *of the cat. Cats'* is a possessive plural, another way of expressing the thought *of the cats.* Note the simplicity of determining whether a word with a possessive apostrophe is singular or plural: just look at the part of the word *before the apostrophe.*

SINGULAR:	cat's claws	machine's speed	racer's edge
PLURAL:	cats' claws	machines' speed	racers' edge

Note, too, that in a phrase like *of the cats,* the word *of* takes care of the idea of possession, and no apostrophe is used.

POSSESSIVES WITH *OF* (NO APOSTROPHE)	POSSESSIVES WITH APOSTROPHES
The claws of a cat are sharp.	A cat's claws are sharp.
The name of my cat is Tigger.	My cat's name is Tigger.
The hunting abilities of cats are well known.	Cats' hunting abilities are well known.
The mysterious glow in the eyes of cats can be frightening.	The mysterious glow in cats' eyes can be frightening.

One more observation is necessary. Possessive pronouns—*my, mine, our, ours, your, yours, his, her, hers, its, their, theirs*—are already possessive in themselves and *never take apostrophes.*

When a possessive apostrophe is required, the rules are relatively simple.

A. Singular or plural nouns that do not end in *s* form their possessives by adding *'s:*

John's car	the boy's book	Women's Lib
the teacher's notes	New York's mayor	children's games

B. Plural nouns that end in *s* form their possessives by adding only an apostrophe:

the students' teacher	Californians' freeways
oil companies' profits	the two boys' mother
automobiles' engines	the two teachers' classes

C. Singular nouns that end in *s* ordinarily form their possessives by adding *'s.* The exceptions are words that already have so many *s* or *z* sounds in them (*Massachusetts, Jesus*) that a final *'s* would create awkward hissings or buzzings. The possessive of such words is often formed by adding only an apostrophe, and individual writers sometimes have to use their own judgment:

the octopus's tentacles	the press's responsibilities
Keats's poetry	the business's profits
Dickens's novels	Massachusetts' excise tax

> Charles's bowling ball   Jesus' disciples
> Mr. Jones's new roof   Moses' journey

D. Indefinite pronouns form their possessives by adding **'s:**

> nobody's fool   someone's knock
>
> anyone's guess   everybody's business

E. In the case of joint possession—possession by two or more—the possessive is formed by adding an apostrophe or '*s,* as appropriate, to the last noun:

> the girls and boys' school   John and Bob's car

> *Note:* To show individual possession, write "John's and Bob's cars" and "the girls' and boys' schools." Here John has a car and Bob has a car; the girls have a school and the boys have a school.

Exercise A

Rewrite the following phrases to form possessives, using an apostrophe or '*s.*

1. the tears of the widow
2. the tears of the widows
3. the suspense of the story
4. the suspense of the stories
5. the hunger of the man
6. the hunger of the men
7. the ambition of the actress
8. the ambition of the actresses
9. the orders of the boss
10. the orders of the bosses
11. the choice of the person
12. the choice of the people
13. the protest of the masses
14. the mother of Sarah and Jess
15. the mothers of Sarah and Jess (two mothers—individual possession)
16. the playing of the orchestra
17. the desire of one to excel
18. a break of an hour
19. a notice of a moment
20. the price of success

Exercise B

In the following sentences, decide which of the *italicized* words are plural and which are possessive. Then make the necessary corrections and be prepared to justify them.

1. *Ball players* contractual *disputes* have achieved the impossible; they have aroused the *publics* sympathy for the *owners*.
2. *His* romantic *conquests* have stimulated his one *friends* envy and his hundred *enemies* disgust.
3. The *Devils* Triangle *refers* to a region in the Atlantic Ocean of many unexplained *accidents*.
4. *Beethovens* nine *symphonies* have intrigued *listeners minds* and enraptured *their souls*.
5. The *Smiths* went to the *Joneses* house for dinner.
6. Considering his record of *knockouts*, Muhammed *Alis* punching ability was consistently underrated by *sports commentators*.
7. Your behavior is worse than *theirs; yours* can't be excused by your *fathers* neglect.
8. It takes only a *moments* thought to realize that *televisions absurdities* are *reflections* of the *absurdities* of American society as a whole.
9. *Bettys plants* are late *bloomers*, but her *roses colors* are all sensational.
10. *Expenditures* for treatment of solid *wastes* will almost double the *towns* budget over the next five *years*.

Appositive. See *Comma, F.*

Blocked quotations. See *Quotation Marks, A, 1.*

Brackets. Use brackets ([ ]) to indicate comments or added information that you have inserted into a direct quotation. Do not use parentheses instead of brackets, or the reader will assume that the inserted material was part of the original quotation.

> "While influenced by moral considerations, Lincoln signed it [the Emancipation Proclamation] primarily to further the war effort."

> "The music column had the altogether intimidating title of *Hemidemisemiquavers* [sixty-fourth notes]."

Capital letters. Use a capital letter for the first word of a sentence or direct quotation, the first word and all important words of titles, the first word and all nouns of a salutation, the first word of a complimentary close, some pronouns, and all proper nouns—the names of particular persons, places, or things.

A. *The first word of a sentence or direct quotation.*

> *A* popular television show featured a detective whose most characteristic line was, "*We* just want the facts, ma'am."

B. *The first and all important words of titles of books, magazines, plays, short stories, poems, essays, and chapters.* Unimportant words include *a, the,* and short prepositions such as *of, in, to,* etc.

A Streetcar Named Desire	"Ode to a Nightingale"
Time	"Such, Such Were the Joys"
Roget's College Thesaurus	

C. *The first word and all nouns of a salutation.*

Dear Sir: My dear Sir:

D. *The first word of a complimentary close.*

Sincerely yours,   Respectfully yours,

E. *Some pronouns:*

1. First person singular: I

2. References to the Judeo-Christian Deity, where necessary to avoid confusion:

God told Moses that he must carry out His commandments.

F. *Proper nouns.*

1. Names and titles of persons and groups of persons:

   a. Persons: James Baldwin, Chris Evert, Albert Einstein, President Roosevelt

   b. Races, nationalities, and religions: Caucasian, Chinese, Catholic

   c. Groups, organizations, and departments: League of Women Voters, Chrysler Corporation, United States Senate, Department of Agriculture

   d. Particular deities: God, Allah, Buddha, Zeus

2. Names of particular places:

   a. Cities, counties, states, and countries: Cleveland, Cuyahoga County, Ohio, United States of America

   b. Particular geographical regions: Pacific Northwest, the South

   c. Streets: East Ninth Street, El Cajon Avenue

   d. Buildings: RCA Building, Union Terminal

   e. Heavenly bodies (except the sun and moon): Mars, Milky Way, Andromeda, Alpha Centauri

3. Names of particular things:

   a. Days and months: Friday, August

   b. Holidays: Easter, May Day

   c. Historical events and periods: the Civil War, the Middle Ages

   d. School courses: Biology 101, History 102 (but "a *history* course")

   e. Languages: English, Russian

   f. Schools: Cornell University, Walt Whitman High School (but "I graduated from *high school*.")

g. Brands: Buick, Peter Pan Peanut Butter (but "I had a peanut butter sandwich for lunch.")

Collective nouns. See *Subject-verb agreement, E.*

Colon. A colon (:) is commonly used after a clause introducing a list or description, between hours and minutes, in the salutation of a formal letter, between biblical chapter and verse numbers, and between the title and subtitle of a book. Less commonly, a colon may be used between independent clauses and before quotations.

A. *List.* A colon is used between a general statement and a list or description that follows:

> We shall never again find the equals of the famous three B's of music: Bach, Beethoven, and Brahms.

> He plans to take five courses: history, English, psychology, French, and physical education.

> *Note:* A colon should appear after a complete statement. A colon should *not* be used after a form of the verb *to be* (*be, am, is, are, was, were, been,* etc.) or after a preposition.

WRONG	RIGHT
Perennial contenders for the NFL championship are: Pittsburgh, Oakland, Minnesota, and Los Angeles.	Several teams are perennial contenders for the NFL championship: Pittsburgh, Oakland, Minnesota, and Los Angeles.
	OR
	Perennial contenders for the NFL championship are Pittsburgh, Oakland, Minnesota, and Los Angeles.
F. Scott Fitzgerald is the author of: *This Side of Paradise, The Beautiful and Damned, The Great Gatsby,* and *Tender is the Night.*	F. Scott Fitzgerald wrote the following books: *This Side of Paradise, The Beautiful and Damned, The Great Gatsby,* and *Tender is the Night.*
	OR
	F. Scott Fitzgerald is the author of *This Side of Paradise, The Beautiful and Damned, The Great Gatsby,* and *Tender is the Night.*

B. *Time.* A colon is used between hours and minutes when a specific time is written in numerals:

> 8:00 P.M.   8:10 A.M.

C. *Salutation.* In formal letter writing, a colon is used after the salutation:

> Dear Dr. Johnson: Dear Sir:

D. *Bible.* A colon is used to separate chapter from verse:

> Genesis, chapter 1, verse 8—Genesis 1:8

E. *Title and subtitle.* A colon is used between the title and subtitle of a book:

> *Johnson's Dictionary: A Modern Selection*

F. *Independent clauses.* A colon may be used between independent clauses when the second clause explains the first:

> She brought up her children on one principle, and one principle only: do unto others what they would like to do unto you—and do it first.

G. *Quotations.* A colon *can* be used before a short quotation and often is used before a long blocked quotation:

> Whenever I try to diet, I am reminded of the bitter truth of Oscar Wilde's epigram: "I can resist everything but temptation."

> In commenting on his function as a writer, Joseph Conrad put every writer's dream into words:

>> My task which I am trying to achieve is, by the power of the written word to make you hear, to make you feel—it is, before all, to make you *see.* That—and no more, and it is everything. If I succeed, you shall find there according to your deserts: encouragement, consolation, fear, charm—all you demand—and, perhaps, also that glimpse of truth for which you have forgotten to ask.

Comma. Using a comma correctly is almost never a matter of taste or inspiration. It is even less a matter of following the ancient junior high school formula of tossing in a comma "to indicate a pause." Different people pause for breath and emphasis in different places. When errors turn up, they are most often the result of the writer's being comma happy—putting in too many commas. Our basic rule, then, is *never use a comma unless you know it is necessary.* It is necessary in the following cases:

- between elements in a list or series
- between independent clauses joined by *and, but, yet, for, or, nor, so*
- after long introductory elements
- before and after interrupting elements
- between coordinate adjectives
- before and after nonrestrictive elements
- between certain words to prevent misreading
- in conventional elements such as dates, numbers, addresses, titles, correspondence, direct quotations

A. *Series.* Three or more items in a list or series must be separated by commas for the sake of clarity.

> The potential buyer should take special care to inspect the roof, basement, and ceilings.

Make sure you read parts one, two, and three before completing the assignment.

The three novels in Dos Passos' *USA* trilogy are *The 42nd Parallel*, *Nineteen Nineteen*, and *The Big Money*.

Note: In all three of these examples, the comma before *and* is optional. Most experienced writers use the comma, however, because it reinforces the idea of a series in the reader's mind.

B. *Independent clauses.* Independent clauses joined by a coordinate conjunction—*and, but, for, yet, or, nor, so*—require a comma *before* the conjunction:

Connotations are not usually entered next to a word in a dictionary, but they still exist in people's minds.

Each writing assignment requires a different kind of organization, and each may be a different length.

You should not use a comma after a conjunction, nor should you use one at the end of a series.

Note: No comma would be used if the above sentences were rewritten to have only one independent clause:

Connotations are not usually entered next to a word in a dictionary but still exist in people's minds.

Each writing assignment requires a different kind of organization and may be a different length.

You should not use a comma after a conjunction or at the end of a series.

C. *Introductory elements.* A comma should be used after a long introductory element:

Because the student was having trouble with commas, he read the section on punctuation.

In good writing, there are few punctuation errors.

The *italicized* parts of these two sentences are introductory elements. When the introductory element is extremely short—one word, for example—the comma can sometimes be omitted if the meaning remains clear: *Soon* the term will end.

POOR	CORRECT
Because this is an introductory element it should have a comma after it.	Because this an introductory element, it should have a comma after it.
Despite the best efforts of both parties no agreement was reached.	Despite the best efforts of both parties, no agreement was reached.
Never having seen her before I expected the worst.	Never having seen her before, I expected the worst.

| As soon as he had showered he went straight to bed. | As soon as he had showered, he went straight to bed. |

Note: If any of the above introductory elements are moved so that they come *after* the independent clauses (and thus no longer introduce anything), no commas should be used:

No agreement was reached despite the best efforts of both parties.

He went straight to bed as soon as he had showered.

Exercise

Put a comma after the introductory element where necessary.

1. If I can forget about the senator's words, ideas, and personality I might actually vote for him.
2. Then I woke up.
3. Whenever I hear someone suggest that love is the answer to our problems I wonder why love has usually made me miserable.
4. Feeling as I do I have no alternative.
5. Not happy with having given us the seatbelt interlock system the bureaucrats are looking for still more ways to save us from ourselves.
6. Frequently we worry about mistakes we never made.
7. Considering my shortcomings I have been luckier than I deserve.
8. Later we may need to discuss some exceptions to this rule.
9. If your essay falls apart it probably has no primary idea to hold it together.
10. After a long introductory clause or phrase use a comma.

D. *Interrupting elements.* A comma should be used before and after an interrupting element. Interrupting elements, while often needed for clarity and continuity, are those that break the flow of words in the main thought of a sentence or clause. In the previous sentence, *while often needed for clarity or continuity* is an interrupting element. Some writers find it helpful to think of interrupting elements as asides to the audience or parenthetical insertions. Interrupting elements may be words such as *indeed, however, too, also, consequently, therefore, moreover, nevertheless* and phrases such as *as the author says, of course, after all, for example, in fact, on the other hand.*

WRONG	RIGHT
Suppose for example that you decide to write about your own life.	Suppose, for example, that you decide to write about your own life.
We must bear in mind too that even the best system is imperfect.	We must bear in mind, too, that even the best system is imperfect.
Punctuation as we can see is not exactly fun.	Punctuation, as we can see, is not exactly fun.
The only thing wrong with youth according to George Bernard Shaw is that it is wasted on the young.	The only thing wrong with youth, according to George Bernard Shaw, is that it is wasted on the young.

His pledges for the future however could not make me forget his broken promises of the past.	His pledges for the future, however, could not make me forget his broken promises of the past.

E. *Coordinate adjectives.* A comma is used to separate coordinate adjectives—adjectives of equal rank—that come before the nouns they modify.

WRONG	RIGHT
This poet uses concrete believable images.	This poet uses concrete, believable images.
Her warm enthusiastic energetic behavior was often mistaken for pushiness.	Her warm, enthusiastic, energetic behavior was often mistaken for pushiness.

> *Note:* Coordinate adjectives have two features: you may put *and* between them (concrete *and* believable, warm *and* enthusiastic *and* energetic) and they are reversible (believable, concrete; enthusiastic, energetic, warm). Compare these examples to "This poet uses several concrete images." You cannot say "several and concrete" or "concrete several." Therefore, you do not use a comma between them. Note, too, that if the coordinate adjectives had originally been joined by *and,* no commas would have been necessary: "Her warm and energetic and enthusiastic behavior was often mistaken for pushiness."

F. *Nonrestrictive elements.* A comma should be used before and after a nonrestrictive element.

Nonrestrictive modifiers. Commas are used before and after nonrestrictive modifiers. A nonrestrictive modifier gives additional information about the noun it modifies but *is not necessary to identify or define that noun:*

> The Empire State Building, which I visited last year, is a most impressive sight.
>
> My father, who has worked in a steel foundry for thirty years, has made many sacrifices for me.

A *restrictive* modifier is not set off by commas. It is a necessary part of the meaning of the noun it modifies:

> A person who is always late for appointments may have serious psychological problems.
>
> The novel that Professor Higgins praised so highly is very disappointing.
>
> People who live in glass houses shouldn't throw bricks.
>
> Many jobs for highly skilled technicians are still available.

Proper punctuation of restrictive and nonrestrictive modifiers often can affect meaning:

The sofa, with those huge armrests, is an eyesore.	The writer sees just one sofa. The nonrestrictive modifier merely conveys more information about it.

The sofa with those huge armrests is an eyesore.	The writer sees more than one sofa. The restrictive modifier is necessary to distinguish this sofa from the others.

A special type of nonrestrictive element is called the *appositive*. It is a word or group of words that means the same thing as the element that *precedes* it. In the sentence, "Joseph Terrell, *Mayor of Greenville*, will speak at graduation," the *italicized* phrase is an appositive; that is, it means the same thing as the first element, *Joseph Terrell*. The rules governing the punctuation of modifiers also govern the punctuation of appositives.

Nonrestrictive appositives. Commas are used before and after nonrestrictive appositives. A nonrestrictive appositive gives additional information about the noun it follows but *is not necessary to identify that noun:*

> Miss Susan Swattem, *the meanest person in town*, was my high school mathematics teacher.

> Thomas Jefferson, *third president of the United States*, also founded the University of Virginia.

A *restrictive appositive* is not set off by commas. It is necessary to identify the noun it follows:

> The expression *hitch your wagon to a star* was first used by Emerson.

> He spoke to Susan *my sister*, not Susan *my wife*.

As with modifiers, proper punctuation of nonrestrictive and restrictive appositives often can affect meaning.

My brother, George, is a kindly soul.	The writer has only one brother, so the word *brother* is sufficient identification. *George* is nonrestrictive.
My brother George is a kindly soul.	The writer has more than one brother, so the name of the specific brother he has in mind is a necessary part of the meaning. *George* is restrictive.

Exercise

Use commas where necessary to set off nonrestrictive elements.

1. The person who left the notebook in the classroom went to the instructor's office before the next class.
2. Albert Einstein that legendary figure of modern science was a notable underachiever during his school days.
3. Exxon which is the largest oil company in the world used to be known as Standard Oil Company of New Jersey.
4. Swiss Army knives pocket knives with a dozen or so different blades have become extremely popular in recent years.
5. The Boy Scout knife that I had as a child will always remain my special favorite.

6. My sister Sonya has four children. My sister Judith has none.
7. The man who picked up the packages for the old woman had his wallet stolen when he bent over.
8. Republicans who support their party will try to support the policies of a Republican president.
9. Harold Arlen who wrote such songs as "Stormy Weather" and "Let's Fall in Love" also composed the classic score for *The Wizard of Oz*.
10. The baseball player who has the highest lifetime batting average in the history of the game is Ty Cobb.

G. *Misreading.* Apart from any more specific rules, commas are sometimes necessary to prevent misreading. Without commas, the following examples would be likely to stop readers in midsentence and send them back to the beginning.

CONFUSING	CORRECT
High above the trees swayed in the wind.	High above, the trees swayed in the wind.
High above the trees an ominous thundercloud came into view.	High above the trees, an ominous thundercloud came into view.
At the same time John and Arnold were making their plans.	At the same time, John and Arnold were making their plans.
Hugging and kissing my half-smashed relatives celebrated the wedding.	Hugging and kissing, my half-smashed relatives celebrated the wedding.

H. *Conventions.* Commas are used in such conventional elements as dates, numbers, addresses, titles, correspondence, and direct quotations.

1. Dates. Commas separate the day of the month and the year:

    April 24, 1938   January 5, 1967

    If only the month and year are used, the comma may be omitted:

    April 1938   *or*   April, 1938

    If the year is used in midsentence with the day of the month, it should be followed by a comma. With the month only, the comma may be omitted:

    World War II began for the United States on December 7, 1941, at Pearl Harbor.

    World War II began for the United States in December 1941 at Pearl Harbor.

    World War II began for the United States in December, 1941, at Pearl Harbor.

2. Numbers. Commas are used to group numbers of more than three digits to the left of the decimal point:

$5,280.00   751,672.357   5,429,000

When a number consists of only four digits, the comma may be omitted:

5,280   *or*   5280

3. Addresses. Commas are used to separate towns, cities, counties, states, and districts:

Cleveland, Ohio

Brooklyn, Kings County, New York

Washington, D.C.

Note: A comma is not used to separate the Zip Code from the state.

Pasadena, California 91106

4. Titles. A comma often separates a title from a name that precedes it:

Norman Prange, Jr.   Harold Unger, M.D.   Julia Harding, Ph.D.

5. Correspondence. A comma is used after the salutation in informal letter writing and after the complimentary close:

Dear John,   Dear Jane,

Respectfully yours,   Sincerely yours,

6. Direct quotations. See *Quotation marks, A.*

Comma splice. Often considered a special kind of *run-on sentence* (for which the Handbook provides a separate entry), a comma splice is a punctuation error that occurs when two independent clauses are joined only by a comma. To correct a comma splice, either use a comma *and* a coordinating conjunction, or replace the comma with a semicolon or a period.

There are only seven coordinating conjunctions: *and, but, or, nor, for, yet,* and *so.* When these are used between independent clauses, they should be preceded by a comma:

WRONG	RIGHT
The boy had been crippled since infancy, he still tried to excel in everything he did.	The boy had been crippled since infancy, but he still tried to excel in everything he did.
	OR
	The boy had been crippled since infancy; he still tried to excel in everything he did.
	OR
	The boy had been crippled since infancy. He still tried to excel in everything he did.

Each writing assignment requires a different kind of organization, each may be a different length.

Each writing assignment requires a different kind of organization, and each may be a different length.

OR

Each writing assignment requires a different kind of organization; each may be a different length.

OR

Each writing assignment requires a different kind of organization. Each may be a different length.

It is often tempting to use words such as *however, therefore, nevertheless, indeed,* and *moreover* after a comma to join independent clauses. *Don't!* The only words following a comma that can join two independent clauses are the seven coordinating conjunctions.

WRONG	RIGHT
We started with high hopes, however we were disappointed.	We started with high hopes; however, we were disappointed.
She had been hurt many times, nevertheless, she always seemed cheerful.	She had been hurt many times; nevertheless, she always seemed cheerful.

Although any choice among coordinating conjunctions, semicolons, and periods will be technically correct, the best choice often depends on complex issues of style and thought. If the independent clauses under consideration are surrounded by long sentences, for example, the writer might choose to break the monotony with a period, thus creating two short sentences. If the independent clauses are surrounded by short sentences, the writer can sometimes achieve variety by creating a long sentence with a coordinating conjunction or semicolon. In addition, the more closely connected are the thoughts in two independent clauses, the more likely the writer will be to show that connection by using a coordinating conjunction or semicolon. In such cases, two separate sentences would indicate too great a separation of thought. Obviously, no easy rules work here, and the writer's intentions have to be the main guide.

Comma splices can be acceptable in standard English when each clause is unusually short and when the thought of the whole sentence expresses an ongoing process.

I came, I saw, I conquered.

Throughout the interview, she squirmed, she stammered, she blushed.

Exercise

Rewrite the following sentences, correcting the comma splices where necessary.

1. The politicians complained bitterly, the company's profits had increased by 63 percent.

2. The company replied that figures have to be interpreted in context, the previous year's profits had been down 84 percent from the year before that.
3. It was impossible for him to express the full measure of his indignation, he bit his lip, and he clenched his fists.
4. As man learns to use machines more effectively, he has more leisure time.
5. Jack Nicklaus had a terrible golfing season recently, he won only $102,000.
6. Automation has cost many individuals their jobs, however, it has, on the whole, created jobs.
7. Tennis seems to have become an extraordinarily popular sport, personally, it leaves me cold.
8. Fear can prevent a person from acting, hate, on the other hand, will often cause action.
9. She was a human being. She was born, she lived, she suffered, she died.
10. Do not join two sentences with just a comma, use a comma and a conjunction, a semicolon, or a period to separate sentences.

Comparative and superlative forms. Comparative forms of adjectives and adverbs are used to compare or contrast groups of two—and only two. The comparative form of regular adjectives is formed by adding -er to the ending of the adjective or by using the word *more* before the adjective: *nicer, sweeter, more dramatic, more beautiful.* (Some adjectives are irregular: the comparative of *good* is *better;* the comparative of *bad* is *worse.*) The comparative form of adverbs is formed by using *more* before the adverb: *more nicely, more sweetly, more dramatically, more beautifully.*

Superlative forms of adjectives and adverbs are used to compare or contrast groups of three or more. The superlative form of regular adjectives is formed by adding -est to the ending of the adjective or by using the word *most* before the adjective: *nicest, sweetest, most dramatic, most beautiful.* (Some adjectives are irregular: the superlative of *good* is *best;* the superlative of *bad* is *worst.*) The superlative form of adverbs uses *most* before the adverb: *most nicely, most sweetly, most dramatically, most beautifully.*

In summary, *comparative forms apply to two, and superlative forms apply to more than two.*

WRONG	RIGHT
If I had to choose between Paul Newman and Robert Redford, I would have to say that Robert Redford is the *best* actor.	If I had to choose between Paul Newman and Robert Redford, I would have to say that Robert Redford is the *better* actor.
The high school girl and the junior high school girl competed on the parallel bars. The junior high school girl was given the *highest* scores.	The high school girl and the junior high school girl competed on the parallel bars. The junior high school girl was given the *higher* scores.
I like many people, but I like Betsy *more*.	I like many people, but I like Betsy *most*.

| Although my first and second themes both required hard work, I wrote the second *most* easily. | Although my first and second themes both required hard work, I wrote the second *more* easily. |

Comparisons. Comparisons must be both logical and complete.

A. *Logical.* Do not compare items that are not related. You would not compare horses to safety pins because they have nothing in common. Not all illogical comparisons are this obvious, however, since it is usually the phrasing rather than the thought behind it that is at fault.

WRONG	RIGHT
His appetite is as huge as a pig. (Here the comparison is between *appetite* and *pig*.)	His appetite is as huge as a pig's.
	OR
	His appetite is as huge as a pig's appetite.
	OR
	His appetite is as huge as that of a pig.
Mark Twain is more amusing than any American writer. (Here Mark Twain is excluded from the group that he belongs to.)	Mark Twain is more amusing than any other American writer.

B. *Complete.* A comparison must be complete: the items being compared must be clear, and both items must be stated.

    1. Clarity:

        POOR: I like him more than you.

        RIGHT: I like him more than I like you.

           OR

        I like him more than you like him.

    2. Both items stated:

        POOR: Old Reliable Bank has higher interest rates. (Higher than it had before? Higher than other banks have? Higher on deposits or higher on loans?)

        RIGHT: Old Reliable Bank has higher interest rates on savings accounts than any other bank in the city.

        Note: For further discussion of comparisons, See Chapter 15, pp. 351–353.

Exercise

Correct any faulty comparisons in the following sentences.

    1. Alka-Seltzer commercials are more entertaining than Anacin's.
    2. Her marks were higher than anyone in the class.

3. Pale and deeply stirred, he looked like a dry martini.
4. *The Exorcist* was the worst movie.   *other*
5. *Hamlet* is more interesting than any play ever written.
6. His great big sad eyes are like a cocker spaniel.
7. Her qualifications were as good as John.
8. I get along with my in-laws better than my wife. *does*
9. My mother's temper is harder to deal with than my father.
10. O. J. Simpson makes more money than any *other* professional athlete.

Compound subjects. See *Subject-verb agreement, A.*

Conjunctions, coordinating. See *Comma, B* and *Comma splice.*

Conjunctions, subordinating. See *Fragmentary sentences, C.*

Coordinating adjectives. See *Comma, E.*

Coordinating conjunctions. See *Comma, B* and *Comma splice.*

Dangling modifier. See *Modifiers, A.*

Dash. A dash is used primarily to emphasize a parenthetical or otherwise nonessential word or phrase. It can also highlight an afterthought or separate a list or series from the rest of the sentence. An *introductory* list or series may be separated by a dash from the rest of the sentence if it is summarized by a word that serves as the subject of the sentence.

A. *Parenthetical word or phrase.*

> Only when politicians are exposed to temptation—and rest assured they are almost always so exposed—can we determine their real worth as human beings.

B. *Afterthought.*

> The only person who understood the talk was the speaker—and I have my doubts about him.

C. *List or series.*

> The great French Impressionists—Manet, Monet, Renoir—virtually invented a new way of looking at the world.
>
> *The Scarlet Letter, Moby-Dick, Walden, Leaves of Grass, Uncle Tom's Cabin*—these American classics were all published during the incredible five-year span of 1850–1855.

Use dashes sparingly, or they lose their force. Do not confuse a dash with a hyphen. (See *Hyphen.*) In typing, indicate a dash by striking the hyphen key twice (--), leaving no space between the dash and the two words it separates.

Double negative. Always incorrect in standard English, a double negative is the use of two negative terms to express only one negative idea. Remember that in addition to obvious negative terms such as *no, not,* and *nothing,* the words *hardly* and *scarcely* are also considered negatives.

WRONG	RIGHT
I don't have no memory of last night.	I don't have any memory of last night.
	OR
	I have no memory of last night.
For truly religious people, money cannot mean nothing of value.	For truly religious people, money cannot mean anything of value.
	OR
	For truly religious people, money can mean nothing of value.
His mother could not hardly express her feelings of pride at his graduation.	His mother could hardly express her feelings of pride at his graduation.
Our troubles had not scarcely begun.	Our troubles had scarcely begun.

Ellipsis. An ellipsis (three spaced dots) shows omission of one or more words from quoted material. If the ellipsis occurs at the end of a sentence, there will be four spaced dots; one dot will be the period for the sentence.

ORIGINAL	USE OF ELLIPSIS
"The connotation of a word is its implicit meaning, the meaning derived from the atmosphere, the vibrations, the emotions that we associate with the word."	"The connotation of a word is its implicit meaning . . . the emotions we associate with the word."

End marks. The three end marks are the period, question mark, and exclamation point.

A. *Period.* A period is used at the end of all complete sentences that make a statement, after abbreviations, and in fractions expressed as decimals.

1. Sentences. If a complete sentence makes a statement, use a period at the end:

   Please give unused clothing to the Salvation Army.

   Place pole *B* against slot *C* and insert bolt *D*.

   The class wants to know when the paper is due.

2. Abbreviations. A period is used after some abbreviations:

   Mr. R. P. Reddish   Mt. Everest   Ph.D.

   Note: A period is not used in abbreviations such as UNESCO, CORE, FCC, and AAUP. See *Abbreviations*.

3. Decimals. A period is used before a fraction written as a decimal.

   $\frac{1}{4} = .25$ $\frac{1}{20} = .05$

Note: If a decimal is used to indicate money, a dollar sign is also necessary.

B. *Question mark.* A question mark is used to indicate a direct question or a doubtful date or figure.

1. Direct question. Use a question mark at the end of a direct question. Do not use a question mark with indirect questions such as "They asked when the paper was due."

   When is the paper due?

   Did the teacher say when the paper is due?

A question mark is also used when only the last part of a sentence asks a question, and when a quotation that asks a question is contained within a larger sentence.

   I know I should go to college, but where will I get the money for tuition?

   The student asked, "When is the paper due?"

   After asking, "When is the paper due?" the student left the room.

   Note: In the last example, the question mark replaces the usual comma inside the quotation.

2. Doubtful date or figure. After a doubtful date or figure, a question mark in parentheses is used. This does not mean that if you are giving an approximate date or figure you should use a question mark. Use it only if the accuracy of the date or figure is doubtful.

   The newspaper reported that the government said it cost $310 (?) to send a man to the moon. (Here a question mark is appropriate because it is doubtful if $310 is the figure. Perhaps there has been a misprint in the paper.)

   Chaucer was born in 1340(?) and died in 1400. (Here historians know when Chaucer died but are doubtful of exactly when he was born, even though most evidence points to 1340. If historians were completely unsure, they would simply write, "Chaucer was born in the mid-1300s and died in 1400."

A question mark in parentheses should never be used to indicate humor or sarcasm. It is awkward and childish to write "He was a good (?) teacher," or "After much debate and sectarian compromise, the legislature approved a satisfactory (?) state budget."

C. *Exclamation point.* An exclamation point is used at the end of emphatic or exclamatory words, phrases, and sentences. In formal writing, exclamation points are rare. They most often occur in dialogue, and even there they should be used sparingly lest their effect be lost.

1. Word or phrase:

   My God! Is the paper due today?

   No! You cannot copy my exam.

2. Sentence:

The school burned down!

Stop talking!

Note: Comic book devices such as !?! or !! are signs of an immature writer. Words, not the symbols after them, should carry the primary meaning.

Exclamation point. See *End mark, C.*

Fragmentary sentences. A fragmentary sentence is a grammatically incomplete statement punctuated as if it were a complete sentence. It is one of the most common basic writing errors.

To avoid a sentence fragment, make sure that your sentence contains at least one independent clause. If it does not contain an independent clause, it is a fragment.

Here are some examples of sentences, with the independent clause *italicized;* sometimes the independent clause *is* the whole sentence, and sometimes the independent clause is part of a larger sentence.

> *Jack and Jill went up the hill.*
> *He sees.*
> If you don't stop bothering me, *I'll phone the police.*
> Tomorrow at the latest, *we'll have to call a special meeting.*
> *He straightened his tie* before he entered the room.
> Discovering that he had lost his mother, *the little boy started to cry.*

An independent clause is a group of words which contains a subject and verb and expresses a complete thought. This traditional definition is beyond criticism except that it can lead to messy discussions about the philosophical nature of a complete thought. Such discussions can usually be avoided by concentrating on the practical reasons for a missing independent clause. There are three major reasons: omission of subject or verb, confusion of verb derivatives (verbals) with verbs, and confusion of a dependent clause with an independent clause.

A. *Omission of subject or verb.* This is the simplest kind of fragment to spot:

> There are many events that take place on campus. *Such as plays, concerts, and many other things.*
> My father finally answered me. *Nastily and negatively.*
> Mrs. Jones has plenty of activities to keep herself busy. *Nagging, scolding, snooping, and drinking.*
> The new department head had a brand new pain in the neck. *In addition to the old ones.*
> We had many blessings. *Like love, nature, family, God, and television.*

These fragments should be obvious even without the italics, and the remedies should be just as obvious. Simple changes in punctuation will solve the problems. Here are the same sentences with the fragments eliminated:

> There are many events that take place on campus, such as plays, concerts, and many other things.
>
> My father finally answered me nastily and negatively.
>
> Mrs. Jones has plenty of activities to keep herself busy: nagging, scolding, snooping, and drinking.
>
> The new department head had a brand new pain in the neck in addition to the old ones.
>
> We had many blessings, like love, nature, family, God, and television.

B. *Confusion of verb derivatives (verbals) with verbs.* Verbals are words derived from verbs. Unlike verbs, they cannot function *by themselves* as the predicate of a sentence. Infinitive forms are verbals (*to do, to see, to walk*). So are gerunds and present participles (*-ing* endings: *doing, seeing, walking*). Study the *italicized* sentence fragments below.

> I decided to take her to the game. *Susan enjoying football a lot.*
>
> Nobody ought to vote. *The government being corrupt.*
>
> We should take pleasure in the little things. *A boy petting his dog. Lovers holding hands. Soft clouds moving overhead.*
>
> *To make the world a better place. To help people be happy.* These are my goals.

In the last example, the fragments lack subjects as well as verbs and can readily be identified. Inexperienced writers, however, looking at the fragments in the first three examples, see a subject and what appears to be a verb. They assume, consequently, that the words make up an independent clause. They are wrong. A present participle all by itself cannot serve as a verb, and an independent clause must have a verb. Study these corrected versions of the fragments.

> I decided to take her to the game. Susan has been enjoying football a lot.
>
> Nobody ought to vote. The government is corrupt.
>
> We should take pleasure in the little things: a boy petting his dog, lovers holding hands, soft clouds moving overhead.
>
> I want to make the world a better place. I want to make people happy. These are my goals.

C. *Confusion of a dependent (subordinate) clause with an independent clause.* All clauses contain a subject and a verb. Unlike an independent clause, however, a dependent or subordinate clause does not express a complete thought and therefore cannot function as a sentence. A subordinate clause at the beginning of a sentence must always be followed by an independent clause. A subordinate clause at the end of a sentence must always be preceded by an independent clause. Fortunately, subordinate clauses can be readily identified if you remember that *they always begin with subordinating conjunctions*—a much easier approach than trying to figure out whether your sentence conveys a complete thought. Here, in alphabetical order, is a list of most of the subordinating conjunctions you are likely to encounter. *Whenever one of these words immediately precedes a clause (subject + verb), that clause becomes a subordinate clause and cannot stand alone as a complete sentence.*

after	because	once	until
although	before	provided that	whenever
as	even if	since	wherever
as if	even though	so that	while
as long as	how	than	
as soon as	if	though	
as though	in order that	unless	

Note: Except when used as question words, *who, which, when* and *where* also introduce a subordinate clause.

In the left column, examples of subordinate clauses used as sentence fragments are *italicized*. In the right column, *italics* indicate corrections to repair these sentence fragments.

FRAGMENTS	CORRECTED
If I ever see home again.	If I ever see home again, *I'll be surprised.*
Keats was a great poet. *Because he was inspired.*	*Keats was a great poet* because he was inspired.
I will never apologize. *Unless you really insist.*	*I will never apologize* unless you really insist.
Provided that the contract is carried out within thirty days.	Provided that the contract is carried out within thirty days, *we will not sue.*
This is the man who will be our next governor. *Who will lead this state to a better tomorrow.*	*This is the man who will be our next governor,* who will lead this state to a better tomorrow.

The major difficulty anyone is likely to have with sentence fragments is in identifying them. They are usually child's play to correct. Sentence fragments occur, in many cases, because of a misunderstanding of complex grammatical issues, but they can almost always be corrected with elementary revisions in punctuation.

Sentence fragments should nearly always be avoided. In rare situations, they can sometimes be justified, especially if the writer wants a sudden dramatic effect.

> I shall never consent to this law. Never!
> Oh, God!

Scared? I was terrified.

Lost. Alone in the big city. Worried. The boy struggled to keep from crying.

Exercise

Some of the following are sentence fragments. Rewrite them to form complete sentences.

1. Whenever I have a bad headache. *I begin to cry.*
2. Because first impressions are often wrong impressions. *don't use them.*
3. After he had studied for several hours and felt fully confident of his ability to do well. *he then went to sleep*
4. Having extremely poor eyesight, I keep an extra pair of glasses at home.
5. The managing editor, an excellent journalist and former reporter. *does a great job.*
6. Being the most popular actor of his generation. *he is a great influence*
7. At 5:00 P.M. the train was due. *so we waited*
8. *The watch.* Which he had lost several times before. *he found*
9. *For hrs but* Before long, the fire died down.
10. Clearing away all of the wreckage, helping victims of the storm, and still finding time to operate the communications network.
11. Unless we all work together for a better world, we may have no world at all.
12. To mention just a few items of relatively minor importance.
13. A man who can approach problems with a unique combination of vision and practicality. *is very versatile*
14. Shuffling papers and looking busy are the only requirements of the job.
15. Who does he think he is? *to act that way*

Fused sentence. See *Run-on sentence.*

Hyphen. A hyphen (-) is used in some compound words and in words divided at the end of a line.

A. *Compound words.*

1. As a general rule, you should consult a recent dictionary to check the use of the hyphen in compound words. Many such words that were once hyphenated are now combined. The following are some compound words that are still hyphenated:

   mother-in-law   court-martial
   knee-deep   water-cooled

2. All numbers from twenty-one to ninety-nine are hyphenated:

   forty-three   one hundred fifty-six

3. A hyphen joins two or more words that form an adjective *before* a noun:

well-known teacher	first-rate performance
but	*but*
The teacher is well known.	The performance was first rate.

B. *Divided words.* Divide words at the end of a line by consulting a dictionary and following accepted syllabication. A one-syllable word cannot be divided. In addition, a single letter cannot be separated from the rest of the word; for example, *a-bout* for *about* would be incorrect. The hyphen should come at the very end of the line, not at the beginning of the next line.

Indirect question. See *End marks, B, 1.*

Italics (underlining). In manuscript form—handwriting or typing—underlining represents printed italics. The rules for underlining and italics are the same. Underline titles of complete works; foreign words and phrases; words used emphatically; and letters, words, and phrases pointed to as such.

Note: When a word or phrase that would usually be italicized appears in a section of text that is already italicized, the word or phrase is typed or written with no italics.

A. *Titles of complete works.*

1. Books: *The Great Gatsby, Paradise Lost, Encyclopedia Britannica, Webster's New Collegiate Dictionary*

2. Newspapers: the *New York Times,* the *Chicago Tribune*

3. Plays: *Raisin in the Sun, Macbeth*

4. Movies: *Easy Rider, The Maltese Falcon*

Note: The titles of poems are put in quotation marks except for book-length poems such as Milton's *Paradise Lost* or Homer's *Iliad.* The titles of small units contained within larger units, such as chapters in books, selections in anthologies, articles or short stories in magazines, etc., are put in quotation marks. See *Quotation marks, B.*

B. *Foreign words and phrases not assimilated into English: vaya con Dios, paisano, auf Wiedersehen.*

C. *Words used emphatically:*

Ask me, but don't *tell* me.

Under *no* circumstances can this be permitted to happen.

Except in special situations, good word choice and careful phrasing are far more effective than underlining to show emphasis.

D. *Letters, words, and phrases pointed to as such:*

Words such as *however* and *therefore* cannot be used as coordinating conjunctions.

The letter *x* is often used in algebra.

The phrase *on the other hand* anticipates a contrast.

Manuscript correction symbols. When you have finished writing a paper or examination in class and are reading it over, you will often find a number of small mechanical errors. For example, in your haste you wrote one word as two or two words as one; perhaps you left out a word here and there, or you forgot to indent for a paragraph. You might have reversed the letters in a word—*e* before *i*, for example. You need not copy the whole paper over. There are a group of neat and easy-to-use symbols for correcting these mistakes. On papers written at home, however, be careful! Correcting a *few* slips of the pen or typewriter is fine; making four or five corrections per paragraph is something else. If you have numerous corrections, it is best to recopy or retype.

A. ⌣ This device joins one word written as two or connects a word in which a space has mysteriously appeared:

Ever‿yone finished writing the paper on time.

Use manu‿script symbols where necessary.

B. / The slash line has two functions.

1. It can separate two words written as one:

Don't write two/words as one.

2. It shows that a capital letter should be lowercased:

the English /language

the Museum /Of Modern Art

C. ¶ This symbol means paragraph. Perhaps you forgot to indent a new paragraph or you simply ran two paragraphs together. Put a ¶ at the beginning of the new paragraph.

D. ∧ The caret indicates that the words written *above* the line are to be inserted at the point the caret is used. The caret is always inserted at the bottom of the line.

first published in 1851,
Herman Melville's *Moby-Dick*,∧is considered one of America's greatest novels.

E. ∽ This device indicates that letters or words are in the wrong order. It should be used *very* sparingly—usually it's better to erase and correct the error.

I recieved an *A* in the course.

I do always well in English.

F. ≡ Three lines under a lowercase letter show that it should be a capital.

He became a presbyterian minister.

I'll see you next friday.

Misplaced modifier. See *Modifiers, B*.

Modifiers. The most frequent errors involving modifiers are dangling modifiers and misplaced modifiers.

A. *Dangling modifiers.* A dangling modifier is a group of words, often found at the beginning of a sentence, that does not refer to anything in the sentence or that seems to refer to a word to which it is not logically related. Dangling modifiers usually include some form of a verb which has no subject, either implied or stated. This construction results in statements that are often humorous and always illogical. To correct this error, either change the modifier into a subordinate clause, or change the main clause so that the modifier logically relates to a word in it. On occasion, it may be necessary to change both clauses.

INCORRECT	CORRECT
Climbing the mountain, the sunset blazed with a brilliant red and orange. (This sentence says that the sunset is climbing the mountain.)	As we were climbing the mountain, the sunset blazed with a brilliant red and orange. (Subordinate clause)
	OR
	Climbing the mountain, we saw the sunset blazing with brilliant red and orange. (Main clause)
After looking in several stores, the book was found. (In this sentence, the book is looking in stores.)	After looking in several stores, we found the book.
To become an accurate speller, a dictionary should be used. (In this sentence, the dictionary is becoming an accurate speller.)	If you want to become an accurate speller, you should use a dictionary.
	OR
	To become an accurate speller, you should use a dictionary.
While talking and not paying attention, the teacher gave the class an assignment. (This sentence says that the teacher is talking and not paying attention while giving an assignment. If that is what the writer meant, then this sentence is correct. If, however, the writer meant that the class was talking and not paying attention, then it is incorrect.)	While the class was talking and not paying attention, the teacher gave an assignment.
	OR
	While talking and not paying attention, the class was given an assignment by the teacher.

B. *Misplaced modifiers.* Since part of the meaning of the English language depends on word order—some other languages depend mostly on word endings—you must make sure that phrases serving as modifiers and adverbs such as *only, always, almost, hardly,* and *nearly* are placed in the position that will make the sentence mean what you intend. Misplaced modifiers, unlike dangling modifiers, can almost always be corrected simply by changing their positions.

1. Phrases serving as modifiers:

The teacher found the book for the student in the library.

This sentence indicates that the student was in the library. If, however, the writer meant that the book was found in the library, then the modifier *in the library* is misplaced. The sentence should read:

The teacher found the book in the library for the student.

The writer of the following sentence seems to be saying that the college is near the lake:

His parents met his friend from the college near the lake.

If, however, the writer meant that the meeting took place near the lake, the modifier is misplaced and the sentence should read:

Near the lake, his parents met his friend from the college.

2. Adverbs like *only, always, almost, hardly* and *nearly*. Words like these usually qualify the word that comes after them. Therefore, the position of these words depends on what the writer wishes to say.

Only is a notorious troublemaker. Observe how the sentence *I want a son* changes meaning significantly with the change in position of *only:*

I *only* want a son.	(I don't yearn for or long for a son; I only *want* one.)
I want *only* a son.	(I have no other wants.)
I want an *only* son.	(One son is as many as I want.)
I want a son *only*.	(I do not want a daughter.)

Exercise

Rewrite the sentences below, correcting any dangling or misplaced modifiers.

1. The man looked at the car he had just fixed while rubbing his hands with satisfaction.
2. Sitting on the edge of the bed, the blanket was wrinkled.
3. While driving through Yosemite, a bear stopped our car.
4. The student left for the college with excess baggage.
5. Running toward second base, we saw the runner make a daring slide.
6. John wants Judy to love him badly.
7. Walking through the park, the trees were in full bloom.
8. Speaking in a moderate tone, the lecture was much more successful.
9. The quarterback was removed from the game before he was permanently injured by the coach.
10. Leaving assignments until the last minute is bad policy.

Modifiers, nonrestrictive. See *Comma, F.*

Modifiers, restrictive. See *Comma, F.*

Nonrestrictive modifiers. See *Comma, F.*

Numerals.

A. *Numerals are used to indicate dates, times, percentages, money, street numbers, and page references.*

> On January 21, 1974, at 5:00 A.M., a fire broke out at 552 East 52nd Street, and before the Fire Department brought the flames under control, 75% of the building had been destroyed.

B. *In other cases, if a number is one hundred or under, spell it out; if it is over one hundred, use the numeral.*

> In the big contest yesterday, forty-five young boys were able to eat 152 hot dogs in two minutes.

C. *Spell out all numbers that start a sentence.*

> Four thugs assaulted an old lady last night.

> Three hundred thirty-one deaths have been predicted for the Labor Day weekend.

Parallelism. Ideas and facts of equal importance should be expressed in the same grammatical form:

INCORRECT	CORRECT
You can get there by *car, bus,* or *fly.* (noun, noun, verb)	You can get there by *car, bus,* or *plane.* (noun, noun, noun)
I thought the climactic episode in the story was *shocking, off-beat,* and *I found it very amusing.* (adjective, adjective, independent clause)	I thought the climactic episode in the story was *shocking, offbeat,* and very *amusing.* (adjective, adjective, adjective)
She *liked* people and *was liked* by people. (active voice, passive voice)	She *liked* people and people *liked* her. (active voice, active voice)
The teacher told us *to work* fast and *that we should write on only one side of the paper.* (infinitive, clause)	The teacher told us *to work* fast and *to write* on only one side of the paper. (infinitive, infinitive)

For further treatment of parallelism, see Chapter 16, pp. 365–367.

Parentheses. Parentheses can enclose incidental comments, provide explanatory details, and sometimes set off numerals that accompany the points of a paper. Parentheses are also used in footnotes. In many cases, parentheses serve to mark afterthoughts that should have been incorporated into the writing elsewhere. Therefore, use parentheses sparingly.

A. *Incidental comments:*

> The movie *The Killers* (its plot had little resemblance to Hemingway's short story) won an award.

B. *Explanation of details:*

> The cornucopia (the horn of plenty) is a Thanksgiving symbol.

C. *Enumerated points:*

> This essay has four main pieces of advice: (1) know your professors as people, (2) attend college-sponsored events, (3) attend student-sponsored events, and (4) use the library.

D. *Footnotes:*

> Kurt Vonnegut, Jr., *Slaughterhouse-Five* (New York: Dell Publishing Co., Inc., 1969), p. 43.

Period. See *End marks, A.*

Possessives. See *Apostrophe, C.*

Pronouns: agreement. A pronoun must agree with its antecedent in number (singular or plural) and gender (masculine, feminine, or neuter). The antecedent of a pronoun is the word or words to which the pronoun refers. For example, in the sentence *John lost his book,* the pronoun *his* refers to the antecedent *John.* Another example is *John could not find his book. He had lost it.* In the second sentence there are two pronouns—*he* and *it.* The antecedent of *he* is *John* and the antecedent of *it* is *book.* With the exception of constructions such as *it is nearly eight o'clock,* in which *it* has no antecedent, all pronouns should have antecedents.

A. *Gender.* If the gender of a singular antecedent is unknown or general, as in *student,* for example, then the antecedent is treated as if it were masculine. (This usage, which is still standard, has come under attack in recent years. See GLOSSARY, *He, his, him, himself,* pp. 453–454.)

Antecedent		*Pronoun*	
The boy	lost	his	book.
The girl	lost	her	book.
The briefcase	lost	its	handle.
The student	lost	his	book.
The students	lost	their	books.

B. *Number.* Most pronoun agreement errors occur when the pronoun does not agree with its antecedent in number. If the antecedent is singular, the pronoun must be singular; if the antecedent is plural, the pronoun must be plural.

1. Indefinite pronouns. Words like *anybody, somebody, everybody, nobody,* and *each* are always singular. Others like *few* and *many* are always plural. Indefinite pronouns such as *all, any, most,* and *more* can be either singular or plural, depending on the object of the preposition which follows them: *All of my concern is justified;* but, *All of my concerns are justified.*

   INCORRECT: Somebody lost *their books.*

   No one turns their paper in on time.

   CORRECT: Somebody lost *his* books.

   No one turns *his* paper in on time.

2. Collective nouns. Some singular nouns refer to more than one thing: *group, youth, family, jury,* and *audience,* for example. If the noun acts as a unit, it takes a singular pronoun. If the individuals within the unit act separately, the noun takes a plural pronoun.

The jury reached its decision.

The jury divided bitterly on their decision.

The audience rose to its feet to show its approval.

The audience straggled to their seats through the entire first act.

3. Antecedents joined by *either . . . or* and *neither . . . nor.* When two antecedents are joined by *either . . . or* or *neither . . . nor,* the pronoun agrees with the antecedent closer to it:

Either John or *Bill* lost *his* book.

Either the father or the *sons* lost *their* books.

Either the sons or the *father* lost *his* book.

Neither the boys nor the *girls* lost *their* books.

4. Compound antecedents. Except when the words function as a single unit—*Macaroni and cheese is my favorite dish; I make it often,* for example—antecedents joined by *and* take a plural pronoun:

The owl and the pussycat shook *their* heads sadly.

Exercise

Correct any errors in pronoun agreement in the following sentences.

1. Nobody can ever tell what the future has in store for them.
2. Everybody passed their paper forward.
3. Neither the governor nor the mayors could explain their tax-reform proposal.
4. Everyone wants to feel some measure of control over their own life.
5. Each of the players signed their contracts.
6. All of the soup was tainted, so they were recalled by the manufacturer.
7. The crowd of sports fans shouted their disapproval of the umpire's decision.
8. Both Jenny and Marie had to make their plans carefully.
9. Either the boss or the workers will have to make up his mind about medical benefits.
10. Someone is certain to lose their temper.

Pronouns: case. Pronoun case refers to the change in form of pronouns which corresponds with their grammatical function. There are three cases, and their names are self-explanatory: *subjective* (when the pronoun acts as a subject), *objective* (when the pronoun acts as an object), and *possessive* (when the pronoun acts to show possession). Following is a list of case changes for the most common pronouns:

Subjective	*Objective*	*Possessive*
I	me	my, mine
you	you	your, yours
he	him	his
she	her	her, hers
it	it	its
we	us	our, ours
they	them	their, theirs
who	whom	whose

Case rarely presents problems for native speakers. Nobody says or writes *He gave I the book* or *Me like she.* Complications turn up in relatively few situations:

A. *Compound subjects and objects (subjects and objects connected by* and*).* Do not be misled by a compound subject or object. Use the pronoun case that shows the pronoun's grammatical role.

WRONG	RIGHT
My father scolded Jim and I.	My father scolded Jim and me.
Betty and her had many good times.	Betty and she had many good times.

A simple test for getting the right word is to eliminate one of the compound terms and see which pronoun works better. No one would write *My father scolded I*—so *My father scolded me* is correct. No one would write *Her had many good times*—so *She had many good times* is correct.

B. *Object of a preposition.* In a prepositional phrase, any pronoun after the preposition always takes the objective case.

WRONG	RIGHT
This match is just between you and I.	This match is just between you and me.
I went to the movies with she.	I went to the movies with her.
This present is for John and he.	This present is for John and him.

C. *After forms of* to be *(is, am, are, was, were, has been, had been, might be, will be, etc.).* A pronoun after forms of *to be* is always in the subjective case. This rule still applies rigorously in formal written English. It is frequently ignored in informal English and has all but disappeared from most conversation.

It was she.

This is he.

The murderer might be he.

The winners will be they.

D. *After* as *and* than. In comparisons with *as* and *than,* mentally add a verb to the pronoun to determine which pronoun is correct. Should you write, for example, *Bill is smarter than I* or *Bill is smarter than me*? Simply complete the construction with the "understood" verb. You could write *Bill is smarter than I am*, but not *Bill is smarter than me am*. Therefore, *Bill is smarter than I* is correct.

WRONG	RIGHT
I am just as good as *them*.	I am just as good as *they*.
Her mother had more ambition than *her*.	Her mother had more ambition than *she*.
Bill liked her more than *I*.	Bill liked her more than *me*. (Meaning *Bill liked her more than he liked me*.)
Bill liked her more than *me*.	Bill liked her more than *I*. (Meaning *Bill liked her more than I liked her*.)

E. We *or* us *followed by a noun*. Use *we* if the noun is a subject, *us* if the noun is an object. If ever in doubt, mentally eliminate the noun and see which pronoun sounds right. Should you write, for example, *The professor had us students over to his house* or *The professor had we students over to his house?* Mentally eliminate *students*. No one would write *The professor had we over to his house*, so *us* is correct.

WRONG	RIGHT
After the demonstration, *us* students were exhausted.	After the demonstration, *we* students were exhausted.
The company's reply to *we* consumers was almost totally negative.	The company's reply to *us* consumers was almost totally negative.

F. *Gerunds*. A gerund is an *-ing* verb form that functions as a noun. In *Swimming used to be my favorite sport*, *swimming* is a gerund. A pronoun before a gerund takes the possessive case.

WRONG	RIGHT
Us nagging him did no good.	*Our* nagging him did no good.
His parents do not understand *him* reading so poorly.	His parents do not understand *his* reading so poorly.
Them believing what she says does not mean that she is telling the truth.	*Their* believing what she says does not mean that she is telling the truth.

G. Who *and* whom. See Glossary, pp. 467–468.

Exercise

Choose the correct pronoun, and be prepared to explain your choice.

1. You are fully as selfish as (I, me), but you do not have the courage to admit it.
2. To (he and she, him and her), the marriage counselor seemed to be speaking nonsense.
3. I think George and (I, me) will always be friends.

4. Twenty or thirty years from now, the president of the United States will be (she, her).
5. The judge then assessed an additional fine for (them, their) cursing.
6. Having to choose between (he and she, him and her) will make Election Day a worse burden than usual.
7. I honestly don't know what he expects (we, us) poor students to do.
8. The winning contestants were no brighter or quicker than (I, me).
9. (Him, His) lying had become part of his character.
10. Bennett hated Stephen and (she, her) with a jealous passion.

Pronouns: reference. A pronoun must not only agree with its antecedent, but that antecedent must be clear. An ambiguous antecedent is as bad as no antecedent at all. Generally two types of ambiguity occur: a pronoun with two or more possible antecedents, and one pronoun referring to different antecedents.

A. *Two or more possible antecedents. When Stanton visited the mayor, he said that he hoped his successor could work with him.* In this sentence, the pronouns *he, his,* and *him* can refer to either the mayor or Stanton. This problem can be avoided by making the antecedent clear: *When Station visited the mayor, Stanton said that he hoped his successor could work with the mayor.* Here the pronouns *he* and *his* clearly refer to Stanton. Be particularly careful of the potential ambiguity in vague use of the word *this.*

AMBIGUOUS	IMPROVED
I received an *F* in the course and had to take it over again. This was very unfair. (Was the *F* unfair or having to take the course again? Were both unfair?)	I received an *F* in the course and had to take it over again. This grade was very unfair.
Young people are unhappy today and are demanding reform. This is a healthy thing. (What is healthy—being unhappy, demanding reform, or both?)	Young people are unhappy today and are demanding reform. This demand is a healthy thing.

B. *One pronoun referring to different antecedents. John received an F on his term paper and had to write a revision of it. It took a long time because it had many errors.* In these sentences the first *it* refers to the paper, the second to the revision, and the third to the paper. A reader could easily become confused by these sentences. In that case, simply replacing the pronouns with their antecedents would solve the problem. *John received an F on his term paper and had to write a revision of it. The revision took a long time because the paper had many errors.*

Exercise

Rewrite the sentences by correcting any errors in pronoun reference.

1. After the students left their papers on the teacher's desk, they remained in the classroom for an hour.

2. The students left the room in their usual order.   *it's*   *manufact*

3. Cars break down so often because they don't make them the way they used to.

4. John told Bill that he could go.   *Bill*

5. John bought a new station wagon and a travel trailer. It needed several adjustments.

6. The teacher asked the student if he could read his writing.

7. He received his citizenship papers and registered to vote. This made him very happy.

8. It has been a long time since John left home.

9. The prosecutor disagreed with the judge. He felt he was guilty.

10. John's final grades were an *A* and an incomplete. This really saved him.

Question marks. See *End marks, B.*

Questions, indirect. See *End marks, B, 1.*

Quotation marks. Quotation marks are used to indicate material taken word for word from another source; to mark the title of a poem, song, short story, essay, and any part of a longer work; and to point out words used in a special sense—words set apart for emphasis and special consideration, slang and colloquial expressions, derisively used words.

A. *Direct quotations.* Quotation marks indicate what someone else has said in speech or writing:

> The mayor said, "The city is in serious financial trouble if the city income tax does not pass."
>
> "No man is an island," John Donne once wrote.

If there is a quotation within a quotation, use single marks for the second quote:

> The mother commented wryly, "I wonder if Dr. Spock and the other great authorities on bringing up kids have ever seen one look at you, calm as can be, and say, 'I don't wanna.' "

Several rules must be observed in punctuation of direct quotations:

1. Blocked quotation. If a direct quotation other than dialogue is more than five lines long, it should be blocked. Blocked quotations *do not* take quotation marks. They are indented from the left margin and are single spaced.

   In the section of the text on quotation marks, the authors make the following observation:

   > Quotation marks are used to indicate material taken word for word from another source; to mark the title of a poem, song, short

story, essay, and any part of a longer work; and to point out words used in a special sense—words set apart for emphasis and special consideration, slang and colloquial expressions, derisively used words.

Note: Ordinarily a colon, rather than a comma, introduces a blocked quotation. See pp. 314–315.

2. Periods and commas. Periods and commas at the end of quotations always go inside the quotation marks.

"The city will be in serious financial trouble if the city income tax does not pass," said the mayor.

Although the producer used the word "art," the picture was widely considered to be pornographic.

3. Other punctuation. An exclamation point or question mark goes inside the quotation marks *if it is part of the quotation*. If it is part of a longer statement, it goes outside the quotation marks.

The student asked, "Is this paper due Friday?"

Did Robert Frost write "Mending Wall"?

A colon or a semicolon always goes outside the quotation marks.

The text says, "A colon or a semicolon always goes outside the quotation marks"; this rule is simple.

B. *Titles.* Use quotation marks to indicate the title of a work—a poem, a song, a short story, a chapter, an essay—that is part of a larger whole, or a short unit in itself.

William Carlos Williams wrote the short story "The Use of Force."

The chapter is called "Stylistic Problems and Their Solutions."

C. *Words.*

1. Words used as words. Underlining is usually preferred. See *Italics.*

2. Words used as slang or colloquial expressions. This usage is almost always undesirable. (See Chapter 16, pp. 375–376.)

3. Words used derisively. The use of quotation marks to indicate sarcasm or derision is generally a primitive means of showing feelings, and should be avoided:

The "performance" was a collection of amateurish blunders.

Run-on sentence. A run-on sentence is two or more sentences written as one, with no punctuation between them. It is most commonly corrected by rewriting the run-on sentence as separate sentences, by placing a semicolon between the sentences, or by placing a comma *and* a coordinating conjunction between the sentences. A comma alone would create a comma splice, often considered a special kind of run-on sentence. See *Comma splice.*

INCORRECT	CORRECT
This rule sounds easy enough putting it into practice is not so easy.	This rule sounds easy enough. Putting it into practice is not so easy.

OR

This rule sounds easy enough; putting it into practice is not so easy.

OR

This rule sounds easy enough, but putting it into practice is not so easy.

Exercise

Correct the following run-on sentences by using a comma and a coordinating conjunction (*and, but, or, nor, for, yet, so*), a semicolon, or a period.

1. Machines do many jobs that people used to in the future, machines will replace even more people.
2. Cramming is a poor method of studying many students, however, use it.
3. Too few students use the library many do not even know its location.
4. There may be life on other planets perhaps the new satellite will provide an answer.
5. A community college may have students from all over the world most, however, come from the surrounding community.
6. Drunk drivers are dangerous they killed 14,000 people last year.
7. Many houses have hidden defects for example, the plumbing may be bad.
8. Miss Ohio won the title of Miss USA then she won the Miss Universe contest.
9. Make sure you separate sentences with a conjunction, a semicolon, or a period never just run them together.
10. Love does not mean just romantic love there can also be parental love, love of God, love of country, love for a book or a pet or a job.

Semicolon. A semicolon can be used between two independent clauses when the coordinating conjunction has been left out and between separate elements in a list or series when the elements contain punctuation within themselves.

A. *Between independent clauses:*

> Stating the problem is simple enough; solving it is the tough part.
>
> The girl wasn't precisely sure what the bearded stranger wanted; all she knew was that he made her nervous.

Observe that in both of these cases a coordinating conjunction preceded by a comma could be used to replace the semicolon. Under no circumstances could a comma alone be used between these independent clauses. In order to use a comma, you must have a coordinating conjunction (*and, but, or, nor, for, yet, so*) between independent clauses. See *Comma Splice.*

B. *Between separate elements in a list or series:*

> The following American cities have grown enormously in recent years: Houston, Texas; Dallas, Texas; Phoenix, Arizona; and Denver, Colorado.

Shifts in time and person. Do not unnecessarily shift from one tense to another (past to present, present to future, etc.) or from one person to another (*he* to *you*, *one* to *I*, etc.).

A. *Tense shifts.* If you begin writing in a particular tense, do not shift to another unless a change in time is logically necessary. The paragraph below breaks this rule:

> In William Carlos Williams's "The Use of Force," a doctor *was called* to examine a young girl. The doctor *was concerned* about diphtheria and *needs* to examine the girl's throat. The girl *is* terrified and *begins* to resist. As her resistance *continues,* the doctor *is compelled* to use more and more physical force. Though he *knows* the force *is* necessary, the doctor, to his horror, *found* that he *enjoyed* it and really *wanted* to hurt the girl.

Here the writer starts in the past tense *(was called, was concerned)*, shifts to the present tense *(needs, is, begins, continues, is compelled, knows, is)*, and then shifts back to the past tense *(found, enjoyed, wanted)*. Why? There is no reason. No change in time is needed. If writers view the events of a story as happening in the present, they should use the present tense consistently. Writers could also view the events as past actions—over and completed—and write entirely in the past tense. In either case, writers should decide which view they prefer and stick to it throughout.

<table>
<tr><td>ALL VERBS IN PRESENT TENSE</td><td>ALL VERBS IN PAST TENSE</td></tr>
<tr><td>In William Carlos Williams's "The Use of Force," a doctor is called to examine a young girl. The doctor is concerned about diphtheria and needs to examine the girl's throat. The girl is terrified and begins to resist. As her resistance continues, the doctor is compelled to use more and more physical force. Though he knows the force is necessary, the doctor, to his horror, finds that he enjoys it and really wants to hurt the girl.</td><td>In William Carlos Williams's "The Use of Force," a doctor was called to examine a young girl. The doctor was concerned about diphtheria and needed to examine the girl's throat. The girl was terrified and began to resist. As her resistance continued, the doctor was compelled to use more and more physical force. Though he knew the force was necessary, the doctor, to his horror, found that he enjoyed it and really wanted to hurt the girl.</td></tr>
</table>

B. *Shifts in person.* Write from a consistent point of view, making sure that any change in person is logically justified. If, for example, you begin expressing your thoughts in the third person (*he, she, it, they, one, the reader, the student, people,* etc.), avoid sudden shifts to the first person (*I, we*) or the second person (*you*). Similarly, avoid sudden shifts from third or first person singular to third or first person plural.

The *average citizen* thinks *he* is in favor of a clean environment, but *you* may change *your* mind when *you* find out what it will cost. (Shift from third person *average citizen* and *he* to second person *you, your.*)

The *teenager* resents the way *he* is being stereotyped. *We're* as different among *ourselves* as any other group in the population. *They* are tired of being viewed as a collection of finger-snapping freaks who say "cool" all the time. (Shift from third person singular *teenager* and *he* to first person plural *we* to third person plural *they.*)

Readers will find this suspense-filled mystery irresistible, just as *they* have found Mr. Stout's previous efforts. *You* should have a real battle keeping *yourself* from looking ahead to the last page. (Shift from third person *readers* and *they* to second person *you, yourself.*)

One wonders what is going on at City Hall. *We* have put up with flooded basements and lame excuses long enough. (Shift from third person *one* to first person *we.*)

The *average citizen* thinks *he* is in favor of a clean environment, but *he* may change *his* mind when *he* finds out what it will cost.

Teenagers resent the way *they* are being stereotyped. *They* are as different among *themselves* as any other group in the population. *They* are tired of being viewed as a collection of finger-snapping freaks who say "cool" all the time.

Readers will find this suspense-filled mystery irresistible, just as *they* have found Mr. Stout's previous efforts. *They* should have a real battle keeping *themselves* from looking ahead to the last page.

We wonder what is going on at City Hall. *We* have put up with flooded basements and lame excuses long enough.

Spelling. Poor spelling can seriously damage an otherwise fine paper. Faced with any significant number of spelling errors, readers cannot maintain their original confidence in the writer's thoughtfulness and skill.

The one spelling rule every writer needs to know is very simple: *Use the dictionary.* Rules for spelling specific words and groups of words almost always have exceptions and are difficult to learn and remember. Good spellers, almost without exception, turn out to be people who read a great deal and who have the dictionary habit, not people who have memorized spelling rules. The most important spelling rule, then, as well as the quickest and easiest one, is *use the dictionary.*

Despite this good advice, it can sometimes be handy to have available a list of frequently misspelled words. For quick reference, we include such a list. Note that words spelled the same as parts of longer words are not usually listed separately: the list has *accidentally* but not *accident, acquaintance* but not *acquaint.*

absence	comparative	formerly	occurred
accidentally	compelled	forty	occurrence
accommodate	conceivable	fourth	omitted
accumulate	conferred	frantically	opinion
achievement	conscience*	generally	opportunity
acquaintance	conscientious*	government	optimistic
acquire	conscious*	grammar	paid
acquitted	control	grandeur	parallel
advice*	controversial	grievous	paralysis
advise*	controversy	height	paralyze
all right	criticize	heroes	particular
amateur	deferred	hindrance	pastime
among	definitely	hoping	performance
analysis	definition	humorous	permissible
analyze	describe	hypocrisy	perseverance
annual	description	hypocrite	personal
apartment	desperate	immediately	personnel
apparatus	dictionary	incidentally	perspiration
apparent	dining	incredible	physical
appearance	disappearance	independence	picnicking
arctic	disappoint	inevitable	possession
arguing	disastrous	intellectual	possibility
argument	discipline	intelligence	possible
arithmetic	dissatisfied	interesting	practically
ascend	dormitory	irresistible	precede*
athletic	effect	knowledge	precedence
attendance	eighth	laboratory	preference
balance	eligible	laid	preferred
battalion	eliminate	led	prejudice
beginning	embarrass	lightning	preparation
belief	eminent	loneliness	prevalent
believe	encouragement	lose	principal*
beneficial	encouraging	losing	principle*
benefited	environment	maintenance	privilege
boundaries	equipped	maneuver	probably
Britain	especially	manufacture	procedure
business	exaggerate	marriage	proceed*
calendar	excellence	mathematics	profession
candidate	exhilarate	maybe	professor
category	existence	mere	prominent
cemetery	existent	miniature	pronunciation
changeable	experience	mischievous	prophecy (noun)
changing	explanation	mysterious	prophesy (verb)
choose	familiar	necessary	pursue
chose	fascinate	Negroes	quantity
coming	February	ninety	quiet*
commission	fiery	noticeable	quite*
committee	foreign	occasionally	quizzes

*See Glossary

recede	sense	succeed	truly
receive	separate	succession	tyranny
receiving	separation	surprise	unanimous
recommend	sergeant	technique	undoubtedly
reference	severely	temperamental	unnecessary
referring	shining	tendency	until
repetition	siege	than, then*	usually
restaurant	similar	their, there,	village
rhythm	sophomore	they're*	villain
ridiculous	specifically	thorough	weather
sacrifice	specimen	through	weird
sacrilegious	stationary*	to, too, two*	whether
salary	stationery*	tragedy	woman, women
schedule	statue	transferring	writing
seize	studying	tries	

Subject-verb agreement. A verb must agree with its subject in number and person. This rule has most practical meaning only in the present tense; in other tenses, the verb forms remain the same regardless of number or person. (The single exception is the past tense of *to be*; in that one instance the verb forms do change: *I was, you were, he was, we were, they were.*)

In the present tense, the third person singular verb usually differs from the others—most often because an -s *or* -es *is added to the verb stem.* A third person singular verb is the verb that goes with the pronouns *he, she,* and *it* and with *any singular noun.*

TO DREAM

	Singular	Plural
First person	I dream	we dream
Second person	you dream	you dream
Third person	he she it } dreams	they dream

The lovers *dream* of a long and happy future together.
The lover *dreams* of his sweetheart every night.
People often *dream* about falling from great heights.
Jennifer *dreams* about being buried alive.

TO MISS

	Singular	Plural
First person	I miss	we miss
Second person	you miss	you miss
Third person	he she it } misses	they miss

*See Glossary

The children *miss* their father more than they thought they would.

The child *misses* her friends.

The commuters *miss* the bus almost every morning.

The leftfielder *misses* more than his share of easy fly balls.

Even with highly irregular verbs, the third person singular in the present tense takes a special form (always with an *s* at the end).

TO BE

	Singular	Plural
First person	I am	we are
Second person	you are	you are
Third person	he she it } is	they are

TO HAVE

	Singular	Plural
First person	I have	we have
Second person	you have	you have
Third person	he she it } has	they have

The clowns *are* happy.

William *is* sad.

The Joneses *have* a lovely new home.

Mr. Jones *has* a lot to learn.

The few cases in which a present tense verb in the third person singular has the same form as in the other persons come naturally to almost every writer and speaker: *he can, he may, he might,* etc.

Once a writer realizes the difference between third person singular and other verb forms, the only problem is likely to be deciding which form to use in a few tricky situations:

A. *Compound subjects.* If the subject is compound (joined by *and*), the verb is plural unless the two words function as a single unit—*pork and beans is an easy dish to prepare,* for example—or unless the two words refer to a single person, as in *My cook and bottle washer has left me* (one person performed both jobs).

WRONG	RIGHT
Writing and reading *is* necessary for success in college.	Writing and reading *are* necessary for success in college.
The introduction and conclusion *does* not appear in an outline.	The introduction and conclusion *do* not appear in an outline.

B. *Neither . . . nor, either . . . or, nor, or.* If two subjects are joined by any of these terms, the verb agrees with the closer subject.

WRONG	RIGHT
Neither the students nor the teacher *are* correct.	Neither the students nor the teacher *is* correct.
Either the supporting details or the thesis statement *are* wrong.	Either the supporting details or the thesis statement *is* wrong.
Snowstorms or rain *cause* accidents.	Snowstorms or rain *causes* accidents.
Rain or snowstorms *causes* accidents.	Rain or snowstorms *cause* accidents.

C. *Time, money, weight.* Words that state an amount (time, money, weight) have a singular verb when they are considered as a unit *even if* they are plural in form.

WRONG	RIGHT
Two semesters *are* really a short time.	Two semesters *is* really a short time.
Five dollars *are* a modest fee for credit by examination.	Five dollars *is* a modest fee for credit by examination.
Five kilos of soybeans *are* about eleven pounds.	Five kilos of soybeans *is* about eleven pounds.

D. *Titles.* Titles of songs, plays, movies, novels, or articles always have singular verbs, even if the titles are plural in form.

WRONG	RIGHT
The Carpetbaggers were made into a movie.	*The Carpetbaggers was* made into a movie.
"The Novels of Early America" *were* published in *American Literature*.	"The Novels of Early America" *was* published in *American Literature*.

E. *Collective nouns.* Collective nouns such as *family, audience, jury,* and *class* have singular verbs when they are considered as a unified group. If the individuals within the unit act separately, the verb will be plural.

WRONG	RIGHT
The family *plan* a vacation.	The family *plans* a vacation.
The jury *is* divided on the verdict.	The jury *are* divided on the verdict. (The jury *are* acting as individual members, not as a unified group.)
The audience *are* going to give this show a standing ovation.	The audience *is* going to give this show a standing ovation.
The audience *is* divided in their opinion of the show.	The audience *are* divided in their opinion of the show.

F. *Indefinite pronouns.* Indefinite pronouns such as *one, no one, someone, everyone, none, anyone, somebody, anybody, everybody, each, neither,* and *either* take singular verbs:

WRONG	RIGHT
None of the ideas *are* correct.	None of the ideas *is* correct.
Each of the students *have* the time to study.	Each of the students *has* the time to study.
Either *are* a valid choice.	Either *is* a valid choice.

G. *Intervening elements.* No matter how many words, phrases, or clauses separate a subject from its verb, the verb must still agree with the subject in number.

    1. Separated by words:

WRONG: Many state capitals—Carson City, Augusta, Jefferson City, Olympia—is only small towns.

RIGHT: Many state capitals—Carson City, Augusta, Jefferson City, Olympia—are only small towns.

Here the plural *capitals,* not the singular *Olympia,* is the subject.

    2. Separated by phrases:

WRONG: A crate of oranges *are* expensive.

RIGHT: A crate of oranges *is* expensive.

Here *crate,* not *oranges,* is the subject.

WRONG: Agreement of subjects with their verbs *are* important.

RIGHT: Agreement of subjects with their verbs *is* important.

Here *agreement,* not *subjects* or *verbs,* is the subject.

    3. Separated by clauses:

WRONG: Reading well, which is one of the necessary academic skills, *make* studying easier.

RIGHT: Reading well, which is one of the necessary academic skills, *makes* studying easier.

Here *reading,* not *skills,* is the subject.

H. *Reversed position.* If the subject comes after the verb, the verb must still agree with the subject.

    1. There. If a sentence begins with *there* and is followed by some form of *be (is, are, was, were,* etc.), the number of *be* is determined by the subject. *There* is never the subject (except in a sentence like this one).

WRONG: There *is* five students in this class.

RIGHT: There *are* five students in this class.

Here *students* is the subject, and it is plural. Therefore, the verb must be plural.

WRONG: There *is* at least three systems of grammar for the English language.

RIGHT: There *are* at least three systems of grammar for the English language.

2. Prepositional phrases. Sometimes a writer begins a sentence with a prepositional phrase followed by a verb and then the subject. The verb must still agree with the subject.

WRONG: Throughout a grammar book *appears* many helpful writing hints.

RIGHT: Throughout a grammar book *appear* many helpful writing hints.

Here *hints*, not *book*, is the subject.

Exercise

Correct any subject-verb agreement errors in the following sentences.

1. *Smiles of a Summer Night* are among the best-known films of Ingmar Bergman.
2. Either the mayors or the governor has to take the blame for failure of the industrial development program.
3. There is suspense and laughter and romance in this marvelous new novel.
4. Watergate, like Teapot Dome and other political scandals, are likely to have little impact on the long-range future of American government.
5. Each of the students in these schools are concerned about the recent tightening of the job market.
6. Compositions of this one special type requires a detailed knowledge of logical fallacies.
7. The whole board of directors are about to resign.
8. The League of Women Voters sponsor many worthwhile activities.
9. Neither John nor Bill have enough money to buy textbooks.
10. Federal judges and the president constitutes the judicial and executive branches of government.

Subjunctive mood. Once far more common English than it is now, the subjunctive mood is still sometimes used to express "conditions contrary to fact"—hypothetical conditions, conditions not yet brought about, suppositional ideas, and so on. In the subjunctive, the verb form is usually plural even though the subject is singular.

If I *were* you, I would turn down the latest offer.

I move that the chairperson *declare* the meeting adjourned.

He looked as if he *were* going to be sick.

Subordinating conjunctions. See *Fragmentary sentences*, C.

Subordination. The most important idea in a sentence should be in an independent clause. Lesser ideas, explanations, qualifying material, and illustrations should be in subordinate clauses or phrases. See also Chapter 16, pp. 368–370.

POOR	IMPROVED
John is a wonderful person. He is very shy. He is extremely kind to everybody.	Although very shy, John is a wonderful person who is extremely kind to everybody. (The main idea is that John is a wonderful person.)
	OR
	Although he is a wonderful person who is extremely kind to everybody, John is very shy. (The main idea is that John is very shy.)
Professor Jones is terribly sarcastic. He is also a tough grader. It is true that he knows his subject. Most students dislike him, however.	Despite Professor Jones's knowledge of his subject, most students dislike him because of his terrible sarcasm and tough grading.
I am going to start on my new job and I am very optimistic.	I am very optimistic about starting on my new job.

Superlative forms. See *Comparative and superlative forms.*

Tense shifts. See *Shifts in time and person, A.*

Titles, punctuation of. See *Italics, A,* and *Quotation marks, B.*

Underlining. See *Italics.*

Verbs: principal parts. The form of most verbs changes according to which tense is being used, and to get the correct form a writer needs to know the principal parts of each verb. There are generally considered to be three principal parts: the *stem* or *infinitive* (the stem is the present tense form of the verb, and the infinitive is the stem preceded by *to*), the *past tense,* and the *past participle.* The past participle is the form used in perfect tenses (*I have seen, I had seen, I will have seen,* etc.) and in the passive voice (*I am seen, I was seen, I will be seen, I have been seen,* etc.)

The principal parts of *regular verbs* are formed by adding *-ed* or *-d* to the stem: *rush, rushed, rushed; love, loved, loved.* The past tense and past participle of regular verbs are always the same.

The principal parts of *irregular verbs* need to be learned separately—and even for the most experienced writer sometimes require checking in a dictionary or handbook. For quick reference, an alphabetical list of the principal parts of the most common irregular verbs follows:

Stem	*Past tense*	*Past participle*
arise	arose	arisen
be	was	been
bear	bore	borne, born
begin	began	begun
bind	bound	bound
blow	blew	blown

break	broke	broken
bring	brought	brought
burst	burst	burst
buy	bought	bought
catch	caught	caught
choose	chose	chosen
come	came	come
creep	crept	crept
deal	dealt	dealt
dig	dug	dug
dive	dived, dove	dived
do	did	done
draw	drew	drawn
drink	drank	drunk
drive	drove	driven
eat	ate	eaten
fall	fell	fallen
flee	fled	fled
fly	flew	flown
forbid	forbad, forbade	forbidden
freeze	froze	frozen
give	gave	given
go	went	gone
grow	grew	grown
hang	hung	hung
hang (execute)	hanged	hanged
know	knew	known
lay	laid	laid
lead	led	led
lend	lent	lent
lie	lay	lain
lose	lost	lost
mean	meant	meant
ride	rode	ridden
ring	rang	rung
rise	rose	risen
run	ran	run
see	saw	seen
seek	sought	sought
send	sent	sent
shake	shook	shaken
shine	shone, shined	shone, shined
sing	sang	sung
sink	sank, sunk	sunk
sleep	slept	slept
speak	spoke	spoken
spin	spun	spun
spit	spat	spat
spread	spread	spread

steal	stole	stolen
stink	stank	stunk
swear	swore	sworn
swim	swam	swum
swing	swung	swung
take	took	taken
teach	taught	taught
tear	tore	torn
thrive	thrived, throve	thrived, thriven
throw	threw	thrown
wear	wore	worn
weep	wept	wept
write	wrote	written

Confusion of the past tense and past participle of irregular verbs is a frequent cause of writing errors. Remember that the past participle is the correct form after *has, have,* and *had.*

WRONG	RIGHT
The mountaineers *had froze* to death.	The mountaineers *had frozen* to death.
The sprinter *has* just *broke* another track record.	The sprinter *has* just *broken* another track record.
I *begun* the book yesterday.	I *began* the book yesterday.
We *seen* that movie when it first came out.	We *saw* that movie when it first came out.

Verbs: tenses. What is the difference between *I eat* and *I am eating?* What is the difference between *I passed* and *I have passed?* Most verbs can be expressed in any tense, and the many different tenses enable the writer to present fine shades of meaning with great accuracy.

There are *six tenses.* Most verbs can take either the *active voice* or the *passive voice* (see pp. 364–365) in any tense. To make matters even more varied, *progressive constructions* can be used for all tenses of active verbs and some tenses of passive verbs.

TO SAVE

	Active Voice	*Progressive*
Present	I save	I am saving
Past	I saved	I was saving
Future	I will (*or* shall) save	I will be saving
Present Perfect	I have saved	I have been saving
Past Perfect	I had saved	I had been saving
Future Perfect	I will (*or* shall) have saved	I will have been saving
	Passive Voice	
Present	I am saved	I am being saved
Past	I was saved	I was being saved

Future	I will (*or* shall) be saved
Present Perfect	I have been saved
Past Perfect	I had been saved
Future Perfect	I will (*or* shall) have been saved

TO DRIVE

	Active Voice	*Progressive*
Present	I drive	I am driving
Past	I drove	I was driving
Future	I will drive	I will be driving
Present Perfect	I have driven	I have been driving
Past Perfect	I had driven	I had been driving
Future Perfect	I will have driven	I will have been driving
	Passive Voice	
Present	I am driven	I am being driven
Past	I was driven	I was being driven
Future	I will be driven	
Present Perfect	I have been driven	
Past Perfect	I had been driven	
Future Perfect	I will have been driven	

The *present tense* indicates present action, of course, especially continuing or habitual action:

> I *save* ten dollars every week.
>
> I *eat* a good breakfast each morning.
>
> She *drives* carefully.

The present is also used to express permanent facts and general truths, and is often the preferred tense for discussing literary actions:

> The speed of light *is* faster than the speed of sound.
>
> Truth *is* stranger than fiction.
>
> In *The Great Gatsby*, all of the events take place during the 1920s.
>
> Nick Carraway is the only character in the novel who understands Gatsby.

The present can even be called upon to deal with future action:

> Tomorrow she drives to the convention.

The *present progressive* indicates actions occurring—actions "in progress"—at the specific instant referred to.

> I *am eating* a good breakfast, and I do not want to be interrupted.
>
> She *is driving* too fast for these icy roads.

The same principle of action *in progress at the time* applies to *all progressive tenses:*

> Past progressive: The criminal *was shaving* when the police arrested him.

> Future progressive: At this time next week, I *will be surfing* in Hawaii.

The *past* tense describes previous actions, generally actions over and done with.

> The lifeguard *saved* two children last week.

> She *drove* to Florida three years ago.

The *future* tense describes actions after the present:

> From now on, I *will save* fifteen dollars every week.

> Marlene says that her in-laws *will drive* her to drink.

The *present perfect* tense (*have* or *has* plus the past participle) refers to past actions, generally of the fairly recent past, that still go on or have bearing on the present:

> I *have saved* over one thousand dollars so far.

> She *has driven* this short route to work many times.

The preceding sentences expressed in the simple past would suggest different meanings. *I saved over one thousand dollars* would suggest that the saving has now stopped. *She drove this short route to work many times* would suggest that some other route is now being used.

The *past perfect* tense (*had* plus the past participle) is employed for actions previous to the simple past—"more past than past."

> The lifeguard saved two children last week and *had saved* three adults the week before.

> She *had driven* to Florida three years ago, so she felt quite confident about making the trip again.

The *future perfect* tense (*will have* or *shall have* plus the past participle) expresses action that will be completed before some future time.

> By this time next year, I *will have saved* two thousand dollars.

> When she gets to Florida, she *will have driven* through three time zones.

The proper *sequence of tenses* within a sentence or series of sentences when different verbs refer to different time periods is an important consideration for all writers. The simple rule that verb tenses need to express precisely the intended period of time is not always simple to apply to one's own writing.

IMPROPER SEQUENCE	CORRECT SEQUENCE
The witness *told* [past] the court that on the night of the crime he *saw*	The witness *told* [past] the court that on the night of the crime he *had seen*

[past] the accused break the window of the liquor store.

[past perfect] the accused break the window of the liquor store. (The past perfect *had seen* refers to events "more past than past.")

When I *will come* [future] to the lake, you *will* already *be* [future] there for two weeks.

When I *will come* [future] to the lake, you *will* already *have been* [future perfect] there for two weeks. (The future perfect *will have been* refers to events that will be completed before some future time.)

Although the coach *has set* [present perfect] new curfew hours, the players still *have refused* [present perfect] to comply.

Although the coach *has set* [present perfect] new curfew hours, the players still *refuse* [present] to comply. (The coach's rules were set a while ago. The present tense *refuse* is necessary to show that the players' refusal to follow the rules is current.)

Wordiness. Wordiness means using more words than are necessary to convey meaning. Wordiness never makes writing clearer, just longer. After writing a rough draft, be sure to look it over and remove all the unnecessary words you can find. For more information on wordiness, see Chapter 15, pp. 353–358.

A. *Deadwood.*

WORDY WRITING	ECONOMICAL WRITING
Her hair was red in color.	Her hair was red.
Pollution conditions that exist in our cities are disgraceful.	Pollution in our cities is disgraceful.
In this day and age we live in, people seem totally apathetic to everything.	People today seem totally apathetic.

B. *Pointless repetition.*

WORDY WRITING	ECONOMICAL WRITING
The film was very interesting and fascinating.	The film was fascinating.
The author gives examples of different and varied criticisms of the novel.	The author gives examples of different criticisms of the novel.
Some early critics of Jonathan Swift called him an insane madman suffering from symptoms of mental disease.	Some early critics of Jonathan Swift called him insane.

C. *Delay of subject.*

WORDY WRITING

There are too many people who care only for themselves.

It is a fact that there has been a great increase in sensationalism in the theatre.

ECONOMICAL WRITING

Too many people care only for themselves.

Sensationalism in the theatre has greatly increased.

D. *Inadequate clause cutting.*

WORDY WRITING

The girl who has red hair was a flirt.

Some of the students who were more enthusiastic wrote an extra paper.

ECONOMICAL WRITING

The red-haired girl was a flirt.

Some of the more enthusiastic students wrote an extra paper.

GLOSSARY OF PROBLEM WORDS

A, an. Use *a* when the next word begins with a consonant sound. Use *an* when the next word begins with a vowel sound.

a book	a horror film
a rotten apple	a use of soybeans
an element	an urgent request
an honest man	an added attraction

Note that it is the sound that counts, not the actual letter.

a hasty decision	an unusual picture
an hour	a usual routine

Accept, except. *Accept* is a verb meaning *to receive, to agree to, to answer affirmatively. Except* is usually a preposition meaning *excluding.* It is also used infrequently as a verb meaning *to exclude.*

> I accepted the parcel from the mailman.
>
> Senator Jones hoped they would accept his apology.
>
> Should she accept that rude invitation?
>
> I liked everything about the concert except the music.
>
> I except you from my criticism.

Adapt, adept, adopt. *Adapt* means *change or adjust in order to make more suitable or in order to deal with new conditions. Adept* means *skillful, handy, good at. Adopt* means *take or use as one's own* or *endorse.*

> The dinosaur was unable to adapt to changes in its environment.
>
> The new textbook was an adaptation of the earlier edition.
>
> Bill has always been adept at carpentry.
>
> They had to wait six years before they could adopt a child.
>
> The Senate adopted the new resolution.

Advice, advise. *Advice* is a noun. *Advise* is a verb.

> My advice to you is to leave well enough alone.
>
> I advise you to leave well enough alone.

Affect, effect. As a noun, the word you want is almost certainly *effect,* meaning *result.* The noun *affect* is generally restricted to technical discussions of psychology, where it means *an emotion* or *a stimulus to an emotion*. As a verb, the word you want is probably *affect*, meaning *impress, influence*. The verb *effect* is comparatively uncommon; it means *bring about, accomplish, produce*.

> Many of our welfare programs have not had beneficial effects.
>
> This song always affects me powerfully.
>
> The crowd was not affected by the plea to disband.
>
> We hope this new program will effect a whole new atmosphere on campus.

Affective, effective. The word you are after is almost certainly *effective*, meaning *having an effect on* or *turning out well*. *Affective* is a fairly technical term from psychology and semantics meaning *emotional* or *influencing emotions*.

> Only time will tell if Federal Reserve policy is effective.
>
> The affective qualities of sound are difficult to evaluate in laboratory conditions.

Aggravate. The original meaning is *worsen* or *intensify*. The more common meaning of *irritate* or *annoy* is also acceptable in all but the fussiest formal writing.

Ain't. *Ain't* should never be used in written English except in humor or dialogue. Use of the phrase *ain't I*, when asking a question in conversational English, is undesirable, as is the supposedly elegant but totally ungrammatical *aren't I*. *Am I not* is grammatically correct, but awkward and stuffy. The best solution to the problem is to avoid it by expressing the thought differently.

All ready, already. *Already* means *previously* or *by the designated time*. *All ready* means *all set, all prepared*.

> Professor Wills has already told us that twice.
>
> The plane is already overdue.
>
> The meal was all ready by six o'clock.

All right, alright. Many authorities consider *alright* to be nonstandard English. It is good policy to use *all right* instead.

All together, altogether. *All together* means *joined in a group*. *Altogether* means *thoroughly* or *totally*.

> For once, the citizens are all together on an important issue.
>
> The character's motivations are altogether obscure.

Allusion, illusion. An *allusion* is an *indirect mention or reference*, often literary or historical. The verb form is *allude*. An *illusion* is an *idea not in accord with reality*.

> In discussing our problems with teenage marriages, the speaker made an allusion to *Romeo and Juliet*.

The nominating speech alluded to every American hero from Jack Armstrong to Neil Armstrong.

The patient suffered from the illusion that he was Napoleon.

At the end of the story, the character loses his pleasant illusions and discovers the harsh truth about himself.

A lot of. This phrase is more appropriate to conversation than to general written English. Use it sparingly. Remember that *a lot* is *two* words. Do not confuse it with *allot,* meaning *to give out* or *apportion.*

Alright. See *All right, alright.*

Altogether. See *All together, altogether.*

Alumna-alumnae, alumnus-alumni. An *alumna* is a female graduate. *Alumnae* is the plural. An *alumnus* is a male graduate. *Alumni* is the plural. Use *alumni* for a group of male and female graduates.

A.M., P.M. (*or* **a.m., p.m.).** Either capitals or lower-case letters are acceptable, but you should not alternate between the two in any one piece of writing. These abbreviations must be preceded by specific numbers:

RIGHT: His appointment is for 10:30 A.M.

WRONG: We expect him sometime in the A.M.

Among, between. Use *between* when dealing with two units. Use *among* with more than two.

WRONG	RIGHT
It is difficult to choose *between* the many excellent career programs at this school.	It is difficult to choose *among* the many excellent career programs at this school.
The company president had to make an arbitrary decision *among* the two outstanding candidates for promotion.	The company president had to make an arbitrary decision *between* the two outstanding candidates for promotion.
It's impossible to tell the difference *between* all the French names on the menu.	It's impossible to tell the difference *among* all the French names on the menu.
Tension has always existed *among* my parents and me.	Tension has always existed *between* my parents and me.
Tension has always existed *between* my mother, my father, and me.	Tension has always existed *among* my mother, my father, and me.

An. See *A, an.*

And etc. *Etc.* is an abbreviation of *et cetera* which means *and so forth* or *and other things.* Using the word *and* in addition to *etc.* is therefore repetitious and incorrect. See *Etc.*

Anyone, any one. Use *anyone* when you mean *anybody at all.* Use *any one* when you are considering separately or singling out each person or thing within a group.

Anyone can learn how to do simple electrical wiring.

Any one of these paintings is worth a small fortune.

The same principle applies to *everyone, every one* and *someone, some one.*

As. Do not make this word mean *because* or *since.*

POOR: I was late for my appointment as I missed the bus.

As I am a shy person, I find it hard to make new friends.

As far as. This phrase should be followed by a noun *and a verb.* Without the verb, it is incomplete.

POOR: As far as religion, I believe in complete freedom.

BETTER: As far as religion is concerned, I believe in complete freedom.

Askance. This word is an adverb meaning *suspiciously, disapprovingly*—used for looks, glances, etc. It can never be used as a noun.

WRONG: The sportswriters looked with askance at the coach's optimistic prediction.

RIGHT: The sportswriters looked askance at the coach's optimistic prediction.

Aspect. An overused, pseudoscholarly word. Try to avoid it wherever possible. Where you feel you must use it, try to preserve the concept of *looking* as part of the implicit meaning of the word.

We viewed the problem in all its aspects.

As to. Stuffy. Change to *about.*

POOR: We need to talk more as to our late deliveries.

BETTER: We need to talk more about our late deliveries.

Awful. The original meaning of this word is *awe-inspiring, arousing emotions of fear.* Some people insist that this is still its only valid meaning. We see nothing wrong, however, when it is also used to mean *extremely bad, ugly, unpleasant,* etc. The word *dreadful* has evolved in the same way, and we know of no objections to that word. See *Awfully.*

Awfully. Does not mean *very.*

POOR: He's an awfully nice person.

I'm awfully impressed by what you said.

Jim felt awfully bad.

A while, awhile. *Awhile* is an adverb. *A while* is a noun.

Success comes only to those who are prepared to wait awhile.

I thought I saw her a while ago.

Take it easy for a while.

Bad, badly. *Bad* is the adjective, *badly* the adverb. In some sentences, the verbs *look, feel,* and *seem* function as linking verbs and must be followed by the adjectival form.

I play badly.

but

I feel bad.

She looks bad.

The idea seems bad.

Watch the location of *badly* when you use it to mean *very much.* It can often be misread as having its more familiar meaning, and comic disaster can occur.

I want to act badly.

He wanted her to love him badly.

Be. Not acceptable written English in constructions like *I be going, they be ready,* etc. Use *I am going, they are ready,* etc.

Beside, besides. *Beside* means *alongside of.* It can also mean *other than* or *aside from.*

He pulled in beside the Volkswagen.

Your last statement is beside the point.

Besides means *in addition to* or *moreover.*

I'm starting to discover that I'll need something besides a big smile to get ahead.

Besides, I'm not sure I really liked the dress in the first place.

Between. See *Among, between.*

Black, Negro. *Negro* is capitalized. *Black* is not, except for special emphasis.

She was proud of being a black American, but she did not like to be called a Negro.

He was a strong supporter of the Black Identity Movement.

The plural of *Negro* is *Negroes. Negro* is Spanish and Portuguese for *black. Black* is now considered preferable because *Negro* has a long history of use as a genteel social and political euphemism.

Blond, blonde. *Blond* is masculine; *blonde* is feminine. Use *blond* when dealing with both sexes or when sex is irrelevant.

She is a blonde.

His hair is blond.

All the children are blonds.

We chose blond furniture for the recreation room.

Brake, break. *Brake,* verb or noun, has to do with stopping a vehicle or other piece of machinery. For additional meanings, see dictionary.

Frantically, he slammed on the brake.

She braked her car to a complete stop.

Break, verb or noun, has many meanings, most commonly *destroy, damage, exceed, interrupt,* etc. The simple past is *broke;* the past participle is *broken.*

Porcelain can break, so be careful.

His left arm was broken.

Henry Aaron broke Babe Ruth's home run record.

The committee took a ten minute break.

The attempted jail break was unsuccessful.

The brake of the school bus has been broken.

Breath, breathe. *Breath* is a noun. *Breathe* is a verb.

His statement was like a breath of fresh air.

The soprano drew a deep breath.

In some cities it can be dangerous to breathe the air.

The soprano breathes deeply.

But that, but what. Not acceptable standard English. Use *that.*

WRONG: I don't question but that you have good intentions.

I don't question but what you have good intentions.

RIGHT: I don't question that you have good intentions.

Can, may. In formal English questions, *can* asks if the ability is there, and *may* asks if the permission is there.

May I intrude on your conversation? (Not *can*—anyone with a voice has the ability to intrude.)

Outside of formal contexts, few people worry about the distinction.

Censor, censure. *Censor,* as a verb, means *examine mail, art, etc., to see if it should be made public,* or *cut out, ban.* As a noun, *censor* means *a person engaged in censoring. Censure* can be a verb or noun meaning *condemn* or *condemnation, criticize adversely* or *adverse criticism,* etc.

Parts of the movie have been censored.

The prison censor examines all mail.

The Citizens for Good Citizenship Committee recently censured the mayor.

Dickens's deathbed scenes have long been singled out for censure.

Cite, site. *Cite,* a verb, means *mention. Site,* a noun, means *location.*

> He cited many examples to prove his point.
>
> The site of a new housing project has been debated for more than a year.

Climactic, climatic. *Climactic* is the adjectival form of *climax.*

> The hero's death is the climactic moment of the story.

Climatic is the adjectival form of *climate.*

> Climatic conditions in the Dakotas go from one extreme to the other.

Complected. Not standard English. *Complexioned* is preferable, but it's better to reword your sentence so you can avoid using either term.

> ACCEPTABLE: He was a light-complexioned man.
>
> BETTER: He had very fair skin.

Complement, compliment. A *complement* completes or brings to perfection. Also means *the full amount.* Noun or verb. *Compliment* means *praise.* Noun or verb.

> A string of pearls is an excellent complement to a black dress.
>
> The ship had its required complement of officers.
>
> Cheese and wine complement each other.
>
> I don't appreciate insincere compliments.
>
> Don't compliment me unless you mean it.

Compose, comprise. *Compose* means *to make up, to constitute.*

> Thirteen separate colonies composed the original United States.

Comprise means *to be made up of, to encompass.*

> The original United States comprised thirteen separate colonies.

If the distinction between these words gives you trouble, forget about *comprise* and use *is composed of* instead.

Conscience, conscientious, conscious. *Conscience* is the inner voice that tells us right from wrong, makes us feel guilty, etc. *Conscientious* means *painstaking, scrupulous,* or *ruled by conscience,* as in *conscientious objector. Conscious* means *aware.*

> No one should ask you to act against your conscience.
>
> I've tried to do this work as conscientiously as possible.
>
> Jerry became conscious of a subtle change in Mary's attitude.

Conservative, reactionary. *Conservatives* are generally skeptical or cautious in their attitudes toward innovations. They tend to respect and rely on tradition and past experience. They are not against all progress but believe it is usually most effective when brought about slowly. *Reactionaries* are opposed to present conditions and want to restore the past. See *Liberal, radical.*

Console, consul, council, counsel. *Console:* As a verb (accent on second syllable)—*to sympathize with, to comfort.* As a noun (accent on first syllable)—*a radio, phonograph, or television cabinet, usually a combination, resting directly on the floor;* also *a small compartment, as found in an automobile between bucket seats;* for other meanings see dictionary.

Consul: A representative of a nation, stationed in a foreign city, whose job is to look after the nation's citizens and business interests.

Council: A governing body or an advisory group.

Counsel: As a verb—*to advise, to recommend.* As a noun—*advice, recommendation, exchange of ideas.*

> I could find no words to console the grieving widow.
>
> I've lived with this portable phonograph too long. I want a console.
>
> The French consul will answer any of your questions on import duties.
>
> The council met last week in a special emergency session.
>
> The tax expert counselled him on medical deductions.
>
> Sarah knew she could rely on her father's friendly counsel.

Continual, continuous. *Continuous* means *completely uninterrupted, without any pause.*

> The continuous noise at the party next door kept us awake.
>
> The patient received continuous round-the-clock care.

Continual means *frequently repeated, but with interruptions or pauses.*

> He had a bad cold and blew his nose continually.
>
> He changed jobs continually.

Costume, custom. *Costume* means *style of dress.* *Custom* means *conventional practice.* See dictionary for other meanings.

> He decided to wear a pirate's costume to the masquerade.
>
> Trick or treat is an old Halloween custom.

Could care less. See *Couldn't care less.*

Couldn't care less. Means *utterly indifferent to.* The phrase *could care less* is sometimes mistakenly used to mean the same thing. It does not mean the same thing; it makes no sense at all.

> WRONG: I could care less about his opinion of me.
>
> RIGHT: I couldn't care less about his opinion of me.

Could of, should of, would of. Not acceptable written English. Use *could have, should have, would have.*

Council. See *Console, consul, council, counsel.*

Counsel. See *Console, consul, council, counsel.*

Credible, creditable, credulous. *Credible* means *believable. Creditable* means *worthy of praise. Credulous* means *gullible, foolishly believing.*

> His lame excuses were not credible.
>
> Adam's behavior since his parole has been creditable.
>
> She's so credulous she still believes that the stork brings babies.

Criterion. This word (plural: *criteria*) is overused and frequently stuffy. Use *standard,* instead.

Cute. An overused word. Avoid it wherever possible in written English.

Data. Technically, a plural word, the singular of which is *datum.* The word's Latin origins, however, have nothing to do with its current usage. We believe that *data* can be treated as singular in all levels of English—and probably should be.

> CORRECT: This data is accurate and helpful.
>
> CORRECT (but very formal): These data are accurate and helpful.

Decompose, discompose. *Decompose* means *rot,* or *break into separate parts. Discompose* means *disturb, fluster, unsettle.*

> When the police found the body, it had already begun to decompose.
>
> His drunken foolishness discomposed all of us.

Definitely. Nothing is wrong with this word except that it is used far too often to add vague emphasis to weak thoughts and weak words.

Detract, distract. *Detract* means *belittle. Distract* means *divert, confuse.*

> Almost everyone tries to detract from television's real accomplishments.
>
> A mosquito kept distracting his attention.

Different than. *Different from* is much better in all circumstances.

Discompose. See *Decompose, discompose.*

Disinterested, uninterested. Don't confuse these words. *Disinterested* means *impartial, unbiased. Uninterested* means *bored, indifferent.* An audience is uninterested in a poor play. A disinterested judge is necessary for a fair trial.

Disorientate, disorientated. Awkward and ugly variations of *disorient* and *disoriented.*

Distract. See *Detract, distract.*

Each. Takes a singular verb and a singular pronoun. See *He, his, him, himself.*

> Each breed of dog has its own virtues.

Each actress was told to practice her lines.

Each of the ballplayers is taking his turn at batting practice.

Economic, economical. Use *economic* for references to business, finance, the science of economics, etc. *Economical* means *inexpensive* or *thrifty*.

We need to rethink our entire economic program to avert a recession.

Economic conditions are improving in the textile industry.

The economical shopper looks hard for bargains.

It's economical in the long run to use first quality oil in your car.

Effect. See *Affect, effect*.

Effective. See *Affective, effective*.

Either. Use only when dealing with two units.

WRONG: Either the Republican, the Democrat, or the Independent will be elected.

When *either* is the subject, it takes a singular verb and pronoun.

The men are both qualified. Either is ready to give his best.

See *Neither*.

Elicit, illicit. *Elicit* means *draw out*. *Illicit* means *improper* or *prohibited*.

The interviewer was unable to elicit a direct answer.

Where would our modern novelists turn if they were suddenly prohibited from writing about illicit romance?

Ensure, insure. Both words mean the same. The more common spelling is *insure*.

Equally as. Not a standard English phrase. Eliminate the *as* or substitute *just as*.

POOR: My grades were equally as good.

The style was equally as important as the plot.

BETTER: My grades were equally good.

The style was just as important as the plot.

Establishment. Avoid this trite fad word. Basically, it should refer to a ruling group or structure that attempts to preserve the status quo. In practice, the word has become a term of vague abuse that interferes with discussion of complex issues.

Etc. Except where brevity is a major concern, as in this glossary, avoid *etc.* It tends to convey the impression that the writer doesn't want to be bothered with being accurate and specific. See *And etc.*

Every. This adjective makes the noun it modifies take a singular verb and a singular pronoun. See *He, his, him, himself*.

Every student is expected to do his assignments on time.

Every idea has been put into its proper place in the outline.

Every businesswoman needs to learn how to deal with the prejudices of her male counterparts.

Everyone, every one. See *Anyone, any one.*

Except. See *Accept, except.*

Expand, expend. *Expand* means *increase, enlarge, fill out. Expend* means *spend, use up.*

The company needs to expand its share of the market.

The speakers will soon expand on their remarks.

Taxes must not be expended on visionary projects.

The student fell asleep during the final examination because he had expended all his energy in studying.

Facet. An overused, pseudoscholarly word. Avoid it wherever possible.

Farther, further. Not too many people worry about the distinction between these words anymore, but we think it is worth preserving. Use *farther* for geographic distance, *further* for everything else.

Allentown is five miles farther down the road.

Further changes need to be made in the curriculum.

Jim kissed her, but they were further apart than ever.

We need to go further into the subject.

Faze, phase. *Faze* means *disconcert, fluster.*

No great artist is fazed by critical sneers.

Phase means *a stage in development.* It is an overused word. Limit it to contexts in which the passage of time is especially significant.

BAD: One phase of the team's failure is poor hitting.

ACCEPTABLE: The history of the team can be divided into three phases.

Fellow. As an adjective, the word means *being in the same situation* or *having the same ideas.* Make sure you do not use it to modify a noun that already implies that meaning.

CORRECT: My fellow workers and I voted to strike.

WRONG: My fellow colleagues have been hasty.

Figurative, figuratively. See *Literal, literally.*

Flaunt, flout. *Flaunt* means *show off arrogantly or conspicuously. Flout* means *treat scornfully, show contempt,* mostly in attitudes toward morality, social customs, traditions.

They lost no opportunity to flaunt their new-found wealth.

Those hoodlums flout all the basic decencies and then complain that we misunderstand them.

Foreword, forward. A *foreword* is a *preface* or *introduction*. *Forward* is the opposite of backward. It can also mean *bold* or *impertinent*.

The girl thought she was a swinger, but Mr. Tweedle thought she was a forward hussy.

Formally, formerly. *Formally* means *in a formal manner*. *Formerly* means *in the past*.

We were asked to dress formally.

People formerly thought that the automobile would turn out to be just another fad.

Former. Means *the first of two*. Don't use when dealing with more than two.

> WRONG: Grant, McKinley, and Harding were poor presidents. The former was the poorest.
>
> RIGHT: Grant, McKinley, and Harding were poor presidents. The first was the poorest.
>
> Grant and McKinley were poor presidents. The former was the poorer.

See *Latter*.

Further. See *Farther, further*.

Gap. Phrases such as "generation gap," "missile gap," "credibility gap," etc. are media-spawned terms that have tended to lose their original meaning and impact through overuse. Avoid using them wherever possible.

Hanged, hung. Both are past participles of *hang;* technically, they are interchangeable. Traditionally, however, *hanged* is reserved for references to executions, and *hung* is used everywhere else.

The spy was hanged the next morning.

All the pictures hung crookedly.

He, his, him, himself. These common and seemingly inoffensive words have become the source of considerable controversy. Some people declare that the words contribute to sexual discrimination when used, as is traditional and grammatical, to refer to people who can be of either sex or when sex is irrelevant or unknown.

The used-car buyer needs to be careful. In fact, *he* can hardly be too careful, for many dealers are waiting for the opportunity to swindle *him*.

Each citizen can make *his* choice known on Election Day.

Everybody should protect *himself* from the dangers of alcoholism.

Defenders of these usages assert that in addition to being grammatically correct they are no more discriminatory in intent or effect than words like *mankind* or phrases like *no man is an island*. Both points of view are capable of being supported by legitimate logical arguments instead of the more usual hysteria and abuse.

For better or for worse, English has no distinct singular pronoun to refer to either sex. The *italicized* words in the three preceding examples are all technically correct—and if no means of revising them were available, they would have to remain as they are. At the same time, few writers want to run the risk of antagonizing a reader over the choice of pronouns, grammatical or not. Publishers of books, magazines, and newspapers have grown increasingly sensitive to the problem, and it seems safe to predict that the *he* usage will become less frequent as time goes by.

Like many problems, this one can often be solved by running away from it. We suggest that you *change singular phrasing to plural whenever possible*.

> Used car buyers need to be careful. In fact, *they* can hardly be too careful, for many dealers are waiting for the opportunity to swindle *them*.
>
> All citizens can make *their* choice known on Election Day.
>
> People should protect *themselves* from the dangers of alcoholism.

Sentences that do not lend themselves to a plural approach may have to be completely rephrased.

See *He or she, his or hers, him or her*.

He or she, his or hers, him or her. These efforts to achieve sexual equality in language are usually best saved for legal contracts. The phrasing is generally strained and pompous.

> POOR: Everyone needs to make early plans for his or her career.
>
> In cases of fatal illness, should a patient be told the truth about what is wrong with him or her?
>
> BETTER: People should all make early plans for their careers.
>
> In cases of fatal illness, should patients be told the truth about what is wrong with them?

Hopefully. *Hopefully* is an adverb, which means that it modifies and usually appears next to or close to a verb, adjective, or other adverb.

> The farmers searched hopefully for a sign of rain.
>
> Hopefully, the children ran down the stairs on Christmas morning.

Hopefully does *not* mean *I hope, he hopes, it is hoped that*, etc. Avoid using it in sentences like the following:

> Hopefully, we can deal with this mess next weekend.
>
> The new driver's training program, hopefully, will cut down on traffic fatalities.

In fairness, so many educated writers and speakers mishandle *hopefully* that the incorrect usage will probably worm its way into Standard English someday.

Human, humane. *Humane* means *kind, benevolent.*

> Humane treatment of prisoners is all too rare.

I, me. *Me* is the object of a verb or preposition.

> He gave the book to me.
>
> He gave me the business.
>
> For me, nothing can beat a steak and French fries.
>
> Why does she like me so much?

I functions as the subject of a sentence or clause, and as a complement in the extremely formal but grammatically correct *It is I*. To determine which word to use in sentences like *Nobody is more enthusiastic than I* or *Nobody is more enthusiastic than me*, simply complete the sentences with a verb, and see which makes sense.

> WRONG: Nobody is more enthusiastic than me (am).
>
> RIGHT: Nobody is more enthusiastic than I (am).

Illicit. See *Elicit, illicit.*

Illusion. See *Allusion, illusion.*

Imply, infer. To *imply* means *to suggest or hint at something without specifically stating it.*

> The dean implied that the demonstrators would be punished.
>
> The editorial implies that our public officials have taken bribes.

To *infer* means *to draw a conclusion.*

> I inferred from her standoffish attitude that she disliked me.
>
> The newspaper wants its readers to infer that our public officials have taken bribes.

Incredible, incredulous. *Incredible* means *unbelievable*. *Incredulous* means *unconvinced, nonbelieving.*

> The witness gave evidence that was utterly incredible.
>
> I was incredulous at hearing those absurd lies.

Indict. To *indict* means *to charge with a crime*. It does not mean to arrest or to convict.

> The grand jury indicted Fields on a gambling charge.

Individual. Often contributes to stuffiness and wordiness.

> BAD: He was a remarkable individual.
>
> BETTER: He was a remarkable man.
>
> BEST: He was remarkable.

Inferior than. Not standard English. Use *inferior to.*

Ingenious, ingenuous. *Ingenious* means *clever*. *Ingenuous* means *naive, open*.

> Sherlock Holmes was an ingenious detective.
>
> Nothing could rival the ingenuous appeal of the little girl's eyes.

Noun forms: *ingenuity, ingenuousness*.

In reference to. Stuffy business English. Use "about."

In spite of. *In spite* is two separate words.

Insure. See *Ensure, insure*.

Inter-, intra-. *Inter* is a prefix meaning *between different groups*. *Intra* is a prefix meaning *within the same group*.

> Ohio State and Michigan fought bitterly for intercollegiate football supremacy.
>
> The English faculty needs a new department head who can control intradepartmental bickering.

Irregardless. Not standard English. The proper word is *regardless*.

Irrelevant, irreverent. *Irrelevant:* Not related to the subject. *Irreverent:* Scornful, lacking respect.

> Your criticisms sound impressive but are really irrelevant.
>
> America could use some of Mark Twain's irreverent wit today.

Confusion of these words may be responsible for the frequent mispronunciation of *irrelevant* as *irrevelant*.

Its, it's. *Its* is the possessive of *it*. *It's* is the contraction for *it is*.

> The cat licked its paws. It's a wonderfully clean animal.

Its' is not a word. It does not exist, and it never has.

Job. Frequently overused in student writing. It is probably most effective when reserved for simple references to employment for wages.

> POOR: Shakespeare does a great job of showing Hamlet's conflicting emotions.
>
> ACCEPTABLE: Our economy needs to create more jobs.

Kind of. Means what it says: *a type of, a variety of*. It does not mean *somewhat* or *rather* except in the most informal writing.

> POOR: She was kind of pretty.
>
> I was kind of curious about his answer.
>
> CORRECT: He suffered from an obscure kind of tropic fever.
>
> He had a kind of honest stubbornness that could be very appealing.

Latter. Means *the second of two*. Don't use when dealing with more than two.

WRONG: Washington, Jefferson, and Lincoln were great presidents. The latter was the greatest.

RIGHT: Washington, Jefferson, and Lincoln were great presidents. The last was the greatest.

Washington and Lincoln were great presidents. The latter was the greater.

See *Former*.

Lay, lie. *Lay* is a transitive verb. It always takes an object *or* is expressed in the passive voice.

Present	*Past*	*Past Participle*	*Present Participle*
lay	laid	laid	laying

Lie is an intransitive verb. It never takes an object and never is expressed in the passive voice. This problem-causing *lie*, by the way, means *recline*, not *fib*.

Present	*Past*	*Past Participle*	*Present Participle*
lie	lay	lain	lying

Now I lay my burden down.

The hen laid six eggs yesterday.

The mason has laid all the bricks.

Our plans have been laid aside.

The porter is laying down our suitcases.

Now I am going to lie down.

Yesterday he lay awake for five hours.

The refuse has lain there for weeks.

Tramps are lying on the park benches.

Lead, led. As a noun, *lead* has various meanings (and pronunciations).

The student had no lead for his pencil.

The reporter wanted a good lead for her story.

Which athlete is in the lead?

The past of the verb *lead* is *led*.

The declarer always leads in bridge.

I led an ace instead of a deuce.

Is it possible to lead without making enemies?

Grant led the Union to triumph at Vicksburg.

Leave, let. *Let* means *allow*, etc. *Leave* means *depart*.

WRONG: Leave us look more closely at this sonnet.

RIGHT: Let us look more closely at this sonnet.

Lend, loan. *Lend* is a verb; *loan* is a noun.

> Jack was kind enough to lend me ten dollars.
>
> High interest rates have interfered with loans.

Liable, libel. *Liable* means *likely to* or *legally obligated*. *Libel* is an unjust written statement exposing someone to public contempt.

> After a few drinks, that man is liable to do anything.
>
> The owner of the dog was liable for damages.
>
> Senator Green sued the newspaper for libel.

Libel, slander. *Libel* is written. *Slander* is spoken.

Liberal, radical. *Radicals* are extremists. They want drastic changes and usually want them immediately. They are inclined to accept extreme means for bringing about the changes. The word is most frequently used now with leftist connotations, but it need not be. A reactionary who wants to abolish Social Security is taking a radical position. *Liberals* tend to believe in reform more than in drastic change, though they are often strongly against the status quo. They are inclined to work within the system to achieve their goals. As an adjective, *liberal* is still used to mean *open-minded*.

See *Conservative, reactionary*.

Like, as. In agonizing over whether to use *like* or *as* (sometimes *as if*), look first at the words that follow. If the words make up a clause (subject plus verb) use *as*; if not, use *like*.

> He acted like a man.
>
> He acted as a man should.
>
> She treated me like dirt.
>
> She treated me as if I were dirt.

This rule is not foolproof, but it will handle almost all practical problems. *Like* in place of *as* is now fairly well accepted outside of formal written English, and we will have no overpowering regrets when it is accepted at all levels.

Literal, literally. These terms mean *in actual fact, according to the precise meaning of the words*. Some people use *literal, literally* when they mean the opposite: *figurative, figuratively*.

> WRONG: He literally made a monkey of himself.
>
> Some of our councilmen are literal vultures.
>
> I literally fly off the handle when I see children mistreated.
>
> RIGHT: The doctor said Karen's jealousy had literally made her ill.
>
> We were so lost that we literally did not know north from south.
>
> A literal translation from German to English rarely makes any sense.

Loan. See *Lend, loan.*

Loath, loathe. *Loath* is an adjective meaning *reluctant. Loathe* is a verb meaning *hate.*

> I am loath to express the full intensity of my feelings.
>
> I loathe people who use old-fashioned words like *loath.*

Loose, lose. *Lose* means *misplace. Loose* is the opposite of *tight* and *tighten.*

Mad. Use this word in written English to mean *insane,* not *angry.* Also, avoid it in its current slang senses of *unusual, wild, swinging,* etc.

> POOR: Please don't be mad at me.
>
> She wore a delightfully mad little hat.
>
> RIGHT: Shakespeare tends to be sympathetic to his mad characters.
>
> The arms race is utterly mad.

Majority, plurality. A candidate who has a *majority* has more than half of the total votes. A candidate who has a *plurality* has won the election but received less than half the total votes.

Masochist. See *Sadist, masochist.*

Massage, message. A *massage* makes muscles feel better. A *message* is a communication.

May. See *Can, may.*

May be, maybe. *May be* is a verb form meaning *could be, can be,* etc. *Maybe* is an adverb meaning *perhaps.*

> I may be wrong, but I feel that *Light in August* is Faulkner's finest novel.
>
> Maybe we ought to start all over again.

Me. See *I, me.*

Medal, metal, mettle. A *medal* is what is awarded to heroes and other celebrities. *Metal* is a substance such as iron, copper, etc. *Mettle* means *stamina, enthusiasm, vigorous spirit,* etc.

> The American team won most of its Olympic medals in men's swimming.
>
> Future metal exploration may take place more and more beneath the sea.
>
> Until the Normandy invasion, Eisenhower had not really proved his mettle.

Medium. An overused word in discussing communications. The plural is *media.* See the dictionary for its many meanings.

Mighty. Use this word to mean *powerful* or *huge.* It doesn't mean *very.*

> POOR: I was mighty pleased to meet you.

Moral, morale. Moral, as an adjective, means *having to do with ethics* or *honorable, decent, upright,* etc. As a noun, it means *lesson, precept, teaching.* *Morale* means *state of mind, spirit.*

> Not all moral issues are simple cases of right and wrong.
>
> The story has a profound moral.
>
> The new coach tried to improve the team's morale.

More, most. Use *more* when two things are being compared. For any number over two, use *most.*

> Between Sally and Phyllis, Sally was the more talented.
>
> Of all my teachers, Mr. Frederic was the most witty.

Most. Never use this word as a synonym for *almost.*

> WRONG: Most everyone showed up at the party.
>
> I'll be home most any time tomorrow.

See *More, most.*

Mr., Mrs., Miss, Ms., etc. These titles should not be used in referring to figures from the historical, cultural, and scientific past. With living figures, the titles should be used in moderation; the better known the person, the less need for the title.

> POOR: Mr. John Adams was the second president of the United States.
>
> *The Scarlet Letter* was written by Mr. Nathaniel Hawthorne.
>
> The trial of Ms. Patty Hearst received worldwide press coverage.
>
> BETTER: John Adams was the second president of the United States.
>
> *The Scarlet Letter* was written by Nathaniel Hawthorne.
>
> The trial of Patty Hearst received worldwide press coverage.

Ms. Now accepted in standard usage as a title for women, though Miss and Mrs. are still common.

Natural. Means *unartificial,* among other things. It is overused as a term of vague praise. It might be applied to someone's voice or manner, but it sounds absurd in a sentence like

> Brand X eyelashes will give you that natural look.

Negro. See *Black, Negro.*

Neither. Use only when dealing with *two* units.

> WRONG: I like neither collies nor poodles nor dachshunds.

When *neither* is the subject, it takes a singular verb and pronoun.

Both powers are responsible. Neither is doing its best for world peace.

See *Either*.

Nice. An overused word, generally too vague in meaning to have much value. Try to find more specific substitutes.

None. Means *no one* or *not one* and takes a singular verb and pronoun.

None of these police officers understands that he is a public servant.

Not hardly. A double negative. Not standard English. Use *hardly*.

WRONG: He couldn't hardly see his hand in front of his face.

RIGHT: He could hardly see his hand in front of his face.

Often times. Wordy and pointless version of *often*.

Only. A tricky word in some sentences. Make sure that it modifies what you really want it to.

POOR: I only felt a little unhappy. (Only *felt*? Does the writer mean that he did not consciously *think* this way?)

I only asked for a chance to explain. (Does the writer mean that he did not insist on or strongly desire that chance?)

BETTER: I felt only a little unhappy.

I asked only for a chance to explain.

Orientate, orientated. Awkward and ugly variations of *orient* and *oriented*.

Passed, past. *Passed* is the past participle of *pass*. *Past* is used mainly as an adjective or a noun. Never use *passed* as an adjective or noun.

We passed them on the highway.

Valerie had a mysterious past.

History is the study of past events.

Perpetrate, perpetuate. *Perpetrate* means *commit an evil, offensive, or stupid act*. *Perpetuate* means *preserve forever*.

He perpetrated a colossal blunder.

We resolve to perpetuate the ideals our leader stood for.

Perscription. No such word—you want *prescription*.

Persecute, prosecute. *Persecute* means *oppress, pick on unjustly*. *Prosecute* means *carry forward to conclusion* or *bring court proceedings against*.

Persecuting religious and racial minorities is one of the specialties of the human race.

The general believes that the war must be prosecuted intensely.

We must prosecute those charged with crimes as rapidly as possible.

Perspective, prospective. *Perspective* has various meanings, most commonly *the logically correct relationships between the parts of something and the whole* or *the drawing technique that gives the illusion of space or depth. Prospective* means *likely to become* or *likely to happen.*

> Inflation is not our only problem; we need to keep the economy in perspective.
>
> Medieval painting reveals an almost complete indifference to perspective.
>
> The prospective jurors waited nervously for their names to be called.
>
> None of the prospective benefits of the Penn Central merger ever materialized.

Phenomenon. Singular; the standard plural form is *phenomena.*

Plurality. See *Majority, plurality.*

Precede, proceed. *Precede* means *go before. Proceed* means *go on.* See dictionary for other meanings.

> Years of struggle and poverty preceded her current success.
>
> Let us proceed with our original plans.

Prejudice, prejudiced. *Prejudice* is ordinarily a noun. *Prejudiced* is an adjective.

> WRONG: John is prejudice.
>
> The neighborhood is filled with prejudice people.
>
> RIGHT: John is prejudiced.
>
> Legislation alone cannot eliminate prejudice.

Prescribe, proscribe. *Prescribe* means *order, recommend, write a prescription. Proscribe* means *forbid.* See other meanings in dictionary.

> The committee prescribed a statewide income tax.
>
> The authorities proscribe peddling without a license.

Principal, principle. As an adjective, *principal* means *foremost, chief, main.* As a noun, it can mean *a leading person* (as of a school) or *the amount owed on a loan exclusive of interest.* For other meanings see dictionary. *Principle* is a noun meaning *a fundamental doctrine, law, or code of conduct.*

> The principal conflict in the novel was between the hero's conscious and subconscious desires.
>
> For the third time that week, Jeff was summoned to the principal's office.
>
> The interest on a twenty-five- or thirty-year mortgage can often equal or exceed the principal.
>
> Be guided by one principle: "Know thyself."
>
> The candidate is a man of high principles.

Pronunciation. Note the spelling. There is no such word as *pronounciation*.

Quiet, quite. *Quiet* means *silence, to become silent, to make silent. Quite* means *rather* or *completely*, in addition to its informal use in expressions like *quite a guy*.

> The parents pleaded for a moment of peace and quiet.
>
> The crowd finally quieted down.
>
> Throughout the concert, I tried to quiet the people behind me.
>
> April was quite cold this year.
>
> When the job was quite finished, Bill felt like sleeping for a week.

Radical. See *Liberal, radical*.

Raise, rise. *Rise* is an intransitive verb and never takes an object. *Raise* is a transitive verb.

> I always rise at 8:00 A.M.
>
> The farmer raises corn and wheat.

Rationalize. This word is most effective when used to mean *think up excuses for*. It can also mean *to reason*, but in that sense it is just a stuffy word for a simple idea. The noun form is *rationalization*.

> The gangster tried to rationalize his behavior by insisting that his mother had not loved him.
>
> All these rationalizations conceal the unpleasant truth.

Reactionary. See *Conservative, reactionary*.

Really. An overused word. It is especially weak in written English when it serves as a synonym for *very* or *extremely*.

> POOR: We saw a really nice sunset.
>
> That was a really big show.

When you do use *really*, try to preserve its actual meaning, stressing what is *real* as opposed to what is false or mistaken.

> RIGHT: The noises were really caused by mice, not ghosts.
>
> He may have been acquitted through lack of evidence, but everyone knew that Bronson was really guilty.

Reason is because. Awkward and repetitious. Use *reason is that*. Even this phrase is awkward and should be used sparingly.

> POOR: His reason for jilting her was because his parents disapproved of older women.
>
> BETTER: His reason for jilting her was that his parents disapproved of older women.
>
> EVEN BETTER: He jilted her because his parents disapproved of older women.

Relevant. An overused word, frequently relied upon to express shallow thought: "Literature is not relevant to our needs," for example. See *Irrelevant, irreverent* for note on pronunciation.

Respectfully, respectively. *Respectfully* means *with respect*. *Respectively* means *each in the order named*.

> Everyone likes to be treated respectfully.
>
> The speaker discussed education, medical research, and defense spending respectively.

Sadist, masochist. A *sadist* enjoys hurting living creatures. A *masochist* enjoys being hurt.

Seeing as how. Not standard English. Use *since* or *because*.

Seldom ever. *Ever* is unnecessary in this phrase. Avoid it.

> POOR: He was seldom ever angry.
>
> BETTER: He was seldom angry.

Set, sit. *To set* means *to place* or *to put*. The dictionary gives dozens of other meanings as well. Our main concern is that *set* does not mean *sit* or *sat*.

> Set the table.
>
> We sat at the table. (Not *We set at the table.*)
>
> Set down that chair.
>
> Sit down in that chair. (Not *Set down in that chair.*)

Shall, will. Elaborate rules differentiate between these words. Few people understand the rules, and no one remembers them. Our advice on this subject is to use *will* all the time except when *shall* obviously sounds more natural, as in some questions and traditional phrases. Examples: *Shall we dance? We shall overcome.*

Shone, shown. *Shone* is the alternate past tense and past participle of *shine*. Same as *shined*. *Shown* is the alternate past participle of *show*. Same as *showed*.

> The sun shone brightly.
>
> More shocking films are being shown than ever before.

Should of. See *Could of, should of, would of.*

Sic. Means *thus* or *so* in Latin. *Sic* is used in brackets within quoted material to indicate that an obvious error or absurdity was actually written that way in the original.

> The author tells us, "President Harold [sic] Truman pulled one of the biggest political upsets of the century."

Site. See *Cite, site.*

Slander. See *Libel, slander.*

So. When *so* is used for emphasis, the full thought often needs to be completed by a clause. See *Such.*

> POOR: The coffee was so sweet.
>
>   My sister is so smart.
>
> CORRECT: That coffee was so sweet that it was undrinkable.
>
>   My sister is so smart that she does my homework for me every night.

So-called. This word has a specific meaning. Use it to complain about something that has been incorrectly or inaccurately named. Do not use it as a simple synonym for "undesirable" or "unpleasant."

> WRONG: These so-called jet planes make too much noise.
>
>   She wore a so-called wig.
>
> RIGHT: Many of our so-called radicals are quite timid and conservative.
>
>   These so-called luxury homes are really just mass-produced bungalows.

Someone, some one. See *Anyone, any one.*

Somewheres. Not standard English. Use *somewhere.*

Sort of. Does not mean *somewhat* or *rather.* Means *a type of, a variety of.* See *Kind of.*

Stationary, stationery. *Stationary* means *unmoving, unchanging. Stationery* is paper for letter writing.

Story. A *story* is a piece of short prose fiction. Do not use the word when referring to essays and articles, poems, plays, and novels. Remember, too, that the action in any work of literature is *plot*, not story.

Such. When *such* is used for emphasis to mean *so much* or *so great*, etc., the full thought usually needs to be completed by a clause. See *So.*

> POOR: He was such a wicked man.
>
> CORRECT: He was such a wicked man that everyone feared him.
>
>   We had such fun at the picnic, we had to force ourselves to go home.

Supposed to. Don't forget the *d.*

> This poem is supposed to be one of the greatest ever written.
>
> The students are supposed to have a rally tomorrow night.

Than, then. *Than* is the word for expressing comparisons and exceptions. *Then* is the word for all other uses.

> Florida is more humid than California.
>
> John has nothing to worry about other than his own bad temper.

At first I thought the story was funny. Then I realized its underlying seriousness.

We must work together, then, or we are all doomed.

Their, there, they're. *Their* is the possessive form of *they*.

They took their seats.

They're is the contraction of *they are*.

The defensive linemen say they're going to do better next week.

For all other situations, the word you want is *there*.

They. Often used vaguely and meaninglessly, as in "They don't make things the way they used to," or "They really ought to do something about safety." Nowhere is the use of "they" more meaningless and weird than when applied to an individual writer. *Never* write:

This was an excellent mystery. They certainly fooled me with the solution.

I think it was sad that they had Othello die at the end of the play.

This, these. Frequent problem-producers when used imprecisely. Make certain that no confusion or vagueness is possible. To be on the safe side, many writers make a habit of following *this* and *these* with a noun that clarifies the reference: *this idea, these suggestions, this comment,* etc.

To, too, two. *Two* is the number. *Too* means *also* or *excessively*. *To* is the familiar preposition used in diverse ways.

Try and. Acceptable in conversation, but undesirable in print. Use *try to*.

POOR: We must all try and improve our environment.

BETTER: We must all try to improve our environment.

Type of. This phrase frequently contributes to wordiness.

WORDY: He was an interesting type of artist.

I enjoy a suspenseful type of novel.

BETTER: He was an interesting artist.

I enjoy a suspenseful novel.

Under way. Two words, except in special technical fields.

Uninterested. See *Disinterested-uninterested*.

Unique. This word means *one of a kind;* it cannot be made stronger than it already is, nor can it be qualified. Do not write *very unique, more unique, less unique, somewhat unique, rather unique, fairly unique,* etc.

Used to. Don't forget the *d*.

I used (not *use*) to like the tales of Jules Verne.

We are used (not *use*) to this kind of treatment.

Very. One of the most overused words in the language. Try to find one *exact* word for what you want to say instead of automatically using *very* to intensify the meaning of an imprecise, commonplace word.

very bright	*could be*	radiant
very bad	*could be*	terrible
very sad	*could be*	pathetic
very happy	*could be*	overjoyed, delighted

When. In using this word, make sure it refers to *time*.

WRONG: Basketball is when five men on opposing teams . . .

RIGHT: Basketball is a game in which five men on opposing teams . . .

WRONG: New York is when the Democratic Convention was held.

RIGHT: New York is where the Democratic Convention was held.

Where. In using this word, make sure it refers to *place*.

WRONG: I'm interested in seeing the movie where the motorcycle gang takes over the town.

RIGHT: I'm interested in seeing the movie in which the motorcycle gang takes over the town.

WRONG: The class is studying the time where the Industrial Revolution was beginning.

RIGHT: The class is studying the time when the Industrial Revolution was beginning.

Where . . . at, where . . . to. The *at* and the *to* are unnecessary. They show how wordiness can often sneak into our writing almost subconsciously.

POOR: Where are you staying at?

Where is he going to?

BETTER: Where are you staying?

Where is he going?

Whether or not. The one word *whether* means the same as *whether or not*, and is therefore preferable.

WEAK: We wondered whether or not it would snow.

BETTER: We wondered whether it would snow.

Who, that, which. Use *who* or *that* for people, preferably *who*, never *which*. Use *which* or *that* for things, preferably *that*, never *who*.

Keats is one of many great writers who died at an early age.

There's the woman that I was telling you about.

Podunk is a town that people always ridicule.

The play which we are now studying is incredibly difficult.

Who, whom. Formal English still makes a fuss about these words. As teachers, we confess that we feel distinctly uncomfortable when the old rules are broken. We also confess, however, that they may be more trouble than they are worth. We suggest the following guidelines:

1. Immediately after a preposition, use *whom.*

> He asked to whom I had been speaking.
>
> This is the man in whom we must place our trust.

2. At other times, use *who.*

> In my home, it's the man who does the dishes.
>
> Fred Simper is the man who Ethel chose.

3. If *who* sounds "wrong" or unnatural, as it may in the previous sentence about Fred and Ethel, or if you are in a situation that demands extremely formal writing, try to eliminate the problem with one of these techniques:

> A. Change *who* or *whom* to *that.*
>
> Fred Simper is the man that Ethel chose.
>
> B. Remove *who* or *whom.*
>
> Fred Simper is the man Ethel chose.

Who's, whose. *Who's* is a contraction of *who is* or *who has. Whose* is the possessive form of *who.*

> Who's going to get the promotion?
>
> Fenton is a man who's been in and out of jail all his life.
>
> Whose reputation shall we attack today?
>
> Kennedy was a president whose place in history is still in doubt.

Will. See *Shall, will.*

Would of. See *Could of, should of, would of.*

INDEX